Birds of Central America

Birds of Central America

Belize, Guatemala, Honduras, El Salvador, Nicaragua, Costa Rica, and Panama

Andrew C. Vallely and Dale Dyer

PRINCETON UNIVERSITY PRESS

PRINCETON AND OXFORD

For Guy Tudor, with thanks for many years of friendship, encouragement and wisdom.

–A. C. V.

For Elise, who makes all things possible.

–D. D.

Published by Princeton University Press,
41 William Street, Princeton, New Jersey 08540

In the United Kingdom: Princeton University Press,
6 Oxford Street, Woodstock, Oxfordshire OX20 1TR

press.princeton.edu

Jacket images provided by authors

ISBN 978-0-691-13801-5
ISBN (pbk.) 978-0-691-13802-2

Library of Congress Control Number: 2017959777

British Library Cataloging-in-Publication Data is available

This book has been composed in Minion Pro and Myriad Pro

Printed on acid-free paper. ∞

Printed in China

10 9 8 7 6 5 4 3 2 1

Political maps of north and south Central America

contributions and we urge readers to seek out these foundational references, as they remain valuable sources of information. To keep up with and include an increasing stream of new distributional records from the region we relied heavily on the regional accounts published in *North American Birds*, and we owe a debt to the authors and contributors who compiled them (Jones 2001–2005, Jones & Komar 2006–2016). We also availed ourselves of a wide range of information that has accumulated elsewhere in periodicals and scientific journals. A complete list of our published sources on the status and distribution of Central American birds can be found in the bibliography.

Plan of the book

Range maps We compiled range maps from published records, specimen data, and our own observations (see above). Three base maps are used. These are northern Central America, southern Central America, and the entire Central American region. Isla del Coco, a remote, oceanic island, is not shown. Bird distributions in many parts of Central America are imperfectly known, and the range areas presented here represent an estimate of the actual range. Bird distributions are also dynamic, and several Central American species have undergone dramatic and well-documented changes in range area. Continued fieldwork in the region promises to refine our understanding, and we hope that these maps inspire observers to document and report their observations, especially when they do not agree with what is presented here.

Figure 1 presents a key to the range maps. Widespread breeding distributions are indicated by dark green shading. Distributions of breeding visitors are indicated by light green shading. Nonbreeding resident distributions are indicated by brown shading. The distributions of transients (mainly Nearctic-Neotropical migrants) are indicated by tan shading. The distributions of species that are thought to be breeding residents, but are of very local occurrence, are indicated by dark green dots. The distributions of breeding visitors of very local occurrence are indicated by light green dots. Distributions that are documented only by historical records (>50 years before the present) are indicated by a green asterisk. Records of vagrants or birds of unknown status are indicated by a black star. Areas of uncertain or hypothetical occurrence are sometimes indicated by a question mark. Arrows are occasionally used to call attention to narrow or peripheral range areas.

Species accounts Each species account includes four or five main sections. Below the species name is a summary of status and distribution. This is followed by sections concerned with identification, habits, and voice. Where appropriate we include brief remarks describing geographic variation (**GV**) following the **ID** section.

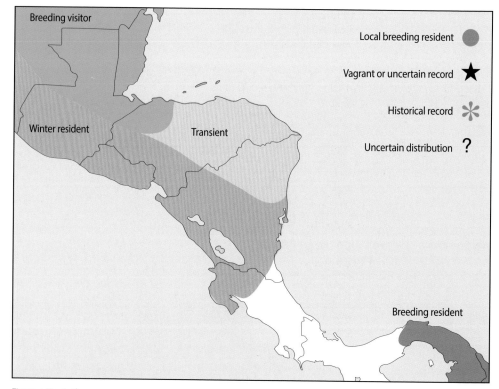

Figure 1. Key to the range maps.

English and scientific names Each species account begins with the English and scientific name of the species treated therein. As noted previously, the nomenclature and species list mostly conforms to the *Check-list of the Birds of North America* (AOU 1998, and supplements through 2017). Because there appears to be no standardized or generally accepted list of Spanish language names, we have not included these.

Taxonomic notes In cases where recent changes to species limits have been introduced or suggested, where our treatment differs from that of the *Check-list*, or where we wish to highlight problems in species-level taxonomy, we use superscript numbers following the English name to direct the reader to individual entries in an appendix (Taxonomic Notes, p. 550). There we provide a brief explanation and bibliographic references to relevant literature.

Lengths To facilitate size comparisons, we provide estimates of total length in centimeters for each species following the species name. For variable species, an intermediate number is usually provided. Two numbers are given in cases where a species exhibits significant sexual dimorphism, and a range is given where a species is geographically variable in size. These figures are based on measurements of well-prepared study skins with reference to wing and tail measurements. In assembling these, we have supplemented our own measurements with data from published sources. Readers should be aware that it is difficult to obtain accurate or reproducible measurements of length from study skins (or even from freshly dead birds), especially of long-necked birds, and these lengths are provided only for the purpose of general comparisons of relative size.

Status and distribution Each species account begins with a concise, general summary of the species global distribution. These are necessarily brief, and we encourage the reader to consult other references for more detailed information on the global distribution of any particular species. For species found only in Central America, the account begins with the phrase "CA endemic." Next we describe the distribution of the species in Central America. These remarks typically include abundance, seasonal status (including months when present), elevational range (in meters above sea level, SL), and a broad summary of geographic occurrence (e.g., "humid Caribbean slope"). Where appropriate, we mention occurrence on various islands and also patterns of vagrancy. For species that are rare, poorly known, of conservation concern, or for which new distributional information is available, we provide the province, district, or indigenous zone for published records, and also numbered references to these publications in the bibliography. These references are not exhaustive, but we hope they can provide at least a convenient entry point to the literature.

We use seven abundance categories. From most to least numerous: abundant, very common, common, fairly common, uncommon, rare, and very rare. These terms refer to the observer's likelihood of encountering a given species in appropriate habitat within its main geographic range.

abundant	Recorded every day in the field, often in large numbers.
very common	Recorded almost every day, but usually not in such large numbers as in the previous category.
common	Recorded on substantially more than half of all days in the field.
fairly common	Recorded on about half of all days in the field.
uncommon	Recorded on substantially fewer than half of all days in the field, but more commonly encountered than species in the following category.
rare	Recorded on fewer than 10% of all days in the field.
very rare	Known from very few records in the region and never encountered in large numbers.

Seasonal status is indicated by one or more of the terms defined below.

breeding resident or **breeder**	A species that breeds in the region and remains there throughout its life cycle.
transient	A species that breeds outside the region and occurs in Central America only during its migrations. A small number of North American birds winter exclusively in South America, or in South American waters, but occur widely in Central America as transients.
winter resident	A species that breeds outside the region (usually in North America) and remains in Central America during its nonbreeding season.
breeding visitor	A species that breeds in Central America and withdraws (usually to South America) outside its breeding season.
visitor	A species with an irregular pattern of occurrence in the region.

Identification In the **ID** section we provide a concise summary of field marks or diagnostic characters for each species. Our emphasis is on features that are useful in field identification. The most critical distinguishing features are *italicized*. The first features mentioned are often those of structure or relative size. Next we describe prominent plumage features. Where known, we mention characters that are useful in distinguishing age and sex classes in the field. Adult males, females, their seasonal changes, and immature plumages are described in that order. Where appropriate, we suggest comparisons with potential confusion species at the end of the ID section. For the names of the parts of a bird and its plumage used in this book, see Figure 2.

Geographic variation For species that are geographically variable we include the section **GV** (geographic variation) wherein we describe broad patterns of geographically structured phenotypic variation in the region. These remarks are based on our studies of museum collections and relevant literature. We have tried to include illustrations representing the range of geographic variation shown by such species in the region. To this end, we have included illustrations of both diagnosable, allopatric forms, and in some cases, figures that represent points within patterns of clinal or continuous variation, typically a midpoint or two extremes. Although our choices of representative figures often correspond to individual named subspecies, in many cases they do not. In some cases, individual figures were chosen to represent broad geographic patterns that involve multiple subspecies. For this reason, we have not used subspecies names, but instead refer to geographic variants in relation to their distributions. To identify patterns of geographic variation deserving illustration, we first compiled a list of subspecies occurring in the region based mainly on *The Howard and Moore Complete Checklist of the Birds of the World* (Dickinson 2003). Next, we assembled a database of diagnostic characters for each subspecies. For this, we consulted many original descriptions, and also relied heavily on other sources including Ridgway (1901–1919), Ridgway & Friedmann (1941–1946), Friedmann (1950), Cory (1918,1919), Hellmayr (1925–1938), and Hellmayr & Conover (1942–1949). We next sought to examine and compare specimens of every subspecies known from the region. We used as our primary resource the collections of Central American birds at the American Museum of Natural History in New York. When necessary, we borrowed specimens from other institutions and visited other collections (see Acknowledgments). Though we were able to locate and examine examples of virtually every named subspecies from the region, we were occasionally forced to base our conclusions on a very small number of skins. In many cases we could not confirm the validity of a particular subspecies or pattern of variation. Such forms are not illustrated or described. We also chose not to illustrate or describe geographic variants that we judged to differ only subtly or inconsistently, and we did not illustrate forms that are diagnosed solely on measurements of size. Our treatment is by no means exhaustive, and much remains to be learned about geographic variation (and species limits) in Central American birds. We hope that our presentation can serve as a useful introduction for naturalists inclined to look more closely at avian diversity in Central America.

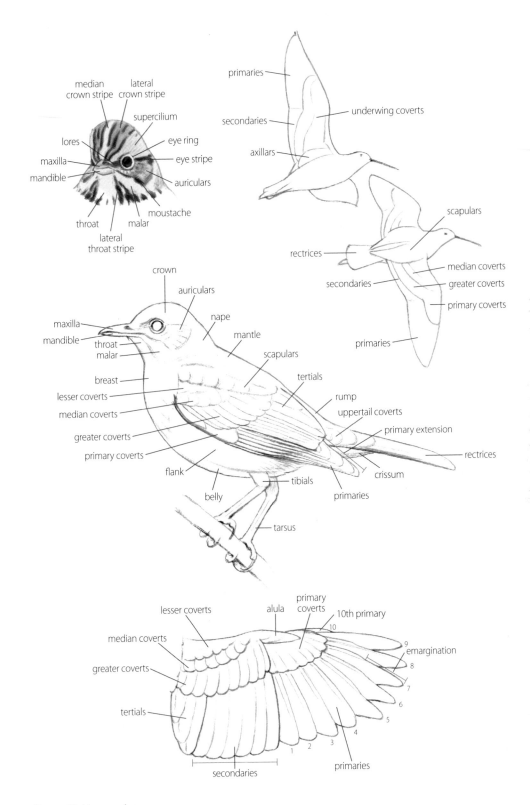

Figure 2. Bird topography.

15

Habits This section provides concise information on ecological and behavioral attributes. Our emphasis is on traits or associations that might aid an observer in locating and identifying a species of interest. We typically first give the vegetation strata (floor, understory, midstory, or canopy) and habitat types in which a species is most likely to be found. We list first the habitats where the species is most often found, or where it can be found in the greatest abundance. Other habitat types are listed in decreasing order of importance. In this, we hope to provide a general sense of where to expect the species. We caution that all habitat categories are approximate and areas can easily be found that combine characteristics of, or are transitional among these categories. See below for a list of habitat terms used in this book. Next, we give some indication of social behavior, for example, whether the species is likely to be encountered as solitary individuals or in pairs or groups. Where appropriate, we note whether a species routinely associates with other species in mixed flocks, in feeding assemblies or at roosts. We also note cases where a species is associated with more specialized social systems. Ant following, for example, is a specialized social system confined to the tropics. Several species of antbirds are dependent for food on nomadic colonies of army ants that flush invertebrate prey from the forest floor. In another specialized association, seabirds may forage in mixed groups or in association with marine mammals or fish.

The following are the most commonly used habitat terms in this book:

lakes and *lagoons*	Lakes are large inland bodies of freshwater. Lagoons are shallow but sometimes extensive bodies of water found in coastal lowlands.
gallery forest	Gallery forests are medium- to high-stature, often evergreen forests that border watercourses in otherwise open areas. Gallery forests often form as ribbonlike extensions of broadleaf vegetation dividing areas of savanna.
scrub	Low-stature plant communities found in areas with poor soils or a long history of continuous disturbance. Scrub is often the result of human disturbance of tall forest but may also form following natural disturbance including erosion or volcanic activity.
thorn forest	Low- or medium-stature plant communities with closed canopy and often dense, impenetrable understory found in arid lowlands or foothills. Thorn forest trees are deciduous, and this forest type is confined to areas with very low annual rainfall and a pronounced or prolonged dry season such as the Nentón Valley in west Guatemala and the Aguán Valley in north Honduras.
littoral forest and *littoral scrub*	Medium- or low-stature plant communities found immediately adjacent to the coast both on islands and on the mainland.
pine-oak forest	Medium-stature plant communities that are dominated by pine (*Pinus*) and oak (*Quercus*) trees. Pine-oak forest is widespread in drier regions of the north Central American highlands, but is also found locally in lowlands where it may occur as gallery forests in regions dominated by savanna.
deciduous forest and *semi-deciduous forest*	Medium- or high-stature plant communities found in areas with a long and pronounced dry season during which all or most canopy trees lose their leaves. Some trees bloom during the dry season. Epiphytes are typically scarce but often include cacti. Terrestrial bromeliads are common in some areas. These forest types are widespread in the Yucatán Shelf and persist in less disturbed areas of the Pacific slope.

humid broadleaf forest	A broad category of high-stature, evergreen plant communities, typically with continuous, closed canopy and open, shaded understory. Humid broadleaf forest is found in areas with very high annual rainfall and is often called "rain forest." Humid broadleaf forest is characterized by a complex vegetation structure, typically featuring well-defined understory, midstory, and canopy strata. Tree species diversity is generally the highest observed among Central American forest types. Large trees (often reaching 30 meters in height) are common and often have buttressed roots. Lianas, understory palms, and epiphytes are often common. In general, humid broadleaf forest hosts the richest bird communities (i.e., with the highest species diversity) found in Central America. Though confined mainly to Caribbean slope lowlands and foothills in north Central America, there is also extensive humid broadleaf forest on Costa Rica's east Pacific slope, and this forest type is widespread on both slopes in eastern Panama.

We use the term "cloud forest" to refer to a type of humid broadleaf forest that is found at higher elevations where local climatic conditions (abundant atmospheric moisture) cause forests to be often or usually enshrouded in mists. Mosses and various epiphytes are typically abundant, particularly at the higher elevation. In north Central America, cloud forest is found mainly on more humid Caribbean-facing slopes, but it is widespread in the highlands of south Central America. |
elfin forest	A low-stature type of broadleaf forest found at high elevations and usually on exposed ridges (above 1200 m) where strong winds result in low, gnarled trees. Elfin forests typically have abundant bamboo, mosses, and epiphytes.
paramo	Open grasslands or shrublands found locally at very high elevations in east Costa Rica and west Panama. Paramo is widespread in the Andes of South America but in Central America is confined to the highest peaks of the Talamancas. Although very limited in extent, Central American paramos host a distinctive bird community.
mangroves	Forested areas dominated by a few species of trees and shrubs with stilted, aerial roots that are tolerant of salt or brackish water. Mangroves are locally distributed on both coasts with the largest stands often associated with estuaries.
savanna and *grassland*	Open areas dominated by grasses and with only scattered trees or shrubs. Large areas of the north Caribbean slope lowlands in Belize and in the Mosquitia region of east Honduras and north Nicaragua host savannas with varying densities of pine trees or stands of low palms. Savannas are often bordered by gallery forests along streams and rivers. Some savannas are managed as low-density pastures, and some are maintained or modified by deliberate setting of fires. Other types of grasslands are found locally in, for example, the cold, arid highlands of the Sierra de los Cuchumatanes in Guatemala, and in the Pacific slope lowlands of west Panama.
pastures	Large areas of cleared land that are managed intensively for livestock and are often maintained through both grazing and fire. Pastures sometimes support or attract species that are more widespread in grasslands or marshes.
marshes	Low, open, often permanently wet or flooded areas that border lakes, rivers, and lagoons and are dominated by grasses, sedges, and other nonwoody emergent vegetation. Marshes are locally distributed in Central America, but some are extensive. As in many other parts of the world, many Central American marshes have been destroyed by conversion for agriculture, especially rice cultivation.
agricultural areas	Lands that are managed for production of plant crops. Although plant diversity is typically low, some management practices (including flooding and tilling) can make agricultural lands locally or briefly attractive to foraging birds. Rice fields may attract birds that are more widely associated with marshes.

plantations	Cultivated areas with tall or relatively complex vegetation structure. Some types of plantations incorporate native trees as shade cover and these areas can host rich bird communities that include species otherwise found mainly in broadleaf forest. Examples include foothill areas managed for "shade coffee" and also cacao plantations in humid lowlands.
gardens	Intensively managed areas that are closely associated with human habitations or other structures. Vegetation typically includes food and ornamental plants.
urban and suburban areas	As in other parts of the world, at least some wild birds can be found in even the most human-dominated areas of Central America. Urban parks and plantings sometimes support a surprising variety of birds, and these can often be new to a first-time visitor in the region.
coastal waters	As in other parts of the world, birds are sometimes abundant and conspicuous in nearshore marine areas on both coasts of Central America. Many widespread or migratory species occur.
pelagic waters	Open ocean waters host specialized communities of birds. The relatively deeper and colder pelagic waters off the Pacific coast of Central America host a relatively rich but poorly studied avifauna. By comparison, relatively few seabirds have been reported from the warm and shallow Caribbean waters.

Voice Knowledge of the sounds produced by birds is essential to effectively locating and identifying them. Once an observer has learned the common sounds in an area of study, he or she will begin to notice unfamiliar sounds, and this often leads to encounters with less common birds. In the voice section we list and describe the most frequent vocal sounds (and in some cases nonvocal sounds or sonations) produced by the species. Distinct, stereotyped sounds are described separately following numbers. Onomatopoeic transcriptions of songs, calls, and sonations are given in *italics*. More complex sounds (songs) are listed and described first, followed by shorter vocalizations (calls). Where possible we point out differences that may be useful in distinguishing these from similar sounds given by other species. In some cases (e.g., some manakins, Pipridae), nonvocal sounds or "sonations" are also described. As a supplement to our descriptions, and as an invaluable aid in comparing and memorizing bird sounds, we urge observers to assemble a collections of sound files, either by recording them directly in the field, or by building a collection of others' recordings.

Plates Illustrations for each species appear on the page opposite the range map and species accounts. Where a single figure is shown it can be assumed to be an adult. Immature plumages, usually drabber than the adult, are placed to the left. The boldest, brightest adult breeding plumages (usually male) are placed farthest to the right. Figures representing geographic variants of the same species are shown in an arrangement that roughly reflects their geographic relations, with northern forms displayed at the top, and figures at the left depicting western populations.

Plumages illustrated Our aim is to facilitate identification to species and also to present a visual summary of broad patterns of geographic variation in Central American birds (see Geographic Variation). Birds of the same species can vary greatly in appearance as the result of many factors in addition to geography. These include sex, season, molt and wear, age (plumage maturation), polymorphism, and individual variation. For species that show significant differences in appearance related to sex, age, or season, these are mentioned in the ID section and the illustrations are labeled to indicate the plumage depicted. Individual figures are intended to allow the user to understand the full range of the species' appearance. For this purpose, typical or representative specimens were selected, and each figure was prepared with a specimen or series of representative specimens at hand.

It is not always possible to identify a live bird to sex and age, and any particular bird may most closely resemble a figure labeled as a different sex or age than its own. In many sexually dimorphic species, older females can appear more male-like, and younger males more female-like. In general, however, as birds mature and molt, their development typically progresses along a range from dullest (often juvenile female) to brightest (usually breeding male). We include illustrations of juvenile plumages in cases where these are confusingly different from adults, are similar to some other species, or are held for an extended period and hence frequently seen.

Plumage, molt, and appearance Many species exhibit annual seasonal changes in their appearance, and for these we use the term "breeding" to refer to their appearance during the portion of the year that includes the species' reproductive activities. We use the term "nonbreeding" to refer to a bird's appearance during the remainder of its annual cycle. When these are different, breeding appearance is typically more intensely or boldly colored. Breeding appearance may result from the replacement of feathers, or from a process of wear that reveals more colorful or contrasting patterns. Breeding appearance may also involve changes in the colors of bare parts such as the bill, legs, or facial skin. In some species, breeding appearance is fairly brief, as in the colorful facial skin of some herons and egrets in breeding condition. In other cases, such as the dull plumage of male ducks, nonbreeding appearance may be of much shorter duration than breeding appearance. In the majority of Central American species, however, breeding appearance is seen roughly from March to August, and nonbreeding appearance from September to February.

Most species molt (replace feathers) at least annually, usually following nesting. In migratory species, this can occur before, during, or after migration. This molt is termed pre-basic molt, and results in the bird's basic plumage. In some species there is a second (usually partial) molt prior to breeding. This is termed pre-alternate molt and results in the alternate plumage, which may give the bird its breeding appearance. Immature birds may undergo a series of molts, sometimes over several years, before attaining adult (or terminal) plumage. The first non-downy plumage is referred to as juvenile. Several molts may follow during a bird's first year (preformative and prealternate molts) before the bird replaces all its feathers a year or more after acquiring juvenile plumage. Some species such as gulls may show, over the course of several years, alternate and basic plumages that are very different from the adult plumage, and these may be sufficiently distinctive to allow an observer to determine the bird's age. We refer generally to birds that have not yet acquired adult plumage as immature (although in some cases these birds may be capable of breeding). We refer to immature birds that have undergone at least some molt following their juvenile plumage as subadults. Note that we use the term "first-year" to refer to the first year of a bird's life, regardless of change in the calendar year.

Scale In general, all portrait (or main) figures on the same plate are presented at the same scale. In a few cases, plates are subdivided by a horizontal black line indicating the use of different scales on the same plate. The scale for each plate (or plate section) is indicated at the upper right. Figures of birds in flight, as well as those shown in behavioral vignettes and the like are presented at much smaller scales than the main figures and scales for these are not given. The scale used for individual plates may vary from plate to plate, sometimes within the same family. The *Glaucidium* pygmy-owls, for example, are shown at a larger scale than the other owls.

Geography of Central America

Topography Central America's physical geography is dominated by its long Pacific and Caribbean coasts and by the mountain ranges that separate these coasts and the Pacific and Caribbean drainages for much of the length of the isthmus. The dominant feature of the northern part of Central America is the Crystalline Highlands, extending east from Mexico between the narrow

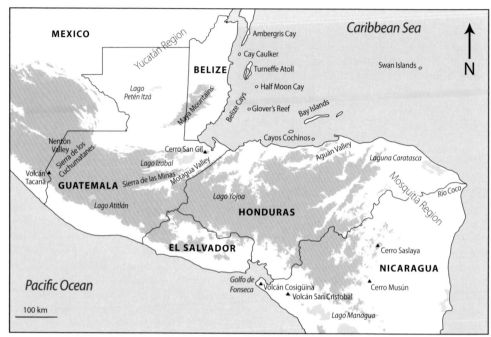

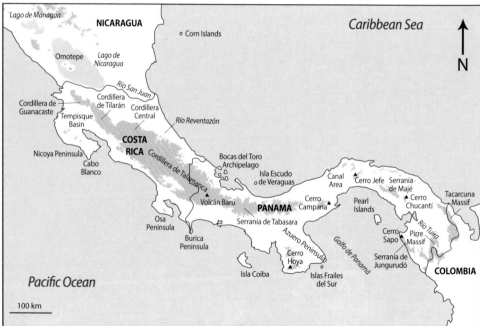

Physical maps of north and south Central America

Pacific coastal plain and the broad lowland expanse of the Yucatán Shelf. Parallel mountain ranges spread across east Honduras and extend to the south, past the Mosquitia region, to lakes Managua and Nicaragua. An active volcanic belt forms the Pacific volcanic highlands and runs nearly parallel to the Pacific coast from Guatemala to west Panama. Several smaller, peripheral highland areas occupy broad peninsulas extending from the Pacific coast. Both the Pacific and Caribbean coastal plains are fairly narrow for much of their length, but become broad in Nicaragua where an area of very low relief dominated by the vast Lago de Nicaragua separates the north and south Central American highlands.

Climate Central America has relatively constant year-round temperatures and seasonally (and locally) variable rainfall. A dry season typically extends from January through April. Rainfall patterns during the wet season are typically bimodal, with peaks occurring during June and September. Rainfall is most seasonal in more arid areas, and those receiving the most rainfall have the least seasonal pattern. With some notable exceptions, the Pacific slope receives far less rainfall and has a more pronounced dry season than the Caribbean slope. Prevailing winds from the Caribbean are present through most of the year. Storms sometimes bring cooler temperatures to north Central America in winter and early spring, but these are usually weak by the time they reach the region. Hurricanes, which approach from the north and east, strike Central America mainly north of Nicaragua, and occur principally from June to the end of October. Severe hurricanes strike the region only every few years.

Vegetation The distributions of the major vegetation formations of Central America correspond closely with the prevailing climate. Deciduous or semi-deciduous forest is the dominant potential vegetation on the Pacific slope while humid broadleaf (evergreen) forest is the dominant potential vegetation over much of the Caribbean slope. In general, Caribbean slope lowlands and foothills receive the highest annual rainfall (in some areas more than four meters) and support taller, more humid, evergreen forests. The Pacific lowlands, with some notable exceptions, receive far less rainfall and host deciduous forest or nonforest vegetation types. In many areas these general distributions are modified locally by soil, fire, wind, or other factors. See habitat terms.

Biogeography and major subregions of Central America

Central America hosts a disproportionate amount of the earth's biological diversity, and actual biodiversity in the region may be higher than is reflected in current regional summaries and checklists. While biogeographic patterns are not yet fully documented, and a complete understanding of the processes that have shaped the Central American avifauna is still emerging, some general insights have emerged. Among the most general patterns in the distribution of Central America's bird life, and in common with many other parts of the world, the richness of local bird communities is inversely correlated with latitude, exemplifying one of the most general global biogeographic patterns, the latitudinal diversity gradient. Looking more closely at the origins of local bird communities in Central America, it is also apparent that the number of bird lineages found locally that have South American affinities decreases as we move from south to north along the isthmus, and that the reverse pattern is apparent in the distributions of bird groups having Nearctic or Palearctic origins. In general, middle- and high-elevation avifaunas in Central America are more diverse, and they also have higher levels of endemism than lowland avifaunas, although evidence suggests that diversification in Central American birds has occurred in both lowland and highland areas.

The richness, local occurrence, and composition of bird communities are often discussed in relation to the web of ecological processes that maintain them in the present, but the origins of large-scale patterns in the spatial and temporal distribution of biological diversity are more fully explained by long-term processes of geological change. These can include erosion, mountain building through volcanism and folding of the earth's crust, as well as changes in the shape of coastlines through marine incursion or retreat. These processes can profoundly alter the distributions of bird lineages and they also drive diversification by enabling successive waves of dispersal, invasion, and subsequent fragmentation or isolation. Even changes in local climate that may limit or enable the expansion of bird distributions can be seen as more proximate manifestations of processes that are ultimately driven by the continuously changing form of the surface of the earth. In Central America, the interactions of six tectonic plates have caused varied, spectacular, and sometimes violent episodes of faulting, volcanism, subduction, and uplift over many millions of years, and these events have shaped the distributions and diversity of bird lineages both within the region, and in the Western Hemisphere as a whole.

Some parts of north Central America, including the Yucatán Peninsula, began taking shape as early as 140 million years before the present (mybp), but the bulk of Central America did not form until much later when that land mass fused with what is now southern Guatemala, Honduras, and north Nicaragua near the end of the Cretaceous. To the south, the highlands of south Central America first appeared as a series of volcanic islands extending toward South America. Declining sea levels further exposed this terrain, creating the present-day lowlands of south Central America. By the end of the Pliocene, the lowlands of east Panama were also exposed, completing the isthmus and forming a connection between North and South America. Below, we briefly describe the major subregions and patterns of endemism in Central America and outline some of the geomorphological processes that have shaped the region and its bird life. The largest and most important of these subregions are the Pacific slope lowlands, the Caribbean slope lowlands, and the north and south Central American highlands. We also describe several smaller areas and island groups that figure prominently in the distributions of Central American birds.

Yucatán Shelf Much of Belize and north Guatemala occupy a broad, low limestone plateau with shallow soils and little or no surface water. Potential vegetation here is mainly deciduous and semi-deciduous forest. Annual precipitation is lower than in other parts of the Caribbean slope, and rainfall, as well as forest stature, decline toward the north along a gradient that continues into adjacent Mexico. Large areas of forest persist, but these are mainly in protected areas in west Belize and north Guatemala. The distinctive avifauna includes Ocellated Turkey, Yucatan Flycatcher, and Rose-throated Tanager. Some range-restricted species are shared between the Yucatán Shelf and the Bay Islands including Caribbean Dove and Yellow-lored Parrot. The Maya Mountains of southern Belize are an older and geologically distinct formation reaching a maximum elevation near 1125 m and hosting isolated populations of several species that are more widely distributed in the north Central American highlands such as Common Chlorospingus, Cabanis's Wren, and Greater Pewee.

Belize Cays A string of small islands runs parallel to the coast of Belize and sits atop a vast coral reef. Many of the Belize Cays are ringed by stands of mangroves and rise only a few feet above sea level. Natural upland vegetation, including littoral forest and scrub, is very limited in extent and is also threatened by development for tourism. Some species found here are shared with the Bay Islands, and some mainly West Indian species occur here, including White-crowned Pigeon and Caribbean Elaenia. Range-restricted species such as Black Catbird and Caribbean Dove also occur on the mainland, but are perhaps most easily found on these islands. Significant seabird colonies are also found locally on more remote cays including those of Red-footed Booby, Roseate Tern, Bridled Tern, and Magnificent Frigatebird.

Bay Islands Located off the north (Caribbean) coast of Honduras, the islands of Útila, Roatán, and Guanaja make up the Bay Islands, and in their geology, form an extension of the Nombre de Dios Mountains on the adjacent Honduran mainland. Upland habitats, including mangroves and littoral woodlands, are more extensive here than in the Belize Cays but are also threatened by development for tourism. Pine woodlands are found locally on Guanaja. Several endemic subspecies have been described from the Bay Islands. Some range-restricted species are shared with the Yucatán Shelf, including Yellow-lored Parrot and Yucatan Woodpecker. Regionally significant tern colonies are found on small nearby islets. The Cayos Cochinos are a smaller group of islands located closer to the Honduran mainland.

North Central American highlands A nearly continuous region of rugged mountains and high plateaus extends from south of the Isthmus of Tehuantepec in Mexico, and stretches across a broad portion of interior Guatemala, Honduras, and north Nicaragua. The north Central American highlands (often called the Crystalline Highlands) have a highly complex topography and reach a maximum elevation above 3000 meters. These mountains were formed from upraised continental crust at the confluence of the North American and Caribbean tectonic plates (Chortis and Maya Terrains) and they are dissected by several deep fault valleys, most notably the long Motagua Valley, and to the east, by the Honduran Depression, a complex set of valleys that stretches from north Honduras to the Gulf of Fonseca on the Pacific coast. These arid intermontane valleys appear to form barriers to dispersal by highland and humid forest birds, and this is reflected in the allopatric, east-west distributions of various geographic variants and sister-species pairs in the region such as Green-throated and Green-breasted mountain-gems.

Much of the north Central American highlands is dominated by pine-oak forest with coniferous forest reminiscent of North American formations found very locally at some of the highest elevations. Humid broadleaf and cloud forest is found locally on some peaks and more humid Caribbean-facing slopes and hosts a set of range-restricted species (some shared with the adjacent Mexican state of Chiapas) that include Bearded Screech-Owl, Blue-throated Motmot, and Pink-headed Warbler. Pine-oak forests and coniferous forests support the range-restricted Belted Flycatcher and Goldman's Warbler. Several widespread and mainly Nearctic bird species reach their southern distributional limits here, including Bushtit, Brown Creeper, and Pine Siskin. Some species are shared between the north and south Central American highlands, including Buffy-crowned Wood-Partridge, Spot-crowned Woodcreeper and Slate-throated Redstart, and these are often represented by distinct geographic forms. In some cases, taxa long treated as widespread species, ranging through both the north and south Central American highlands, have recently been regarded as separate, allopatric species. Examples include the recently revised treatments of Rivoli's and Talamanca hummingbirds, and White-faced and Cabanis's ground-sparrows (see Taxonomic Notes).

Caribbean slope arid valleys Several narrow fault valleys, most notably the Motagua Valley in Guatemala and the Aguán Valley in Honduras, extend from the interior of north Central America to near the Caribbean coast and are shadowed from the prevailing Caribbean winds, resulting in a locally arid climate. Potential vegetation here is thorn or deciduous forest, but this is often scarce, and many areas are overgrazed and hence support low, open scrub. The Central American endemic Honduran Emerald is found only in arid valleys of north Honduras, and disjunct populations of several species that are more widespread on the Pacific slope are found locally here, including Lesser Ground-Cuckoo, Double-striped Thick-knee, and White-lored Gnatcatcher. Some species found in arid areas, and otherwise confined in Central America to the Nentón Valley in west Guatemala, are also found here including Varied Bunting and Russet-crowned Motmot.

Caribbean slope pine savannas Although humid broadleaf forest is the potential vegetation over much of the Caribbean slope, areas with poor, sandy soil in Belize, and over a larger area in the Mosquitia region straddling the borders of east Honduras and north Nicaragua, host open pine and pine-oak woodlands and grassy savannas. Seasonal streams in these areas often support veins of gallery forest, and seasonal wetlands including ponds and marshes are common. The Mosquitia region is remote and poorly known, but large blocks of intact vegetation remain. Characteristic species of Caribbean slope savannas include Black-throated Bobwhite, Botteri's Sparrow, and Grace's Warbler.

Pacific volcanic highlands A volcanic mountain chain runs parallel to the Pacific coast of Central America and dominates much of the landscape on the Pacific slope from Guatemala to Costa Rica, with some peaks reaching elevations above 4000 m. In some areas, such as south Guatemala and central Costa Rica, these volcanoes emerge from within the geologically older formations of the north and south Central American highlands, but for much of the length of the isthmus, they form a distinct and separate mountain chain. Middle elevations on most of these volcanoes have been converted to coffee plantations, but natural habitats often remain at higher elevations. In some regions these "sky islands" of humid broadleaf forest are isolated by relatively arid lowlands from the more extensive humid broadleaf forests of the north and south Central American highlands. Despite the isolated distributions of cloud forest birds on these upper slopes, the region has relatively few endemic species, and many geographic variants described from the Pacific volcanic highlands are only weakly differentiated. Of note, however, are Horned Guan and Azure-rumped Tanager, two very distinctive and range-restricted species confined to the Pacific volcanic highlands of Guatemala and adjacent south Mexico. Central America's only extinct species, Atitlan Grebe, is known only from Lago Atitlán, a deep caldera lake nestled in the Pacific volcanic range of Guatemala.

Isla del Coco Located in the Pacific Ocean some 500 km southwest of mainland Costa Rica, Isla del Coco is a true oceanic island. Habitats found on the island include beaches, littoral woodlands, and humid broadleaf forest. Cocos Cuckoo, Cocos Flycatcher, and Cocos Finch are endemic to the island. Significant seabird colonies are also found here, including those of Red-footed Booby, White Tern, and Great Frigatebird.

North Pacific slope arid lowlands and foothills A dry climate prevails over a large area of lowlands and foothills extending from the Isthmus of Tehuantepec in Mexico, through Guatemala, and south to near the Gulf of Nicoya in Costa Rica. The drier portions of the Costa Rican Central Valley form an interior extension of this area. Potential vegetation is mainly deciduous or semi-deciduous broadleaf forest, or thorn forest in driest areas, but the landscape has been extensively modified through conversion for agriculture and livestock, and the Pacific slope has endured Central America's longest history of settlement and urbanization. Surviving areas of deciduous forest in Central America are scarce, but can be found, for example, at El Impossible National Park in west El Salvador, and at Santa Rosa National Park in west Costa Rica. The few endemic bird species confined to the region include Hoffman's Woodpecker. Characteristic species, of which most are shared with the ecologically continuous Pacific slope of south Mexico, include Lesser Ground-Cuckoo, Pacific Screech-Owl, White-lored Gnatcatcher, and Stripe-headed Sparrow. Significant mangroves and salt marshes are found locally along the Pacific coast.

Caribbean slope humid lowlands and foothills Over most of the Caribbean slope from south Belize to east Panama, the potential vegetation is humid broadleaf forest or "rain forest." The landscape of the Caribbean slope has been widely degraded through conversion for agriculture and livestock, but in some areas large blocks of humid broadleaf forest remain, mainly in remote national parks and indigenous zones. Swamp forest and mangroves are found locally on the Caribbean coast. In the Mosquitia region, a broad alluvial plain spanning the borders of Honduras and Nicaragua, these forests are interdigitated with pine savanna (see Caribbean slope savannas). A broad lowland area, nowhere rising more than 50 m above seal level, occupies south Nicaragua, separating the north and south Central American highlands and uniting the Caribbean slope with the more arid Pacific along a broad humidity gradient. Sometimes called the "Nicaraguan Depression," this area is thought to have been periodically submerged beneath a shallow sea during the Miocene, and this sea may have formed an important barrier influencing the distribution and diversification of lowland birds in the region.

Among the bird species endemic to the Caribbean slope of Central America are Snowcap, Snowy Cotinga, Tawny-chested Flycatcher, and Canebrake Wren. Many species that are widespread in the humid lowlands of South America reach their northern range limits here, including Great Potoo, Broad-billed Motmot, and Long-tailed Tyrant. Although highly biodiverse and harboring some of the region's richest local bird communities, the Caribbean slope has less pronounced endemism in comparison with the south Central American highlands.

Pacific slope humid lowlands and foothills In east Costa Rica and extreme west Panama, the otherwise dry Pacific slope is interrupted by a region with relatively high rainfall and hosting an extensive area of humid broadleaf forest that is not continuous with the more extensive humid forests of the Caribbean slope and east Panama. Much of this forest has been lost to agricultural conversion (with very little remaining in west Panama), but Corcovado National Park on Costa Rica's Osa Peninsula protects a relatively large block of intact forest. Several endemic species are confined to this region, including Fiery-billed Aracari, Riverside Wren, and Black-cheeked Ant-Tanager. The Central American endemic Yellow-billed Cotinga and Mangrove Hummingbird are confined mainly to mangroves that are found locally along the coast here.

South Central American highlands A nearly continuous highland area extends from the Cordillera de Tilarán in west Costa Rica to the Cordillera de Tabasará in central Panama and reaches a maximum elevation of 3800 m in the Cordillera de Talamanca in east Costa Rica. Potential vegetation is mainly humid broadleaf forest or "cloud forest," with elfin forest found locally at higher elevations, and very small areas of paramo confined to the highest peaks in east Costa Rica.

These mountains first began to form as a chain of islands roughly 11 mybp, long before the closing of the land connection with South America (see below), and they were further uplifted later in the Miocene. This early isolation, as well as more recent cycles of expansion and contraction of highland forests in response to climatic change, is thought to have driven diversification by periodically isolating montane forest birds in so-called sky islands. Warmer periods saw a reduction of highland vegetation and the avifauna associated with it, driving diversification and creating the fragmented distributions and endemism seen today in south Central America's highland birds. Colder conditions promoted more continuous highland forests and associated bird communities, and also favored dispersal to the area by bird lineages from the Andes in South America and from North America. In addition, the formation of the Talamancas may have driven diversification in adjacent lowlands by altering local climate and by dividing populations of lowland species on the Caribbean and Pacific slopes.

Today, the south Central American highlands host the highest concentration of endemic bird species in the region, including representatives of both mainly northern (North American) and southern (Andean) lineages. These include no fewer than 8 endemic genera and 39 endemic species. Among them are highly distinctive forms including Prong-billed Barbet, Peg-billed Finch, and Wrenthrush. Some resident breeding species found in the south Central American highlands are shared between this region and the north Central American highlands, and a smaller number are shared with the Darién highlands of east Panama, but the region is most notable for its concentration of endemic bird species. Small areas of paramo in the Talamancas support the endemic Volcano Junco and Volcano Hummingbird. The Cordillera de Tabasará, lying near the easternmost extension of the south Central American highlands in the Panamanian province of Veraguas, hosts a smaller set of poorly known and range-restricted taxa that include Glow-throated Hummingbird and Yellow-green Finch.

South Pacific slope arid lowlands and foothills A relatively dry area extends from the Valle General in interior east Costa Rica, through central Panama, and includes the lowlands of the Azuero Peninsula. The landscape here is widely modified for agriculture and grazing, and very little of the semi-deciduous forests that once dominated there now remain. There are no endemic bird species confined to the region, but several species that are found in open or disturbed habitats, and are widespread in South America, reach their northwestern distributional limits here. These include Ocellated Crake, Savanna Hawk, Bran-colored Flycatcher, and Yellowish Pipit.

Isla Coiba Located off the southwest coast of the Azuero Peninsula in Panama, Isla Coiba is the largest Central American island. Several smaller islands are nearby. Isla Coiba is largely undisturbed and hosts an extensive area of humid broadleaf forest. Maximum elevation is 416 m. One endemic species, Coiba Spinetail, and more than a dozen endemic subspecies are confined to the island. The Central American endemic Brown-backed Dove is common on the island, and some forest-dependent species that were formerly more widespread on the mainland persist here, including Harpy Eagle and Scarlet Macaw.

Azuero highlands Much of the Azuero Peninsula in Panama is composed of arid lowlands, but an isolated foothill and highland region in the south of the peninsula reaches a maximum elevation near 1600 m at Cerro Hoya and hosts a remote and isolated area of humid broadleaf forest. Many widespread highland and humid forest species occur here in isolated populations, including Scaly-throated Leaftosser, Red-capped Manakin, and Shining Honeycreeper. The Central American endemic Azuero Parakeet is found only in this region, and the area may yet prove to hold other endemic bird species.

East Panama highlands A set of isolated mountaintops and ridgelines in east Panama reach a maximum elevation of 2300 meters and support small areas of humid broadleaf (cloud) forest at higher elevations. These include the Serrannia del Darién stretching from Cerro Azul in Panamá Province to the Tacarcuna Massif on the Colombian border, the Serrania de Majé, the Pirre Massif, and Cerro Jungurudó and Cerro Sapo. Higher elevations in these mountains hold a set of endemic species that include Pirre Hummingbird, Beautiful Treerunner, and Pirre Chlorospingus. Several mainly South American foothill and highland species reach their northernmost distributional limits here, including Tooth-billed Hummingbird, Golden-headed Quetzal, and Sharp-tailed Streamcreeper.

East Panama lowlands and foothills Prior to the emergence of the present-day land connection between North and South America, these continents were separated for much of their histories and their avifaunas evolved in isolation. The connection through the Central American isthmus is thought to have formed about 3 to 4 mybp, and this event began a process with unprecedented ecological and evolutionary consequences for the previously isolated avifaunas of both continents. Though the precise date and details are somewhat uncertain, it is clear that the formation of this relatively small land area profoundly affected the global distribution and diversity of birds (and other groups) by enabling them to extend their distributions in both directions. Some bird (and other animal) groups invaded southward from North America and ultimately diversified in South America, and other groups moved north into Central and North America, an event referred to as the Great American Biotic Interchange (GABI). While the GABI is best known for its profound impact on the distributions of land mammals, its role as a driver of diversification in birds, a group with greater dispersal abilities, was probably both more complex and perhaps also more attenuated, as some bird lineages may have dispersed across the narrowing water gap and diversified in isolation while the land-bridge was still incomplete. Further complicating the role of the GABI in shaping the Central American avifauna is evidence that the region simultaneously underwent dramatic changes in climate with alternating periods of high and low humidity. These cycles likely favored dispersion at different times by birds associated with dry or humid habitats and contributed to the assembly of a rich avifauna through a complex or "compound" history.

Today, the lowlands and foothills of east Panama host extensive areas of humid broadleaf forest, and much of this is protected in Darién National Park and in several indigenous zones. Many South American species reach their northern distributional limits here, and many of these are shared with the Choco region on the Pacific slope of northern South America, including the range-restricted and highly distinctive Black-crowned Antpitta, Sapayoa, and Speckled Antshrike. Many forest-dependent species that are now scarce in other parts of Central America persist here, including Crested and Harpy eagles, *Ara* macaws, and Rufous-vented Ground-Cuckoo. In some areas, recent human settlement and local forest loss appears to have enabled invasions by nonforest South American species such as Bicolored Wren.

Pearl Islands Located in the Gulf of Panama, the Pearl Islands have a semiarid climate and habitats include littoral scrub and semi-deciduous forest. An endemic subspecies of White-fringed Antwren, a species found nowhere else in Central America, is confined to Isla San José, Isla Pedro González, and Isla Rey, and is among 16 endemic subspecies described from these islands. Colonial waterbirds nest locally here including Blue-footed Booby.

Species Accounts

TINAMOUS Tinamidae

Short-tailed, terrestrial birds. Tinamous are found mainly in humid broadleaf forest. They are sensitive to hunting pressure and can be difficult to see as they quickly walk away at the approach of an observer. In less humid areas, tinamous can sometimes be located by the scratching sound produced as they walk over dry leaf litter. Most are detected by voice. Great Tinamou is the most common and widespread.

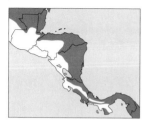

Great Tinamou *Tinamus major* 44 cm

South MX to SA. Fairly common resident in lowlands and foothills (to 1800 m). Confined to Caribbean slope in north. **ID** Largest CA tinamou. *Gray legs* and white throat. Mostly brownish barred with dusky on upperparts and flanks. Grayish below with fine barring on flanks. Compare with smaller Little Tinamou. Note different leg color. **GV** Birds from Pacific east CR and west PA have chestnut-brown crown. Birds from east PA (Darién) have distinct crest. **HABITS** Floor of semihumid to humid broadleaf forest. Most often detected by voice during early morning or dusk. Sometimes calls from elevated roost site. Individuals, pairs, or small groups can be located by listening for rustling sounds produced as they forage or walk in dry leaf litter. **VOICE** Call (1) among the characteristic sounds of humid lowland forests, is two to four paired, long, tremulous whistles. First note usually slightly lower-pitched and sometimes repeated two or three times. Second note drops in pitch. Compare with Little Tinamou.

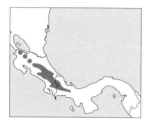

Highland Tinamou *Nothocercus bonapartei* 40 cm

CA and north SA. Uncommon to rare resident in foothills and highlands (above 1200 m) of CR (126, 570, 602, 600) and west PA (89, 657, 512). **ID** Fairly large. *Legs gray. Crown and sides of head dark gray.* Underparts cinnamon, becoming brightest on throat and belly, and narrowly and sparsely barred with dusky. Dark rufous-brown above with fine blackish vermiculations and variable *buff spotting on wings.* Some have buff spotting extending to rump and mantle. Compare with larger Great Tinamou (mainly lower elevations). Note different upperparts and voice. **HABITS** Floor of humid broadleaf forest and adjacent tall second growth. Solitary or in pairs. Secretive and rarely seen. Most often detected by voice. **VOICE** Very different from other CA tinamous. Call (1) a short, hoarse, low-pitched, resonant *huh-wowr* or *unh-heer.* Sometimes repeated steadily.

28%

**Great
Tinamou**

widespread
brown morph

Pacific CR
and west PA

east PA

widespread
typical morph

**Highland
Tinamou**

TINAMOUS Tinamidae

Small tinamous. Observers glimpsing these furtive birds should note leg color and extent of barring on the upperparts. Like other tinamous, their distinctive vocalizations are the best clue to their presence. Females are more brightly colored and more boldly patterned than males. Little Tinamou is the most common and widespread.

Little Tinamou *Crypturellus soui*   23 cm

South MX to SA. Fairly common resident in lowlands and foothills (to 1500 m). Confined to Caribbean slope in north. Also Pearl Islands (Panamá, 58, 611). More common in foothills than Great Tinamou. **ID** Smallest CA tinamou. *Legs dull olive-yellow.* Mostly plain, *uniform brown* (no or little barring) becoming more rufous on rump and tail, whitish on throat, and grayer on head. Some birds are more grayish-brown overall. Female brighter brown, especially below. Leg color and plain pattern distinguish this from other CA tinamous. **HABITS** Floor of semihumid to humid broadleaf forest, tall second growth, shaded plantations, and gallery forest. Widespread in north. Mainly in second growth in south. Walks quietly on ground. Solitary or in pairs. Reclusive. **VOICE** Calls include (1) a series of clear, successively higher-pitched, tremulous whistles that accelerate and increase in volume and usually end abruptly, and (2) a long, tremulous whistle that rises then drops in pitch like Great Tinamou. Less resonant than calls of Great Tinamou.

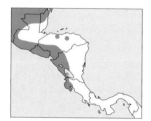

Thicket Tinamou *Crypturellus cinnamomeus*   28 cm

South MX and CA. Uncommon to locally common resident in lowlands and foothills (to 1500 m). Confined mainly to Yucatán region and Pacific slope. Also Aguán and Agalta valleys in north HN (Yoro, Olancho, 442). **ID** *Bold buff barring on upperparts and flanks.* Note reddish legs. Extensively rufous-cinnamon. Female more boldly barred. Variable, but always more boldly patterned than other CA tinamous. Compare with Slaty-breasted Tinamou. Note different habits. **HABITS** Floor of arid to semihumid broadleaf forest, second growth, gallery forest, scrub, pine savanna, and thorn forest. Walks quietly over leaf litter. Shy and retiring (even in comparison to other tinamous) and notably difficult to glimpse. Solitary or in pairs. **VOICE** Call (1) a short, low-pitched, hollow whistle *hoo-oop* or *ooop*. Call often two-syllabled, but may sound like a single note at a distance.

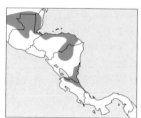

Slaty-breasted Tinamou *Crypturellus boucardi*   28 cm

South MX and CA. Uncommon to locally fairly common resident in Caribbean lowlands and foothills (to 1200 m). **ID** Mostly *gray head, neck, and breast.* Note *reddish legs.* Female has more obvious blackish and buff barring on upperparts and flanks. Barred female similar to Thicket Tinamou but somewhat darker above and grayer below. Note different habits. Choco Tinamou allopatric. **HABITS** Floor of semihumid to humid broadleaf forest and adjacent tall second growth. Secretive like other *Crypturellus* tinamous. Solitary or in pairs. **VOICE** Call (1) a long, hollow, low-pitched *whoo-oo-ooo*. Compare with call of White-tipped Dove.

Choco Tinamou *Crypturellus kerriae*   26 cm

CA and SA. Uncommon resident in foothills (300 to 750 m) of east PA. Reported from cerros Quía, Sambú, Jacqué, upper Río Tuira, and Pirre Massif (Darién, 658, 659, 512, 45). **ID** Small and *dark.* Note *reddish legs.* Head blackish (or slate-gray). Sides of head slate-gray. Otherwise mostly warm dark brown above with indistinct cinnamon barring. Throat white. Remaining underparts dull cinnamon. Resembles allopatric Slaty-breasted Tinamou but Choco is darker and more richly colored below. Compare with Little Tinamou. Note different leg color and upperparts. **HABITS** Floor of humid broadleaf forest. Poorly known. Presumably like other *Crypturellus* tinamous. **VOICE** Call (1) a low-pitched, two-syllable, tremulous whistle *who-oo-ooow*. Much like Slaty-breasted Tinamou.

**Little
Tinamou**

♂

♀

**Thicket
Tinamou**

♂

♀

**Slaty-breasted
Tinamou**

♂

♀

**Choco
Tinamou**

♂

♀

WHISTLING-DUCKS, GOOSE, AND DUCKS Anatidae

A diverse group of waterfowl. Whistling-ducks sometimes perch in trees and fly with long neck held low and long legs projecting beyond tail. Black-bellied Whistling-Duck is the most common and widespread.

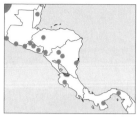

Fulvous Whistling-Duck *Dendrocygna bicolor* 47 cm

Cosmopolitan. Irregular resident in lowlands of GT (Santa Rosa, Retalhuleu, San Marcos, 229, 608), BZ (Belize, Orange Walk, Toledo, 433, 343), SV (San Miguel, Santa Ana, 619), HN (Santa Bárbara, Choluteca, 442), and NI (Matagalpa, Jinotega, Managua, Granada, 419, 420). First reported in CR in 1975 (Guanacaste, Puntarenas, 601) and in PA in 1936 (Panamá, 286) where confirmed breeding (Herrera, Coclé, 41, 42). **ID** Bill and legs gray. *Underparts tawny* with whitish streaks on neck and broad, creamy white stripes on sides and flanks. Ad has rufous edging on upperparts. In flight, *uniform dark wings* contrast with paler buff body and conspicuous white vent and uppertail coverts. Juv (Jun to Nov) has gray edging on upperparts. Compare with Black-bellied Whistling-Duck. **HABITS** Marshes, lagoons, and lake margins. Usually in flocks. May associate with other waterfowl. Sometimes active at night. **VOICE** Often calls in flight. Call (1) a slightly hoarse or buzzy, two-syllable *chee-hee* or *chi-heahw* sometimes with stuttering or chattering introduction *ch-ch-ch che-hew.*

White-faced Whistling-Duck *Dendrocygna viduata* 41 cm

Pantropical. Formerly resident in Pacific lowlands of CR (Guanacaste, 126, 281, 570, 601) and PA (Veraguas, Panamá, 657, 152, 41). Extirpated. **ID** Relatively small. Bill black. Ad has *white sides of head, forehead, and crown* contrasting with black hindcrown and neck (some with white patch on foreneck). Lower neck and breast rufous. Otherwise mostly brown with fine, pale gray barring on flanks and sides of breast. Lower underparts black. In flight, shows plain, all-dark upperwing. Juv mostly gray with buff sides of head. **HABITS** Marshes, lagoons and lake margins. **VOICE** Call (1) a rapid, high-pitched *whee-hee-heeu* with last note downslurred.

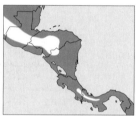

Black-bellied Whistling-Duck *Dendrocygna autumnalis* 45 cm

MX to SA. Locally or seasonally common resident in lowlands. Perhaps increasing. **ID** Bill and legs pink. *Black lower underparts* and *whitish eye ring*. Mostly reddish-brown with grayish sides of head and upper neck. In flight, shows *broad white wing-band*. Juv has gray bill and legs and duller, mottled plumage. Compare with Fulvous Whistling-Duck. Note different underparts and head pattern. **GV** Birds from central and east PA (not shown) have variably gray lower breast. **HABITS** Marshes, lagoons, lake edges, and flooded agricultural fields. Forages mainly at night. Unlike other whistling-ducks, often perches in trees, especially on dead branches. May gather in large flocks. **VOICE** Often calls in flight. Calls (1) a loud, slightly squeaky *cheee-hew wheeeoow* and (2) single *cheeeow* or *cheee.*

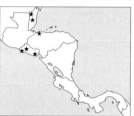

Snow Goose *Chen caerulescens* 70 cm

Breeds Nearctic. Very rare winter visitor (Oct to Feb) to BZ (Orange Walk, Belize, Cayo, 313, 348, 346), SV (La Libertad, Usulután, Ahuachapán, 341, 301), and HN (Cortés, 442). **ID** Large. *White* with *black primaries*. Bill and legs pink. Scarce dark morph mostly gray with white head. **HABITS** Lagoons, ponds, marshes, and agricultural fields. Typically gregarious and forms large flocks on main wintering grounds. CA reports are mostly single birds loosely associated with other waterfowl. **VOICE** Gives (1) hoarse or nasal honking cries.

Muscovy Duck *Cairina moschata* female 60, male 80 cm

MX to SA. Uncommon and local resident in lowlands and foothills. **ID** Large with short legs. *Mostly glossy black* with slight, bushy crest. Ad male has fleshy red carbuncles over eye and at base of bill. Note *white upperwing coverts* and mostly *white undersurface of wing* (conspicuous in flight). Ad female smaller with less red on bill and face and lacks crest. Imm uniform black. In flight, compare with Black-bellied Whistling-Duck. Note different wing pattern. **HABITS** Wooded swamps, river margins, lagoons, and marshes. Shy and retiring. May perch in trees. Solitary or in pairs. Gathers in small flocks at favored foraging areas during dry season. May associate with Black-bellied Whistling-Ducks. Widely domesticated. **VOICE** Calls (1) a series of short, barklike cries *whuk* or *woc* and (2) a short, slightly hoarse *uhr* or *owr.*

Comb Duck *Sarkidiornis melanotos* female 53, male 65 cm

Pantropical. Very rare vagrant with recent records from lowlands of CR (Guanacaste, 187) and historical records from east PA (Panamá, Darién, 650, 657). All records from Mar. **ID** Large. Wings and upperparts mostly iridescent black. Underparts white. Head and neck flecked with black. Ad male has *black protuberance on culmen*. Feathers on head recurved to form slight crest. Female is smaller, has paler flanks and lacks ad male's comb. **HABITS** Wooded swamps, lagoons, ponds, rivers, and marshes. Solitary or in pairs. May associate with other waterfowl. **VOICE** Call (1) a short, low-pitched *errrt.*

15%

Fulvous Whistling-Duck

ad

White-faced Whistling-Duck

ad

Black-bellied Whistling-Duck

imm

ad

Snow Goose

light morph

dark morph

imm

♀

Muscovy Duck

♂

♀

♀

Comb Duck

♀

♂

DUCKS Anatidae

Nearctic breeding migrant ducks. Found almost exclusively on freshwater ponds and lakes. *Anas* ducks typically forage by tipping. Blue-winged Teal is the most common and widespread.

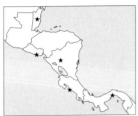

Mallard *Anas platyrhynchos*   60 cm

Holarctic. Rare vagrant to BZ (Cayo, 345, 343), SV (Usulután, 301), CR (Cartago, Puntarenas, 570, 346), and PA (Panamá, 337, 512, 48). **ID** *Orange legs and feet*. Male has *dark green head* and *narrow white collar*. Bill yellow. Female mottled brownish. Note blue wing speculum bordered on both sides with white. Female's bill dusky and orange. **HABITS** Marshes, lakes, lagoons, flooded agricultural fields, and wetlands. Most records of single birds. May associate with other waterfowl. **VOICE** Call (1) a nasal *ahk-ahk-ahk, ahk*.

Northern Pintail *Anas acuta*   female 60, male 70 cm

Holarctic. Nearctic birds winter south USA to WI and CA. Uncommon transient and winter resident in north (Sep to May). Rare in east PA (Panamá, Colón, 206, 512, 41, 346). **ID** *Long, slender neck*. Male has *long, pointed tail*. Note white trailing edge of wing and blue-gray bill. Breeding male (Nov to Jun) has *brown head with narrow white stripe on neck*. Otherwise mostly pale gray. Central underparts white with contrasting black crissum. In flight, male shows green wing speculum. Female is mottled with brown and has shorter, pointed tail. Note female's plain buffy brown head and bill color. **HABITS** Marshes, lakes, lagoons, and wetlands. Most records of single birds or small groups, but may associate with other waterfowl. **VOICE** Call (1) a nasal, rolling *wirrr-k*.

Green-winged Teal *Anas crecca*   36 cm

Holarctic. Nearctic birds winter mainly USA to WI and MX. Rare winter visitor (Nov to Mar) to BZ (Belize, 72, 346), GT (Alta Verapaz, Retalhuleu, Jutiapa, Santa Rosa, 229, 550, 608), SV (Cuscatlán, Chalatenango, La Paz, 619, 346), HN (Choluteca, Cortés, Yoro, 346), NI (RAAN, 413), CR including Isla del Coco (Cartago, Guanacaste, San José, 602, 346, 546, 329), and PA (Herrera, Panamá, 341, 48). **ID** Small with small bill. *Legs gray*. In flight, whitish belly contrasts with gray flanks. Breeding male (Oct to Jun) has *mostly rufous head with green mask*. Female mottled brown and lacks whitish forecheek. Compare female with female Blue-winged Teal. Note different head pattern, leg color, and forewing. **HABITS** Marshes, freshwater ponds and lakes, and flooded agricultural fields. Most records of single birds. May associate with other waterfowl. **VOICE** Male gives (1) a hollow, piping *chrriik* or *krriip*. Female (2) a short, lower-pitched, nasal *ehh*.

Blue-winged Teal *Spatula discors*   38 cm

Breeds Nearctic. Winters USA to north SA. Common transient and winter resident (mainly Aug to May). Locally abundant on Pacific slope. **ID** Small. Bill dark gray. *Pale blue wing coverts* obvious in flight, but usually concealed while swimming. *Legs yellow*. Breeding male has dark gray head with *crescent-shaped white mark on face*. Otherwise mostly golden-brown, densely vermiculated and spotted with blackish. On male, note white mark on flanks and black crissum. Female mostly mottled brown with whitish forecheek and distinct dark eye stripe. **HABITS** Lake margins, marshes, and flooded agricultural fields. May form large flocks and joins mixed associations of waterfowl. Flies in compact flocks with weaving, twisting style. **VOICE** Male's call (1) a reedy *pseep* or *wseep*. May be repeated. Female gives (2) lower-pitched, nasal *ehh-eh*.

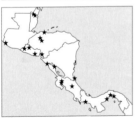

Cinnamon Teal *Spatula cyanoptera*   39 cm

Breeds west NA and disjunctly in SA. Nearctic birds winter mainly MX. Rare visitor (Nov to Feb) in BZ (Orange Walk, Belize, 625, 347, 346), GT (Retalhuleu, 229), SV (Santa Ana, San Miguel, Cuscatlán, La Libertad, La Paz, 301, 346), HN (Atlántida, Cortés, 442, 262), NI (Río San Juan, Managua, 90, 413), CR (Guanacaste, 601, 574, 600), and PA (Panamá, 48). **ID** Small. Legs yellow. Breeding male (Oct to Jun) *mostly chestnut* with black rump and crissum. *Eyes red*. In flight, both sexes show pale blue wing coverts and green wing speculum lacking white trailing border. Female very similar to female Blue-winged Teal but slightly tawnier overall, with less distinct head markings and slightly larger bill. **HABITS** Like Blue-winged Teal. **VOICE** Like Blue-winged Teal.

Northern Shoveler *Spatula clypeata*   49 cm

Holarctic. Nearctic birds winter NA to WI and CA. Uncommon transient and winter resident (mainly Oct to Apr). Rare in PA (512, 346). **ID** *Long, spatulate bill*. In flight, note *pale bluish wing coverts* (grayer in female) divided from green speculum by white stripe. Male has dark green head and neck and white breast. Note male's yellow eyes. Flanks rufous with white patch on rear. In flight, note male's contrasting dark belly. Female mottled brown. No duck has similar bill shape. In flight, compare with Blue-winged Teal. **HABITS** Marshes, freshwater ponds and lakes, and flooded agricultural fields. **VOICE** Usually quiet. Calls include (1) a chattering, nasal *quee-quee-guee . . .* and (2) *chee-up chee-chee chee* etc.

Mallard

♀

breeding ♂

♀

non-breeding ♂

Northern Pintail

breeding ♂

♀

♀

Green-winged Teal

♀

♀

breeding ♂

Blue-winged Teal

♀

♀

breeding ♂

Cinnamon Teal

♀

♀

breeding ♂

Northern Shoveler

♀

non-breeding ♂

♀

breeding ♂

DUCKS Anatidae

Nearctic breeding migrant ducks. Head shape and pattern are useful in separating female *Aythya* ducks.

American Wigeon *Mareca americana*   50 cm
Breeds Nearctic. Winters NA to CA. Locally fairly common but irregular transient and winter visitor (Oct to Apr). Most common on Pacific slope. Uncommon to rare in BZ (Orange Walk, Belize, 345). **ID** Mostly pinkish-brown. *Small bill blue-gray with black tip.* Breeding male's (Oct to Jun) *white forehead and crown* contrast with *dark green facial mask.* Female and nonbreeding male duller with speckled crown and plain brown flanks. In flight, note white belly and center of underwing. Upperwing shows broad white patch on coverts. **HABITS** Marshes, freshwater ponds, lakes, and flooded agricultural fields. May associate with other waterfowl. Often forages by grazing on grassy areas or mudflats. **VOICE** Call (1) a whistled *whee whee whew.*

Lesser Scaup *Aythya affinis*   40 cm
Breeds Nearctic. Winters USA to WI and CA. Uncommon and local transient and winter resident in north (mainly Nov to Mar). **ID** Rounded head and broad, mostly plain, gray bill. In flight, shows white stripe in secondaries. Breeding male (Nov to Jun) has black head, neck, and chest (shows purple gloss in good light). Tail, rump, and crissum also blackish. Otherwise mostly grayish (becoming paler below). Female mostly plain dark brownish becoming darker above with distinct white patch at base of bill. Nonbreeding male has dusky or brownish flanks. Compare with Ring-necked Duck. Note different head shape and mantle color in ad male and different bill and head pattern in other plumages. Also compare female with female Redhead. Note different head and bill pattern. **HABITS** Open water of large lakes, rivers, and lagoons. May form large flocks at favored sites. Dives frequently. Rests and forages mainly on deep water. Rarely seen perched on muddy edges. **VOICE** Usually quiet.

Ring-necked Duck *Aythya collaris*   43 cm
Breeds Nearctic. Winters USA to WI and CA. Uncommon and local transient and winter resident (mainly Oct to Apr). **ID** *Peaked head shape. Bill mostly bluish-gray with transverse white band and black tip.* Breeding male (Oct to Jun) has black head and neck (glossed purple in good light). Chest and mantle black divided from gray flanks by *white vertical mark in front of wing.* Female and juv mostly grayish-brown (darkest on crown and back) with prominent whitish area at base of bill and *narrow whitish eye ring and postocular stripe.* Nonbreeding male similar but has brownish flanks. Compare with Lesser Scaup. Male has different head shape, darker mantle, and different bill pattern. Female differs from similar species in having relatively strong whitish eye ring and postocular streak and dark brownish mantle contrasting more strongly with paler flanks. **HABITS** Open waters of lagoons, lakes, and estuaries. Wintering birds form flocks. Dives frequently. Rarely seen perched on muddy edges. **VOICE** Usually quiet.

Redhead *Aythya americana*   47 cm
Breeds Nearctic. Winters mainly USA and MX. Rare winter visitor (Oct to Apr) to GT (Alta Verapaz, Sololá, 229, 378, 318), BZ (Orange Walk), SV (San Miguel, 341), HN (Cortés, 346), NI (413), and CR (Guanacaste, 264, 543, 346). **ID** Bill bluish-gray with black tip. *Rounded head shape.* Breeding male (Oct to Jun) has *chestnut-red head.* Note *gray flanks and mantle* contrasting with black breast and rump. Nonbreeding male has near-uniform brown mantle and flanks. Female and juv (Aug to Oct) mostly warm brown with variable faint pale eye stripe, pale eye ring, and diffuse pale face. Compare female with females of Ring-necked Duck and Lesser Scaup. Note Redhead's plain head showing only faint whitish forecheek, eye ring, and postocular stripe and lack of contrast between flanks and mantle. **HABITS** Open water of large lakes and lagoons. **VOICE** Wintering birds usually quiet.

Red-breasted Merganser *Mergus serrator*   57 cm
Holarctic. Nearctic birds winter mainly NA. Very rare vagrant to BZ (Belize, Toledo, 345, 346) and SV (San Miguel, 341). **ID** *Long, thin, red bill* and swept-back crest. Breeding male (Nov to May) has dark green head contrasting with white neck-band. Breast tawny with blackish speckling. In flight, note mostly white inner portion of wing contrasting with dark tips. Nonbreeding male and female mostly gray with *orange-rusty head.* **HABITS** Open waters of lakes and lagoons. Dives frequently while foraging. Usually seen swimming. Rarely perches on muddy edges. **VOICE** Usually silent.

♀

breeding ♂

♀

American Wigeon

breeding ♂

♀

Lesser Scaup

♀

breeding ♂

♀

♀

breeding ♂

Ring-necked Duck

♀

♀

breeding ♂

Redhead

♀

breeding ♂

Red-breasted Merganser

♀

breeding ♂

DUCKS Anatidae

Ruddy and Masked ducks have long tails that are sometimes held cocked.

Ruddy Duck *Oxyura jamaicensis* 41 cm

NA to SA. Rare and local breeder in GT (Alta Verapaz, Sololá, 229, 279, 539). Nearctic birds winter mainly USA to CA. Uncommon and local winter visitor to north Pacific. Rare in BZ (Belize, Toledo, 346), HN (Yoro, 442, 346), NI (Matagalpa, Chontales, León, 413, 346), and CR (Guanacaste, Cartago, Alajuela, 346, 543). **ID** Breeding male mostly plain chestnut with plain blue bill. Crown and nape black, contrasting with *white face, auriculars, and throat.* Nonbreeding male has similar pattern with dusky crown and white face, auriculars, and throat. Female has *whitish sides of head divided by single dark line.* Female's dark crown extends below eye (no pale supercilium). In flight, note all-dark upper wing. **HABITS** Open water of lakes and lagoons. Dives frequently. Usually in flocks. **VOICE** Usually quiet.

Masked Duck *Nomonyx dominicus* 34 cm

South USA to SA. Uncommon to rare and local resident in BZ (Belize, Cayo, 313, 343), GT (Petén, 229), GT/SV border (619, 227), SV (San Miguel, 619), HN (Cortés, Francisco Morazán, Choluteca, Olancho, 442, 346), NI (Granada, Jinotega, Matagalpa, 412), CR (Guanacaste, Alajuela, Puntarenas, 474), and PA (Chiriquí, Panamá, Colón, 657, 48, 346). **ID** Breeding male (Jun to Oct) has blue bill with black tip and is mostly chestnut with *black streaking and spotting on mantle and flanks* and *black head.* Nonbreeding male has *pale sides of head crossed by two dark stripes.* Note pale supercilium. Female resembles nonbreeding male but is browner. In flight, shows white on secondaries. Compare with Ruddy Duck. Note different habits and head pattern. **HABITS** Freshwater marshes and ponds with emergent or floating vegetation. Reclusive. Often swims low in water. In pairs or small groups. **VOICE** Song (1) a long, slurred, hollow, low-pitched note followed by two shorter notes *oooo, ood-oo* or *kir-rooo, kirroo-kiroo.* Female gives (2) a short, repeated hiss.

GREBES Podicipedidae

Grebes are small aquatic birds that may swim low in the water, often with only the head and neck visible. Least Grebe is the most common and widespread.

Pied-billed Grebe *Podilymbus podiceps* female 31, male 34 cm

NA to SA. Nearctic breeding and resident birds thought to occur (619). Uncommon and very local breeder, transient, and winter resident in lowlands and foothills. **ID** *Short, stout bill* (whitish with vertical black bar in breeding ad). Eyes dark. Ad grayish-brown becoming somewhat paler below, with black throat (in breeding plumage) and white crissum. Nonbreeding ad has whitish throat and variably plain, dull yellowish bill. Dimorphic with males larger. Least Grebe has different bill shape and eye color. **HABITS** Ponds and lakes with emergent or floating vegetation. Uses open or deep water more than Least Grebe. May swim partly submerged with only head and neck exposed. Solitary or in pairs. **VOICE** Call (1) typically a series of loud, hoarse notes that drop in pitch *cuk-cuk, cuk-cuk, cukcuk, cow-cow-cow.* Also (2) a repeated *cah-cow, cah-cow . . .* Compare with call of Least Bittern.

Atitlan Grebe *Podilymbus gigas* female 46, male 50 cm

CA endemic. Formerly an uncommon and local resident at Lago Atitlán, GT (Sololá, 276, 647, 102, 103). Extinct since 1980s (290, 333, 252). **ID** Like Pied-billed Grebe but with relatively deeper, heavier bill. Also similar in plumage, but Atitlan Grebe darker and grayer with more extensive black on throat and nape. Larger than Pied-billed, but dimorphic with smaller female close in size to male Pied-billed Grebe. **HABITS** Like Pied-billed Grebe. **VOICE** Calls lower-pitched than Pied-billed Grebe.

Least Grebe *Tachybaptus dominicus* 22 cm

NA, WI, and SA. Uncommon to locally fairly common resident (to 1600 m). **ID** Small with *pale eyes* and *fine, pointed bill.* Breeding ad has black bill and blackish cap and throat. Sides of head and neck sooty gray. Nonbreeding ad has dull yellowish mandible, paler gray neck and sides of head, and whitish throat. Juv has whitish throat and brown stripes on sides of head and neck. In flight, shows white wing patch. Compare with Pied-billed Grebe. **HABITS** Ponds, lakes, marshes. Solitary or in pairs. Hides in vegetation at edges of (sometimes very small) bodies of freshwater. Dives frequently and for long periods. **VOICE** Calls (1) a short, harsh *tsew* or *tsii* that may be repeated, (2) a long, crake-like rattle on steady pitch, and (3) coarse *kwrek* and *eh kehr.*

Eared Grebe *Podiceps nigricollis* 31 cm

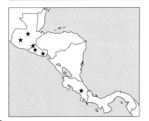

Holarctic. Nearctic birds winter mainly USA and MX. Rare winter visitor (Nov to Apr) to GT (227) and SV (619, 301). **ID** *Steep, peaked forehead.* Note *sharp, slightly upturned bill.* Eyes red. Nonbreeding ad mostly dusky gray with blackish crown and auriculars and whitish crescent extending behind auriculars. Breeding ad (Apr to Sep, not shown) mostly blackish with yellow facial plumes. In flight, shows white patch on wing. Compare with Pied-billed Grebe. Note different head pattern, structure, and habits. **HABITS** Open water of bays, lakes, and estuaries. May form small flocks. Dives frequently and for long periods. **VOICE** Usually quiet.

♀

Ruddy Duck

breeding ♂

nonbreeding ♂

♀

♀

Masked Duck

breeding ♂

nonbreeding ♂

♀

Pied-billed Grebe

juv

nonbreeding ad

breeding

Atitlan Grebe

ad

Least Grebe

juv

nonbreeding ♂

breeding ♀

Eared Grebe

nonbreeding ad

CHACHALACAS AND GUAN Cracidae

Chachalacas are long-tailed, arboreal birds with small, red dewlap. Frequently seen in groups that fly single-file across gaps making long glides. Often noisy. Groups call in chorus (mainly at dawn). Most are allopatric, though White-bellied and Plain chachalacas may be locally syntopic. Crested Guan is a large, arboreal species confined to regions with extensive humid broadleaf forest.

Plain Chachalaca *Ortalis vetula*   53 cm
South Texas to north CA. Fairly common resident in lowlands and foothills (mainly below 1500, locally to 2200 m). Uncommon to rare and local on Pacific slope in SV (Santa Ana, 494) and Nicoya Peninsula, CR (Guanacaste, 570, 574). Also Isla Útila and Roatán in Bay Islands (94, 442, 559). **ID** Plain grayish-brown becoming paler and more buff below. Small patch of bare red skin on throat. Note narrow buff terminal band on tail. Plain may be locally syntopic with White-bellied on Pacific slope. **GV** Birds from north BZ, as well as those from Bay Islands (not shown), are paler below, especially on crissum. **HABITS** Floor to subcanopy and edge of open or semi-open wooded habitats, including forest edge, plantations, pine savanna, and scrub. In pairs or groups. Vocalizes from elevated perch. Typically seen clambering through foliage, but may forage on ground. **VOICE** Song (1) a loud, percussive series of hoarse cries often given by several birds in chorus *rhaw-paw-haw, rhaw-paw-haw . . .*

White-bellied Chachalaca *Ortalis leucogastra*   48 cm
South MX and CA. Fairly common resident in north Pacific lowlands and foothills (to 1500 m). **ID** Mostly plain grayish-brown with small patch of bare red skin on throat. *Head and neck distinctly gray.* Underparts relatively pale with whitish scaling on breast and *white belly and crissum.* Note white terminal band on tail. Resembles Plain Chachalaca but White-bellied has grayer head and neck and browner breast contrasting with white crissum and belly. **HABITS** Midstory to subcanopy and edge of open or semi-open woodland, forest edge, plantations, and scrub. Usually in pairs or small groups. **VOICE** Groups vocalize in chorus giving (1) a hoarse, rhythmic *kuk uh-ruh, kuk uh-ruh . . .* Thinner and higher-pitched than Plain Chachalaca.

Gray-headed Chachalaca *Ortalis cinereiceps*   53 cm
CA and north SA. Fairly common resident in lowlands and foothills (to 1200 m) from east HN (Gracias a Dios, 401) south to PA. Also Isla San Miguel in Pearl Islands (Panamá, 58). **ID** Mostly plain grayish-brown with small patch of bare red skin on throat. Head and neck distinctly grayish. Note *rufous primaries* (visible in folded wing and conspicuous in flight). **HABITS** Midstory to subcanopy and edge of open or semi-open wooded habitats including forest edge, riparian tangles, plantations, and scrub. Often in pairs but may assemble in groups. Visits fruiting trees. **VOICE** Groups vocalize in chorus producing (1) a cacophony of hoarse, slurred *kloik* or *kleeuk* cries. Also (2) a series of higher-pitched cries *whee-uk, whee-uk, whee-uk . . .*

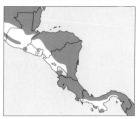

Crested Guan *Penelope purpurascens*   78–94 cm
South MX to north SA. Uncommon and local resident in extensively forested lowlands and foothills (to 1500 m, locally to 2500 m). Historically perhaps more widespread on north Pacific slope in GT (Retalhuleu, Escuintla, Sacatepéquez, 539, 279, 550, 227) and SV (183, 619). **ID** Large with long neck, *short, bushy crest,* and long tail. Prominent bare red throat and dewlap. Mostly dark brown. *Neck and underparts narrowly streaked with white.* At close range note pink legs and bare gray facial skin. Compare with smaller *Ortalis* chachalacas. Note different underparts. Also compare with male Highland Guan. **GV** Birds from north CA (not shown) have variable whitish edging on upperparts and more rufous rump. **HABITS** Subcanopy to canopy of semihumid to humid broadleaf forest. Arboreal. Walks or hops along large limbs. Usually in pairs (less often small groups). May gather in numbers at fruiting trees. **VOICE** Typical call (1) a long series of loud, slightly hoarse, piping notes *pow, pow, pow . . .* or *pleeh pleeh pleeh . . .* that may accelerate briefly and rise slightly in pitch before slowing at end. Also (2) soft whistles *whew* or *who.* Dawn song (3) a loud whistle followed by a lower-pitched growl *ku leerrr!* In gliding display, produces (4) a loud, drumming sonation with wings.

Plain Chachalaca

White-bellied Chachalaca

Gray-headed Chachalaca

Crested Guan

GUANS Cracidae

Large, long-tailed birds found in humid broadleaf forests in highlands. All are range-restricted. Like other members of the family these are sensitive to hunting pressure. Black and Highland guans both produce loud, distinctive sonations as they make long glides between perches in display.

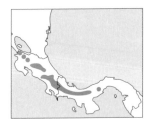

Black Guan *Chamaepetes unicolor*   66 cm

CA endemic. Uncommon to locally fairly common resident in foothills and highlands (above 1000 m) of CR and west PA. **ID** Sexes similar. Medium-sized with plain blackish plumage, red legs, and *blue bare facial skin*. At close range note red or reddish-brown eyes. Highland Guan allopatric. **HABITS** Upper midstory to subcanopy of very humid broadleaf (cloud) forest. Arboreal. Forages by walking or hopping along large tree limbs. Feeds on foliage and fruit. Usually solitary and secretive but can be confiding and easily approached where protected from hunting. **VOICE** Usually quiet. Calls include (1) a low-pitched *ro-rooo*, (2) muffled, groaning *kowr*, and (3) series of ticking notes *tsik tsik tsik* . . . Rarely gives (4) a series of piping cries like Crested Guan but softer and lower-pitched. In display produces (5) a loud, rattling sonation with wings as it glides between perches.

Highland Guan *Penelopina nigra*   62 cm

South MX and north CA. Resident in north highlands (500 to 3000, but mainly above 1000 m). Locally fairly common in GT (229). Uncommon to rare and local in HN and SV (Santa Ana, 503, 619). Recently reported from Cerro Musún in central NI (Matagalpa, 137). **ID** Medium-sized cracid. Legs red. Sexually dimorphic. Male *uniform glossy black* with large red dewlap. Female *mostly rufous, intricately barred and vermiculated with brown*. Black Guan allopatric. Crested Guan can appear very dark, and also has red dewlap. **HABITS** Floor to canopy of humid montane (cloud) forest. Usually solitary. **VOICE** Call in breeding season (1) a loud, clear, upslurred *oooooowheeeeeet*. In male's display this is followed by (2) an abrupt, loud, "crashing" sonation produced with wings as male glides between perches. Alarm call given throughout the year, (3) a long series of two-syllable cries *whi-uh whi-uh-whi-uh* . . . May accelerate to become a loud rattle.

Horned Guan *Oreophasis derbianus*   80 cm

South MX and CA. Uncommon and very local resident in humid highlands (mainly 2000 to 3000 m) of GT (37, 127, 149, 229, 232). **ID** Very large and bulky with small, flat head. Sexes similar. Mostly plain black above with *broad white tail-band* and *bare red horn on crown*. Breast mostly white with *fine black streaks*. Note white eye, red legs, and red bare skin on throat. Imm resembles ad but has smaller horn. **HABITS** Midstory to subcanopy of humid broadleaf (cloud) forest. Rarely or locally in mixed pine-broadleaf forest. Mainly arboreal. Occasionally descends to ground. Generally solitary and reclusive. May gather in numbers at fruiting trees. Sometimes sluggish and may permit an observer to approach closely. **VOICE** In Feb to May male gives (1) a very low-pitched, three- or four-note booming call usually repeated several times per minute *ho hoom ho hoom* . . . Also (2) a two-note *hoo-hoooo*. Alarm call (3) a long series of coarse, croaking notes followed by a downslurred cry *rah rah rah rah . . . oh-whaaaa*.

Black Guan

Highland Guan

♂

♀

Horned Guan

CURASSOW Cracidae

A large, mainly terrestrial bird that is sensitive to hunting pressure and persists mainly in remote or protected areas. Great Curassow has variable female plumage including light, dark and barred morphs.

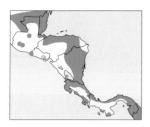

Great Curassow *Crax rubra*   female 82, male 90 cm
South MX to north SA. Locally common to rare resident in extensively forested lowlands and foothills (to 1200 m). Rare, but formerly perhaps more widespread on north Pacific slope in GT (Suchitépequez, 550, 227) and SV (Ahuachapán, 183, 619, 362). **ID** Very large and bulky. Male near-uniform black with rounded crest of recurved feathers and prominent, globular yellow knob on base of culmen. Male has *white lower underparts and crissum*. Female lacks knob and has variable plumage. Typical female mostly rufous-brown with head, neck, and crest barred with black and white and tail barred with buff and brown. Belly buff. Scarce barred morph extensively barred above. Dark morph female has blackish neck. Subad male lacks knob on bill. **HABITS** Floor to subcanopy of broadleaf forest. Mainly terrestrial when foraging. Walks quietly over forest floor, usually in pairs or small groups. Often feeds on fallen fruit. May attend ant swarms. Roosts in trees and sometimes ascends to high perch when disturbed. **VOICE** Male's call (1) a long, extremely low-pitched, booming or humming sound. In south Caribbean foothills compare with call of Bare-necked Umbrellabird. Also (2) a high-pitched, whistle *wheep, wheep, wheeeew* or (3) upslurred *whee-eep?*

TURKEY Phasianidae

Ocellated Turkey is endemic to the Yucatán region. Like Great Curassow, it is found mainly in remote or protected areas.

Ocellated Turkey *Meleagris ocellata*   female 75, male 90 cm
South MX and CA. Uncommon and local resident in lowlands of BZ (Cayo, Orange Walk, 343, 355) and north GT (Petén, 272, 227, 583). Confined mainly to protected areas. Formerly perhaps more widespread. **ID** *Very large* and bulky with long neck and small head. Mostly dark plumage with striking, multicolored iridescence. Head and neck bare, exposing *blue skin with orange wartlike protuberances*. Remiges white with brown bars. Legs reddish. Female smaller and duller. **HABITS** Floor of semihumid broadleaf forest and adjacent clearings and plantations. Mainly terrestrial. Roosts in groups in trees. Often in pairs or groups. Shy and reclusive in most areas, but some local populations (where protected from hunting) can be bold and confiding. **VOICE** Male's call (1) a series of low-pitched, slightly nasal cries that begin slowly and accelerate to become a rattle *puhk, puhk-puhk, puhk . . .* or *puht-puht-puht . . .*

barred morph ♀

dark morph ♀

rufous morph ♀

Great Curassow

♂

breeding ♂

♂

Ocellated Turkey

Displaying male with female

WOOD-PARTRIDGE AND QUAIL Odontophoridae

Reclusive birds found on floor of broadleaf forest and woodland. Voice is important for detection and identification and often provides the only evidence of the bird's presence. When extended views can be obtained, observers should note details of head and underparts pattern.

Buffy-crowned Wood-Partridge *Dendrortyx leucophrys* 33–35 cm

South MX and CA. Locally fairly common resident in north highlands (400 to 3000 m). Also volcanic highlands of SV (San Vicente, San Miguel, Chalatenango, Sonsonate, Morazán, 539, 183, 341). Disjunctly in highlands (1000 to 2800 m) of CR (Alajuela, Cartago, Puntarenas, 126, 570, 600) where uncommon and local. **ID** Large and *long-tailed*. Tail typically held slightly cocked. Note *buffy white forecrown, supercilium, and throat*. Ad has orange-red legs and bare orbital skin and pale eyes. Nape and neck chestnut streaked with white. Juv might suggest an *Odontophorus* wood-quail. Note long tail. Also compare juv with female Singing Quail. **GV** Birds from CR have mostly plain gray underparts. **HABITS** Floor and understory of semihumid to humid pine-oak and humid broadleaf (cloud) forest. Also agricultural areas and plantations with dense hedgerows. Terrestrial. Usually remains hidden beneath brushy understory. Reclusive and usually detected by voice. Usually in pairs. **VOICE** May vocalize in chorus. Song (1) a rapid series of loud, slightly hoarse cries *wuk-cheer-weeuu, wuk-cheer-weeuu, wuk-cheer-weeuu . . .*

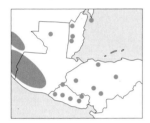

Singing Quail *Dactylortyx thoracicus* 23 cm

MX and north CA. Uncommon to locally common resident in north foothills and highlands (800 to 3000 m). Rare near SL in BZ (Orange Walk, Cayo, 313, 433, 250) and north GT (Petén, 579, 346). Also highlands of SV (San Miguel, Santa Ana, San Vicente, Morazán, 183, 364). **ID** *Black speckled collar* and broad, pale supercilium. Wing coverts and tertials intricately patterned with black, chestnut-brown, and buff. Ad male has *tawny supercilium and throat*. Male's underparts grayish-brown with *fine white streaking*. Ad female has grayish head, whitish throat and supercilium, and dull cinnamon breast with fine whitish streaking. Individually and perhaps geographically variable. Compare female with female Tawny-faced Quail. Note different underparts and habits. Also compare with female Ocellated Quail. Note different habits. **HABITS** Floor of semihumid to humid pine-oak and broadleaf forest. Usually in pairs or small groups. **VOICE** Song (1) begins with accelerating series of quavering *preeeer* notes that gradually become louder, followed by loud, rapid *chi-cheeroweer, chi cheeroweer . . .* or *wheep-cha weeereer, wheep-cha weeereer . . .* repeated three or four times.

Tawny-faced Quail *Rhynchortyx cinctus* 19 cm

CA and north SA. Uncommon to rare and local resident in humid lowlands and foothills (to 750, locally to 1000 m) of HN (Atlántida, Colón, Gracias a Dios, 483, 442, 35), NI (Jinotega, RAAS, 511, 413), north CR (Guanacaste, Alajuela, Heredia, 570, 600, 253), and PA (Colón, Panamá, Kuna Yala, Darién, 67, 350, 512, 522, 42). **ID** Small with heavy bill. Grayish-brown upperparts and wings intricately patterned with black, rufous, and buff. Variable rump may be cool gray or rufous with fine black and buff speckling. Male has *orange-tawny sides of head* with *narrow dark eye stripe*. Male's lower underparts tawny with gray throat and breast. Female mostly brown with *narrow white supercilium* and whitish throat. Female's *plain brown breast* contrasts with *black-and-white barred lower underparts*. **HABITS** Floor of humid broadleaf forest. Usually in pairs, sometimes in groups. Very shy and usually difficult to observe at length. May freeze or flee into dense vegetation when approached. **VOICE** Song (1) a short series of clear, hollow, tinamou-like notes. First two to four notes longer and followed (after a pause) by a more rapid series of two or three shorter, upslurred notes *whooou-whooou-whooou, whoo-whoo*.

juv

north CA
ad

Buffy-crowned Wood-Partridge

CR
ad

Singing Quail   ♀   ♂

Tawny-faced Quail   ♀   ♂

WOOD-QUAIL Odontophoridae

Shy birds of broadleaf forest floor. Usually found in small groups. All give loud, repetitive calls in chorus. Observers should note details of the head and underparts pattern.

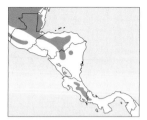

Spotted Wood-Quail *Odontophorus guttatus*   25 cm

South MX and CA. Uncommon resident in north Caribbean lowlands and foothills (to 1800, locally to 2500 m). Confined to middle elevations in Pacific GT. Locally fairly common in upper foothills and highlands in CR and west PA (above 800 m). **ID** Dark brown overall, intricately patterned with black, rufous, and buff. Throat and sides of neck black with white streaks. Lower underparts variably grayish-brown or chestnut brown with black-bordered white spots. Male has *rufous-orange crest* (sometimes held erect). **GV** Individually variable, especially in south CA, where some have chestnut underparts and rufous crown. **HABITS** Floor and edge of humid broadleaf forest, second growth, and plantations. **VOICE** Song (1) a series of loud phrases *wheet-a-towheoo . . .* or *wheet-to-whao*. Also (2) mournful, whistled notes.

Black-eared Wood-Quail *Odontophorus melanotis*   24 cm

CA endemic. Uncommon resident in humid lowlands and foothills (mainly SL to 500, locally to 2000 m in north). **ID** Dark. Bare facial skin gray. Note *plain rufous crown and underparts* and *plain blackish auriculars, throat, and foreneck*. Female has grayer auriculars. Marbled Wood-Quail has barred underparts, lacks rufous crest and has orange (not gray) bare facial skin. **HABITS** Floor of humid broadleaf forest and adjacent tall second growth. **VOICE** Song (1) a loud, repeated phrase *klawcoo, klawcoo, klawcoo . . .* sometimes reversed as *kooklawk*.

Marbled Wood-Quail *Odontophorus gujanensis*   26 cm

CA and SA. Rare to locally fairly common resident in lowlands and foothills (to 1500 m) of CR (Puntarenas) and PA. Perhaps most common in central and east PA. **ID** *Orange bare orbital skin.* Grayish-brown with fine blackish barring on underparts. Individually variable, but generally very intricately barred and vermiculated with black, rufous, and buff both above and below. Short crest blackish or brown. Compare with Black-eared Wood-Quail. Note different head pattern. **GV** Some birds from east PA (not shown) have grayish mantle and collar. **HABITS** Floor of humid broadleaf forest and adjacent tall second growth. **VOICE** Call (1) a long series of loud, rhythmic phrases *oowac, oowac, oowac . . .* or *corco what-too, corco what-too . . .*

Tacarcuna Wood-Quail *Odontophorus dialeucos*   24 cm

CA and north SA. Poorly known resident in foothills and highlands (1050 to 1450 m) of east PA (Darién). Reported to be fairly common at Cerro Mali, Tacarcuna Massif and Serranía del Darién (657, 512, 643). **ID** Crown and auriculars mostly black (spotted very lightly with white). Note *white supercilium, face and band on throat*. Hindneck buff. Otherwise dull brown above vermiculated with black. Remaining underparts rather plain dull brown. Compare with Marbled Wood-Quail. **HABITS** Floor of humid broadleaf forest. Poorly known. Presumably similar to other wood-quails. **VOICE** Call (1) a long series of loud, rhythmic phrases *corco-wheetu, corco-wheetu, corco-wheetu..* May be given by pairs or groups in chorus.

Black-breasted Wood-Quail *Odontophorus leucolaemus*   24 cm

CA endemic. Uncommon to rare and local resident in highlands (700 to 1850 m) of CR and west PA. **ID** Sexes similar. Dark with variable (sometimes inconspicuous) white throat or white mark on lower throat. Most of underparts black with variable white mottling or barring on lower breast. Upperparts dark brown (darker on crown) with heavy blackish spotting and barring. Compare with locally syntopic Black-eared and Spotted wood-quails. **HABITS** Floor and edge of humid broadleaf forest, and adjacent second growth. **VOICE** Song (1) given by groups in chorus, includes individual phrases *kee-a wowa kee-a wowa . . .* Similar to song of Black-eared Wood-Quail. Also (2) a long series of short notes *chu chu chu chu . . .* Juv's (3) two-syllable alarm call may recall Collared Trogon.

brown ♀

rufous ♀

brown ♂

rufous ♂

Spotted Wood-Quail

Black-eared Wood-Quail ♂   ♀

Marbled Wood-Quail

Tacarcuna Wood-Quail

Black-breasted Wood-Quail

QUAIL Odontophoridae

Quails found in savannas and grassy understory of dry, open woodland. Usually in groups. Secretive and usually flee on foot or make short, rapid flights when disturbed. Most often detected by voice. May take low perch to vocalize. Geographic variation in Crested Bobwhite is complex.

Northern Bobwhite *Colinus virginianus* 20 cm

USA to north CA. Fairly common in Nentón-Comitán Valley of west GT (900 to 1850 m, Huehuetenango, 229, 279, 460). **ID** Male has *blackish head* with variable white supercilium, and plain cinnamon underparts. Female resembles females of other (allopatric) CA bobwhites but has some cinnamon on flanks. Other bobwhites allopatric. **HABITS** Floor and understory at edges or in clearings in thorn or dry (deciduous) forest, brushy or scrubby areas, and agricultural fields. **VOICE** Call (1) a harsh, hoarse, upslurred *haa-wow, haa-wow, haa-wow,* and (2) harsh *kreh-kreh . . .* when disturbed.

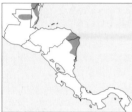

Black-throated Bobwhite *Colinus nigrogularis* 20 cm

South MX and CA. Uncommon to locally fairly common resident in Caribbean lowlands of BZ (529, 235). Rare in north GT (Petén, 229, 637). Also Mosquitia region of east HN and northeast NI. **ID** Male has black throat and mask and white malar and supercilium. Note *bold black-and-white scaling on underparts.* Female has buff throat and supercilium. Other bobwhites allopatric. **HABITS** Floor and understory of pine savanna, scrub, and borders of agricultural fields. Behavior much like Crested Bobwhite. **VOICE** Call (1) an upslurred *huu-wheeeeeet* and (2) harsh *kreh-kreh . . .* when disturbed.

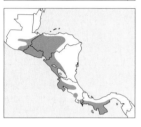

Crested Bobwhite[1] *Colinus cristatus* 20 cm

CA and SA. Fairly common resident in Pacific lowlands and foothills (to 1000, locally to 1500 m). Local in arid Caribbean slope valleys of GT (Valle de Motagua, 279), HN (Yoro, 442, 316), and central CR (Cartago, 600). Perhaps expanding. **ID** and **GV** Both individually and geographically variable. Male from Pacific east CR and PA has *cinnamon-rufous* supercilium and lower throat contrasting with whitish foreface, and has *prominent, pointed crest.* Underparts buff to chestnut with bold white spotting on breast and flanks. Female has grayish streaked head. Males from Pacific GT and west SV have extensively white underparts. Males from east SV have white throat, grayish upper breast, and black-and-white scaled lower underparts. Males from HN to west NI have throat marked with black. Male from CR has rufous breast with black- and- white spotting on lower underparts. **HABITS** Floor and understory of savanna, open scrub or brushy areas and agricultural fields. **VOICE** Call (1) an upslurred *huu-wheeeeeet* or *pwit pwit pweet!* much like other *Colinus* bobwhites, but perhaps clearer (less hoarse or scratchy). Also (2) a sneezelike *whee!-cheer* repeated four to six times and (3) high-pitched, clucking *chut-chut-chuturrr . . .*

Ocellated Quail *Cyrtonyx ocellatus* 20 cm

South MX and CA. Uncommon and local resident in foothills and highlands (750 to 3700 m) of GT and HN (Francisco Morazán, Santa Bárbara, Yoro, Olancho, 279, 442, 236). Historical records from SV (Chalatenango, 183, 619). Rare in NI (Jinotega, Nueva Segovia, 517, 413, 236). **ID** Broad, low crest and *black collar.* Male has complex black-and-white head pattern and pale brownish crest (sometimes held flat). Upperparts mostly gray blotched and spotted with black. Male's buff central breast grades into chestnut belly. Female has mostly pale cinnamon underparts with sparse, fine dark markings. Female's supercilium and throat whitish. Note *pale streaking on mantle.* Compare female with female Singing Quail. Note different head shape, underparts pattern, and habits. **HABITS** Floor and understory of brushy pine-oak woodland and grassy clearings in coniferous forest. In pairs or small groups. More reclusive than *Colinus* bobwhites. **VOICE** Song (1) a long, trilled whistle that is steady or drops slightly in pitch followed by a series of short notes that drop in pitch *trrrrrrrrrrrrreu cheu chu chu chu chu.*

Northern Bobwhite ♀ ♂

Black-throated Bobwhite ♀ ♂

GT ♀

SV ♂

HN ♂

GT ♂

Crested Bobwhite

east CR and PA ♀

east CR and PA ♂

west CR ♀

west CR ♂

Ocellated Quail ♀ ♂

PIGEONS Columbidae

Large pigeons found mainly in forest canopy and edge. All are strong fliers and are often seen on high, open perch. Often detected by voice.

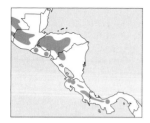

Band-tailed Pigeon[2] *Patagioenas fasciata* 35 cm
NA to SA. Locally fairly common in highlands (above 800 m). Also volcanic highlands of SV (Sonsonate, San Miguel, 183) and west CR (Guanacaste, 600). May undertake seasonal or irregular movements (253).Very rarely wanders to lowlands. **ID** Large. Mostly grayish above and mostly pale vinaceous brown below. Ad has *white band on nape*. In good light note metallic bronzy green on hindneck. In flight, note bicolored tail and pale crissum and belly. Imm duller and browner and lacks white collar. **GV** Birds from CR and PA are darker, especially below, and have entirely yellow bill. **HABITS** Canopy of broadleaf and coniferous forests. Gregarious. At least formerly occurred in large flocks in favored areas. In flight, produces a loud, whooshing sound with wings. **VOICE** Song (1) a very low-pitched, slightly hoarse *wooo wo-hooor, wo-hooor* or *coo-cooo, coo-cooo* often repeated in long series. Also (2) a low-pitched *gurrr*.

White-crowned Pigeon *Patagioenas leucocephala* 33 cm
Mainly WI and CA. Breeds (Jul to Aug) on Caribbean islands including BZ Cays (535, 313, 343), Bay Islands and Cayos Cochinos off HN (94, 442, 622, 560), Isla Providencia, Isla San Andres, and Corn Islands off NI (484, 531), and islands in Bocas del Toro Archipelago off west PA including Isla Escudo de Veraguas (Bocas del Toro, 275, 657, 48). Rare visitor (mainly Oct to Feb) to mainland in BZ (Corozal, 346), GT (Izabal, Petén, 220, 229), CR (Limón, 600, 346, 546), and PA (Ngäbe-Buglé, 346). **ID** Ad near-uniform dark bluish-gray with *white crown*. Note pale yellow eyes, white eye ring and green and dusky iridescent scaling on neck (visible in good light). Bill mostly deep pink with yellow tip. Juv mostly plain drab sooty gray. Note juv's diffuse pale grayish forehead and pale eyes. No other CA pigeon is as extensively plain gray (without any reddish or vinaceous color) and none has similar head pattern. **HABITS** Canopy of mangroves, littoral scrub and riparian forest. Breeds in loose colonies on mangrove islets. May commute from island breeding sites to forage in littoral forests on mainland. **VOICE** Song (1) a clear, loud, low-pitched *cooo, coo-coo cooo* or *cooo-cura-cooo.*

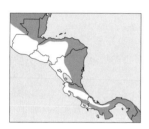

Scaled Pigeon *Patagioenas speciosa* 31 cm
South MX to SA. Fairly common resident in lowlands and foothills (to 1200 m). **ID** *Dull rufous head* and *scaled pattern on neck and underparts*. Note red bill with yellow tip and red orbital ring. Male has mostly dark rufous mantle and wings. Female duller with dusky brown mantle and wings. In poor light appears mostly dark with paler (whitish) lower underparts. In flight from below, note dark tail contrasting with whitish crissum. **HABITS** Subcanopy to canopy and edge of semihumid to humid broadleaf forest and adjacent plantations, gardens, and clearings with scattered trees. Often in pairs. Does not form large flocks but may gather in numbers at fruiting trees. Pairs may perch together on high, exposed branches. **VOICE** Song (1) a low-pitched, three- or four-note *coooo-cu-coooo* or *hwooo hip-hoowooh.* May be repeated several times.

juv

♀

north CA
♂

Band-tailed Pigeon

CR and PA
♂

juv

ad

**White-crowned
Pigeon**

♂

♀

Scaled Pigeon

PIGEONS Columbidae

Large pigeons found mainly in upper levels of broadleaf forest and woodland. Often detected by voice, and voice is important for identification. Short-billed and Pale-vented pigeons are the most common and widespread.

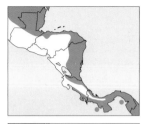

Pale-vented Pigeon *Patagioenas cayennensis* 31 cm

South MX to SA. Fairly common resident in lowlands (to 750 m). Also Isla Coiba and Pearl Islands (Veraguas, Panamá, 611, 470). **ID** Bill blackish. Mostly purple-rufous with gray head. Note *white belly and crissum* (conspicuous in flight). Red-billed Pigeon has different bill and underparts. Short-billed Pigeon more uniformly patterned. Also note different habits and voice. **HABITS** Subcanopy to canopy and edge of riparian woodland, savannas, plantations, mangroves, and gardens. Most common in semi-open areas near water. Pairs or single birds loiter and call from high, exposed perches. **VOICE** Song (1) a three-syllable phrase with last note longest and slurred. Often repeated in series *cu cu wooooo, cu-cu wooooo . . .* Compare with four-syllable call of Red-billed Pigeon.

Red-billed Pigeon *Patagioenas flavirostris* 34 cm

South Texas to CA. Fairly common resident in lowlands and foothills (to 1200, locally to 2000 m). Most common in arid to semihumid regions. Perhaps undertakes seasonal movements. **ID** *Red bill with yellow tip.* Feet, eyes, and narrow, bare eye ring red. *Rufous wing coverts contrast with bluish-gray of remaining wing.* Bluish-gray rump and crissum contrast with *dark tail.* Pale-vented Pigeon has whitish crissum, pale gray tail, and dark bill. **HABITS** Subcanopy to canopy and edge of open woodland, second growth, plantations, forest, urban areas, and mangroves. Typically seen on high exposed perch. Sometimes forages on ground. Often in pairs. Does not form large flocks. May gather in numbers at fruiting trees. **VOICE** Song (1) typically a long, upslurred note followed by three shorter notes *woooo, cu cucu-cooo, woooo, cu cucu-cooo . . .* or *cooooo cu cu coo, cooooo cu cu coo . . .*

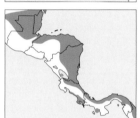

Short-billed Pigeon *Patagioenas nigrirostris* 29 cm

South MX and CA. Fairly common resident in lowlands and foothills (to 1200, locally to 1800 m). **ID** Dull brown above becoming paler vinaceous-gray on head, neck, and underparts. At close range note *red eyes.* Ruddy Pigeon (south CA) is more reddish-brown above and is found mainly at higher elevations. In east PA (Darién) compare with Plumbeous Pigeon. Note different eye color and voice. **HABITS** Subcanopy to canopy and edge of semihumid to humid broadleaf forest and adjacent plantations. Solitary or in pairs. May gather at fruiting trees. Often remains concealed in canopy foliage and most are detected by voice. **VOICE** Song (1) a four-syllable *cuk cukcuk cwoo* with accent on second and fourth syllables. Also (2) a hoarse, low-pitched, rolling *krooouw.*

Ruddy Pigeon *Patagioenas subvinacea* 30 cm

CA and SA. Uncommon to locally fairly common resident in south foothills and highlands (breeds mainly above 1500 m, but may move lower in breeding season). Ranges to SL in east PA. **ID** Uniform *reddish-brown above* and slightly paler vinaceous-gray on head, neck, and underparts. At close range note *red eyes.* Short-billed Pigeon mainly at lower elevations. Note different voice. **HABITS** Subcanopy to canopy and edge of humid broadleaf forest. Often in pairs. Usually remains concealed in vegetation. Usually detected by voice. Takes grit from ground at roadsides. **VOICE** Song (1) a clear, four-syllable *coo c'coo coo* with accent on third syllable (not second and fourth as in Short-billed Pigeon). Also (2) a coarse growl. Harsher than call of Short-billed Pigeon.

Plumbeous Pigeon *Patagioenas plumbea* 32 cm

CA and SA. Uncommon resident in lowlands and foothills (to 1100 m) of east PA (Darién, 45, 42, 117). **ID** Closely resembles Short-billed, Ruddy, and Dusky pigeons. Uniform dull brown above with slightly paler uniform vinaceous-gray on head, neck, and underparts. At close range note *pale eyes* and *gray orbital skin.* Dusky Pigeon has red eyes. Compare with Ruddy and Short-billed pigeons. Note different eye color and especially voice. **HABITS** Subcanopy to canopy and edge of humid broadleaf forest. Like Short-billed Pigeon. **VOICE** Song (1) a low-pitched, three-syllable *whit hut-hooo.* Compare with four-syllable songs of Short-billed and Ruddy pigeons.

Dusky Pigeon *Patagioenas goodsoni* 27 cm

CA and north SA. Poorly known. Perhaps resident in lowlands and foothills of east PA (Darién, 659, 116). **ID** In close view shows *red eyes.* Note, gray head and chestnut flanks and crissum. Plumbeous Pigeon has pale eyes. **HABITS** Subcanopy to canopy and edge of humid broadleaf forest. Like Short-billed Pigeon. **VOICE** Song (1) a clear, three-syllable, low-pitched *wook, coo-coo.* Often repeated persistently. Compare with four-note songs of Short-billed and Ruddy pigeons.

Pale-vented
Pigeon

Red-billed Pigeon

Short-billed
Pigeon

Ruddy Pigeon

Dusky Pigeon

Plumbeous
Pigeon

PIGEON AND DOVES Columbidae

Pigeons and doves found mainly in open or disturbed areas. Eurasian Collared-Dove is an Old World species that has recently become established in the region. White-winged Dove is the most common and widespread.

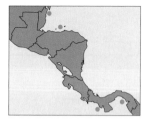

Rock Pigeon *Columba livia*   32 cm

Palearctic species widely introduced. Locally common resident in urban areas. Also various islands. **ID** Variable. All CA populations have been subject to some degree of selective breeding. Variants range from uniform white to near-uniform dusky blackish. Many birds are dark gray with a contrasting paler gray mantle and wings and show two broad blackish wingbars. At close range note violet or purple iridescence on neck. Tail typically banded or broadly tipped with blackish. Compare with Band-tailed Pigeon. Note different habits. **HABITS** Urban areas, parks, gardens, and agricultural areas. Usually in small, compact flocks closely associated with human habitations, domestic animals, and agricultural lands. Forages mainly on ground. Roosts, often in large numbers, on elevated perches on buildings or in trees. **VOICE** Call (1) a low-pitched, hollow *coo, cucoo-coooor*. May be repeated persistently.

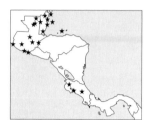

Eurasian Collared-Dove *Streptopelia decaocto*   32 cm

Palearctic species introduced in NA, WI, and CA. Uncommon and local but increasing in GT (229), BZ, including Belize Cays (Belize, Corozal, Orange Walk, 347, 346), and CR (Guanacaste, San José, Puntarenas, 341). **ID** Fairly large and slender. Mostly *plain pale brownish-gray* with *blackish collar* and pinkish breast. Bill blackish. Note contrasting dark primaries and dark base of square, mostly white tail. Compare with smaller Mourning Dove. **HABITS** Gardens, agricultural areas, plantations, scrub, urban and suburban areas. Often forages on ground but may perch at any level in vegetation or on utility wires. Solitary or in pairs. May associate with other dove species. **VOICE** Song (1) a mournful, hollow, three-syllable *wha-hoooo who* or *kukkoooo-kook* with second note longest. Also (2) a harsh *mew* or *rehh*. May be repeated.

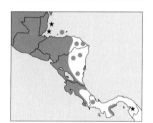

White-winged Dove *Zenaida asiatica*   27 cm

South USA to WI and CA. Fairly common breeding resident (SL to 500, locally to 3200 m in north). Nearctic breeding birds perhaps also occur. Very common transient and winter resident (Nov to May) on Pacific slope. Perhaps expanding on Caribbean slope in north GT (Petén, 227, 346) and BZ (Belize, 71). Also Bay Islands (346). Local in Pacific lowlands of PA (Coclé, Herrera, 274, 657). May undertake seasonal movements in some regions. **ID** Fairly large with square tail. *White on wing coverts* forms long, narrow white bar and contrasts with dark primaries. Note short black streak below auriculars. Outer rectrices gray with black subterminal band and broad white tip. At close range note blue bare orbital ring and red eyes. Bill blackish. Compare with Mourning Dove. Note different tail shape and wing pattern. White-tipped Dove also has blue facial skin in CR and PA populations. Note different wing pattern. **HABITS** Arid woodland, open or disturbed areas with scattered trees, plantations, agricultural fields, littoral scrub, mangroves, urban areas, and gardens. Forages mainly on ground. Calls from elevated perch. Often in pairs. May assemble in large numbers to roost. **VOICE** Song (1) a repeated phrase of hollow, hoarse notes *cuu-cuu-cuwooo*. Commonly given call (2) a simple *cu-cuk-woo*.

Mourning Dove *Zenaida macroura*   29 cm

NA, WI, and CA. Nearctic migrant and breeding resident birds occur (11). Locally common breeding resident on Pacific slope in GT (Santa Rosa, Retalhuleu, 229, 378, 539), CR (Cartago, 600), and west PA (Los Santos, Herrera, Coclé, 207). Locally or seasonally common transient and winter resident (Oct to Mar) in north Pacific slope and interior valleys. Uncommon to rare on Caribbean slope. **ID** *Long, graduated tail* with white-tipped rectrices. Underparts pinkish-tan. Upperparts light brown with *black spots on coverts and tertials*. Juv mostly drab brownish with fine buff scaling and dark spotting. Compare with White-winged Dove. Note different tail shape and wing pattern. **HABITS** Arid woodland, open or disturbed areas with scattered trees, savannas, agricultural fields, plantations, scrub, gardens, and urban areas. Forages mainly on ground but regularly perches in crowns of shrubs or on utility wires. Often in pairs. May form small flocks outside breeding season. **VOICE** Song (1) a long, low-pitched, slurred note followed by a series of shorter, hollow notes on lower pitch *ooooooow-woow, oo oo oo . . .*

Rock Pigeon

Eurasian Collared-Dove

White-winged Dove

Mourning Dove

juv

ad

DOVES Columbidae

Small doves that forage mainly on the ground. Often in pairs or small groups. May sing from low perch. Ruddy Ground-Dove is the most common and widespread *Columbina*. Maroon-chested Ground-Dove is rarely encountered.

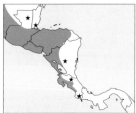

Inca Dove *Columbina inca*   21 cm
South USA to CA. Fairly common resident in Pacific lowlands and foothills (to 2000 m). Local on Caribbean slope in north. Perhaps expanding in BZ (Toledo, 347), north GT (Petén, 279, 78), and Pacific CR (Puntarenas, 567, 346). **ID** Long tail with *white outer rectrices*. Bill blackish. Pale brownish-gray (pinkish on chest) with *extensive fine dusky scaling*. Rufous concealed in folded wing, but conspicuous in flight. Imm browner with indistinct scaling on underparts and pale supraloral spot. Common Ground-Dove has shorter, square tail. **HABITS** Open or disturbed areas with scattered trees, agricultural fields, savannas, plantations, scrub, and gardens. **VOICE** Calls (1) an emphatic, hollow, two-syllable *caw-coo* repeated persistently and (2) harsher, hoarse *grr-hrrrr*.

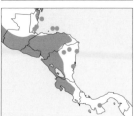

Common Ground-Dove *Columbina passerina*   17 cm
South USA to SA. Common resident in lowlands and foothills (to 2000 m). Also Belize Cays (343) and Bay Islands off HN (442). Poorly known in Caribbean NI (RAAN, 327). Local in PA (Coclé, Herrera, Los Santos). **ID** Short square tail. *Scaled and speckled breast*. Wing coverts and tertials spotted with dark violet. Red bill with dark tip (duskier in female). Female slightly duller with less pinkish underparts. In flight, rufous primaries contrast with brownish-gray upperparts. Inca Dove has longer tail. Compare with Plain-breasted and Ruddy ground-doves. Note different bill and underparts. **HABITS** Floor and understory of open or disturbed areas with scattered trees, agricultural fields, savannas, plantations, scrub, and gardens. **VOICE** Call (1) a low-pitched, soft, clear *coo-oop* or *cowoot* repeated persistently. Compare with shorter song phrases of Ruddy Ground-Dove.

Plain-breasted Ground-Dove *Columbina minuta*   15 cm
MX to SA. Uncommon and local resident in lowlands and foothills (to 500 m). Poorly known in HN (247, 341) and NI (RAAN, 327). **ID** Small with short tail. Grayer than other *Columbina*. Note *plain underparts* with no scaling or iridescence. Bill pale pinkish or yellowish with dark tip. Wing coverts and *tertials spotted with dark violet*. Male has gray crown, nape, and forehead. Female very plain with dull grayish underparts. Female Common Ground-Dove has different head and underparts pattern. Also compare with female Ruddy Ground-Dove. **HABITS** Floor and understory of grassy clearings, savannas, and agricultural areas. **VOICE** Song (1) a rapidly repeated, hollow, two-syllable *towoo towoo towoo . . .* Compare with call of Ruddy Ground-Dove.

Ruddy Ground-Dove *Columbina talpacoti*   18 cm
MX to SA. Common resident in lowlands and foothills (to 1400 m). Also Isla Coiba and Pearl Islands (Veraguas, Panamá, 611, 649, 470). **ID** Long-tailed. Bill dusky-yellow. Male *mostly rufous* (becoming paler below) with gray crown. Female duller. Compare with female Blue Ground-Dove. Note different wing pattern. **HABITS** Floor to midstory in open areas, agricultural fields, savannas, plantations, scrub, and gardens. **VOICE** Call (1) a repeated, soft *oo-woot, oo-woot, oo-woot . . .* Faster, lower-pitched and more hoarse than Common Ground-Dove. Also (2) a simple, low-pitched *coo*.

Blue Ground-Dove *Claravis pretiosa*   20 cm
MX to SA. Fairly common resident in lowlands and foothills (to 1200, locally to 2000 m). Uncommon in north Pacific lowlands (619, 182). Also Isla Coiba (Veraguas, 470). **ID** *Bill dull yellow*. Male *bluish-gray* (paler below) with black spotting on wing coverts and tertials. Female mostly pale brown and rufous with chestnut spotting on wings (outlined whitish). In flight, shows bright rufous rump and tail coverts. Female resembles female Ruddy Ground-Dove. Note different wing and head pattern. **HABITS** Floor and understory of second growth, riparian tangles and hedgerows in agricultural areas. Pairs or solitary birds forage on ground, usually beneath cover. **VOICE** Call (1) a soft, resonant, flat *boop* repeated several times. Compare with call of Gray-fronted Dove. Less often (2) a short, hoarse *khoor*.

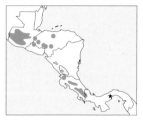

Maroon-chested Ground-Dove *Claravis mondetoura*   21 cm
CA and SA. Rare in foothills and highlands (900 to 3000 m) of GT (229, 539, 279, 375), SV (Chalatenango, Morazán, 296, 619, 341), HN (Francisco Morazán, La Paz, Olancho, 442, 346), CR (Cartago, 600, 346), and PA (Chiriquí, Panamá, 160, 473, 657, 512). Perhaps nomadic. **ID** *Unmarked tertials*. Male mostly gray with *whitish forehead, face, and throat* and *maroon breast*. Compare with Blue Ground-Dove. Note different wing pattern and female's tawny crown. **HABITS** Floor, understory, and edge of humid broadleaf forest and second growth, especially with extensive bamboo. Reclusive. Forages on ground. May take an elevated perch when disturbed. Vocalizes from midstory. Solitary or in pairs. **VOICE** Song (1) a resonant, slightly upslurred, two-syllable *buwoop* repeated several times. Compare with song of Blue Ground-Dove.

Inca Dove

Common Ground-Dove
♂
♀

Plain-breasted Ground-Dove
♂
♀

Ruddy Ground-Dove
♂
♀

Blue Ground-Dove
♂
♀

Maroon-chested Ground-Dove
♂
♀

DOVES Columbidae

Five similar doves resident in lowlands and foothills. All forage by walking on the ground and may vocalize from an elevated perch. Solitary or in pairs. Details of the head and underparts pattern are useful for identification. Voice and habitat are also helpful. White-tipped Dove is the most widespread and common.

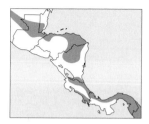

Gray-chested Dove *Leptotila cassinii*   24 cm
South MX to SA. Uncommon to locally fairly common resident in lowlands and foothills (to 750, locally to 1400 m). Confined to Caribbean slope in north.
ID Darkest *Leptotila* dove. Note dark gray underparts becoming brownish on flanks (whitish confined to crissum) and *brown or rufous nape and hindcrown*. Gray-headed Dove has gray nape. White-tipped Dove has different eye ring color (in south CA), underparts, and habits. **GV** Birds from Pacific CR are paler and have reddish-brown nape. Widespread form is darker and duller with brown nape. **HABITS** Floor and understory of broadleaf forest. **VOICE** Call (1) a series of long, attenuated, downslurred *woooooooouuu* or *crrooooo* phrases (no introductory note). Individual phrases often loudest in middle. Compare with shorter, upslurred phrases of White-tipped Dove. Also compare with Ruddy Quail-Dove.

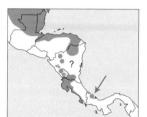

Gray-headed Dove *Leptotila plumbeiceps*   25 cm
MX to north SA. Fairly common resident in north Caribbean lowlands and foothills (to 1000, locally to 1500 m). Local in north highlands and Pacific NI (Matagalpa, Granada, 413) including Isla Mancarroncito (Río San Juan, 548) and in Pacific CR on Nicoya Peninsula and Cordillera de Guanacaste (Guanacaste, Puntarenas, 570, 600, 346). Rare and poorly known in Caribbean lowlands of west PA and Bocas del Toro Archipelago (Bocas del Toro, 486, 512, 48). **ID** *Bluish-gray hindcrown, nape, and sides of neck.* Breast paler and lower underparts more extensively whitish than Gray-chested Dove. Compare with White-tipped Dove. Note different upperparts color and head pattern (also different eye ring color in south). **HABITS** Floor and understory of semihumid to humid broadleaf forest, shaded plantations, and second growth. **VOICE** Call (1) a repeated *groooo* or *whroooo*. Lower-pitched, shorter, and huskier than other *Leptotila* doves. Often repeated. Compare with smoother, shorter phrases of Blue Ground-Dove.

Brown-backed Dove[3] *Leptotila battyi*   24 cm
CA endemic. Rare and local resident in Pacific lowlands and foothills (to 500 m?) of Azuero Peninsula, PA (Veraguas, Herrera, Los Santos, 274, 470, 425). Fairly common on Isla Coiba and Isla Cébaco (Veraguas, 653, 40). **ID** *Rufous-brown upperparts* and *bluish-gray hindcrown*, nape, and sides of neck. Compare with White-tipped Dove. Note different head color, upperparts color, and habits. Other *Leptotila* doves allopatric. **GV** Mainland birds (not shown) slightly duller. **HABITS** Floor and understory of semihumid to humid broadleaf forest, shaded plantations, and second growth. **VOICE** Call (1) a low-pitched, resonant *whoo-oooo*. Compare with higher-pitched call of White-tipped Dove.

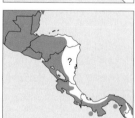

White-tipped Dove *Leptotila verreauxi*   27 cm
MX to SA. Common resident in lowlands and foothills (to 1500, locally to 2500 m). Also Isla Coiba and Pearl Islands off PA (Veraguas, Panamá, 58, 649, 470). **ID** Shows more extensive white on rectrices than other *Leptotila* doves. Breast *pale pinkish-gray* becoming whitish on lower underparts. Upperparts dull brown (paler than other *Leptotila*). Often appears drab but pinkish iridescence on nape and sides of neck sometimes visible. Gray-headed Dove has darker upperparts and always has red eye ring. **GV** Birds from north CA have red or pink bare eye ring and lores like other *Leptotila*. Birds from CR and PA have blue eye ring and lores. **HABITS** Floor and understory of open or disturbed areas including broadleaf forest edge, second growth, scrub, plantations, and gardens. Favors more open habitats than other *Leptotila* doves but also found inside deciduous forest. **VOICE** Call (1) a low-pitched, mournful, slightly ascending *wu huwooooo*. Soft introductory note may not be audible at a distance.

Caribbean Dove *Leptotila jamaicensis*   26 cm
South MX, WI, and CA. Poorly known. Uncommon to rare and local resident in north GT (Petén, 110, 229) and BZ including Ambergris Cay (Belize, Corozal, 318, 343, 341). Also Bay Islands and Cayos Cochinos (442, 317, 560). **ID** *Whitish forehead, face, and underparts.* In favorable light shows extensive pinkish-rufous and green iridescence on nape, sides of neck, and breast. Compare with White-tipped Dove. Note different head pattern. **HABITS** Floor, understory, and edge of littoral forest, gallery forest, and scrub. **VOICE** Call (1) a short, descending series of hollow notes *who-wowoo-huuuu*. Last note longest.

30%

Gray-chested Dove

juv

Pacific CR
ad

widespread
ad

Gray-headed Dove

Brown-backed Dove

White-tipped Dove

north CA

CR and PA

Caribbean Dove

QUAIL-DOVES Columbidae

Large doves usually seen walking on floor of broadleaf forest. All are shy and difficult to observe at length. Most are detected by voice. Details of upperparts and head pattern are important field marks. All have plain tails and never show white "corners" as do *Leptotila* doves. Ruddy Quail-Dove is the most common and widespread.

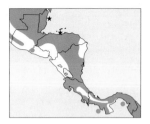

Ruddy Quail-Dove *Geotrygon montana*   23 cm

MX and WI to SA. Fairly common resident in lowlands and foothills (to 1200, locally to 1650 m in north). Uncommon to rare and local in north Pacific slope in SV (Ahuachapán, 619, 341). Reported from islands including BZ Cays (347, 341), Cayos Cochinos (560), and Isla Coiba and Pearl Islands off PA (Veraguas, Panamá, 649, 653, 470). **ID** Bulky. Low, sloping forehead. Base of bill, bare lores, and *eye ring red to deep pink*. Eyes yellow. Ad male deep rufous above including crown. Note *buff moustachial stripe*. Breast grayish-pink becoming buff on lower underparts. Ad female has similar pattern but is olive-brown above and on breast. Imm has fine rufous scaling on breast and wing coverts. Chiriqui Quail-Dove (mainly higher elevations) has gray crown and black malar. **HABITS** Floor and understory of humid to humid broadleaf forest. Solitary or in pairs. Generally shy, but somewhat more confiding than other CA quail-doves. **VOICE** Call (1) a repeated, hollow *cooo, cooo, cooo . . .* with steady, low pitch. Compare with longer, slightly downslurred phrases of Gray-chested Dove. Also compare with call of White-faced Quail-Dove.

Violaceous Quail-Dove *Geotrygon violacea*   24 cm

CA and SA. Rare and local resident in humid lowlands and foothills (to 1500 m) of NI (Jinotega, Matagalpa, RAAN, 413, 626), CR, including Pacific volcanic range (Guanacaste, Puntarenas, 624, 126, 570, 341, 346), and PA (Colón, Panamá, Darién, 512). **ID** Relatively slender. *White lower underparts* and *plain gray sides of head* (dark malar faint or lacking). Legs, loral line, eye ring, and *bill red*. Eyes amber. Male has *rufous-brown upperparts* with deep violet on mantle and back. Note male's *pale violet-gray breast*. Female olive-brown above with rufous-brown rump and tail and gray head. Juv still duller and more brownish overall with rufous edging on wings and cinnamon scaling on drab brownish breast. Imm may show faint dusky malar stripe. Compare with *Leptotila* doves. Note different tail pattern and upperparts color. **HABITS** Floor and understory of humid broadleaf forest. Forages on ground but may take low, open perch. Solitary or in pairs. Bobs hindquarters as it walks. **VOICE** Call (1) a repeated, short, hollow *ooo* or *ooou*.

White-faced Quail-Dove *Zentrygon albifacies*   30 cm

South MX and north CA. Uncommon to locally fairly common resident in north highlands (800 to 2800 m). Local in volcanic highlands of SV (Ahuachapán, Usulután, Santa Ana, San Vicente, 341). Recently reported from Cerro Musún in central NI (Matagalpa, 137). **ID** Large and robust. Ad rufous-brown above with *grayish crown*. In close view note purple iridescence on mantle and *pale neck with fine dusky scaling*. Underparts pale grayish-brown becoming brownish on flanks. Note plain whitish sides of head and throat (no dark malar). Bill blackish. Imm browner with dusky markings. Chiriqui Quail-Dove allopatric. **HABITS** Floor and understory of humid broadleaf and pine-broadleaf forest and shaded plantations. Solitary or in pairs. Walks deliberately over forest floor. **VOICE** Call (1) a single, low-pitched, hollow note *whoooo* or *whooʻoo* that rises slightly in pitch and ends abruptly. Sometimes repeated persistently. Compare with calls of Ruddy Quail-Dove and White-tipped Dove.

Chiriqui Quail-Dove *Zentrygon chiriquensis*   30 cm

CA endemic. Uncommon and local resident in highlands (600 to 2500 m) of CR and west PA. **ID** Large and robust. Mostly *rufous-brown including breast* with *contrasting gray head*. Note narrow blackish malar streak. In close view shows purple iridescence on mantle. Bill black. Superficially resembles widespread Ruddy Quail-Dove (mainly lower elevations). Note different crown color and head pattern. Also compare with Buff-fronted Quail-Dove. Note different head pattern. **HABITS** Floor and understory of humid broadleaf forest. Solitary or in pairs. **VOICE** Call (1) a downslurred *whooooo* becoming loudest in middle and fading softly at end. Often repeated at intervals of one or two seconds. Compare with call of Ruddy Quail-Dove.

Ruddy Quail-Dove

juv
♀

ad
♀

ad
♂

Violaceous Dove

♀

♂

White-faced Quail-Dove

juv

ad

Chiriqui Quail-Dove

QUAIL-DOVES Columbidae

Uncommon quail-doves found in humid broadleaf forest in south Central America.

Olive-backed Quail-Dove *Leptotrygon veraguensis*   23 cm
CA and north SA. Uncommon to rare and local resident in south lowlands and foothills (to 500, locally to 900 m). Rare in Caribbean NI (Río San Juan, 452). **ID** Small and dark. Breast dark gray. Note *white facial stripe* and *whitish forehead.* Mostly olive-brown. Compare with Purplish-backed Quail-Dove (mainly higher elevations). Also compare with ad female and imm Ruddy Quail-Dove. Note different head pattern. **HABITS** Floor and understory of humid broadleaf forest. Terrestrial. Very shy and usually difficult to observe at length. Solitary or in pairs. **VOICE** Call (1) a short, very low-pitched, resonant *uum* or *oowm.*

Buff-fronted Quail-Dove *Zentrygon costaricensis*   24 cm
CA endemic. Uncommon and local resident in highlands (1000 to 3000 m) of CR and west PA. **ID** Large and robust. Note *buff forehead contrasting with gray crown* and narrow, black malar. Upperparts pattern features iridescent green nape contrasting with deep purple mantle and chestnut wings and tail. Breast bluish-gray. Purplish-backed Quail-Dove shows less contrasting nape and mantle and has white forehead. **HABITS** Floor and understory of humid broadleaf forest. Terrestrial. Solitary or in pairs. **VOICE** Call (1) a low-pitched, hollow, slightly upslurred *hooooo* that becomes louder toward end. Often repeated in long series.

Purplish-backed Quail-Dove *Zentrygon lawrencii*   25 cm
CA endemic. Uncommon to rare and local resident in south foothills (400 to 1000 m). Poorly known in east PA (Darién, 657). **ID** Mostly dull brown upperparts with iridescent purple mantle (visible in good light). Note *grayish nape becoming blue-gray on crown.* Compare with Buff-fronted Quail-Dove. Note different head pattern. **HABITS** Floor and understory of humid broadleaf forest. Often in hilly terrain. Walks deliberately over ground. May call from elevated perch. Reclusive, but may emerge from cover to forage along muddy trails or edges. **VOICE** Call (1) a relatively high-pitched, two- or three-syllable *oo-a'ooooow* or *coo-ka-krrrw* with cooing quality. Last note longest and strongly downslurred. Sometimes only last note is audible. Compare with Buff-fronted and Chiriqui quail-doves.

Russet-crowned Quail-Dove *Zentrygon goldmani*   25 cm
CA and north SA. Uncommon and local resident in highlands (mainly 750 to 1600 m) of central and east PA (Panamá, Kuna Yala, Darién, 519, 45). **ID** Large and robust. Note *rufous crown and nape* and dark malar contrasting with white throat. Remaining upperparts mostly dull brown with purple iridescence on mantle (visible in good light). Breast gray. Ruddy Quail-Dove mainly at lower elevations. Note different head pattern. **GV** Birds from Serranía de Majé (not shown) are darker. **HABITS** Floor and understory of humid broadleaf forest. Mainly terrestrial. Forages on ground while walking deliberately over leaf litter. May call from elevated perch. Solitary or in pairs. **VOICE** Call (1) a very low-pitched, downslurred *wooooo* repeated at four- to five-second intervals in long series. Compare with longer call of Gray-chested Dove.

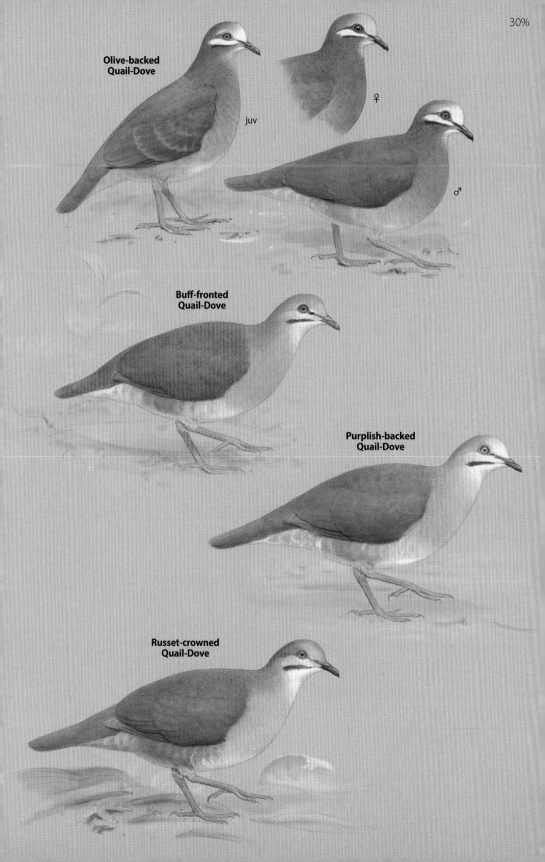

Olive-backed Quail-Dove

juv

♀

♂

Buff-fronted Quail-Dove

Purplish-backed Quail-Dove

Russet-crowned Quail-Dove

CUCKOOS Cuculidae
Slender, long-tailed birds found mainly in middle and upper levels of forest edge and woodland.

Black-billed Cuckoo *Coccyzus erythropthalmus* 28 cm
Breeds Nearctic. Winters SA. Uncommon to rare fall transient (mainly Sep to Oct). Very rare in spring (Apr to May). **ID** *Slender, black bill* with gray base. Ad has *red eye ring.* Dull grayish-brown above including auriculars (no dark mask). May show some rufous-brown in folded primaries but this is much less conspicuous than in Yellow-billed Cuckoo. Underparts whitish with variable faint buff on throat. Note *pale undertail surface* with narrow whitish tips on rectrices. Juv (Jun to Sep) has more extensive buff on underparts and inconspicuous pale eye ring. Yellow-billed Cuckoo has brighter rufous on wing, dark mask, and yellow mandible. **HABITS** Prefers midstory to subcanopy of humid broadleaf forest, second growth, and plantations. Transients can occur in a wide variety of arboreal habitats. Usually solitary. Shy and retiring. **VOICE** Transients usually silent.

Yellow-billed Cuckoo *Coccyzus americanus* 30 cm
Breeds Nearctic and WI. Winters mainly SA. Passage mainly in WI. Uncommon to rare transient (mainly Apr to May and Sep to Nov). Very rare in winter (341). **ID** Bill has mostly *yellow mandible.* Mostly dull brown above and whitish below. Note *rufous on primaries.* Undersurface of ad's tail shows large white tips on rectrices and white outer edge at base. Juv has less contrasting tail pattern. Black-billed Cuckoo has dark bill and little or no rufous on wings. Mangrove Cuckoo has heavier bill, plain grayish wings, and buff underparts. **HABITS** Prefers midstory to subcanopy and edge of humid broadleaf forest, second growth, and plantations, but transients can occur in wide variety of arboreal habitats. Usually solitary, but transients may form small flocks. Shy and retiring. **VOICE** Transients and wintering birds usually silent.

Pearly-breasted Cuckoo *Coccyzus euleri* 27 cm
CA and SA. Poorly known in central PA where recently found breeding (Panamá, 118). **ID** Closely resembles Yellow-billed Cuckoo but has *plain brownish primaries.* **HABITS** Upper understory to midstory of humid broadleaf forest, second growth, and gardens. **VOICE** Song (1) a rapid, hollow series of six to eight notes with last notes slower *cucucucucucu-cu-cu.* Sometimes repeated several times.

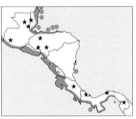

Mangrove Cuckoo *Coccyzus minor* 31 cm
South USA to WI and SA. Uncommon and irregular breeding resident in coastal lowlands and islands of both slopes (69) including BZ Cays (343), Bay Islands (480, 442), Swan Islands (480), Corn Islands (RAAS, 484, 413), and Isla Coiba (Veraguas, 657, 470). Rare in foothills and highlands (to 2400 m) of GT (Quetzaltenango, 229), SV (Sonsonate, 183, 341), CR (Guanacaste, Heredia, 474), and PA (Bocas del Toro, 469). Perhaps undertakes seasonal movements. Most records Oct to Apr. **ID** Black mask and variably *pale buff or cinnamon underparts.* Base of mandible yellow. Undertail surface black with large white spots. Note *plain grayish upperparts and wings.* Cocos Cuckoo allopatric. **HABITS** Midstory to subcanopy of mangroves, gallery and littoral forest, arid woodland, gardens, and scrub. Transients sometimes found in arid to humid broadleaf forest and edge. Solitary and secretive. **VOICE** Calls (1) a slightly nasal rattle that slows and drops slightly in pitch *grrtdtdtdtdtdtdtdt-dt-dt*, (2) short series of dry, low-pitched, froglike *owr* notes, (3) single, barking *whip!* or *whik!.*

Cocos Cuckoo *Coccyzus ferrugineus* 32 cm
Endemic to Isla del Coco off Pacific CR. Uncommon resident (163, 268, 571, 600). **ID** Black mask and *rich cinnamon underparts.* Upperparts grayish-brown with extensive rufous in wings. Imm has pale brownish undersurface of tail with indistinct whitish tips on rectrices. Mangrove Cuckoo allopatric. **HABITS** Understory to subcanopy of forest, second growth, and scrub. **VOICE** Calls (1) a series of five to eight low-pitched, dry, coughing *kcha* notes sometimes preceded by rolling or rattling notes and (2) resonant, guttural *k'k'k'k'k'ru'hoo.*

Gray-capped Cuckoo *Coccyzus lansbergi* 26 cm
SA. Rare vagrant (Dec to Feb) to central and east PA (Panamá, Darién, 104, 512). **ID** Richly colored. *Gray cap and auriculars* (no dark mask) and *cinnamon-buff throat.* Note relatively *rich brown upperparts* and rufous panel on wings. Mangrove Cuckoo (usually) has paler underparts and blackish mask. **HABITS** Upper understory to midstory of forest edge, second growth, and gardens. Vagrants may occur in wide variety of arboreal habitats. **VOICE** Song (1) a rapid, hollow *cucucucucucu-cu* (six to eight notes) with last notes slower. Sometimes repeated several times.

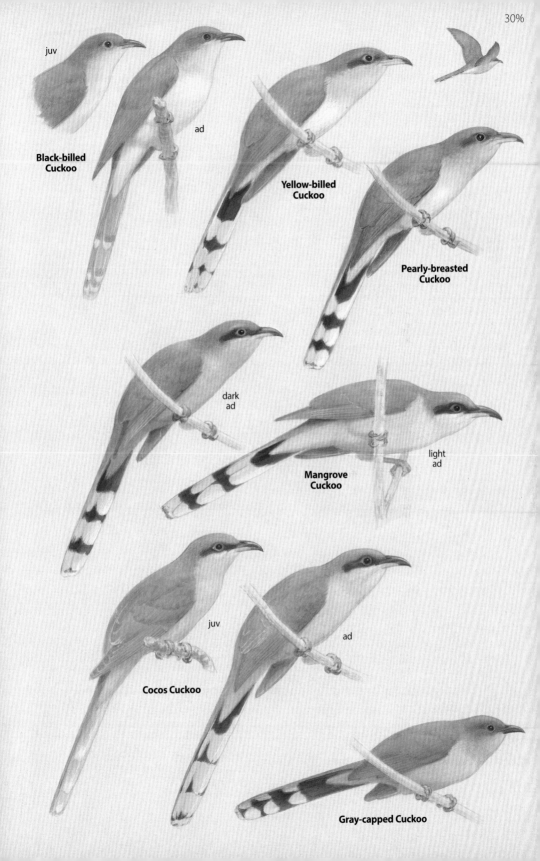

30%

juv

**Black-billed
Cuckoo**

ad

**Yellow-billed
Cuckoo**

**Pearly-breasted
Cuckoo**

dark
ad

**Mangrove
Cuckoo**

light
ad

juv.

Cocos Cuckoo

ad

Gray-capped Cuckoo

CUCKOOS AND ANIS Cuculidae

A diverse group of cuckoos found in a wide variety of habitats. Squirrel Cuckoo is a widespread and often conspicuous bird in the region. The *Crotophaga* anis form a distinctive and fairly uniform group found in open areas where they are often common and conspicuous. Bill shape and range are useful in separating anis.

Squirrel Cuckoo *Piaya cayana* 46 cm

MX to SA. Common resident in lowlands and foothills (to 1500, locally to 2500 m). **ID** Large. Very long tail shows bold black-and-white pattern on undersurface. Plain rufous above. Pinkish throat and breast and pale gray lower underparts. Note *greenish-yellow bill and bare orbital skin.* Juv (not shown) slightly paler and duller. **HABITS** Midstory to subcanopy and edge in a wide variety of arboreal habitats including arid to humid broadleaf forest, second growth, gallery forest, plantations, and gardens. Conspicuous. Forages actively. Hops along larger limbs. Makes short, gliding or undulating flights through vegetation. Usually solitary. Sometimes follows mixed flocks. **VOICE** Varied calls (1) a loud, hard, explosive *kip!* or *dik!* often given in flight, (2) loud *kip! wheeeu* or *whik-wheeer*, (3) dry, nasal *wid-d-dear* or *hic-a-roo*, (4) long, steady series of loud, bright *whip* or *pwit* notes, (5) an abrupt, loud, squeaky *med-ahr!* and (6) a long, dry rattle that drops in pitch.

Little Cuckoo *Coccycua minuta* 26 cm

CA and SA. Uncommon and local resident in lowlands and foothills (to 750 m) of central and east PA (Darién, Panamá, 657). **ID** Resembles much larger Squirrel Cuckoo but has *red bare orbital skin* and *yellow bill.* Juv mostly plain rufous-brown with gray lower underparts. **HABITS** Upper understory to midstory and edge of humid broadleaf forest, second growth, and adjacent semi-open areas. Secretive and usually solitary. **VOICE** Song (1) a nasal, upslurred note followed by a rattle that rises in pitch *errrrr-eheheheheh.* Calls include (2) a single, sharp *ehk* or *czek,* (3) nasal *nyaa-nyaa-nyaa,* and (4) downslurred, slightly hollow *goowp* or *ooow.*

Groove-billed Ani *Crotophaga sulcirostris* 31 cm

South USA to SA. Common resident in lowlands and foothills (to 1800, locally to 2300 m). Also Islas Cébaco and Gobernadora off PA (Veraguas, 470). **ID** Long, broad, graduated tail. Often appears disheveled. Glossy black scaled and streaked with grayish. Note *arched culmen with lengthwise grooves.* Imm may lack grooves. Compare with Smooth-billed Ani (locally syntopic in south). Note different bill shape. **HABITS** Understory to midstory in open areas, particularly pastures, agricultural fields, marshes, scrub, and gardens. Gregarious. Usually in small groups perched in shrubbery or on backs of cattle. **VOICE** Typical call (1) a bright, liquid *tijo* or *tee-oh.* When excited gives (2) a series of similar phrases *tee ooh tee ooh ho tee ooh . . .* often preceded by soft, clucking *tuc* notes. Also (3) a rapid series of long, whistled *kiw* notes that drop in pitch.

Smooth-billed Ani *Crotophaga ani* 34 cm

WI, CA, and SA. Common resident in south lowlands and foothills (to 1200 m). Also islands including BZ Cays (Corozal, 313, 343), Bay Islands and Swan Islands (94, 480, 442), Corn Islands (RAAS, 484, 413), and Isla Coiba and Pearl Islands (Veraguas, Panamá, 58, 455, 470). **ID** Long, broad, graduated tail. Often appears disheveled. Near-uniform glossy black scaled and streaked with grayish. *Bill has narrow, keel-like process on high, smooth, arched culmen.* Compare with slightly smaller Groove-billed Ani. Note different bill shape. **HABITS** Understory to midstory in open areas, particularly pastures, agricultural fields, scrub, and gardens. Gregarious and usually in small groups. Perches in shrubbery or on backs of cattle. Often descends to ground to forage in open, grassy areas. **VOICE** Calls include (1) a whining, upslurred *oooenk* or *wooyeek* or *eeee-yik.* May call in flight.

Greater Ani *Crotophaga major* 47 cm

CA and SA. Uncommon to rare and local resident in lowlands of PA. Vagrant to Caribbean lowlands of CR (Limón, 287). **ID** Very large. Long, graduated tail. Proportionally *long, pointed bill* with sharply angled, low "keel" rising from culmen. Note prominent *whitish eyes.* Mostly black with blue-green gloss visible in favorable light. Imm has dark eyes. Smaller Smooth-billed and Groove-billed anis have dark eyes and different bill shape. **HABITS** Understory to midstory of forested riverbanks, margins of lagoons, marshes, damp second growth and mangroves. Small groups, pairs, or solitary birds perch conspicuously and often loiter on branches overhanging water. **VOICE** Calls (1) a low-pitched, dry, rasping *errrrrrrrr,* (2) short, abrupt *gow* or *gowk,* and (3) higher-pitched, slurred *keew* or *k-kew.* Groups may vocalize in chorus.

Squirrel Cuckoo

Little Cuckoo

juv

ad

Groove-billed Ani

Smooth-billed Ani

Greater Ani

CUCKOOS, GROUND-CUCKOOS, AND ROADRUNNER Cuculidae

Mainly terrestrial cuckoos found in a variety of habitats. Voice is helpful in locating some of these secretive species. The rare and local Rufous-vented Ground-Cuckoo is confined to areas with extensive humid broadleaf forest.

Pheasant Cuckoo *Dromococcyx phasianellus* 35 cm

MX to SA. Uncommon and local resident in lowlands and foothills (to 1000, locally to 2000 m). Mainly Pacific slope in south. **ID** Slender bill and *small head*. Long, broad, graduated tail and whitish speckling on long uppertail coverts. Note *white stripe behind eye*. Pointed, rufous crest may be raised in display, but usually held low against nape. Upperparts brown with fine pale scaling. Underparts white with *dark speckling on upper breast*. Imm lacks speckling and has brown crest. **HABITS** Floor to midstory and edge of semihumid to humid broadleaf forest and tall second growth. Favors dense, tangled areas. Reclusive. May forage or display on ground. Attends ant swarms. Bobs rump and tail as it walks. Solitary or in pairs. Usually detected by voice. May sing at night. **VOICE** Typical call (1) a two- to four-note phrase with first two or three notes clear, and last lower-pitched and quavering *who who who-h-h-h-h*. Compare with songs of Great and Little tinamous. Also compare with song of Striped Cuckoo.

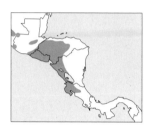

Lesser Ground-Cuckoo *Morococcyx erythropygus* 26 cm

South MX and CA. Fairly common resident in Pacific lowlands and foothills (to 1500 m). Local on Caribbean slope in Motagua Valley, GT (229), and in north HN (Yoro, 442). **ID** Slender and long-tailed. *Cinnamon underparts*. Blue and yellow bare facial skin outlined with black. Bill mostly orange-yellow with dusky culmen. Legs rosy pink. Juv duller and has buff tips on outer rectrices. Compare with Mangrove Cuckoo. Note different head pattern and habits. **HABITS** Floor, understory, and edge of arid to semihumid (deciduous) forest, hedgerows, scrub, and overgrown plantations. Favors areas with terrestrial bromeliads. Reclusive. Sings from elevated, concealed perch. Forages on ground. Solitary or in pairs. **VOICE** Song (1) a series of ten or more loud, slightly hoarse, quavering whistles that start rapidly and gradually slow. Series may be even in pitch or may descend slightly and gradually at end. May include two or three introductory notes *pree, prree-prree-prreeprrree pree, pree, pree, pree, pree*. Also (2) a slightly hoarse, upslurred *wreeep* and (3) a clear whistle with steady pitch *tweeeee*. Compare with softer, lower-pitched call of Thicket Tinamou.

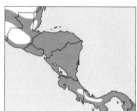

Striped Cuckoo *Tapera naevia* 29 cm

South MX to SA. Locally fairly common resident in lowlands and foothills (to 1500 m). **ID** Long, graduated tail. Dark eye stripe and *shaggy black-and-rufous crest* (often raised) contrast with *white supercilium*. Light ochre-brown upperparts and tail with *blackish streaking*. Note black alula. Juv has gray crown with buff scaling. **HABITS** Understory to lower midstory of scrub, low second growth, and open areas with scattered shrubs. Reclusive. Usually detected by voice. May sing persistently from hidden perch. Raises and lowers crest as it sings. Solitary. **VOICE** Song (1) typically five whistled notes *pee-peep-peepeedee*. Most frequent call (2) two loud, clear, whistles with second higher-pitched. Often repeated persistently.

Lesser Roadrunner *Geococcyx velox* 48 cm

South MX to north CA. Locally fairly common resident in foothills and highlands (mainly 300 to 3000 m). Local on Caribbean slope in Motagua Valley, GT (127, 376) and in north HN (442). **ID** Shaggy crest. Long tail often cocked or briefly spread. *Dusky brown upperparts streaked and spotted with white*. Ad has pale blue bare facial skin. Juv has grayish facial skin. **HABITS** Floor, understory, and edge of arid to semihumid (deciduous) woodland, hedgerows, scrub, plantations, and gardens. Mainly terrestrial. Runs rapidly over ground. Skulks beneath cover. Occasionally loiters in open at edges. Takes elevated perch when vocalizing. Solitary. **VOICE** Call (1) a long, slow series of three to seven low-pitched, downslurred cries *oowah, oowah, oowah, ooowah . . .* Compare with call of Mourning Dove.

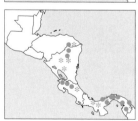

Rufous-vented Ground-Cuckoo *Neomorphus geoffroyi* 50 cm

CA and SA. Rare and local resident in lowlands and foothills (to 1450 m) of east HN (Gracias a Dios, 191), and north NI (RAAN, Chontales, Matagalpa, 537, 326, 139, 299). In CR, mainly in west Caribbean foothills and volcanic slopes (Cartago, Heredia, Limón, Guanacaste, 624, 126, 600). Most recent reports from PA (Coclé, Panamá, Colón, Kuna Yala, Darién, 539, 280, 657, 519, 512, 48). **ID** Very large. *Shaggy crest* and *heavy, greenish-yellow bill*. Long tail often cocked or raised. Note narrow *black breast-band* and blue bare facial skin. Juv (not shown) is much darker with trace of ad's breast-band. **HABITS** Floor and understory of humid broadleaf forest. Runs or hops rapidly over ground. Secretive, but forages boldly at ant swarms. **VOICE** Call (1) a very low-pitched, hollow *ooooooooooo* that is steady or rises slightly in pitch. Compare with call of Great Curassow. Also (2) snaps bill loudly in short, rapid series.

Pheasant Cuckoo

ad

juv

ad

Lesser Ground-Cuckoo

juv

ad

Striped Cuckoo

Lesser Roadrunner

Rufous-vented Ground-Cuckoo

NIGHTHAWKS Caprimulgidae

A distinctive group of nightjars that forage on the wing. *Chordeiles* nighthawks have long, pointed wings that are very different from the rounded wings of other nightjars. The distinctive shape of Short-tailed Nighthawk is usually obvious, but Common and Lesser nighthawks can present identification problems.

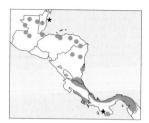

Short-tailed Nighthawk *Lurocalis semitorquatus*   20 cm

South MX to SA. Rare and local resident in humid lowlands and foothills (to 1000 m) of BZ (Cayo, 347, 343, 346), GT (Petén, Quiché, Alta Verapaz, Izabal, 317, 229), HN (Atlántida, Yoro, Gracias a Dios, 317, 346, 629), and NI (RAAS, RAAN, Río San Juan, 331, 413). Uncommon and local in CR and PA. Rarely reported from islands including BZ Cays (343) and Isla Cébaco (Veraguas, 470) where status uncertain. **ID** In flight, note *short tail* and *broad wings*. When perched (often lengthwise on branch) folded wings extend well beyond tail. Shows inconspicuous white forecollar and throat. Plumage dark including remiges and tail (*no white on wing*). Lower underparts pale cinnamon with dusky barring. Compare with Lesser and Common nighthawks. Note different structure and wing pattern. **HABITS** Crepuscular. Solitary birds or pairs forage over canopy of humid broadleaf and gallery forest with erratic, bounding and fluttering flight style. Favors forested river valleys. **VOICE** In flight, gives (1) a short, upslurred, liquid *whoit* or *uwoit*. Usually repeated. Also (2) a louder, upslurred *uhweeeet*.

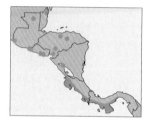

Lesser Nighthawk *Chordeiles acutipennis*   21 cm

South USA to SA. Nearctic migrant and breeding birds occur. Uncommon and local breeder on Pacific slope in GT (Jutiapa, 229), SV (San Vicente, Usulután, 369, 346), NI (Managua, 368), CR (Guanacaste, 600), and PA (657). Breeds on Caribbean slope in BZ (Corozal, Belize, 70, 343) and perhaps north HN (318). Uncommon to (briefly or locally) very common transient (Sep to early Nov and Apr to May) in lowlands and foothills (to 1200 m). **ID** Ad grayish with narrow white or buff forecollar. Male has *white band on primaries*. Female has buff band. Very similar to Common Nighthawk but note *white on primaries nearer wingtip*. Also note more rounded wingtips of Lesser and (usually) browner or buff underwings with dusky bands on base of primaries. At rest, Lesser Nighthawk's wingtips extend just to tail tip (beyond tail tip in Common Nighthawk). Also note pale wing patch extends to tips of tertials in resting Lesser Nighthawk (more proximal in Common Nighthawk). **HABITS** Crepuscular. Roosts on ground on beaches, gravel bars in rivers, scrub, and savanna during daylight hours. May roost in trees including mangroves. Typically flies lower than Common Nighthawk, often close to ground. **VOICE** Calls from low perch or ground. Call (1) a long, low-pitched, toadlike trill *urrrrrrrrr . . .* or *trrrrrrrrr*. Very different from Common Nighthawk. Also compare with call of Vermiculated Screech-Owl. Also (2) a shorter *whik* in flight.

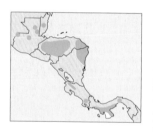

Common Nighthawk *Chordeiles minor*   22–24 cm

NA to SA. Winters SA. Nearctic migrant and breeding visitors occur. Uncommon and local breeder in GT (Huehuetenango, Baja Verapaz, Petén, 229), BZ (Cayo, 529, 343), HN (210, 442), NI (RAAN, 327), CR (Guanacaste, Puntarenas, 600, 570, 210), and PA (Panamá, Chiriquí, 200, 210, 472, 657, 512). Transients may be briefly or locally abundant (Mar to May and Aug to Nov, with peak passage mid-Sep). Rare in winter. **ID** Grayish (including underparts) with white or buff throat and forecollar. Male has white band on tail. In flight, note *flared white wing patch broadest near trailing edge of wing* and midway between tip and bend of wing (compare with Lesser Nighthawk). At rest *wingtips usually extend beyond tail tip*. In close view also note that both whole wing and individual primaries are relatively more pointed in Common Nighthawk. Tenth (outermost) primary longest in Common Nighthawk (ninth longest in Lesser Nighthawk). **GV** Birds from North American breeding migrant population are individually and geographically variable. Birds from north CA breeding populations are similar to NA breeders. Birds breeding in PA are smaller and more buffy and thus more similar to Lesser Nighthawk. **HABITS** Nests (and may roost) on ground in open areas with coarse gravel or very sparse grass. May perch lengthwise on branch. In north CA breeds in pine woodland or savanna. Crepuscular. Transients may form loose flocks or foraging associations. **VOICE** Call (1) a sharp, nasal *eeenk* or *peehn* given in flight. Compare with trilled call of Lesser Nighthawk. In diving display flight wings produce (2) a low-pitched, booming or whooshing sonation.

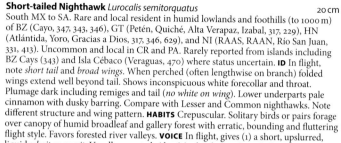

38%

Short-tailed Nighthawk

Lesser Nighthawk

♂

♀

♂

pale
northern migrant
♂

Common Nighthawk

♀

dark
northern migrant
♂

♂

PA breeder
♂

♂

PAURAQUE AND NIGHTJARS Caprimulgidae

Nightjars are nocturnal birds with large mouths and cryptic plumage. These species are found mainly in open or semi-open areas. All have rounded wings that are very different from the pointed wings of *Chordeiles* nighthawks. Each has distinctive vocalizations. Common Pauraque is the most common and widespread nightjar in Central America.

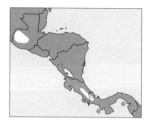

Common Pauraque *Nyctidromus albicollis*   28 cm

South Texas to SA. Common resident in lowlands and foothills (to 1800 m). Also Pearl Islands (Panamá, 58, 611, 649). **ID** *Large* with *long, rounded tail.* Variably gray or brownish-rufous with coarse blackish, white, and buff variegations. White throat and forecollar often conspicuous. *Cinnamon face and auriculars* often contrast with gray crown. Scapulars boldly patterned with dark centers and buff edging. Underparts variably gray to buff with very fine black barring. Male has *white band on primaries* (often visible on folded wing) and mostly white outer rectrices (conspicuous in flight). Female has restricted white forecollar (often tinged buff). Female's outer rectrices have narrow white tips. Female's wing-band narrower and buff. **HABITS** Open areas with short or sparse vegetation including savannas, road margins, lawns, pastures, and agricultural fields. Forages from ground. May allow close approach. Typically flies a short distance when disturbed then settles back on ground. **VOICE** Sings persistently during dry season. Call (1) an abrupt, loud *pur-eeeuu* or *por-eeeeyu* or *per weeh-yu* with middle syllable sharply higher-pitched. Sometimes with stuttering introduction *puc-puc-pureeeuu.*

White-tailed Nightjar *Hydropsalis cayennensis*   21 cm

CA, WI, and north SA. Uncommon to rare and local resident in Pacific lowlands and foothills (to 800 m) of CR and PA (Chiriquí, Coclé, Panamá, Darién, 657). Poorly known in Caribbean lowlands of CR (Limón, 600). **ID** Pale. Long, straight, notched tail. *Pale supercilium* contrasts with dusky eye stripe. Grayish overall with coarse whitish and dusky markings above. Note pale rufous hindcollar and whitish throat. Male has narrow *white band on primaries* and *mostly white tail* (center two rectrices dark). Female has narrow rufous band on primaries. Female's tail barred with rufous and blackish. Compare with Spot-tailed Nightjar. Note different head pattern. Also compare with Common Pauraque. **HABITS** Savannas, pastures, low scrub, large clearings such as airstrips. Nocturnal. Roosts on ground, often under low shrub. Rarely perches on branch. **VOICE** Song (1) a thin, high-pitched *ptcheeeeeeeee* or *chip-weeeeuu.* Second note an attenuated whistle that rises steeply then falls in pitch. Compare with Spot-tailed Nightjar.

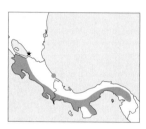

Spot-tailed Nightjar *Hydropsalis maculicaudus*   20 cm

South MX to SA. Very rare, local, and poorly known breeding visitor (or resident?) in lowlands and foothills (to 600 m). Recorded from Lake Yojoa in HN (Cortés, 442, 262) and in lowlands of Mosquitia region in north NI (RAAN, 327). **ID** Grayish with coarse whitish and dusky markings. *Whitish supercilium* contrasts with *dusky face and auriculars.* Note broad buff or white markings on scapulars and whitish spots on wing coverts. Shows broad cinnamon-buff collar. Remiges dusky barred with rufous. Male has white-tipped rectrices. Female has barred rectrices with pale tips. **HABITS** Savannas, marshes, and open areas with short grass and scattered shrubs. Calls from ground or low perch. Also vocalizes in flight. Often flies low. Forages both by sallying from ground and in flight. May begin calling before dark. **VOICE** Song (1) a high-pitched, songbird-like *pitt-seet* or *pitt-see-it* or *chit-eeeit.* Repeated. Compare with song of White-tailed Nightjar.

Common Pauraque

rufous morph ♂

gray morph ♂

♀

♂

♂

White-tailed Nightjar

♂

Spot-tailed Nightjar

♀

POORWILLS AND NIGHTJARS Caprimulgidae

Rare or range-restricted nightjars found mainly in broadleaf forest and edge. All have distinctive vocalizations.

Yucatan Poorwill *Nyctiphrynus yucatanicus* 19 cm

South MX and CA. Uncommon resident in lowlands (to 250 m) of north BZ (529, 313, 343) and north GT (Petén, 637, 378). **ID** Small. Note feathered brow or ridge over eye and *pale breast* often distended to form a *broad "bib."* Variable plumage includes rufous and brown morphs. Note *dark marks on scapulars*. Outer rectrices tipped white. Compare with Yucatan Nightjar. Note different structure and underparts. **HABITS** Floor to midstory and edge of semihumid to humid broadleaf forest, second growth, scrub, and adjacent clearings and plantations. Usually sings and forages from elevated perch inside foliage but may also forage from ground. Perches crosswise on branch. **VOICE** Call (1) given mainly Feb to Oct a loud, rapidly repeated, short, slightly resonant *wheeuu* or *whirrrr*. Also (2) a slightly liquid, clucking *puk-puk-puk* . . .

Ocellated Poorwill *Nyctiphrynus ocellatus* 20 cm

CA and SA. Very rare and local resident in Caribbean lowlands and foothills (to 750 m) of east HN (Gracias a Dios, OlanchO, 34, 33). Historical records from north NI (Jinotega, 412, 413, 429). Recent reports from south Caribbean NI (Río San Juan, 76) and adjacent CR (Alajuela, 594, 546, 76, 346). A report from central PA is unconfirmed (Colón, 512). **ID** Small. Rather plain. Note feathered brow or ridge over eye. Variable plumage includes rufous and dark morph. Breast feathers often distended to form a *broad "bib."* White forecollar often concealed. Outer rectrices tipped white. Note round or triangular *dark spots on scapulars* and sparse *whitish spotting on wing coverts and belly*. **HABITS** Midstory and edge of humid broadleaf forest, second growth, and clearings. Nocturnal. May roost on ground. Calls from perch at midstory in vegetation. Perches crosswise on branch. **VOICE** Call (1) an emphatic, strongly downslurred, slightly quavering *preeeo* or *weerrroo*. Repeated at intervals of about five seconds, sometimes steadily.

Yucatan Nightjar *Antrostomus badius* 25 cm

South MX and CA. Uncommon and local resident in north BZ (Corozal, Orange Walk) and GT (Petén, 229). Nonbreeding resident (Dec to Feb) in south BZ (Cayo, Toledo, 68, 529, 241, 343), east GT (Izabal, 218), and west HN (Atlántida, 318, 100). Transient in BZ Cays (529, 343). **ID** Large-headed. *Blackish breast with coarse white mottling* and whitish malar. Dark and grayish overall with broad cinnamon hindcollar and white forecollar. Male has mostly white outer rectrices (tail mostly white from below). Female has buffy white tips of rectrices. Compare with Yucatan Poorwill. Note different structure, underparts, and voice. Buff-collared Nightjar allopatric. **HABITS** Understory and edge of semihumid broadleaf forest, scrub, brushy woodland, and second growth. Forages from low, open perch and may return there on consecutive nights. **VOICE** Call (1) a rapid, loud, clear *puc ree-u-reeeu* or *ruc weeu-wee-weeuu*. Sometimes repeated rapidly and steadily. First note may not be audible at a distance.

Buff-collared Nightjar *Antrostomus ridgwayi* 23 cm

South USA to CA. Locally fairly common resident in foothills and highlands (500 to 1600 m) of Motagua Valley, GT (276, 376) and south HN (Comayagua, Francisco Morazán, 442). Also west GT (Huehuetenango, 229). Historical records from NI (Chontales, Matagalpa, 413). **ID** Grayish with fine blackish and whitish speckling and vermiculations and *buff hindcollar*. Fine dark streaking on crown. Male has broad white tips on outer rectrices (tail mostly white from below). Female has buff tips on rectrices. Compare with Mexican Whip-poor-will and Common Pauraque. Yucatan Nightjar allopatric. **HABITS** Arid to semihumid brushy woodland, scrub, thorn forest, and edge. Poorly known. Calls and hunts from ground (sometimes on roads) or from stump or bare branch at forest edge. **VOICE** Call (1) a rapid series of notes that rise in pitch and end with a sharp note or short phrase *kuk-kukukuku-uu-ee*. Also (2) a low, coarse *chuuk* or (3) *kruk kruk kruk* . . .

Dusky Nightjar *Antrostomus saturatus* 24 cm

CA endemic. Uncommon to locally fairly common resident in highlands (above 1500 m) of CR and west PA. **ID** *Fairly small and dark*. Mostly brownish with coarse dusky vermiculations and barring. Narrow buff forecollar usually concealed. Male has broad white tips on outer rectrices. Female has buff tips. Compare with Common Pauraque (lower elevations). **HABITS** Midstory and edge of humid broadleaf forest including forest-paramo transition and pastures with scattered trees. Calls from open branch or fence post (rarely from ground). **VOICE** Call (1) a rapidly repeated *chup-wheer-purrwheeew* or *chuck, wheer-purreee*. First note low-pitched and sometimes faint.

Yucatan Poorwill

rufous morph

brown morph

Ocellated Poorwill

rufous morph

dusky morph

Yucatan Nightjar

imm ♀

ad ♀

♂

♀

Buff-collared Nightjar

♂

♂

Dusky Nightjar

♀

♂

♂

38%

NIGHTJARS Caprimulgidae

Two pairs of very similar nightjars that are best separated by voice.

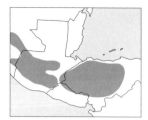

Mexican Whip-poor-will *Antrostomus arizonae* 24 cm

South USA to CA. Uncommon to locally common resident in foothills and highlands (1400 to 3800 m, locally or seasonally to near SL). **ID** Fairly small. Dark brown or gray overall with blackish and gray vermiculations. Note narrow white forecollar and *blackish central crown stripe.* Male has mostly blackish tail with broad white tips on outer three rectrices. Central rectrices gray with blackish barring. Female has mostly gray tail with small buff tips on outer rectrices. Compare with larger Chuck-wills-widow. Note different tail, throat, and crown pattern. **HABITS** Understory to midstory and edge of arid to humid broadleaf and coniferous forest edge, pine-oak woodland, second growth and clearings with scattered trees, and plantations. May forage from ground or perch, sometimes by sallying from dirt roads. Roosts on elevated perch, usually on tree branch. Solitary. **VOICE** Call (1) given mainly Feb to Aug a rapidly repeated, burry *pwurr-p-wiuh, pwurr-p-wiuh . . .* or *whirr-p-wiir, whirr-p-wiir . . .* Slower and lower-pitched than Eastern Whip-poor-will. Calls with (2) low-pitched, hollow, clucking notes.

Eastern Whip-poor-will *Antrostomus vociferus* 24 cm

Breeds east Nearctic. Winters south USA to CA. Rare and poorly known winter visitor to BZ (Stann Creek, Toledo, 529, 341, 343, 346), GT (Izabal, 229, 377), SV (Santa Ana, Cuscatlán, Usulután, San Miguel, Morazán, 183), HN (Copán, Cortés, 442), NI (Chinandega, Matagalpa, 413), CR (Guanacaste, San Jose, Puntarenas, 570, 474), and PA (Chiriquí, 657, 512). Also Bay Islands (346). **ID** Very similar to Mexican Whip-poor-will and probably not separable except by voice. Male Eastern Whip-poor-will typically has more extensive white on tail. Compare with larger Chuck-will's-widow. **HABITS** Semihumid to humid broadleaf and pine-oak forest and edge. Transients may occur in a variety of forested or wooded habitats. Like Mexican Whip-poor-will. **VOICE** Wintering birds usually silent. Call (1) a repeated, three-syllable phrase like Mexican Whip-poor-will but faster and higher-pitched. May give (2) a simple, short *quirt.*

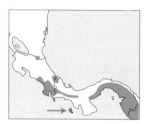

Rufous Nightjar *Antrostomus rufus* 25 cm

CA, WI, and SA. Uncommon to rare and local resident in lowlands and foothills (to 1000 m) of both slopes in south NI (Río San Juan, 452), CR (Puntarenas, Limón, 353, 570), and west PA (Chiriquí, Bocas del Toro, 512). Perhaps most common in east PA (Panamá Dist, Kuna Yala, 129, 512). Also Isla Coiba (Veraguas, 653, 470). **ID** Large, with *large head and flat crown.* Rufous-brown with *narrow white forecollar.* Often shows pale grayish scapulars bordered with large blackish-brown spots. Male has large buff or white spots on outer rectrices (smaller than in Chuck-wills-widow). Female has white confined to inner webs of rectrices. Compare with Chuck-wills-widow. Note different tail pattern. **HABITS** Broadleaf forest edge, second growth, and thickets in savannas. Often in hilly terrain. Perches low or on ground at edges or in clearings. Roosts by day on ground beneath dense vegetation or on low perch. Sings from low perch. **VOICE** Call (1) a repeated, resonant phrase *chuck, wheet-wheet-wee-oo or.* More slurred than Chuck-wills-widow. Often repeated persistently. First syllable often not audible.

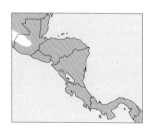

Chuck-will's-widow *Antrostomus carolinensis* 30 cm

Breeds east Nearctic. Winters WI, MX, and CA. Rarely reported transient and winter resident (Sep to Apr) in lowlands and foothills (to 1500 m). Also BZ Cays (347, 341). **ID** *Large,* with long wings. *Large head with flat crown.* Variably rufous-brown or gray overall with blackish and gray vermiculations. Sharp, even blackish streaking on crown and narrow white forecollar. Often shows pale grayish scapulars. Underparts variably rufous or grayish-brown (rarely as gray as Eastern Whip-poor-will). Note pale bill with dark tip. Male has large buff markings on outer rectrices (more extensive than those on Rufous Nightjar). Female has barred rectrices. Compare with Eastern Whip-poor-will. Note different bill, head, and tail. Also compare with Rufous Nightjar. Note different tail pattern. **HABITS** Floor to midstory and edge of forest, second growth, and tall hedgerows and thickets in savannas, marshes, and agricultural areas. Transients or vagrants might appear in a wide variety of habitats. Solitary. Nocturnal. **VOICE** May sing in spring migration. Call (1) a repeated, resonant phrase *chuck, wick-wick-wee-o.* Faster and more clipped than Rufous Nightjar. Also (2) a low-pitched *chuck.* In north compare with song of Yucatan Nightjar.

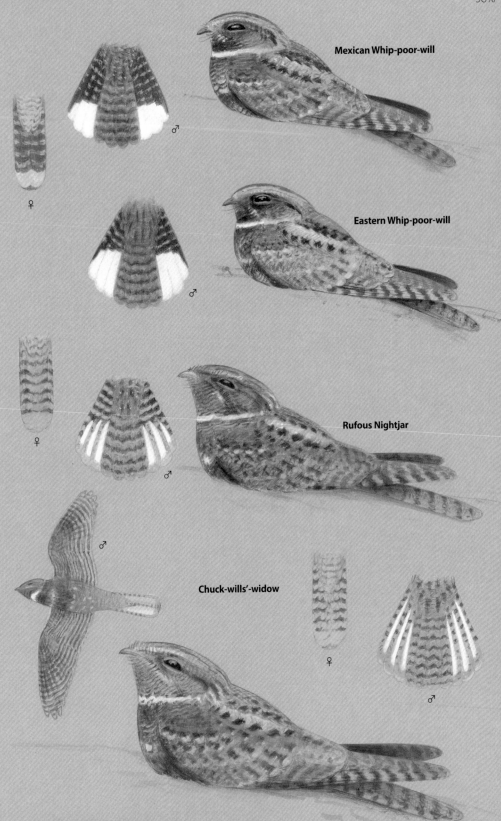

Mexican Whip-poor-will

♀

♂

Eastern Whip-poor-will

♂

Rufous Nightjar

♀

♂

♂

Chuck-wills'-widow

♀

♂

POTOOS Nyctibiidae

Large nocturnal birds that are remarkably cryptic as they perch motionless, with eyes closed, on their day roosts. Their loud, eerie, nocturnal vocalizations are often the best clue to their presence.

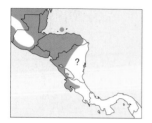

Northern Potoo *Nyctibius jamaicensis*   38 cm
MX, WI, and CA. Uncommon resident in north Caribbean lowlands and foothills (to 1500 m). Rare and local on Pacific slope in GT (Santa Rosa, Suchitepéquez, 279, 182), SV (Usulután, San Miguel, 183, 341, 346), and west CR (Guanacaste, Puntarenas, 570, 666, 546). Also Isla Roatán in Bay Islands (538, 94, 442). **ID** *Large yellow eyes*, broad mouth, and small bill. Mostly gray-brown with fine blackish vermiculations, barring, and streaking. Usually shows long blackish malar and irregular band of blackish spots on breast. Parapatric Common Potoo very similar. Note different voice. Larger Great Potoo is plainer and paler. Note different voice. **HABITS** Midstory to canopy and edge of broadleaf forest, second growth, lake margins, mangroves, and clearings in forest. Nocturnal. Sometimes found in agricultural areas adjacent to forest. Forages by sallying from exposed perch on high, bare limb or fence post. Solitary. Roosts by day in cryptic posture with head steeply inclined and suggesting a broken tree limb. **VOICE** Typical call (1) a loud, hoarse, wailing cry followed by a series of one to four shorter cries on a lower pitch *kwaaah, kwa-kwa-kwa* or *rrrah, rah rah rah*. Also (2) a variety of other low-pitched cries, including an attenuated *awhrrr* or *rroh-rr*.

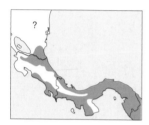

Common Potoo *Nyctibius griseus*   35 cm
CA and SA. Uncommon resident in south lowlands and foothills (to 1250 m). **ID** Large, with large, *yellow eyes*. As with other potoos, note small bill and broad mouth. Mostly pale gray with fine, blackish or dusky streaking and vermiculations. Usually shows *long, narrow, blackish malar* and irregular band of blackish spots on breast. Parapatric Northern Potoo very similar (and probably not separable in field). Note different voice. Great Potoo larger with larger head. Note different voice. **HABITS** Midstory to canopy and edge of semihumid to humid broadleaf forest, tall second growth, and adjacent clearings and plantations. Much like Northern Potoo. **VOICE** Call (1) a series of plaintive cries that are successively shorter and lower-pitched *whhaaaaa waaaa waaa waa wa*.

Great Potoo *Nyctibius grandis*   50 cm
South MX to SA. Rare and local resident in Caribbean lowlands and lower foothills (to 500 m) of GT (Petén, Alta Verapaz, Izabal, 380, 379, 227), south BZ (Toledo, Cayo, 341, 343, 346), HN (Atlántida, 341, 346), NI (RAAN, Río San Juan, Rivas, RAAS, 413), CR (482, 602, 572), and PA (512). Also Pacific lowlands of east CR (Puntarenas, 602, 600). **ID** *Very large* with large head. Paler than other potoos. *Eyes dark brown*. Variable plumage mostly pale gray and buff (some birds nearly whitish) with very fine, sparse, dusky barring and vermiculations. Smaller Common and Northern potoos have more prominent dark markings and more slender structure with proportionally smaller head. **HABITS** Canopy and edge of semihumid to humid broadleaf forest and tall second growth. Nocturnal. Forages by sallying from exposed perch, usually in forest subcanopy or canopy. Roosts by day on branch or snag. Solitary. **VOICE** Calls (1) a single, loud, far-carrying, barking cry *bwow!* or *gwok!* and (2) longer, loud, guttural, snoring *gwawwrrrr* or *bwaaaarrr*.

OILBIRD Steatornithidae

A large, nocturnal, frugivorous bird with no close relatives.

Oilbird *Steatornis caripensis*   42 cm
CA and SA. Poorly known. Perhaps a rare vagrant or rare and local resident. Breeding unknown in CA. Reported Jun to Sep in CR. Reports (some involving several birds) from CR (Cartago, Puntarenas, Guanacaste, San José, 594, 53, 346) and PA (Panamá, Colón, Darién, 512, 341, 346). **ID** Distinctive. Large and long-tailed. Mostly *rufous with fine white spotting*. **HABITS** Nocturnal. Nests colonially in large caves in humid forested regions. Often appears "front heavy" as it perches with head held awkwardly below body. Frugivorous. Feeds primarily on palm fruits. **VOICE** In flight, gives (1) repeated, dry, clicking sounds *chk-chk chk* or *kerr kerr kerr . . .* Foraging birds sometimes give clicking sounds as at nest cave.

juv

ad

Northern Potoo

Common Potoo

At night showing eyeshine.

Great Potoo

At day roost in cryptic pose.

Oilbird

SWIFTS Apodidae

Large swifts. Resident species nest and roost in colonies, often in caves or on cliffs, and often behind waterfalls. White-collared and Chestnut-collared swifts are widespread and relatively easily recognized. The three *Cypseloides* swifts are poorly known and rarely identified.

White-collared Swift *Streptoprocne zonaris*   22 cm

MX and WI to SA. Fairly common resident in foothills and highlands. Often wanders to SL. Also Isla Coiba (Veraguas, 470). **ID** Largest CA swift. Tail notched. Ad black with *white collar*. Imm has white confined to nape. In soaring flight note distinctive wing shape with bulging inner primaries. **HABITS** Usually in flocks (sometimes several hundred birds). Circles while foraging high over a wide variety of terrestrial landscapes including broadleaf or pine-oak forests, plantations, and agricultural lands. **VOICE** In flight, gives (1) loud, slightly burry or buzzy calls *tchee tcheee cheee cheee*.

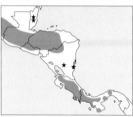

Chestnut-collared Swift *Streptoprocne rutila*   13.5 cm

MX to SA. Uncommon resident in foothills and highlands (mainly 1500 to 2400 m). Wanders to near SL. Rare in BZ (Stann Creek, Cayo, 625, 343, 346), south NI (RAAS, 346), and central PA (Panamá, 341). **ID** Nearly square tail. Male blackish-brown with *chestnut collar*. Female may have collar reduced or lacking and may not be separable in field from Black and White-chinned swifts but note that Chestnut-collared never appears as broad-headed as *Cypseloides* swifts. **HABITS** Usually in flocks flying high overhead. May associate with other swifts. Glides frequently, but perhaps less than White-collared Swift. Often flies with wings below horizontal. Makes short glides alternating with rapid bursts of shallow wingbeats like *Cypseloides* swifts. **VOICE** Gives (1) short busts of very buzzy notes *beez-zee-zee-zee-zee*.

Black Swift *Cypseloides niger*   16.5 cm

NA to SA. Nearctic and resident breeding birds occur. Rare and local breeder in foothills and highlands of CR (Cartago, 599) and perhaps also GT (229) and west PA (Chiriquí, 42). Nonbreeding distribution of CA breeding birds unknown (77). Nearctic birds winter SA and occur as rare transients (Apr to May and Sep to Oct) mainly on Pacific slope and at sea over Pacific (577, 161, 353, 600, 317, 405, 599, 182, 413, 548). Very rare in BZ (Cayo, 346). **ID** *Near-uniform blackish*. Male's *tail long and notched*. Female's tail square. Female and imm typically have extensive whitish markings on belly and crissum. Chestnut-collared Swift smaller and never shows deeply notched tail of male Black Swift. Spot-fronted and White-chinned swifts very similar (and also have square tail) but have less direct, more fluttering flight style. **HABITS** Solitary or in small groups. Makes long glides. May associate with other swifts. **VOICE** Transients usually quiet. Infrequent call (1) a series of sharp, clear notes *chi-chi-chi-chit* or *chip chip chi-dititittt*. Not buzzy.

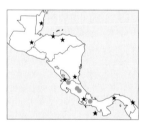

White-chinned Swift *Cypseloides cryptus*   14.5 cm

CA and north SA. Rare and local resident with reports mainly from foothills and highlands (100 to 1900 m) of GT (Chiquimula, 229), BZ (Belize, 529, 313), HN (Olancho, 216, 442), NI (RAAS, 322), CR (Guanacaste, Cartago, Alajuela, Puntarenas, 676, 353, 600, 406, 253, 341), and PA (Chiriquí, Kuna Yala, and near Isla Coiba, 524, 512, 308). Breeds at higher elevations but wanders widely. **ID** Square tail. Near-uniform blackish. Variable, diffuse whitish markings on forehead and chin (rarely discernible in field). Female may show variable whitish markings on lower belly. Similar to Spot-fronted Swift in structure. **HABITS** Forms tight, fast-moving flocks while commuting between roosting and foraging areas. Flight more powerful and direct than Chestnut-collared Swift with rapid wingbeats. Foraging birds may associate with other swifts. **VOICE** Call (1) a short, rapid series of hard, buzzy notes *zazazazeezeezee*.

Spot-fronted Swift *Cypseloides cherriei*   13.5 cm

CA and SA. Poorly known. Rare and local resident in foothills and highlands (mainly 1100 to 2200 m) of east CR (Cartago, San José, Puntarenas, 353, 150, 406, 407) and west PA (Chiriquí, 308). Perhaps also Caribbean slope in west CR (Alajuela, 253). Very rare in east PA (Darién, 346). Most records from upper Pacific slope but wanders to near SL. **ID** Near-uniform blackish with *white spots on lores and behind eye*. Female may show variable whitish markings on lower belly. Structure much like Black Swift but head broader with different tail shape. Very similar to White-chinned Swift but note different head pattern and slightly shorter wings. **HABITS** Favors forested, mountainous areas with steep valleys or gorges. Like White-chinned Swift. **VOICE** Call (1) a twittering, slightly buzzy *ch-ch-ch-chiichii*.

Chestnut-collared Swift

♀

♀

White-collared Swift

imm

♂

ad

Black Swift

♂

♀

White-chinned Swift

Spot-fronted Swift

SWIFTS Apodidae

Small swifts with plain blackish or brownish plumage. The distinctive shape of Short-tailed Swift is often obvious but other *Chaetura* swifts are similar in structure and can present identification problems. Voice is sometimes helpful. Vaux's Swift is the most common and widespread.

Vaux's Swift *Chaetura vauxi*   11–12 cm

NA to SA. Nearctic migrant and resident breeding birds thought to occur. Locally common in foothills and highlands (mainly 600 to 2200 m, locally near SL). Poorly known in NI (Río San Juan, Granada, Rivas, 548). Also Isla Coiba and Pearl Islands off PA (Veraguas, Panamá, 649, 653). **ID** Near-uniform brownish-gray with (variably) *paler gray throat and breast*. Note slightly paler rump. Closely resembles Chimney Swift. Note Vaux's paler underparts and slightly different structure with shorter wings and tail. Flies with more rapid and constant wingbeats than Chimney Swift. **GV** Birds from breeding resident population are darker overall with more contrasting pale throat in comparison with Nearctic migrants. Birds from Azuero Peninsula, PA (not shown) have paler rump. **HABITS** Often forages in flocks over open or semi-open areas.
VOICE Call (1) frequently given in flight, a rapid, high-pitched liquid or soft *treet-treet-treet* or *tseep cheecheechee*. Compare with harder, lower-pitched, more staccato call of Chimney Swift.

Chimney Swift *Chaetura pelagica*   12.5 cm

Breeds Nearctic. Winters SA. Uncommon to briefly or locally common transient (Mar to Apr and Sep to Nov). Passage mainly in Caribbean lowlands (602) and foothills (to 500, rarely to 1000 m). Uncommon on north Pacific slope in SV (La Paz, 365) and GT (Santa Rosa, 182). Winter reports from Caribbean lowlands of CR (Heredia, 341) require verification. **ID** *Near-uniform, brownish-gray* with (variably) very slightly paler gray throat and breast. Compare with Vaux's Swift. Note different underparts and voice. **HABITS** Poorly known in CA. Flocks have been reported migrating along coastlines and interior ridges. **VOICE** Call frequently given in flight (1) a staccato series of sharp, hard notes that accelerate to become a trill *cheet cheet cheet chetetetetetete*. Compare with softer, higher-pitched call of Vaux's Swift.

Chapman's Swift *Chaetura chapmani*   12.5 cm

SA. Rare and poorly known in east PA (Colón, Kuna Yala, Darién, 657, 512, 48). Status uncertain. Perhaps a rare breeding resident or perhaps reaches PA as a nonbreeding visitor. **ID** Glossy blackish. Slightly larger-bodied and shorter-winged than Chimney Swift but probably not separable in field. **HABITS** Very poorly known in CA. **VOICE** Call (1) a hard, metallic *chi-chi-chi-chi . . .*

Short-tailed Swift *Chaetura brachyura*   10.5 cm

CA and SA. Uncommon resident in lowlands of central and east PA. Poorly known in Pacific central PA (Coclé, 46). **ID** Small with *short tail*. Note bulging rear contour of primaries. Near-uniform bluish-black. Extensively pale rump and uppertail coverts conceal the short, dark tail. Also note pale undertail coverts. Other CA *Chaetura* swifts, including widespread Gray-rumped Swift, have different structure with longer tail and different wing shape. **HABITS** Flocks forage high over canopy of humid broadleaf forest. Often in vicinity of rivers or wetlands. **VOICE** Call (1) a high-pitched, very sharp *tsee* or *seet* repeated rapidly and often becoming a hard trill.

northern
migrant

Vaux's Swift

CA
resident

Chimney
Swift

Chapman's
Swift

Short-tailed
Swift

SWIFTS Apodidae

Gray-rumped Swift *Chaetura cinereiventris*   11.5 cm
CA and SA. Uncommon to locally fairly common resident in lowlands and foothills (to 1500, but mainly below 1000 m). Local in Caribbean east HN (Colón, Gracias a Dios, 629) and NI (RAAN, RAAS, 413, 358). **ID** Small. Blackish mantle and wings and diffuse *grayish rump and uppertail coverts*. Band-rumped Swift has similar structure but shows more sharply defined pale rump. In PA compare with Short-tailed Swift. Note different structure. **HABITS** Forages over canopy of humid broadleaf forest. Often near rivers or wetlands. Flies with long periods of rapid wingbeats. Gregarious, usually in flocks of twenty to forty. May forage with other swifts or with swallows. Hovers briefly to glean insects from vegetation. **VOICE** Call (1) a short, rapid series of piercing, very high-pitched notes *seeseeseesee*.

Band-rumped Swift *Chaetura spinicaudus*   11.5 cm
CA and SA. Locally fairly common resident in lowlands and foothills (to 1200 m) of central and east PA (Veraguas, Colón, Panamá, Darién, 657, 404). **ID** Small. Blackish mantle and wings contrast with *pale gray rump-band*. Gray-rumped Swift has more extensive gray extending from rump through tail. Costa Rican Swift allopatric. Also compare with Short-tailed Swift. Note different structure. **HABITS** Forages over canopy of humid broadleaf forest and adjacent open areas. Often near rivers or wetlands. Perhaps crepuscular. In small flocks. May forage with other swifts. May hover briefly while foraging. **VOICE** In flight, gives (1) a series of high-pitched notes *chiip* or *cheep*. May accelerate into a short, thin trill.

Costa Rican Swift *Chaetura fumosa*   11 cm
CA endemic. Confined to humid Pacific lowlands and foothills (to 1200 m) of CR (Puntarenas, 66, 657, but see 404) and west PA. Uncommon to locally common in CR. Poorly known in PA (Chiriquí, 512). **ID** Small. Mostly blackish. *Pale gray rump-band*. Band-rumped Swift has slightly narrower rump-band but is thought to be allopatric. **HABITS** Usually in flocks flying high over canopy of humid broadleaf forest. Often near rivers or wetlands. **VOICE** In flight, gives (1) high-pitched, slightly squeaky notes that may accelerate into a soft trill *cheepa-cheepa-tr-r-r-r-r*.

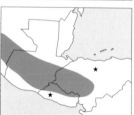

White-throated Swift *Aeronautes saxatalis*   15 cm
NA to SA. Uncommon resident in north foothills and highlands (mainly above 600 m). **ID** Shallow forked tail (often closed to form a point). Mostly dark brown with white throat and center of breast and belly and *white marks on rear flanks*. No other CA swift has such extensive white on underparts. Compare with Lesser Swallow-tailed and Great Swallow-tailed swifts. Note different underparts and structure. Also compare with Violet-green Swallow. **HABITS** Forages over arid to humid areas, including steep mountain slopes, canyons and cliff faces. In pairs or small groups. Flies fast with fairly rapid wingbeats. Also soars and makes long, fast glides. **VOICE** Often noisy. Call (1) a loud, shrill *klee-klee-klee . . .*

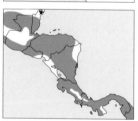

Lesser Swallow-tailed Swift *Panyptila cayennensis*   13 cm
MX to SA. Uncommon resident in humid lowlands and foothills (to 1000 m). Rare and local in Pacific GT (Santa Rosa, Escuintla, 182) and SV (Ahuachapán, Chalatenango, Santa Ana, 363, 341, 346). **ID** Small and slender. *Long, deeply forked tail* usually closed in narrow point. Mostly black with *white throat and collar* and *white patch on flanks*. Compare with White-throated Swift (highlands). Note different underparts. Great Swallow-tailed Swift is larger. **HABITS** Pairs forage high over canopy of broadleaf forest and adjacent open areas. Displays erratic, swallow-like flight with long glides, abrupt turns, and short bursts of slow wingbeats. **VOICE** Gives (1) buzzy, thin, high-pitched calls in flight *pssi zzizziizzi* or *pzi zii sii-sii-sii*.

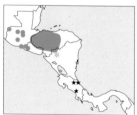

Great Swallow-tailed Swift *Panyptila sanctihieronymi*   20 cm
South MX and CA. Uncommon to rare and local resident in north highlands (mainly above 1000, rarely or locally as low as 500 m) of GT (Baja Verapaz, Alta Verapaz, Huehuetenango, Sacatepéquez, Chiquimula, Quiché, 182, 229, 279, 539), SV (Santa Ana, Libertad, Chalatenango, 341), and HN (Francisco Morazán, El Paraíso, Santa Bárbara, Olancho, Choluteca, 125, 442). Rare in NI (Nueva Segovia, Matagalpa, Jinotega, 413). Vagrant to CR (Heredia, Limón, Puntarenas, 602, 600, 265). **ID** Large. *Long, deeply forked tail* usually closed in narrow point. Mostly black with *white throat and collar* and *white patch on flanks*. Pattern like smaller Lesser Swallow-tailed Swift, but shows more white on trailing edge of wing. Note different habits. Great Swallow-tailed Swift has steadier flight with longer glides. Compare with White-throated Swift. Note different underparts. **HABITS** Pairs or small groups forage over rugged, forested or partly forested highland terrain. **VOICE** Call (1) a short series of loud, shill cries. Often accelerate and end with an emphatic note *kree kri-kri-kri-kri kree-kreeh*. Compare with call of Killdeer.

Gray-rumped
Swift

Band-rumped
Swift

Costa Rican
Swift

Lesser
Swallow-tailed
Swift

White-throated
Swift

Great
Swallow-tailed
Swift

JACOBIN, SICKLEBILL, AND HERMITS Trochilidae

Hummingbirds found in humid broadleaf forest. Most have strongly decurved bill. White-tipped Sicklebill is highly distinctive in plumage, structure, and habits. Tail and underparts pattern are useful in identifying Band-tailed Barbthroat and *Glaucis* hermits.

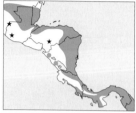

White-necked Jacobin *Florisuga mellivora* 11.5 cm

South MX to SA. Fairly common resident in lowlands and foothills (to 500, locally to 750 m). Rare visitor (Oct to Feb) to Pacific slope in GT (Suchitepéquez, 229). **ID** Fairly large with square tail. Male has *blue hood* and *mostly white tail*. Variable female has *scaled breast* and *white on tail*. Scaly-breasted Hummingbird is less boldly patterned below and has white postocular spot. **HABITS** Midstory to canopy and edge of semihumid to humid broadleaf forest, second growth, plantations, and gardens. Hawks insects from perch or over water. Hovers with tail cocked. **VOICE** Usually quiet. Song (1) a long, rapid series of high-pitched, thin *tseep* notes. Call (2) a high-pitched, thin *tseet* or *tseep*. May be repeated.

White-tipped Sicklebill *Eutoxeres aquila* 13 cm

CA and north SA. Uncommon to rare and local resident in south humid lowlands and foothills (300 to 1000 m, rarely or locally higher). Rare in Pacific west PA (Chiriquí, 657). Perhaps undertakes local or elevational movements (593, 670). **ID** Large and robust. *Long, heavy, and very strongly decurved bill* with yellow mandible. Note *underparts streaked* with whitish and dusky. Graduated tail with white-tipped rectrices. **HABITS** Understory and edge of humid broadleaf forest and tall second growth. Clings (rarely hovers) while feeding at *Heliconia* flowers. **VOICE** Variable song (1) a long, rhythmic series of squeaky notes *chwee chee tzee cheea zet zet zeezeezee ee-ee-ee.* Call (2) a piercing, high-pitched thin *tseet.*

Bronzy Hermit *Glaucis aeneus* 10.5 cm

CA and north SA. Uncommon to locally fairly common resident in humid lowlands and foothills (to 750 m). Poorly known in Caribbean east HN (Gracias a Dios, 34) and north NI (RAAN, Jinotega, 413). **ID** Long, decurved bill with yellow base of mandible. Upperparts bronzy green. *Underparts dull rufous* including crissum. *Rounded, graduated tail* with broad rufous band at base, blackish subterminal band and white-tipped rectrices. Rufous-breasted Hermit mainly allopatric but note different upperparts. Resembles Band-tailed Barbthroat (often syntopic). Note different tail pattern, bill shape, and underparts. **HABITS** Understory of humid broadleaf forest, tall second growth, and adjacent shaded plantations. **VOICE** Song (1) a series of thin, slurred, very high-pitched notes followed by a long, steeply descending, liquid trill *schee cheew chee cht-t-t-t-t-t-tu-tutu-tu.* May be repeated persistently. Call (2) a thin *tseew* or *tseet* often given in series.

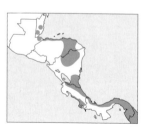

Rufous-breasted Hermit *Glaucis hirsutus* 11 cm

CA and SA. Uncommon to fairly common resident in humid lowlands of PA. Confined to Caribbean slope in west PA (Bocas del Toro, 469). **ID** Long, decurved bill with *yellowish mandible*. Note *rounded tail* with broad rufous band at base and white-tipped rectrices. Upperparts green. Underparts mostly plain dull cinnamon with grayish crissum. Female has short, whitish malar and whitish postocular spot. Male duskier. In west Caribbean PA compare with Bronzy Hermit. Note different upperparts color. Resembles Band-tailed Barbthroat (often syntopic). Note different tail pattern, bill shape, and underparts pattern. **HABITS** Understory and edge of humid broadleaf forest and tall second growth. Favors stands of *Heliconia* and other large-leaved herbs. **VOICE** Song (1) a long series of *tcheep* or *cheep* notes. Call (2) a rich, slightly trilled or rolled *chreeup.*

Band-tailed Barbthroat *Threnetes ruckeri* 11 cm

CA and north SA. Uncommon to locally fairly common resident in humid lowlands and foothills (to 700 m). At north limit in south BZ (Toledo, Stann Creek, 72, 313, 343). **ID** *Rounded, graduated tail.* Long decurved bill with yellow mandible. *Dusky throat* contrasts with *rufous breast* and whitish malar. Note white band at base of tail and blackish subterminal band. Bronzy Hermit has different tail pattern and paler throat. **GV** Birds from east PA are greener (less coppery) above. **HABITS** Understory of humid broadleaf forest, second growth, and adjacent shaded plantations and gardens. Favors stands of large-leaved herbs such as *Heliconia.* Twitches tail up and down while perched. Sings persistently. **VOICE** Song (1) a long, complex series of very high-pitched, squeaky or buzzy phrases *swee wee tsee zee tse tse squee . . .* On Pacific slope includes buzzy trills and high-pitched, whistled phrases. In flight, gives (2) a sharp *sqzzk.* Lower-pitched and buzzier than calls of hermits.

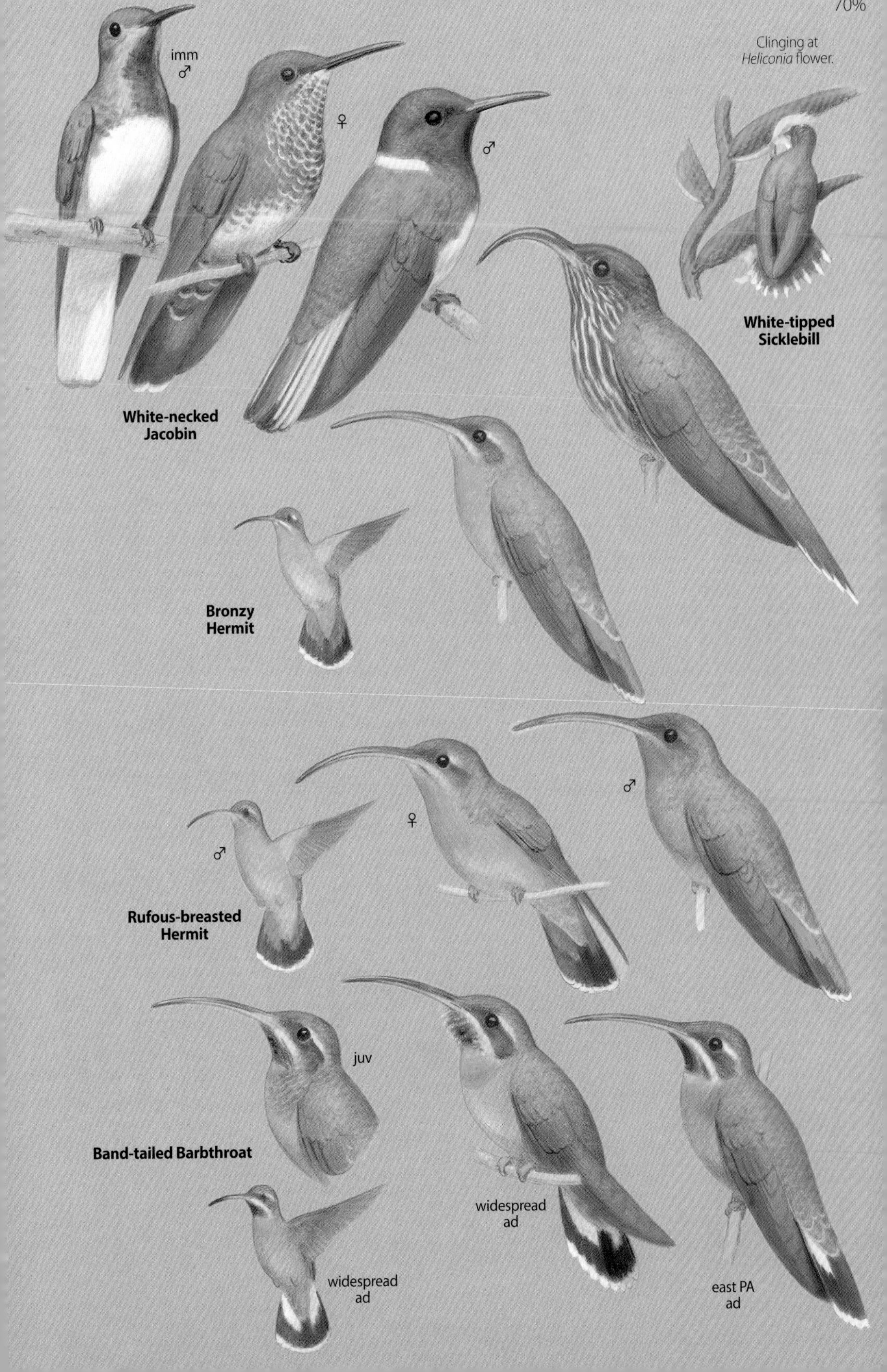

70%

imm
♂

♀

♂

Clinging at
Heliconia flower.

**White-tipped
Sicklebill**

**White-necked
Jacobin**

**Bronzy
Hermit**

♂

♀

♂

**Rufous-breasted
Hermit**

juv

Band-tailed Barbthroat

widespread
ad

widespread
ad

east PA
ad

HERMITS AND LANCEBILL Trochilidae

Hummingbirds found mainly at lower levels in humid broadleaf forest. *Phaethornis* hermits all have decurved bill and long central rectrices. Often inquisitive. Male hermits flick their tail as they sing at leks in shaded understory. Long-billed and Stripe-throated hermits are the most common and widespread.

White-whiskered Hermit *Phaethornis yaruqui* 14.5 cm

CA and SA. Poorly known. Perhaps a rare and local resident in lowlands and foothills of east PA (Darién, 558) **ID** Large and dark. Long bill less decurved than in other hermits and with reddish mandible. Dark auriculars contrast with buff supercilium. Note *whitish malar* and variable *whitish central throat stripe. Sides of breast and upperparts dark green.* Crissum white. Compare with Pale-bellied and Long-billed hermits. Green Hermit found mainly at higher elevations. **HABITS** Understory to midstory and edge of humid broadleaf forest. **VOICE** Song (1) a harsh, rapidly repeated *zreet-eet zreet-eet zreet-eet . . .* Call (2) a high-pitched *seeek* or *tseeet.*

Green Hermit *Phaethornis guy* 14 cm

CA and north SA. Fairly common resident in south foothills and highlands (700 to 2000 m, locally near SL). Perhaps undertakes local or elevational movements (593, 670). **ID** Large. Long, strongly decurved bill. Male mostly *deep iridescent green.* Note male's faint pale malar and long, white-tipped central rectrices. Female has longer central rectrices and buff supercilium, throat, and malar. Breast and belly grayish. Long-billed Hermit (mainly lower elevations) has paler, golden-brown upperparts. **HABITS** Understory to midstory of humid broadleaf forest. Forages mainly at low levels but may visit flowers in subcanopy. Males produce a snapping sonation with wings. **VOICE** Song (1) a long series of nasal, squeaky notes *byup, byup, byup, byup, byup . . .* or *yip yip yip yip, yip . . .*

Long-billed Hermit *Phaethornis longirostris* 15 cm

CA and north SA. Fairly common resident in lowlands and foothills (to 1300, mainly below 600 m in north). Confined to Caribbean slope in north. **ID** Large and slender with *long, strongly decurved bill* and *long white central rectrices.* Note buff belly, grayish breast and tawny rump with dusky barring. Compare with Green Hermit (higher elevations). Smaller Stripe-throated Hermit widely syntopic. Note different underparts. **HABITS** Understory to lower midstory of semihumid to humid broadleaf forest and adjacent tall second growth. **VOICE** Song (1) a rapidly repeated, buzzy *zzreep zzreep zzreep* or *weesp weesp wseep.* Often given persistently. Call (2) a high-pitched, sharp *sweek.*

Pale-bellied Hermit *Phaethornis anthophilus* 14 cm

CA and SA. Uncommon resident in lowlands of central and east PA. Fairly common in Pearl Islands (Panamá, 58, 611, 649). **ID** Long, decurved bill and long white central rectrices. Greenish-olive above and *whitish below including streaked throat.* Note reddish mandible. Long-billed Hermit is more bronzy above, has more contrasting rump, and has more strongly decurved bill. Green Hermit (higher elevations) has darker underparts. **GV** Birds from Pearl Islands (not shown) are slightly greener above. **HABITS** Midstory at edge of semihumid to humid broadleaf forest, tall second growth, mangroves, and scrub. More often in open areas than other CA hermits. **VOICE** Song (1) a long, halting series of thin, high-pitched phrases *tseee-eet tseee-eee eee-it . . .*

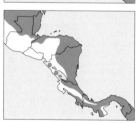

Stripe-throated Hermit *Phaethornis striigularis* 9 cm

CA and north SA. Common resident in lowlands and foothills (to 1200 m, seasonally or locally to 1600 m). Mainly Caribbean slope in north but reported from Pacific volcanic highlands of NI (Chinandega, Granada, 413). **ID** *Smallest* CA hermit. Note long, decurved bill and long, graduated tail. Long central rectrices tipped with buff or whitish. *Underparts typically cinnamon* (some are grayish below). Other CA hermits larger and none have similar underparts. **HABITS** Understory to midstory of semihumid to humid broadleaf forest, gallery forest, and tall second growth. **VOICE** Song (1) a long series of high-pitched, rapidly repeated phrases *wseep-eep tseep wseep tseet . . .* Call (2) a high-pitched *tcheep* or *tseet.*

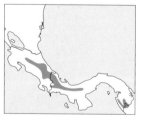

Green-fronted Lancebill *Doryfera ludovicae* 11.5 cm

CA and SA. Uncommon to rare and local resident in south foothills and highlands (750 to 2300 m). Moves to lower elevations outside breeding season (593). **ID** *Very long, slightly upturned bill,* rounded crown and *rounded, all-dark tail.* Note *small white postocular spot.* In good light male shows glittering blue-green forecrown and brownish or coppery cast on head, nape. and mantle. Lower underparts dull gray. Appears very dark in poor light. **GV** Birds from east PA are paler with green forecrown. **HABITS** Understory to subcanopy of humid broadleaf forest. Favors shaded streamsides or ravines. Feeds at hanging, tubular flowers by probing from below. Sallies for insects and returns to same low perch. **VOICE** Call (1) a very sharp, slightly dry *snick* or *chiit.* Sometimes doubled or given in rapid, stuttering series.

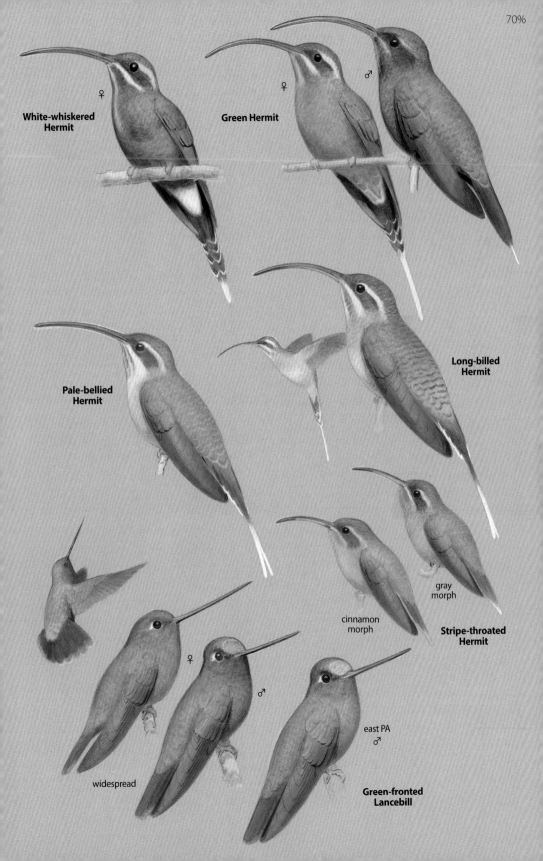

White-whiskered Hermit ♀

Green Hermit ♀ ♂

Long-billed Hermit

Pale-bellied Hermit

gray morph

cinnamon morph

Stripe-throated Hermit

widespread ♀ ♂

east PA ♂

Green-fronted Lancebill

VIOLETEARS, BRILLIANT, AND PUFFLEG Trochilidae

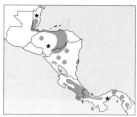

Brown Violetear *Colibri delphinae*   11 cm

CA and SA. Uncommon in lowlands and foothills (to 1000, occasionally to 1400 m). Wanders to lower elevations outside breeding season. **ID** Fairly large. *Short, near-straight bill.* Mostly drab, grayish-brown with variable *whitish or buff malar.* In good light note glittering violet auriculars and restricted green gorget. Near-square tail with *dark subterminal band.* Uppertail coverts and crissum cinnamon barred with dusky. **HABITS** Midstory to canopy and edge of humid broadleaf forest, tall second growth, and shaded plantations. Sings from open perch while fanning tail. **VOICE** Song (1) a series of five to ten emphatic, squeaky *tseeup* or *ksip* notes. Compare with songs of Lesser and Mexican violetears. Call (2) a short, hard, dry *tchip* or *tchichip* or *chidit.*

Mexican Violetear[4] *Colibri thalassinus*   11 cm

MX and CA. Common resident in north foothills and highlands (1400 to 3800, locally or seasonally as low as 500 m). Uncommon and local in volcanic highlands of SV and in north NI (Chinandega, Jinotega, Matagalpa, 411, 413). **ID** Fairly large with *decurved bill* and square tail. Mostly iridescent green with blue central underparts. Note *blue-violet auriculars* and *broad, dark tail-band.* Juv duller and lacks violet auriculars. Lesser Violetear allopatric. **HABITS** Midstory to canopy of forest edge, plantations, gardens, and urban areas. Males vocalize persistently from favored perch on high, exposed snag or utility line. **VOICE** Song (1) a long series of emphatic, short phrases *cheep cheet-chup, chip cheet-chup . . .* Call (2) a sharp, dry, low-pitched *chute* or *buut.* Sometimes given in long, rapid series. May accelerate into a chatter.

Lesser Violetear[4] *Colibri cyanotus*   11 cm

CA and SA. Common resident in south foothills and highlands (1400 to 3000, locally or briefly as low as 500 m). **ID** Fairly large with *decurved bill* and square tail. Iridescent green including underparts (may appear all-dark). Note *blue-violet auriculars* and *broad, dark tail-band.* Juv duller and lacks violet auriculars. Mexican Violetear allopatric. **HABITS** Midstory to canopy of forest edge, plantations, gardens and urban areas. Much like Mexican Violetear. **VOICE** Song (1) a long series of short notes that may alternate slightly in pitch *cheep chiit, cheep chiit, . . .* Call (2) a sharp, dry, low-pitched *chute* or *chut.* Sometimes given in long, rapid series. May accelerate into a chatter.

Green-crowned Brilliant *Heliodoxa jacula*   female 12, male 14.5 cm

CA and north SA. Locally common resident in highlands (700 to 2000 m) of CR. Uncommon and local in PA. **ID** Large. Bill shape sexually dimorphic. *Low, sloping forehead* and *long, dark, forked tail.* Ad male mostly iridescent green with small white postocular spot. Small gorget glittering blue-violet. Ad female has white postocular spot and *white moustachial streak.* Female's underparts densely spotted or scaled with white and dark green. Note white-tipped rectrices. Imm male has *rufous malar and chin.* Compare female and imm with female White-necked Jacobin (mainly lower elevations). Note different structure and habits. **GV** Birds from east PA (Darién, not shown) have greenish central rectrices. **HABITS** Midstory to canopy and edge of humid broadleaf forest. Feeds while perched or hovering. **VOICE** Call (1) a loud, squeaky *kyew* or *tyew.* May be repeated rapidly.

Greenish Puffleg *Haplophaedia aureliae*   female 10, male 11.5 cm

CA and SA. Locally common resident in highlands (above 900 m) of east PA including Serranía de Jungurudó, Pirre Massif, Cerro Malí, and Tacarcuna Massif (Darién, 657, 519, 45). **ID** Straight black bill, rounded forehead and white postocular spot. Mostly deep iridescent green with coppery crown and rump. Often appears all-dark. Note white tibial tufts and faint whitish scaling on breast. Notched tail dark with slight violet gloss. Female has more whitish scaling below and whitish belly. Compare male with Bronze-tailed Plumeleteer (lower elevations). **HABITS** Understory to lower midstory and edge of humid broadleaf (cloud) forest and second growth. **VOICE** Call (1) a high-pitched *tsit.* May be repeated in long, monotonous series.

Scaly-breasted Hummingbird *Phaeochroa cuvierii*   12 cm

CA and north SA. Uncommon resident in lowlands and foothills (to 1200 m). Also Isla Coiba (Veraguas, 470). **ID** Large and plain with *white-tipped outer rectrices* and *white postocular spot.* Underparts green with *fine buff scaling.* Belly dingy buff. Compare with female White-necked Jacobin. **GV** Birds from south CA have pinkish mandible and greenish base of rectrices. Birds from Isla Coiba (not shown) are darker. **HABITS** Understory to midstory and edge of humid broadleaf forest, plantations, gardens, and mangroves. Males form small singing assemblies in which they vocalize from an open perch. **VOICE** Song (1) a variable, long, complex series of loud, squeaky or slurred phrases including four to eight notes *tseee chew tseetsee teew.* Typically includes sharp squeaks alternating with short trills. Call (2) a piercing *cheet.*

65%

Brown
Violetear

Mexican
Violetear

Lesser
Violetear

Green-crowned
Brilliant

imm
♀

imm
♂

ad
♂

ad
♀

♀

♂

Greenish Puffleg

♀

north
CA

south
CA

White-necked Jacobin
for comparison
(text and map p. 88)

Scaly-breasted
Hummingbird

HUMMINGBIRDS, FAIRY, AND MANGOS Trochilidae

Hummingbirds found mainly in humid broadleaf forest. *Anthracothorax* mangos are large hummingbirds found mainly at middle and upper levels of forest edge, second growth, and woodland. All have slightly decurved bill and magenta tail. Green-breasted Mango is the most common and widespread.

Tooth-billed Hummingbird *Androdon aequatorialis*   12.5 cm
CA and north SA. Uncommon to rare and local resident in lowlands and foothills (to 1450 m) of east PA (Darién, 657, 519, 45). **ID** Large. *Very long, slightly upturned bill.* At close range note yellow base of mandible and fine hook on bill tip. Tail rounded. Underparts and auriculars *streaked with black and white.* Note *white lateral rump patches* and white tips of rectrices. In favorable light shows coppery crown. **HABITS** Midstory to subcanopy and edge of humid broadleaf forest. Favors light gaps and small clearings. Forages by traplining. **VOICE** Song (1) a series of very high-pitched, thin notes *tseet tsit tsee-it* . . . Call (2) a lower-pitched, sharp, penetrating *tcheep* or *tchit.* Sometimes repeated persistently. May be doubled as *tcheep-it.*

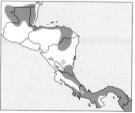

Purple-crowned Fairy *Heliothryx barroti*   female 14, male 12 cm
South MX to north SA. Fairly common resident in lowlands and foothills (to 1250, rarely or locally to 1650 m). **ID** *Long tail.* Straight bill and low, sloping forehead. Note black mask. *Underparts and underside of tail immaculate white.* Above mostly iridescent green. Ad male has glittering violet crown. Female and imm may have fine, dark spotting on throat and upper breast. **HABITS** Midstory to canopy and edge of semihumid to humid broadleaf forest and tall second growth. Bathes at puddles or forest pools by hovering over water and dipping briefly at surface. Sallies to take insects in flight. Spreads and flips tail in flight. **VOICE** Usually quiet. Calls include (1) a high-pitched, staccato series of thin metallic or tinkling *tsit* notes. May accelerate to form a trill.

Green-breasted Mango *Anthracothorax prevostii*   12 cm
South MX and CA. Disjunctly in north SA. Uncommon resident in lowlands (to 300, occasionally or locally to 1100 m). South to Caribbean west PA (Bocas del Toro, 469, 42). Most common on coasts and Caribbean islands including BZ Cays (535, 529) and Bay Islands (94, 442, 622). Perhaps undertakes seasonal movements (365). **ID** Fairly large. Long, slightly decurved bill and low, rounded crown. Tail rounded. Ad male mostly deep green with *black central throat stripe.* Tail mostly magenta. Female has black throat stripe and blue-green breast stripe contrasting with otherwise mostly white underparts. Female's tail boldly patterned with magenta base, blackish subterminal band, and white-tipped rectrices. Black-throated Mango allopatric. **HABITS** Midstory to subcanopy in semi-open areas including forest edge, savannas, mangroves, littoral scrub, plantations, and gardens. **VOICE** Song (1) a short, rhythmic series of buzzy phrases. Calls (2) a repeated, liquid *tsup* or *tseep* and (3) buzzy *pzzt.*

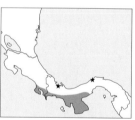

Veraguan Mango *Anthracothorax veraguensis*   12 cm
CA endemic. Uncommon resident in Pacific lowlands and foothills (to 500 m) of east CR (Puntartenas, 114) and west PA. Vagrant to Caribbean PA (Colón, Bocas del Toro, 42). **ID** Structure like other mangos. Ad male mostly deep green below (no black) with *entirely glittering green throat.* Female has *blue-green stripe* (appears blackish in poor light) contrasting with white sides of breast. Compare with Green-breasted Mango. **HABITS** Understory to canopy of open and semi-open areas including hedgerows, disturbed woodland, plantations, mangroves, and gardens. Visits flowering trees in dry season. **VOICE** Call (1) a high-pitched *tsi tsi* or *chi chi* or *tsi, tsi-chichichit.*

Black-throated Mango *Anthracothorax nigricollis*   12 cm
CA and SA. Locally fairly common resident in lowlands and foothills (to 500 m) of central and east PA. **ID** Fairly large. Long, slightly decurved bill and low, rounded crown. Mostly *magenta tail* rounded. Ad male mostly deep green with *broad, black, central stripe* extending to belly and bordered with glittering blue on throat. Female's broad, *blackish breast-stripe* contrasts with white sides of breast. Note narrowly white-tipped outer rectrices and black subterminal band on tail. Imm male resembles female but has rufous on neck and upper breast. Green-breasted Mango allopatric. **HABITS** Midstory of semi-open areas including forest edge, savannas, mangroves, plantations, and gardens. Forages at flowering trees. Sallies for insects from exposed perch. **VOICE** Call (1) a slightly dry *tchup* or *tseep.*

Ruby-topaz Hummingbird *Chrysolampis mosquitus*   10 cm
CA and SA. Poorly known. Rare in lowlands and foothills of east PA (Darién, 104, 346). **ID** Small. *Short, near-straight bill* and low sloping forehead. Note mostly rufous tail. Ad male has *glittering magenta crown* and *orange gorget* (may appear greenish in poor light). Otherwise mostly dark, dusky brown. Female mostly drab gray below and dull greenish above with dusky auriculars. Note female's *mostly rufous outer rectrices with white tips* and *dark subterminal band.* **HABITS** Understory to midstory of humid broadleaf forest, savannas, woodland, mangroves, plantations, and gardens. **VOICE** Call (1) a rich, clear *cleep* or *cheep.* Given singly or in series.

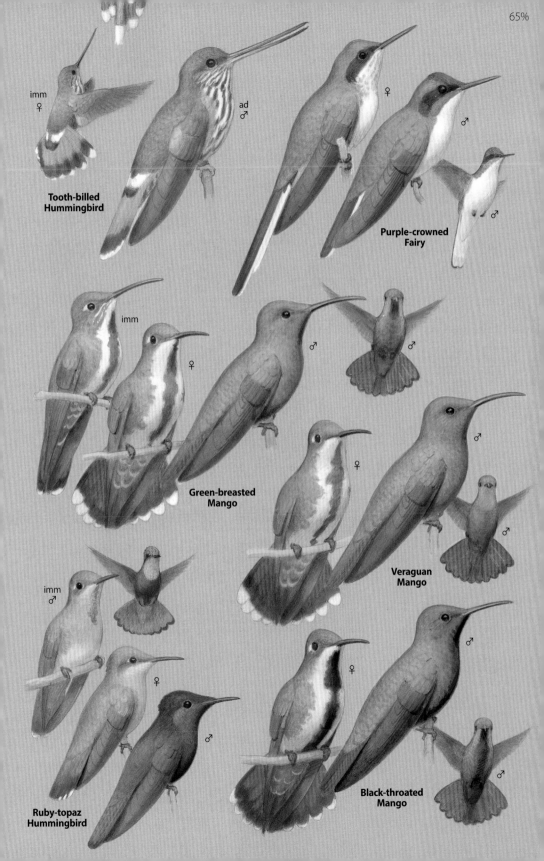

imm ♀

Tooth-billed
Hummingbird

ad ♂

♀

♂

♂

Purple-crowned
Fairy

imm

♀

♂

♂

Green-breasted
Mango

♀

♂

♂

Veraguan
Mango

imm ♂

♀

♂

♀

♂

Ruby-topaz
Hummingbird

♂

Black-throated
Mango

THORNTAIL, COQUETTES, AND HUMMINGBIRDS Trochilidae

Tiny hummingbirds found mainly in middle and upper levels of humid broadleaf forest. All have weaving, insect-like flight with horizontal aspect and often hold tail cocked. All have white on rump or white postocular spot.

Green Thorntail *Discosura conversii* female 7, male 11 cm

CA and north SA. Uncommon resident in foothills (700 to 1400 m, rarely or briefly to near SL). **ID** Tiny. Straight bill. Tail often cocked while hovering. *White rump-band* contrasts with blackish tail and uppertail coverts. Male has *long, wiry tail.* Female has *white markings on* underparts. Female has forked tail with white edging. *Lophornis* coquettes also have whitish rump-band. Note different tail shape. Also compare with *Calliphlox* woodstars. **HABITS** Midstory to canopy and edge of humid broadleaf forest, adjacent tall second growth, plantations, and clearings with scattered trees. Takes prominent perch on high, bare twig. Visits flowering *Inga* trees. **VOICE** Often quiet. Call (1) a high-pitched, liquid *tsit* or *tseep*. Displaying male produces a buzzy sonation.

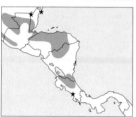

Black-crested Coquette *Lophornis helenae* 7.5 cm

South MX and CA. Uncommon to rare resident in Caribbean lowlands and foothills (to 1500 m). Local in Pacific foothills of GT (Quetzaltenango, Retalhuleu, Suchitepéquez, 378, 105, 346). Vagrant to north BZ (Corozal, Orange Walk, Belize, 346) and Pacific slope in east CR (Puntarenas, 346). Perhaps undertakes seasonal or local movements. **ID** Tiny. *Short, straight mostly red bill.* Tail mostly rufous. Male has green gorget bordered with black. *Black and buff plumes extend from below gorget and long green plumes extend from forecrown.* Female has bronze spotting on breast and flanks and *buff throat.* Other *Lophornis* coquettes allopatric. **HABITS** Midstory to canopy and edge of humid broadleaf forest, second growth, and adjacent clearings. Pumps tail while hovering. Males perch on high, bare twigs and return there after foraging or pursuing intruders. Visits flowering *Inga* trees. **VOICE** Usually quiet. Calls (1) a sweet, slightly metallic *cheep* or *tseek* and (2) clear, upslurred *tsuweee*. Chase call (3) a high-pitched twittering.

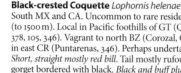

White-crested Coquette *Lophornis adorabilis* 7.5 cm

CA endemic. Uncommon to rare and local resident in Pacific lowlands and foothills (to 1300 m) of east CR (Puntarenas, 142, 600) and west PA (Chiriquí, 657, 512). Rare in Caribbean foothills of CR (Cartago, 341), where status uncertain. Perhaps undertakes local or seasonal movements. **ID** Tiny. Note white rump-band. Ad male has *white plumes extending from forecrown* and green plumes extending from gorget. Note male's *white breast-band* and *mostly rufous tail.* Female has *white throat* and rufous lower underparts. Black-crested Coquette mainly allopatric. **HABITS** Midstory to canopy and edge of humid broadleaf forest. **VOICE** Usually quiet. Call (1) a soft, liquid *tseep.*

Rufous-crested Coquette *Lophornis delattrei* 7 cm

CA and SA. Uncommon to rare resident in lowlands and foothills (to 1300 m) of PA. Rare in highlands of Azuero Peninsula (Veraguas) and on Caribbean slope in CR (Limón, Cartago, 66, 600, 346). **ID** Tiny. *Short, straight mostly red bill.* Note white rump-band. Male has broad, glittering green gorget and *long rufous crest.* Female has *rufous crown and face.* Female's underparts drab greenish. Other *Lophornis* coquettes allopatric. **HABITS** Midstory to canopy and edge of humid broadleaf forest, second growth, and adjacent clearings or gardens. **VOICE** Usually quiet. Call (1) a soft, liquid *tseep.* May be repeated rapidly.

Emerald-chinned Hummingbird *Abeillia abeillei* 8 cm

South MX and north CA. Uncommon to locally common resident in highlands (1000 to 2200 m) of GT (229). Rare and local in HN and NI. **ID** Tiny and short-tailed. *Short, straight bill* and *white postocular spot.* Short, broad, dark tail with gray-tipped outer rectrices. Male has glittering green gorget and dark, dusky green underparts. Female has mostly gray underparts including throat. **GV** Birds from south HN and NI are more coppery. **HABITS** Understory to midstory and edge of humid broadleaf and pine-oak forest and shaded plantations. Forages low. **VOICE** Song (1) a series of very high-pitched phrases *tseet ch-cheet tsee-tseet.* Also (2) a simple, rapid, monotonous *tseetseetseetseet.*

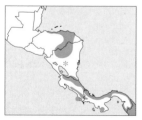

Violet-headed Hummingbird *Klais guimeti* 8 cm

CA and SA. Uncommon resident in humid lowlands and foothills (to 1200, rarely to 1350 m). Rare in HN (Olancho, Atlántida, 449, 442). Nests in foothills, may move to lowlands outside breeding season (570). **ID** Tiny. *Short, straight black bill* and *white postocular spot.* Short, square tail with partial dark subterminal band and white-tipped outer rectrices. Male has *glittering violet crown and gorget.* Remaining upperparts iridescent green. Female has grayish underparts and bluish-green crown. **HABITS** Understory to canopy and edge of humid broadleaf forest, tall second growth, plantations, and gardens. Hovers with body horizontal. Flicks cocked tail. Calls from high, open perch. **VOICE** Song (1) a rapid series of high-pitched, squeaky phrases *che-teewii tsee-tee tsi* or *tsi-chi si-chi chi-si-chi.* Call (2) a short, high-pitched, sharp, dry *chit* or *pwik.* May accelerate into shrill, sputtering trill.

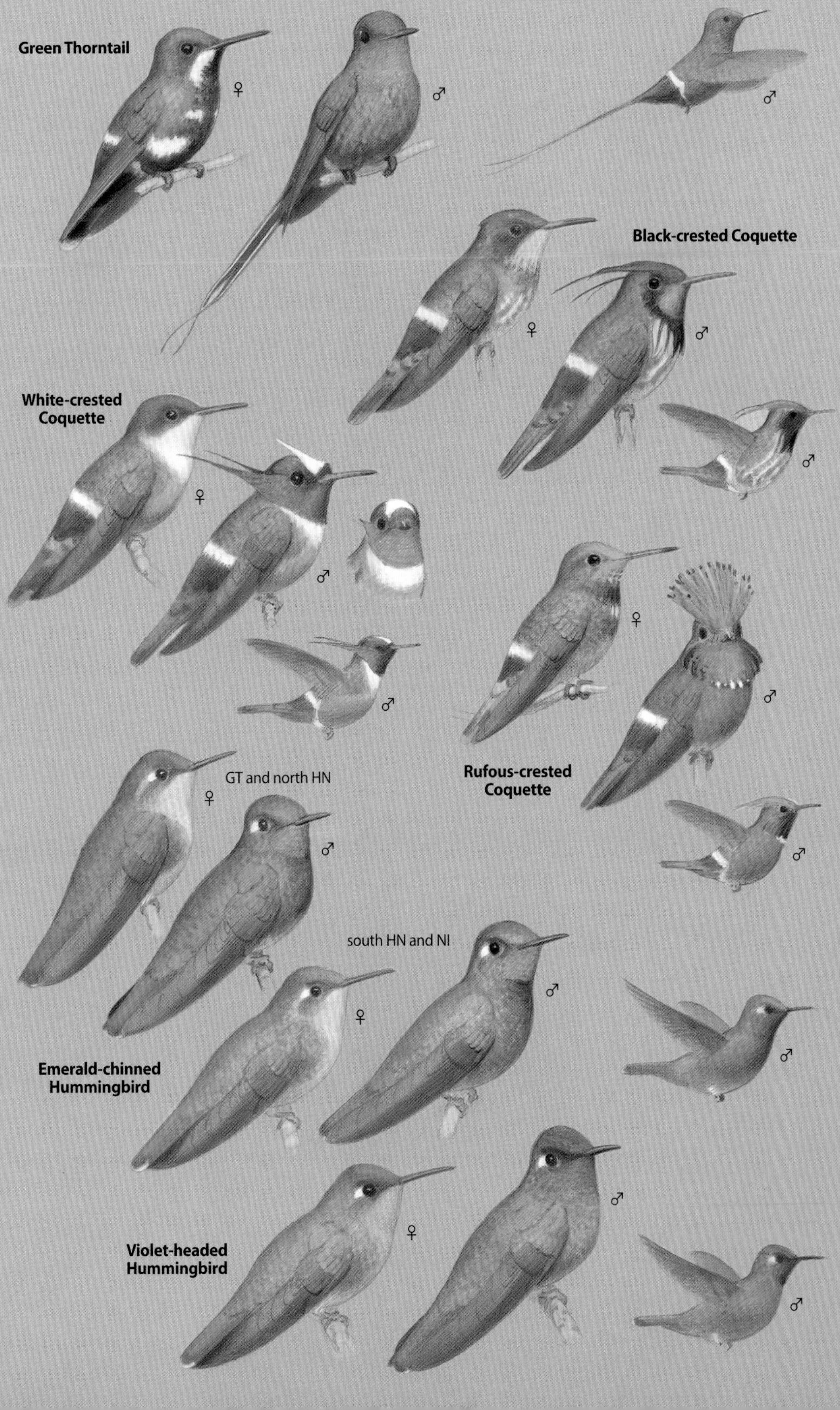

Green Thorntail ♀ ♂ ♂

Black-crested Coquette ♀ ♂ ♂

White-crested Coquette ♀ ♂ ♂

Rufous-crested Coquette ♀ ♂ ♂

GT and north HN ♀ ♂

south HN and NI ♀ ♂ ♂

Emerald-chinned Hummingbird

Violet-headed Hummingbird ♀ ♂ ♂

75%

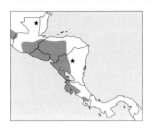

Plain-capped Starthroat *Heliomaster constantii* 12.5 cm

MX and CA. Uncommon resident in Pacific lowlands and foothills (to 1000, locally to 1500 m in north). Rare in Térraba Valley of east Pacific CR (Puntarenas, 600). Perhaps undertakes seasonal movements (253). **ID** *Very long bill.* Note *black spots in white tips of rectrices.* Dark auriculars contrast with *long white postocular stripe* and whitish malar. *Dull green crown* and near-uniform grayish underparts. Both sexes have glittering red gorget. Long-billed Starthroat has different tail pattern and male has different crown color. **HABITS** Midstory to canopy and edge of arid to semihumid pine-oak and deciduous forest, second growth, arid scrub, gardens, and plantations. Perches on prominent exposed snag. Sallies for insects. **VOICE** Call (1) a single or long, monotonous series of high-pitched, metallic or slightly slurred notes *tseet tseet tseet tseet . . .*

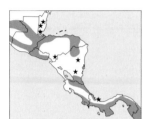

Long-billed Starthroat *Heliomaster longirostris* 12 cm

MX to SA. Uncommon resident in lowlands and foothills (to 1400, mainly below 1200 m). Rare in south Caribbean slope. Vagrant to BZ (Cayo, Belize, Toledo, 343, 345, 346). **ID** *Very long bill,* white malar and *white postocular spot.* Mostly dark bronzy green above and whitish below with dusky green flanks. Note white tips of rectrices and irregular white mark on rump. Both sexes have glittering violet-pink gorget and *blue crown.* Compare with Plain-capped Starthroat. Note different head and tail pattern. **GV** Male from north CA has green crown. **HABITS** Midstory to canopy and edge of semihumid to humid forest, open woodland, plantations, and gardens. Takes prominent perch on high, bare twig. **VOICE** Usually quiet. Calls (1) a rapid trill or rattle *breet-t-t-t-t* and (2) series of liquid notes *sip* or *tseep.*

Fiery-throated Hummingbird *Panterpe insignis* 12 cm

CA endemic. Locally fairly common resident in highlands (mainly above 1400 m) of CR and west PA. Perhaps undertakes elevational movements (592, 670). May descend to 750 m outside breeding season. **ID** High, slanted crown and *straight bill.* Note dark tail and white postocular spot. In favorable light shows glittering blue breast, *red and yellow gorget,* and blue crown. Juv has rusty scaling on face and nape. **GV** Birds from Volcán Miravalles in west CR (Guanacaste, not shown) are reported to have more extensive blue on throat and breast and shorter bill. **HABITS** Understory to subcanopy and edge of humid broadleaf (cloud) forest, adjacent clearings, gardens, and plantations. Aggressive. **VOICE** Call (1) a long, staccato series of sharp, high-pitched *tit* or *tsik* notes.

Garnet-throated Hummingbird *Lamprolaima rhami* 12.5 cm

South MX and CA. Fairly common resident in north highlands (1200 to 2800, mainly above 2000 m). Poorly known in east HN. **ID** Large and dark. *Short, straight bill* and *mostly rufous wings.* Notched tail purple. White postocular spot (in male) or postocular stripe (in female) contrasts with black sides of head. Male's glittering red gorget and blue-violet breast visible in favorable light. Female has grayish tips on outer rectrices and dull gray underparts. **HABITS** Midstory to subcanopy and edge of humid broadleaf and pine-oak forest, adjacent second growth, and plantations. Sallies to take flying insects. Flies with slow wingbeats. **VOICE** Calls (1) a sharp, slightly buzzy *tss-ty, tyu* or *tyu-tyu* and (2) single nasal *nyu* or *chew.*

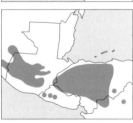

Rivoli's Hummingbird[5] *Eugenes fulgens* female 13, male 13.5 cm

South USA to CA. Common resident in north foothills and highlands (mainly 1500 to 3200, locally as low as 400 m). Also Pacific volcanic range in SV (San Vicente, San Salvador, Santa Ana, 341). **ID** Large with *long bill* and sloping forehead. Note white postocular mark. Male has glittering *violet crown* and blue-green gorget. Tail dark. Female has grayish underparts, *short whitish malar,* and dusky auriculars. Tail black with gray terminal band. Imm resembles female. **HABITS** Midstory to canopy and edge of humid broadleaf (cloud) forest, pine-oak woodland, second growth, and plantations. Often feeds while perched. **VOICE** Song (1) a long series of short, slightly squeaky notes *tseet-tweet, tseet-tweet . . .* or single notes *tseet, tseet, tseet . . .* Calls include (2) a buzzy, rolling *zrrrt.*

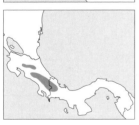

Talamanca Hummingbird[5] *Eugenes spectabilis* female 14, male 13.5 cm

CA endemic. Common resident in south highlands (mainly above 1400 m). **ID** Large with *long bill* (especially female) and sloping forehead. Note white postocular mark. Male has glittering *violet crown* and blue-green gorget. Tail dark. Female has grayish underparts, *short whitish malar* and dusky auriculars. Tail black with gray terminal band. Imm resembles female. Compare with smaller Purple-throated Mountain-gem. Note different head pattern. **HABITS** Midstory to canopy and edge of humid broadleaf (cloud) forest, second growth, and plantations. Often feeds while perched. **VOICE** Song (1) a long, varied series of short, coarse, buzzy phrases. Calls include (2) a buzzy, hard *chrrt, chrrt, chrrt . . .* or double *chrrt-chrrt.*

65%

imm

Plain-capped
Starthroat

ad ♂

♂

north CA
♀

north CA
♂

north CA
♂

south CA
♂

Long-billed Starthroat

♂

♀

♂

Garnet-throated
Hummingbird

Fiery-throated
Hummingbird

♀

♂

♀

♂

Rivoli's
Hummingbird

♂

Talamanca
Hummingbird

HUMMINGBIRDS Trochilidae

Lampornis hummingbirds with near-straight bill and white eye stripe. Males are fairly distinctive. Females of these species are very similar. These are among the most common hummingbirds in humid highlands of Central America.

Amethyst-throated Hummingbird *Lampornis amethystinus*   11.5 cm
MX and north CA. Fairly common resident in north highlands (900 to 3000, but mainly above 2000 m). **ID** Large. Male has white eye stripe and dusky mask bordered by *faint buff malar*. Male's *gorget glittering purplish-pink*. Female and imm *grayish below* with dull buff throat. Compare female with females of Magnificent and Garnet-throated hummingbirds. Note different wing pattern, underparts, and bill shape. **HABITS** Midstory to subcanopy and edge of humid broadleaf and pine-oak forest and adjacent second growth. Males sing from favored perch. **VOICE** Song (1) a long, dull, staccato rattle *te-te-te-te-te* . . . Call (2) a sharp *cheep* or *tchip*. May be repeated persistently.

Green-throated Mountain-gem *Lampornis viridipallens*   10.5 cm
CA endemic. Locally fairly common resident in highlands (900 to 2700 m) of GT and west HN. Also volcanic highlands of SV (San Vicente, San Salvador, Santa Ana, 183, 341). **ID** White postocular streak, dusky mask, and near-straight bill. Note *grayish outer rectrices*. Male has green mottled throat divided from lower underparts by *white breast-band*. Female has mostly plain white underparts (including throat) with green confined to flanks. Green-breasted Mountain-gem (allopatric) has different tail pattern. Compare with Amethyst-throated Hummingbird and with female Magnificent Hummingbird. Note different tail pattern. Also compare with White-eared Hummingbird. **HABITS** Understory to canopy and edge of humid broadleaf forest, second growth, and plantations. **VOICE** Song (1) a long series of low-pitched, squeaky and buzzy notes *cheeet-d-d-d-d-d* or *tseet titititi tseet*. Call (2) a high-pitched, clear *seet* or *pseet*.

Green-breasted Mountain-gem *Lampornis sybillae*   10.5 cm
CA endemic. Uncommon to locally fairly common resident in highlands (750 to 2400 m) of central HN and north NI. **ID** White postocular streak, blackish mask, and near-straight bill. Both sexes have *extensive pale gray on inner webs of outer rectrices* (conspicuous in flight). *Tail mostly pale gray below*. Male has *extensive green spotting and mottling on throat and breast*. Female has *pale cinnamon throat* and mostly white underparts. Green-throated Mountain-gem allopatric. Compare female with female Magnificent Hummingbird. Note different tail pattern. Also compare with White-eared Hummingbird. **HABITS** Similar to Green-throated Mountain-gem. **VOICE** Song (1) a long, monotonous series of short, hard, buzzy notes *zrrt, zrrt, zrrt, zrrt, zrrt* . . .

White-bellied Mountain-gem *Lampornis hemileucus*   10.5 cm
CA endemic. Uncommon and local resident in Caribbean foothills (700 to 1400 m) of CR and west PA. **ID** Both sexes have *white breast*. Note gray tail with dark subterminal band and whitish tip. Male has glittering violet gorget. Female has white throat with fine green spotting at sides. Purple-throated Mountain-gem mainly higher elevations. White-bellied Emerald mainly lower. **HABITS** Understory to canopy of humid broadleaf forest, second growth, and adjacent plantations and clearings. **VOICE** Song (1) a series of squeaks and dry or liquid trills and sputters. Call (2) a high-pitched *deet* or *deedee-deet*.

White-throated Mountain-gem *Lampornis castaneoventris*   10.5 cm
CA endemic. Common resident in foothills and highlands (above 1800 m) of east CR and west PA (Chiriquí). **ID** Male mostly iridescent green with glittering green crown, white postocular streak, and *white throat*. Male has blue-black or gray tail. Female cinnamon below with white tail tips and closely resembles female Purple-throated Mountain-gem. **GV** Male from Cordillera de Talamanca, CR has gray tail. Male from west PA has dark blue tail. **HABITS** Midstory to canopy and edge of humid broadleaf forest, second growth, and plantations. **VOICE** Calls (1) a high-pitched, squeaky *pick* or *pipipick* and (2) short, very buzzy, rolling *zeet* or *breet*.

Purple-throated Mountain-gem *Lampornis calolaemus*   10.5 cm
CA endemic. Common resident in south foothills and highlands (800 to 3900, rarely as low as 300 m). Local in Pacific volcanic highlands of NI (Granada, Rivas, 413). An undescribed *Lampornis* hummingbird has been reported from highlands of the Azuero Peninsula, PA (Veraguas, Los Santos, 425). May move to lower elevations outside breeding season. **ID** Notched tail. Male has glittering green breast, *violet gorget*, and green crown. Female has cinnamon underparts and white tail tips and closely resembles female White-throated Mountain-gem. Compare male with larger Magnificent Hummingbird. Note different head pattern. **HABITS** Understory to canopy and edge of humid broadleaf forest, second growth, gardens, and plantations. **VOICE** Song (1) a complex series of high-pitched, thin, dry, buzzy and warbling notes. Call (2) a short, very buzzy *zeet* or *zeep*. May be repeated in long series.

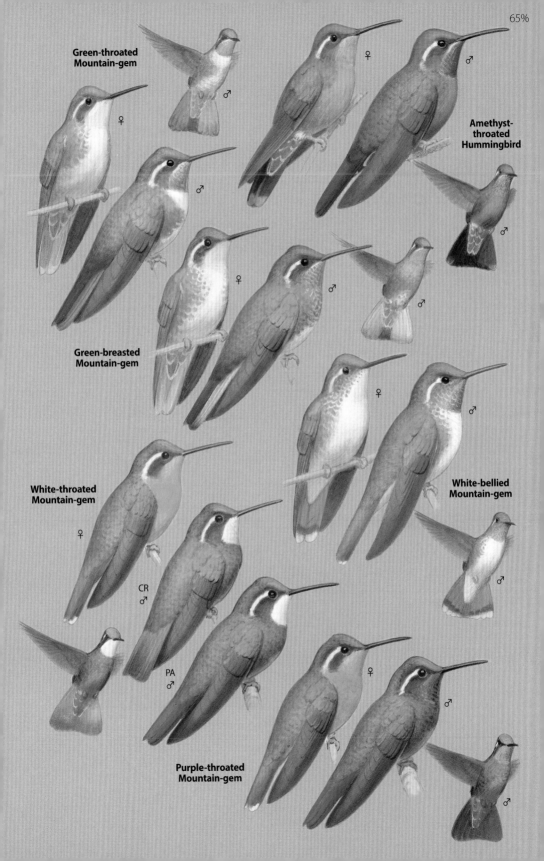

65%

Green-throated Mountain-gem

♀

♂

♂

Amethyst-throated Hummingbird

♀

♂

♂

♂

Green-breasted Mountain-gem

♀

♂

♂

♀

♂

White-throated Mountain-gem

♀

CR
♂

PA
♂

White-bellied Mountain-gem

♂

♀

♂

Purple-throated Mountain-gem

♂

HUMMINGBIRDS, WOODSTARS, AND SHEARTAIL Trochilidae

Small, mostly uncommon hummingbirds found mainly in highlands. Ruby-throated Hummingbird, a Nearctic migrant, is the most common and widespread.

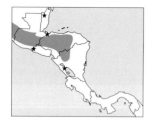

Sparkling-tailed Hummingbird *Tilmatura dupontii*   female 6.5, male 9.5 cm
MX and CA. Uncommon to rare and local resident in north foothills and highlands (SL to 2500, mainly above 750 m). Perhaps undertakes local or regional movements. Reports from BZ are unconfirmed (Orange Walk, 343). **ID** *Bill near-straight.* Hovers with tail cocked. Note white on sides of rump. Male's white breast contrasts with *blue gorget* and green lower underparts. Male's *long, forked tail banded with white.* Female has *uniform cinnamon sides of head, neck and underparts.* Compare with female Slender Sheartail. Note different bill and tail shape. **HABITS** Understory to canopy of semiarid to humid forest edge, brushy second growth, and scrubby woodland. Weaving, beelike flight style. Sallies for insects from high, exposed perch. **VOICE** Usually quiet. Rarely gives (1) high-pitched, sharp, twittering notes. Song (2) a long series of thin, very high-pitched, squeaky notes.

Magenta-throated Woodstar *Calliphlox bryantae*   female 8, male 9 cm
CA endemic. Uncommon resident in Pacific foothills and highlands (700 to 1850 m) of CR and west PA. Perhaps undertakes local or elevational movements (249, 593, 253, 670). **ID** Very small. Fairly short, near-straight bill. Male has glittering purple-red gorget and *long, deeply forked tail* (usually held closed). Note *white breast and white or buff marks on sides of rump.* Lower underparts rufous. Male has glittering purple gorget. Female mostly green above and cinnamon below with white band across breast and postocular stripe. Purple-throated Woodstar allopatric. Compare with Green Thorntail. **HABITS** Canopy and edge of humid broadleaf forest, second growth, and plantations. Rapid, weaving, beelike flight with audibly whirring wings. Hovers with tail cocked or pumps tail up and down. **VOICE** Song (1) a rapid, sputtering series of low-pitched notes. Calls (2) a dry *cht* and (3) rolling *chrrrt.*

Purple-throated Woodstar *Calliphlox mitchellii*   female 7, male 8.5 cm
CA and north SA. Rare and local resident in foothills and highlands (450 to 1400 m) east PA (Darién, 519). Reported from slopes of Pirre Massif above Cana. **ID** *Very small.* Fairly short, straight bill. Male has purple-red gorget and *long, deeply forked tail* (usually held closed). Note white band on breast and white markings on sides of rump. Female mostly green above and cinnamon below with buffy white markings including band across upper breast and postocular stripe. Magenta-throated Woodstar allopatric. Compare with Green Thorntail. **HABITS** Subcanopy to canopy and edge of humid broadleaf forest. Perches on high, exposed snag. **VOICE** Usually quiet. Call (1) a short series of clear, high-pitched notes followed by a short rattle or trill *tew-tew-tew tetetete.*

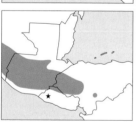

Slender Sheartail *Doricha enicura*   female 8, male 9.5 cm
South MX and north CA. Uncommon to rare and local resident in highlands (1000 to 2200 m) of GT (229). Reported from HN (La Paz, Ocotepeque, 448, 442) and SV (Chalatenango, Morazán, Santa Ana, 183, 619). Perhaps undertakes seasonal movements. **ID** Small. *Long, decurved bill* and white postocular spot. Male has *very long, slender, forked tail* (often held closed). Upperparts and flanks uniform iridescent green. Male's gorget mostly glittering violet with green area extending from chin to eye. Note white band on breast. Female has cinnamon underparts. Female's long tail has cinnamon, black, and white on outer rectrices. Compare female with female Sparkling-tailed Hummingbird. Note different bill shape and tail pattern. **HABITS** Understory to midstory of arid to humid forest edge, second growth, and brushy scrub. Males hover while foraging with tail held closed and nearly vertical. Female wags tail in flight. May take high, exposed perch. Wings produce low-pitched, humming sonation. **VOICE** Call (1) a rapid series of hard *tcheet* notes. Often repeated steadily.

Ruby-throated Hummingbird *Archilochus colubris*   8.5 cm
Breeds east Nearctic. Winters MX and CA. Uncommon to locally fairly common (SL to 3000 m) transient and winter resident (Oct to Apr). Most common in Pacific lowlands and foothills. Rare in PA (mainly Chiriquí, 512, 346). **ID** Medium-length, near-straight, all-black bill. Ad male has forked tail and *glittering red gorget.* Female has square tail with white tips on outer rectrices and whitish postocular spot. Female's underparts mostly whitish. Compare female with White-bellied Emerald. Note different bill color, tail pattern, and habits. **HABITS** Understory to canopy in semi-open or disturbed areas including arid to semihumid broadleaf forest edge, second growth, plantations, scrub, littoral woodland, and gardens. May hover with tail cocked like a woodstar. **VOICE** Call (1) a liquid, downslurred *tyew* or *tew.* Sometimes combined with short, buzzy note as *tyew ttttttt.*

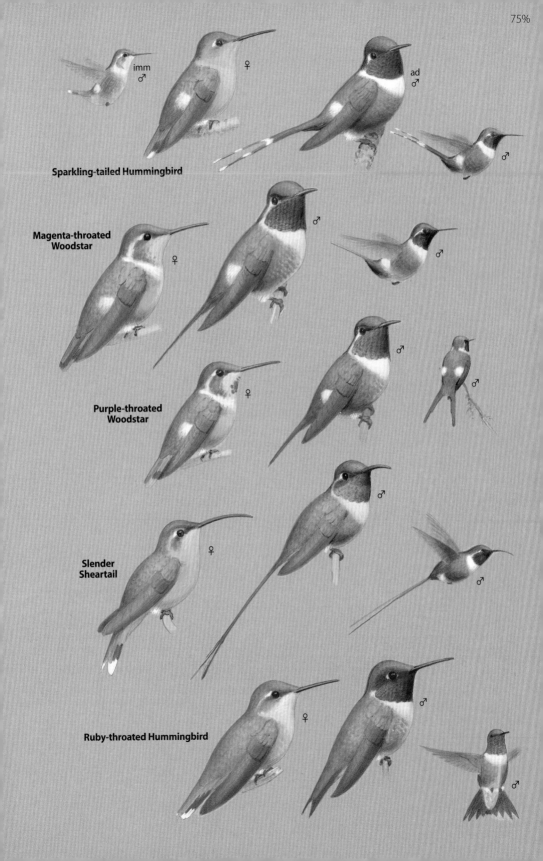

Sparkling-tailed Hummingbird

imm ♂

♀

ad ♂

♂

Magenta-throated Woodstar

♀

♂

♂

Purple-throated Woodstar

♀

♂

♂

Slender Sheartail

♀

♂

♂

Ruby-throated Hummingbird

♀

♂

♂

HUMMINGBIRDS Trochilidae

Small highland hummingbirds. Some populations of these species are thought to undertake elevational movements. All may forage low in open areas or at forest edge with weaving, beelike flight. Some are locally syntopic and may present identification challenges. Glow-throated Hummingbird is very poorly known and the female of this species is undocumented. Observers should note gorget color, tail pattern, and geographic range in separating *Selasphorus* hummingbirds.

Broad-tailed Hummingbird *Selasphorus platycercus*　　　9 cm
NA to CA. Locally common resident in highlands (2700 to 4100 m) of GT. Rare in SV (Santa Ana, Chalatenango, 364, 301). **ID** Long bill. Ad male has glittering *rose-red gorget*. Female has fine dark spotting on throat and cinnamon flanks. Tail mostly dark green with *rufous base, blackish subterminal band*, and white-tipped rectrices. Female Wine-throated Hummingbird smaller with shorter bill. Other *Selasphorus* allopatric. Compare with Ruby-throated Hummingbird. **HABITS** Understory to subcanopy and edge of pine and pine-oak woodland, clearings, and gardens. Perches at low to mid-levels. **VOICE** Call (1) a hard, sharp *cheet*. Wings produce (2) a high-pitched, trilling sonation.

Wine-throated Hummingbird *Atthis ellioti*　　　7 cm
MX and north CA. Locally fairly common resident in north highlands (1400 to 3000, mainly above 1800 m). Also volcanic highlands of SV (Santa Ana, 619). **ID** *Very small. Short, straight bill*. Ad male has elongated glittering *purple gorget* (flared laterally in display). Both sexes have rufous base of tail and white-tipped rectrices. Female has spotted throat and cinnamon flanks contrasting with white breast-band. Compare with larger Broad-tailed Hummingbird. Other *Selasphorus* hummingbirds allopatric. **HABITS** Understory to canopy and edge of pine-oak and broadleaf forest, second growth and scrub. At lek males vocalize persistently from low perch and flare gorget laterally to form broad triangle. **VOICE** Song (1) a complex medley of high-pitched, squeaky and slurred notes *cheeew tseeuu tsucheecheechee tsuu tse . . .*

Volcano Hummingbird *Selasphorus flammula*　　　8 cm
CA endemic. Common resident in highlands (mainly above 1850, rarely as low as 1200 m) of CR and west PA (Chiriquí, 657, 512). **ID** Very small. Short, straight bill. Ad male's gorget varies geographically. Note male's mostly blackish tail with acutely pointed central rectrices. Female has fine dark speckling on throat, white breast-band, and greenish flanks. Note female's white or whitish-tipped outer rectrices. Glow-throated Hummingbird allopatric. Compare with Scintillant Hummingbird (mainly lower elevations). Note female's different flank color and *tail pattern*. **GV** Male from volcáns Poás and Barva, CR, has purple gorget. Male from Volcán Irazú, CR, has paler gorget. Male from Cordillera de Talamanca in CR and west PA has variable dull gorget. **HABITS** Understory and edge of elfin forest, brushy roadsides, and paramo. **VOICE** Usually quiet. Song (1) a long, very high-pitched, thin note that drops steadily in pitch *teeeeeeuuu*. Also (2) a more complex phrase that ends with thin, downslurred, buzzy note *che-chuchu-chutzeeeeeuuu* and (3) rapid series of high-pitched, sharp *chip* or *tip* notes. May accelerate into a short twitter.

Glow-throated Hummingbird *Selasphorus ardens*　　　7.5 cm
CA endemic. Very rare, local and poorly known resident in highlands (750 to 1850, but mainly above 1200 m) of west PA (Chiriquí, Ngäbe-Buglé, Veraguas, 657, 588, 512, 149, 197). Historically known from Cerro Santiago and highlands above Santa Fe. Recently reported from Cerro Hoya on Azuero Peninsula (Los Santos, 425). **ID** Ad male has glittering *purple-red gorget*. Note more extensive black on tail in comparison with Scintillant Hummingbird. Female undocumented but probably resembles female Scintillant Hummingbird but with broader green median stripe on central rectrices, paler tips on outer rectrices, and more rufous-bronze above. The plate figure is based on a specimen likely of this species. Compare ad male with Scintillant Hummingbird. Note different gorget color. Also compare with Magenta-throated Woodstar. **HABITS** Understory to midstory and edge of humid broadleaf forest. Poorly known. **VOICE** Unknown.

Scintillant Hummingbird *Selasphorus scintilla*　　　7 cm
CA endemic. Locally fairly common resident in highlands (mainly 900 to 2450 m) of CR and west PA east to Cerro Santiago (Chiriquí, Ngäbe-Buglé, 657, 588, 512). **ID** Very small. Near-straight bill. Ad male has glittering *orange-red gorget* and extensive rufous in tail. Female has white breast-band, rufous flanks, and fine speckling on throat. Note female's buff or cinnamon tips on outer rectrices. Note narrow dark or green median stripes on central rectrices of both sexes. Compare with Volcano Hummingbird (mainly higher elevations). Note female's different underparts and tail. **HABITS** Understory to midstory and edge of humid broadleaf forest, second growth, plantations, hedgerows, and gardens. Often forages low. Males take exposed perch at medium levels. Performs diving, aerial display. **VOICE** Call (1) a series of very high-pitched, thin, clear, liquid notes *tseet chew-ch-ch-seet . . .* Also (2) a sharp chatter. In display, wings produce (3) a high-pitched, buzzy, insect-like sonation.

Broad-tailed Hummingbird

♀

♂

♂

Wine-throated Hummingbird

♀

♂

♂

♀

♂

Poas and Barva

Volcano Hummingbird

♀

♀

♂

Irazú

♂

♂

♂

Talamancas

♀?

♀?

♂

♂

Glow-throated Hummingbird

Scintillant Hummingbird

♀

♀

♂

♂

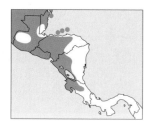

Canivet's Emerald[6] *Chlorostilbon canivetii* — female 8, male 8.5 cm

South MX and CA. Locally fairly common resident in north lowlands and foothills (to 1500, locally to 1900 m). Also Bay Islands and Cayos Cochinos (94, 560). **ID** Small and long-tailed. Red bill with black tip. Male has *dark, deeply forked tail* and is near-uniform glittering green including most of underparts. Female has notched tail with *grayish band* and tips on outer rectrices. *Dusky mask* contrasts with *whitish postocular stripe*. Underparts grayish-white. Female may suggest a female *Lampornis* mountain-gem. Compare male with larger Crowned Woodnymph. Note different head pattern and habits. **GV** Males from north GT, BZ, and Bay Islands, HN have more deeply forked tail with grayish tips on rectrices. **HABITS** Understory to midstory at edge of arid to semihumid broadleaf forest, gallery forest, second growth, pine savanna, scrub, plantations, and gardens. Forages restlessly, making short, rapid flights. Habitually pumps tail. **VOICE** Song (1) a long series of high-pitched, thin, phrases *tsippy-tsee tsee . . .* or *tseee tseeeree . . .* Call (2) a dry, scratchy *chut* or *chit*. May be repeated and sometimes accelerates into a soft, staccato chatter.

Garden Emerald[6] *Chlorostilbon assimilis* — 8 cm

South MX and CA. Locally fairly common resident in south lowlands and foothills (to 1500 m). Also Isla Coiba and Pearl Islands (Veraguas, Panamá, 58, 649, 470). **ID** Small and long-tailed. Bill black. Male has plain, dark *forked tail* and is near-uniform glittering green including most of underparts. Female has blackish notched tail with grayish or whitish tips on outer rectrices and dusky mask contrasting with *whitish postocular stripe*. Female's underparts plain, dull grayish-white. Female's head pattern suggests female *Lampornis* mountain-gems but these are all larger, have different underparts, and are found at higher elevations. **HABITS** Understory to midstory at edge of semihumid broadleaf forest, gallery forest, second growth, scrub, plantations, and gardens. Like Canivet's Emerald. **VOICE** Song (1) a long series of high-pitched, thin phrases *tsippy-tsee tsee . . .* or *tseee tseeeree . . .* Call (2) a dry, scratchy *chut* or *chit*. May be repeated or accelerate into soft, staccato chatter.

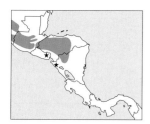

White-eared Hummingbird *Hylocharis leucotis* — 8.5–9.5 cm

Southwest USA to north CA. Common resident in foothills and highlands (1000 to 3300 m). Rare in volcanic highlands of SV (Morazán, 183) and NI (Chinandega, 413). **ID** Steep forehead and slightly peaked crown. *Bold white postocular stripe* and *red bill with dark tip*. Male has glittering violet chin and forehead and glittering green lower gorget. Female has dull crown, *spotted throat* and breast, and grayish tail tips. **GV** Birds from HN and NI are more coppery on rump and nape. **HABITS** Understory to midstory and edge of humid broadleaf, pine-oak and pine forest, second growth, plantations, and gardens. Males form small singing assemblies in which they vocalize persistently from favored perch. **VOICE** Song (1) a long, monotonous series of high-pitched *t-chew* or *teechew* phrases. Call (2) a low-pitched *chut* or *choot*. May be repeated in rapid, stuttering series.

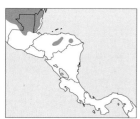

Wedge-tailed Sabrewing *Campylopterus curvipennis* — 13 cm

South MX and CA. Uncommon and local resident in lowlands and foothills of BZ and north GT (Petén). Rare and local in foothills (400 to 700 m) of east HN (Olancho, Gracias a Dios, 442, 35, 341). **ID** Fairly large with long, slightly decurved bill and *long, dark, graduated tail*. Note *white postocular spot*, plain gray underparts and glittering violet crown. **HABITS** Understory to subcanopy and edge of semihumid to humid broadleaf forest, tall second growth, plantations, and riparian woodland. Sings from bare branch in midstory. **VOICE** Song (1) a loud, complex series that includes squeaky *chip* notes and garbled, warbling phrases. Also (2) a steady series of sharp notes *chip chip chip chip-ip chip . . .* In flight (3) a loud *pweek* or *preet*.

Rufous Sabrewing *Campylopterus rufus* — 13 cm

South MX and north CA. Uncommon to fairly common resident in Pacific GT (mainly 900 to 2000, locally to 2500 m). Local in volcanic highlands of SV (San Miguel, San Vicente, 341). **ID** Sexes similar. Large with long, slightly decurved bill. White postocular spot and *uniform cinnamon sides of head and underparts*. Tail mostly cinnamon with dusky subterminal band. **HABITS** Understory and edge of semihumid to humid broadleaf forest, second growth, gardens, and shaded plantations. Forms small singing assemblies. May sing persistently from perch inside cover. **VOICE** Calls (1) very sharp, slightly nasal *squik* or *chiik*. May be given singly or doubled as *chid-iik*. In what may be the song (2) these notes are repeated rapidly in long monotonous series *chiik-chiik-chiik-chiik . . .*

♀

north GT and BZ
♂

widespread
♂

♂

Canivet's Emerald

♀

♂

♂

Garden Emerald

♀

GT

♂

GT
♂

White-eared Hummingbird

♀

HN and NI

♂

Wedge-tailed Sabrewing

Rufous Sabrewing

SABREWING, PLUMELETEERS, AND WOODNYMPH Trochilidae

Large hummingbirds found mainly at lower levels in humid broadleaf forest. Bronze-tailed Plumeleteer and Crowned Woodnymph show complex geographic variation in Central America.

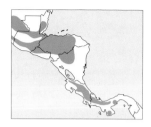

Violet Sabrewing *Campylopterus hemileucurus*   14.5 cm

South MX and CA. Fairly common resident in foothills and highlands (1000 to 3300, rarely or locally as low as 100 m). Also highlands of Azuero Peninsula in PA (Herrera, Los Santos, 425). **ID** *Large* with fairly long, decurved bill. Note *bold white markings on outer rectrices.* Ad male *mostly violet* below and on head. Female has plain gray underparts, white postocular spot, and violet confined to throat. Wedge-tailed Sabrewing has similar pattern. Note different bill and tail shape. **HABITS** Understory to midstory of semihumid to humid forest, plantations, and tall second growth. Often aggressive. Males form small singing assemblies in which they vocalize persistently from perches in midstory. **VOICE** Song (1) a long, variable series of high-pitched, evenly spaced notes *cheep tsew cheep tik-tik tsew cheep . . .* While foraging gives (2) sharp, penetrating twitters or dry chatters.

White-vented Plumeleteer *Chalybura buffonii*   11.5 cm

CA and SA. Fairly common resident in Pacific lowlands and foothills (to 600 m) of central and east PA. Local on Caribbean slope (Colón, Coclé). **ID** Fairly large with slightly curved bill and low, rounded crown. *Feet dusky.* Both sexes have small white postocular spot and *white crissum* contrasting with *blue-black tail.* Male mostly green. Female has grayish underparts and white tips on rectrices. Bronze-tailed Plumeleteer has pinkish feet, pinkish mandible, and bronzy tail. **HABITS** Midstory and edge of humid broadleaf forest and tall second growth. Occasionally visits adjacent open areas. **VOICE** Call (1) a slightly dry *chit* or *ch-t-t-t.* In interactions may give (2) a long, decelerating rattle or trill *cheetttttt t-t-t-t-t.*

Bronze-tailed Plumeleteer *Chalybura urochrysia*   11.5 cm

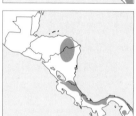

CA and north SA. Uncommon resident in humid lowlands (to 750 m). **ID** Fairly large with slightly curved bill and low, rounded crown. Both sexes have small white postocular spot. Long, broad, dark tail. Note *pinkish feet* and pinkish base of mandible. Male mostly green. Female grayish on throat and breast and has gray tips on outer rectrices. In PA compare with White-vented Plumeleteer. Note different underparts. **GV** Birds from north CA have dark crissum and blackish tail. Birds from PA have bronzy tail and dark mottled crissum becoming white in Pacific east PA. **HABITS** Understory to midstory and edge of humid broadleaf forest, tall second growth, and riparian thickets. **VOICE** Song (1) a series of slightly scratchy, short rattles *ter-pleeleeleelee ter-pleeleeleelee ter-pleeleeleelee-lee ter-pleee.* Call (2) a loud, metallic *breet* or *briit.* May be repeated rapidly in long series. Also (3) a rapid, scolding chatter.

Crowned Woodnymph *Thalurania colombica*   11 cm

CA and SA. Common to locally very common resident in humid lowlands and foothills (to 800, locally to 1300 m). May disperse to higher elevations after breeding. At north limit in Caribbean foothills of south BZ where uncommon and local (Toledo). **ID** Fairly long, slightly decurved bill and low, sloping forehead. Male has *deeply forked dark violet tail.* Note male's glittering green throat (often appears dark) and violet forecrown (in north). Female has notched tail with gray tips on outer rectrices. Note female's *grayish-white throat and breast contrasting with green lower underparts.* Compare male with smaller Fork-tailed Emerald. Note different head pattern, habits, and structure. **GV** Male from north CA has green belly becoming violet in Caribbean NI south through PA. Female in north has mostly whitish underparts. Male from east PA has green crown. **HABITS** Humid broadleaf forest, tall second growth, and edge. Males typically feed at epiphytes in canopy. Females forage mainly in understory. **VOICE** Song (1) a long, monotonous series of squeaky *tseep* or *cheep* notes. Calls (2) a high-pitched, squeaky *kip* or *kyip* and (3) dry scratchy *chut-t-t-t.*

65%

imm ♀

♀

ad ♂

ad ♂

Violet Sabrewing

♀

♂

♂

White-vented Plumeleteer

north CA

Bronze-tailed Plumeleteer

♀

north CA ♂

north CA ♂

Caribbean PA ♂

east Pacific PA ♂

north CA ♀

north CA ♂

NI to central PA ♂

NI to central PA ♂

south CA ♀

east PA ♂

Crowned Woodnymph

EMERALDS, SNOWCAP, AND HUMMINGBIRDS Trochilidae

Small hummingbirds found mainly at lower levels in humid broadleaf forest. All have white markings on tail. Most are endemic to Central America. Stripe-tailed Hummingbird is the most common and widespread.

Coppery-headed Emerald *Elvira cupreiceps*   8.5 cm
CA endemic. Common resident in highlands (mainly 700 to 1500 m) of west CR. May move to lower elevations outside breeding season. **ID** Small with rounded crown. *Bill decurved.* Male mostly iridescent green with *coppery crown, uppertail coverts, and tail.* Note white on tail and white crissum. Female green above and dull white below with green flanks. Compare with White-tailed Emerald. Note different habits and bill shape. **HABITS** Understory to canopy and edge of humid broadleaf forest, adjacent second growth, and gardens. Forages low. Weaving, insect-like flight style with sweeping, side-to-side movements. Flips or spreads tail to display white rectrices. **VOICE** Song (1) a short, rapid, high-pitched trill or twitter. May be repeated persistently. Call (2) a high-pitched, thin, liquid *quip* or *quit.*

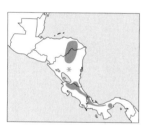

White-tailed Emerald *Elvira chionura*   8.5 cm
CA endemic. Uncommon and local resident in Pacific foothills and highlands (800 to 1700 m, but mainly below 1400 m) of east CR and west PA. **ID** Small with rounded crown and *near-straight bill.* Tail has *extensive white on outer rectrices* (conspicuous in flight) and black terminal band (male) or subterminal band (female). Flight feathers plain dusky. Male otherwise mostly iridescent green with white crissum. Female has extensively whitish underparts and white-tipped rectrices. Resembles Coppery-headed Emerald. Note different upperparts and bill shape. Compare with Stripe-tailed Hummingbird. Note different wing pattern. **HABITS** Understory to canopy and edge of humid broadleaf forest, shaded plantations, and gardens. **VOICE** Song (1) a long series of thin, scratchy or buzzy notes that rise and fall in pitch. Gives (2) high-pitched, buzzy notes and (3) soft, scratchy chip notes in flight.

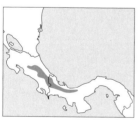

Snowcap *Microchera albocoronata*   6.5 cm
CA endemic. Uncommon and local resident in Caribbean foothills (mainly 300 to 1000 m, rarely to 1600 m). May wander to lower elevations outside breeding season. **ID** Very small and short-tailed. *Short, near-straight bill* and slightly peaked crown. Male coppery purple (often appears very dark) with *white crown.* Female mostly green above with plain whitish underparts and whitish tips on outer rectrices. Note fine whitish tips on secondaries. Molting imm males are pied with green and red and can have dark central underparts. Female resembles several other small hummingbirds. Compare especially with female White-tailed Emerald (mainly higher elevations). Note different underparts. **GV** Male from PA is blacker below. **HABITS** Understory to canopy and edge of humid broadleaf forest, adjacent second growth, and gardens. Forages low. Often takes an open perch in forest interior. **VOICE** Call (1) a high-pitched, liquid *tseep.*

Stripe-tailed Hummingbird *Eupherusa eximia*   9.5 cm
MX and CA. Uncommon to locally common resident in highlands and foothills (800 to 2000, rarely or locally as low as 400 m). Perhaps undertakes local or elevational movements (593, 670). **ID** Small with near-straight bill and rounded crown. Note *rufous secondaries* and *black-and-white patterned tail* (conspicuous in flight). Male mostly green. Female grayish-white below with plain grayish face (small postocular spot). In south compare with Black-bellied Hummingbird. Note different underparts. **GV** Female from CR and PA is less buff below, and has more white on tail. **HABITS** Understory to canopy and edge of humid broadleaf (cloud) forest. Males forage higher in forest strata than females. **VOICE** Call (1) a slightly buzzy *cheep* or *tcheep* often given in flight.

Black-bellied Hummingbird *Eupherusa nigriventris*   8.5 cm
CA endemic. Uncommon resident in foothills and highlands (900 to 2000 m) of east CR and west PA. **ID** Small with rounded crown and *near-straight bill.* Note rufous secondaries and white outer rectrices. Male has *black crown, sides of head, and underparts.* Female has buff-white underparts. Compare with larger Stripe-tailed Hummingbird. **HABITS** Understory to canopy and edge of humid broadleaf forest, second growth, and adjacent clearings. Males tend to forage higher in forest strata than females. Weaving, beelike flight. **VOICE** Call (1) a high-pitched, sharp, liquid *tseet* or *pseet.* Repeated.

Coppery-headed Emerald

White-tailed Emerald

Snowcap

imm ♂

widespread ad ♂

PA ad ♂

♀

north CA ♀

south CA ♀

♂

♂

Stripe-tailed Hummingbird

♀

♂

Black-bellied Hummingbird

HUMMINGBIRDS Trochilidae

A diverse group of hummingbirds found mainly in Panama.

Pirre Hummingbird *Goethalsia bella*   9 cm

CA and SA. Uncommon and local resident in foothills (500 to 1500, but mainly above 1000 m) of east PA. Recorded from Cerro Sapo, Serranía de Jungurudó, and Pirre Massif (Darién, 657, 519, 45, 426). **ID** Near-square tail with *mostly cinnamon outer rectrices*. Note rufous secondaries and *rufous lores, face, and chin*. Male mostly green above and below with glittering green throat and breast. Male has blackish terminal band on tail. Female has cinnamon underparts. **HABITS** Understory to lower midstory and edge of humid broadleaf forest and tall second growth. Forages by traplining at understory shrubs. **VOICE** Call (1) a sharp *tew* or *tchew*. May be repeated rapidly and persistently.

Violet-capped Hummingbird *Goldmania violiceps*   9 cm

CA and north SA. Uncommon to locally common resident in foothills and highlands (mainly 600 to 1200 m) of central and east PA (Panamá, Colón, Darién, Kuna Yala, 461, 657, 512, 44). **ID** Small. Near-straight black bill. Male mostly green with *violet-blue crown* and glittering green underparts. Notched *bronzy tail with chestnut centers of rectrices*. Female plain iridescent green above and mostly whitish below with sparse green speckling on sides of breast. Female has white-tipped rectrices. Compare female with female Snowcap (allopatric). **HABITS** Midstory and edge of humid broadleaf forest and second growth. Males take prominent, open perch. **VOICE** Song (1) a rapid series of short, buzzy, very nasal notes *dzee-deedee dee zee-deedee . . .* or *chee-deedeedee-chut, dee.*

Humboldt's Sapphire *Hylocharis humboldtii*   10 cm

CA and north SA. Uncommon and local resident in Pacific coastal lowlands of east PA (657, 512, 595). **ID** Notched or near-square green tail. *Red bill with broad base* (visible at close range) and black tip. Male has *glittering blue forecrown and throat*. Breast glittering green. Crissum and central belly white. Female has white postocular spot and mostly whitish underparts with green spotting on flanks and sides of breast. Female has whitish tips on rectrices. Compare with Sapphire-throated Hummingbird and Blue-throated Goldentail. **HABITS** Understory to canopy of mangroves, adjacent woodland, and littoral scrub. **VOICE** Call (1) a rapid, high-pitched, descending trill.

Sapphire-throated Hummingbird *Lepidopyga coeruleogularis*   8 cm

CA and north SA. Locally fairly common resident in lowlands of east PA (Darién). Also Isla Coiba (Veraguas, 653, 470). Poorly known in lowlands of Pacific east CR (Puntarenas, 82). **ID** Small. *Dark, forked tail* and near-straight bill. Male has violet gorget becoming blue on chest. Female has grayish underparts with green spotting on sides of breast and flanks. Female Violet-bellied Hummingbird has different tail shape. Compare male with male Crowned Woodnymph. Note different head pattern and habits. **HABITS** Interior understory (occasionally forages in canopy) of mangroves, second growth, gardens, and scrub. **VOICE** Song (1) a long, slightly descending trill *peetetetetetetetet.*

Violet-bellied Hummingbird *Juliamyia julie*   7.5 cm

CA and SA. Uncommon to locally common resident in lowlands and foothills (to 1200 m) of central and east PA. **ID** Small. *Short, straight bill* with mostly red mandible. *Long, square tail*. Male has glittering green gorget and *violet-blue underparts*. Female has white throat, small white postocular spot, and mostly whitish underparts. Note female's gray-tipped outer rectrices. Compare with larger female Crowned Woodnymph. Note different tail shape and bill color. Also compare with female Sapphire-throated Hummingbird. Note different tail shape and habits. **HABITS** Understory and edge of humid broadleaf forest, second growth, plantations, and gardens. **VOICE** Song (1) a repeated, buzzy or rolling *whiiirrrr* or *brrrrrrr*. Call (2) a downslurred *tchewii*.

Pirre Hummingbird

Violet-capped Hummingbird

Humboldt's Sapphire

Sapphire-throated Hummingbird

Violet-bellied Hummingbird

GOLDENTAIL AND HUMMINGBIRDS Trochilidae

Hummingbirds found mainly in lowlands and foothills. *Amazilia* hummingbirds may present identification challenges. Males have more strongly notched tails. Tail color, wing and underparts pattern, as well as geographic range are useful in identification.

Blue-throated Goldentail *Hylocharis eliciae* 8 cm

South MX and CA. Uncommon resident in lowlands and foothills (to 1000, rarely or locally to 2000 m). Most common in south Pacific slope. Also Isla Coiba (Veraguas, 653, 470). Rare in BZ (Cayo, Toledo, 435, 625) and in south Caribbean slope. Perhaps undertakes seasonal movements (593, 670). **ID** *Red bill* with dark tip slightly broad at base. *Tail metallic golden-green.* Male has *violet-blue sides of head and gorget* (appears dark in poor light). Female slightly duller with throat variably spotted or flecked violet-blue. Note drab buff lower underparts. May suggest an *Amazilia* hummingbird but tail color distinctive. Compare with Rufous-tailed Hummingbird. **HABITS** Upper understory to midstory and edge of broadleaf forest, tall second growth, and shaded plantations. Males form small singing assemblies in which they vocalize persistently from favored perches inside cover. **VOICE** Song (1) a short, rapid series of clear, high-pitched, metallic notes *tsi tsi tsi tsi* or *psi psi psi psi psi*. Often repeated persistently. Call (2) a slightly buzzy *zip* or *tzip*.

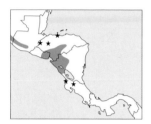

Blue-tailed Hummingbird *Amazilia cyanura* 9 cm

MX and north CA. Uncommon resident in lowlands and foothills (to 1500 m) of Pacific GT (378). Disjunctly in SV (Morázon, 341), HN, and NI (413). Reaches Caribbean slope in foothills of central NI where uncommon and local (Matagalpa) and in HN (600 to 1200 m, 442). Rare in Pacific CR (Guanacaste, Puntarenas, 346). **ID** *Dark blue tail.* Bill mostly dusky. Often appears very dark. In favorable light note coppery rump and lower back. Female has grayish lower underparts. Similar to Steely-vented Hummingbird but note *rufous on wing*. Also compare with Berylline Hummingbird. Note different tail color. **GV** Birds from Pacific GT are greener and have less coppery above. **HABITS** Midstory to canopy and edge of broadleaf forest, second growth, plantations, and gardens. Visits flowering *Inga* trees. **VOICE** Song (1) a repeated, short, squeaky phrase. May include buzzy and whistled notes. Also a repeated, hard, buzzy *bzzzrt*. Call (2) a high-pitched, sharp *siik*.

Berylline Hummingbird *Amazilia beryllina* 9 cm

Southwest USA to north CA. Fairly common resident in north Pacific and interior (to 2000 m). A report from north GT is dubious (Petén, 78). **ID** Mandible mostly red with dark tip. Note *magenta tail* and *rufous on secondaries*. Male mostly glittering green below. Female has dull buff belly. Rufous-tailed Hummingbird has plain wings. Compare with Blue-tailed Hummingbird. **HABITS** Midstory to subcanopy of semihumid to humid broadleaf forest, woodland, scrub (especially with oaks), clearings, and plantations. Perches and forages at all levels. **VOICE** Song (1) a variable, high-pitched rattle or twitter. May include one or two lisping introductory notes *ssi-si t-t-t-t-t-t-u* or *sssi-ir sssiirr chit-chit chit-chit chit*. Calls (2) a steady series of sharp *chit* or *tsit* notes and (3) dry, buzzy *dzzzzir* or *drrzzzt* that may be repeated.

Steely-vented Hummingbird *Amazilia saucerottei* 9 cm

CA and (disjunctly) SA. Uncommon to locally very common resident in Pacific lowlands and foothills (to 1800 m) of NI and west CR. **ID** Bill mostly dusky. Blue-black notched tail. Mostly glittering green below with white tibial tufts, dark blue vent, and coppery lower back. *Wings plain dusky.* Sexes similar. Compare with Blue-tailed Hummingbird. **HABITS** Midstory to subcanopy and edge of arid to semihumid broadleaf forest, second growth, gardens, and plantations. **VOICE** Song (1) a soft, high-pitched *bzz wee-wup* or *deeh-deeh duu* that drops in pitch. Calls (2) a high-pitched, sharp *tsik* or *chit*. May accelerate into a rattle.

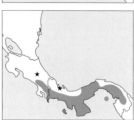

Snowy-bellied Hummingbird *Amazilia edward* 9 cm

CA and north SA. Uncommon resident in south Pacific lowlands and foothills (to 1800 m). Also Isla Coiba (Veraguas, 653, 470) and Pearl Islands (Panamá, 58, 274, 657). Vagrant to Caribbean foothills of CR (Cartago, 346, 123) and PA (Bocas del Toro, 512). **ID** Glittering *green head and breast* contrast sharply with *white belly*. Lower back and rump iridescent coppery in favorable light. Female less coppery above. Imm slightly duller with grayish flanks. **GV** Birds from CR and west PA typically have blackish tail becoming variably coppery magenta in birds from central and east PA and Pearl Islands. **HABITS** Midstory in semi-open or disturbed areas including broadleaf forest edge, second growth, plantations, mangroves, and gardens. May take conspicuous perch on high, bare snag. Usually solitary. **VOICE** Song (1) a soft, buzzy *tzeer* or *tseer tir tir*. Call (2) a short, slightly buzzy *tip* or *tsip* that may be repeated.

Blue-throated Goldentail

♀

♂

♂

Blue-tailed Hummingbird

Pacific GT
♂

♀

widespread
♂

♂

♀

♂

Berylline Hummingbird

♂

Steely-vented Hummingbird

east CR and west PA

central and east PA

Snowy-bellied Hummingbird

HUMMINGBIRDS Trochilidae

Medium-sized hummingbirds found mainly in north lowlands and foothills. Observers should note head and underparts pattern as well as geographic range. Rufous-tailed Hummingbird is the most common and widespread.

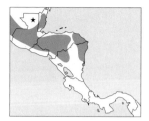

Azure-crowned Hummingbird *Amazilia cyanocephala*   10 cm
South MX and north CA. Common resident in north (SL to 2500 m). Uncommon in Caribbean lowlands of east HN (Gracias a Dios) and north NI (RAAN). **ID** Fairly large *Amazilia* with relatively long bill (mandible mostly red). Mostly bronzy above with *glittering blue crown* (in most of range). Note white central underparts and *plain brown tail* (no dark subterminal band). White-bellied Emerald smaller with different tail and habits. **GV** Birds from Mosquitia region of east HN and north NI have green crown and are brighter coppery above. **HABITS** Midstory to canopy and edge of pine savanna, scrub, pine-oak woodland, gardens, and plantations. **VOICE** Call (1) a low-pitched, slightly buzzy *zzeer* or *tzur*. May be repeated or may accelerate into sputtering rattle.

Green-fronted Hummingbird *Amazilia viridifrons*   9.5 cm
South MX and GT. Uncommon resident in Nentón Valley (100 to 1300 m) of west GT (Huehuetenango, 229). **ID** Fairly large *Amazilia*. Bill bright red with dark tip. Plain green crown and *mostly white underparts*. Dark flanks less extensive than in Azure-crowned Hummingbird. Tail plain bronzy (no dark subterminal band). **HABITS** Understory to canopy and edge of arid to semihumid forest, second growth, gardens, and plantations. May take prominent, exposed perch on bare twig. **VOICE** Call (1) a low-pitched, slightly buzzy *zzeer* or *tzur* like Azure-crowned Hummingbird.

Buff-bellied Hummingbird *Amazilia yucatanensis*   9 cm
MX and north CA. Locally fairly common resident in lowlands of north BZ and GT (Petén). **ID** Mostly red bill with dark tip. *Rufous tail* with bronzy terminal band. Green throat and breast contrast with *cinnamon lower underparts*. Compare with Cinnamon and Rufous-tailed hummingbirds. Note different underparts. Berylline Hummingbird allopatric. **HABITS** Understory to canopy of arid scrub, pine savanna, and open or disturbed areas including second growth, plantations, gardens, and urban areas. **VOICE** Song (1) a brief series of thin, high-pitched notes *ts-eeuw tsew tsew*. Calls (2) a hard *tic* that may be repeated or may accelerate into a rattle (like Rufous-tailed Hummingbird) and (3) high-pitched, sharp *siik* or *tsik*. May be repeated.

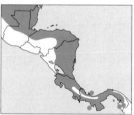

Rufous-tailed Hummingbird *Amazilia tzacatl*   10–12 cm
South MX to north SA. Common to very common resident (SL to 1850 m). Confined to Caribbean slope in north. Also Isla Coiba off Pacific PA (Veraguas, 653, 470) and Isla Escudo off Caribbean west PA (Bocas del Toro, 427). **ID** Mostly red bill with dark tip. Eye ring reddish. Mostly green below with dull grayish belly. Similar Berylline Hummingbird has rufous on secondaries. In north, compare with Cinnamon and Buff-bellied hummingbirds. Note different underparts color. **GV** Birds from Isla Escudo off Caribbean west PA are larger than widespread form. **HABITS** Understory to canopy and edge in wide variety of habitats including semihumid forest, open or disturbed areas including second growth, plantations, scrub, gardens, and urban areas. Perches and forages at all levels. Males sing persistently from favored perch. **VOICE** Song (1) a descending series of high-pitched, slurred notes *tsseeew ti-tu tu* or *tsseew ti-tititi-tu*. Calls (2) a sharp, slightly buzzy *tew* or *t-tew* and (3) hard *tic*. May be repeated or accelerate into a rattle.

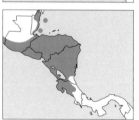

Cinnamon Hummingbird *Amazilia rutila*   10 cm
MX to north CA. Fairly common to very common resident in lowlands and foothills (to 500, locally to 1800 m). Widespread on Pacific slope. Locally common on Caribbean coast and islands including BZ Cays (535, 343). Also Caribbean lowland savannas of east HN and NI. **ID** Slightly decurved red bill with dark tip. Relatively long rufous tail slightly forked. *Entirely pale cinnamon underparts*. Male Buff-bellied Hummingbird has green throat and breast. Rufous-tailed Hummingbird has different underparts color. **HABITS** Understory to canopy and edge of scrub, littoral and deciduous forest, savanna, open or disturbed areas including second growth, mangroves, plantations, and gardens. Perches and forages at all levels. May gather in large numbers at flowering trees during dry season. **VOICE** Song (1) a short series of high-pitched, short, slurred notes *tsee ee-ee ee cheeeechee* may be repeated persistently.

73%

Azure-crowned Hummingbird

widespread

Mosquitia

Green-fronted Hummingbird

Buff-bellied Hummingbird

Rufous-tailed Hummingbird

♂

♀

♂

Escudo
♂

♂

widespread

Cinnamon Hummingbird

HUMMINGBIRDS Trochilidae

Amazilia hummingbirds found mainly in lowlands and foothills. Honduran Emerald, Mangrove Hummingbird, and Charming Hummingbird are endemic to the region and have narrow ecological associations. White-bellied and Blue-chested emeralds are the most common and widespread.

White-bellied Emerald *Amazilia candida*   9 cm

South MX and CA. Fairly common to very common resident in Caribbean lowlands and foothills (to 1500 m). Uncommon and local in Pacific foothills of GT (276, 279, 608, 341). One record from SV (San Salvador, 341). **ID** Small and plain. Short, near-straight bill with red base of mandible. Olive-green above and whitish below with greenish mottling on sides of breast. Note *faint, dark subterminal band on notched tail*. Female Ruby-throated Hummingbird has different tail pattern. Mangrove Hummingbird and Honduran Emerald are allopatric. **HABITS** Midstory to canopy of semihumid to humid broadleaf forest and tall second growth. Males sing persistently at leks in subcanopy. Feeds at flowering trees. **VOICE** Song (1) a long, monotonous series of short, squeaky phrases and single notes *chip cha chee-chee chip chink . . .*

Honduran Emerald *Amazilia luciae*   9.5 cm

CA endemic. Uncommon to very locally common resident on Caribbean slope (200 to 500 m) of north HN (Santa Bárbara, Cortés, Yoro, Olancho, Lempira, 447, 488, 442, 316, 317, 149). Most often reported from vicinity of Olanchito (Yoro). Recently found in west HN (Santa Bárbara, Lempira, 36, 346). **ID** Dark, notched tail with dark subterminal band. Fairly long, slightly decurved bill mostly dusky with reddish mandible and dark tip. Mostly green above (becoming bronzy on uppertail coverts) and dull whitish below. Glittering *turquoise-blue gorget*. Some (imm male or ad female?) have gorget fringed with white. Note whitish postocular and smaller preocular spot. **HABITS** Understory to midstory and edge of arid woodland, thorn forest, and scrub. **VOICE** Song (1) a series of very high-pitched, thin, insect-like notes and soft, warbled phrases. Calls (2) a series of hard, slightly metallic *tsic* or *chik* notes. May be repeated steadily *chik, chik-chik, chik chik . . .* Also (3) a rapid series of high-pitched, slightly buzzy notes *zzii-zzii-zzii-zzchi-chi-chi* or *chik chi zzhi-zzchi-zzchi-zzchi* and (4) high-pitched, sharp *siik* or *tzeer* in interactions.

Mangrove Hummingbird *Amazilia boucardi*   9 cm

CA endemic. Uncommon to locally fairly common resident in Pacific coastal lowlands of CR (Guanacaste, Puntarenas, 126, 570, 574, 600, 149). Perhaps most common in east CR. **ID** Rather plain. Male has blackish *slightly forked tail*. Male's glittering green throat and olive flanks contrast with white central lower underparts. Female has mostly whitish underparts and gray tips on outer rectrices. Compare with Snowy-bellied Hummingbird (foothills). **HABITS** Understory to canopy and edge of mangroves and adjacent littoral scrub, second growth, and gardens. **VOICE** Song (1) a short, soft, slightly descending trill or rattle *chu-tu-tu-tu-tututututu*. Call (2) a short, soft *dot* or *tut*.

Blue-chested Hummingbird *Amazilia amabilis*   8.5 cm

CA and north SA. Fairly common resident in Caribbean lowlands and foothills (to 500 m, occasionally or locally higher). Rare and poorly known in east HN (Gracias a Dios, 341, 346) and north NI (RAAN, 413). **ID** Small with near-straight bill. *Blackish tail*. Male mostly green above and has glittering *blue-violet gorget* and grayish lower underparts. Female has white throat speckled with bluish-green. Female's outer rectrices tipped grayish. Imm resembles female. Charming Hummingbird allopatric. **HABITS** Understory and edge of humid broadleaf forest, second growth, gardens, and clearings. **VOICE** Song (1) a long series of squeaky notes or short phrases *tsip tsew tsew tseek tsew tseek . . .* Calls (2) metallic *tsink* or *tsit* sometimes given in short series and (3) short, descending trill *dir-r-r-r-rup*.

Charming Hummingbird *Amazilia decora*   8.5 cm

CA endemic. Uncommon resident in Pacific lowlands and foothills (SL to 1800, mainly 300 to 1200 m) of CR and west PA. **ID** Small with near-straight bill. *Tail brown*. Male mostly green above and has glittering *blue-violet gorget* and grayish lower underparts. Female has white throat speckled with bluish-green. Imm resembles female. Blue-chested Hummingbird allopatric. **HABITS** Midstory in semi-open or disturbed areas including humid broadleaf forest edge, second growth, plantation, and gardens. May take conspicuous perch on bare snag. Usually solitary. **VOICE** Song (1) a soft, buzzy *tzeer* or *tseer tir tir*. Call (2) a short, slightly buzzy *tip* or *tsip*. May be repeated.

White-bellied Emerald

Honduran Emerald

imm
♂

ad
♂

♂

Mangrove Hummingbird

♀

♂

♂

Blue-chested Emerald

♀

♂

♂

♀

♂

Charming Hummingbird

CRAKES AND RAIL Rallidae

Small rails found on ground in grassy or tangled wetland vegetation. All are secretive and are most often detected by voice. When birds are glimpsed, observers should note details of head and underparts pattern. Ruddy and White-throated crakes are the most common and widespread.

Ruddy Crake *Laterallus ruber*   15.5 cm

South MX and CA. Locally common resident in lowlands and foothills (to 1500, rarely to 2200 m). Vagrant to CR (Guanacaste, Heredia, 570, 584) and PA (Bocas del Toro, 346, 42). **ID** Small with dusky bill and dull greenish legs. Eyes red. Rufous-brown with gray crown and auriculars. No other small crake has *plain rufous underparts*. Larger Uniform Crake has red legs and dull greenish bill. **HABITS** Floor and understory of wetlands, flooded agricultural fields, marshes and margins of ponds and lakes. **VOICE** Call (1) a long rattle that rises and falls in pitch. Often with high-pitched introductory notes *viit, viit, urrrrrrrrrrrrrrrr* . . . Compare with calls of Gray-breasted and White-throated crakes. Also (2) a series of short, hard, ticking *chk* or *tek* notes. May be doubled as *chk-chk*.

White-throated Crake *Laterallus albigularis*   14 cm

CA and north SA. Locally common resident in lowlands and foothills (to 1500 m). Poorly known in east HN (Gracias a Dios, 442, 34) and NI (RAAN, 322). Also Isla Coiba (Veraguas, 653, 470). **ID** Small with dull greenish bill. *Black-and-white barred flanks* and *rufous-brown breast*. Ruddy Crake has plain underparts. **GV** Birds from east PA have rufous head. **HABITS** Floor and understory of wetlands, marshes, and margins of ponds and lakes. **VOICE** Call (1) a long rattle that rises and falls in pitch. Much like Ruddy Crake but higher-pitched and thinner. Compare with rattle of Gray-breasted Crake and with call of Least Grebe. Also (2) a series of sharp, metallic *cheep* or *tchip* notes.

Gray-breasted Crake *Laterallus exilis*   14 cm

CA and SA. Uncommon and local resident in lowlands and foothills (to 1400 m). Confined to Caribbean slope in north. Also Isla Coiba (Veraguas, 653, 470). **ID** *Yellow-green base of bill* and red eyes. *Rufous nape and sides of neck* contrast with gray crown and brown upperparts. Juv whitish below with duller bill and dusky eyes. **HABITS** Floor and understory of wetlands, marshes, and margins of ponds and lakes. **VOICE** Calls include (1) a short series of metallic, high-pitched notes *tinc ti-ti-ti-ti-ti*. Also (2) a descending rattle like other *Laterallus* crakes. Usually with two or three harsh introductory notes *chr-chr trrrrrrrrrr*. Compare with longer, higher-pitched rattles of White-throated and Ruddy crakes.

Black Rail *Laterallus jamaicensis*   14 cm

USA to Chile. Rare and local near SL in BZ (Orange Walk, Belize, Toledo, 529, 530, 313), HN (Cortés, Gracias a Dios, 442, 628), and CR (Guanacaste, Puntarenas, Alajuela, 474, 600). Historical records from GT highlands (1800 m, Sacatepéquez, 229, 536). One record from PA (Panamá, 657, 293). **ID** Blackish head and breast contrast with rufous-brown nape. Eyes red. Bill black. Note *fine white spotting on upperparts*. Gray-breasted Crake has plain brownish mantle. **HABITS** Floor and understory of dry or seasonally flooded grasslands. May call at night. **VOICE** Call (1) one or two sharp notes followed by gruff, rolled note *kee-kee-durr*. Also (2) a short, coarse rattle *gurrrr-rrrr* and (3) quiet, low-pitched *kuk* or *cwuc*.

Yellow-breasted Crake *Hapalocrex flaviventer*   13 cm

South MX and WI to SA. Rare and local resident in lowlands and foothills (to 650 m, but mainly near SL) of BZ (Belize, Cayo, 347, 343), GT (San Marcos, Santa Rosa, 171, 178, 182), SV (San Miguel, 183, 619), HN (Cortés, 346), NI (Río San Juan), CR (Guanacaste, Alajuela, Heredia, 474, 574, 600, 346), and PA (Bocas del Toro, Chiriquí, Herrera, Panamá, Colón, Veraguas, 512, 346). **ID** *Broken white supercilium* contrasts with *dark crown and eye stripe*. Eyes red. Boldly streaked above. Note buff sides of breast and barred flanks. Legs and long toes yellow. Juv Sora larger with plainer head pattern and heavier, yellowish bill. **HABITS** Floor and understory of freshwater wetlands with emergent or floating vegetation. Walks or climbs through tangled growth. Secretive. **VOICE** Calls (1) two short, high-pitched notes *chee-jeep or jee-jeep*, (2) a short descending series of harsh notes *jeee-jeee-jeer-jeer*, and (3) harsh *kweer*.

Ocellated Crake *Micropygia schomburgkii*   13 cm

Mainly SA. Rare and local resident in east Pacific foothills (near 1500 m) of CR near Buenos Aires (Puntarenas, 170). **ID** Very small. Legs and eyes red. Tawny ochre below and on sides of head. Upperparts, including hindcrown, brown with *black-bordered, white spots*. In flight, shows white on wing. **HABITS** Floor and understory of damp or dry grasslands. Secretive. **VOICE** Call (1) a slightly descending rattle with a ticking quality. Drier and higher-pitched than rattles of *Laterallus* crakes. Also (2) a series of loud notes *pir-pir-pir* and (3) harsh, buzzy *pjrrrrrrrr* or *wheeiiiiiiiiur* that drops slightly in pitch.

38%

Ruddy Crake

juv

ad

White-throated Crake

juv

widespread
ad

east PA
ad

Gray-breasted Crake

juv

ad

Black Rail

Ocellated Crake

Yellow-breasted Crake

RAILS Rallidae

Poorly known, medium-sized rails found in marshes and mangroves. Virginia Rail is known in Central America only from historical records in the highlands of Guatemala. Clapper and Mangrove rails were formerly considered conspecific.

Virginia Rail *Rallus limicola*   21 cm

USA to MX. Disjunctly in SA. Known only from historical record in highlands (near 1000 m) of GT (Sacatepéquez, Guatemala, 539). At least formerly perhaps a rare and local resident. **ID** Fairly long, mostly *orange-red bill. Gray face* and auriculars contrast with rufous breast and blackish crown. Note rufous wing coverts. Lower underparts boldly barred with black and white. Legs dull pink or reddish. Clapper and Mangrove rails (coastal regions) are larger and have paler, brownish head and breast. **HABITS** Floor and understory of freshwater marshes, lakeshores, and flooded agricultural fields or savannas. Terrestrial, walks over muddy banks or through dense marsh vegetation. Solitary or in pairs. **VOICE** Calls (1) a short, slightly descending, rhythmic series of coarse, grunting notes *rreh-rreh-rreh-rreh-rreh-rreh* . . . or *nyuh-nyuh-nyuh-nyuh* . . . and (2) single short, sharp *kriik* or *riik* or *reek*.

Clapper Rail⁊ *Rallus crepitans*   34 cm

NA and WI to CA. Uncommon to locally common resident in coastal BZ and BZ Cays (68, 96, 529, 343, 346). **ID** Long red-orange bill. *Pale cinnamon breast and brownish head*. Note short, whitish supercilium and black-and-white barred lower underparts. Mangrove Rail allopatric. **HABITS** Floor of coastal marshes and mangroves. Walks on mudflats beneath vegetation. Secretive. Occasionally forages in the open. Solitary or in pairs. **VOICE** Poorly known in region. In NA, gives (1) a series of dry, laughing cries *kah-kah-kah kah-kah* . . . or *cah-cah-cah-cah* . . . Compare with call of Least Bittern. Also (2) a sharp *kek*. May be repeated.

Mangrove Rail⁊ *Rallus longirostris*   32 cm

CA and SA. Uncommon to locally common resident on Pacific coast of SV (La Unión, 346), HN (Choluteca, Valle, 346, 631, 399), NI (Chinandega, León, 346), and CR (Guanacaste, Puntarenas, 546, 346, 266). **ID** Long red-orange bill. *Dull gray neck* and brownish head. Note short, whitish supercilium and black-and-white barred lower underparts. Clapper Rail allopatric. **HABITS** Floor of coastal marshes and mangroves. Favors low-stature mangroves and adjacent mudflats. Like Clapper Rail. **VOICE** Calls (1) a very long, rhythmic series of dry, rattling phrases *eh-arh-eh-arh-eh-arh* . . . and (2) a short, sharp grunt *kek*. May be repeated.

Virginia Rail

Clapper Rail

Mangrove Rail

WOOD-RAILS Rallidae

Large, long-necked rails. Some are found in upland habitats including broadleaf forest. All have loud and distinctive vocalizations. Russet-naped and Gray-cowled wood-rails were until recently considered conspecific. Although both are widespread and frequently encountered, the precise distributions, as well as the nature of vocal differences between these species are poorly known.

Rufous-necked Wood-Rail *Aramides axillaris*   32 cm

MX to north SA. Rare and local resident in coastal lowlands of BZ (343), GT (San Marcos, Izabal, 220, 229), HN (Valle, 346), CR (Puntarenas, 114), and PA (Bocas del Toro, Coclé, Panamá, 657, 512, 48). Also islands including BZ Cays (343) and Bay Islands (94, 317). Perhaps undertakes seasonal movements (343). Rarely reported from Pacific foothills in SV (Santa Ana, 619) and NI (Chinandega, Granada, 413). **ID** Long-necked with fairly long, greenish-yellow bill. Note *rufous head and breast* and *gray mantle*. Lower underparts black. More common Gray-cowled and Russet-naped wood-rails have mostly gray head and neck. **HABITS** Floor and understory of mangroves, littoral scrub, and adjacent beaches and mudflats. Also reported to use broadleaf forest in upland areas. Usually remains inside cover. Occasionally forages in open on mudflats during low tide. Solitary or in pairs. **VOICE** Calls (1) a long series of loud *pik* or *pyik* notes on steady pitch, sometimes combined with *chew* notes as *pyik-pyik-pyik-pyik-chew-pyik-chew* . . . and (2) a high-pitched *tiik* or *kik*. May be repeated persistently.

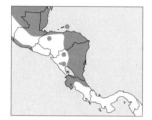

Russet-naped Wood-Rail[8] *Aramides albiventris*   35–40 cm

MX and CA. Common resident in north lowlands and foothills (to 900 m). Local on Pacific slope (428, 619, 400). Also Isla Guanaja in Bay Islands (94). **ID** Large and long-necked. Fairly long, stout, yellow bill with greenish tip. *Gray head and neck* contrast with rufous lower underparts. **GV** Birds from GT, SV and BZ are larger, paler and have white border on belly patch. Nape russet. **HABITS** Floor and edge of humid broadleaf forest, second growth, plantations, and dense riparian thickets. Often near water but also ranges into uplands. Walks deliberately while nervously twitching tail. Usually remains inside cover but sometimes forages in open along quiet roadsides or in small clearings. Solitary or in pairs. **VOICE** May vocalize at night. Pairs call in duet, producing (1) loud, rapid and rhythmic series of two to five pairs of notes *kajack kajack kajack* . . . with second note of each pair louder and longer; and alternating with series of two to six pulsing notes *koo koo koo* . . . The entire sequence may last as long as thirty seconds. Compare with calls of *Odontophorus* wood-quails. Also (2) a low-pitched, repeated *gup, gup, gup* . . . and (3) loud, harsh cackle.

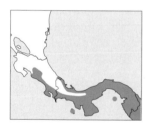

Gray-cowled Wood-Rail[8] *Aramides cajaneus*   35 cm

CA and SA. Common resident in south lowlands and foothills (to 1400 m). Also Isla Coiba and Pearl Islands (Veraguas, Panamá, 400, 611, 470). **ID** Large and long-necked. Fairly long, stout, yellow bill with greenish tip. *Gray head and neck* contrast with rufous lower underparts. Nape dull brown. **HABITS** Floor and edge of humid broadleaf forest, second growth, plantations, and dense riparian thickets. Like Russet-naped Wood-Rail. **VOICE** May vocalize at night. Pairs call in duet, producing (1) loud, rhythmic series of three to eight three-note phrases *kiddik kur, kiddik kur, kiddik kur* . . . with last note of each phrase on lower pitch; and alternating with series of three to five pulsing notes *koo koo koo* . . . The entire sequence may last as long as thirty seconds. Compare with calls of *Odontophorus* wood-quails. Also (2) a very low-pitched *huup, huup huup-hup-hup-hup* and (3) loud, harsh cackle.

Rufous-necked Wood-Rail

juv

ad

Russet-naped Wood-Rail

GT, SV and BZ

HN, NI, and Caribbean CR

Gray-cowled Wood-Rail

CRAKES AND RAIL Rallidae

The two *Neocrex* crakes are poorly known inhabitants of freshwater wetlands and flooded agricultural fields. Observations of the enigmatic Colombian Crake should be carefully documented. The Nearctic migrant Sora is a winter resident and can be briefly or locally common. Spotted Rail is rarely encountered.

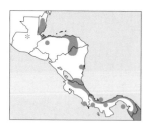

Uniform Crake *Amaurolimnas concolor*   21 cm

South MX to SA. Rare and local resident in lowlands and foothills (to 1100 m) of BZ (Stann Creek, Orange Walk, Cayo, 313, 346), GT (Izabal, 539, 218, 229), HN (Atlántida, Gracias a Dios, 35), NI (Río San Juan, 324), CR (Guanacaste, Heredia, Puntarenas, 55, 474, 353, 586, 346), and PA (Chiriquí, Bocas del Toro, Colón, Darién, 512, 153, 48). Locally common on Isla Escudo de Veraguas off Caribbean west PA (Bocas del Toro, 48). Also Isla San José in Pearl Islands (Panamá, 649). **ID** Structure like a small *Aramides* wood-rail. *Plain rufous-brown* with *red legs*, red eyes, and *dull greenish bill*. Ruddy Crake is smaller and has dull greenish legs and dark bill. Also note different habits. **HABITS** Floor and understory of wet or flooded broadleaf forest, dense tangled second growth, and stands of large-leaved herbs in ravines or at streamside margins. Walks over muddy or cluttered forest floor with neck erect and tail cocked. Solitary and secretive. Usually remains inside cover. Pumps tail like a wood-rail when disturbed. **VOICE** Call (1) a series of clear, upslurred whistles that accelerate and gradually become louder before fading at the end *tooeee toooeee toooeee tooeee tooee tooee-tueetui*. Compare with song of Northern Barred-Woodcreeper. Also (2) a sharp, nasal *kek*.

Sora *Porzana carolina*   19 cm

Breeds Nearctic. Winters USA to WI and SA. Uncommon transient and winter resident (Oct to May) in lowlands and foothills (to 1500 m, rarely to 2000 m). Irregular. May be briefly or locally common. Vagrant to Isla del Coco (329). **ID** *Black face*. Breeding ad (Mar to Aug) has black throat and *deep-based, yellow bill*. Gray sides of head contrast with brown crown and nape. Upperparts brown with blackish spotting and fine white streaking. Juv (Jul to Nov) has mostly buff head and breast. **HABITS** Floor and understory of damp grasslands, margins of lakes and ponds, and flooded agricultural fields. Forages in open more often than other small rails. Mainly terrestrial, but may climb into low shrubs or tangled vegetation at borders of wetlands. **VOICE** Usually silent in winter.

Colombian Crake *Neocrex colombiana*   18 cm

CA and north SA. Very rare and local in lowlands of central PA where reported breeding (Colón, Panamá, 79, 659, 48). **ID** *Dusky yellow bill with reddish base*. Red legs and eyes. Plain brown above and mostly gray below. Note *plain tan rear flanks and crissum*. Resembles Paint-billed Crake. Note darker bill and different rear underparts (may be difficult to discern in field). **HABITS** Floor and understory of marshes, pond edges, drainage ditches, and flooded agricultural fields. Poorly known. Secretive. **VOICE** Unknown.

Paint-billed Crake *Neocrex erythrops*   18 cm

CA and SA. Rare and local resident in lowlands of CR (Heredia, Limón, Puntarenas, 641, 341, 346) and PA (Bocas del Toro, Herrera, Panamá, 79, 659, 512, 346). **ID** Greenish-yellow bill with red base. Red legs and eyes. Plain brown above and gray below. Note dark rear flanks and undertail with fine whitish barring. Compare with larger Sora. Note Paint-billed's plain head and pale throat. **HABITS** Floor and understory of marshes, pond edges, drainage ditches, grassy or brushy pastures, and flooded agricultural fields. Secretive. Occasionally forages in open in early morning. **VOICE** Call (1) a loud, slightly accelerating series of hollow notes *qurk qurk qurk auk-auk-auk* or *purk, purk, purk purk purk-prk-prk-prk*. Very different from rattles of *Laterallus* crakes. Also (2) a long, rhythmic series of slightly hoarse, pumping phrases *quee-urrk-quee-urrk-quee-urrk* and (3) single note *twuk* or *uk*.

Spotted Rail *Pardirallus maculatus*   26 cm

MX and WI to SA. Rare and local resident in lowlands and foothills (mainly near SL, rarely or locally to 1600 m) of GT (Alta Verapaz, Baja Verapaz, Izabal, Jutiapa, 229, 300), BZ (Orange Walk, Toledo, Belize, 68, 630, 343, 346), SV (La Paz, San Miguel, 619), HN at Lago Yojoa (Cortés, 262), NI (Rivas, 412), CR (Guanacaste, Puntarenas, Cartago, 88, 474, 600, 346), and PA (Panamá, Colón, 239, 512, 346). **ID** Blackish-brown *extensively streaked, barred, and spotted with white. Long green bill with red spot at base*. Note red eyes and rose-red legs. **HABITS** Floor and understory of marshes, tangled lakeshores, and flooded agricultural fields or savannas. Walks over muddy banks or through dense vegetation. Secretive. May forage in open during early morning. Solitary. **VOICE** Varied calls include (1) a loud, decelerating series of rhythmic, nasal, grunting cries that each start with a pop or grunt *g'reech, g'reech g'reech . . .* or *pum-kreep pum-kreep pum-kreep . . .* (2) a nasal, groaning screech that drops in pitch *wiiiiiiiiiiahhh*, (3) an accelerating series of low *pum* notes, (4) a sharp, high-pitched *gheek* or *g-deek* that may be repeated, and (5) a series of loud, harsh *rehk* notes.

35%

Uniform Crake

juv

ad

Sora

juv

nonbreeding
ad

Colombian Crake

Paint-billed Crake

Spotted Rail

GALLINULES AND COOT Rallidae

Gallinules and coots are heavy-bodied relatives of rails found in freshwater marshes and margins of lakes where they are often seen swimming.

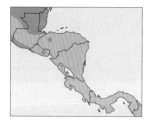

Purple Gallinule *Porphyrio martinicus* 28 cm

USA to SA. Uncommon and local breeding resident in north (to 1500 m). Nearctic breeding birds occur as uncommon and local winter residents. **ID** Fluffy white crissum. Yellow legs and long toes. Ad has short, stout red bill with yellow tip and *pale blue frontal shield*. Upperparts deep green. *Head and underparts deep violet-blue.* Juv has dusky bill tip, buffy brown head and neck, and whitish lower underparts. Compare with Common Gallinule. Note different bill pattern and crissum. **HABITS** Dense vegetation of marshes and lake, pond, and lagoon margins with floating or flooded vegetation. Usually solitary when not breeding. Swims like American Coot or Common Gallinule but more often seen walking or climbing over tangled vegetation. **VOICE** Varied calls (1) a series of high-pitched *ik* or *pik* notes *pikit-it-it-it-pik* . . . (2) a short, very nasal *eeeht* or *eeeen* that may be repeated, and (3) single, loud *ghik*.

Common Gallinule *Gallinula galeata* 32 cm

USA to SA. Uncommon to locally fairly common resident in lowlands and foothills (to 1000, rarely to 2000 m). Nearctic breeding birds may also occur as transients and winter residents (Nov to Mar). **ID** *Dark gray underparts* including center of crissum. Note white stripe extending along flanks and white lateral crissum. Ad has red bill with yellow tip and *red frontal shield*. Juv mostly grayish with pale throat and usually shows some suggestion of ad's bill pattern (juv American Coot has plain bill). Also compare with Purple Gallinule. Note different bill pattern. **HABITS** Dense vegetation of marshes, lake, pond and lagoon margins, and flooded agricultural fields. Usually solitary when not breeding. Forages mainly while swimming. Also walks or climbs over tangled vegetation. **VOICE** Varied calls (1) a nasal, laughing *weh-heh-heh-heh-he-he-he* that gradually slows and may drop slightly in pitch, (2) an abrupt, nasal, barking *nep!* or *bip!* that may be repeated, (3) lower-pitched, explosive *kup*, (4) a low-pitched *kloc-kloc-kloc*, and (5) strident *kr-r-r-r, kruc-kruc*.

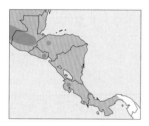

American Coot *Fulica americana* 38 cm

NA, WI, CA, and SA. Uncommon and local breeding resident in lowlands and foothills of GT (279) south to CR (Guanacaste, 600). Nearctic breeding birds are locally abundant winter residents in north. **ID** Ad mostly plain slaty gray (becoming darkest on head) with *white bill and frontal shield*. Note red eyes and pale green legs with long, lobed toes. Juv drab grayish-brown becoming paler below. Note dusky sides of head. Compare with juv Common Gallinule. Note different bill. **HABITS** Marshes, lakes, and lagoons. Forages while swimming or walks over open grassy or muddy areas near water. Gregarious. May form rafts of several hundred birds on open water at favored wintering sites. **VOICE** Usually quiet. May give (1) a series of very low-pitched grunts or (2) short, nasal, barking cries.

SUNGREBE Heliornithidae

Sungrebe is a highly distinctive species with no close relatives in the region.

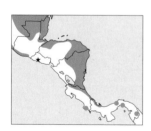

Sungrebe *Heliornis fulica* 29 cm

MX to SA. Uncommon and local resident mainly in lowlands. Rare in Pacific GT (Santa Rosa, Escuintla, San Marcos, Retalhuleu, 182) and SV (La Libertad, 341). **ID** Long, white-tipped tail (held low on water's surface) and long, slender neck. Note *bold black-and-white markings on head and neck*. Female has buff auriculars. Female's bill red in breeding condition. Lobed feet banded with dusky. Compare with Least and Pied-billed grebes. **HABITS** Slow-moving watercourses including streams, rivers and oxbow lakes. Usually solitary. Favors shaded areas with dense vegetation overhanging water. Swims with jerking motion, pumping head forward like a coot. Sometimes alights on branch or other low perch. **VOICE** Calls (1) a series of three or four slightly hollow hoots or barks that drop slightly in pitch *huu-huu huu-huu*, (2) single, quiet, barking *kek* or *wek*, and (3) quiet, sharp *plik*.

Purple Gallinule

imm

ad

Common Gallinule

imm

ad

American Coot

imm

ad

Sungrebe

breeding
♀

♂

LIMPKIN Aramidae

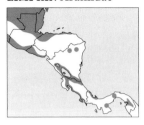

Limpkin *Aramus guarauna* 62 cm
MX and Florida to SA. Locally common in lowlands (mainly near SL, locally to
1500 m). Resident, but may undertake local movements. Perhaps most common in
lowlands of BZ and north GT (Petén). Local at higher elevations, as for example at
Lago Yojoa in HN (Santa Bárbara, Cortés, 442) and in central CR (Cartago, 346).
ID Long bill slightly decurved at tip. Mostly *dark brown with white spotting on mantle,
wing coverts, and neck.* **GV** Birds from central and east PA have white markings
confined to head and neck. **HABITS** Freshwater marshes and borders of lakes and
lagoons. Wades deliberately through submerged, grassy vegetation, constantly
twitching tail. Usually remains hidden inside cover but occasionally takes an elevated
perch in open. Often active and may vocalize persistently at night. Flies with shallow,
rapid wingbeats and short glides. Feeds on snails. Usually solitary. **VOICE** Calls (1)
a series of low-pitched, resonant cries that gradually fade *kleeeeo* or *krrleeeeoo* or
krowww, (2) a harsher, *kyarrrr* ending in a dry rattle, and (3) short, sharp, barking
keew.

SUNBITTERN Eurypygidae

Sunbittern is a highly distinctive species with no close relatives in the region.

Sunbittern *Eurypyga helias* 45 cm
CA and SA. Uncommon and local resident in foothills and adjacent lowlands (mainly
100 to 1500 m). Very rare on north Caribbean slope of GT at Cerro San Gil (Izabal,
227) and historically at Cobán (Alta Verapaz, 539). **ID** Long, slender neck, *orange legs,*
and *long bill with orange-yellow mandible.* Plumage mostly grayish with cinnamon
and dusky vermiculations and barring and *bold white spotting on wings.* Head blackish
with white markings. In flight (and in display) shows spectacular black, gold, and
rufous wing pattern. **HABITS** Margins of streams and rivers inside or adjacent to
humid broadleaf forest. Walks along banks of streams or wades deliberately in shallow
water. May perch on boulder or branch overhanging water. Usually solitary except
when breeding. Often secretive. **VOICE** Call (1) a ringing, clear, high-pitched whistle
hurrrrrrrrrrrrree that may drop slightly in pitch. May be repeated several times. Also
(2) a short, dry, rattle *k-rrrrrrrr*, (3) a ringing *ko way*, and (4) a hissing, bubbling *churr.*

JACANAS Jacanidae

Jacanas are charadriiform birds with short bills and very long toes. They are locally common in wetlands, particularly those
with tangled or floating vegetation.

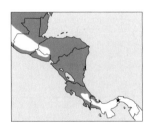

Northern Jacana *Jacana spinosa* 22 cm
MX and CA. Fairly common resident in lowlands and foothills (to 1500 m). Vagrant
to central PA (Panamá, 48). **ID** Very long, greenish-gray toes. Yellow bill and frontal
shield. In flight (or in display) shows *citrine-yellow remiges.* Ad mostly *deep rufous with
blackish head, neck, and breast.* Juv mostly whitish below with dark eye stripe
and crown. Compare juv with various crakes. Wattled Jacana mainly allopatric but
hybrids reported from Pacific east CR (Puntarenas). **HABITS** Marshes, ponds, and lake
margins and wetlands with floating vegetation and flooded agricultural fields. Forages
while walking over floating vegetation or on ground near water. Frequently lifts or
stretches wings displaying yellow flight feathers. Gregarious. In pairs or small groups.
VOICE Calls (1) a buzzy *jeeeah*, (2) series of short, buzzy *jik* or *jer* notes that may
accelerate into a rattle, and (3) loud *jaak* or *jeek.*

Wattled Jacana *Jacana jacana* 22 cm
CA and SA. Locally fairly common resident in lowlands of PA. Vagrant to east CR
(Puntarenas, 594, 346) and NI (Jinotega, Río San Juan, 419). **ID** Yellow bill and *red
frontal shield.* Very long greenish-gray toes. Mostly *blackish including mantle and lower
underparts.* Bill yellow with short, fleshy red wattles at base. Flight feathers citrine-
yellow. Juv similar to juv Northern Jacana but may show trace of ad's red frontal shield.
HABITS Marshes, pond and lake margins, wetlands with floating vegetation, and
flooded agricultural fields. Similar to Northern Jacana. **VOICE** Calls similar to Northern
Jacana but coarser, lower-pitched, and more nasal.

Limpkin

widespread

central and
east PA

Sunbittern

Sunbittern displaying.

Northern Jacana

juv

ad

ad

ad

Wattled Jacana

THICK-KNEE Burhinidae

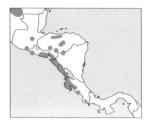

Double-striped Thick-knee *Burhinus bistriatus* 46 cm

South MX and WI to SA. Uncommon to rare and local resident in arid Pacific lowlands and foothills (to 1500 m). Local in arid Caribbean slope valleys of north HN (Cortés, Yoro, Francisco Morazán, 609, 442). Formerly perhaps more widespread, now rare and local in SV (San Miguel, 183, 619) and GT (Baja Verapaz, Santa Rosa, Escuintla, Zacapa, 229, 279, 182). Perhaps most common in west CR (Guanacaste, Puntarenas, 600). **ID** Fairly large. Note *stout bill*, large yellow eyes, and whitish supercilium with black border. Mostly pale brownish, heavily streaked with dusky. Lower underparts whitish. In flight, shows *white markings on wing* and tail. **HABITS** Open, arid, rocky areas including savanna, grasslands, pastures, and agricultural fields. Usually in pairs or small groups. Mainly nocturnal. In daylight loiters motionless in shadow of shrub or tree. Shy and difficult to approach. **VOICE** Often calls at night, especially when moonlit. Call (1) long series of short *heh* or *eh* notes. Often doubled as *heh-heh, heh-heh, heh-heh, heh, heh, heh* . . . Compare with call of Southern Lapwing.

STILT AND AVOCET Recurvirostridae

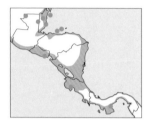

Black-necked Stilt *Himantopus mexicanus* 35 cm

USA to SA. Nearctic breeding and resident birds occur. Uncommon and very local breeding resident on coasts. Also Caribbean islands including BZ Cays and Bay Islands (442). Locally common transient and winter resident (Oct to May). **ID** Slender with *long, fine, slightly upswept bill* and *very long red legs* Mainly black above and white below with white forehead and white spot above eye. Female more brownish above. Juv brown above with fine buff scaling. **HABITS** Marshes, lagoon margins, mangroves, mudflats, and flooded agricultural fields. Wades through water when foraging. Usually in pairs or small groups. **VOICE** Often noisy. May call at night. Frequently gives (1) a nasal *pep* or *yip*. Also (2) a clear, high-pitched *peek* that may be repeated persistently and (3) coarse, grating *jaahr*.

American Avocet *Recurvirostra americana* 42 cm

Breeds Nearctic. Winters (Sep to May) mainly MX. Uncommon to rare winter visitor (Aug to Apr) in Pacific coastal lowlands of SV (San Salvador, La Paz, 346), HN (Choluteca, 346), NI (León, Masaya, 135, 346), CR (Puntarenas, Cartago, 602, 346), and PA (Coclé, 108). Rare on Caribbean slope in BZ (Belize, Toledo, 529, 347, 346), HN (Gracias a Dios, Atlántida, 346, 263), and CR (Limón, 341, 346). **ID** *Long, slender, upturned bill* and long, bluish-gray legs. Note bold black-and-white pattern on upperparts. Breeding ad (Mar to Aug) has mostly cinnamon head and neck. Ad female has more sharply upturned bill. Nonbreeding ad has mostly pale gray head and neck. **HABITS** Marshes, mudflats, and margins of lagoons. Solitary or in small groups. Often forages actively while wading in water. Occasionally swims. **VOICE** Call (1) a sharp *keep* or *keek*.

Double-striped Thick-knee

Black-necked Stilt

ad
♂

juv

ad
♀

American Avocet

nonbreeding
♂

nonbreeding
♀

breeding
♂

OYSTERCATCHER Haematopodidae

American Oystercatcher *Haematopus palliatus*   44 cm
USA to SA. Nearctic breeding and resident birds thought to occur. Uncommon and local breeding resident on Pacific coast of SV (Usulután, 346, 368), NI (Chinandega, 346), CR (Guanacaste, 145), and PA (Los Santos, 512). Also Pearl Islands and Isla Coiba (Veraguas, Panamá, 512, 41). Transients and winter resident (mainly Sep to May) are most common on Pacific coast. Rare on Caribbean coast in BZ (313, 343) and GT (Izabal, 222). **ID** Black head and neck and plain white lower underparts. Note *long, straight, red bill* and *red orbital ring.* Eyes yellow. Legs pink. In flight, shows *broad white wing stripe.* Imm has duller, dark-tipped bill, dark brown eyes, and grayish scaling on upperparts. **HABITS** Beaches and estuaries, particularly with rocky intertidal or coarse sandbars. Solitary or in pairs. **VOICE** Calls (1) a clear, downslurred *keeeew* or *wheeeeu* often repeated, (2) a sharper *wreeek,* and (3) sharp *pik.*

LAPWING AND PLOVERS Charadriidae
Black-bellied and American Golden-Plovers have distinctive breeding plumages but can present identification problems in nonbreeding or juvenile plumages. Bill shape and details of the head pattern are useful in separating these. Black-bellied Plover is more common.

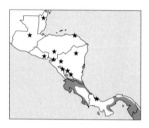

Southern Lapwing *Vanellus chilensis*   32 cm
CA and SA. Uncommon breeder in lowlands (rarely to 1300 m) of PA where first reported in 1936 (Herrera, Colón, Panamá, Darién, Bocas del Toro, 286, 42, 346) and CR (Guanacaste, San José, Heredia, Limón, Puntarenas, 542, 341, 346, 546). Rare visitor to north CA with records from BZ (Belize, 341, 346), GT (Alta Verapaz, 229), SV (San Miguel, 346), HN (Gracias a Dios, Francisco Morazán, 346), and NI (Río San Juan, RAAN, Matagalpa, Chontales, 83, 418, 346). **ID** Large and boldly patterned with *thin, black crest.* Mostly grayish-brown above with iridescent rufous and green on wing coverts. White lower underparts contrast with *broad black breast-band.* Whitish markings on head contrast with black forehead and throat. Eyes red. Legs dull pink. In flight, note broad wings with black primaries and *bold white wing stripe.* Underwings mostly white. Tail black with broad white base. **HABITS** Short grass marshes, lake margins, pastures, and agricultural fields. Usually solitary or in pairs. May form small flocks outside breeding season. Active at night. **VOICE** Often noisy. Call (1) a very loud, metallic *keek, keek, keek . . .* or *kee, kee, kee . . .* Compare with call of Double-striped Thick-knee.

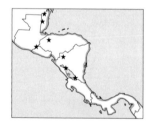

Black-bellied Plover *Pluvialis squatarola*   28 cm
Breeds Holarctic. Nearctic birds winter south to SA. Widespread and common transient and uncommon winter resident (Aug to May) on coasts. May be locally or briefly abundant in passage on Pacific coast. Uncommon nonbreeding summer resident. **ID** Fairly large, robust plover. Note *black axillars* (visible in flight), whitish tail and rump, and relatively heavy bill. Breeding ad (Apr to Sep) has mottled black-and-white upperparts and mostly black sides of head, throat, and underparts. Crown appears mostly white. Nonbreeding ad drab grayish with pale edging and spotting on back and plain grayish-white breast. Fall ad may show traces of black on underparts. Juv (Jul to Nov) more crisply patterned and has diffuse area of fine streaking on breast and flanks. **HABITS** Beaches, mudflats, and estuaries. Forms small flocks and joins mixed associations of shorebirds. **VOICE** Often calls in flight. Call (1) a mellow, downslurred *peeeuweeee* or *wheeeeur.*

American Golden-Plover *Pluvialis dominica*   25 cm
Breeds Nearctic. Winters mainly SA. Uncommon to rare transient (Aug to Nov and Apr to May). Very rare in winter (602). Most records from Pacific lowlands and foothills (to 1500 m). Also Isla del Coco (571). **ID** *Relatively fine bill* and rounded, dark crown. Breeding ad has buff, white, and black mottled upperparts and mostly black sides of head, throat, and underparts extending to vent. Nonbreeding ad mostly gray with distinct whitish supercilium. Juv (Jult to Nov) more crisply patterned. Compare nonbreeding ad and juv with more common Black-bellied Plover. Note different structure (especially bill), underwing pattern, and head pattern. **HABITS** Transients favor areas with extensive short grass including sod farms and airfields. May share this habitat with Killdeer or Pectoral Sandpipers. Also uses beaches and mudflats where may occur with Black-bellied Plover. **VOICE** Often calls in flight. Call (1) a clear, whistled *keet!* or *pleet!* Sometimes doubled as *keeleeet.*

American Oystercatcher

Southern Lapwing

nonbreeding

Black-bellied Plover

breeding

nonbreeding

nonbreeding

breeding
♂

nonbreeding

nonbreeding

American Golden-Plover

PLOVERS Charadriidae
Small plovers. Collared and Wilson's plovers breed locally in Central America.

Snowy Plover *Charadrius nivosus*   16.5 cm
USA to SA. West Nearctic birds winter MX and CA. Uncommon to rare winter resident (Sep to May) in BZ (Corozal, Cay Caulker, 347, 345, 343), GT (Santa Rosa, 178, 182), HN (Cortés, 442), NI (Masaya, Granada, León, 420, 421), CR (Limón, Puntarenas, 570, 602, 346), and PA (Panamá, Herrera, 512, 128, 346). **ID** Small with fine black bill. *Legs gray.* Breeding ad (Feb to Aug) *pale grayish-brown above* and white below with *broken black breast-band*, black bar on crown, and *black on auriculars*. Nonbreeding ad mostly lacks black markings. Compare with Collared Plover. **HABITS** Dry or rocky beaches. May join mixed groups of waders on mudflats. **VOICE** Call (1) a sharp, hard *quip* or *keep*. In flight (2) a slightly nasal *koor-wij*.

Collared Plover *Charadrius collaris*   15 cm
MX to SA. Uncommon and local breeding resident near coasts. Rare in interior. **ID** Very small. *Slender, all-black bill.* Long legs pinkish. Ad has black and rufous on crown and neck and grayish hindneck (no white band). Imm has less rufous on head and white supercilium. Juv has white collar. Compare with Semipalmated Plover. Note different head pattern and bill shape. **HABITS** Gravel bars in rivers, estuaries, and drier areas of beaches. Usually in pairs or small groups. Rarely in large flocks. **VOICE** Call (1) a simple *peet* or *dreep*. Sometimes repeated several times or varied as two-syllable *dreedup* with second note lower-pitched.

Piping Plover *Charadrius melodus*   17.5 cm
Breeds NA. Winters USA and WI. Very rare vagrant to HN (Atlántida, 346), NI (RAAS, 412), and CR (Guanacaste, 115). **ID** Small and very pale with stout bill. Legs yellow. Breeding ad (Feb to Aug) has short yellow bill with dark tip and pale gray auriculars. Note *pale gray upperparts* and black bar on crown. Nonbreeding ad plain grayish above with broken gray breast-band. Juv (Jul to Oct) similar to nonbreeding ad. Compare with Snowy Plover. **HABITS** Sandy or rocky beaches. May join mixed groups of waders on mudflats. **VOICE** Call (1) a sharp, hard *quip* or *keep*. In flight (2) a slightly nasal *koor-wij*.

Semipalmated Plover *Charadrius semipalmatus*   17.5 cm
Breeds Nearctic. Winters south USA and WI to SA. Fairly common transient and winter resident (Aug to Jun). May be briefly or locally abundant. **ID** Small with *short, stout bill.* Note brown upperparts, *yellow legs*, and single black breast-band. Breeding ad (Mar to Sep) has base of bill yellow-orange. *Sides of head and band on crown black.* Nonbreeding ad (Sep to Mar) has whitish supercilium and dusky bill. Juv (Aug to Nov) similar to nonbreeding ad, but has fine whitish scaling above. Larger Wilson's Plover has different head pattern and bill. Also compare with Killdeer and Collared Plover. **HABITS** Marshes, beaches, mudflats. Runs rapidly, stopping abruptly to glean from surface. Often in flocks and joins mixed associations of shorebirds. **VOICE** Calls (1) a variable, short, fairly low-pitched *chu-wee* or *kuweet*, (2) low-pitched, husky *kwiip*, and (3) rapid, descending series *wyeep wyeep yeep yip yipyiyiyi*. In flight, gives (4) a whistled *too-ee, too-ee . . .* or *chee-up, chee-up*.

Wilson's Plover *Charadrius wilsonia*   17.5 cm
USA to SA. Resident breeders and Nearctic migrants occur. Uncommon and local breeding resident. Uncommon to locally fairly common winter resident on coasts. **ID** *Long, heavy bill*, brown upperparts, and dull pink legs. Male has single black breast-band, black bar on crown, and white supercilium and forehead. Female paler with brown breast-band. Juv has pale buff fringing on upperparts. Semipalmated Plover smaller with different bill shape, leg color, and head pattern. Also compare with Killdeer. Note different rump pattern. **HABITS** Beaches, rocky coasts, and mudflats. **VOICE** Call (1) a loud, liquid *quit*. May be doubled as *quitit*. Also (2) a sharper, higher-pitched *peet* or *kweet*.

Killdeer *Charadrius vociferus*   25 cm
NA to SA. Resident breeders and Nearctic breeding migrants occur. Uncommon and very local breeding resident in Pacific NI (Managua, 346), CR (Cartago, 594), and west PA (Herrera, 42). Uncommon transient and winter resident (Aug to May). **ID** Large with slender black bill and long tail. *Two black bands on breast.* Note red orbital ring. In flight, shows *rufous rump and base of tail.* Juv (Jun to Sep, not shown) has buff edging on upperparts. Compare with Wilson's Plover. Note different bill shape, underparts, and rump pattern. **HABITS** Gravel bars, drier portions of beaches, grassy lake margins, airstrips, savannas, and pastures. Often in pairs. May form small groups or join mixed associations of shorebirds. **VOICE** Often noisy. Calls (1) a high-pitched, strident *dee, deeeyeee tyeeeeeee deew deew*, (2) clear, repeated *teeee di di*, and (3) high-pitched, rapid *didideeerr didideeer . . .*

Snowy Plover

nonbreeding

nonbreeding

breeding ad

juv

ad

Collared Plover

ad

Piping Plover

nonbreeding

breeding

nonbreeding   juv

breeding

Semipalmated Plover

♀

♀

♂

Wilson's Plover

Killdeer

WHIMBREL, CURLEW, SANDPIPER, AND GODWITS Scolopacidae

Large shorebirds found mainly in coastal regions. Whimbrel is the most common.

Whimbrel *Numenius phaeopus*　　　　　　　　　　　　female 45, male 42 cm

Holarctic. Winters in tropics. Uncommon to locally common transient and winter resident (Aug to early May) on coasts. Uncommon in summer. Transients may be briefly or locally common. **ID** *Large* with long neck and *very long, decurved bill*. Note dark brown eye stripe and *brown-and-white striped crown*. In flight, shows brown-barred underwings (compare with Long-billed Curlew). Juv has crisp pale spotting or spangling above. Juv may have shorter bill. **HABITS** Marshes, beaches, mudflats, and rocky coasts. Often solitary. May form small groups. Gleans or probes from muddy or stony areas at water's edge. Joins mixed groups of shorebirds at roosts. **VOICE** Call (1) a short, rapid, staccato series of liquid whistles *qui-qui-qui-qui-qui* on even pitch.

Long-billed Curlew *Numenius americanus*　　　　　　female 60, male 50 cm

Breeds west Nearctic. Winters mainly south USA to MX. Uncommon transient and winter resident (mainly Aug to May) on Pacific coast. Rare in BZ (667, 313, 346), Caribbean CR (Limón, 346), and PA (Panamá, Colón, 391, 659, 41). **ID** Very large. *Extremely long, decurved bill* and *plain crown*. In flight, note *cinnamon undersurface of wings*. Juv may have shorter bill than ad. Compare with Whimbrel. Note different head and underwing pattern. Also compare with Marbled Godwit. Note different bill shape. **HABITS** Marshes, beaches, and mudflats. May wade in shallow water (unlike Whimbrel). **VOICE** Calls (1) a clear to hoarse upslurred whistle *coooli* or *quuu-dee* or *whoo-ee-deedee*. Sometimes gives (2) *kwid wid wid wid* or (3) loud, whistled *wrrreeep*.

Upland Sandpiper *Bartramia longicauda*　　　　　　　　　　　　28 cm

Breeds Nearctic. Winters south SA. Uncommon to rare transient (Aug to Nov and Mar to May) mainly in interior and Pacific lowlands. Vagrant to Isla del Coco (163). **ID** Long legs, long tail, and small head. *Short, straight bill* mostly yellowish with black tip. Note plain head pattern with large, dark eyes. Legs dull yellowish. In flight, note barred underwing surface and dark rump. Juv (Jul to Nov) has fine scaling on upperparts. Compare with Pectoral and Buff-breasted sandpipers. Note different structure. **HABITS** Grassy areas including fields, lawns, pastures, sod farms, and airfields. Holds wings extended after landing. Solitary or in small groups. Usually not with other shorebirds. **VOICE** Often calls in flight, giving (1) a low-pitched, loud, liquid *qui-di-di-du* or *whee-dud-du* with last note slightly lower-pitched.

Marbled Godwit *Limosa fedoa*　　　　　　　　　　　　　　42 cm

Breeds Nearctic. Winters mainly south USA to MX. Rare transient and winter resident (Aug to May) on coasts (202, 602, 48, 412, 347). **ID** Large. *Long, upswept bill* pinkish with dark tip. In flight, shows *cinnamon underwing surface*. Breeding ad has fine blackish barring on underparts. Worn birds can be very plain and pale. Juv and nonbreeding ad plainer below. Compare with Hudsonian Godwit. Note different tail and wing pattern. Plumage similar to Long-billed Curlew. Note different bill and dark legs. **HABITS** Marshes, beaches, mudflats. Usually solitary, sometimes in small groups. Joins mixed groups of waders at roost sites. Probes vertically in mud or gleans from surface. **VOICE** Call (1) a slightly hoarse or nasal *kweh* or *kaa-wek* or *ka-weh-eh-eh*. Compare with call of Laughing Gull.

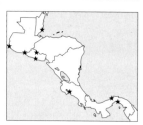

Hudsonian Godwit *Limosa haemastica*　　　　　　　　　　　　37 cm

Breeds Nearctic. Winters south SA. Rare transient and winter visitor (Sep to May), mainly on coasts in GT (San Marcos, Santa Rosa,182), SV (La Paz, 346), BZ (Belize, Toledo, 347), CR (Puntarenas, 601), and PA (Colón, Panamá, 107, 48, 346). **ID** Fairly large with *long, upswept bill*. Note *short, whitish supercilium and narrow, dark eye stripe*. In flight, note black-and-white wing stripe, mostly black tail, and black wing linings. Breeding ad (Apr to Sep) has mostly rufous breast and gray neck. Nonbreeding ad (Oct to Mar) mostly plain gray. Juv (Aug to Nov) has dull brownish-buff breast and whitish lower underparts. Compare with Marbled Godwit. Note different head and wing pattern. **HABITS** Marshes, beaches, and mudflats. Probes vertically in mud. Often wades in deep water. **VOICE** In flight, gives (1) a variable, high-pitched *kwid-wid* or *kweh-weh*. Also (2) a high-pitched *week* or *yeep*. Compare with harsher call of Black-necked Stilt.

Whimbrel

ad

ad

Long-billed Curlew

ad

juv

ad

Upland Sandpiper

nonbreeding

Marbled Godwit

breeding

Hudsonian Godwit

nonbreeding

juv

breeding ♂

nonbreeding

SANDPIPER, YELLOWLEGS, AND WILLET Scolopacidae

Medium- to large-sized shorebirds with long neck and legs. Leg color, bill shape, and head pattern are useful in separating these.

Solitary Sandpiper *Tringa solitaria*   20 cm
Breeds Nearctic. Winters MX to SA. Uncommon to fairly common transient and winter resident (Aug to May). Very rare in summer. **ID** Straight bill and long *olive legs*. Note *whitish spectacles*. Brown above with fine white spots. In flight, note dark underwing surface, dark rump, and dark barring on central rectrices. Greater and Lesser yellowlegs have yellow legs. **HABITS** Freshwater habitats including streamsides, riverbanks, marshes, and lake and pond margins. Transients may occur in littoral habitats. When disturbed may circle overhead and call. **VOICE** Usually quiet. Call (1) a clear, whistled *peet-weet* or *peet weet weet*. Compare with call of Spotted Sandpiper. Also (2) a very hard, sharp *plic, plic* . . . May be repeated in long series.

Lesser Yellowlegs *Tringa flavipes*   25 cm
Breeds Nearctic. Winters Middle and SA. Fairly common transient and winter resident (Aug to May) on coasts. **ID** Yellow legs. *Fairly long, near-straight bill.* Breeding ad has fine gray streaking on neck and breast contrasting with plain white lower underparts. Nonbreeding ad (Oct to Apr) has faintly speckled gray upperparts. Juv (Jul to Nov) has gray neck and breast indistinctly streaked with dusky and upperparts boldly speckled with white. Greater Yellowlegs has different bill shape and voice. **HABITS** Marshes, mudflats, and lake margins. Forages actively while wading in water. Typically picks from surface rather than probing. Often in small groups. **VOICE** Calls (1) a single *tiip* or (2) doubled *too-too*. Compare with (typically) longer call of Greater Yellowlegs. Also (3) a repeated *tiw, tiw* and (4) upslurred, slightly trilled *kleet* . . .

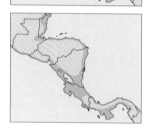

Greater Yellowlegs *Tringa melanoleuca*   32 cm
Breeds Nearctic. Winters Middle and SA. Fairly common transient and winter resident (Aug to May). Mainly on coasts. Rare in summer. **ID** Yellow legs and long, *very slightly upswept bill*. Breeding ad (Mar to Aug) has extensive dark barring on breast and flanks. Nonbreeding ad has faint speckling above (best told from Lesser by structure and voice). At close range note gray base of bill. Juv (Jul to Nov) has upperparts boldly speckled with white. Lesser Yellowlegs smaller with shorter, straighter bill. Note different voice. **HABITS** Marshes, mudflats, and lake margins. Forages actively, usually while wading in water. Often in small groups. **VOICE** Calls (often given in flight) include (1) a rapid phrase of three or four short whistles *tiip-tiip-tiip* or *too-too-too-too* or *deewdeew-deew*. Typically higher-pitched than calls of Lesser Yellowlegs. May give (2) a long series of single notes on even pitch *tew, tew, tew* . . .

Willet⁹ *Tringa semipalmata*   30–37 cm
NA to SA. Nearctic birds winter south USA to CA. Uncommon transient, winter resident, and nonbreeding summer resident on coasts. **ID** Fairly long, heavy, *near-straight bill* (grayish with black tip). Note narrow whitish eye ring. In flight, shows bold *black-and-white pattern on wings*. Breeding ad (Apr to Aug) has extensive fine blackish checkering. Nonbreeding ad (Sep to Mar) is plain gray above and whitish below. Juv (Jul to Nov) has fine, pale edging on upperparts. **GV** Birds from population breeding in coastal eastern NA are smaller, less lanky, and have shorter bill. They are also darker and more heavily marked, and the bill may have a pinkish base. **HABITS** Marshes, beaches, mudflats. Gleans from surface or probes in mud. Also wades in water. Solitary. **VOICE** Calls include (1) a loud, clear, ringing *kyaah yah* or *klee lii*, (2) downslurred *haaaa*, (3) rapid, rhythmic *kawee-a-wee-weeee*, and (4) monotonously repeated *wik, wik* . . .

23%

Solitary Sandpiper

nonbreeding

breeding

nonbreeding

Lesser Yellowlegs

nonbreeding

juv

nonbreeding

breeding

Greater Yellowlegs

juv

nonbreeding

breeding

nonbreeding

Willet

juv

west NA
breeding ad

west NA
nonbreeding ad

coastal east NA
breeding ad

SANDPIPER, TATTLER, TURNSTONE AND SURFBIRD Scolopacidae

Small to medium-sized shorebirds. Spotted Sandpiper, often found inland and near freshwater, is the most common and widespread. The remaining species are found mainly on rocky coastlines.

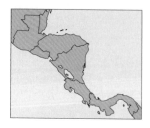

Spotted Sandpiper *Actitis macularius*   17.5 cm

Breeds Nearctic. Winters Middle America and SA. Common transient and winter resident (Aug to May). Rare in summer. **ID** Short-necked with straight bill. Breeding ad (Apr to Aug) has *black spotting on white underparts* and mostly orange bill. Nonbreeding ad and juv (Jul to Oct) have mostly plain white underparts with *brown mark on sides of breast*. Compare with Solitary Sandpiper (often in same habitat). Note different structure and flight style. **HABITS** Uses a wide variety of aquatic habitats including streamsides, riverbanks, marshes, beaches, mudflats, and lake margins. More likely near freshwater than most other shorebirds. Walks with bobbing gait. Flies with rapid bursts of shallow wingbeats and short glides. Usually solitary. Transients may form small flocks. **VOICE** Usually quiet. Calls (1) a clear, high-pitched, whistled *twii twii* or *peet-weet* and (2) descending series *peet weet weet*. Compare with higher-pitched calls of Solitary Sandpiper.

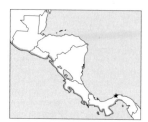

Wandering Tattler *Tringa incana*   26 cm

Breeds west Nearctic. Winters mainly on Pacific islands and on Pacific coast of NA south to north SA. Uncommon to rare and local transient and winter visitor (Sep to Mar) on Pacific coast (601, 659, 341, 336, 48, 346). One report from Caribbean slope in PA (Colón, 512). **ID** Distinctive structure with short legs, long wings, and fairly long, straight bill. Note *yellow legs* and *short whitish supercilium*. Breeding ad (Apr to Oct) has *gray barring on underparts*. Nonbreeding ad more uniform gray. In flight, shows *plain gray upperwing*. Juv (not shown) similar. Compare with Solitary Sandpiper. Note different structure and habits. Also compare with Surfbird. Note different bill shape and head pattern. **HABITS** Rocky or pebble-strewn coasts, islets, and beaches. Solitary or in small groups. **VOICE** Calls (1) a clear, high-pitched *lidididi* or *wi-di-di-di-di* on even pitch and (2) sharp, high-pitched *klee-lik . . .*

Ruddy Turnstone *Arenaria interpres*   22 cm

Holarctic. Nearctic birds winter USA to SA. Uncommon transient and winter resident on coasts (Sep to Apr). Uncommon in summer. **ID** Stocky and short-necked. *Bill short, pointed, and slightly upswept.* Note dark-patterned head and breast and *short orange-red legs*. Lower underparts immaculate white. In flight, shows bold black, white, and rufous pattern on mantle and upperwing and mostly clean white underwing. Tail mostly white with broad black subterminal band. Breeding ad (Apr to Sep) has rufous and black upperparts. Nonbreeding ad (Sep to Apr) has brownish head and upperparts. Juv (Aug to Nov) similar, but has fine buff scaling above. **HABITS** Rocky or pebble-strewn beaches, breakwaters, and islets. Occasionally on muddy or sandy beaches. Solitary or in small groups. **VOICE** Calls often given in flight (1) a low-pitched *chew-chch-ch*, (2) single-note, sharp *klew* or *chew*, and (3) hard, rattling *graerrrrrt*.

Surfbird *Calidris virgata*   24 cm

Breeds west Nearctic. Winters Pacific coast from NA to south SA. Uncommon transient and winter resident (601) on Pacific coast (mainly Aug to Apr). Very rare in summer (199, 202). **ID** Bulky and short-necked. Note *short, stout, straight bill* with orange or yellow base of mandible. *Legs yellow.* Breeding ad (Mar to Aug) has fine black-and-white streaking and spotting on head, neck, and throat and bold black chevrons on white breast and flanks. Nonbreeding ad and juv (Jul to Sep) mostly plain brownish-gray above and on breast. Note whitish supraloral spot and whitish lower underparts with dark streaking or spotting on flanks. In flight, shows white tail with broad black terminal band and white wing stripe. **HABITS** Beaches, rocky and pebble-strewn coasts and islets. Gleans from rocks in intertidal zone. Usually in small groups. Often confiding. **VOICE** Usually quiet. Calls (1) often given in flight, a soft *iff-iff-iff*. Also (2) a short, slightly squeaky rattle *wreep*. May be repeated.

28%

Spotted Sandpiper

nonbreeding

breeding

nonbreeding

nonbreeding

breeding

Wandering Tattler

nonbreeding

Ruddy Turnstone

nonbreeding

nonbreeding

breeding

nonbreeding

breeding

Surfbird

nonbreeding

SANDPIPERS Scolopacidae

Medium-sized *Calidris* sandpipers. Sanderling, found mainly on sandy coastlines, is the most common and widespread.

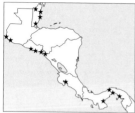

Dunlin *Calidris alpina* 19 cm

Breeds Holarctic. Nearctic birds winter mainly USA. Rare transient and winter visitor (Sep to early May) to BZ (Orange Walk, Stann Creek, Belize, Toledo, 313, 341, 346), GT (San Marcos, 180, 227, 226), SV (La Paz, Usulután, 346), CR (Guanacaste, 601), and PA (Panamá, Colón, Coclé, 657, 512, 48). **ID** Short-necked with *long, decurved bill*. Legs black. Breeding ad (Apr to Aug) has mostly rufous upperparts and fine, sharp blackish streaking on neck and breast. *Black central belly* contrasts with white flanks. Nonbreeding ad (Aug to Mar) plain gray-brown including head and breast. Compare with smaller Western Sandpiper. Also compare with Stilt Sandpiper. Note different structure and rump pattern. **HABITS** Beaches and mudflats. Forages mainly by probing in mud while wading in shallow water. **VOICE** Flight call (1) a buzzy or trilled *pree-uw* or *treeep*. In interactions gives (2) a low-pitched, hoarse *gwrr-drr-drr-drr..*

Curlew Sandpiper *Calidris ferruginea* 19 cm

Palearctic. Winters Old World tropics and subtropics. Very rare fall vagrant (Oct to Nov) in CR (Guanacaste, 594, 346) and PA (Panamá, 346). **ID** Robust with *long, decurved black bill*. Breeding ad has *deep chestnut head and breast*. Upperparts boldly checkered with blackish, white, and rufous. Nonbreeding ad mostly pale gray-brown (paler below) and resembles Dunlin. Note Curlew Sandpiper's evenly curved bill and *white rump*. Juv resembles juv Stilt Sandpiper. Note different structure and leg color. **HABITS** Lagoons, mudflats, lake margins, and grassy pools. Forages by wading and probing in mud beneath shallow water. Usually solitary but readily joins mixed groups of shorebirds. **VOICE** Call (1) a soft, slightly rolled or trilled *cheerit* or *cheerit-it*.

Stilt Sandpiper *Calidris himantopus* 21 cm

Breeds Nearctic. Winters MX to SA. Uncommon transient and winter resident (Jul to May). Mainly on Pacific coast. **ID** Slender. Note fairly *long decurved bill*. Legs dull yellow. Breeding ad (Apr to Aug) has *barred underparts* and *rufous auriculars*. Nonbreeding ad mostly plain gray above and plain whitish below. In flight, shows *white rump*. Juv (Jul to Sep) has neatly scaled upperparts. **HABITS** Lagoons, mudflats, lake margins, and grassy pools. Wades and probes rapidly in mud beneath water. Forms small flocks. May associate with Short-billed Dowitchers but tends to forage in deeper water. **VOICE** Flight calls (1) a low-pitched, soft *toof* or *jeew* and (2) shorter, slightly nasal *cuwee* or *koowi*.

Red Knot *Calidris canutus* 24 cm

Breeds Holarctic. Nearctic birds winter mainly SA. Uncommon transient on Pacific coast (mainly Aug to Oct and Mar to May). Rare on Caribbean slope in BZ Cays, mainland BZ coast (Stann Creek, 343), and GT (Izabal, 222). **ID** Bulky with fairly short, straight bill. Breeding ad (May to Aug) has rufous sides of head, neck, and underparts. Upperparts checkered with blackish and rufous. Nonbreeding ad plain gray above and mostly whitish below with gray barring and speckling on flanks. Juv (Aug to Oct) similar, but has fine pale edging and dark submarginal lines on upperparts. **HABITS** Beaches, mudflats, coastal marshes. Forages mainly by gleaning from surface. **VOICE** Usually silent. May give (1) a low-pitched, slightly hoarse *ee-ee-ew* or *urr-ew-ew*.

Sanderling *Calidris alba* 19 cm

Breeds Holarctic. Nearctic birds winter NA to SA. Common transient and winter resident (Aug to May) on coasts. Rare inland (419). **ID** Short, relatively heavy, straight black bill. Legs black. Note mostly white underwings and *bold black-and-white pattern on upperwing* (conspicuous in flight). Breeding ad (May to Aug) has mostly *rufous head, neck, and upperparts*. Nonbreeding ad (Sep to Apr) is *clean white below* and mostly plain pale gray above. Juv (Jul to Nov) has blackish central crown, boldly mottled black-and-white upperparts, and mostly clean white underparts. **HABITS** Favors sandy or gravel-strewn intertidal of beaches. Occasionally in muddy areas of estuaries. Runs rapidly at water's edge and gleans prey from surface. May form large flocks. Often confiding. **VOICE** Calls (1) a short, hard *klit* or *kwit* and (2) high-pitched, scratchy *tiv*.

nonbreeding

nonbreeding

nonbreeding

nonbreeding

breeding

Dunlin

nonbreeding

breeding

Curlew Sandpiper

nonbreeding

juv

nonbreeding

breeding

Stilt Sandpiper

nonbreeding

juv

nonbreeding

breeding

Red Knot

nonbreeding

juv

Sanderling

nonbreeding

breeding

SANDPIPERS Scolopacidae

Small *Calidris* sandpipers. White-rumped and Baird's sandpipers winter mainly in South America and are rare transients. These two species can be separated from other small *Calidris* by their long wings extending well beyond the tail at rest. Least and Western sandpipers are the most common and widespread.

Least Sandpiper *Calidris minutilla*   13.5 cm

Breeds Nearctic. Winters south USA to SA. Fairly common transient and uncommon winter resident (Jul to May) on coasts. Most common on Pacific slope. **ID** Smallest CA *Calidris*. Slightly crouched posture. *Fine, slightly decurved bill* and *greenish or dull yellowish legs.* Folded wing tips even with tail. Breeding ad (Apr to Sep) has breast-band of fine dark streaking or speckling. Nonbreeding ad grayer with brownish-gray breast-band. Juv (Jul to Oct) has dark upperparts with rufous edging. Juv's breast-band faint or incomplete. Compare with Western and Semipalmated sandpipers. Note different leg color and bill shape. Also compare with Pectoral Sandpiper. **HABITS** Drier portions of beaches, mudflats, lake margins, and fields with short grass. Gleans prey from surface. **VOICE** Flight call (1) a high-pitched, slightly trilled *prreep*.

Semipalmated Sandpiper *Calidris pusilla*   15 cm

Breeds Nearctic. Winters MX and WI to SA. Common transient and winter resident (Jul to May) on coasts. **ID** *Near-straight bill with slightly swollen tip.* Legs black. Folded wings extend only slightly beyond tail. Breeding ad (Mar to Sep) lacks flank spots and rufous scapulars of Western Sandpiper. Upperparts feathers have dark centers and paler whitish or buff edgings. Nonbreeding ad similar to nonbreeding Western Sandpiper but is slightly darker, especially on breast. Note different bill. Juv (Jul to Sep) has mostly brownish-gray upperparts with neat pale edging. Juv has relatively strong whitish supercilium and dark auriculars. Compare with Western Sandpiper. Note different bill shape. **HABITS** Beaches, mudflats, lake margins, and fields with damp, short grass. Gleans prey from mud or wades and probes in shallow water. Gregarious. Forms large flocks. **VOICE** Flight call (1) a short, husky *chrup* or *chrif*. Also (2) a sharp, thin *cheet* similar to Western Sandpiper.

Western Sandpiper *Calidris mauri*   16 cm

Breeds Nearctic. Winters south USA to SA. Common transient and winter resident (Jul to May) on coasts. **ID** *Long bill with fine, slightly drooped tip* (longer in female). Folded wings extend only slightly beyond tail. Breeding ad (Mar to Aug) has rufous auriculars, crown, and scapulars. Breeding ad has sparse, dark, arrow-shaped markings on flanks and breast. Nonbreeding ad plain pale gray above and mostly whitish below. Some retain a few dark markings on underparts, but in general, breast paler than in nonbreeding Semipalmated Sandpiper. Juv (Jul to Sep) has mostly gray upperparts with white edging. Note rufous edging on upper scapulars and pale head and breast. Resembles Semipalmated Sandpiper. Note different bill shape. Also compare with Least Sandpiper. Note different leg color. **HABITS** Beaches, mudflats, lake margins, or damp areas with short grass. Gleans from surface of mud or wades and probes beneath shallow water. **VOICE** Flight call (1) a thin, high-pitched, harsh *cheet* or *jeet*. Flocks produce (2) chorus of quiet, scratchy notes *twee twee twee twee . . .*

White-rumped Sandpiper *Calidris fuscicollis*   17 cm

Breeds Nearctic. Winters south SA. Uncommon to rare transient (Apr to May and Sep to Oct) mainly on coasts but also found inland and in highlands. **ID** Large with slightly *decurved bill.* Note whitish supercilium. *Wings extend well beyond tail at rest.* In flight, shows *all-white rump.* At close range note small orange spot on base of mandible. Breeding ad (Apr to Sep) has *fine dark streaking on breast* and white lower underparts. Nonbreeding ad plain grayish above with whitish supercilium and flanks. Juv (Aug to Nov) has neatly scaled upperparts and grayish breast-band. Compare with rare Baird's Sandpiper. Note different bill. **HABITS** Beaches, mudflats, lake margins, and fields with damp, short, grass. Wades and probes in shallow water. **VOICE** Flight call (1) a high-pitched, scratchy *tzeet* or *seet*. In interactions gives (2) a very high-pitched rattle *t-k-k-k-k-k.*

Baird's Sandpiper *Calidris bairdii*   17.5 cm

Breeds Nearctic and Siberia. Winters SA. Rare transient (Apr to Jun and Aug to Nov). Mainly highlands and Pacific coast (570, 180, 346). Very rare on Caribbean slope in BZ (Orange Walk) and GT (Izabal, 222). Formerly perhaps regular in Central Valley of CR (Cartago, 126, 602). Rare in PA (334). **ID** Slender with *fine, straight bill. Wings extend well beyond tail* at rest. Legs black. Breeding ad (Apr to Sep) brownish-gray above with black spotting on scapulars. Dull buff breast contrasts with whitish chin. Nonbreeding ad plain above. Juv (Aug to Nov) warm buffy brown with *bold scaling on upperparts.* Compare with White-rumped Sandpiper. Note plain flanks and different bill shape. Also compare with Buff-breasted Sandpiper. Note different leg color and head pattern. **HABITS** Favors damp, short grass. Less often on mudflats or at water's edge. Gleans from surface. **VOICE** Call (1) a low-pitched, coarse *grrrt* or *kreep*. Compare with Pectoral Sandpiper.

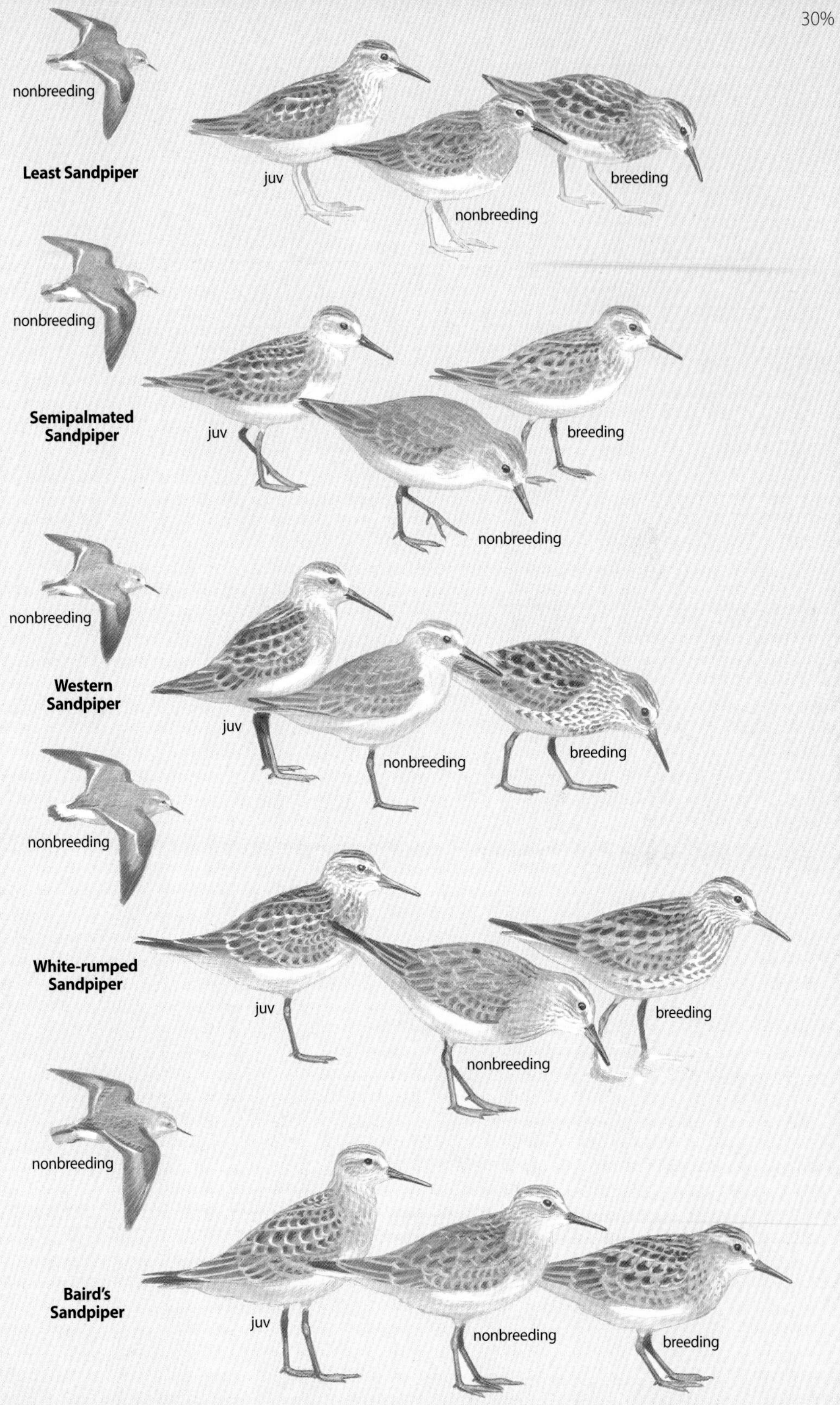

nonbreeding

Least Sandpiper

juv

nonbreeding

breeding

nonbreeding

Semipalmated Sandpiper

juv

nonbreeding

breeding

nonbreeding

Western Sandpiper

juv

nonbreeding

breeding

nonbreeding

White-rumped Sandpiper

juv

nonbreeding

breeding

nonbreeding

Baird's Sandpiper

juv

nonbreeding

breeding

SANDPIPERS, RUFF, AND SNIPE Scolopacidae

Medium-sized shorebirds found mainly on muddy shores, marshes, and damp fields.

Pectoral Sandpiper *Calidris melanotos*   female 21, male 23 cm
Breeds Holarctic. Winters SA. Fairly common transient (Apr to May and Aug to Nov).
ID Medium to large and stocky (males larger). Slightly decurved bill with orange base.
Bib of dark streaking on neck and breast contrasts with plain white lower underparts.
Juv has white edging above. Compare with smaller Least Sandpiper. **HABITS** Favors
flooded or damp areas with short grass. Gleans from surface, rarely probes. Less likely
to forage on open mudflats or by wading in water than other *Calidris*. Often solitary.
May form small flocks. **VOICE** Flight call (1) a low-pitched *drrip* or *jriff*. In interactions
(2) a low-pitched, soft *goit goit goit* . . .

Buff-breasted Sandpiper *Calidris subruficollis*   21 cm
Breeds Nearctic. Winters south SA. Uncommon to rare transient (Mar to May and Aug
to Oct). Favors inland and highland areas. Formerly regular in CR (Cartago, 126, 602,
346). Very rare in winter in SV (San Miguel, 341). **ID** Slender with small, rounded head.
Note short, fine bill, *plain buff sides of head* and *whitish eye ring*. Underparts mostly
plain deep buff. Legs yellow. In flight, clean white underwing contrasts with buff flanks.
Juv has white edging above. Pectoral Sandpiper has distinctly streaked breast-band and
different bill shape. **HABITS** Grassy areas including damp fields, lake beds, pastures, sod
farms, and airstrips. Solitary or in small flocks. Gleans from vegetation. Rarely probes
in mud. **VOICE** Calls (1) *jurp* or *jiirt* and (2) quiet *tik*.

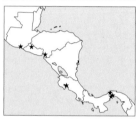

Ruff *Calidris pugnax*   female 23, male 30 cm
Palearctic. Winters Old World tropics and subtropics. Very rare vagrant or transient
(May to Apr and Aug to Oct). Most reports from Pacific slope including GT (Santa
Rosa, 178), SV (Chalatenango, 346), HN (Choluteca, 263), CR (Puntarenas, 602), and
PA (Panamá, Colón, 659, 512, 48). **ID** Fairly long-legged with smallish head, longish
neck, and *fairly short, near-straight bill*. Sexually dimorphic in plumage and size with
male larger. Breeding male (Mar to Jul) has variably colored and patterned head tufts
and bulky ruff (variation includes black, rufous, and white morphs). Legs variably
pink to yellow. Breeding female has variable black mottling on breast and upperparts.
Nonbreeding ad mostly grayish above with dark centers on feathers. Note white at base
of bill. In flight, note divided white uppertail coverts and mostly white underwing.
Compare with Upland Sandpiper. Note different habits. **HABITS** Lagoons, mudflats,
lake margins, and grassy pools. Wades and probes in mud beneath shallow water.
VOICE Usually quiet. Call (1) a short, slightly hoarse, laughlike *ah-ah-ahh* or *eh-ah-ah*.

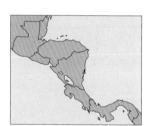

Wilson's Snipe *Gallinago delicata*   27 cm
Breeds Nearctic. Winters south USA to north SA. Uncommon to locally common
winter resident (Oct to Apr). May be briefly or locally abundant. **ID** Bulky and
short-necked with *very long, near-straight bill*. Fairly long tail extends beyond wingtips
at rest. *Dark stripes on crown and sides of head* are distinctive. Note buff stripes on
mantle. Juv similar to ad. Compare with dowitchers. Note different head pattern.
HABITS Freshwater marshes, flooded agricultural fields, lake margins, and grassy pools.
Wades and probes in mud or shallow water. Solitary. Skulks in damp vegetation.
VOICE In flight, gives (1) a dry, harsh, buzzy *scresh* or *kriish*.

Pectoral Sandpiper

juv ♀

ad ♂

Buff-breasted Sandpiper

ad ♂

juv ♀

nonbreeding ♂

Ruff

breeding ♂

juv ♂

nonbreeding ♂

nonbreeding ♀

Wilson's Snipe

DOWITCHERS AND PHALAROPES Scolopacidae

Dowitchers are medium-sized shorebirds with long bills. Voice is often helpful in separating these two species. Phalaropes are a distinctive group of small shorebirds that show reversed sexual dimorphism. Wilson's Phalarope is often seen on the Pacific coast of Central America in migration. Red and Red-necked phalaropes are pelagic outside their breeding season.

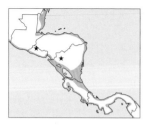

Short-billed Dowitcher *Limnodromus griseus*   26 cm
Breeds Nearctic. Winters USA to SA. Locally common transient and winter resident (Aug to May). Most common on Pacific slope. **ID** Short-necked with long, straight bill. Breeding ad (Apr to Aug) has cinnamon breast spotted with black (cinnamon more extensive in Pacific and central NA breeding birds) and dark barring on flanks (less extensive on some). Note blackish scapulars with narrow bars and tips. Nonbreeding ad mostly plain grayish with dusky barring and *dark speckling on breast*. Juv (Jul to Nov) has bold, internal buff markings on tertials (compare with narrow rufous edging in juv Long-billed Dowitcher). **HABITS** Lagoons, mudflats, lake margins, and grassy pools. Probes rapidly in mud with vertical motion while wading in shallow water. Forms tight flocks. **VOICE** Calls (1) a rapid, liquid *tututu* or *kewtutu* or *tlututu* that drops slightly in pitch and (2) harder, *kitititi* on even pitch. Compare with call of Lesser Yellowlegs.

Long-billed Dowitcher *Limnodromus scolopaceus*   27 cm
Breeds Nearctic. Winters USA to CA. Uncommon to rare transient and winter resident (Aug to May) mainly in north Pacific slope. Rare on Caribbean slope in BZ (347) and south to NI (Granada, Managua, 412, 420), CR (Guanacaste, 570, 574, 474, 602), and PA (Bocas del Toro, Colón, Herrera, 346). **ID** Closely resembles Short-billed Dowitcher. Bill typically longer. Breeding ad (Apr to Aug) has extensively cinnamon underparts (including belly). Blackish scapulars with buff bars and white tips. Less spotted and more barred below than Short-billed Dowitcher. Nonbreeding ad has mostly *plain gray breast* (darker than Short-billed Dowitcher). Whitish lower underparts tend to contrast more with grayish breast. Most adults cannot be distinguished by plumage from Short-billed Dowitcher. Voice more useful. Juv has dark-centered tertials and scapulars with rufous edging. **HABITS** Like Short-billed Dowitcher but more frequent in freshwater habitats. **VOICE** Call (1) a sharp, high-pitched *keek* or *pweek*. May be repeated in short series *kik-kik-kik-kik*.

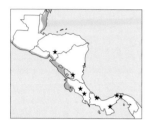

Wilson's Phalarope *Phalaropus tricolor*   22 cm
Breeds Nearctic. Winters mainly SA. Uncommon transient (Mar to May and Aug to Sep). May be briefly or locally common on Pacific coast. Rare at other seasons and on Caribbean slope. **ID** Long-necked with *fairly long, fine, straight bill*. Breeding female (Apr to Jul) has black legs, *chestnut on foreneck*, and black stripe on sides of head and neck. Breeding male less boldly marked. Nonbreeding ad plain pale gray above and mostly white below. Legs bright yellow. **HABITS** Lagoons, mudflats, lake margins, and grassy pools. Picks restlessly from mud or shallow water while walking, wading, or swimming. Solitary or in small groups. Joins mixed associations of shorebirds. **VOICE** Call (1) a low-pitched, very nasal *wemf* or *rehn* or *vimp*. Compare with call of Black Skimmer.

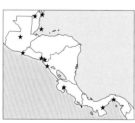

Red-necked Phalarope *Phalaropus lobatus*   18 cm
Breeds Holarctic. Winters at sea in equatorial oceans including waters off Pacific SA. Common to (briefly or locally) abundant fall transient (Aug to Nov) in Pacific offshore. Rare on coast (151) and on Caribbean slope in BZ (Corozal, Cayo, Orange Walk, 347, 346). **ID** *Fine, straight bill*. Note dark central rump. Breeding female (Apr to Sep) has black sides of head and white throat contrasting with rufous-red neck. Breast dark gray. Breeding male paler. Nonbreeding ad has narrow black mask (mostly below and behind eye) and gray upperparts with whitish streaking on scapulars. Juv (Jul to Oct) has narrow black mask and blackish upperparts with bold buff stripes. Compare with Red Phalarope. Note different bill. **HABITS** Mainly pelagic away from breeding range but may visit coastal lagoons, mudflats, lake margins. Wades or swims and probes in water. Forms large flocks at sea. Often in areas with floating vegetation or debris. **VOICE** Call (1) a short, nasal *kett* or *kick*.

Red Phalarope *Phalaropus fulicarius*   21 cm
Breeds Holarctic. Winters mainly at sea including waters off Pacific SA. Rarely reported but perhaps a widespread transient in offshore Pacific (Sep to Nov and Mar to Apr, 600, 346, 672). Rare on Pacific coast (544). **ID** *Bill straight and heavy with blunt tip*. Breeding female (Apr to Sep) has mostly yellow bill, rufous underparts, and white auriculars. Breeding male paler. Nonbreeding ad has narrow black mask and *plain gray upperparts*. Juv (Jul to Oct) has dull yellow base of mandible, narrow black mask, and buff breast and flanks. Upperparts mostly blackish with neat buff edging. Compare with Red-necked Phalarope. **HABITS** Pelagic away from breeding range. Flocks rest on water in areas with floating vegetation or debris. **VOICE** Call (1) a high-pitched *piik*. Higher-pitched and less nasal than Red-necked Phalarope. Also (2) a softer *dreet*.

Short-billed Dowitcher

central
breeding

nonbreeding

juv

eastern
breeding

nonbreeding

Long-billed Dowitcher

nonbreeding

nonbreeding

juv

breeding

nonbreeding

nonbreeding

Wilson's Phalarope

breeding
♀

nonbreeding
♀

nonbreeding

breeding
♂

Red-necked Phalarope

nonbreeding

breeding
♀

juv

nonbreeding

Red Phalarope

nonbreeding

breeding
♀

juv

nonbreeding

JAEGERS AND SKUA Stercorariidae

Mainly pelagic birds. Jaegers present considerable identification problems, especially with distant or difficult views. Jaegers are polymorphic (variation includes light and dark morphs). Identification of light morph adult jaegers in breeding plumage is relatively straightforward, but these plumages are rarely seen in the region. Adults in nonbreeding plumage are more variable. Jaegers require four years to develop adult plumage. During that time, they progress through a variable series of juvenile and subadult plumages. Juvenile and first-year birds are heavily barred with highly contrasting barring on the underwing coverts and axillars. Most jaegers seen in the region are in these variable juvenile and immature plumages. These range from nearly solid dark brown to quite pale. Many birds seen in Central America are subadults and these are often in extremely worn plumage. Birds in their second or third year are intermediate between juveniles and adults and always show some barring on the underwing coverts. Details of structure, bill pattern, and head pattern are helpful, but plumage characters are variable and many individuals will not be identifiable in the field. Lengths given are without adult's long central rectrices.

Pomarine Jaeger *Stercorarius pomarinus*   46 cm

Breeds Holarctic. Perhaps a locally or seasonally uncommon transient in Pacific offshore waters. Uncommon visitor to coastal waters. Small numbers (mostly subads) may linger around harbors and estuaries during winter (Sep to May). **ID** Broad-based wings, deep belly, large head, and large bill. Always shows extensive white shaft streaks on upper primaries. Base of bill usually pink. Ad has long, *spatulate central rectrices.* Breeding ad's dark cap often slightly lighter on face and forecrown (head shows less contrast with base of bill than Parasitic). Breeding ad has variable *barred breast-band* (sometimes incomplete with only barring on sides of breast). Note extensive dark barring on flanks in comparison with Parasitic Jaeger and dark cap extending to face and malar. Nonbreeding ad has dark face and distinct barring or spotting on sides of head and nape. Dark morph ad entirely dark brown except for white "flash" on underwing. Variable juv typically has dark nape and heavy dark barring below. Juv has *white on primary coverts* creating distinctive "double flash" on underwing. **HABITS** Pelagic but may loiter near shore to harass terns or gulls. Often solitary. **VOICE** Usually silent. Transients may form small flocks at sea. **VOICE** Usually silent.

Parasitic Jaeger *Stercorarius parasiticus*   42 cm

Breeds Holarctic. Locally or seasonally fairly common in offshore Pacific. Uncommon to rare visitor (Oct to Apr) to coastal waters. **ID** Intermediate in structure between Pomarine and Long-tailed jaegers. Always shows extensive white shaft streaks on upper primaries. Ad has long pointed central rectrices. Rarely seen light morph breeding ad has slightly diffuse dark brownish-black cap (dark does not extend below bill to malar). All ads have white feathering at base of maxilla (ad Pomarine Jaeger has black extending to base of maxilla) and gray bill. Typical breeding ad has white belly, solid gray-brown breast-band, and plain (unbarred) flanks. Some lack dark breast-band and show only gray-brown smudge on sides of breast. Nonbreeding ad has extensive dark barring below and diffuse head pattern with pale malar. Compare with dark face of nonbreeding ad Pomarine Jaeger. Dark morph ad (more common in Parasitic Jaeger) is entirely medium brown except for white "flash" on underwing. There is also an intermediate morph. Variable juv can be light or dark (most are intermediate) and is entirely barred above and below with buff edging. Head and nape show fine dark streaking. Note *barred primary coverts* on underwing surface. **HABITS** Like Pomarine Jaeger. **VOICE** Usually silent.

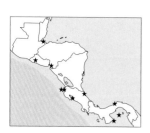

Long-tailed Jaeger *Stercorarius longicaudus*   36 cm

Breeds Holarctic. Rare transient in coastal waters. Most likely in Pacific offshore. Very rare in Caribbean with records from GT (Izabal, 346), CR (Limón, 237), and PA (Colón, 390). Wrecked birds very rarely found inland in SV (La Libertad, 346). **ID** Small with long, slim wings and short bill. Shows fewer white shaft streaks on upperwing surface than other jaegers. Ad has very long central rectrices. Ads have *entirely dark underwing surface* and pale upperwing coverts contrasting strongly with dark flight feathers. Breeding ad has plain breast (no breast-band) and dark rear underparts. Nonbreeding ad (Oct to Mar) has brown breast and speckled throat and breast. Variable imm grayish and has sharp contrasting barring on underwing, crissum, and axillars. Juv grayish overall and sometimes very pale, especially on head, and may have whitish collar. **HABITS** Highly pelagic. Very rarely seen inshore. Reported to specialize in parasitism of Arctic Tern and Sabine's Gull over deep ocean water. Usually solitary. **VOICE** Usually silent away from breeding grounds.

South Polar Skua *Stercorarius maccormicki*   50 cm

Austral breeding species. Very rare visitor to Pacific waters off GT (229), Caribbean coast of CR (Limón, 74), and Pacific waters in Gulf of Panamá (657, 512). **ID** Very robust with heavy bill and short tail. In all plumages shows *large white patch at base of primaries.* Compare with juv and subad jaegers. Note different structure and wing pattern. **HABITS** Pelagic. Rarely seen inshore. Solitary. **VOICE** Usually silent away from breeding grounds.

15%

Pomarine Jaeger

intermediate juv

dark morph ad

nonbreeding

breeding

Parasitic Jaeger

intermediate juv

dark morph ad

nonbreeding

breeding

Long-tailed Jaeger

intermediate juv

light juv

nonbreeding

breeding

South Polar Skua

dark morph ad

light morph ad

intermediate ad

GULLS Laridae

A large, cosmopolitan group of waterbirds. Large gulls reach adult plumage in their fourth year. Though adults of different species can be quite similar, immature and adult birds of the same species are very different in appearance. Immature birds are also individually variable. Useful features for separating gulls include structure, upperwing pattern and head pattern. Ring-billed and Herring gulls, while generally scarce in Central America, are the most commonly encountered large gulls in the region.

Herring Gull *Larus argentatus*   56 cm

Breeds Holarctic. Nearctic birds winter mainly USA and Canada. Uncommon to rare but widespread transient and winter resident on coasts. Rare inland. **ID** Four-year gull. Large with *short primary extension* and *long legs.* Note *slanted forehead and fairly long, heavy bill.* Legs dull pink. Ad has *pale gray saddle* and pale eyes. Imm's bill variable but usually blackish with pinkish base. First-year variably pale to dark brown with extensive, soft dusky mottling on saddle and wing coverts. Note pale inner primaries. Subad gradually acquires plain gray saddle and plain white tail. Compare with Ring-billed Gull. Note different structure, leg color, and bill pattern in ad. Note different tail and underparts pattern in imm. **HABITS** Beaches, river mouths, and harbors. Often solitary. Readily associates with other gulls.

California Gull *Larus californicus*   50 cm

Breeds west Nearctic. Winters mainly USA to MX. Rare winter visitor to Pacific coast of SV (La Unión, La Paz, 363, 346), HN (Choluteca, 346), NI (Managua, Chinandega, León, 346), and CR (Puntarenas, 346). **ID** Four-year gull. Slightly smaller than Herring Gull with more rounded head, longer wings, and shorter legs. Long bill yellow with black and red subterminal spots in ad or pink with dark tip in imm. Legs yellow in ad and variably dull pinkish to gray in imm. Nonbreeding ad has variable hood of fine dusky streaking often concentrated on nape. First-year has dark brown-and-white checkering on upperwing coverts and rather bold dark barring or speckling on underparts (compare with softer, more mottled imm Herring Gull). Subad has mostly plain gray mantle. First- and second-year has dark primaries and usually coarse blackish mottling on nape. In comparison with Herring Gull, California Gull has shorter legs, slimmer bill, and longer wing projection beyond tail. Ad resembles Herring Gull but has dark eye and different leg color and bill pattern. **HABITS** Harbors, lagoons, beaches, mudflats, and estuaries. All records solitary birds. May associate with other gulls.

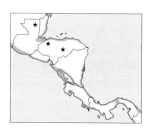

Ring-billed Gull *Larus delawarensis*   44 cm

Breeds Nearctic. Winters mainly USA and MX. Uncommon transient or winter visitor to coasts. Rare inland. **ID** Three-year gull. Medium-sized with *rounded crown.* Ad has pale eyes. *Small bill yellow with dark subterminal band* in ad or pinkish with dark tip in imm. First-winter already has mostly gray back and has brown markings on upperwing coverts. Subad has mostly plain gray saddle. Both first- and second-year have mostly white tail with blackish subterminal band (broad in first-year and becoming narrower and incomplete in second-year). First- and second-year birds show extensive black wingtips extending to wrist on leading edge of wing and usually have very coarse dark mottling on nape. Nonbreeding ad has variable hood of fine dusky streaking concentrated on nape. Ad resembles larger Herring and California gulls. Note different structure, leg color, and bill pattern. **HABITS** Harbors, lagoons, beaches, mudflats, estuaries, and lakes. Often solitary but may associate with Laughing Gulls. **VOICE** Call (1) a nasal *kyow* or *kwow.*

Herring Gull

first year

Subadult
Herring Gulls.

first year

breeding

first year

nonbreeding
ad

California Gull

first year

first year

breeding

nonbreeding
ad

Ring-billed Gull

first year

first year

breeding

nonbreeding
ad

GULLS Laridae

Gulls often wander outside their "normal" ranges. Identification of gulls is potentially complex and determination of vagrant or irregular species requires close scrutiny and careful consideration of a large set of rare but possible species. Adults of the various species of large white-headed gulls are closely similar. These three species are all rare in the region; each is known from just a handful of records. Increased study of gulls in the region should help clarify patterns of occurrence in Central America.

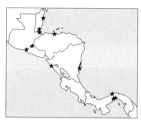

Lesser Black-backed Gull *Larus fuscus*   52 cm

Mainly Palearctic. Recently established breeding in Nearctic and perhaps increasing. Rare visitor with records from BZ (Belize, 346), SV-GT border area (346), HN, NI (León, RAAS, 346), and PA (Panamá, Colón, 578, 512, 48, 341, 346). **ID** Four-year gull. Slightly smaller, shorter-tailed, and longer-winged than Herring Gull, but with similar head structure. Ad's legs usually yellow. Ad has *dark gray saddle* (darker than ad Herring Gull). Juv has variably pinkish legs, and head and underparts are spotted and streaked with brown and white. Sometimes looks masked. Primaries all black. Tail often looks banded dark, contrasting with barred base and rump. Bill all black. Compare with Ring-billed and Herring gulls. Note different mantle color and structure. Also compare with Kelp Gull. **HABITS** Coastal areas such as rocky coasts, harbors, inlets, estuaries, beaches, mudflats. Readily associates with other gulls.

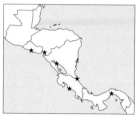

Kelp Gull *Larus dominicanus*   52 cm

Southern Hemisphere. Very rare vagrant to SV (La Paz, 346), HN (Choluteca, 346), NI (Granada, 346), CR (Limón, Puntarenas, 99), and PA (Panamá, 341, 346). **ID** Three-year gull. Large, with short wings, long legs, and *short, heavy bill*. Eyes variably yellow to brown. Ad has yellow bill with red spot near gonys. Ad has slaty black saddle, white head, and underparts. Juv has mostly whitish head with diffuse dark mask. Underparts heavily streaked and spotted with brown. Bill mostly black, sometimes pinkish at base. Compare with Belcher's and Lesser Black-backed gulls. Note Kelp Gull's heavier bill, shorter wings, and darker mantle. **HABITS** Coastal areas such as rocky coasts, harbors, etc.

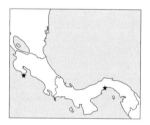

Belcher's Gull *Larus belcheri*   46 cm

Pacific SA. Very rare vagrant (Aug to Dec) to PA (Panamá, 659, 512) and CR (Puntarenas, ACV). Also reported from Isla del Coco (99). **ID** Three-year gull. Fairly large. Long bill mostly yellow with black subterminal band (and red tip in ad). Eyes dark. Breeding ad has slaty black saddle, white head and underparts and broad white trailing edge on wing. Nonbreeding ad has *dusky hood* and *white eye crescents*. Ad's white tail has *broad black subterminal band*. First-year has dusky brownish head, neck, and breast forming dark hood. Lower underparts dingy grayish white. Imm has mostly pinkish bill with blackish tip and dull pinkish or yellow legs. Compare ad with Kelp Gull. **HABITS** Coastal areas such as rocky coasts, harbors, etc.

Lesser Black-backed Gull

first year

breeding

first year

nonbreeding

Kelp Gull

first year

breeding

first year

nonbreeding

Belcher's Gull

juv

nonbreeding

breeding

GULLS Laridae

Laughing Gull is the most common and widespread gull in the region. Franklin's Gull, a long-distance migrant, forms large flocks and can be briefly or locally abundant along the Pacific coast in spring and fall. Heermann's and Gray gulls are very rare in the region.

Heermann's Gull *Larus heermanni*   48 cm
Breeds west Nearctic. Winters USA and MX. Very rare visitor to Pacific coast with records from GT (Retalhuleu, Escuintla, 535, 539), HN (Choluteca, 346), and PA (Veraguas, 653). **ID** Three-year gull. Slender and long-winged with black legs. Slender bill usually red in ad. Ad has gray mantle and paler gray underparts. Primaries mostly blackish (with no or very small white spots). Breeding ad has *whitish head.* Nonbreeding ad has head streaked brownish. Juv (Aug to Nov) near-uniform dark brown with pinkish base of bill. Juv and subad resemble corresponding plumages of Gray Gull. Note different bill color. **HABITS** Beaches, harbors, mudflats, river mouths. May join Laughing Gulls at favorite foraging or roosting areas. **VOICE** Wintering birds usually quiet.

Gray Gull *Leucophaeus modestus*   42 cm
Breeds Pacific SA. Vagrant to Pacific PA (Nov to Mar, Panamá, 512, 341) and Isla del Coco (570). **ID** Three-year gull. Slender with *fine, all-black bill.* Dark. Nonbreeding ad *near-uniform dark gray with brown head.* Breeding ad has *whitish head* and white band on trailing edge of secondaries. Juv and first-winter near-uniform brownish with all-black bill. Compare juv with juv Laughing Gull and juv Heermann's Gull. **HABITS** Sandy beaches, rocky coasts, river mouths, inshore waters.

Laughing Gull *Leucophaeus atricilla*   41 cm
Breeds Nearctic. Winters USA to CA. Locally common transient, winter resident, and nonbreeding summer resident on coasts. Uncommon inland on lakes or lagoons. Perhaps breeds in Belize Cays (344). Most common and widespread CA gull. **ID** Three-year gull. Slender and long-winged with long legs. Long, slender bill slightly drooped. Bill usually black (red in breeding ad). Note breeding ad's (Mar to Sep) dark gray hood and *narrow white eye crescents.* Breeding ad's wingtips extensively blackish (no or very small white tips on primaries). Subad resembles corresponding plumages of Franklin's Gull. Note complete dark tail-band (extending to outer rectrices) and relatively pale head with diffuse dark markings. Molting birds may have partial hood (never as dark or sharply defined as Franklin's Gull). Juv (Aug to Nov) mostly brown scalloped with pale edging with broad, complete black tail-band. Note extensively dark upperwing surface and brownish face and breast. **HABITS** Beaches, harbors, mudflats, river mouths. Gathers at favorite foraging or roosting areas. **VOICE** Wintering birds usually quiet.

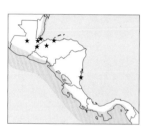

Franklin's Gull *Leucophaeus pipixcan*   36 cm
Breeds west Nearctic. Winters mainly Pacific SA. Briefly or locally abundant transient (Apr to May and Sep to Nov) on Pacific coast and offshore (672). Uncommon to rare in winter on Pacific coast. Rare on Caribbean slope in BZ (Corozal, Belize, Toledo, 347) and NI (RAAN, 413). **ID** Three-year gull. Small with rounded crown. Relatively short legs and small, fine, dark bill (smaller and straighter than Laughing Gull). Breeding ad (Apr to Aug) has red bill and black hood. Note *large white eye crescents* (meeting or nearly meeting behind eye) and white spots on wingtips (reduced by wear in late summer). Also white band between gray saddle and black on primaries and light gray (not white) tail. Underwing mostly whitish. Nonbreeding ad and subad have sharply defined, partial dark hood and pale hindneck (usually gray in Laughing Gull). Subad has partial dark tail-band (outer rectrices mostly white). Compare with tail of Laughing Gull. Juv mostly brownish above with whitish face, neck, and breast (juv Laughing Gull darker). **HABITS** Pelagic and coastal waters. Transients form large flocks. May forage over ponds, marshes, or agricultural fields. May loaf on beaches or mudflats with other gulls. **VOICE** Wintering birds usually quiet. Flocks of transients give (1) a chorus of high-pitched, nasal cries.

Heermann's Gull

first year

first year

breeding

nonbreeding

Gray Gull

juv

juv

breeding

nonbreeding

Laughing Gull

juv

first year

breeding

nonbreeding

Franklin's Gull

first year

first year

breeding

nonbreeding

GULLS Laridae

Mostly small gulls with dark hood in breeding plumage. Adults in nonbreeding plumage and immature birds have a dark mark on auriculars. Immatures of these species have a bold dark pattern on the upperwing. Useful features for identification include bill shape and pattern, upperwing pattern, and head pattern. Most of these are rare vagrants to the region and are documented by only a few records. Sabine's Gull is sometimes common off the Pacific coast in migration but is rarely seen on land in Central America.

Gray-hooded Gull *Chroicocephalus cirrocephalus* 38 cm
SA and Africa. Rare vagrant to GT (Petén, 346), Pacific coast and Pearl Islands of PA (Panamá, 659, 512, 341, 48, 346), and Isla del Coco (265). **ID** Three-year gull. Ad has *white on base of outer primaries* and *fairly long red bill with dark tip*. Legs red. Eyes yellow. Breeding ad has gray hood with narrow black border. Nonbreeding ad has mostly white head with gray spot on auriculars and may show grayish on hindcrown. Imm has diffuse brownish hood and carpal bar. **HABITS** Beaches, harbors, and river mouths as well as lakes and large rivers.

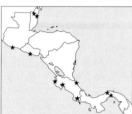

Bonaparte's Gull *Chroicocephalus philadelphia* 33 cm
Breeds Nearctic. Winters mainly NA. Rare winter visitor (mainly Dec to May) to coasts of GT (Escuintla, 346), BZ (Orange Walk, Belize, 347), SV (La Paz, 346), CR (Puntarenas, Guanacaste, Limón, 602, 346), and PA (Panamá, Colón, 501, 659, 346). **ID** Two-year gull. Small with rounded crown and *slender, black bill* (may show some red near base). In flight, ad shows *white outerwing coverts and white primaries* with dark tips. Short legs red. Breeding ad (Apr to Aug) has black hood and very narrow white eye crescents. Nonbreeding ad and first-winter has mostly whitish head with *small dark spot on auriculars* and dark terminal band on tail. First-winter has dark carpal bar and *dark trailing edge on wing* and *dark terminal band on tail*. Note dark spot on auriculars. Compare with Sabine's Gull. Note different upperparts and tail shape. Also compare with Black-legged Kittiwake. **HABITS** Mainly coastal waters outside breeding season but has been recorded at inland lagoons and lakes. **VOICE** Wintering birds usually quiet.

Black-legged Kittiwake *Rissa tridactyla* 41 cm
Breeds Holarctic. Winters mainly NA and Europe. Very rare winter visitor (mainly Dec to May) to BZ Cays (345), CR (Limón, 346), and PA (Panamá, 346). **ID** Three-year gull. Small with rounded crown and square tail. Note *all-black wingtips*. Ad has *yellow bill* and black legs. Nonbreeding ad has *large dark mark on auriculars*. First-winter has blackish bill and dark mark on auriculars. Note imm's *black collar*, gray saddle, and black carpal bar in flight. Sabine's Gull has different tail shape. Compare with Black-legged Kittiwake. Note different wing pattern. **HABITS** Coastal or pelagic waters. **VOICE** Wintering birds usually quiet.

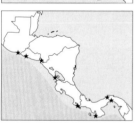

Sabine's Gull *Xema sabini* 33 cm
Breeds Holarctic. Winters Southern Hemisphere. Fairly common to locally or seasonally very common transient (mainly Aug to Nov and Mar to Jun) in Pacific pelagic waters (229, 672). Rarely seen on coast. Vagrant to Caribbean PA (Colón, 46). **ID** Two-year gull. Small with small-headed structure. Short, slender *bill black* (with yellow tip in ad). Note *slightly forked or notched tail*. In flight, shows extensive black on outer primaries and coverts contrasting with *white inner primaries*. Breeding ad (Apr to Sep) has dark gray hood with black border. Nonbreeding ad has variable partial hood confined mostly to nape (compare with Laughing Gull). First-winter has *black terminal band on tail* and is mostly brownish-gray above including nape and hindcrown. Compare with imm Laughing Gull. **HABITS** Pelagic. Transients may form flocks. **VOICE** Usually quiet.

Swallow-tailed Gull *Creagrus furcatus* 53 cm
Pacific SA. Breeds on Galápagos Islands and Isla Malpelo. Disperses mainly to waters off north SA. Rare visitor to waters off Pacific CR (346, 672), Isla del Coco (2, 446, 346), and PA (521, 505, 346). Most records from spring (Mar to early May, 671). **ID** Large. Note *forked tail* and *long, drooping bill*. Legs pink. Bold wing pattern with mostly white remiges contrasting with black primary tips and outer webs. Mantle and wing coverts gray. Breeding ad has sooty-gray hood and red eye ring. Ad's *bill black with whitish spot at base of maxilla and pale tip*. Nonbreeding ad lacks hood and has black around eye and small dark mark on auriculars. Juv has gray spot on auriculars, black around eye, and dark saddle and *wing coverts scaled with whitish*. Compare with Sabine's Gull. Note different structure, wing pattern, and bill. **HABITS** Pelagic when not breeding. Nocturnal. Most records of solitary birds but may form flocks. Follows ships. **VOICE** Usually silent.

first year

Gray-hooded Gull

breeding

first year

nonbreeding

first year

Bonaparte's Gull

first year

nonbreeding

breeding

first year

Black-legged Kittiwake

nonbreeding

breeding

first year

Sabine's Gull

first year

nonbreeding

breeding

juv

nonbreeding

breeding

Swallow-tailed Gull

TERNS Laridae

Pantropical terns. These species are pelagic. Most are rare and poorly known in the region. Black Noddy formerly bred on islands off Belize. White Tern is common near its only Central American breeding site on Isla del Coco off Pacific Costa Rica.

Bridled Tern *Onychoprion anaethetus* 37 cm

Pantropical. Uncommon and very local breeding resident (Mar to Sep) in BZ Cays (158, 529, 341), islands in Gulf of Fonseca (Los Farallones, 370, 346), Bay Islands (442, 613, 561), islands off west Pacific CR (Guanacaste, 600, 194), and Los Frailes del Sur off PA (Los Santos, 41, 42, 47). Rare visitor elsewhere. Reported to be most common in Gulf of Panamá during Oct and Nov (390). **ID** Pale collar divides black cap from dark mantle. Note extensively white outer rectrices. Breeding ad (Mar to Sep) has white supercilium extending to behind eye. Nonbreeding ad (not shown) has more extensive white on forehead. Juv has brown mantle with fine white barring. First-summer imm (not shown) has extensively whitish crown. Compare with Sooty Tern. **HABITS** Pelagic except when breeding. Breeds colonially on remote islands. Often solitary but may form loose feeding associations that include up to 50 birds. May forage in association with cetaceans or predatory fishes. Rests on drifting debris or turtle carapace. **VOICE** Usually quiet. At nesting colonies gives (1) a repeated, nasal *kawik-kawik-kawik* . . . and (2) harsher *kahrrr*.

Sooty Tern *Onychoprion fuscatus* 40 cm

Pantropical. Very local breeding resident (Feb to mid-Aug) on Tobacco Cay off south BZ (341), Isla del Coco off Pacific CR (571, 600, 446) and Los Frailes del Sur off PA (Los Santos, 41, 42, 47). Formerly bred on Middle Snake Cay and perhaps other islands off BZ (535, 536, 529, 343). Uncommon to very rare transient or visitor elsewhere. Locally or seasonally common in Pacific pelagic waters. Very rare in Caribbean waters away from breeding sites (594, 346). **ID** Breeding ad (Jan to Sep) blackish-gray above and white below with short white supercilium. Nonbreeding ad has pale collar. Note restricted white on outer rectrices (shows mostly black tail). Juv mostly blackish (including breast) with extensive white spotting on upperparts. Compare with Bridled Tern. **HABITS** Pelagic except when breeding. Breeds colonially on remote islands. May forage in association with schools of predatory fish. Seizes prey from surface of water in swooping flight. Does not dive. **VOICE** Usually quiet at sea. Sometimes gives (1) a nasal, barking *ka-wake or ka-a-ah*. At nesting colonies gives (2) harsh, attenuated *kraaaaa-ah* and (3) a distinctive *ke weh-de-wek*.

Brown Noddy *Anous stolidus* 40 cm

Pantropical. Uncommon to rare and very local breeding resident (Apr to Aug) on Pacific islands including Isla del Coco (600, 446) and Los Frailes del Sur off PA (Los Santos, 41, 42, 47). Extirpated or now very rare at Caribbean breeding sites in BZ Cays (535, 529, 341, 343, 346, 344). Rare visitor elsewhere (622, 672). **ID** Shares lobed tail shape only with Black Noddy. When perched, appears more hunched or shorter-necked than Black Noddy. Ad mostly dull brown with whitish forecrown. Juv all brown. Subad has whitish supercilium. Worn coverts may form pale wing panel in imm. **HABITS** Pelagic and rarely encountered except at sea or near breeding colonies. **VOICE** Usually quiet. At breeding colonies gives (1) nasal barks *keh-eh-eh* or *eh eh*. In flight gives (2) a low-pitched, slightly upslurred rattle *reeeeh*.

Black Noddy *Anous minutus* 33 cm

Pantropical. Locally abundant breeding resident (Oct to Jan or Feb) on Isla del Coco (163, 571, 600, 446). Formerly bred in BZ Cays at Glover's Reef, Tom Owen's Cay, and Half Moon Cay (535, 529, 415, 347, 343, 344). Very rare visitor elsewhere including Bay Islands (401) and Pacific coast of PA (Los Santos, 41). **ID** Ad resembles ad Brown Noddy but is smaller and darker with straight, narrow bill and longer neck. Juv has sharply defined white cap. **HABITS** Pelagic and rarely encountered except at sea or near breeding colonies. Breeds on small, remote islands. **VOICE** Usually quiet. At breeding colonies gives (1) guttural, growling *ahrrrr* or *garrr*.

White Tern *Gygis alba* 26 cm

Pantropical. Locally abundant breeding resident (Feb to Sep) on Isla del Coco (163, 256, 571, 600, 446). Very rare visitor to Pacific pelagic and inshore waters away from breeding sites (602, 341, 672). **ID** Small. *Immaculate white* with *large dark eyes*. **HABITS** Pelagic and rarely encountered except at sea or near breeding colonies. Breeds colonially on small, remote islands. **VOICE** Usually silent away from breeding colonies. At nest or at roosting sites, gives (1) dry, harsh *jeer-jeer-jeer-jurr-jur-jur* . . . At sea may give (2) a shrill *cheep* or *keek*.

Bridled Tern

juv

ad

juv

ad

juv

Sooty Tern

ad

juv

ad

Brown Noddy

ad

juv

ad

ad

Black Noddy

juv

ad

juv

ad

ad

juv

ad

White Tern

Black Tern *Chlidonias niger* 24 cm

Breeds Nearctic. Winters mainly at sea off Middle and South America. Locally (or briefly) abundant transient and winter resident (mainly Sep to Jun) on coasts and offshore. Uncommon to rare at larger inland lakes and marshes. **ID** *Short tail*. Breeding ad (Mar to Aug) has mostly *black head and underparts*. Nonbreeding ad and juv have *round, blackish spot on auriculars* and *blackish mark on sides of breast*. **HABITS** Forms loose flocks that fly low over coastal or pelagic waters. May fly low over marshes or mangrove channels. When foraging, displays erratic, buoyant flight style. At sea, perches on floating debris or turtle carapace. May join mixed groups of terns at roost. **VOICE** Calls (1) a short, metallic *kik* or *kek* and (2) *k-seek*.

Least Tern *Sternula antillarum* 22 cm

NA, WI, and SA. Breeds locally in BZ Cays at Tobacco Cay (341, 344), in HN at Trujillo Bay and Barra Muerta (Gracias a Dios, 106, 346), and on islets off Útila (622, 562, 561). Breeds on Pacific slope in SV (Usulután, 341, 346, 368) and NI (León, 346, 84). Nearctic breeding birds occur as uncommon transients and winter visitors (mainly Sep to May) on coasts. **ID** Small with long wings and short, forked tail. In flight, shows dark outer primaries. Breeding ad has *yellow bill* with black tip. Note black cap and *narrow white forehead*. Nonbreeding ad has mostly white crown and dusky mask and nape. Bill black. Juv has gray scaling on upperparts. **HABITS** Beaches, sandy islets, seacoasts and estuaries. May join mixed groups of terns at roost sites. **VOICE** Calls (1) high-pitched, metallic *kip* or *keep* and (2) harsh *chir-ee-eep*.

Yellow-billed Tern *Sternula superciliaris* 24 cm

SA. Rare visitor to PA (Colón, Herrera, Coclé, 512, 41, 346). Most records Apr to Oct. **ID** Small. Resembles Least Tern but has *longer and heavier bill*. Ad's *bill all yellow*. Breeding ad has black cap and narrow white forehead Nonbreeding ad has mostly grayish crown with fine streaking and dusky mask and nape. **HABITS** Favors rivers and other large bodies of freshwater in main SA range. May use other aquatic habitats. Often solitary. **VOICE** Call (1) a series of high-pitched, laughlike cries *chee-hee-hi-hi-hi . . .*

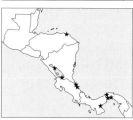

Large-billed Tern *Phaetusa simplex* 37 cm

SA. Rare visitor to HN (Gracias a Dios, 341), NI (Granada, Río San Juan, 346), CR (Limón, 546), and PA (Colón, Herrera, 659, 512, 346). Most reports from spring (Mar to Jun). **ID** Large, with *short, forked tail* and *long, heavy yellow bill*. Upperwing pattern features mostly *black primaries contrasting boldly with white secondaries*. Legs yellow. Juv has upperparts scaled with gray. **HABITS** Favors rivers and other large bodies of freshwater in main SA range. May use other aquatic habitats. Often solitary. **VOICE** Often noisy. Call (1) a loud, slightly squeaky *keee-ow* or *kaay-rak*.

Black Skimmer *Rynchops niger* 46 cm

NA to SA. Birds from breeding populations in NA and SA reach coastal CA as uncommon transients and nonbreeding residents. Nearctic birds thought to be present during Sep to May. SA birds reach CR and PA in spring (May to Oct). Breeds locally on Pacific coast in SV (Usulután, 368, 346). Rare visitor to inland lakes and lagoons. **ID** *Large*. Note *long, mostly red bill with protruding mandible*. Mostly plain black above and white below. Nonbreeding ad (Sep to Mar) has white hindneck. Juv has extensive dusky and whitish scaling on upperparts. **GV** Birds from SA breeding population have gray underwing surface and narrower white trailing edge on wing. SA birds appear not to have the white collar of NA breeding birds in nonbreeding plumage. **HABITS** Beaches, seacoasts, and river mouths. While foraging, flies low over water with wings held high and mandible dipping below surface. Gregarious. May join groups of terns at roost sites. **VOICE** Call (1) loud, clipped, very nasal *oow* or *ehh*. Often repeated.

Inca Tern *Larosterna inca* 38 cm

SA. Rare visitor to Pacific waters off CR (Guanacaste, Puntarenas, 346, 672) and PA (Panamá, Veraguas, Los Santos, 505, 346). **ID** Mostly *dark sooty gray* including underparts. Note ad's *long curling white plumes extending from sides of head* and dark tail. Bill and legs red. Juv mostly drab gray. **HABITS** Favors littoral waters in expected SA range. Wandering birds may use other aquatic habitats. Flight erratic with stiff wings. Usually solitary. May associate with other terns. **VOICE** Calls (1) a series of short, nasal notes *eh-eh-eh-eh-eh . . .* or (2) longer *ehhhh-ah*.

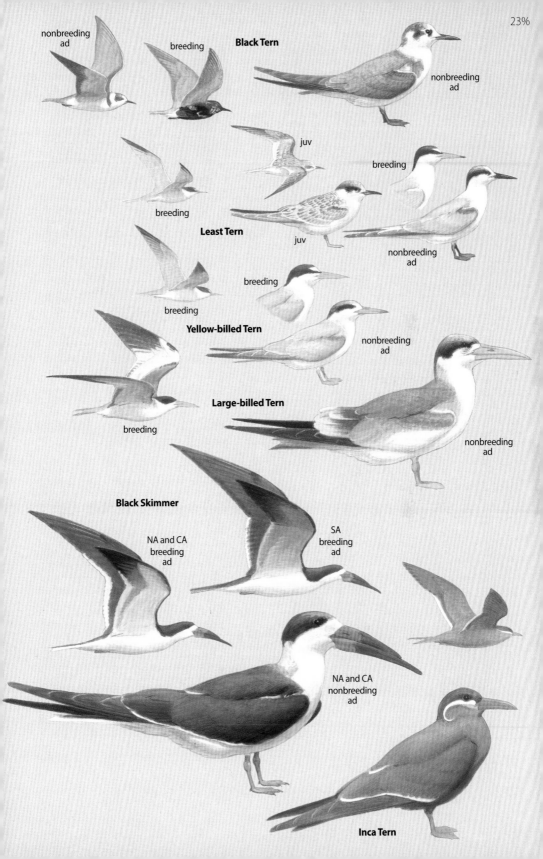

nonbreeding ad

breeding

Black Tern

nonbreeding ad

juv

breeding

breeding

nonbreeding ad

Least Tern

juv

breeding

breeding

nonbreeding ad

Yellow-billed Tern

breeding

nonbreeding ad

Large-billed Tern

breeding

nonbreeding ad

Black Skimmer

NA and CA breeding ad

SA breeding ad

NA and CA nonbreeding ad

Inca Tern

TERNS Laridae

Medium-sized terns. All *Sterna* terns are similar and identification is often complicated by patterns of age and seasonal variation in plumage. Useful features for separating these species include head shape, bill shape, and wing pattern. Common Tern is the most common and widespread.

Gull-billed Tern *Gelochelidon nilotica*   33 cm

Cosmopolitan. Nearctic birds winter south USA to CA. Uncommon transient and winter resident (mainly Aug to May) on Pacific coast. Uncommon to rare on Caribbean coast. **ID** Round crown, *heavy black bill*, and *short tail* with shallow fork. In flight, long outer primaries create curved, pointed wing shape. Upperwing surface mostly white. Nonbreeding ad has narrow dark mask that is grayer than mask of nonbreeding Forster's Tern. Juv very pale (similar to nonbreeding ad) and never as boldly marked as other juv terns. **HABITS** Coastal wetlands, beaches, mudflats, and estuaries. Forages more frequently over land and at freshwater sites than other terns. Sometimes hawks insects over fields or wetlands. Usually solitary. May join mixed groups of terns at roosts. **VOICE** Call (1) a nasal *kee-yah, kee-kee-kee . . .* Compare with lower-pitched call of Black Skimmer.

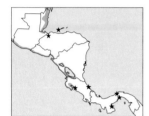

Forster's Tern *Sterna forsteri*   39 cm

Breeds Nearctic. Winters mainly south USA and MX. Uncommon to rare winter resident or visitor (mainly Aug to Apr). Reported mainly from GT (227) and SV (346) on Pacific slope and from BZ (347, 346) on Caribbean slope. Rarely reported south to CR (Guanacaste, Limón, 600, 346) and PA (Panamá, Colón, 512, 346). **ID** Longer bill and legs than other *Sterna* terns. Tail usually extends beyond wings while perched. In flight, shows *pale wings* with white primary coverts and mostly white primaries. Pale rump contrasts with darker tail and mantle. Nonbreeding ad has sharply defined black mask contrasting with pale nape and black bill. Gull-billed Tern has heavier bill and usually shows dark trailing edge on outer primaries. Also compare with Common and Arctic terns. Note different head and upperwing pattern. **HABITS** Coastal wetlands, beaches, river mouths, marshes, and lagoons. May join mixed groups of terns at roost sites. **VOICE** Call (1) a short, hoarse, buzzy *keeh* or *kyarr*. Lower-pitched and shorter than call of Common Tern

Common Tern *Sterna hirundo*   33 cm

Holarctic. Nearctic birds winter widely in coastal regions of Neotropics and reach CA as uncommon transients, winter residents (mainly Nov to Apr). Rare inland. **ID** In flight, all plumages show some extent of distinctive *dark wedge on primaries*. Rump gray. Nonbreeding ad and subad have *dark carpal bar* and *dark gray primaries*. Ad's tail extends nearly to wingtips while perched. **HABITS** Beaches, seacoasts, and river mouths. **VOICE** Call (1) a low-pitched, coarse, attenuated *kee-arrr*. Compare with shorter call of Forster's Tern.

Arctic Tern *Sterna paradisaea*   35 cm

Holarctic. Winters at sea in Antarctic. Pelagic in migration and perhaps a transient (Aug to Oct and Apr to May) on Pacific offshore. Very rare visitor to Pacific coast and inshore waters of SV (La Paz, 365), NI (Rivas, 52), and PA (Panamá, 46). A historical record from "Grassy Cay" perhaps refers to BZ (158). **ID** Resembles Common Tern. Note rounded crown, and *short bill*. In flight, ad shows *near-uniform gray upperwing surface*. While perched, displays short legs and tail extending past wingtips. Ad's primaries appear near-uniform pale gray on folded wing. Breeding ad slightly grayer below than other *Sterna* terns and has white mark on lower auriculars contrasting with dark neck and red bill. Nonbreeding or molting ad has whitish forehead and may be mottled with gray below. **HABITS** Pelagic in migration. **VOICE** Calls (1) a buzzy *tree-arrrrh* that is higher-pitched than Common Tern and (2) short, nasal *kyip*.

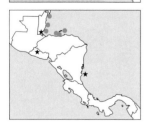

Roseate Tern *Sterna dougallii*   38 cm

Cosmopolitan. New World birds winter coastal SA (270). Uncommon and local breeding visitor (Apr to Sep) in BZ Cays at Sapodilla Cay and Tobacco Cay (535, 481, 341) and in HN on Cayos Cochinos and Bay Islands (623, 622, 562, 561, 346). Very rarely reported from mainland. **ID** Resembles Common Tern. Note slender bill and *long, all-white tail* (extends well beyond wings when perched). Paler than other *Sterna* terns. When perched shows white inner edges of primaries on upper surface of folded wing. In flight, short wings show mostly white upper surface. Juv barred and scalloped with dusky on upperparts and has black bill and legs. **HABITS** Beaches, sandy islets, seacoasts, and river mouths. May join mixed groups of terns at roost sites. Flies with rapid wingbeats. **VOICE** Calls (1) a soft *chi-weep* or *chee-dip* and (2) attenuated, buzzy *zrra-ap*.

breeding

Gull-billed Tern

nonbreeding
ad

nonbreeding
ad

Forster's Tern

breeding

nonbreeding
ad

nonbreeding
ad

Common Tern

first year

breeding

breeding

nonbreeding
ad

breeding
ad

breeding

Arctic Tern

first year

juv

breeding

breeding

juv

Roseate Tern

nonbreeding
ad

TERNS Laridae

Large terns that occur mainly as transients or winter residents in coastal regions. Wing pattern, head pattern, and bill color are useful in separating these species. Terns often gather in large numbers to roost on sandbars or estuaries. Sandwich and Royal are the most common large terns in Central America.

Sandwich Tern *Thalasseus sandvicensis* 38 cm

Cosmopolitan. Uncommon and very local breeding resident in BZ Cays at Tobacco Cay (342, 343, 344). Perhaps also breeds in Bay Islands (562). Fairly common transient and nonbreeding resident on coasts (Sep to May). **ID** Medium-sized with relatively short legs. *Slim, slightly decurved, black bill with small yellow tip.* Breeding ad (Mar to Aug) has black crown and shaggy crest. Nonbreeding ad has white forehead and forecrown. Resembles other large terns but Sandwich Tern is more slender than Caspian or Royal terns and has paler gray mantle. Juv (Jul to Sep) resembles juv Caspian and Royal terns. Note smaller size, paler upperwing, and different bill. **HABITS** Beaches, seacoasts, and river mouths. Often in small groups. Readily associates with other terns especially Royal Terns. **VOICE** Calls include (1) harsh, two-syllable *gwit gwit* or *skee-rick*. May be repeated.

Elegant Tern *Thalasseus elegans* 43 cm

Breeds west Nearctic. Winters Pacific south USA to SA. Uncommon to rare transient and nonbreeding visitor (Aug to May). Mainly in north Pacific. Rare in CR (Guanacaste, Puntarenas, 474, 600, 672) and PA (Panamá, Coclé, 659, 346). Vagrant to Caribbean CR (Limón, 600). **ID** *Long, slightly downcurved bill* with slightly paler tip and relatively long, shaggy hindcrest. Breeding ad (Mar to Aug) has orange bill. Nonbreeding ad (Aug to Feb) has more yellow-orange bill, white forehead, and sharply defined black hindcrown and mask. Note black area extending forward to encircle eye (compare with restricted black on head of nonbreeding Royal Tern). In flight, note blackish primaries (paler in Royal Tern). Juv (Jul to Oct) has yellowish bill and relatively plain upperparts. Compare with Caspian and Royal terns. Note different bill shape and wing and head pattern. **HABITS** Beaches, seacoasts, and river mouths. May associate with Royal Terns. **VOICE** Calls include (1) a sharp, harsh *kee-rick*. Similar to Sandwich Tern.

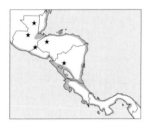

Royal Tern *Thalasseus maximus* 46 cm

NA to SA. Also west Africa. Nearctic birds winter south USA, to WI and SA. Fairly common transient and nonbreeding visitor to coasts (Sep to Jun). Rare visitor to interior lakes and rivers. Breeds locally in Cayos Cochinos, HN (Atlántida, 560). **ID** Large and robust. Ad has *heavy red-orange bill* (more slender than bill of Caspian Tern). In flight, shows mostly *pale underside of primaries* (upperside dusky). Juv (Jul to Nov) and nonbreeding ad (Jun to Mar) have restricted dark mask and *white forehead and lores.* Juv has obvious dark carpal bar and mostly dark primaries (compare with plain wings of Caspian). Caspian Tern has different bill and head pattern. Also compare with Sandwich Tern. **HABITS** Beaches, seacoasts, and river mouths. Loafs in small groups on beaches, rocks, or sandbars. Readily associates with other terns. **VOICE** Calls include (1) a coarse, slightly trilled *kee-areer* and (2) shorter *keer*. Often repeated.

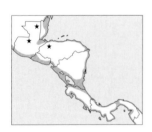

Caspian Tern *Hydroprogne caspia* 51 cm

Cosmopolitan. Nearctic birds winter mainly south USA to CA. Uncommon transient and winter resident (Aug to May). Rare in summer. **ID** Largest tern. Bulky with *very heavy, deep red bill.* Resembles Royal Tern but has broader wings and less deeply forked tail. In all plumages (especially juv) has *extensive blackish on underside of primaries* (upperside pale). Breeding ad has complete black crown and shaggy rear crest. Nonbreeding ad (Oct to Feb) has *white speckling on dark forehead* and crown (nonbreeding Royal and Elegant terns have white forehead). Juv (Jul to Oct) has relatively plain upperwing and lacks obvious carpal bar of juv Royal and Elegant terns. In all plumages note larger size and heavier bill. **HABITS** Lagoons and large bodies of fresh or brackish waters including lakes, rivers, and marshes but also occurs in littoral habitats including beaches and estuaries. Often forages by hovering over tidal waters in inlets. May join mixed groups of terns at roost sites. **VOICE** Calls include (1) a low-pitched, harsh *kowk* and (2) longer *ca-arr* or *cawarhh.*

21%

Sandwich Tern

breeding ad

juv

nonbreeding
ad

breeding ad

Elegant Tern

nonbreeding
ad

juv

breeding ad

Royal Tern

nonbreeding
ad

Caspian Tern

juv

breeding ad

nonbreeding
ad

ALBATROSS Diomedeidae

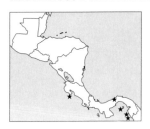

Waved Albatross *Phoebastria irrorata* 80 cm

Breeds on Galápagos Islands and other islands off Ecuador. Disperses mainly to waters off SA. Rare vagrant to waters off south Pacific or wrecked inland (512, 2, 390, 346). **ID** *Very large*, short-tailed, and very long-winged. Note mostly whitish head and long neck and *large yellow bill*. Appears bulky while resting on water. Mostly dark grayish-brown above. Underwing surface mostly whitish. **HABITS** Pelagic. Often feeds at night. Flight style languid with slow wingbeats alternating with low glides. In stronger winds, flies rapidly and often banks in high arcs. Often solitary but may join mixed foraging associations with other seabirds. **VOICE** Silent away from breeding grounds.

PETRELS Procellariidae

Large Pacific seabirds. Patterns of distribution and seasonal occurrence are poorly known in these species.

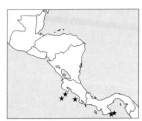

Tahiti Petrel *Pterodroma rostrata* 40 cm

Breeds southwest Pacific. Disperses widely in equatorial Pacific. Poorly known, but perhaps a regular visitor to Pacific waters. Reported off GT (229), CR (346, 672), and PA (346). **ID** Heavy-bodied with narrow wings. Tail fairly long. Note *very heavy, dark bill*. Mostly dark brown above. *Dark brown hood contrasts with white lower underparts.* Underwing surface variable but typically dark and usually with *whitish median stripe*. **HABITS** Pelagic. Most reports from well offshore. Often solitary but may join mixed groups of seabirds. Flight languid with long glides and short periods of flapping. Often flies low over water. In strong winds may soar or bank higher like an albatross. **VOICE** Silent away from breeding grounds.

Galapagos Petrel *Pterodroma phaeopygia* 38 cm

Breeds on Galápagos Islands. Disperses mainly to equatorial east Pacific. Poorly known, but perhaps a regular visitor to Pacific waters. Several records from off CR (570, 346, 115, 672) and PA (346). **ID** Long-tailed with heavy bill. *White throat and forehead* contrast with dark hood. Plain sooty brown above with *bold black-and-white pattern on underwing surface.* Underparts mostly white with dark mark at sides. Compare with Tahiti Petrel. **HABITS** Pelagic. Usually seen well offshore. May fly low over water on stiff wings. Flaps only occasionally, banking to change direction. In calm weather often seen swimming. **VOICE** Silent away from breeding grounds.

Parkinson's Petrel *Procellaria parkinsoni* 42 cm

Breeds on islands off New Zealand. Disperses widely in south Pacific. Rarely reported, but perhaps a regular visitor (Mar to Sep) to Pacific waters off GT (229, 335), CR (672), and PA (659, 512). **ID** Bulky and short-tailed. *Near-uniform sooty brown. Bill white with dark tip.* Compare with Christmas Shearwater. Note different bill and structure. Also compare with dark morph Wedge-tailed Shearwater. **HABITS** Pelagic. Most reports from well offshore. May forage in association with cetaceans. **VOICE** Silent away from breeding grounds.

Waved Albatross

Tahiti Petrel

Galapagos Petrel

Parkinson's Petrel

SHEARWATERS Procellariidae

Larger shearwaters found on Pacific waters. Distribution and patterns of seasonal occurrence in these species are poorly known. Identification sometimes challenging. Observers should note details of structure as well as head and underwing pattern. Wedge-tailed Shearwater is the most common and widespread.

Pink-footed Shearwater *Ardenna creatopus*   47 cm

East Pacific. Breeds Juan Fernández Islands and Isla Mocha off Chile. Disperses (mainly northward) outside breeding season. Poorly known. Probably reaches CA as a transient (Jan to early Nov) and perhaps summer resident in offshore Pacific waters (229, 672). **ID** Large, robust, and broad-winged. Appears bulky and large-headed when resting on water. Near-uniform dark grayish-brown above with grayish-brown hood. Central underparts and throat mostly white. Note *extensive dusky mottling on whitish underwing*. Bill mostly pink with dark tip. Feet pink. Compare with pale morph Wedge-tailed Shearwater. Note different bill pattern, underwing pattern, and structure. **HABITS** Generally pelagic, but small numbers sometimes seen from shore and prefers shallow shelf waters. The flight style is languid with slow wingbeats alternating with low glides. In stronger winds, flies rapidly and often banks in high arc. Often solitary but may form mixed foraging associations with other seabirds. **VOICE** Silent away from breeding grounds.

Wedge-tailed Shearwater *Ardenna pacifica*   43 cm

Breeds Pacific and Indian oceans. Disperses widely outside breeding season. Widespread transient (Jan to Oct) and perhaps summer resident in Pacific offshore waters. May be locally or seasonally abundant (Jan to Mar, 600, 512, 335, 672). **ID** Slender-bodied and small-headed with broad wings. *Tail rather long* and wedge-shaped. When swimming, tail extends beyond wingtips. Bill typically gray. Feet pink. Variable plumage includes light and dark morphs. Dark morph entirely dark brown including underwing. Pale morph brown above with contrasting white underparts. Flanks and crissum mottled brownish-gray. *Underwing surface mostly white* with leading and trailing edges brown and some brown mottling on coverts. Compare with smaller Christmas Shearwater. Compare pale morph with Pink-footed Shearwater. Note different underwing pattern, structure, and bill color. **HABITS** Pelagic. Often gathers in large flocks and may join mixed associations that include Galapagos Shearwaters and Black Terns. **VOICE** Silent away from breeding grounds.

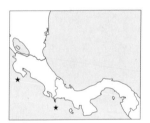

Christmas Shearwater *Puffinus nativitatis*   35 cm

Breeds tropical Pacific. Disperses widely outside breeding season. Poorly known. Uncommon to rare nonbreeding visitor to Pacific waters off GT (229), CR (114, 346), and west PA (582) in Apr and May. **ID** Small. *Near-uniform sooty brown* including underwing surface. Feet and bill black. Compare with dark morph Wedge-tailed Shearwater. Note different bill and foot color. **HABITS** Pelagic. May associate with Wedge-tailed Shearwaters. Typically flies low with fast, stiff wingbeats and long, low glides. **VOICE** Silent away from breeding grounds.

Pink-footed Shearwater

dark
morph

Wedge-tailed Shearwater

Christmas Shearwater

SHEARWATERS Procellariidae

Small, blackish-brown and white shearwaters. These species are small with broad wings and thickset body. Distribution and patterns of seasonal occurrence are poorly understood. Details of the head and underside pattern are useful in identification. Galapagos Shearwater is the most common and widespread.

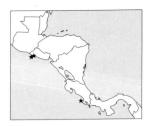

Black-vented Shearwater *Puffinus opisthomelas* 36 cm

East Pacific. Breeds on islands off west MX. Disperses mainly to north outside breeding season. Rare visitor (Oct and Nov) to waters off SV (346) and CR (606). **ID** Small and relatively short-tailed. Head less rounded than Galapagos Shearwater. Mostly dusky brownish above and whitish below. Note *diffuse or mottled dusky sides of head* (not contrasting sharply with white throat). Crissum mostly dark. Legs grayish-pink. Underwing mostly whitish with dark mark on axillars. Worn birds can appear very pale-headed. At rest on water, tail falls short of folded wings. Compare with Galapagos Shearwater. Note different head and neck pattern. Also compare with larger Pink-footed Shearwater. Note different underwing and underparts. Audubon's Shearwater allopatric. **HABITS** Forages over inshore waters and sometimes seen from land. Typically flies fast and low with bursts of rapid wingbeats and short glides. **VOICE** Silent away from breeding grounds

Audubon's Shearwater *Puffinus lherminieri* 30 cm

Pantropical. Breeds WI and locally on Tiger Cay off Caribbean west PA (Bocas del Toro, 655, 42) and on Crab Cay near Isla Providencia off Caribbean NI (42). Very rare elsewhere (345, 346). **ID** Very small and long-tailed. Crown high and rounded. Bill black. Legs grayish-pink. Plumage brownish-black above and *sharply demarcated on sides of head from white underparts*. Underwing surface mostly white. At rest on water, *long tail projects beyond folded wings*. Galapagos and Black-vented shearwaters allopatric. **HABITS** Pelagic. Distinctive, floppy flight style. Makes several shallow flaps followed by short glides. May follow ships. Frequently forages over schools of small fish. May form mixed feeding associations with terns and other seabirds. **VOICE** Silent away from breeding grounds.

Galapagos Shearwater *Puffinus subalaris* 29 cm

Breeds on Galápagos Islands. Disperses north to waters off CA and MX. Widespread and common transient and nonbreeding visitor to Pacific coastal and offshore waters (521, 335, 390, 672). Perhaps most common in spring. **ID** Small and fairly long-tailed. Crown high and rounded. Bill black. Legs pinkish. Plain brownish-black above, *sharply demarcated on sides of head from white underparts*. Underwing pattern variable, but usually whitish mottled with dusky. Dark morph has mostly dark underwing surface. At rest on water, long tail projects slightly beyond folded wings. Audubon's Shearwater allopatric. Compare with Black-vented Shearwater. Note duskier underwing and more contrasting hood. **HABITS** Mainly pelagic but sometimes seen near shore. Distinctive, floppy flight with five to ten shallow flaps interspersed with short glides. May approach and circle boats. Often forages over schools of small fish with terns and other seabirds. **VOICE** Silent away from breeding grounds.

Black-vented Shearwater

Audubon's Shearwater

dark
morph

Galapagos Shearwater

STORM-PETRELS Hydrobatidae

Very small pelagic seabirds. Storm-petrels present considerable identification difficulties and may require comparative experience and favorable views for confident determination. Observers should note flight style, size, rump pattern, and tail shape. Status and seasonal movements poorly known. Black, Least, and Wedge-rumped storm-petrels are the most common and widespread.

Black Storm-Petrel *Oceanodroma melania*   22 cm

East Pacific. Breeds on islands off Pacific MX. Disperses to Pacific waters off south USA to north SA. Fairly common (Jan to Dec) to locally or seasonally abundant visitor (mainly Feb to Jun and Sep to Nov, 521, 335, 602, 390, 672). **ID** *Large* and long-winged. *Tail deeply forked.* Legs long. Near-uniform brownish-black including rump with slightly paler brown wing coverts forming faint carpal bar. Shares dark rump only with smaller Least and Leach's storm-petrels. Note different tail shape. **HABITS** Sometimes seen near shore. Flight languid and graceful (may recall Black Tern) with steady, slow, deep wingbeats and relatively little gliding. Usually flies well above surface. Usually solitary. May gather in small, loose groups. May follow ships. **VOICE** Silent away from breeding grounds.

Leach's Storm-Petrel *Oceanodroma leucorhoa*   20 cm

Cosmopolitan. Pacific populations breed west NA. Atlantic populations breed USA, Canada, and west Europe. Disperses widely at sea. Poorly known. Reported off north CA (335) and Pacific CR (601, 573, 346, 672). A report from Caribbean coast of CR is uncertain (Limón, 341). **ID** Medium-sized. *Forked tail.* Fairly prominent pale carpal bar. Rump variably dark or white. Note restricted white on sides of crissum. Resembles larger Black Storm-Petrel but note shorter wings and less deeply forked tail. Leach's flight style more bounding and erratic. **HABITS** Erratic, batlike flight with deep wingbeats. Glides less often than Black Storm-Petrel. **VOICE** Silent away from breeding grounds.

Least Storm-Petrel *Oceanodroma microsoma*   14.5 cm

East Pacific. Breeds on islands off Baja, MX. Disperses north to waters off south USA and south to waters off SA. Uncommon to (seasonally or locally) fairly common visitor (Sep to Jun) to Pacific offshore waters. Reported to be most common in Gulf of Panamá during Feb to Mar and in Nov (672). Recently reported off Pacific Nicaragua in Golfo de Fonseca (Chinandega, 346). **ID** Smallest CA storm-petrel. *Note wedge-shaped tail.* Wings relatively long and narrow. Near-uniform brownish-black (including rump) becoming slightly paler on wing coverts. **HABITS** Often with Wedge-rumped Storm-Petrels. Fluttery, somewhat erratic flight, usually close to surface. **VOICE** Silent away from breeding grounds.

Wedge-rumped Storm-Petrel *Oceanodroma tethys*   15 cm

East Pacific. Breeds on Galápagos Islands and islands off Peru. Disperses widely in east Pacific. Widespread transient and nonbreeding visitor (229, 657, 390, 672). Most numerous storm-petrel in Pacific waters (161, 521). Peak numbers in Gulf of Panamá in Jun to Aug. Rare in winter (Jan and Feb). **ID** Very small. Tail notched. Mostly brownish-black with pale grayish carpal bar and triangular white rump patch extending to sides of crissum and nearly to tip of tail. Leach's Storm-Petrel has dark rump or less extensive whitish rump. **HABITS** Rapid, steady flight style with deep wingbeats and occasional glides. Forages with bounding flight style. Often drops to water and trails feet at surface. In calm weather may rest in flocks on water. Less wary than other storm-petrels. Sometimes attracted to boats. **VOICE** Silent away from breeding grounds.

Band-rumped Storm-Petrel *Oceanodroma castro*   17 cm

Cosmopolitan. Galápagos Islands breeders disperse to pelagic waters of equatorial Pacific. Poorly known in CA. Records from off Pacific CR (664, 672) and PA (346). **ID** Bill relatively long and heavy. Tail notched. Mostly brownish-black with pale carpal bar and *narrow white rump patch.* Compare with Wilson's Storm-Petrel. Note different structure. Leach's Storm-Petrel has different rump pattern. **HABITS** Usually far offshore. Flies with steady, slow, rhythmic wingbeats. Glides infrequently, often low over water. Patters feet on surface and holds wings horizontally, not at angle like Wedge-rumped and Leach's storm-petrels. **VOICE** Silent away from breeding grounds.

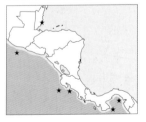

Wilson's Storm-Petrel *Oceanites oceanicus*   17 cm

Cosmopolitan. In east Pacific breeds on islands off south SA and disperses north. Poorly known but reported from waters off Pacific GT (335) and CR (335, 601, 672). One specimen from near Pearl Islands off Pacific PA (Panamá, 659, 390, 346). A report from BZ is dubious (Stann Creek, 346). **ID** *Square tail.* Note *long legs extending beyond tail* in direct flight. Wings short and broad with straight trailing edge. Long legs black with yellow on webs of feet (sometimes visible at close range when held dangling over water's surface). Mostly brownish-black with pale carpal bar and *bold, rounded white rump-band* extending to sides of crissum. **HABITS** Patters feet on surface. **VOICE** Silent away from breeding grounds.

Black
Storm-Petrel

Leach's
Storm-Petrel

dark-
rumped
morph

Least
Storm-Petrel

Wedge-rumped
Storm-Petrel

Band-rumped
Storm-Petrel

Wilson's
Storm-Petrel

TROPICBIRDS Phaethontidae

Tropicbirds are pelagic.

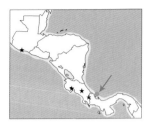

Red-billed Tropicbird *Phaethon aethereus* 90 cm

Pantropical. Breeds in east Pacific at Isla Mapelo and Galápagos Islands. Perhaps also islands off Pacific west CR (Guanacaste, 193). Breeds in south Caribbean at Swan Cay off west PA (Bocas del Toro, 486, 657, 41, 48). Elsewhere a rare visitor to Pacific waters (657, 390, 346, 672). Wrecked birds rarely found inland (341, 547). **ID** Ad has heavy *red bill* and very long, white, central rectrices. In all plumages, wings mostly white with *black primary coverts* and outer primaries. Note black stripe through eye and fine, black barring on back and rump. Juv lacks ad's long rectrices and has yellowish bill and coarser barring on mantle. Ad White-tailed Tropicbird has different upperparts pattern and yellow bill. Juv White-tailed Tropicbird has white primary coverts. **HABITS** Pelagic. Usually solitary. Strong dove-like flight. While swimming holds tail above water. Plunges into water to seize prey. **VOICE** Silent away from breeding grounds.

White-tailed Tropicbird *Phaethon lepturus* 75 cm

Pantropical. Breeds in WI. Disperses widely at sea outside breeding season. Very rare visitor to BZ (Belize, 347, 346), GT (Izabal, 647), CR (Limón, 371), and PA (Bocas del Toro, 275, 469, 42). One report from Pacific at Isla del Coco (192). **ID** *Yellow bill* (may vary to deep orange) and short, narrow, black facial stripe. Ad has very long, white central rectrices. Otherwise mostly white with boldly patterned black primaries and long carpal bar. In all plumages note white primary coverts. Juv lacks ad's long rectrices and carpal bar and has coarse blackish barring on mantle. Compare with Red-billed Tropicbird. Note White-tailed's short black eye stripe (not extending to nape). **HABITS** Pelagic. Similar to Red-billed Tropicbird. **VOICE** Silent away from breeding grounds.

FRIGATEBIRDS Fregatidae

Magnificent Frigatebird is widespread in coastal waters, where it is often seen soaring overhead.

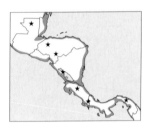

Magnificent Frigatebird *Fregata magnificens* 95 cm

Pantropical. Locally common resident on coasts and islands. Wandering or displaced birds sometimes seen inland. **ID** Very large and slender with *very long, narrow, sharply pointed wings* and *very long, deeply forked tail* (often closed to form a single point). Ad male mostly blackish with faint purple iridescence on back. Male's bare red throat pouch is inflated in display (otherwise inconspicuous). Female lacks red throat pouch and has white breast and sides. Note female's pale brown carpal bar. Imm has white head and more conspicuous whitish carpal bar. **HABITS** Coastal and pelagic waters. Soaring birds may wander inland. Breeds in colonies on small islands. Soars high on motionless wings. Gathers in large congregations at nesting and roosting sites. Harasses other waterbirds on the wing, forcing them to disgorge prey. **VOICE** Usually silent.

Great Frigatebird *Fregata minor* 90 cm

Pantropical. Common breeder on Isla del Coco (256, 571, 600, 446). Very rare visitor elsewhere with records from waters off Pacific CR (Puntarenas, 600) and PA (Veraguas, 42, 346). **ID** Ad male has *brown carpal bar* (sometimes shown faintly by male Magnificent Frigatebird), green iridescence on back, and reddish or brown (not black) legs. Female has whitish or pale gray (not black) throat and narrow pinkish-red (not blue) orbital ring. Juv has *head (and often breast) tinged with rusty*. Very similar to more common and widespread Magnificent Frigatebird. Note Great's pale edging on axillars (all black in Magnificent Frigatebird). **HABITS** Pelagic and coastal waters. **HABITS** Similar to Magnificent Frigatebird. **VOICE** Usually silent.

Red-billed Tropicbird

juv

ad

juv

White-tailed Tropicbird

ad

Displaying adult.

ad
♂

♀

ad
♂

juv

Magnificent Frigatebird

ad
♂

♀

juv

Great Frigatebird

ad
♂

CORMORANTS Phalacrocoracidae

Cormorants swim low in the water and present a distinctive silhouette in flight with outstretched head and neck. Neotropic Cormorant is common and widespread.

Neotropic Cormorant *Phalacrocorax brasilianus*　　　　　　65–70 cm

TX and Cuba to SA. Locally common resident in lowlands and foothills. Also islands including BZ Cays, Bay Islands, and islands off Pacific PA. **ID** Ad near-uniform glossy black with narrow line of *white feathers at rear border of bare gular patch*. Bare facial skin yellow-orange. At close range note blue-green eyes. Imm grayish-brown above and variably paler below. In coastal north Caribbean compare with Double-crested Cormorant. Note different head pattern and structure. **GV** Birds from south CA are larger with longer bill. **HABITS** Uses a wide variety of aquatic habitats including rivers, lagoons, lakes, and estuaries. Prefers fresh or brackish water habitats. Swims low in water, sometimes with only head and neck showing above surface and bill tilted upward. Flies strongly with outstretched head and neck projecting slightly upward. Perches upright, often with wings outstretched. Gregarious. Often gathers in small groups, especially at roost sites. Dives frequently and may remain submerged for long periods. **VOICE** Usually quiet. Sometimes gives (1) a low-pitched, coarse grunting *rru rru rru . . .*

Double-crested Cormorant *Phalacrocorax auritus*　　　　　　75 cm

NA to CA. Locally fairly common resident in coastal lowlands and islands off BZ (96, 529, 343, 346). Perhaps expanding in south BZ (Toledo, 346), Caribbean GT (Izabal, 229), and Isla Guanaja in Bay Islands (346). **ID** Ad entirely glossy black with orange throat pouch and *bare orange facial skin extending to lores*. In breeding condition ad has two wispy black tufts on hindcrown. At close range note blue-green eyes. Imm grayish-brown above and variably paler below. Widespread Neotropic Cormorant has longer tail and shorter, more slender bill. Note *pointed rear margin of gular patch* (not rounded as in Double-crested Cormorant) bordered with white. **HABITS** Prefers salt or brackish water environments including coastlines, mangroves, lagoons, and estuaries. Dives frequently and often remains submerged for long periods. Typically perches upright, often with wings outstretched. Gregarious. Gathers in small groups, especially at roost sites. **VOICE** Usually quiet. Sometimes gives (1) a low-pitched, nasal *err err err . . .*

ANHINGA Anhingidae

Like cormorants, anhingas swim low in the water, sometimes with only head and neck visible and bill tilting upward.

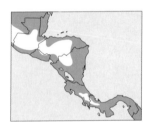

Anhinga *Anhinga anhinga*　　　　　　85 cm

South USA to SA. Uncommon to locally fairly common resident, mainly in lowlands. Uncommon and local in north Pacific. **ID** *Long, pointed bill*, very long neck, *long, square tail* and large white area on wing. Scapulars and inner wing feathers streaked with white. Tail tipped with brown. Ad male mostly glossy black. Ad female has pale brown head, neck, and chest. Compare with cormorants. Note Anhinga's longer and more slender pointed bill (not hooked), broad white wing patch and square (not graduated) tail. **HABITS** Freshwater aquatic habitats including marshes, ponds, lakes, lagoons, and wooded rivers. Perches on branches over or near water, often with wings held outstretched. In flight, makes long glides alternating with flapping. Also soars in spirals with wings held flat. May swim low in water with only head and neck above surface. Solitary or in pairs. **VOICE** Usually quiet. Sometimes gives (1) a low-pitched, nasal *err-err-err-err . . .*

Neotropic Cormorant

imm

north CA
ad

south CA
ad

Double-crested Cormorant

imm

nonbreeding
ad

breeding
ad

Anhinga

♀

♀

nonbreeding
♂

breeding
♂

♀

BOOBIES Sulidae

Large birds of offshore and coastal marine habitats. Status and distribution, including pattern and timing of migrations poorly understood. *Sula* boobies present identification problems that are compounded by rarity and complex patterns of individual, geographic, and age-related variation. Brown Booby is generally the most common and widespread and also the species most likely to be encountered in coastal waters.

Brown Booby *Sula leucogaster*   70–72 cm

Pantropical. Uncommon to locally fairly common resident. Breeding sites include Los Farallones in Gulf of Fonseca, islands off west Caribbean HN (Atlántida), Swan Islands and Cayos Vivorillos (442, 263), Isla Santa Catalina and Cabo Blanco off Pacific CR (Puntarenas, Guanacaste, 601, 141), near Isla Uvita off Caribbean CR (Limón 600) and islands off Bocas del Toro and Chiriquí, and Pearl Islands in PA (512, 40, 41). Also Isla del Coco (163, 256). **ID** Ad has *dark brown neck and breast contrasting with white lower underparts*. Upperparts plain dark brown including tail. In flight, ad's white underwing coverts contrast with dark brown flight feathers. Feet yellowish. Ad male has blue facial skin. Imm has dark brown neck and breast *sharply demarcated from slightly paler lower underparts*. Compare with imms of Red-footed, Masked, and Nazca boobies. Note different underparts. **GV** Ad male from Pacific population has whitish head. **HABITS** Pelagic and nearshore waters. More often near shore than other CA *Sula*. May loiter near fishing boats or in harbors. Buoyant flight with deep wingbeats. Usually solitary away from breeding sites. May join other seabirds in mixed foraging associations. **VOICE** Usually silent.

Red-footed Booby *Sula sula*   68 cm

Pacific and Indian oceans and Caribbean Sea. Breeds at Half Moon Cay off BZ (535, 96, 640, 529, 292, 343), Swan Islands off Caribbean HN (251, 442), and Isla Violín and Isla del Coco off Pacific CR (Puntarenas, 163, 256, 600, 571, 446). Disperses widely at sea. Rare and irregular visitor to coastal and offshore waters elsewhere. **ID** Small with long tail, slender bill, and rounded crown. Ad has pale bluish-gray bill and bare pinkish facial skin. *Legs and feet red*. Variable. White morph ad mostly white with dark flight feathers and variable *dark carpal mark on underwing*. Ad may have golden-buff wash on head and neck. Tail usually white (dark in white morph from Pacific islands). Brown morph ad mostly *pale brown* with white rump, crissum, and tail. Some brown morph birds have brown rear parts. Imm variably brown or grayish-brown with variable, indistinct *dark breast-band* and plain brown underwing surface. Lower underparts paler. Imm has variably dusky or dull pinkish legs and feet. Imm may be difficult to separate from imm Brown Booby. Note different underwing and underparts pattern. **HABITS** Pelagic and often seen far from land. Crepuscular or perhaps nocturnal. May form mixed foraging associations with other seabirds. Follows ships. **VOICE** Usually silent.

Masked Booby *Sula dactylatra*   72 cm

Pantropical. Breeds on islands off Pacific MX and in small numbers on Isla del Coco (2, 163, 256, 346, 446). Disperses widely at sea. Uncommon nonbreeding visitor to offshore Pacific (521, 495, 602, 520). Rare in Caribbean (570, 106, 341, 347, 433) but breeding reported at Cayos Vivorillos off HN (263). **ID** Large and short-tailed. Ad mostly white with black tail and black on upperwing extending to inner wing (compare with Red-footed Booby). Note black face and chin. *Bill dull yellow*. Legs and feet olive-gray. Juv has grayish-brown hood and dull-yellow bill. Juv typically has *white collar* contrasting with brown head and mantle. Subad intermediate. Compare juv with Brown Booby. Note different underparts and underwing pattern. In Pacific compare with Nazca Booby. Note ad's different bill color. Juvs not always separable, but note different upperparts. See also juv Blue-footed Booby. **HABITS** Pelagic. Rarely near shore. Forms small groups. May follow ships. May perch on floating debris or carapace of sea turtle. **VOICE** Usually silent.

Nazca Booby *Sula granti*   73 cm

Pacific SA. Breeds on Galápagos Islands (Oct to Jun) and on Isla Mapela off north SA (495, 520). Rare to (briefly or locally) common visitor (Apr to Nov) to Pacific waters (390, 495, 42, 346, 672). **ID** Large and short-tailed. *Very similar to Masked Booby*. Ad has *orange bill*. Note black face and chin. Ad mostly white with black tail and black on upperwing extending to inner wing (compare with Red-footed Booby). Legs and feet greenish-gray. Juv has brown upperparts and hood (usually lacks white collar). Subad intermediate but usually shows trace of ad's bill color. Juv also resembles Brown Booby. Note less extensive hood not cut straight across breast. Also note different bill color. See also juv Blue-footed Booby. **HABITS** Like Masked Booby. **VOICE** Usually silent.

10%

Brown Booby

juv

Pacific
ad
♂

ad
♀

juv

ad
♀

brown-tailed
white morph
ad

Red-footed Booby

juv

brown
morph ad

white-tailed brown morph
ad

white
morph ad

juv

brown-tailed
white morph
ad

Masked Booby

juv

ad

juv

ad

juv

ad

juv

Nazca Booby

juv

ad

juv

ad

BOOBIES Sulidae

Blue-footed Booby *Sula nebouxii* 72 cm

East Pacific. Breeds on islands in Gulf of Fonseca (442, 336) and off PA including Islas Frailes del Sur, Farallón del Chirú, Isla Camote and Pearl Islands (Los Santos, Coclé, Panamá, 649, 40, 41, 47). Uncommon to rare and irregular visitor to Pacific waters off CR (Guanacaste, Puntarenas, 600, 672). **ID** Ad has blue facial skin and *blue legs and feet* (duller in juv). Eyes pale. Note small white patches on rump and upper mantle and plain brown upperwing surface. Ad has *fine brown-and-white streaking on head and neck*. Mantle mostly brown with white barring and spotting. Juv has dusky brown hood and white belly. Brown Booby more uniform above. Compare ad with Peruvian Booby. Note different head and upperwing pattern. Also compare juv with juv Masked Booby. Note different underwing pattern and bill color. **HABITS** Pelagic and inshore waters. Often in small groups that fly single-file. Perhaps crepuscular. Perches inactively through most of day. **VOICE** Usually silent.

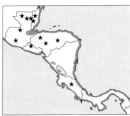

Peruvian Booby *Sula variegata* 68 cm

East Pacific. Breeds on coast and islands off SA. Rare and irregular visitor to Pacific waters of Panamá Bay (512, 6, 505, 346). **ID** Bill and legs gray. Bare facial skin blackish. Eyes red. Ad has *entire head and neck white* (lacks streaked hood of Blue-footed Booby). Upperparts brown with *conspicuous white scaling on mantle and upperwing surface*. Underparts entirely white. Juv similar but has head, neck and underparts brownish. Juv's upperparts show less white. Resembles Blue-footed Booby. Note different leg color, head color, and upper wing pattern. **HABITS** Coastal marine waters. Solitary or in small groups. **VOICE** Usually silent.

PELICANS Pelecanidae

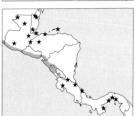

Brown Pelican *Pelecanus occidentalis* 130 cm

NA to SA. Locally common resident on coasts. Rare inland. May undertake seasonal or local movements. **ID** Very large and bulky with long bill and *deep pouch hanging below mandible*. Mostly gray above with whitish streaking. Dark brown below. Breeding ad has brown stripe on neck. Nonbreeding ad has mostly whitish head and neck. Juv brownish above and on head and neck with whitish underparts. American White Pelican larger with different habits. **HABITS** Coastal waters including harbors, beaches, and estuaries. Head typically held drawn back with bill resting on neck. Flies with characteristic pattern of two or three wingbeats followed by short glide. Forms small flocks. May fly low over water or soar high overhead on thermals. **VOICE** Usually silent.

American White Pelican *Pelecanus erythrorhynchos* 150 cm

Breeds west Nearctic. Winters south USA to CA. Locally common transient and winter visitor in north Pacific (mainly Sep to Apr). Rare on Caribbean slope in BZ (Orange Walk, Belize, 343) and GT (Petén, Sololá, 225, 346). Uncommon to rare but perhaps increasing in NI (Granada, León, 602, 346), CR (Guanacaste, Alajuela, Limón, 602, 341, 546), and PA (Panamá, Herrera, 512, 341, 48, 48, 346). **ID** Very large. Bulky with long bill, long broad wings, and *deep pouch hanging below mandible*. Ad *mostly white* with black outer secondaries and primaries. Note *yellow-orange bill and legs*. Juv (not shown) has brownish mottling on head, neck, and wing coverts. **HABITS** Marshes, lakes, flooded agricultural fields. More often on freshwater than Brown Pelican. Many records of single birds but gregarious and regularly forms large flocks. Forages while swimming. Does not dive. **VOICE** Usually silent.

Blue-footed Booby

juv

ad

ad

juv

ad

Peruvian Booby

juv

ad

ad

juv

ad

Brown Pelican

juv

nonbreeding

breeding

ad

American White Pelican

BITTERNS Ardeidae

Secretive herons with broad neck. Bitterns often perch with the bill held upward at a steep angle.

Least Bittern *Ixobrychus exilis*   30 cm

NA to SA. Rare and local breeding resident. Nearctic breeding birds perhaps also occur as rare transients and winter residents. Reported from BZ (Orange Walk, Belize, Toledo, Ambergris Cay, 529, 341), GT (Santa Rosa, Petén, Sololá, 279, 182, 341), SV (Ahuachapán, Chalatenango, 619, 346), HN (Atlántida, 167, 262), CR (Alajuela, Guanacaste, 55, 474, 176, 574, 600), and PA (Panamá, Colón, Chiriquí, Bocas del Toro, Herrera, Darién, 346, 48). **ID** Smallest CA heron. *Pale wing coverts* contrast with dark brown flight feathers (conspicuous in flight). Individually variable. Also varies by age and sex. Typical ad male has black crown, mantle, and tail. Hindneck rich chestnut. Male's underparts variably ochre to whitish. Female similar to male but has reddish-brown back. Female's underparts mostly whitish with variable streaking on throat and breast. Imm has fine buff edging on upperparts. Compare with Green Heron. **HABITS** Freshwater marshes and lake edges with tall emergent or floating vegetation. Solitary and secretive. Usually remains concealed in vegetation. May stand motionless with neck and bill almost vertical. Makes short, low flights over marshes. **VOICE** Call (1) a variable, short series of low-pitched, gruff notes *whu whu-huhu* or *huhuhuhu*. Other calls include (2) a very low-pitched *huuw* or *gruuuh* that may be repeated. In interactions gives (3) an abrupt *kek* or *kuk* that may be repeated.

American Bittern *Botaurus lentiginosus*   62 cm

Breeds Nearctic. Winters USA, WI, MX, and CA. Rare winter visitor (Sep to Mar) to BZ (Corozal, Orange Walk, Belize, Toledo, Cayo, 667, 343, 346), GT (Alta Verapaz, Sacatepéquez, Retalhuleu, 229, 539, 279), SV (San Miguel, 183), HN (Cortes, Swan Islands, 480, 341, 346), NI (Matagalpa, Jinotega, 346, 133), and CR (Cartago, Puntarenas, Alajuela, Limón, 65, 126, 600, 341, 346). One historical record from PA (Panamá, 383). **ID** Long, broad neck and short legs. Mostly buffy brown with *long dark malar* extending to stripe on sides of neck. Note brown and white streaking on foreneck and breast. In flight, dark flight feathers contrast with paler wing coverts. Imm lacks dark neck stripe. Imms of both night-herons are superficially similar but lack dark neck stripe and have different wing pattern. Also compare with Pinnated Bittern. Note different head pattern. Also compare with more coarsely marked imms of *Tigrisoma* tiger-herons. **HABITS** Freshwater marshes and margins of lakes and ponds. Usually remains concealed in vegetation. Sometimes raises head and neck above tall grass. Solitary and reclusive. **VOICE** Call (1) a very low-pitched, hollow phrase *bloonk-adonk* that is repeated. When disturbed, gives (2) a rapid, coarse *kok-kok-kok*. In flight (3) a loud, hoarse, nasal *squark*. Compare with calls of night-herons.

Pinnated Bittern *Botaurus pinnatus*   68 cm

South MX to SA. Uncommon to rare and local resident, mainly in lowlands (to 1000 m) of BZ (Orange Walk, Belize, 72, 433, 343), GT (Petén, Izabal, Retalhuleu, Jutiapa, Santa Rosa, 229, 279, 182), SV (San Miguel, La Unión, 173, 341, 346), HN (Choluteca, Cortes, 336, 263), NI (Río San Juan, RAAS, Matagalpa, Jinotega, 506, 173, 346), and CR (Guanacaste, Puntarenas, Cartago, Alajuela, 88, 172, 173, 474, 574, 600). **ID** Typical bittern structure with long, broad neck and short legs. Mostly buffy brown with *fine dusky barring on crown and neck*. Upperparts, including wings, show bold blackish streaking and barring. In flight, note contrasting dark flight feathers. Compare with American Bittern. Note different crown and neck pattern. Also compare with more coarsely marked imms of *Tigrisoma* tiger-herons. Note different head and neck pattern. **HABITS** Freshwater marshes. Solitary and secretive. Sometimes raises head and neck above concealing vegetation. **VOICE** Call (1) similar to American Bittern but higher-pitched and less hollow.

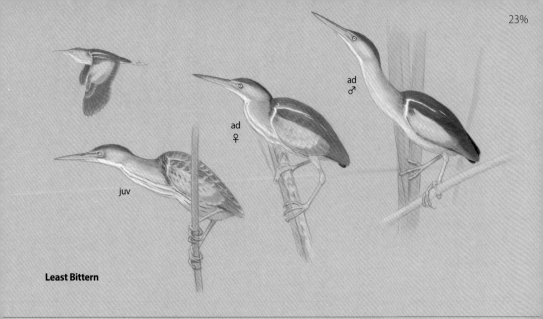

Least Bittern

ad ♀

ad ♂

juv

American Bittern

Pinnated Bittern

TIGER-HERONS Ardeidae

Broad-necked herons. Often crepuscular or nocturnal. Tiger-herons require several years to reach definitive adult plumage. While adults are fairly distinctive, immatures can be difficult to separate and are often misidentified. Juvenile Rufescent and Fasciated tiger-herons are especially similar, and young birds may not be separable in the field. Each has a fairly narrow habitat association and this can be an important clue for identification. Juvenile, immature, and subadult birds encountered away from their typical habitat may present identification problems. Immature birds should also be compared with Pinnated Bittern. Bare-throated Tiger-Heron is the most common and widespread tiger-heron in Central America.

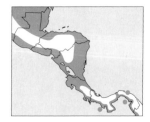

Bare-throated Tiger-Heron *Tigrisoma mexicanum*   76 cm

MX to north SA. Fairly common resident in lowlands and foothills (to 700 m, rarely or locally higher). Also Isla Coiba (Veraguas, 653, 470) and Pearl Islands (Panamá, 649, 374). **ID** *Entirely bare (unfeathered) throat* variably orange-yellow to yellow. Ad has black malar and crown contrasting with plain (unmarked) light gray sides of head. Sides of neck and upperparts mostly blackish-brown narrowly barred and vermiculated with buff or light gray. Median neck stripe rufous bordered with black and white. Remaining underparts plain rufous. Subad resembles ad but is more coarsely barred and vermiculated and often has dark barring on crown and auriculars. Juv mostly buff and variably barred and vermiculated with black (more coarsely patterned on wings). Juv Rufescent and Fasciated tiger-herons similar but tend to have warmer, brighter cinnamon-colored neck, coarser dark barring on upperparts, and feathered central throat and chin. Compare ad Bare-throated with ad Fasciated Tiger-Heron. Note different head pattern and extent of feathering on throat. **HABITS** Uses a wide variety of aquatic habitats including marshes, flooded agricultural fields, lakeshores, and forested riverbanks. Occasionally or locally in coastal areas with rocky shorelines. Solitary. Forages on ground, usually near water. May remain motionless for long periods. Often perches in trees, especially when vocalizing. Like other tiger-herons, habitually twitches tail. **VOICE** Often vocalizes at night. Call (1) a very low-pitched, guttural *roowhr* or *woowhr* or two-syllable *rowoh-wrr* usually repeated in long series. When disturbed gives (2) a rapid series of low-pitched, coarse croaks *wok-wok-wok* or *ruhk-ruhk-ruhk*.

Fasciated Tiger-Heron *Tigrisoma fasciatum*   64 cm

CA and SA. Rare to locally uncommon resident in Caribbean foothills and highlands (250 to 2400 m). On Pacific slope locally in CR and PA. Rare in Caribbean foothills of east HN (Gracias a Dios, 629). One report from NI (Río San Juan, 136). **ID** Ad resembles ad Bare-throated but is grayer on neck and has *narrow fringe of whitish feathers on central throat*. Bill typically shorter than bills of other CA tiger-herons. Ad's lower underparts pale cinnamon with (usually concealed) gray-and-white barring on flanks. Imm resembles ad but has coarser barring and vermiculations (extending to auriculars and crown) and more brownish plumage. Juv Fasciated and Rufescent tiger-herons very similar and may not be separable. With adequate view all plumages of Fasciated can be distinguished from Bare-throated by the presence of feathering on the central throat. **HABITS** Margins of rocky, fast-flowing rivers. Solitary. Perches motionless for long periods on boulders or gravel bars at water's edge. May alight on high, open branch when disturbed. **VOICE** Undescribed.

Rufescent Tiger-Heron *Tigrisoma lineatum*   68 cm

CA and SA. Uncommon to rare resident in lowlands and foothills (to 500 m). Poorly known in Caribbean lowlands of east HN (Gracias a Dios, 513, 442, 401, 341) and NI (RAAN, RAAS, 548, 346). Recently documented from BZ (Orange Walk, 346) where status uncertain. **ID** In all plumages note *narrow fringe of whitish feathers on central throat*. Ad has *rufous head, neck, and chest* and rufous median throat stripe bordered with black and white. Ad's upperparts mostly brownish-gray with fine black barring and vermiculation. Lower underparts mostly pale cinnamon with (mostly concealed) black-and-white barring on flanks. Subad has extensive fine barring on neck and sides of head and gradually acquires ad's rufous head and neck. Juv mostly cinnamon-buff with variably sparse to bold black barring on upperparts. Juv Bare-throated Tiger-Heron similar to juv Rufescent, but always shows bare (unfeathered) throat. Juv Rufescent Tiger-Heron closely resembles juv Fasciated (and may not be separable) but Rufescent typically has longer bill. Also note different habits. **HABITS** Flooded or swampy forest and forested streams or pools. Occasionally in more open wetlands, flooded savannas or on forested banks of slow-moving rivers. Reclusive and usually solitary. Typically freezes with neck hunched and does not elevate bill when disturbed. May perch in trees. **VOICE** Often vocalizes at night. Gives (1) a series of low-pitched, slightly nasal cries *waaaah haaah haaaaaaaww* or *honh-honh-honh-honh . . . honnhhh-hh*. Usually includes two or more shorter introductory notes followed by a longer, more attenuated note. When disturbed gives (2) a long series of low-pitched, gruff, clipped croaks *rheeh-heh-heh-heh-heh, heh*.

15%

Bare-throated Tiger-Heron

juv

subad

ad

juv

Fasciated Tiger-Heron

juv

subad

ad

Rufescent Tiger-Heron

juv

subad

ad

EGRET AND HERONS Ardeidae

Large herons. Great Egret and Great Blue Heron are widespread winter residents and also breed very locally. Cocoi Heron is a mainly South American species confined to east Panama.

Great Egret *Ardea alba*
90 cm

Cosmopolitan. Nearctic breeding and resident birds occur. Common transient and winter resident (Oct to Apr) on coasts. Less common inland. Very local breeder in lowlands and (occasionally) foothills of GT (Santa Rosa, 182), BZ (Corozal, Belize, Toledo, 343), CR (Guanacaste, 600), and PA (Chiriquí, Herrera, Los Santos, 512, 40). At least formerly bred in SV (San Miguel, 183, 619). Probably breeds elsewhere in region but status poorly documented. **ID** Large and long-necked. Uniform white. Note *yellow bill* and *all-black legs and feet*. Ad's briefly held breeding plumage features long white plumes extending from mantle. During courtship ad's bare facial skin briefly becomes bright green. Compare with smaller Snowy Egret and with imm Little Blue Heron. Note different bill pattern. **HABITS** Marshes, borders of ponds and lakes, flooded agricultural lands, river margins, beaches, mangroves, and mudflats. Stands motionless for long periods. Solitary when foraging. Forms communal roosts in trees. **VOICE** Usually quiet. May give (1) a hoarse *guuk* or *guuk-uuk-uuk* or (2) attenuated *gruuuuuuuk*.

Great Blue Heron *Ardea herodias*
120 cm

Breeds mainly Nearctic. Uncommon and very local breeder in north BZ (Corozal, 343). Widespread and uncommon to locally fairly common winter resident (mainly Dec to Jun) in lowlands. Uncommon nonbreeding summer resident. Most common in north. **ID** *Very large*. In all plumages (except rare white morph) note *rufous tibials*. Ad mostly gray and has black crown with white central stripe and white sides of head. Ad's briefly held breeding plumage features two long black plumes extending from crown. In brief courtship period ad's bill becomes bright orange and bare facial skin blue. In flight, pale upperwing contrasts with blackish flight feathers. White morph reported from breeding population in north BZ. Imm duller with dark sides of head and crown. In east PA compare with Cocoi Heron. Note different head and underparts. Also compare white morph with smaller Great Egret. Note proportionally larger bill and gray lores of Great Blue Heron. White morph Great Blue Heron also distinguished by paler grayish (not black) legs. **HABITS** Marshes, borders of ponds and lakes, flooded agricultural lands, and riverbanks. Also coastal habitats including beaches, marshes, mangroves, and estuaries. Usually solitary and often wary. **VOICE** Usually quiet. When disturbed gives (1) a very coarse, low-pitched *gruuuk* or *guuuk*.

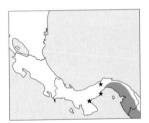

Cocoi Heron *Ardea cocoi*
110 cm

SA and PA. Uncommon resident in lowlands of east PA (Panamá, Darién). Vagrant west to Herrera. **ID** *Very large*. Note *entirely black crown* and white tibials. Ad has long black occipital plumes tipped with white. Neck and chest white. In flight, pale upperwing contrasts with blackish flight feathers. Imm grayer below with *white tibials* and solid dark crown and face. Structure and size similar to Great Blue Heron. Note different underparts and head pattern. **HABITS** Freshwater marshes, mangroves and riverbanks. Much like Great Blue Heron. Solitary. **VOICE** Usually quiet. Call (1) a guttural, low-pitched *gruuk*.

Great Egret

nonbreeding

breeding

Great Blue Heron

imm

white morph
ad

typical
ad

Cocoi Heron

imm

ad

EGRETS AND HERONS Ardeidae

Widespread herons. Several are migratory. Little Blue and Tricolored herons are widely and routinely encountered, but the breeding status of these species is poorly understood and few nesting sites have been documented in the region.

Cattle Egret *Bubulcus ibis*
50 cm

Cosmopolitan. Common resident in lowlands and foothills. Also islands including BZ Cays and Bay Islands (442). Nearctic breeding birds perhaps occur in winter. Formerly confined to Old World. First recorded in CA in 1950s and has expanded rapidly (202, 580, 569, 159). **ID** Small with *bulky neck*. Nonbreeding ad uniform white. Breeding ad has variable patches of cinnamon on crown, back, and breast. Bill yellow becoming (briefly) mostly orange when breeding. Legs gray (orange when breeding). Juv has gray bill. Snowy Egret and imm Little Blue Heron are larger with different structure and bill color. **HABITS** Agricultural fields, pastures, marshes, ponds, and lakeshores. Groups forage or loiter in vicinity of livestock. Follows farm equipment. Forms large roosts in trees. **VOICE** Usually quiet. At nest gives (1) low-pitched, guttural cries.

Snowy Egret *Egretta thula*
60 cm

NA to SA. Nearctic breeding and resident birds occur. Fairly common transient and winter resident on coasts. Less common inland. Uncommon and local breeder in coastal lowlands. Also islands including Bay Islands and BZ Cays. **ID** *Yellow or yellow-green lores*. Ad has *slender black bill*. Note ad's *black legs and yellow feet*. Breeding ad has long plumes extending from crown and back. Imm has greenish-yellow rear surface of legs and grayish base of bill. Great Egret is larger with yellow bill. Imm Little Blue Heron has different bill pattern and leg color. **HABITS** Mainly coastal saltwater and brackish habitats including beaches, estuaries, mudflats, marshes, and shores of lakes and rivers. Forages actively in shallow water. Solitary when foraging. Forms communal roosts in trees. **VOICE** Usually quiet. Occasionally gives (1) a soft, guttural *gwah*.

Little Blue Heron *Egretta caerulea*
60 cm

NA to SA. Nearctic breeding and resident birds occur. Uncommon and very local breeder in Pacific CR (Guanacaste, 600) and PA (Coclé, Herrera, Veraguas, Panamá, 42, 47, 346). Fairly common transient and winter resident on coasts. Less common inland. Also islands including BZ Cays and Bay Islands (442). **ID** Mostly *bluish-gray bill with black tip*. Legs greenish (blacker when breeding). Ad mostly slaty gray with maroon head and neck. Breeding ad head has long plumes extending from crown, foreneck, and back. Subad mostly white splotched irregularly with slaty gray. Juv white with dusky tips of primaries. *Pale base of bill* yellowish to grayish. Compare imm with Snowy Egret and with white morph Reddish Egret. Note different bill and leg color. **HABITS** Beaches, estuaries, mudflats, marshes, and shores of lakes and rivers. Forages actively, often in shallow water. Usually solitary. May gather in numbers at favored foraging sites. Joins mixed roosts with other herons. **VOICE** Usually quiet.

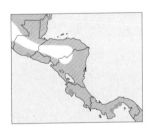

Tricolored Heron *Egretta tricolor*
62 cm

NA to SA. Nearctic breeding and resident birds thought to occur. Uncommon and very local breeding resident in Pacific GT (Santa Rosa, 182), SV (at least historically, 183), CR (Guanacaste, 600), and PA (Panamá, Herrera, 512, 47). Breeds on Caribbean coast in north BZ (Corozal, 343). Fairly common transient and winter resident on coasts. Less common inland. Also Bay Islands (94) and BZ Cays. **ID** Long, slender bill. Dark breast contrasts with white lower underparts. In flight, note *white underwing coverts*. Ad mostly bluish-slate above with white occipital plumes (when breeding) and long, light brown scapulars. Imm has rufous head, hindneck, and wing coverts. Ad Little Blue Heron bulkier with dark underparts. **HABITS** Mainly saltwater and brackish coastal habitats including marshes, estuaries, and lagoons. Forages actively. Sometimes makes rapid, dashing movements like Reddish Egret. May spread wings while foraging. Often solitary but may gather in numbers at favored foraging sites. Joins mixed roosts with other herons. **VOICE** Usually quiet.

Reddish Egret *Egretta rufescens*
75 cm

South USA to CA, WI, and north SA. Uncommon to rare transient and winter resident (mainly Sep to May) in coastal regions. Also BZ Cays (344). Breed locally in coastal north BZ (Corozal, 343). Very rare vagrant inland (354, 343, 262, 346). **ID** Ad has shaggy hindcrest and *heavy, pinkish bill with black tip* (bill brighter and lores blue in breeding season). Legs gray. Typical ad has variably rufous to cinnamon head, neck, and breast and gray posterior. In flight, shows pale band on underwing. Note pale eyes. Light morph ad uniform white. Subad resembles ad but has shorter plumes and duller bare parts. Juv mostly pale gray-brown with all-dark bill and bare gray facial skin. Compare with smaller Little Blue Heron. **HABITS** Rocky coasts and islets, exposed reefs and sandbars. Occasionally on mudflats in estuaries. Forages actively with crest raised and wings spread. Usually solitary. **VOICE** Usually quiet.

nonbreeding ad

breeding ad

juv

Cattle Egret

breeding ad

imm

Snowy Egret

juv

breeding ad

subad

Little Blue Heron

breeding ad

Tricolored Heron

nonbreeding ad

breeding ad

juv

dark morph nonbreeding ad

white morph breeding ad

Reddish Egret

HERONS Ardeidae

Herons found mainly in freshwater habitats. The two *Butorides* herons have sometimes been regarded as conspecific. The widespread Green Heron is represented in Central America by both Nearctic migrant birds and resident breeding birds. Striated Heron is confined mainly to Panama but vagrants have been found north to Nicaragua.

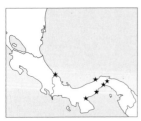

Whistling Heron *Syrigma sibilatrix* 57 cm

SA. Rare vagrant to CR (Limón, 8) and PA (Panamá, Herrera, Coclé, Colón, 346). **ID** Large. *Heavy pink bill with dusky tip.* Bright blue skin around eye. Mostly dull buff with gray mantle. White rump and tail conspicuous in flight. Compare with Capped Heron. **HABITS** Marshes, agricultural fields, pastures, and savannas. Often far from water and rarely wades. Solitary. May stand motionless for long periods. **VOICE** Usually quiet. Call (1) often given in flight, a repeated *wheeee, wheeee . . .*

Capped Heron *Pilherodius pileatus* 57 cm

CA and SA. Rare to locally uncommon resident in lowlands of east PA (Panamá, Darién). **ID** Stocky with fairly short legs. Base of bill, lores, and bare facial skin blue (becoming brighter during breeding season). Legs gray. Mostly whitish with *mostly black crown* (forecrown gray) and two to four long white occipital plumes. In breeding season neck and underparts become buff and bill brighter. In flight, displays bulky structure with wings strongly curved and may suggest a night-heron. **HABITS** Riverbanks, freshwater swamps, ponds, and marshes. Solitary and shy. While foraging often stands motionless for long periods. **VOICE** Call (1) in display, a series of soft, low-pitched, two-syllable notes *wa-huu wa-huu, wa huu, wa huu . . .*

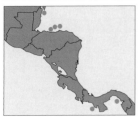

Green Heron *Butorides virescens* 43 cm

NA to SA. Nearctic breeding and resident birds occur. Locally fairly common breeder in lowlands and foothills, particularly in coastal regions. Less common in highlands. Common transient and winter resident (Sep to May). Also BZ Cays, Bay Islands, and Pearl Islands. **ID** Small and stocky with dark plumage. Short, shaggy crest usually held flat against nape. Ad's legs orange in breeding season (yellow in other seasons). Crown black. *Sides of head, neck, and chest maroon-chestnut.* Foreneck streaked with white. Upperparts gray-green with wing coverts edged buff-whitish. Some birds from resident population in Caribbean lowlands (including Bay Islands and Swan Island) are very dark with reduced white on foreneck. Imm is duller than ad and has browner upperparts and variable coarse brown streaking on white underparts. Compare ad with ad Striated Heron. Note different neck color. Imms are very similar and probably not separable in field. **HABITS** Marshes, shores of lakes, lagoons, rivers, and mangroves. Usually solitary. Typically forages by still-hunting from partially submerged limb or other low perch at water's edge. Often flicks tail and raises short crest. **VOICE** Gives (1) loud, hoarse *kyow* in flight or when disturbed.

Striated Heron *Butorides striata* 43 cm

Cosmopolitan. Locally fairly common breeding resident in central and east PA. Also Pearl Islands (Panamá, 611). Vagrant to west PA (Veraguas, Chiriquí), mainland CR (Guanacaste, Alajuela, Puntarenas, 600, 341, 546), Isla del Coco (571) and Caribbean NI (Río San Juan, 548). **ID** Structure like Green Heron and also has orange legs in breeding condition. Ad typically has *sides of head, neck, and chest gray.* Note that Striated Heron (in fresh plumage) typically has *whiter and more contrasting pale edging on wing coverts* (these buff in Green Heron). Ads with light brown neck (thus appearing intermediate toward Green Heron) are thought to represent a plumage variant of Striated Heron. Imm very similar to imm Green Heron and probably not separable in field. **HABITS** Similar to Green Heron. **VOICE** Similar to Green Heron.

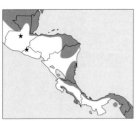

Agami Heron *Agamia agami* 68 cm

South MX to SA. Uncommon resident in Caribbean lowlands. Rare and local in Pacific CR (Puntarenas, 602, 600). Also Pearl Islands (Panamá, 58). One report from north Pacific slope in SV (Santa Ana, 346). Poorly known in Caribbean NI (Río San Juan, 412, 452). **ID** Rather short legs, long neck, and *very long, slender bill.* Ad mostly dark glossy green above with black head. Neck and most of underparts rich chestnut. Throat and stripe down front of neck white. Note silvery blue fringing on lower neck and chest. In breeding season, long bluish-gray plumes extending from crown and mantle and bright red facial skin. Imm dark brown with blackish crown, white throat, and whitish belly. **HABITS** Shaded margins of small streams, pools, and flooded areas inside broadleaf forest. Occasionally (or locally) in marshes or mangroves. Usually solitary and reclusive but may form small colonies when breeding. Often forages at night. Roosts by day in trees. Stands motionless for long periods. When disturbed, twitches tail nervously. **VOICE** Rarely gives (1) coarse, low-pitched, rattling or snoring cries *kur'r'r'r'r* or *ku'd'd'd'd.*

Capped Heron

Whistling Heron

typical
ad

juv

dark
ad

Green Heron

typical
ad

brown
ad

Striated Heron

Agami Heron

ad

breeding
ad

imm

HERONS Ardeidae

Nyctanassa and *Nycticorax* night-herons have similar immature plumages. Details of structure, upperparts pattern, and bill color are helpful in separating these. Boat-billed Heron is a highly distinctive resident species.

Black-crowned Night-Heron *Nycticorax nycticorax* 62 cm

Cosmopolitan. Nearctic breeding and resident birds occur. Uncommon and local breeder. Mainly in lowlands. Also Bay Islands and BZ Cays. Nearctic birds thought to reach CA as widespread and uncommon to locally common winter residents (Oct to Mar). **ID** Bulky with short, thick neck and short bill. Legs yellowish. Ad's legs briefly rosy pink in breeding season. Ad's crown, nape, and back glossy black with long white occipital plumes (becoming longer when breeding). Wings and tail gray. Sides of head, neck, and underparts white. Imm browner. Juv and subad have mostly dull yellow mandible (compare with dark bill of juv Yellow-crowned Night-Heron). Juv mostly brown above, *streaked and spotted with white* (especially on wing coverts) and streaked with brown and white below. Compare with Yellow-crowned Night-Heron. **HABITS** Uses a wide variety of aquatic habitats including freshwater marshes, swamps, mudflats, lagoons, and riverbanks. More often in freshwater habitats than Yellow-crowned Night-Heron. Mainly nocturnal. Solitary when foraging. Roosts in small groups in dense foliage. **VOICE** Usually quiet. When disturbed or in flight, gives (1) an abrupt *quok*.

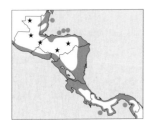

Yellow-crowned Night-Heron *Nyctanassa violacea* 60 cm

NA to SA. Nearctic breeding and resident birds occur. Uncommon to locally fairly common breeder in coastal lowlands. Also islands including Bay Islands and BZ Cays. Nearctic birds thought to reach CA as uncommon to locally fairly common winter residents (mainly Oct to Apr). **ID** Structure like Black-crowned Night-Heron but with *shorter, heavier, all-dark bill*. Note longer neck and legs (projecting well beyond tail in flight). Ad mostly gray. Head black with pale yellow crown and *white mark on auriculars*. Legs orange-yellow. Subad duskier than subad Black-crowned Night-Heron and usually shows at least trace of ad's head pattern. Juv brown with *fine, sharply defined, whitish edging and spotting on upperparts*. Compare with broad, soft markings on upperparts of juv Black-crowned Night-Heron. Also note different bill. **HABITS** Uses wide variety of aquatic habitats including mangroves, marshes, beaches, tidal flats, and rocky shorelines. Less common inland on larger rivers and lakes. More closely associated with coastal or saltwater habitats than Black-crowned Night-Heron. Mainly nocturnal. Solitary when foraging. Roosts in small groups in dense foliage. **VOICE** Usually quiet. When disturbed or in flight, gives (1) a low-pitched, very coarse *rehk* or *ruk*.

Boat-billed Heron *Cochlearius cochlearius* 50 cm

MX to SA. Uncommon and local resident in lowlands. Uncommon to rare and local in SV (619). **ID** Short-necked, night-heronlike structure with *very broad bill* and *large eyes*. Long black plumes extend from crown and often held flat against hindneck. *Upperparts mostly uniform gray*. Sides of head, neck, and chest variably whitish to cinnamon. Belly rufous. Gular pouch usually yellow-green but becomes black during breeding season. In flight seen from below, all forms show black flanks and wing linings. Imm brownish and lacks ad's crest. Compare with Black-crowned Night-Heron. **GV** Birds from both Pacific and Caribbean slope in north (GT and BZ) are paler than widespread CA form. Birds from far southeast PA (Río Jaqué, Darién) are also pale above, and have white face, foreneck, and breast. **HABITS** Mangroves, freshwater swamps, and riparian woodland. Shy, retiring, and strictly nocturnal. Roosts by day in groups in dense foliage. Often found on branches overhanging water. **VOICE** Calls include (1) a low-pitched, laughlike *bwa-ha-ha-ha* and (2) low-pitched, ducklike *quack*.

breeding ad

juv

nonbreeding ad

Black-crowned Night-Heron

juv

ad

Yellow-crowned Night-Heron

north CA ad

widespread ad

Boat-billed Heron

imm

east PA ad

IBISES Threskiornithidae

Wading birds with long, curved bill. These species are found mainly in marshes and mangroves, but Green Ibis prefers forested river margins. Glossy and White-faced ibises are closely similar at all ages and present some identification problems. Observers should note details of eye color and head pattern. White Ibis is the most common and widespread.

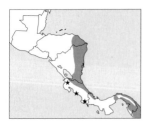

Green Ibis *Mesembrinibis cayennensis*   56 cm

CA and SA. Uncommon resident in lowlands (mainly near SL, locally to 1200 m). Poorly known in HN (Gracias a Dios, 401) and NI (RAAN, Río San Juan, 662, 413). Vagrant to Pacific lowlands of CR (Guanacaste, Puntarenas, 341, 346). **ID** Short neck and short grayish legs. Mostly *dark bronzy green* with inconspicuous *short, bushy crest on hindneck*. Superficially similar *Plegadis* ibises have more slender bill and no crest, and ads have chestnut sheen visible in good light. Also note different habits. **HABITS** Forested riverbanks, swampy or flooded woodland and savannas. Mainly nocturnal. Solitary or in pairs. Reclusive, but sometimes forages in open on gravel bars or riverbanks. May perch in bare trees at dusk. Probes in mud and among rocks. Flies with stiff, rapid wingbeats. **VOICE** Vocalizes mainly at dawn and dusk. Call (1) a long, accelerating series of loud, croaking cries *kro, kro, kro, kro . . .* or *koro, koro, koro, koro . . .*

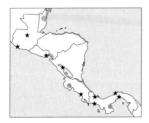

Glossy Ibis *Plegadis falcinellus*   56 cm

Cosmopolitan. Uncommon and local breeding resident in CR (Guanacaste, 600) and PA (Herrera, 650, 42, 48). Rare transient and winter visitor (Sep to May) elsewhere. **ID** Long, decurved bill. Breeding ad mostly chestnut with bronzy green and purplish iridescence (may appear blackish). Nonbreeding ad duller with fine whitish streaking on head and breast. *Eyes brown.* Ad's bare gray facial skin edged with pale blue (pale area never extends behind eye). Juv resembles nonbreeding ad but is duller and grayer (may appear plain brownish). Compare with White-faced Ibis. Green Ibis has shorter neck and legs, slight bushy crest, and is greener on neck. Also note different habits. **HABITS** Marshes, borders of ponds and lakes, flooded agricultural fields, and riverbanks. Wades in shallow, muddy water. Gregarious and typically forms small flocks when foraging or roosting. **VOICE** Usually quiet.

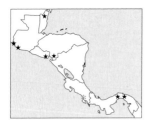

White-faced Ibis *Plegadis chihi*   56 cm

Breeds in NA and disjunctly in SA. One record from BZ (Belize, 346). Uncommon to rare transient and winter resident in Pacific GT and SV. One old record from CR (Puntarenas, 600). Recently first recorded in PA (Colón, 346). **ID** Long, decurved bill. Breeding ad mostly chestnut with bronzy green and purplish iridescence visible in good light (appears blackish in poor light). Nonbreeding ad duller with fine whitish streaking on head and breast. *Eyes red.* Closely resembles Glossy Ibis but breeding ad has *bare red or pink facial skin* and *lores bordered with white (extending behind eye)*. Nonbreeding ad has dull red facial skin and lacks white border. Juv (unlikely in region) very similar to juv Glossy Ibis and probably not separable in field. **HABITS** Marshes, borders of ponds and lakes, flooded agricultural lands, and riverbanks. Like Glossy Ibis. May form small flocks or may associate with Glossy Ibis. **VOICE** Usually quiet.

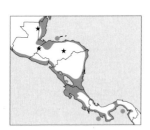

White Ibis *Eudocimus albus*   60 cm

NA to SA. Locally fairly common breeding resident in lowlands and foothills (to 500, locally to 1000 m). Some populations may undertake seasonal or local movements. Also BZ Cays (96), Bay Islands (318) and islands off Pacific PA. **ID** Long, decurved *red bill* and *bare red facial skin*. Ad mostly plain white with *red legs*. In flight, note *black wingtips*. Imm mostly grayish-brown somewhat streaked with white and has contrasting *white rump* and belly. *Plegadis* ibises and Green Ibis have dark rump. **HABITS** Freshwater marshes, mangroves, tidal flats, borders of ponds and lakes, riverbanks, and flooded agricultural lands. Forages by wading in shallow, muddy water. Gregarious. May form large roosts. Commutes in flocks between foraging and roosting areas. **VOICE** Usually quiet. Sometimes gives (1) a nasal *urnk*.

15%

Green Ibis

Green Ibises perched in tree at dusk.

Glossy Ibis

nonbreeding ad

breeding ad

White-faced Ibis

nonbreeding ad

breeding ad

White Ibis

imm

ad

SPOONBILL Threskiornithidae

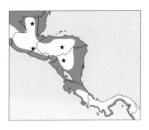

Roseate Spoonbill *Platalea ajaja* 76 cm
South USA to SA. Uncommon and local resident. Mainly in coastal lowlands.
ID Fairly large. *Long, spatulate bill.* Ad has bare grayish head and white neck. *Mostly pink.* Bar on wing coverts red. Tail buffy orange. Imm has mostly feathered head and is mostly whitish. **HABITS** Mangroves, lagoons, mudflats, and marshes. Forages by swinging bill from side to side as it wades slowly in shallow water and mud. Somewhat gregarious and often in small groups. Joins mixed associations of large wading birds at favored foraging and roosting sites. **VOICE** Usually silent.

FLAMINGO Phoenicopteridae

American Flamingo *Phoenicopterus ruber* 100 cm
Pantropical. Nearest breeding population in north Yucatán, MX. Very rare and irregular visitor to BZ (Corozal, Toledo, 343, 250) and HN (Cortes, Atlántida, Gracias a Dios, 442, 263). **ID**. Very large with distinctive structure. Long, slender neck and very long legs. Note *very deep, decurved bill* with black tip. Ad's plumage and legs *near-uniform pink with black remiges.* Juv mostly gray. **HABITS** Salt lagoons, mudflats, mangroves, and estuaries. Forages by wading in shallow, muddy water. **VOICE** Usually quiet.

JABIRU AND STORK Ciconiidae

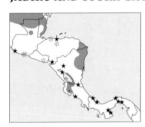

Jabiru *Jabiru mycteria* 135 cm
South MX to SA. Rare and local resident in lowlands. Breeding confined mainly to north BZ (Orange Walk, Belize, 343, 73), GT (Petén, 227), and Caribbean savannas of east HN (Gracias a Dios) and adjacent NI (RAAN, 258). Rare and local in CR (Guanacaste, Limón, 574, 600, 346, 437) and NI (Chontales, Río San Juan, 327, 413). Wanders widely. Vagrants reported from PA (Bocas del Toro, Coclé, Herrera, Panamá, Colón, 657, 512, 41, 42) and historically from SV (San Miguel, 183). Recently reported from Pacific HN (Choluteca, 336, 346) where status uncertain. Very rare in Pacific GT where known mainly from historical records (Santa Rosa, Escuintla, 539, 165, 608).
ID *Very large* with *very heavy, slightly upturned bill.* Ad has entirely white plumage and *bare blackish head and neck.* Note bare red skin on lower neck. Imm somewhat browner. Wood Stork smaller with black flight feathers. Also note different bill shape.
HABITS Freshwater marshes, lake margins, savannas, and flooded or recently plowed agricultural lands. Usually solitary or in pairs. Often soars, sometimes spiraling to great heights on thermals. Joins concentrations of herons and other wading birds at favored foraging sites during dry season. May follow farm machinery or walk in advance of grassfires. **VOICE** Usually silent.

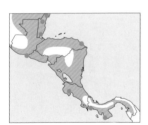

Wood Stork *Mycteria americana* 95 cm
South USA to SA. Uncommon to locally fairly common in lowlands. Considered resident, but wanders widely and may undertake seasonal movements. **ID** Very large with *heavy, decurved bill.* Ad mostly white with bare dusky head and upper neck and *black tail and flight feathers.* Juv has mostly feathered neck and dull yellow bill. White Ibis is much smaller, and has red bill and facial area and black restricted to wingtips. Soaring birds may suggest King Vulture. Note different structure. **HABITS** Freshwater marshes and swamps, mangroves, estuaries, flooded or plowed agricultural fields. Gregarious. Joins mixed associations of large wading birds at favored foraging and roosting sites. Often soars. **VOICE** Usually silent away from nest.

Roseate Spoonbill

imm

ad

American Flamingo

Wood Stork

Jabiru

ad

ad

juv

VULTURES Cathartidae

Black and Turkey vultures are common in most of the region. Lesser Yellow-headed and King vultures are much less common and have narrower ecological associations. Large carcasses may attract assemblages that include three or four vulture species.

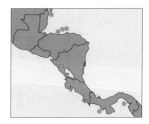

Turkey Vulture *Cathartes aura* 65–70 cm

NA to SA. Nearctic and resident birds occur. Common to locally abundant breeder in lowlands and foothills. Transients may be briefly or locally abundant (85, 86). Also BZ Cays, Bay Islands and islands off Pacific PA. **ID** Uniform brownish-black plumage. Ad has *bare, mostly red head and neck*. Ad's legs pink. Soars with *long wings held above horizontal*. From below, black underwing coverts contrast with gray remiges. On upperwing, shows brownish shafts on primaries. Imm has dull blackish head and neck. Black Vulture has shorter tail, broader wings, and white on primaries. Lesser Yellow-headed Vulture is smaller, has mostly yellow head, and usually shows whitish shafts on primaries. Imm King Vulture shows at least some white below except when very young. Zone-tailed Hawk smaller with feathered head and white bands on tail. **GV** Birds from breeding population in PA have whitish nape and are blacker overall. **HABITS** Uses a wide variety of terrestrial habitats. Most numerous in agricultural and urban areas. Flaps slowly and loosely during brief powered flight. Soars for long periods, often circling to great heights. Transients may associate loosely with Broad-winged and Swainson's hawks to form large mixed groups along favored migration routes. **VOICE** Usually silent.

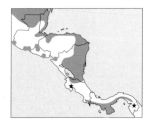

Lesser Yellow-headed Vulture *Cathartes burrovianus* 58 cm

South MX to SA. Uncommon to locally fairly common resident in lowlands. Most numerous in north Caribbean. Poorly known in north GT (Petén, 78). Rare and local in north Pacific slope (574, 600, 341, 182, 419, 346) and in east PA (Darién, 346). **ID** Smaller than Turkey Vulture. Ad uniform dull black (darker and less brownish than Turkey Vulture). *Bare head and neck multicolored with mostly yellow sides.* Legs gray. In flight, shows *whitish shafts of primaries* on upperwing surface. Imm has dusky head and whitish collar. Turkey Vulture is larger and paler with browner plumage. At close range note different head and leg color. **HABITS** Savannas and marshes. Occasionally found foraging over flooded agricultural fields. Glides low with tilting or weaving flight style. Usually solitary. May perch on low branch or fence post. Typically flies lower than Turkey Vulture. **VOICE** Usually silent.

Black Vulture *Coragyps atratus* 63 cm

USA to SA. Very common to locally abundant breeding resident. Nearctic birds perhaps occur as transients and winter residents. Also BZ Cays, Bay Islands, and islands off Pacific PA. **ID** In flight, shows *short tail* and broad wings held flat. Mostly dull black with *bare black head and neck*. In flight, note broad whitish patch on underside of primaries. Ad Turkey Vulture has red (not black) head and lacks pale wing patch. **HABITS** Uses a wide variety of mainly nonforest terrestrial habitats. Particularly abundant around human settlements and agricultural lands of all kinds. Also partial to lowland riverbanks and estuaries. Forms large concentrations at favored foraging sites. Holds wings level while soaring. Flaps rapidly during brief powered flight. **VOICE** Usually silent.

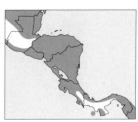

King Vulture *Sarcoramphus papa* 76 cm

South MX to SA. Locally fairly common resident in forested lowlands and foothills (to 1200 m). Now uncommon to rare and local in north Pacific slope in GT (Sacatepéquez, Suchitepéquez, Escuintla, 182) and SV (Santa Ana, Morazán, 364, 346) where formerly more widespread (413, 183, 279). Also Isla Coiba (Veraguas, 653). **ID** Very large. In flight, shows *long, broad wings* held flat and *short tail*. Ad mostly *creamy white with mostly black wings and tail*. At close range note ad's white eyes and bare head with red or yellow fleshy wattle at base of bill. Subad has white underparts and dark mantle and wings. Imm mostly blackish-brown and gradually attains white plumage over several years. Compare soaring ad with Wood Stork and American White Pelican. **HABITS** Semihumid to humid broadleaf forest and adjacent second growth, plantations, and agricultural areas. Most often seen while soaring, often very high overhead. May gather in groups at large carcasses. **VOICE** Usually silent.

Turkey Vulture

widespread
ad

PA
ad

ad

juv

**Lesser Yellow-headed
Vulture**

ad

ad

Black Vulture

ad

juv

ad

juv

King Vulture

juv

ad

ad

OSPREY Pandionidae

Osprey is a highly distinctive fish-eating raptor that winters widely in the region.

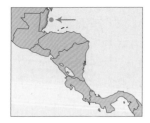

Osprey *Pandion haliaetus*   58 cm

Cosmopolitan. Nearctic birds winter MX and WI to SA. Fairly common transient and winter resident (Sep to Apr). Widespread but most passage is on coasts. Uncommon nonbreeding summer resident. Uncommon and local breeding resident on BZ coast and BZ Cays (529, 343). **ID** Slender and long-legged. In flight, shows long, narrow wings with "crooked" or bent shape. Underside of wing mostly whitish with *black carpal mark*. Mostly dark brown above and white below with white crown. Note *dark eye stripe*. Imm (not shown) more extensively edged with white above and speckled with brown below. **GV** Birds from breeding population in BZ have extensively white head, neck, and underparts. **HABITS** Vicinity of large bodies of water including lakes, lagoons, marshes, rivers, and seacoasts. Transients can occur overhead in a wide variety of habitats. Soars frequently, often high. Often takes high, exposed perch. Hunts fish by hovering briefly over water, then plunging abruptly below the surface to seize prey. Solitary away from nest. **VOICE** Call (1) a loud, slightly hoarse whistle *cleeeeeyp*. Sometimes repeated in short series.

KITES Accipitridae

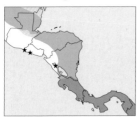

Swallow-tailed Kite *Elanoides forficatus*   60 cm

NA to SA. Uncommon and local breeding visitor (Jan to Sep) in foothills and lowlands (to 1800 m). Nearctic breeding birds also occur. Passage of Nearctic transients mainly on Caribbean slope. Rare on north Pacific slope in SV (Ahuachapán, La Libertad, 346). **ID** Slender with *very long, deeply forked tail* and long, pointed wings. *Head, neck and underparts white*. Back, wings, and tail black, glossed with green or violet on mantle and wing coverts. **HABITS** Canopy of broadleaf or mixed forest, pine savanna and adjacent open areas. Feeds on wing. Often in groups that circle slowly over forest canopy. Rarely seen perched. **VOICE** Usually quiet. Calls (1) a variable, shrill *kwee-kwee-kwee-kwee* and (2) rapid, slightly hoarse *ewit-ewit-ewit-ewit-ewit*. Often repeated in accelerating series. Compare with White-collared Swift.

White-tailed Kite *Elanus leucurus*   41 cm

NA to SA. Locally fairly common resident in lowlands and foothills (to 1500 m). Recent invader from SA. First recorded in CA during 1950s (213). First reported in PA in 1967 (659), in CR in 1965 (570, 574, 666), in SV in 1963 (423, 618), and in NI in 1961 (97). Also Isla Útila in Bay Islands (317). **ID** Slender with long, pointed wings and square *white tail*. Wingtips extend to tail tip when perched. Ad mostly white with gray mantle and wings and *black wing coverts*. Underwing mostly white with black carpal mark. At close range note red eyes and dark lores. Imm mostly brownish above with white scaling on tertials and streaking on crown. *Ictinia* kites are much darker and have different tail pattern and habits. **HABITS** Savannas, agricultural fields, pastures, and marshes. Flies with deep, graceful wing strokes. Often hovers while foraging with body held at steep angle. Does not soar. Perches for long periods on open branch or utility pole. Solitary or in pairs. **VOICE** Usually quiet. Call (1) a series of short, high-pitched *keep* or *wreep* cries sometimes combined with low-pitched, rasping squeal as *wreep-wreep-wreeep raaaaaah*.

BZ

widespread

Osprey

19

Swallow-tailed Kite

imm

ad

Adult White-tailed Kite hovering.

White-tailed Kite

KITES Accipitridae

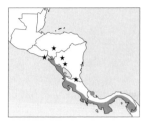

Pearl Kite *Gampsonyx swainsonii* 23 cm
CA to SA. Uncommon and local resident in Pacific slope lowlands and foothills (rarely or locally as high as 1300 m) of NI (428), CR, and PA (502). Perhaps expanding. Recently confirmed breeding in CR where first reported in 1996 and recently found on Caribbean slope (Puntarenas, Alajuela, 546). Recently reported from SV (La Unión, 346, 632) and HN (Choluteca, Valle, Francisco Morazán, 346, 632). **ID** *Very small* with falconlike, pointed wings. Legs and feet yellow. Ad male mostly slaty black above and white below. In flight, shows variably rufous flanks and axillars and whitish underwing. Note *white collar*, narrow dark mask, and buff forecrown and auriculars. Imm has rufous spotting on crown and scaling on mantle. Compare with larger White-tailed Kite and with American Kestrel. **HABITS** Open savannas, agricultural fields, pastures, and marshes. Perches in the open on utility wire or bare branch. May hover briefly while hunting. Solitary or in pairs. **VOICE** Usually quiet. Calls (1) a rapid *cheedit-cheedit-cheedit-cheedit . . .* and (2) simpler *tew tew tew tew . . .*

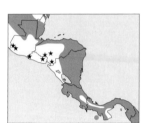

Double-toothed Kite *Harpagus bidentatus* 32 cm
South MX to SA. Uncommon resident in lowlands and foothills (to 1200 m). Perhaps undertakes seasonal movements in some regions. Very rare in north Pacific where perhaps a seasonal visitor (Nov to Mar). Also Isla Coiba (Veraguas, 657). **ID** Small bill, large red eyes, and rounded crown. Note white throat with *dark central stripe*. Ad has mostly rufous breast and whitish lower underparts barred with rufous. In flight, pale underwing coverts contrast with darker body and barred flight feathers. White crissum conspicuous in flight, sometimes protruding laterally. Tail often held closed while soaring. Imm brown above and mostly creamy whitish below, variably (usually heavily) streaked and spotted with dusky brown on breast and flanks. Compare with *Accipiter* hawks. Note different structure and throat pattern. Also compare with Broad-winged and Roadside hawks. **HABITS** Midstory to canopy and edge of broadleaf forest, second growth, and plantations. Solitary or in pairs. Often stolid. Perches in open. Soars during late morning, typically circling low over forest canopy, sometimes higher. Follows monkeys to seize prey disturbed by their passage. **VOICE** Call (1) a weak, high-pitched, thin *weeoo-weest* or *weeoo-wheep*.

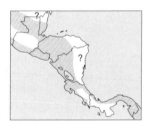

Mississippi Kite *Ictinia mississippiensis* female 36, male 33 cm
Breeds Nearctic. Winters south SA. Uncommon to briefly or locally common transient (Mar to Apr and Sep to Oct). Passage mainly on Pacific slope in north and on Caribbean in CR and west PA. Reported from north Caribbean in fall (345, 346). **ID** Slender with *long, pointed wings*. Legs yellow. Ad plain gray becoming *pale on head* and darker on mantle. Note *plain black tail* and pale secondaries (usually visible in folded wing and forming pale trailing edge in flight). Imm *streaked with rufous below*. Often shows white spots on scapulars and wing coverts. Resembles Plumbeous Kite. Note ad's different tail and wing pattern. Imm has different underparts. **HABITS** Transients can occur overhead in wide variety of terrestrial habitats. Aerial. Often soars. Migrants form large groups and may join mixed concentrations of transient raptors. Rarely seen perched. **VOICE** Usually quiet.

Plumbeous Kite *Ictinia plumbea* female 35, male 32 cm
MX to SA. Fairly common breeding visitor in lowlands and foothills (mainly Feb to Sep, 212, 557). Winters SA. Also Bay Islands (538, 94). Status poorly known. **ID** Slender with *long, pointed wings*. Legs orange. Ad mostly gray becoming darker on mantle. *Tail black with two white bands*. Note *rufous on primaries*. Imm blackish above with narrow pale edging. Imm's underparts *streaked with brown*. Compare with rufous streaking on imm Mississippi Kite. Compare ad with ad Mississippi Kite. Note different tail pattern. **HABITS** Canopy and edge of semihumid to humid broadleaf forest, plantations, and second growth. Transients can occur overhead in a wide variety of terrestrial habitats. Aerial. Soars or circles low over forest canopy in late morning. Forms small groups. May associate with Swallow-tailed Kites. Perches prominently on high, exposed snag. **VOICE** Usually silent. Calls (1) a shrill, thin, whistle *sheeeeeeeuu* that drops steeply in pitch and (2) a breathy phrase that also drops in pitch *sheee-chuuuu*.

20

Pearl Kite

Double-toothed Kite

imm

imm

ad

ad

imm

imm

ad

Mississippi Kite

imm

ad

imm

ad

ad

Plumbeous Kite

imm

KITES AND HARRIERS Accipitridae

Snail Kite is found very locally in marshes, where it can be common. Slender-billed Kite is a mainly South American species known in the region from a handful of records in eastern Panama. Harriers are found in open areas, where they often hunt by flying low over the ground with tilting flight. Northern Harrier is a scarce Nearctic migrant. Long-winged Harrier is a rare visitor from South America.

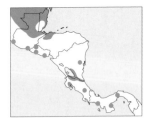

Snail Kite *Rostrhamus sociabilis*   41–45 cm
NA to SA. Locally common resident in lowlands and foothills (mainly near SL, locally to 700 m) of north BZ (Orange Walk, Belize, 529, 343), Pacific GT (Santa Rosa, San Marcos, Jutiapa, Retalhuleu, 182, 229, 645) and SV (Ahuachapán, Cuscatlán, Chalatenango, San Miguel, 301), Caribbean foothills of HN at Lake Yojoa (Cortés, 483, 442), and Tempisque Basin of Pacific CR (Guanacaste, 281, 600). Perhaps expanding in PA (Panamá, Colón, Chiriquí, Herrera, 38, 42). **ID** *White rump, crissum, and base of tail.* Note *fine, sharply hooked bill* and orange bare facial skin. Ad male mostly plain slate-gray. Ad female brownish-black above. Female's underparts whitish-buff, *heavily streaked and mottled with brown.* Imm browner above with less heavily streaked underparts. Slender-billed Kite allopatric. **HABITS** Freshwater marshes and swamps, lagoon and lake margins. Flies low over water or flooded vegetation with long, tilting glides and slow, loose wingbeats. Gregarious. Perches in the open on bare snag, shrub, or utility wire. Feeds on snails. **VOICE** Usually quiet. Calls (1) a rapid series of nasal cries that rise in pitch *whi-i-i-i-i-i-i-i*, (2) low-pitched, nasal, rasping *ahrrrr* or *sheerrrrr*, and (3) very low-pitched, nasal cackle *wah-ah-ah-ah-ah*.

Slender-billed Kite *Helicolestes hamatus*   38 cm
CA and SA. Rare and local in Pacific lowlands of east PA (Darién, 657, 346). Perhaps resident. **ID** *Short tail* barely extends beyond wings in flight. Note sharply hooked bill. Ad uniform dark gray with *plain black tail.* Eyes yellow. Bare facial skin; cere and legs orange. Imm similar but has two or three narrow white bands on tail and whitish tail tip. Snail Kite (allopatric) has longer tail and wings and shows obvious white area at base of tail in all plumages. Compare with dark morph Hook-billed Kite. **HABITS** Swamp forest, river margins, and forested lagoons. Pairs or small groups perch at varying heights in dense foliage near water. Like Snail Kite feeds mainly on snails. May soar low over forest canopy. **VOICE** Call (1) a buzzy, nasal *wheeeaaaaaaaah* that rises then falls in pitch. Compare with call of Snail Kite.

Northern Harrier *Circus hudsonius*   female 50, male 44 cm
Breeds Holarctic. Nearctic birds winter mainly NA and MX. Uncommon to rare and irregular transient and winter resident (mainly Oct to Apr). **ID** Slender with long wings and tail. Wings often held above horizontal in gliding flight. *Rump white.* Note dark trailing edge on secondaries. Ad male (rare in region) mostly pale gray. Male has mostly white underwing contrasting with black tips of primaries. Ad female mostly dark brown above with brown and white streaked underparts. Imm near-uniform tawny rufous below with less streaking on underparts. Compare female and imm with female and imm Snail Kite. Note different structure and habits. **HABITS** Open grassy areas including agricultural lands, pastures, savannas, beaches, and marshes. Flies low while foraging, often tilting, weaving, and changing direction abruptly. Sometimes soars on level wings. Rarely seen perched (usually on ground in tall grass). Solitary. **VOICE** Usually silent.

Long-winged Harrier *Circus buffoni*   female 55, male 48 cm
SA. Vagrant (Jan to Aug) to central and east PA (Panamá, Darién, 512, 42, 43, 346). **ID** Large with long wings and long tail. Highly variable plumage includes light and dark morphs. Light morph ad has mostly white underparts with *dark breast-band.* Upperparts dark with white rump. Note *whitish forehead, supercilium, and face* and *gray on upperwing surface* and contrasting gray flight feathers with black barring. Dark morph ad mostly black on head, body, and wing coverts. Variable imm resembles light morph ad female but is streaked below and may show dark barring on whitish rump. Some imms have rufous lower underparts including tibials. Compare with Northern Harrier (especially imm). Note different head and wing pattern. **HABITS** Marshes, flooded agricultural fields, scrub, and grasslands. Flies with wings raised in dihedral. May hover briefly. Solitary. **VOICE** Usually silent.

imm

ad ♀

♂

ad ♂

imm

Snail Kite

imm

ad

ad

Slender-billed Kite

ad ♀

ad ♂

imm

Northern Harrier

ad ♀

imm

♂

black morph ad

♀

Long-winged Harrier

♂

KITES AND CRANE HAWK Accipitridae

Uncommon, mainly forest-inhabiting raptors. Hook-billed and Gray-headed kites have highly variable immature and adult plumages including dark and light morphs. All have distinctive vocalizations, and voice can be helpful in locating these scarce birds. Structure and habits are often useful for identification.

Gray-headed Kite *Leptodon cayanensis* 48 cm

South MX to SA. Uncommon resident in lowlands and foothills (to 1500, mainly below 750 m). Rare in north Pacific (182, 346, 413). **ID** Long, broad tail. In flight, note broad, rounded, *black-and-white barred wings* and plain pale underparts. Ad has *pale gray head*, *dark gray upperparts*, and white underparts. Note pale gray lores and bare facial skin. Variable imm plumage with several morphs. All have yellow cere and legs. Note *pale lores*. In pale morph imm (most common) has most of head, neck, and underparts white with brown patch on crown and black eye stripe. Imm's underwing coverts white (not black as in ad) and primaries barred with dusky. Scarce dark morph imm is mostly plain, dusky brown above (including sides of head and neck) and buffy whitish below, variably (usually heavily) streaked with dusky brown. In some the chest is all dark. Some imms have rufous auriculars and neck. Pale morph imm may suggest Black-and-white Hawk-Eagle but note kite's smaller size and yellow lores. Compare with imms of Hook-billed Kite and Ornate Hawk-Eagle. **HABITS** Subcanopy to canopy and edge of semihumid to humid broadleaf forest, tall second growth, and adjacent clearings and plantations. Unobtrusive. Typically perches inside subcanopy. May take exposed perch in early morning. Soars in late morning with wings bowed slightly downward. **VOICE** Call (1) an accelerating series of slightly wooden or nasal cries *kek kek kek kek . . .* or *eheheheheheh . . .* and (2) loud, nasal, catlike *eeeeeh-ooow* that rises rapidly then suddenly drops in pitch.

Hook-billed Kite *Chondrohierax uncinatus* 44 cm

South USA and Cuba to SA. Uncommon and local in lowlands and foothills (to 2300, mainly below 500 m). Rare in north Pacific (279, 341, 346). Considered resident but may undertake local movements (87, 346, 343, 660). Also Pearl Islands (Panamá, 611). **ID** In flight, shows *broad, rounded wings constricted at base* (more pronounced than in *Spizaetus* hawk-eagles). Variably *heavy and strongly hooked bill*. Note yellow cere, green facial skin, and orange spot in front of *whitish eye*. Legs yellow or orange. Plumage variable. Light morph ad male usually slaty gray above and lightly barred with white or buff on underparts. Uppertail coverts whitish. Tail dark gray with two whitish bands and narrow whitish tip. Ad female variably dark brown to slaty gray above with rufous collar. Underparts coarsely barred with rufous and white. Imm dark brown above and whitish below with whitish collar. Dark morph ad may suggest various dark-plumaged hawks and kites. Compare imm to pale morph imm Gray-headed Kite, imm Bicolored Hawk, and Collared Forest-Falcon. Also compare dark morph with larger Black Hawk-Eagle. **HABITS** Midstory to canopy and edge of semihumid to humid broadleaf forest. Solitary or in pairs. Transients may form small groups. Often sluggish and unsuspicious. Soars briefly in late morning, usually circling low over forest canopy. **VOICE** Call (1) a rapid, slightly nasal, laughlike series that rises steeply then gradually drops in pitch *wiiiiiiiiieeeeeeee-uh.*

Crane Hawk *Geranospiza caerulescens* 43–52 cm

MX to SA. Uncommon and local resident in lowlands and foothills (to 500, locally to 1500 m in north). **ID** Slender, with small head, long wings, and long tail. Note *long, orange-red legs*. Eyes red. Cere grayish. Ad mostly *plain slaty black* in north. Ad's underparts may be variably barred with fine white markings on lower belly, tibials, and crissum. Tail black with two white bands. In flight, note *white band at base of primaries*. Holds wings slightly bowed. Imm slightly browner with whitish streaking on auriculars and throat and buff mottling or barring on lower underparts. Compare with *Buteogallus* black hawks and Zone-tailed Hawk. Note different structure, leg color, and habits. **GV** Birds from east PA are paler gray. **HABITS** Upper midstory to canopy and edge of semihumid to humid broadleaf forest, second growth, swamps, mangroves, and marshes. Most common in gallery forest in arid or semihumid regions. When foraging may hop and flutter actively along large branches. Occasionally hangs upside down. Probes with long legs in epiphytes or tree cavities to extract prey. Also walks on ground and may fly low over open areas. Occasionally soars in late morning. Usually solitary. **VOICE** Usually quiet. Call (1) a shrill *kweeeuur* or *weeee-urr* that drops in pitch. Compare with longer, lower-pitched call of Roadside Hawk. Also (2) a long, steady series of low-pitched phrases *oo-oow oo-oow oo-oow oo-oow . . .*

imm

imm

imm

imm

ad

ad

imm

Gray-headed Kite

imm

ad ♀

ad ♂

black
morph

Hook-billed Kite

♀

widespread ad

Crane Hawk

PA
ad

PA
imm

widespread imm

HAWKS Accipitridae

Slender, long-tailed, and short-winged hawks. Two species are scarce winter visitors or transients. Observers should note that structure and underparts pattern are helpful in separating Sharp-shinned and Cooper's hawks. Like many other hawks, *Accipiters* are sexually dimorphic in size, with females larger than males.

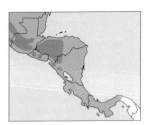

Sharp-shinned Hawk[10] *Accipiter striatus*   female 33, male 28 cm
Nearctic breeding birds winter NA to CA. Uncommon to rare transient and winter resident (Oct to Apr). Mainly in foothills and highlands. CA breeding birds are confined to north highlands (mainly above 700 m) where uncommon. **ID** Small with slender tarsi. In flight, shows long, *square tail* and small head (not projecting far forward from wing). Ad dark bluish-gray above, becoming slightly darker on crown. Underparts barred with rufous and white (or plain white in CA breeding birds). Imm mostly dusky brown above and often shows whitish spotting on scapulars. Underparts whitish heavily streaked with rufous-brown. Compare with very similar Cooper's Hawk. Note rounded shape of individual streaks on imm Sharp-shinned Hawk (compare with narrower streaks on imm Cooper's Hawk). Note different structure in ad. **GV** Ad from breeding population in north CA is plain white below. Imm has faint, fine, dark streaking below. **HABITS** Open woodland, forest edge, and clearings with scattered trees. CA breeders use broadleaf (cloud) forest, pine-oak woodland and adjacent plantations, and second growth. Inconspicuous and usually perches inside foliage. Makes rapid, short flights, weaving through dense vegetation. Often soars. Solitary. **VOICE** Transients and wintering birds usually silent. Call of breeding form (1) a rapid *eey, yip-yip-iyip-yip-yip . . .*

Cooper's Hawk *Accipiter cooperii*   female 46, male 42 cm
Breeds Nearctic. Winters NA to CA. Uncommon transient and winter visitor in north (mainly Oct to Apr). Rare in south. **ID** Very similar to smaller Sharp-shinned Hawk but with slightly different structure. When perched note graduated tail and heavy tarsi. In flight, note longer, *rounded tail* and larger head projecting forward from wing. Ad often shows blackish crown contrasting with pale nape. Imm closely resembles imm Sharp-shinned Hawk but has finer, darker individual streaks on underparts and often has cinnamon wash on neck and auriculars. **HABITS** Open woodland, forest edge, and clearings with scattered trees. Transients may occur in a wide variety of habitats. May perch in open. Often soars. Solitary. **VOICE** Usually silent.

Sharp-shinned Hawk

CA breeder

imm
♀

ad
♂

ad

northern migrant

imm
♀

ad
♂

ad

imm

Cooper's Hawk

imm
♀

ad
♂

ad

imm

HAWKS Accipitridae

Resident *Accipiter* hawks. Bicolored Hawk, though rarely seen, is the most widespread. Immatures of Bicolored and Tiny hawks are variable and some plumages resemble *Micrastur* forest-falcons. Like many other hawks, these species are sexually dimorphic in size, with females larger than males.

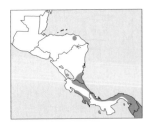

Tiny Hawk *Accipiter superciliosus*   female 26, male 22 cm
CA and SA. Rare resident in lowlands and foothills (to 1200 m). Poorly known in NI (RAAN, Río San Juan, 514, 413). Recently reported from east HN (Gracias a Dios). **ID** Very small. Eyes red (yellow in imm). Cere yellow. Legs and feet yellow to orange. Ad has *fine, dark barring on white underparts*. Slaty gray above. Tail blackish with gray bands. Imm variable. Brown morph imm dusky brown above and buff below barred with rufous brown. Tail dusky brown with grayish bands. Rufous morph rufous-brown above becoming darker on crown and with dusky barring on mantle. Underparts barred with buff and rufous. Tail brighter rufous with dusky bands. Compare with larger Sharp-shinned Hawk and Barred Forest-Falcon. **HABITS** Canopy and edge of humid broadleaf forest. Secretive but may take prominent perch on bare snag in early morning or late afternoon. Solitary. **VOICE** Usually quiet. Calls (1) a variable, long, rapid series *wheee-ee-ee-eee-ee-ee* . . . that accelerates slightly and falls slightly in pitch and (2) series of high-pitched, squeaky, passerine-like notes *cheet, cheet-cheet, cheet* . . . or *chut, chut, chut-chut* . . .

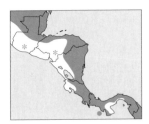

Bicolored Hawk *Accipiter bicolor*   female 44, male 38 cm
MX to SA. Uncommon to rare resident in lowlands and foothills (to 2000, mainly below 1000 m). Also Isla Coiba (Veraguas, 653). Historical records from Pacific GT (Escuintla, 539) and HN (Francisco Morazán, 539). **ID** Ad plain slaty gray above with blackish crown. *Underparts plain pale to medium gray* with *rufous tibials* (often concealed). Long, blackish tail with grayish bands. Variable imm has *buffy white to rufous collar*. Underparts variably buffy white to rufous with dusky sometimes darker or mottled with rufous. Compare imm with *Micrastur* forest-falcons. Note yellow eyes and different tail shape. Compare ad with Semiplumbeous Hawk. **HABITS** Midstory to subcanopy of broadleaf forest and woodland. Reclusive. May perch in open in early morning. Solitary. **VOICE** Usually quiet. Calls (1) a squealing *waaah* and (2) barking *keh keh keh keh* or *kra-kra-kra-kr-kr-kr-kr-ka*. Compare with call of Slaty-tailed Trogon.

Gray-bellied Hawk *Accipiter poliogaster*   female 46, male 40 cm
Mainly SA. Rare vagrant or visitor (Apr to Aug) to CR (Heredia, Alajuela, 346, 49) and PA (Panamá, Darién, 346). **ID** Large. Variable ad *mostly plain gray above* with *black crown* and variably light gray to white underparts. Cere, eyes, and legs yellow. Sides of ad's head variably black or gray and may have black malar. Imm has rufous neck and sides of head and barred underparts and thus closely resembles ad Ornate Hawk-Eagle. Compare ad with smaller Bicolored Hawk. Note different underparts. **HABITS** Midstory to canopy of humid broadleaf forest. Solitary. **VOICE** Usually quiet. Calls include (1) a short series of upslurred whistles *uh-wheet-uh-wheet-uh-wheet* . . .

rufous morph
imm
♀

brown morph
imm
♀

ad
♂

Tiny Hawk

pale morph
imm
♀

buff morph
imm
♀

ad
♂

Bicolored Hawk

Collared Forest-Falcon
for comparison
(text and map p.276)

white-bellied
morph
ad ♀

gray-bellied
morph
ad ♂

imm
♀

Gray-bellied Hawk

HAWKS Accipitridae

Forest-inhabiting raptors. White and Barred hawks soar for long periods and so are often conspicuous. Plumbeous and Semiplumbeous hawks are reclusive and do not soar or often fly above forest canopy. Voice is helpful in locating and identifying these.

Plumbeous Hawk *Cryptoleucopteryx plumbea*   female 35, male 32 cm
CA and SA. Uncommon to rare resident in humid forested lowlands and foothills (to 600 m) of central and east PA. **ID** Compact structure with short, broad, rounded wings. Ad *plain slaty gray above and below*. Note *orange legs, cere, and lores*. Eyes red. Tail mostly blackish with one white band. In flight, shows white underwing with blackish trailing edge and tips of primaries. Imm has whitish barring on tibials, underwing, and belly. Compare with other dark-plumaged hawks. Dark morph Hook-billed Kite has different bill shape, head pattern, and underwing pattern. Plumbeous Kite has gray cere and different structure. Also compare with Crane Hawk. **HABITS** Midstory to canopy of humid broadleaf forest. Usually perches inconspicuously in shaded forest interior. May vocalize from exposed perch in canopy in early morning. Rarely or never soars. **VOICE** Call (1) a long, piercing, downslurred *wheeeeeeeeeer* or *kiyeeeeeeeee* and (2) quavering, woodpecker-like *wh-i-i-i, wh-i-i-i, whi-i-i-i*.

Semiplumbeous Hawk *Leucopternis semiplumbeus*   33 cm
CA and SA. Uncommon resident in humid lowlands and foothills (to 800 m). Most common in CR and PA. Rare in east HN (Gracias a Dios, 401, 34) and north NI (RAAN, RAAS, 413, 548). **ID** Short, broad, rounded wings. Ad mostly plain gray above and *plain white below*. Note *orange legs, cere, and base of bill*. Tail blackish with single, prominent white band (a second, narrower band may be visible near base). Undersurface of wing mostly white. Imm has fine streaking on head and chest. Compare with light morph Short-tailed Hawk. Note different cere color, tail pattern, and habits. Slaty-backed Forest-Falcon has different tail pattern and cere color. **HABITS** Midstory to canopy of humid broadleaf forest and adjacent tall second growth. Perches quietly for long periods. Often stolid or unsuspicious. May take high, exposed perch in early morning or evening. Does not soar. Usually solitary. **VOICE** Call (1) a long, slightly upslurred *kiteeeeeeeeeeah* or *uhweeeeeet*. Sometimes doubled or given in short series. Compare with Broad-winged Hawk.

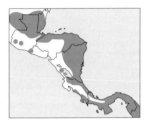

White Hawk *Pseudastur albicollis*   48 cm
South MX to SA. Uncommon to locally fairly common resident in lowlands and foothills (to 1200 m, occasionally or locally higher). Rare and local in Pacific GT (Escuintla, Suchitepéquez, 539), SV (Ahuachapán, 619, 366), and NI at Volcán Mombacho (Granada, 413). **ID** Broad, rounded wings and short tail (often spread while soaring). *Mostly white* with black markings on primaries and secondaries and broad black subterminal band on tail. Imm has more extensive black markings on wings and black postocular stripe. **GV** Ad from north CA (GT and BZ) has mostly white upperwing and narrower dark tail-band. **HABITS** Midstory to canopy and edge of semihumid to humid broadleaf forest. Most common along forested rivers. Soars frequently and for long periods in late morning. May perch fairly low at forest edge. Solitary or in pairs. **VOICE** Call (1) a flat, slightly hissing, semi-whistled or buzzy *sheeeeeeer* or *wheeeeeer*.

Barred Hawk *Morphnarchus princeps*   52 cm
CA and SA. Uncommon to rare resident in south foothills and highlands (450 to 2500 m). **ID** Large and bulky with *very broad, rounded wings* and *short tail*. Gray hood contrasts with fine gray-and-white barring on breast and belly. Underparts and undersurface of wings appear mostly pale gray on soaring birds, but note blackish-bordered wings. Cere and legs yellow. Imm (not shown) browner with fine whitish edging on wing coverts. Compare with smaller, paler Gray-lined Hawk. Note different structure, underparts pattern, and habits. **HABITS** Subcanopy to canopy of humid broadleaf forest. Solitary or in pairs. Usually seen soaring over forested ridges. Rarely seen perched. **VOICE** Call (1) a loud, scream *kee-yaaaar*. Sometimes repeated or (2) followed by series of *wheep* notes. Compare with calls of *Spizaetus* hawk-eagles.

Plumbeous Hawk

imm

ad

Semiplumbeous Hawk

ad

imm

White Hawk

imm

GT and BZ
ad

widespread
ad

GT and BZ
ad

widespread
ad

ad

Barred Hawk

ad

BLACK HAWKS AND SOLITARY EAGLE Accipitridae

The smaller *Buteogallus* black hawks are widespread and often common. Details of underparts and head pattern are useful in separating these. Solitary Eagle is a very rare and local resident in mountainous regions. Observers should be careful to eliminate the very similar and more common Great Black Hawk when identifying this scarce species. Observations of Solitary Eagle should be carefully documented.

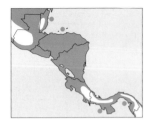

Common Black Hawk *Buteogallus anthracinus* 46–54 cm

South USA to SA. Fairly common resident in lowlands and foothills (mainly below 1800 m). Most common near coasts. Also BZ Cays (343), Bay Islands (442), Isla Coiba, and Pearl Islands (Veraguas, Panamá, 611, 470). **ID** Very broad wings, short tail, and long legs. Ad has yellow base of bill, facial skin, and legs. Ad mostly *plain black including tibials*, with single white tail-band. In flight from below, usually shows whitish on base of primaries. Some ads have flight feathers variably barred with gray or rufous. In all plumages shows dark uppertail coverts. Imm brown above and mostly buff below with brown streaking, and *broad dark malar*. Rare variant can be extremely pale. Compare with Great Black Hawk. In all plumages note Common's shorter legs, shorter tail, and dark uppertail coverts. Imm Great Black Hawk has different head pattern, structure, and voice. Also compare ad Common Black Hawk with other black-plumaged hawks, including Zone-tailed, Crane, and dark morph Short-tailed Hawk. Imm Common Black Hawk also resembles imm Gray Hawk. Note different tail pattern and structure and other details. **GV** Individually and geographically variable in CA. Some birds have extensively rufous wings. Very pale (leucistic) birds are occasionally seen. Birds from Pacific coast of CA are smaller. **HABITS** Broadleaf forest and woodland, second growth, mangroves, marshes, and lakeshores. Most common near water. Often sluggish and may allow close approach. Perches at all heights. Walks on ground or wades in shallow water. Frequently soars. Solitary or in pairs. **VOICE** Call (1) a series of loud, high-pitched, whistles *whi whi whi whi . . .* May rise and fall in pitch. May suggest Osprey. Very different from long scream of Great Black Hawk.

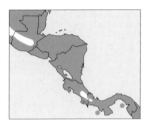

Great Black Hawk *Buteogallus urubitinga* 57 cm

MX to SA. Uncommon resident in lowlands and foothills (to 1200 m). Most common in north Caribbean. Rare in north Pacific and in south. **ID** Resembles Common Black Hawk but has longer legs and longer tail. Cere and legs yellow. *Facial skin ashy gray, and pale area does not extend under eye.* Note white uppertail coverts. Ad of widespread form mostly black with fine *white barring on tibials* and two white bands on tail (upper band narrow and often concealed). Imm brown above and mostly buff below with brown streaking. Compare imm with imm Common Black Hawk. Note typically paler head (lacking dark malar) and different structure. **GV** Birds from east PA have white base of tail and lack white barring on tibials. **HABITS** Semihumid to humid broadleaf and pine-oak forest, second growth woodland, plantations, agricultural areas, and savanna. Less tied to aquatic habitats than Common Black Hawk and more often inside forest. May forage on ground. Often soars. Solitary or in pairs. **VOICE** Calls (1) a long, slightly hoarse whistle or scream *oooooooo-leeeeeeer* that first rises then drops slightly in pitch and (2) rapid series of excited, high-pitched, piping or whistled cries *whi whi hi-i-i-i-i . . .* or *whi pi pi pi-pi-pi-pi-pi..* May accelerate into a roll or trill

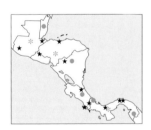

Solitary Eagle *Buteogallus solitarius* 70 cm

MX to SA. Very rare and local resident in foothills and highlands (mainly 500 to 2000 m). Confirmed breeding in BZ (Cayo, 146, 667, 347, 465). Records from GT (Suchitepéquez, Quetzaltenango, Alta Verapaz, Baja Verapaz, 539, 378, 221, 227, 346), SV (Chalatenango, Santa Ana, 346, 364), HN (Atlántida, Yoro, Francisco Morazán, 442), NI (Nueva Segovia, Matagalpa, RAAN, 412, 419, 626), CR (Alajuela, Heredia, Puntarenas, 674, 570, 600, 346), and PA (Bocas del Toro, Veraguas, Panamá, Darién, 657, 512, 48, 346). **ID** Very large and bulky. Note very broad wings and *very short tail*. In flight, tail barely extends beyond trailing edge of wing. When perched, *wingtips extend beyond tail.* Ad mostly grayish-black. Tail black with single white band. Imm near-uniform brown above and has *extensive, solid dark brown on breast and tibials.* Imm's tail gray *speckled* with dusky (*no distinct barring*). In flight from below, note imm's plain whitish undersurface of primaries. Compare with Great Black Hawk. Note different structure and imm's different underparts and tail pattern. Imm Great Black Hawk has banded tail, barred tibials, and lacks dark chest patches. **HABITS** Canopy of semihumid to humid forest and adjacent open areas. Usually seen soaring over steep mountain ridges. Solitary or in pairs. **VOICE** Calls, often given in flight, include (1) a rapid, hawk-eagle-like series of piping whistles that fall then rise in pitch *wheet-wheet-wheet-wheet . . .* and (2) a long, hoarse whistle that drops slightly in pitch.

13

Common Black Hawk

imm

ad

ad

imm

rufous ad

Great Black Hawk

imm

widespread ad

widespread ad

east PA ad

imm

Solitary Eagle

imm

ad

ad

imm

HAWKS Accipitridae

Uncommon raptors found very locally in open areas and wetlands.

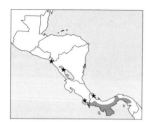

Savanna Hawk *Buteogallus meridionalis* 52 cm

CA and SA. Uncommon resident in Pacific lowlands of PA. Rare in Pacific east CR (Puntarenas, 346, 546). Vagrant to NI (Carazo, Chinandega, 346) and Caribbean west PA (Bocas del Toro, 206). **ID** Large with long, broad wings, short tail, and long neck. Note *long yellow legs*. Ad mostly pale cinnamon and rufous. In flight, shows rufous wings with black-tipped primaries. Imm brown above with rufous mottling on wings. Imm's head and underparts mostly white, mottled and streaked with brown. Tibials rufous. Black-collared Hawk has different tail and underparts. Compare imm with imms of Common and Great black hawks and with imm Harris's Hawk. **HABITS** Savannas, marshes, pastures, roadsides, and agricultural areas. Takes low perch or walks on ground. Attends grass fires and follows farm machinery. Often soars. Solitary or in pairs. **VOICE** Usually quiet. Calls (1) a shrill, slightly hoarse scream *keeeeeeeuu* that drops in pitch and (2) steady series of short, high-pitched notes *eet eet eet . . .* or *eep eep eep . . .*

Black-collared Hawk *Busarellus nigricollis* 48 cm

MX to SA. Uncommon to rare and local resident in lowlands and foothills (to 600 m). Perhaps most numerous in BZ. Rare and local in north Pacific GT (San Marcos, Santa Rosa, Escuintla, Sacatepéquez, 182) and SV (San Miguel, Usulután, Ahuachapán, 183), HN where historically reported from Lake Yojoa (Cortés, 442), and CR (Guanacaste, Puntarenas, Alajuela, 602). **ID** Large with *short tail*. Ad mostly *buffy whitish head* and *black patch on upper chest*. In flight, note rufous underwing coverts and black primaries. Imm duller and paler below with heavier streaking and barring below. Compare with imms of Great and Common black hawks. Note different head pattern. In PA compare imm with Savanna Hawk. **HABITS** Gallery forest, marshes, and margins of rivers and lakes, especially oxbow lakes with emergent or floating vegetation. Perches at medium height near water or on ground at muddy edges. Soars in late morning. Solitary or in pairs. **VOICE** Typical call (1) an abrupt, harsh, hoarse *breeeeyurr* or *weeeee-urr*. Also (2) a variety of very low-pitched, coarse growls *br-eehhhh* or *reh-hehe.*

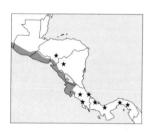

Harris's Hawk *Parabuteo unicinctus* female 56, male 52 cm

South USA to SA. Uncommon to rare and local resident in Pacific lowlands (to 200 m). Records from Pacific GT (Escuintla, 539, 346, 227), SV (La Paz, Usulután, San Miguel, Santa Ana, Ahuachapán, 183, 619), HN (Choluteca, 34), NI where mainly on Pacific slope but reaches Caribbean slope locally (Río San Juan, 413), and CR where mainly in west Pacific lowlands and confirmed breeding (Guanacaste, Puntarenas, Alajuela, 570, 574, 474, 600, 346). Nonbreeding visitor to PA (Chiriquí, Bocas del Toro, Panamá, 657, 512). **ID** Lanky with long tail and wings and long, dull-yellow legs. Ad mostly blackish-brown with *rufous wing coverts and tibials*. Note ad's *white rump* and white undertail coverts and white terminal band on tail. In flight from below, shows rufous underwing coverts and blackish remiges. Imm has upperparts paler and mottled. Underparts streaked with brown. Note *rufous wing coverts*. Imm's tail grayish with dusky barring. **HABITS** Savannas, pastures, and open near areas with scattered trees. Often near water or marshes in arid regions. Flies low with tilting glides. Occasionally soars. Takes low, open perch. May forage on ground. Sometimes in pairs or small groups. **VOICE** Call (1) a harsh, nasal scream *jaaahr* or *nyaaah.*

14

Savanna Hawk

imm

ad

ad

imm

Black-collared Hawk

imm

ad

ad

imm

Harris's Hawk

imm

ad

ad

imm

HAWKS Accipitridae

Small hawks with rounded wings. Adult plumages are fairly distinctive. Details of head and underparts pattern are useful in separating immature birds. Short-tailed Hawk is usually seen soaring. Roadside, Gray-lined, and Gray hawks soar less often and are usually found perched in the open at medium levels. Broad-winged Hawk can be briefly abundant in migration as large numbers pass through the region in spectacular flights.

Short-tailed Hawk *Buteo brachyurus*   female 44, male 39 cm
South USA to SA. Uncommon resident in lowlands and foothills (to 2000 m). **ID** Pointed wings. Light morph ad has *blackish-brown hood* and upperparts. Throat and *underparts white*. Dark morph ad uniform blackish with white forehead. In flight, light morph mostly whitish below with faint grayish barring on black-tipped primaries. Tail whitish with narrow blackish bands and broader subterminal band. In dark morph, *dark wing linings contrast with paler flight feathers*. Imm has narrow bars on tail. Light morph imm has whitish streaked head. Dark morph imm has white markings below. **HABITS** Canopy of semihumid to humid broadleaf forest and adjacent plantations and open areas. Soars high in late morning. Rarely seen perched. Stoops into forest canopy to take prey. Solitary or in pairs. **VOICE** Calls (1) a shrill scream *sheeerreeeea* with second part piercing and (2) shorter, more nasal *kleee-ah*.

Gray Hawk" *Buteo plagiatus*   42 cm
South USA to CA. Uncommon resident in north lowlands and foothills (to 1800 m). Also Bay Islands (317). **ID** Fairly long tail. Cere and legs yellow. Ad gray above with faint barring. Underparts white narrowly barred with gray. Tail black with white bands. In flight, underwing mostly gray with indistinct dark trailing edge. Imm has pale supercilium, brown moustache, and *pale auriculars*. Note barred tibials. In flight, shows white rump. Compare with imm Roadside Hawk. Note different underparts and wing pattern. Also compare with imm Broad-winged Hawk. Note Gray's Hawks *barred (not speckled) tibials*, different head pattern and shorter primary projection. **HABITS** Forest edge, second growth, open woodland, and clearings or plantations with scattered trees. Soars briefly, usually low. Often sluggish. Solitary or in pairs. **VOICE** Call (1) a loud, clear, downslurred *schweeeeeer*.

Gray-lined Hawk" *Buteo nitidus*   40 cm
CA and SA. Uncommon resident in south lowlands and foothills (to 1000 m). **ID** Fairly long tail. Ad gray above with *distinct darker gray barring*. Underparts white narrowly barred with gray. Tail black with white bands. In flight, underwing mostly gray with indistinct dark trailing edge. Imm dark brown above with buff or whitish edging. Imm has heavy brown streaking on breast. Note pale supercilium, brown moustache, *pale auriculars*, and *plain cinnamon tibials*. In flight, shows white on rump. Compare with imm Roadside Hawk. Note different underparts and wing pattern. Also compare imm with imm Broad-winged Hawk. Note different structure and different head and underparts pattern. **HABITS** Like Gray Hawk. **VOICE** Call (1) a loud, clear, downslurred *schweeeeeer*.

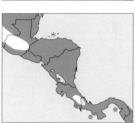

Roadside Hawk *Rupornis magnirostris*   37–40 cm
MX to SA. Fairly common resident in lowlands and foothills (to 1200, rarely to 2100 m). Also Isla Coiba and Pearl Islands (Panamá, Veraguas, 455, 649, 470). Rare in Bay Islands (94) **ID** Small. Ad has *pale eyes* and dull rufous barring on belly. In flight, note *rufous on primaries*. Imm streaked with brown on breast and barred with dull rufous on belly and tibials. Compare with imms of Broad-winged, Gray, and Gray-lined hawks. Note different head pattern and underparts. **GV** Birds from north CA (not shown) are typically larger and browner than birds from south CA. Birds from Bay Islands are brownest and darkest. Birds from central CR to central PA have mostly rufous tail-bands. **HABITS** Forest edge, plantations, second growth, woodland, and scrub. Perches low, often on utility pole or wire. Flies with rapid wingbeats and short, slow glides. Soars in display with tail closed. Solitary or in pairs. **VOICE** Call (1) a squealing, buzzy *kzweeeeeeeo* or *zhweeeeeyo*. In display (2) a rapid series of nasal cries *heh-heh-heh . . .* or *keh heh-hehheh* or *reh, reh, heh-heh-heh*. Compare with Lineated Woodpecker. At nest (3) a short whistle *wheet* or *whee-wheet*.

Broad-winged Hawk *Buteo platypterus*   38 cm
Breeds Nearctic. Winters CA and SA (mainly Sep to May). Transients may be briefly or locally abundant (85, 86). Most passage on Caribbean slope in north. Uncommon winter resident, mainly in south. **ID** *Long primary projection*. Ad dark brown above and whitish below barred with rufous. Ad's *tail black with broad white bands*. Underside of wings mostly whitish with black-tipped flight feathers. Imm has *streaked auriculars*, brown malar, and whitish supercilium. Note imm's plain or speckled tibials. Compare with imm Gray Hawk. Note different head and underparts pattern. **HABITS** Forest edge, plantations, second growth, woodland, and scrub. Often seen soaring. Perches inconspicuously at midlevels. Wintering birds solitary. Migrants gregarious. **VOICE** Gives (1) a loud, shrill whistle *p-teeeeeee*. Steady or dropping slightly in pitch.

Short-tailed Hawk

imm

ad

dark morph
imm

dark morph
ad

light morph
ad

imm

ad

imm

ad

Gray Hawk

imm

ad

imm

ad

widespread
ad

Roadside Hawk

imm

ad

Gray-lined Hawk

imm

ad

Bay Islands
ad

PA
ad

imm

ad

Broad-winged Hawk

ad

imm

HAWKS Accipitridae

Large hawks often seen soaring. Details of structure and habits can be helpful in identification. Zone-tailed Hawk resembles several other black-plumaged hawks but has a distinctive, Turkey Vulture-like shape and flight style. Swainson's Hawk can be briefly abundant in Central America as large numbers pass through the region in spectacular flights.

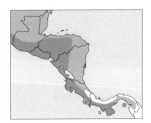

Zone-tailed Hawk *Buteo albonotatus*　　　　female 53, male 50 cm

NA to SA. Uncommon resident in Pacific slope and interior (to 3000 m). Uncommon transient and winter visitor (mainly Oct to Apr) on Caribbean slope. Wanders widely. Also Pearl Islands (Panamá, 611). **ID** Long, slender wings and tail. Yellow cere and legs. Ad *near-uniform black* with white tail-bands. In flight, black underwing coverts contrast with paler flight feathers. Imm browner with variable white spotting below. Imm's tail grayish-brown above with narrow black bars. Inner webs whitish or pale gray (tail appears whitish from below). Tilting flight with upraised wings and black plumage suggest Turkey Vulture. Note Zone-tailed's smaller size, white tail-bands and larger, feathered head. Also compare with dark morph Short-tailed Hawk. Note different structure and tail pattern. Great and Common black hawks have yellow facial skin and different structure. **HABITS** Savannas, pastures, agricultural fields, and plantations. Flies lower than other buteos when hunting. Solitary. **VOICE** Calls (1) a series of short, high-pitched cries *kra kree-kree-kree* or *whee-ah, whee-ah, whee-ah* and (2) longer, lower-pitched, slightly nasal scream that rises then drops in pitch *raaaaaaaauu*.

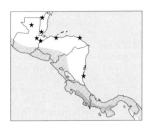

Swainson's Hawk *Buteo swainsoni*　　　　female 50, male 48 cm

Breeds west Nearctic. Winters mainly SA (359). Uncommon to briefly or locally abundant (85, 86) transient (mainly Mar to May and Oct to early Nov). Uncommon to rare and irregular winter resident on Pacific slope (619, 413). Vagrant to north Caribbean (341, 346). **ID** Long, pointed wings extend to or just beyond tail tip when perched. Variable. Light morph ad (more common) has *dark brown bib* contrasting with white throat. Tail brownish-gray with fine dark bands. In flight, whitish underwing coverts contrast with dark flight feathers. Intermediate morph is barred below. Dark morph near-uniform brown with brown or chestnut underwing. Imm typically brown above and buffy whitish below with variable dusky streaking. Imm often has extensive white on uppertail coverts. Dark morph imm resembles imm White-tailed Hawk. Note different underparts. Dark morph Short-tailed Hawk smaller with different underwing pattern. Compare with dark morph Red-tailed Hawk. **HABITS** Favors arid to semihumid open areas including savannas, agricultural fields, and marshes. May roost on ground. Occasionally follows farm equipment. Transients possible overhead in wide variety of habitats. May associate with migrating Broad-winged Hawks. While soaring may hold wings in slight dihedral and rock from side to side like Turkey Vulture. **VOICE** Usually quiet. Call (1) a high-pitched scream.

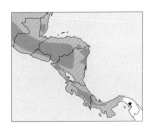

Red-tailed Hawk *Buteo jamaicensis*　　　　54–58 cm

NA to CA. Uncommon breeder in north highlands (including Maya Mountains of BZ), Caribbean savannas of NI and HN, and south highlands (mainly above 2000 m). Uncommon to rare in lowlands. Nearctic birds occur as rare transients and winter visitors. **ID** Broad wings. Ad has *rufous tail* (brighter above) with dark subterminal band. Imm's tail has faint dark barring. In all plumages note dark leading edge on inner wing. Imm resembles other large imm buteos. Compare with Swainson's Hawk. Note different structure. **GV** Birds from both migrant and resident populations are variable and have light and dark morphs. Resident light morph ad has rufous tibials and usually has pale rufous belly, flanks, and underwing coverts and has little or no streaking on underparts. Some in north CA are nearly white below. Migrant light morph has variable brown streaking, especially on belly (often forming a band). Dark morphs ad is mostly blackish with rufous tail. **HABITS** Open pine-oak woodland, pastures, savannas, agricultural lands, and paramo. Soars frequently. Solitary or in pairs. **VOICE** Call (1) a long, hoarse, scream *wheeee-eahr* or *wheeeeihr* and (2) shorter, hoarse *wheeir*. May be repeated.

White-tailed Hawk *Geranoaetus albicaudatus*　　　　53 cm

NA to SA. Uncommon and local resident in lowlands and foothills (to 1200 m). **ID** Large. Long, broad, pointed wings project beyond tail when perched. Ad has mostly white underparts, *dark slaty hood* and *rufous wing coverts. Rump and tail mostly white.* Tail has broad black subterminal band. Variable imm has whitish rump barred with brown and pale brownish or grayish tail. Some are mostly brownish with *variable white patch on breast.* Imm's underwing may be entirely dark or mottled with white. Compare ad with Short-tailed Hawk. Note different tail. Imm White-tailed Hawk resembles imm buteos but usually has pale rump and tail suggesting ad's pattern. **HABITS** Savannas, grasslands, pastures, and agricultural fields. May perch low or on ground. Frequently soars (often with wings in dihedral). May hover. Solitary or in pairs. **VOICE** Call (1) a short series of two-syllable, buzzy, nasal cries *whee-ahh, whee-ah* or *keela, keela, keela* and (2) harsher, barking *aaack, aaaack, aaaack.*

13%

Zone-tailed Hawk (right)
with Turkey Vulture (left).

ad

imm

ad

Zone-tailed Hawk

intermediate
morph
ad

light morph
ad

imm

imm

dark morph
ad

ad

Swainson's Hawk

imm

Red-tailed Hawk

dark morph
ad

light morph
north CA
ad

light morph
CR
ad

imm

migrant ad

White-tailed Hawk

imm

ad

ad

imm

imm

EAGLES Accipitridae

Very large hawks. Both are very rare and local species confined to extensively forested regions. Several years are required to attain adult plumage. Crest shape, structure, and underparts pattern are helpful in identification but differences can be subtle and difficult to discern in the field.

Crested Eagle *Morphnus guianensis*   78 cm

South MX to SA. Very rare and local resident in forested lowlands and foothills. More often in foothills regions than Harpy Eagle. Records from BZ (Orange Walk, Cayo, Toledo, 433, 347), GT (Petén, 238, 78, 227, 346), HN (Gracias a Dios, 442, 34), NI where very poorly known (Río San Juan, RAAN, 452, 413), CR (Limón, San José, Heredia, 126, 570, 113, 346), and PA (Veraguas, Darién, Colón, Kuna Yala, 657, 512, 48). **ID** Very large with broad, rounded wings and long tail. In all plumages note *narrow, single-pointed crest*. In flight, from below note *all-white underwing coverts* and broad black-and-gray bands on flight feathers. Variable ad plumage includes light and dark morphs. Light morph ad (much more common) has immaculate white underwing coverts (note dark markings on underwing in Harpy Eagle) and *pale, brownish-gray chest* contrasting with white lower underparts. Some birds show tawny barring on lower underparts. Dark morph ad has dark gray head, neck, and chest, and lower underparts boldly barred with black. Intermediates (and very rare black morph) also occur. Subad has pale head, neck, and underparts (gradually becoming grayer with age). Juv entirely white with some dark barring on wings. Closely resembles Harpy Eagle (especially imm). Crested Eagle differs in smaller size, more slender structure (especially tarsi and feet), proportionally longer tail, smaller bill, and single (not double) pointed crest. Compare imm with smaller *Spizaetus* hawk-eagles (note feathered tarsi in those species). **HABITS** Subcanopy to canopy of humid broadleaf forest. Similar to Harpy Eagle. Rarely soars. Occasionally makes long glides over forest canopy. When perched can sometimes be approached closely. Solitary except at nest. **VOICE** Usually quiet. Call (1) a long, hoarse whistle.

Harpy Eagle *Harpia harpyja*   95 cm

South MX to SA. Very rare and local resident in forested lowlands and (formerly) foothills of GT (Petén, formerly Alta Verapaz, 539, 279, 639, 227), BZ (Cayo, Toledo, Orange Walk, 529, 347, 343, 526), HN (Gracias a Dios, Olancho, 34, 346), NI (Río San Juan, Rivas, Matagalpa, 452, 413), CR (Limón, Puntarenas, 570, 113, 346), and PA (Bocas del Toro, Colón, Los Santos, Kuna Yala, Darién, 554, 657, 512, 639, 638). **ID** Very large and robust with *heavy tarsi*. Very broad rounded wings and long tail. In all plumages shows *broad, often divided crest* and massive bill. Ad has gray head and neck contrasting with black chest-band. Lower underparts mostly white with black barring on tibials. Tail black with three broad gray bands and narrow gray tip (whiter from below). In flight from below, shows white underwing with *black mottling* on coverts and axillars. Juv almost entirely white. Very similar to Crested Eagle. Note different structure, underparts pattern, and crest shape. **HABITS** Subcanopy to canopy and edge of humid broadleaf forest. Inconspicuous despite enormous size. Solitary except at nest. Does not soar. Sometimes takes an exposed perch. **VOICE** Usually quiet. Call (1) a long, hoarse whistle.

Crested Eagle

imm

dark morph
ad

typical
ad

ad

imm

subad

ad

ad

imm

Harpy Eagle

13%

HAWK-EAGLES Accipitridae

Large, scarce hawks confined to extensively forested regions. Hawk-eagles are most often seen as they soar during late morning. Ornate and Black hawk-eagles display a distinctive structure in flight with long tail and broad, relatively short wings that narrow near the body. Black-and-White Hawk-Eagle has a more *Buteo*-like structure. All have feathered tarsi. Hawk-eagles often call in flight and voice is often helpful in locating and identifying hawk-eagles.

Black-and-white Hawk-Eagle *Spizaetus melanoleucus* female 56, male 52 cm

MX to SA. Rare and local resident in lowlands and foothills (to 1200 m) of BZ (Orange Walk, Cayo, Toledo, 343), GT (Petén, Alta Verapaz, 317), HN (Atlántida, Gracias a Dios, 442, 317, 629), NI (RAAN, Matagalpa, 413, 626), CR (Limón, Heredia, Puntarenas, 539, 126, 570), and PA (Chiriquí, Bocas del Toro, Veraguas, Los Santos, Panamá, Darién, 89, 657, 45). Very rare or perhaps extirpated in Pacific GT (San Marcos, Escuintla, 539). **ID** Large. In flight, shows *Buteo*-like silhouette with broad-based wings and *relatively short tail*, mostly white underwing surface and *white on leading edge of inner wing*. Striking ad has mostly white head and underparts, *narrow black mask*, and short black crest. Note *yellow eyes, orange cere and black lores*. Imm has brownish-gray mantle with white edging. Imm Ornate Hawk-Eagle has different head and underparts. In flight, note different structure. Pale morph imm Gray-headed Kite has similar pattern to ad Black-and-white Hawk-Eagle. Note kite's more slender structure, unfeathered tarsi, pale lores, and more boldly patterned flight feathers. **HABITS** Canopy and edge of humid broadleaf forest. Soars frequently, particularly during late morning. Solitary or in pairs. May perch on high, exposed limb. **VOICE** Not as vocal as other *Spizaetus* hawk-eagles. Call (1) a shrill *kree-owow* or (2) accelerating series of piping notes recalling Ornate Hawk-Eagle *whee whi-whi-whiwhi-wheee-eer*.

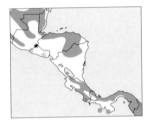

Ornate Hawk-Eagle *Spizaetus ornatus* female 63, male 60 cm

MX to SA. Uncommon to rare resident in forested lowlands and foothills (to 1500 m, occasionally or locally higher). Now rare and local in north Pacific where formerly perhaps more widespread (183). **ID** Large. In flight, note rounded, broad-tipped wings and long tail. *Undersurface of wings pale* and less boldly patterned than Black Hawk-Eagle. Ad has black crown and long, pointed crest. *Rufous sides of head and neck* contrast with white throat and center of chest. *Lower underparts barred with black and white*. Imm has mostly white head, neck, and underparts (usually with some dark barring). Imm's crest usually white with black tip. Imm might be confused with Black-and-white Hawk-Eagle. Note different head, underparts, and structure. Black Hawk-Eagle has similar structure but is darker below in all plumages. **HABITS** Semihumid to humid broadleaf forest. Often seen soaring in late morning. Solitary or in pairs. In display flight, pairs make short, swooping dives and flutter wings rapidly. Sometimes found perched inside subcanopy. **VOICE** Call (1) often given in flight *where-er, whip, whip, whip, whip* with long, slurred note given first (not last as in Black Hawk-Eagle).

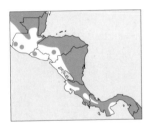

Black Hawk-Eagle *Spizaetus tyrannus* female 66, male 63 cm

MX to SA. Uncommon resident in forested lowlands and foothills (to 1000 m, occasionally or locally higher). Most common and widespread *Spizaetus* hawk-eagle. Rare and local in north Pacific foothills of SV (Santa Ana, Ahuachapán, 619) and GT (Quetzaltenango, Suchitepéquez, Sacatepéquez, 633). Historical records from Pacific NI at Volcán Mombacho (Granada, 413). **ID** Large. In flight, shows *rounded, broad-tipped wings*. Note *long tail and undersurface of wings boldly banded with black and white*. Ad mostly black with some white markings on crest and white barring on tarsi. Note short, bushy crest. Imm mostly dark brown with white to buff mottling and streaking. Note imm's whitish throat and dark auriculars. Ornate Hawk-Eagle has pale underparts and is never as dark or boldly patterned as Black Hawk-Eagle. **HABITS** Semihumid to humid broadleaf forest and adjacent open areas. Often soars during late morning, sometimes circling to great heights. Solitary or in pairs. **VOICE** While soaring or in undulating flight display gives (1) a loud, clear, whistled *wheep-wheep-wheep-waheee-er* with last note attenuated and downslurred. This longest note is given in the middle or at the end (not first as in Ornate Hawk-Eagle). May call once or several times without pause.

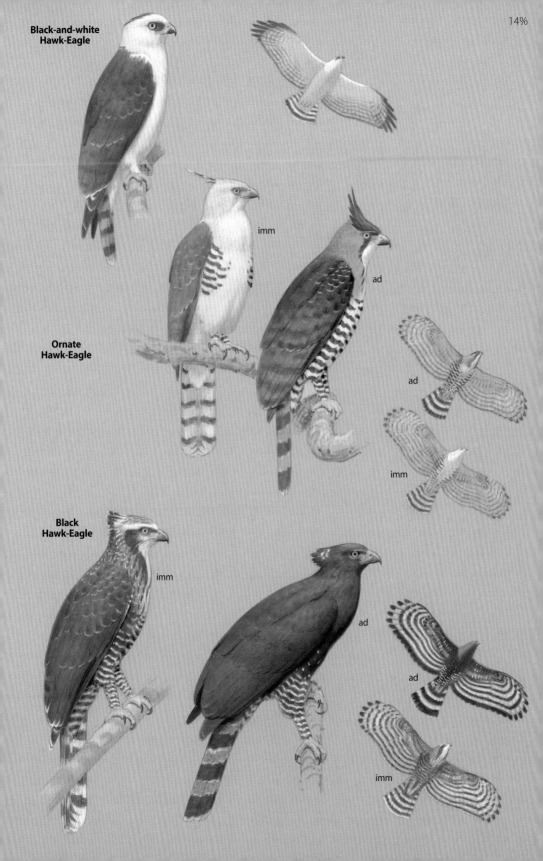

Black-and-white Hawk-Eagle

14%

imm

Ornate Hawk-Eagle

ad

ad

imm

Black Hawk-Eagle

imm

ad

ad

imm

BARN OWL Tytonidae

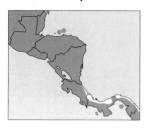

Barn Owl *Tyto alba* 36 cm
Cosmopolitan. Widespread and locally common resident in lowlands (to 1850 m). Also Bay Islands (94, 479) and Pearl Islands (Panamá, 649). **ID** Long legs, short tail, and large, rounded head. Rather pale (often appears whitish) with *heart-shaped, whitish face*. Eyes dark. Compare with Striped Owl. Note different structure and underparts pattern. **HABITS** Uses a wide variety of habitats but favors semi-open or disturbed areas including agricultural fields, plantations (especially palm plantations), urban areas, and marshes. Nocturnal. Roosts in daylight in dense vegetation, tree cavity, or abandoned building. **VOICE** Call (1) a very harsh, squealing scream *shaaahr* or *shwiiike*. In interactions may give (2) a persistent series of sharp *eenk* notes.

OWLS Strigidae

Striped Owl *Pseudoscops clamator* 38 cm
South MX to SA. Uncommon and local resident in lowlands and foothills (to 1400 m). Formerly considered rare but widely reported in recent decades. Perhaps expanding. **ID** Medium-sized. Conspicuous black ear tufts bordered with white. *Eyes dark*. Boldly patterned plumage features *white facial disk bordered with black* and *broad blackish streaking on white underparts*. Upperparts tawny with dark brown streaking and barring. Compare with Barn Owl. Note different facial and underparts pattern. **HABITS** Agricultural fields, grasslands, scrub, palm plantations, and marshes. Nocturnal. Roosts on ground in tall grass or at lower levels in dense vegetation. May hunt from open perch at dusk. **VOICE** Calls (1) a clear, emphatic, downslurred *heeeeeer* or *scheeeeeer*, (2) short, hoarse, downslurred scream that is harsher than previous, (3) irregular series of low-pitched, muffled single or doubled hoots on an even pitch *hooooooh* or *hoo-hoo, hoo-hu*. Also (4) a long series of short hoots with steady pitch that gradually slow. Pairs may call in duet. Compare screaming or hissing call with call of Barn Owl.

Short-eared Owl *Asio flammeus* 37 cm
Cosmopolitan. Very rare vagrant to BZ (Toledo, 347), GT (Sacatepéquez, 536), and CR (San José, 600). **ID** Small, inconspicuous ear tufts. Eyes yellow. In flight, shows whitish underwing. On upperwing note buff base of primaries and blackish mark near wrist. Compare with Striped and Stygian owls. Note different head pattern. **HABITS** Open areas including grasslands, beaches, and agricultural fields. Roosts on ground or very low in concealing vegetation. May forage in daylight. **VOICE** Quiet away from breeding areas.

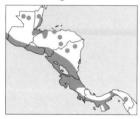

Stygian Owl *Asio stygius* 45 cm
MX and WI to SA. Rare and local resident in north (to 3000 m) with records from BZ (Cayo, Orange Walk, Belize, 529, 667, 313, 343, 491), GT (Alta Verapaz, Baja Verapaz, Quetzaltenango, Suchitepéquez, Sacatepéquez, Sololá, 516, 228, 346, 306), HN (Cortés, Atlántida, Francisco Morazán, Olancho, Gracias a Dios, 346, 1), and north NI (Estelí, Jinotega). **ID** Closely spaced ear tufts. Eyes yellow. Mostly *dark brown, heavily barred and streaked with blackish*. Note *whitish forehead* and *dark facial disks*. Juv paler, more barred, and with more contrasting dark facial disks. Compare with larger Great Horned Owl. Note different head pattern. **HABITS** Poorly known. Midstory to subcanopy of pine-oak forest, pine savanna broadleaf forest, and plantations. Elsewhere in range also uses marshes, mangroves, and urban areas. Nocturnal. Roosts in dense, shaded vegetation. **VOICE** Calls (1) a single, very low-pitched, booming *whoooo* repeated at long intervals and (2) slightly hoarse or squeaky, upslurred *eeee-ya* or *eeeeyup*.

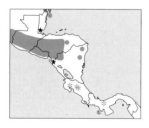

Great Horned Owl *Bubo virginianus* 50 cm
NA to SA. Uncommon resident in north highlands (to 3000 m). Rare and local in coastal lowlands of north BZ (Corozal, Belize, 68, 642, 529, 343), and in foothills and highlands of SV (San Vicente, Santa Ana, Morazán, Chalatenango, 183, 408, 619, 346). Poorly known in NI (Matagalpa, Chinandega, RAAN, 327, 413). Very rare in CR (Guanacaste, Puntarenas, Cartago, San José, 126, 600, 341) and PA (Veraguas, 653, 512, 470). **ID** Large. Long ear tufts. Eyes yellow. Note cinnamon facial disks and white throat and breast. Compare with smaller Stygian Owl. Note different head pattern. **HABITS** Savanna, deciduous and pine-oak forest or woodland, arid or litoral scrub, plantations, and urban areas. Nocturnal. **VOICE** Song (1) a rhythmic phrase of three to six short, very low-pitched hoots. Second note often attenuated *hu-huuuu, huu huu huu*. Compare with song of Mottled Owl.

Barn Owl

light morph

dark morph

Striped Owl

Short-eared Owl

Stygian Owl

Great Horned Owl

OWLS Strigidae

Large owls found mainly in broadleaf forest. All are strictly nocturnal and can be difficult to locate in the dense vegetation of their favored haunts. Most are detected by voice, and vocalizations are often important clues to identification. Mottled Owl is the most common and widespread.

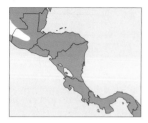

Mottled Owl *Ciccaba virgata*   35 cm
MX to SA. Common resident in lowlands and foothills (to 1800, locally to 2500 m in north). **ID** Fairly large. Slightly cowl-necked with rounded crown. Note dark eyes and mostly *dark facial disk* outlined by pale supercilium and whiskers. Underparts variable. Usually has dark barring on breast and variably tawny to whitish lower underparts streaked with brown. Fulvous Owl larger, with different head pattern. Smaller *Megascops* screech-owls have yellow eyes. **HABITS** Midstory to subcanopy and edge of semihumid to humid broadleaf forest, second growth, scrub, and plantations. **VOICE** Most frequent call (1) a series of two or three very low-pitched, muffled, downslurred hoots *ho hoo whooo*. Compare with call of Black-and-white Owl. Also (2) a long, harsh, downslurred, catlike scream and (3) descending whinny.

Fulvous Owl *Strix fulvescens*   42 cm
South MX and CA. Locally common resident in north highlands (1800 to 3000 m, rarely lower). **ID** Large. Bulky, cowl-necked structure. Dark eyes contrast with *pale gray facial disk*. Crown, nape, and breast tawny scalloped and scaled with dark brown. Belly buff streaked with dark brown. Mottled Owl smaller with dark face and different underparts. **HABITS** Midstory to subcanopy and edge of humid broadleaf and pine-oak forest. **VOICE** Song (1) a series of loud, barking cries on steady pitch. Typically three or four notes given in rapid series followed by one or two notes after a slightly longer interval *oot-oot-oot oot oot* or *hut-hut-hut-hut huu*. Also (2) a hoarse scream *jaaaaaai*. Compare with songs of Black-and-white and Great Horned owls.

Black-and-white Owl *Ciccaba nigrolineata*   42 cm
MX to north SA. Uncommon resident in lowlands and foothills (to 2000 m). Most widespread on Caribbean slope. Rare and local on Pacific slope in GT (Quetzaltenango, Suchitepéquez, 539, 228), SV (Ahuachapán, San Miguel, Usulafter, 183, 408), HN (Choluteca, 34), and volcanic highlands of NI (Chinandega, Granada, 413). **ID** Large with bulky, rounded structure. Ad's *black-and-white barred underparts* are distinctive. Note *blackish crown and facial disks* and narrow supercilium of whitish speckling. Eyes dark. Yellow bill conspicuous against dark face. Juv mostly whitish with black face. **HABITS** Midstory to subcanopy and edge of semihumid to humid broadleaf forest, adjacent plantations, and gardens. Locally in urban areas. **VOICE** Song (1) a series of three to six short, slightly hoarse hoots that ascend in pitch and are followed by a single, longer, louder, downslurred note *huu-hoo-hoo-hoo whuuuua*. Last note sometimes given alone.

Crested Owl *Lophostrix cristata*   38 cm
South MX to SA. Uncommon resident in lowlands and foothills (to 1500, rarely or locally to 2000 m). Most widespread on south Caribbean slope. Rare and local in Pacific GT (Escuintla, Retalhuleu, 228) and SV (Morazán, 183). Rare in BZ (433, 477). Poorly known in NI, with historical records from central highlands (Jinotega, Matagalpa, 413) and recent reports from Caribbean lowlands (Río San Juan, 548). **ID** Fairly large. *Very long, prominent, white supercilium*. White ear tufts sometimes held low and drooping laterally or raised to form a white V. Note *chestnut facial disks*. Eyes dark amber. Variable underparts with very fine dusky vermiculations (may appear plain). Juv has extensively white underparts and crown contrasting with brown facial disks and upperparts. Spectacled Owl also has bold white facial markings. Note different underparts and structure. **HABITS** Midstory to subcanopy and edge of humid broadleaf forest. Roost in pairs in dense tangles. **VOICE** Call (1) a short, very low-pitched, gruff, rolling growl *grrrrrrr*. Rises slightly in pitch then drops at end.

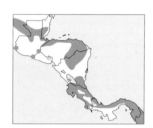

Spectacled Owl *Pulsatrix perspicillata*   48 cm
South MX to SA. Uncommon resident in lowlands and foothills (to 1500 m). Rare and local on north Pacific slope in GT (San Marcos, Santa Rosa, Sacatepéquez, Escuintla, San Marcos, 539, 516, 279, 608, 228) and SV (Santa Ana, Ahuachapán, 619). **ID** Large with bulky, rounded structure. Bold head pattern and *solid dark breast-band are distinctive*. Lower underparts usually plain buff. Eyes yellow. Juv has mostly white head and underparts and black facial disks. **GV** Some birds from north CA show fine dark barring below. **HABITS** Midstory to subcanopy and edge of humid broadleaf forest, tall second growth, and shaded plantations. **VOICE** Call (1) a short, rapid series of very low-pitched, hollow notes that drop progressively in pitch *pum-pum-pumpum*. Female's call higher-pitched. Also (2) a hawk-like *ker-wheeeeer*.

Mottled Owl

dark morph

light morph

Black-and-white Owl

Fulvous Owl

Crested Owl

light morph

dark morph

ad

juv

Spectacled Owl

SCREECH-OWLS Strigidae

Megascops owls with mainly allopatric distributions in lowlands and foothills. All are strictly nocturnal. These species are closely similar in plumage and structure, and voice is the best means of identification. Vermiculated Screech-Owl is the most widespread.

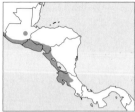

Pacific Screech-Owl *Megascops cooperi* 22 cm

South MX and CA. Uncommon to fairly common resident in Pacific lowlands and foothills (to 1000 m). Local on GT Caribbean slope in Motagua Valley (Zacapa, 228). Also reaches the Caribbean slope locally in north CR and south NI. **ID** Large, pale *Megascops* owl. Eyes yellow. Monomorphic (no rufous or brown morph). Vermiculated Screech-Owl (mainly Caribbean slope) has different voice. **HABITS** Midstory and edge of arid to semihumid forest, second growth, littoral woodland, mangroves, and adjacent clearings. **VOICE** Song (1) a rapid series of five to ten abrupt, nasal, hooting, or barking notes. Series sometimes begins with short, purring trill, becomes loudest in middle and slows slightly at end *prrr pu-pu-PU-PU-PU-pu-pu*. Also (2) hoarse growl *raaaaw*.

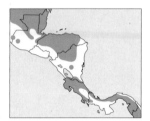

Vermiculated Screech-Owl[12] *Megascops guatemalae* 22 cm

MX to SA. Fairly common resident in lowlands and foothills (to 1000, locally to 1800 m). In north, confined mainly to Caribbean slope and interior. Very rare in Pacific foothills of GT (Retalhuleu, 228, 229). Uncommon and local on Nicoya Peninsula, CR. **ID** Variable *Megascops* owl with several color morphs. Eyes yellow. Note plain head pattern with no or little dark outline on auriculars. In south compare with Tropical Screech-Owl. Note different voice. In north, compare with Whiskered Screech-Owl. Pacific Screech-Owl allopatric. **GV** Shows poorly understood variation with several color morphs. Several examples are shown. Birds of both brown and rufous morphs from south CA are more reddish than those from north CA. It is unclear how this variation may be related to geographic variation in voice. **HABITS** Midstory to subcanopy and edge of broadleaf forest, tall second growth, pine-oak forest, gardens, and plantations. Also pine-oak woodland and arid scrub in north. **VOICE** Song (1) of north CA populations a long, hollow, flat, toadlike trill *prrrrruuu*. Song of south CA populations (south NI to west PA) very similar but perhaps slightly higher-pitched. Song in central and east Panama shorter and distinctly downslurred.

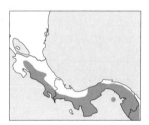

Tropical Screech-Owl *Megascops choliba* 22 cm

CA and SA. Fairly common resident in lowlands and foothills (to 1000, locally to 1600 m). Also Pearl Islands (Panamá, 611, 507, 657). **ID** Note *pale gray facial disks* with *distinct dark outline* and narrow black streaking on underparts. Eyes yellow. Plumage variable (rufous morph scarce). Vermiculated Screech-Owl has relatively plain head pattern and different voice. **GV** Birds from Pearl Islands (not shown) are somewhat darker. **HABITS** Midstory to subcanopy in a wide variety of arboreal habitats including forest edge, second growth, plantations, suburban areas, and gardens. **VOICE** Song (1) a short, hollow trill followed by two (sometimes one or three) louder notes *prrrr pu poo* or *prrrr poo poo, prrrr poo*. Calls include (2) a short series of abrupt barking cries *kwah-hwah-kwah*.

Pacific Screech-Owl
at day roost with
ear tufts raised.

Pacific Screech-Owl

**Vermiculated
Screech-Owl**

north CA
brown morph

north CA
rufous morph

south CA
brown morph

Tropical Screech-Owl

south CA
rufous morph

rufous morph

brown morph

OWLS Strigidae

Small owls found mainly in highlands. All are strictly nocturnal and roost inside shaded vegetation in daylight. Most are detected by voice, and vocalizations are often the best means of identification. *Megascops* owls have variable plumage, often including rufous and brown or gray morphs. Unspotted Saw-whet Owl is a distinctive small owl with no close relatives in the region. Whiskered Screech-Owl and Bare-shanked Screech-Owl are the most common and widespread.

Whiskered Screech-Owl *Megascops trichopsis*　　　　20 cm

South USA to north CA. Uncommon to locally fairly common resident in north foothills and highlands (750 to 3000 m). Poorly known in NI with records from north central highlands (Nueva Segovia) and Volcán Casita (Chinandega, 413). **ID** Small *Megascops* owl with rounded crown. Shows no (or very inconspicuous) ear tufts. Note coarse, black streaks and fine bars on underparts. Eyes yellow. Variable plumage includes gray and rufous morphs. Compare with Vermiculated Screech-Owl. Note different voice and habits. **HABITS** Midstory to subcanopy and edge of pine-oak and broadleaf forest. **VOICE** Song (1) an irregular series of four to ten hoots *hoo-hoo-hoo-hoo hoo-hoo* or *hoo-hoo hoo-thoo hoo-hoo hoo*. Pairs may call in duet.

Bearded Screech-Owl *Megascops barbarus*　　　　18 cm

South MX and CA. Fairly common but local resident in Caribbean highlands (1700 to 2300 m) of GT (Quiché, Alta Verapaz, Baja Verapaz, El Progreso, Huehuetenango, 555, 279, 232, 228, 229). Poorly known. **ID** Small. Shows no or very inconspicuous ear tufts and often shows white band encircling crown. Underparts white, streaked and scalloped with black. Individual breast feathers have black median streaks that curve outward to form terminal bars. Variable plumage includes gray and rufous morphs. Eyes yellow. Resembles Whiskered Screech-Owl and best separated by voice. Vermiculated Screech-Owl found mainly at lower elevations. Note different underparts. **HABITS** Poorly known. Midstory to subcanopy and edge of humid broadleaf and pine-oak forest. **VOICE** Song (1) a long, soft, low-pitched trill that rises then drops very slightly in pitch *trrrrrrrrrrrrrr*. Repeated after a short pause. Also (2) a soft *hu*.

Bare-shanked Screech-Owl *Megascops clarkii*　　　　25 cm

CA and SA. Resident in south highlands (900 to 2100 m). Locally fairly common in CR. Rare in west PA and highlands of east PA (Darién, 657, 519). **ID** Fairly large *Megascops* owl. Variably rufous to brown plumage (an intermediate bird is shown). Facial disk with indistinct border. Underparts barred with white and streaked with black. Small, inconspicuous ear tufts. Eyes yellow. Other *Megascops* owls mainly at lower elevations. **HABITS** Interior midstory and edge of very humid broadleaf (cloud and elfin) forest. **VOICE** Song (1) a short phrase of low-pitched whistles on steady pitch *hu-huu huu-huu* or *hoo-WOO hoo-hoo*. Second or third notes loudest.

Flammulated Owl *Psiloscops flammeolus*　　　　16 cm

NA to CA. Very rare and poorly known breeder in highlands (1500 to 3700 m) of GT (Huehuetenango, 231). Historical records from highlands of central GT (Sacatepéquez, Chimaltenango, 539, 164). **ID** Small with very small, inconspicuous ear tufts. *Eyes dark.* Note *rufous on facial disks* and white scapular spots tipped with rufous. Long wings project beyond tail while perched. Variably rufous or brown plumage. Underparts barred and streaked with black. Compare with Whiskered and Bearded screech-owls. Note different voice and eye color. **HABITS** Midstory and edge of pine forest. **VOICE** Song (1) a single, short, low-pitched *ooot*. May be repeated in long series.

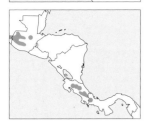

Unspotted Saw-whet Owl *Aegolius ridgwayi*　　　　20 cm

South MX and CA. Disjunct populations in north and south CA. Fairly common resident in highlands (1400 to 3700 m) of GT (228). Rare in SV (Chalatenango, 408, 5). Rare and local in highlands of CR (San José, Cartago, 7, 576, 255, 600). Poorly known in PA where documented only from Volcán Barú (Chiriquí, 657, 346). **ID** Small. Compact, large-headed structure (no ear tufts) and short, broad, whitish supercilium. Ad has *plain brown breast and buff belly.* Eyes dark. No other small CA owl has *plain underparts* without streaking or barring. **HABITS** Midstory of pine and pine-oak woodland and edge of humid broadleaf (cloud) forest. **VOICE** Typical call (1) a rhythmic series of four to ten mellow *hoo* notes on steady pitch. Compare with voice of Northern Pygmy-Owl. Also (2) a short, higher-pitched scream.

Whiskered Screech-Owl

brown
morph

rufous
morph

brown
morph

rufous
morph

Bearded Screech-Owl

Bearded Screech-Owl
showing crown band.

**Bare-shanked
Screech-Owl**

Flammulated Owl

**Unspotted
Saw-whet Owl**

PYGMY-OWLS Strigidae

Small owls. Often active in daylight. Flight is rapid and direct. Pygmy-owls are often mobbed by small birds. Most are individually variable in plumage and brown and rufous morphs occur. Head pattern, range, habitat, and vocalizations are useful for identification. The number and spacing of white bars on the underside of the tail is sometimes helpful. Ferruginous Pygmy-Owl is the most common and widespread.

Northern Pygmy-Owl[13] *Glaucidium gnoma* 15 cm

NA and CA. Fairly common resident in highlands of GT (1500 to 3400 m, 229) and HN (Lempira, Santa Bárbara, Francisco Morazán, 442, 346). **ID** Variable plumage includes brown and rufous morphs. Brown morph ad has *narrow rufous nuchal collar*. Rufous morph ad near-uniform above with *plain crown*. Compare with Ferruginous Pygmy-Owl. **HABITS** Subcanopy of broadleaf and coniferous forest. **VOICE** Call (1) a long series of short, soft hoots *hoo-hoo-hoo hoo-hoohoo hoo-hoo hoo-hoo* . . . with notes often doubled or tripled. Compare with calls of Ferruginous Pygmy-Owl and Unspotted Saw-whet Owl.

Costa Rican Pygmy-Owl *Glaucidium costaricanum* 16 cm

CA endemic. Uncommon to rare and local resident in foothills and highlands (above 900 m) of CR (576, 570, 600) and west PA (Chiriquí, Ngäbe-Buglé, Bocas del Toro, Veraguas, 351, 657, 48). Recently reported from Cordillera de Tilarán in west CR (Alajuela, 122). **ID** Variable plumage includes brown and rufous morphs. Brown morph has bold white spotting on crown. Rufous morph mostly deep rufous with faint spotting on sides of breast and crown. In all plumages note spotted (not streaked) crown and forehead. *Pale barring on flanks* is distinctive but may be obscure in rufous morph. Central American and Ferruginous pygmy-owls found at lower elevations. Note different crown pattern. **HABITS** Midstory to canopy and edge of humid montane forest. **VOICE** Song (1) a long series of short notes that are usually doubled *hao hao, hao hao, hao hao*. Higher-pitched than Ferruginous Pygmy-Owl.

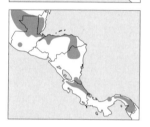

Central American Pygmy-Owl *Glaucidium griseiceps* 15 cm

CA endemic. Uncommon to rare resident in humid forested lowlands and foothills (to 800, locally to 1300 m). Confined mainly to Caribbean slope but also reported (very rarely) from Pacific foothills of GT (Suchitepéquez, 312, 228). Poorly known and perhaps disjunct population in central and east PA (Panamá, Colón, Darién, 346). **ID** Small and short-tailed. Typically has less contrasting pattern than other CA *Glaucidium*. Note *fine white spotting on grayish crown*. Pale spotting on sides of breast is distinctive. Flanks coarsely streaked with rufous-brown. Compare with Ferruginous Pygmy-Owl. Note different structure, crown, and tail pattern. **HABITS** Midstory to subcanopy of humid broadleaf forest, tall second growth, and adjacent plantations and small clearings. **VOICE** Call (1) a series of two to ten clear, even or downslurred notes *hoo hoo hoo hoo hoo* . . . Compare with lower-pitched call of Ferruginous Pygmy-Owl.

Ferruginous Pygmy-Owl *Glaucidium brasilianum* 16.5 cm

South USA to SA. Locally fairly common resident in lowlands and foothills (to 1600 m). Also Pearl Islands (Panamá, 58). Poorly known in NI. **ID** Long tail. Variable plumage with brown and rufous morphs. Pale when worn. Note *fine pale streaking on crown* and relatively fine brown streaks on flanks. Compare with Central American Pygmy-Owl. Note different crown and tail pattern. **HABITS** Midstory to subcanopy of forest edge, second growth, savannas, gardens, plantations, littoral scrub, and suburban areas. **VOICE** Typical song (1) a long series of evenly spaced, slightly upslurred notes *oot oot oot oot oot* . . . Notes sometimes doubled and series may end with sharp barking note. Compare with higher-pitched song of Central American Pygmy-Owl.

Burrowing Owl *Athene cunicularia* 22 cm

NA, WI, and SA. Very rare winter visitor known mainly from historical records in BZ (Belize, Toledo, 529, 347), GT (Retalhuleu, Escuintla, Sacatepéquez, Sololá, Huehuetenango, Alta Verapaz, Zacapa, 539, 164, 279, 647), SV (La Unión, Cuscatlán, 183, 619), HN (Francisco Morazán, 442), CR (Cartago, 570), and west PA (Chiriquí, 657). Formerly perhaps more regular in the region. **ID** Short tail, rounded crown, and long legs. Note white forehead and supercilium. In flight, ad shows grayish-white wing linings. **HABITS** Floor of arid to semihumid open areas, including savannas, grasslands, and agricultural fields. Terrestrial and often diurnal. May take an elevated perch when hunting. Displays undulating flight style and typically lands by swooping upward to perch. CA records are of solitary birds. **VOICE** Call (1) a hollow, two-syllable, dove-like phrase repeated persistently *hu-huuu* or *coo-cooh*.

Northern Pygmy-Owl

rufous
morph

brown
morph

Costa Rican Pygmy-Owl

brown
morph

rufous
morph

**Central American
Pygmy-Owl**

Ferruginous Pygmy-Owl

rufous
morph

brown
morph

Burrowing Owl

Pygmy-owls
have "eye-spots"
on nape.

TROGONS Trogonidae

Trogons with red underparts found mainly in lowlands and foothills. Details of head pattern including eye ring and bill color, as well as tail pattern and voice are helpful in identification. Slaty-tailed Trogon is the most common and widespread.

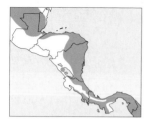

Slaty-tailed Trogon *Trogon massena* 33 cm

CA and north SA. Widespread and fairly common resident in lowlands and foothills (to 1200 m). Confined to Caribbean slope in north but reported from Volcán Mombacho in NI (Granada, 413). **ID** Large. Red lower underparts, dark eyes and *plain, dark gray undersurface of tail*. Ad male has green hood, *orange bill*, and red eye ring. Female has lead-gray hood and upperparts and *orange mandible*. Juv has quetzal-like white barring on undersurface of tail. Black-tailed Trogon has yellow bill and different underparts. **HABITS** Midstory of semihumid to humid broadleaf forest and tall second growth. Solitary or in pairs. **VOICE** Song (1) a series of fairly low-pitched, nasal, barking *uk* or *ow* notes repeated steadily on even pitch. Less frequently gives (2) an accelerating series with notes running together to produce a rattle.

Black-tailed Trogon *Trogon melanurus* 33 cm

CA and SA. Common resident in lowlands and foothills (to 550 m) of east PA. **ID** Large. Red lower underparts, plain dark gray undersurface of tail and *partly or all-yellow bill*. Eyes dark. Male has white band dividing green hood and red lower underparts. Female mostly lead-gray with yellow confined to base of bill. Male similar to smaller Collared Trogon. Note different tail pattern. Male of similar Slaty-tailed Trogon lacks white chest-band and both sexes have different bill color. **HABITS** Midstory of humid broadleaf forest, tall second growth and mangroves. Solitary or in pairs. **VOICE** Song (1) a steady series of hollow notes *kwow kwow kwow kwow . . .* Compare with song of Slaty-tailed Trogon (often syntopic).

Lattice-tailed Trogon *Trogon clathratus* 31 cm

CA endemic. Uncommon to rare and local resident in Caribbean foothills (100 to 1100 m, rarely or locally as low as SL). **ID** Large. *Pale eyes*, red lower underparts and *fine whitish barring on underside of tail*. Ad male has green breast contrasting with red lower underparts. Female mostly lead-gray above and on breast with red lower underparts. Pale eyes and pale yellow bill separate this species from Slaty-tailed Trogon. Juv brownish with bold white spots on wing coverts. Black-tailed Trogon allopatric. **HABITS** Midstory of humid broadleaf forest. Solitary or in pairs. **VOICE** Song (1) a rapid series of low-pitched, slightly hoarse *kwa* notes that rise in pitch then drop and slow slightly at end. Also (2) a short, low-pitched rattle on even pitch.

Baird's Trogon *Trogon bairdii* 30 cm

CA endemic. Confined to Pacific lowlands and foothills (to 1200, locally to 1600 m) of east CR (San José, Puntarenas) and west PA (Chiriquí). Common resident in CR. Formerly perhaps more widespread in west PA (60, 657). **ID** *Pale blue eye ring* and orange lower underparts. Male has blue hood, pale bill, *white underside of tail*, and plain (unbarred) blackish wings. Note male's dark breast contrasting with orange-red lower underparts (no white breast-band). Female has dark gray hood and fine white barring on gray wing coverts. Undersurface of female's tail shows fine white barring and white tips on rectrices. Female's bill gray with dusky culmen. Juv resembles female but has more white on tips of rectrices. Lattice-tailed and White-tailed trogons allopatric. **HABITS** Understory to subcanopy and edge of humid broadleaf forest and adjacent tall second growth. Solitary or in pairs. **VOICE** Song (1) a long, rapid, accelerating series of hollow notes *tok, tok, tok, tok, tok tok tok tok toktoktoktoktok*. Sometimes ends with several widely spaced notes on lower pitch. Compare with song of Black-crowned Antshrike. Also (2) an accelerating series of softer notes that are clearer and more melodious than call of Slaty-tailed Trogon.

29

Slaty-tailed Trogon

imm ♂

ad ♀

ad ♂

♂

Black-tailed Trogon

♀

♂

♂

♀

♂

Lattice-tailed Trogon

♀

♂

♂

♂

Baird's Trogon

TROGONS Trogonidae

Trogons with yellow underparts. Solitary birds or pairs perch at medium heights and often appear sluggish. More active at fruiting trees. Sometimes nervously raise and lower the tail. Useful features for identification include eye ring and bill color as well as tail pattern. Voice is also helpful.

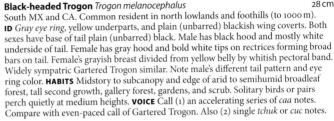

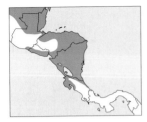

Black-headed Trogon *Trogon melanocephalus*   28 cm

South MX and CA. Common resident in north lowlands and foothills (to 1000 m). **ID** *Gray eye ring*, yellow underparts, and plain (unbarred) blackish wing coverts. Both sexes have base of tail plain (unbarred) black. Male has black hood and mostly white underside of tail. Female has gray hood and bold white tips on rectrices forming broad bars on tail. Female's grayish breast divided from yellow belly by whitish pectoral band. Widely sympatric Gartered Trogon similar. Note male's different tail pattern and eye ring color. **HABITS** Midstory to subcanopy and edge of arid to semihumid broadleaf forest, tall second growth, gallery forest, gardens, and scrub. Solitary birds or pairs perch quietly at medium heights. **VOICE** Call (1) an accelerating series of *caa* notes. Compare with even-paced call of Gartered Trogon. Also (2) single *tchuk* or *cuc* notes.

White-tailed Trogon *Trogon chionurus*   28 cm

CA and north SA. Uncommon resident in lowlands and foothills (to 400 m) of PA. **ID** *Blue-gray eye ring*, pale grayish bill, and *extensive white on undersurface of tail*. Ad male's violet breast contrasts with yellow lower underparts (no white breast-band). Male has mostly white underside of tail. Female plain gray above and has gray hood extending to breast. Female's lower underparts yellow. Black-headed and Baird's trogons allopatric. Compare with Gartered Trogon. Note different underparts and tail pattern. **HABITS** Midstory to subcanopy and edge of humid broadleaf forest and tall second growth. **VOICE** Call (1) a series of soft *coo* notes that accelerate into a roll. Series may end with several slower notes. Resembles song of allopatric Black-headed Trogon. Also (2) a short, deliberate series of lower-pitched notes *chuck, chuck, ckuck* . . .

Gartered Trogon *Trogon caligatus*   23 cm

South MX to north SA. Common resident in lowlands and foothills (to 1200, locally to 1800 m in north). **ID** Relatively small with rounded crown. Note fine gray barring or vermiculations on wings and yellow lower underparts. Both sexes have black-and-white barring on underside of tail (including base). Male has *yellow eye ring* set in blackish sides of head, *violet-blue hood*, and fine black-and-white barring on underside of tail. Female has broad, broken gray eye ring, gray hood and breast, and fine black-and-white barring on outer webs of rectrices. Compare with Black-headed Trogon. Note different tail pattern and eye ring color. **HABITS** Midstory to subcanopy and edge of broadleaf forest, second growth, plantations, gallery forest, and scrub. Solitary birds or pairs perch motionless for long periods. More active at fruiting tress. **VOICE** Call (1) a long, steady series of short, downslurred notes on even pitch *kwer kwer kwer kwer* . . . or *kew kew kew kew* . . . Compare with accelerating call of Black-headed Trogon and lower-pitched call of Slaty-tailed Trogon. When disturbed, gives (2) a nasal *nyrrrrrp*.

Black-throated Trogon *Trogon rufus*   24 cm

CA and SA. Uncommon to locally fairly resident in lowlands and foothills (to 1000, locally to 1250 m). Confined to Caribbean slope in north. **ID** Small. Male has blue eye ring, *green hood*, and *yellow lower underparts*. Female has unique combination of *brown hood* and *yellow lower underparts*. Note female's *rufous tail*. Male resembles Gartered Trogon. Note different eye ring, breast color, and habits. **HABITS** Midstory of humid broadleaf forest and tall second growth. Solitary or in pairs. **VOICE** Call a short series of two to five (usually three) soft *caaw* notes on even pitch. Compare with shorter song of Collared Trogon. Also (2) a churning or rattling *krrrr* and (3) nasal *nyurrrrrp*.

Black-headed Trogon

♀

♂

30%

White-tailed Trogon

♀

♂

♂

♂

imm
♂

ad
♀

ad
♂

ad
♀

Black-throated Trogon

♀

♂

Gartered Trogon

♀

♂

TROGONS Trogonidae

Trogons with red underparts found mainly in foothills or highlands. Head pattern, including eye ring and bill color, as well as tail pattern and voice are helpful in identification. Collared Trogon is the most common and widespread.

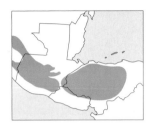

Mountain Trogon *Trogon mexicanus*   30 cm

MX and north CA. Fairly common resident in north highlands (1800 to 3200 m, rarely lower). Poorly known in SV. **ID** Male's tail mostly green above with black tip. From below, male's *tail mostly black with broad white tips on rectrices*. Note male's *red eye ring* and yellow bill. Shows dark primaries on folded wing. Female brown above with *broad, pale brownish chest-band* and *broken white eye ring*. Note female's dusky culmen. From below female's tail shows fine black-and-white barring along outer edge and is mostly coppery from above. Juv mostly tawny brown with bold white spots on wing coverts. Female resembles female Collared Trogon (mainly humid broadleaf forest). Note Mountain Trogon's different tail and underparts pattern. Also compare with Elegant Trogon. Note different head pattern. **HABITS** Midstory of humid pine-oak and broadleaf forest, tall second growth, and adjacent plantations. May venture into open to feed at fruiting trees. Solitary or in pairs. **VOICE** Most frequent call (1) a short series of five to seven slightly hoarse *caw* or *oow* notes delivered slowly with even tone and spacing. From a distance may suggest a *Glaucidium* pygmy-owl. Also (2) a descending and accelerating series *ow ow ow-owow-ow owowow.*

Elegant Trogon *Trogon elegans*   29 cm

South USA to north CA. Locally fairly common resident in north Pacific slope and interior (to 1800 m). Uncommon in arid Caribbean valleys of GT (229, 376) and north HN (Yoro, 316). **ID** Fairly large. Both sexes have yellow bill, pale edges on primaries (visible in folded wing), and fine barring on underside of tail. Male has green upperparts, golden-green uppertail surface, and red eye ring. Upper surface of tail shows broad black terminal band. Female has grayish-brown upperparts and *white mark extending from below eye*. Also note female's pale brownish breast. Compare with Mountain and Collared trogons. Note female's different head pattern and male's different tail. **HABITS** Midstory of arid (deciduous) to semihumid broadleaf, pine-oak, and oak forest. Solitary or in pairs. **VOICE** Call (1) four to six hoarse, two-syllable phrases *krawah krawah krawah krawah krawah . . .* or *cawah-cawah-cawah-cawah . . .* given rapidly with steady pitch and speed. Also (2) a gruff, chattering *wehrr-rr-rr rr-rr-rr* or *wuc uc uc uc uc uc* and (3) steady, gruff *ahrr, ahrr . . .*

Collared Trogon[14] *Trogon collaris*   25 cm

MX to SA. Uncommon resident in lowlands and foothills (to 2800 m). Breeds mainly in foothills (700 to 2000 m). In north, wanders to lower elevations outside breeding season. **ID** Underside of male's *tail shows black-and-white barring and narrow white tips*. Female has broken whitish eye ring, narrow white band across chest, and all-red lower underparts. Imm male's tail may be more similar to Elegant Trogon. In north compare with Elegant Trogon. Note ad male's different tail and female's different head pattern. Also compare with Mountain Trogon. **GV** Male from Pirre Massif in east PA (Darién) has red eye ring and more extensive white on rectrices. **HABITS** Midstory of humid broadleaf forest and adjacent tall second growth. Seems most common in broken or hilly terrain. Ventures into semi-open to feed at fruiting trees. Solitary or in pairs. **VOICE** Call (1) a simple, two- or three-syllable phrase with second note slightly shorter and more clipped *cawcow* or *keeu-keu*. Sometimes varied as *caaw-cowcow*. Compare with longer song of Black-throated Trogon. Also (2) a short, low-pitched rattle.

Orange-bellied Trogon[14] *Trogon aurantiiventris*   25 cm

CA endemic. Uncommon resident in foothills and highlands (to 2800 m) of CR and west PA. **ID** *Orange lower underparts*. Underside of male's *tail shows black-and-white barring and narrow white tips*. Female (not shown) resembles female Collared Trogon and has broken whitish eye ring, narrow white band across chest, and all-orange lower underparts. **HABITS** Midstory of humid broadleaf forest and adjacent tall second growth. Like Collared Trogon. **VOICE** Like Collared Trogon.

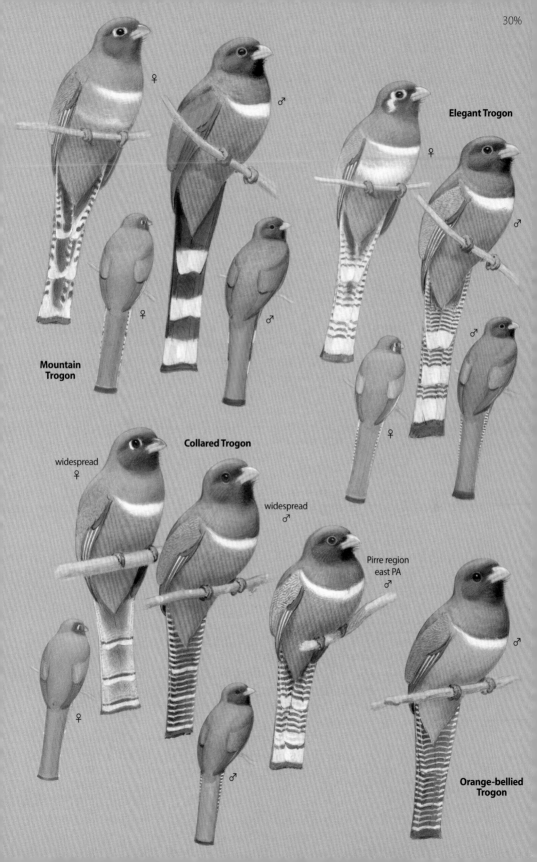

30%

Elegant Trogon

♀

♂

♀

♂

♀

♂

Mountain Trogon

♀

♂

Collared Trogon

widespread
♀

widespread
♂

♀

Pirre region
east PA
♂

♂

♂

Orange-bellied Trogon

QUETZALS Trogonidae

Large, spectacular trogons found in humid highland forests. In all plumages quetzals have distinctive, elongated wing and uppertail coverts.

Resplendent Quetzal *Pharomachrus mocinno*   female 37, male 90 cm
South MX and CA. Uncommon to rare and local resident in foothills and highlands (1000 to 3000, rarely or locally as low as 200 m). In CR, breeds at high elevations during Jan to Aug. Outside breeding season moves to lower elevations on both Caribbean and Pacific slopes (393, 498, 497, 221). Rare vagrant or seasonal visitor to lowlands (near SL) in CR (Limón, 287) and HN (Atlántida). Recently reported from Cerro Musún in central NI (Matagalpa, 137). **ID** Large with tapered (not square) tail. In all plumages note *long, pointed wing coverts.* Ad male has bushy green crest and *very long uppertail coverts extending beyond tail to form long, dangling train.* Underside of ad male's tail white. Female mostly brilliant green with red lower underparts and dull olive head. Female has black-and-white barring on underside of tail. Golden-headed Quetzal allopatric. **HABITS** Midstory to canopy and edge of humid broadleaf (cloud) forest, adjacent tall second growth, and plantations and pastures with scattered large trees. Generally secretive and easily overlooked. Most active and easily located when feeding at fruiting trees or while males perform spectacular aerial courtship display. **VOICE** Calls (1) a soft, upslurred *kwa* or *quuo*, (2) two-syllable *ah-wahc, ah-wahc . . .* , and (3) nasal *ahhk ahhk ahhk . . .* May accelerate to become a short, nasal laugh. Also (4) a series of short, nasal notes with woodpecker-like quality *kwehk-kewhk-kewhk.*

Golden-headed Quetzal *Pharomachrus auriceps*   37 cm
CA and SA. Uncommon to rare and local resident in highlands (1200 to 1500 m) of east PA (Darién, 512). **ID** Undersurface of tail black. Belly and crissum red. Ad male mostly *brilliant metallic green* on breast and upperparts (including long pointed wing coverts and long uppertail coverts). Male's head shows brilliant coppery green in good light. Female generally duller with mostly brownish-gray head and breast and lacks male's long uppertail coverts. Black-tailed and Slaty-tailed trogons also have green upperparts and plain dark tails but are found at lower elevations and have different bill color and underparts. Resplendent Quetzal allopatric. **HABITS** Midstory to subcanopy of very humid broadleaf (cloud) forest. Solitary or in pairs. Retiring and inconspicuous. Hover-gleans to take fruit. **VOICE** Calls (1) a loud, repeated *wheeu, we-weeeoo, weweeeoo* and (2) descending, laughlike *wa-ha-ha-ha-ha.*

imm
♀

ad
♀

ad
♀

♂

Resplendent Quetzal

♀

ad
♀

♂

**Golden-headed
Quetzal**

KINGFISHERS Alcedinidae

Large and medium-sized kingfishers. Amazon and Green kingfishers are widespread and common. Head shape and wing pattern are helpful in separating these.

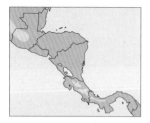

Belted Kingfisher *Megaceryle alcyon*   31cm

Breeds Nearctic. Winters USA to WI and north SA. Fairly common transient and winter resident (mainly Sep to May) in lowlands and foothills. Rare in summer. **ID** *Large* with bushy crest. Both sexes have blue-gray upperparts with very fine whitish spotting on wing coverts and *mostly white lower underparts including crissum*. Both sexes have blue-gray breast-band. Female also has rufous flanks and rufous band across lower breast. Compare with larger Ringed Kingfisher. Note different underparts. **HABITS** Borders of lakes, ponds, and rivers, marshes, mangroves, estuaries, and seacoasts. Solitary. Perches prominently on bare branch or utility wire. Often noisy and conspicuous. More partial to saltwater habitats than Ringed Kingfisher. Hovers briefly before plunging into water to seize prey. **VOICE** Call (1) a loud, rough, laughing rattle *ehehehehehehehehehe*. Higher-pitched, faster, and smoother than call of Ringed Kingfisher. Also (2) a higher-pitched, buzzy *rrrrrrrr*.

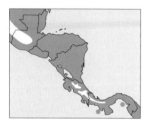

Ringed Kingfisher *Megaceryle torquata*   40cm

South Texas to SA. Locally common resident in lowlands and foothills. Also Isla Coiba and Pearl Islands (Veraguas, Panamá, 611, 470). **ID** *Very large* with bushy crest. Note heavy bill with slightly upswept mandible. Blue-gray upperparts and extensively rufous underparts. Male has *rufous breast, belly, and flanks*. Female has blue chest divided from entirely rufous lower underparts by narrow white band. Female has rufous wing linings. Similar Belted Kingfisher is smaller with different underparts. **HABITS** Borders of lakes, ponds, and rivers, marshes. Solitary or in pairs. Usually noisy and conspicuous. Perches prominently on bare branch or utility wire. Hovers briefly before plunging into water to seize prey. **VOICE** Call (1) a loud, gravelly rattle *ehkehkehkehkehkehk*. Lower-pitched and often shorter than Belted Kingfisher. In flight (2) a gruff, low-pitched *rrruk* or *krek*.

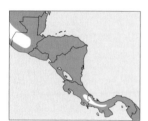

Amazon Kingfisher *Chloroceryle amazona*   30cm

MX to SA. Locally common resident. Mainly in lowlands and foothills. Uncommon to rare and local in north Pacific. **ID** Long, heavy, bill and *shaggy, pointed crest*. Mostly plain green above (no or very little white spotting on wings and tail). Note *green streaking (not barring) on flanks*. Male has broad rufous chest-band. Female lacks rufous and has single broken green breast-band. Juv (not shown) resembles female but has variable extent of cinnamon wash on underparts. Compare with smaller Green Kingfisher. Note different head shape and wing pattern. **HABITS** Borders of lakes, ponds, and rivers, marshes. Perches on open, low branches overhanging water or on boulders in watercourses. Solitary or in pairs. **VOICE** Calls (1) a rapid series of sharp notes that drop gradually in pitch *chi-chi-ch-ch-ch-chrchrchr* and (2) low-pitched, harsh *krrrik* and (3) hard, buzzy *zzrt* that may be repeated.

Green Kingfisher *Chloroceryle americana*   19cm

South USA to SA. Locally common resident in lowlands and foothills. Also Isla Coiba (Veraguas, 470). **ID** Fairly small. *Very short, rounded crest* (not as long or pointed as crest of Amazon Kingfisher). Mostly green above and white below with extensive *white spotting and barring on wings* and white on base of tail. Male's mostly whitish underparts show variable *green mottling or barring on flanks*. Female resembles male but has mostly whitish underparts with green spots forming two narrow chest-bands and green spotting on flanks. Some females are faintly buffy below. Amazon Kingfisher larger with mostly plain green wings. **HABITS** Borders of lakes, ponds, and rivers, marshes. Perches on open, low branches overhanging water or exposed boulder in watercourse. Solitary or in pairs. **VOICE** Calls (1) a series of dry, hard, double notes *chi chi . . .* May accelerate to become (2) a short rattle *chi chi ch-ch-chchch*. Also (3) a coarse, rolling *zurrk*.

Belted Kingfisher

♀   ♂

Ringed Kingfisher

♀   ♂

♂

♀

Amazon Kingfisher

♂

♀

Green Kingfisher

KINGFISHERS Alcedinidae

Small kingfishers.

Green-and-rufous Kingfisher *Chloroceryle inda* 22 cm

CA and SA. Uncommon resident in lowlands. Rare in HN (Gracias a Dios, 34) and NI (RAAN, RAAS, Río San Juan, 413). Also Pearl Islands (Panamá, 58, 611, 657). **ID** *Entirely rufous lower underparts including belly and crissum.* Throat and neck tawny. Upperparts mostly green with faint white spotting on wings and tail. Male has all rufous underparts. Female has green chest-band with white mottling. Green and American Pygmy kingfishers have white on lower underparts. **HABITS** Understory to lower midstory of wooded swamps, mangroves, and forested river margins. Solitary or in pairs. Perches in shaded vegetation overhanging water. **VOICE** Song (1) a descending series of six to eight shrill, thin, high-pitched notes *tseek tseek eek eek . . .* or *wich wich weech weech . . .* Calls (2) a very hard, sharp *drriit,* (3) single, high-pitched, sharp, ticking notes *tic, tic* or *tsic, tsic,* and (4) rapid bursts of ticking *dic-dic-dic-dic* or *tric-tric-tric-tric.*

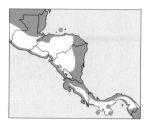

American Pygmy Kingfisher *Chloroceryle aenea* 13 cm

MX to SA. Uncommon and local resident in lowlands and foothills (to 600 m). Also Isla Coiba (Veraguas, 653, 470) and Bay Islands (442). **ID** *Very small. Supraloral streak and neck-band tawny.* Upperparts green with very fine white spotting on wing coverts. Both sexes have *white central belly* and crissum. Female has narrow green chest-band with variable white speckling. Compare with larger Green and Green-and-rufous kingfishers. Note different underparts. **HABITS** Margins of small streams and pools in semihumid and humid broadleaf forest, gallery forest, marshes, and mangroves. Perches very low in vegetation over shallow, slow-moving or still water. Solitary or in pairs. **VOICE** Calls (1) a dry, clicking *tsk* or *ik* and (2) lower-pitched, slightly hoarse, repeated *eh eh eh eh* or *eh-eheh-ho.* Also (3) a shrill, high-pitched *chrreiiiik* or *chrreeiiii.*

MOTMOTS Momotidae

Blue-throated Motmot is endemic to north Central America. Turquoise-browed Motmot, found mainly in arid to semihumid areas, is common and widespread.

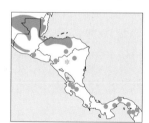

Tody Motmot *Hylomanes momotula* 17 cm

CA and SA. Uncommon to rare and local resident in lowlands and foothills (to 1500, but mainly 400 and 1000 m). Most common in BZ and north GT. Rare and local in SV (Ahuachapán, 619, 341), Pacific HN (Choluteca, 346), NI (Jinotega, RAAN 413, 626), CR (Guanacaste Alajuela, 624, 600), and PA (Veraguas, Panamá, Colón, Coclé, Kuna Yala, Darién, 67, 657). **ID** Small with long bill and relatively short, graduated tail (no racquets). *Whitish lateral throat and moustachial stripes.* **GV** Birds CR and PA are more olive above and more brownish below. **HABITS** Understory to midstory of semihumid to humid broadleaf forest. Often in or near dark, tangled vegetation in ravines or hilly areas. Makes short, fluttering sallies to seize prey from vegetation or forest floor. Solitary or in pairs. Twitches tail from side to side. **VOICE** Often calls in predawn darkness, giving (1) a long series of loud, hoarse cries *kwaaa, kwaaa, kwaaa, kwaaa . . .* Compare with call of Crested Guan. In south compare with call of Prong-billed Barbet.

Turquoise-browed Motmot *Eumomota superciliosa* 35 cm

South MX and CA. Common resident in Pacific lowlands and foothills (to 800, locally to 1400 m in north). Local in arid Caribbean slope valleys of HN and GT. Recently found in north GT (Petén, 229). **ID** *Throat black.* Blue tail with *large, black-tipped racquets* and *broad bluish-white supercilium.* Rufous mantle and turquoise-blue flight feathers also distinctive. Lesson's Motmot is greenish (never rufous) above and has mostly green wings. Note different tail shape and habits. **GV** Birds from north GT have tawny breast blending into rufous belly. Birds from Caribbean HN are more richly colored with deep turquoise supercilium. **HABITS** Midstory of arid to semihumid forest edge, second growth, scrub, plantations, and gardens. Perches conspicuously on open branch or utility wire. Solitary or in pairs. **VOICE** Call (1) a low-pitched, hoarse *kowk* or *cawah.* May be repeated in long series. Compare with voices of Keel-billed and Broad-billed motmots. Also (2) a rapid, multisyllable *kawhok-kwok-kawok-kawok* and (3) longer *kup-kup-kup-kup.*

Blue-throated Motmot *Aspatha gularis* 27 cm

South MX and CA. Resident in north highlands (mainly above 1800, locally as low as 1500 m). Fairly common in GT. Uncommon to rare and local in HN. **ID** Distinctive. Fairly small. Mostly green. Note short bill, *blue throat and belly,* and *black mark on auriculars.* Face buff. Legs dull pink. **HABITS** Midstory to subcanopy and edge of semiarid to humid broadleaf and pine-oak forest, tall second growth, and plantations. Solitary or in pairs. **VOICE** Typically gives (1) a single, low-pitched, hollow *ooow* or *whoot.* Not as nasal as hooting calls of other motmots. Often repeated every few seconds. Also (2) a rapid series of (usually) ten to twenty hoots *whood a whooda whoooda loodloodloodl . . .* May accelerate briefly and slow slightly at end.

Green-and-rufous Kingfisher ♂

♀

American Pygmy Kingfisher

♂

♀

north CA

Tody Motmot

CR and PA

north GT

Caribbean GT and HN

widespread

Turquoise-browed Motmot

Blue-throated Motmot

MOTMOTS Momotidae

Large-billed birds found at middle levels in forest and woodland. Motmots often perch motionless on open branches for long periods, but several species habitually twitch their tails from side to side. Lesson's Motmot is the most widespread and common.

Russet-crowned Motmot *Momotus mexicanus* 36 cm

South MX and CA. Uncommon and local resident in arid foothills (200 to 1300 m) of west GT in Nentón Valley (Huehuetenango, 229) and on Caribbean slope in Motagua Valley (El Progreso, Zacapa, Chiquimula). **ID** *Rufous crown* and nape and *pale green underparts*. Narrow black mask. Compare with widespread Turquoise-browed Motmot (often syntopic). Note different head and underparts pattern. **GV** Birds from west GT have violet moustache. **HABITS** Midstory and edge of arid to semihumid woodland, broadleaf forest, scrub, and semi-open areas. Solitary or in pairs. More retiring than Turquoise-browed Motmot. Rarely perches in open. **VOICE** Call (1) a low-pitched very hollow, rolling *wurrrp* or *krrrup* and *wharrr-up*. Rarely (2) a single hollow *ook* suggesting Lesson's Motmot.

Lesson's Motmot¹⁵ *Momotus lessonii* 42 cm

MX and CA. Uncommon to locally common resident. In north mainly in lowlands and foothills (to 1600 m). In south mainly foothills and highlands (to 2000 m). **ID** Large. Note *blue band encircling black crown* and narrow band of blue or violet outlining black mask. Eyes red. Underparts variably rufous or green. Turquoise-browed Motmot has rufous mantle and turquoise flight feathers. Note different habits. **HABITS** Midstory and edge in semihumid to humid broadleaf forest, second growth, clearings with scattered trees, plantations, and gardens. May drop to ground to take prey. Sometimes forages at ant swarms. Solitary or in pairs. Perches stolidly for long periods. **VOICE** Call (1) a two-syllable, low-pitched, hollow phrase *whoot-whoot* or *ooot oot*.

Whooping Motmot¹⁵ *Momotus subrufescens* 41 cm

CA and SA. Uncommon to locally common resident in lowlands and foothills (to 1500 m) of central and east PA. **ID** Very similar to parapatric Lesson's Motmot. Note *blue head-band with no black border*. Belly more rufous than breast. **HABITS** Like Lesson's Motmot. **VOICE** Call a short, single-note *who*.

Rufous Motmot *Baryphthengus martii* 48 cm

CA and SA. Uncommon to fairly common resident in humid lowlands and foothills (to 1000, locally to 1400 m). Uncommon and local in Pacific west PA (Veraguas, Coclé, 657, 46. **ID** Large. *Rufous head and underparts including chin and belly*. Broad black mask. Resembles smaller Broad-billed Motmot. Note different underparts and *blue primaries* of Rufous Motmot. **HABITS** Midstory to subcanopy of humid broadleaf forest. Solitary or in pairs. Takes an exposed perch on branch or vine. Remains motionless for long periods. **VOICE** Call (1) a series of very hollow, resonant notes. Call (2) two or three loud, distinct notes followed by rapid, rolling series on lower pitch *hoop hoop huhuhuhuhu.*

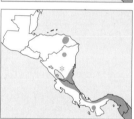

Keel-billed Motmot *Electron carinatum* 32 cm

South MX and CA. Uncommon to rare and local resident in Caribbean lowlands and foothills (mainly 300 to 900, locally to near SL, or as high as 1550 m) of BZ (Cayo, Toledo, Stann Creek, 529, 434, 343), GT (Petén, Izabal, Alta Verapaz, 539, 579, 149, 317, 221), HN (Santa Bárbara, Atlántida, Gracias a Dios, 609, 63, 483, 442, 35, 629), and north NI (RAAN, Jinotega, Nueva Segovia, Matagalpa, 413, 332, 626). At south limit in foothills of west CR (Guanacaste, Alajuela, 570, 600, 253). **ID** Mostly green becoming variably tawny below. Note rufous forehead and *short, blue supercilium*. Broad-billed Motmot has rufous hood and breast. Also compare with Lesson's Motmot. Note different head pattern. **HABITS** Midstory of humid broadleaf forest in steep or hilly terrain. Often perches quietly but may call persistently in early morning. Solitary or in pairs. **VOICE** Call (1) a single, low-pitched, nasal *ooow* or *huuuk* or *kawk* repeated every few seconds. Very similar to call of Broad-billed Motmot. Also compare with call of Turquoise-browed Motmot.

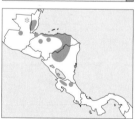

Broad-billed Motmot *Electron platyrhynchum* 32 cm

CA and SA. Uncommon to locally common resident in humid lowlands and foothills (to 1500, but mainly below 1100 m). Very rare in Caribbean foothills of GT at Cerro San Gil (Izabal, 227). Rare in Pacific foothills of west PA (Veraguas, Chiriquí, 657). **ID** Narrow black mask. Rufous hood and breast with *green chin and lower underparts*. Compare with larger Rufous Motmot (often syntopic). Note different underparts including Broad-billed's larger black breast spot. **HABITS** Midstory of humid broadleaf forest. Solitary or in pairs. **VOICE** Call (1) a series of low-pitched, very hoarse, croaking cries *cwaa, cwaa, cwaa . . .* or *kawk, kawk, kawk . . .* Very similar to call of Keel-billed Motmot.

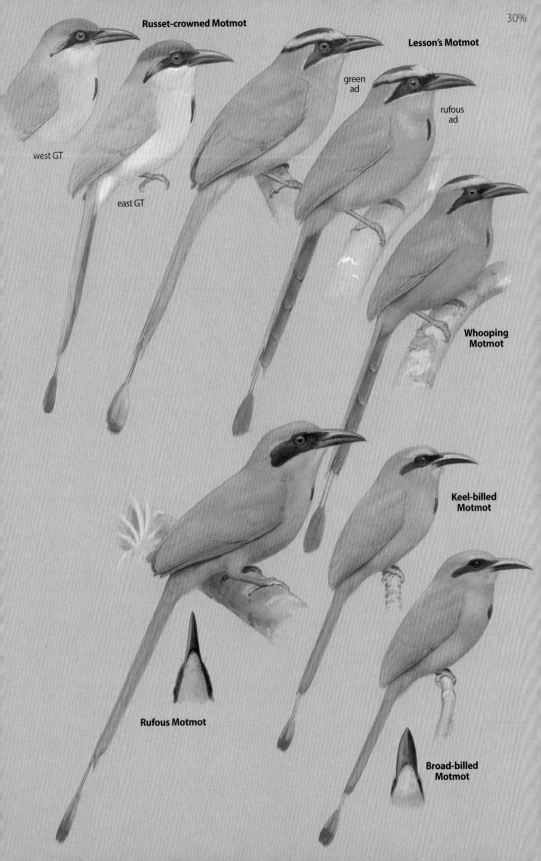

Russet-crowned Motmot

Lesson's Motmot

30%

green
ad

rufous
ad

west GT

east GT

**Whooping
Motmot**

**Keel-billed
Motmot**

Rufous Motmot

**Broad-billed
Motmot**

JACAMARS Galbulidae

Large-billed birds found mainly at middle levels in humid broadleaf forest. With long, pointed bills and long, graduated tails, jacamars present a distinctive silhouette as they perch motionless in the open. Rufous-tailed Jacamar is the most common and widespread.

Dusky-backed Jacamar *Brachygalba salmoni*   18 cm
CA and SA. Rare and local resident in lowlands and foothills (to 600 m) of east PA (Darién, 657, 519, 512). **ID** Small and dark with *long, pointed bill* and *blackish, square-tipped tail*. Upperparts and breast dark, glossy green. Belly and crissum rufous. Throat variably white or buffy white. Smaller and darker than Rufous-tailed Jacamar. Note shorter tail. **HABITS** Subcanopy to canopy and edge of humid broadleaf forest, tall second growth, and clearings with scattered trees. Often along rivers. Pairs or solitary birds perch on high, exposed snags. Sallies to capture flying insects and usually returns to same or nearby perch. **VOICE** Usually quiet. Call (1) a high-pitched, thin, upslurred *psee* or *wsee*. Sometimes repeated in long series.

Rufous-tailed Jacamar *Galbula ruficauda*   24 cm
South MX to SA. Fairly common resident in lowlands and foothills (to 800, rarely or locally to 1200 m). Uncommon to rare in east PA (Darién). **ID** Long, graduated tail and long, near-straight bill (typically upraised). Metallic green above and cinnamon-rufous below (including crissum) with *iridescent green breast-band*. Male has white throat. Female has buff throat. **GV** Birds from east PA have white chin and more rufous on tail. **HABITS** Midstory and edge of semihumid to humid broadleaf forest, tall second growth, and shaded plantations. Usually near gaps or edges. Pairs or solitary birds forage by sallying from exposed perch. In east PA mainly in semi-open and disturbed areas. **VOICE** Song (1) begins with several sharp, staccato *beek* or *eek* notes then suddenly accelerates into a very fast, hard trill or rattle *beek beek beek beebeebeeebeebeebeebee* or *beek, beekbeekbeek beebeebeebeebee-ee-ee-ee*. In simpler variation may give (2) long, rapid series of sharp *bee* or *beek* notes. Calls include (3) emphatic, two-syllable phrases that may be repeated *bee-yuk* or *ee-yuk*. Compare with softer call of Royal Flycatcher. Also (4) a sharp whistle that ends abruptly *wheeeert* or *peeeeur*.

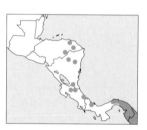

Great Jacamar *Jacamerops aureus*   30 cm
CA and SA. Uncommon to rare and local resident in Caribbean lowlands and foothills (to 500 m) in HN (Colón, Gracias a Dios, 341, 629), NI (RAAN, Río San Juan, 452, 626), CR (Cartago, Heredia, Limón, 126, 600), and PA (Bocas del Toro, Darién, 67, 486, 657). **ID** Large and bulky with long, heavy, graduated tail. *Long, heavy, decurved bill with arched culmen* typically held raised. Iridescent coppery green above and on chin and upper throat. Underparts including *breast cinnamon-rufous*. Male has white on lower throat. Widespread Rufous-tailed Jacamar smaller with different bill and underparts. **HABITS** Midstory to subcanopy of humid broadleaf forest and adjacent tall second growth. Pairs or solitary birds perch on slender horizontal limb or vine. Sits motionless for long periods then suddenly reverses position on perch. **VOICE** Often quiet. Call (1) a loud, clear, high-pitched whistle *keeeyeeeeeew!* that drops in pitch and is slightly trilled at end.

NUNLET AND PUFFBIRD Bucconidae

Gray-cheeked Nunlet and Barred Puffbird are both distinctive puffbirds found in Panama.

Gray-cheeked Nunlet *Nonnula frontalis*   14 cm
CA and SA. Uncommon and local resident in lowlands (to 500 m) of east PA (Panamá, Darién, 276, 657). At least formerly in central PA (Colón, Coclé, Panamá, 657, 522, 512). **ID** Sexes similar. Small and slender with upright posture. Note rounded head and slightly curved bill. Sides of head gray with *narrow red eye ring*. Breast cinnamon-buff. **HABITS** Understory to midstory at edge or in gap of humid broadleaf forest and tall second growth. Solitary. Inconspicuous and easily overlooked. Perches quietly for long periods in shaded vine tangle or bamboo. **VOICE** Calls include (1) a long series of loud, slightly nasal notes *wii, wii, wii, wii* . . . (2) a squeaky, rolling *cheee-churr, churr, churr* . . . and (3) single *chur* notes.

Barred Puffbird *Nystalus radiatus*   20 cm
CA and north SA. Uncommon resident in lowlands and foothills (to 600 m) of east PA. Rare in central PA (Colón, Coclé, 657, 48, 346). **ID** Bulky with very heavy, slightly hooked bill. Chestnut-rufous *mantle and wings heavily barred with blackish*. Underparts variably whitish to cinnamon with *fine dusky barring*. Note broad buff hindcollar. **HABITS** Midstory to subcanopy and edge of humid broadleaf forest, tall second growth, and adjacent clearings or plantations with scattered trees. Solitary or in pairs. Perches motionless on exposed, shaded branch. **VOICE** Call (1) two long, hoarse whistles. First note rises in pitch and second drops *wheeeet wheeeeooo*.

40%

Dusky-backed Jacamar

Rufous-tailed Jacamar

widespread ♂

widespread ♀

east PA ♂

Great Jacamar

♀

♂

Gray-cheeked Nunlet

Barred Puffbird

PUFFBIRDS AND MONKLET Bucconidae

Large-billed birds found at middle and upper levels of humid broadleaf forest and edge. Puffbirds present a distinctive, bulky silhouette as they sit motionless on open perch. White-whiskered and White-necked puffbirds are the most common and widespread.

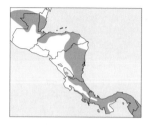

White-whiskered Puffbird *Malacoptila panamensis*   19 cm
South MX to north SA. Uncommon resident in lowlands and foothills (to 1200 m). **ID** Bulky and large-headed with heavy, curved bill and narrow tail. Most have *white plumes* projecting from base of bill and lores. Variable. Male typically rufous-brown above with *fine pale spotting on crown, mantle, and wing coverts*. Breast cinnamon with variable extent of dusky streaking on breast and flanks. Some males are rufous below. Female grayer with variably cinnamon to whitish throat. Imm resembles female. **HABITS** Midstory of semihumid to humid broadleaf forest, tall second growth, and adjacent shaded plantations. Retiring and inconspicuous. Pairs or solitary birds sit motionless for long periods on open vine or branch. Makes abrupt sallies to seize prey from vegetation or ground. **VOICE** At long intervals gives (1) a high-pitched, thin, hissing call. May begin or end as a rapid trill *pssssssiiiiiiii* or *iiiiiiiiiisssssssh*.

Lanceolated Monklet *Micromonacha lanceolata*   13 cm
CA and SA. Rare and local resident in foothills (400 to 1350 m) of CR (Alajuela, Cartago, 195, 570, 600, 253, 670, 346) and west PA (Chiriquí, Veraguas, Bocas del Toro, 657, 512, 346). Very rare in east PA (Darién, 46). **ID** Small and large-headed with heavy bill. Note complex black-and-white head pattern. Mostly brown above. *White underparts streaked with black*. **HABITS** Midstory at edge or in gaps in humid broadleaf forest and adjacent tall second growth in hilly or steep terrain. Usually solitary. Perches quietly on open branch or vine. Sallies to capture (sometimes large) insects. Retiring and easily overlooked but can be confiding. **VOICE** Usually quiet. Call (1) a series of high-pitched, upslurred cries *wheeeeup wheeeeup wheeeeup-wheeeeup-wheeeeupwheeeeup* . . . Series is variable in duration and gradually increases in tempo and volume.

Pied Puffbird *Notharchus tectus*   15 cm
CA and SA. Uncommon resident in lowlands and lower foothills (to 300 m). Confined mainly to CR and PA. Recently reported from Pacific NI (Granada, 419, 413). **ID** Small and large-headed. *Narrow white supercilium* and white speckling on crown. From behind usually shows white on scapulars. Recalls larger White-necked Puffbird but note *white spots on tail* and different head pattern. **HABITS** Subcanopy to canopy and edge of semihumid to humid broadleaf forest, adjacent clearings and plantations, tall second growth, and mangroves. Pairs or solitary birds perch on high, open snag. Somewhat more active than larger puffbirds. **VOICE** Song (1) a long series of high-pitched, thin notes that begin rapidly and gradually slow at end *wee-weeda-weeda-weeda, weee-a, wee-a, wee-a* . . . Compare with song of Rufous-tailed Jacamar.

Black-breasted Puffbird *Notharchus pectoralis*   22 cm
CA and north SA. Uncommon resident in lowlands and foothills (to 1000 m) of central and east PA. **ID** Robust with heavy bill and *black crown*. Mostly black with *white auriculars*, throat, and lower underparts. Ad has deep red eyes. Larger White-necked Puffbird has different head pattern and narrower black breast-band. **HABITS** Upper midstory to subcanopy of humid broadleaf forest. Perches motionless for long periods on exposed branch or vine, usually in shaded forest interior. Usually solitary, sometimes in pairs. **VOICE** Loud song (1) a very long series of whistles that usually end with three two-syllable phrases on lower pitch *kweee-kweee-kweee-kweee-kweee-kweee-a, kwey-a, kyoo-a*. May suggest song of Bright-rumped Attila.

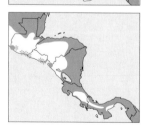

White-necked Puffbird *Notharchus hyperrhynchus*   25 cm
CA and SA. Uncommon resident in lowlands and foothills (to 750 m). Rare in north Pacific where historically perhaps more widespread in GT (Santa Rosa, Escuintla, Retalhuleu, 539, 279, 608) and SV (Ahuachapán, San Miguel, 183, 619). **ID** Large and bulky with heavy, black bill. Note *white forecrown*. Mostly black above and white below with *black pectoral band*. Ad has deep red eyes. **HABITS** Subcanopy to canopy in arid to humid broadleaf forest, second growth, clearings with scattered trees, plantations, mangroves, and gallery forest. Usually solitary, sometimes in pairs. Perches on high, bare snag. May sit motionless for long periods. **VOICE** Usually quiet. Song (1) a long trill on steady pitch *trtrtrtrtrtrtrtrtrtrtrtrtrt*. Infrequently gives (2) a strongly downslurred, slightly hissing cry *wheeeeeeeuuur*. Compare with call of White-whiskered Puffbird.

40%

White-whiskered Puffbird

typical ♂

rufous morph ♂

♀

Lanceolated Monklet

Pied Puffbird

Black-breasted Puffbird

White-necked Puffbird

NUNBIRD Bucconidae

White-fronted Nunbird is a distinctive, large puffbird found locally in humid broadleaf forest.

White-fronted Nunbird *Monasa morphoeus* 28–30 cm

CA and SA. Uncommon to rare and local resident in humid lowlands and foothills (to 500, locally to 700 m). **ID** Large and long-tailed. Long, slightly curved and pointed *red bill* and white or cream forehead, chin, and lores. Imm brownish with buff facial bristles. **GV** Birds from north CA are mostly dark slate-gray. Birds from east PA lack white on throat and have pale gray wing coverts. **HABITS** Midstory of humid broadleaf forest, adjacent tall second growth, and shaded plantations. Often near gaps, at edges, or in riparian forests. Pairs or groups sometimes follow mixed flocks that may include fruitcrows, caciques, *Celeus* and *Piculus* woodpeckers, and Speckled Mourners. Often noisy and conspicuous. Groups vocalize together in loose, cacophonous chorus while raising and lowering their tails. Sallies abruptly to seize prey from vegetation or ground. Flies gracefully with swooping glides. **VOICE** Varied repertoire includes (1) a descending whistle followed by short trill *peeeurr-r-r-r*. Also (2) a variety of loud, slurred cries *how how how* or *ooit ooit ooit*.

BARBETS Capitonidae

Barbets are smaller relatives of the toucans confined to southern Central America.

Red-headed Barbet *Eubucco bourcierii* 15 cm

CA and SA. Fairly common resident in south foothills and lower highlands (900 to 1500 m). May undertake local or altitudinal movements (92). **ID** Stout and large-headed with *heavy, pale bill*. Note *coarse olive streaking on flanks*. Ad male has mostly *red head* and yellow bill. Ad female has *blue auriculars* and brow contrasting with dark face. Imm male (not shown) has less red on head. **GV** Male from east PA has more red (less orange) on breast. **HABITS** Midstory to subcanopy of humid broadleaf forest, adjacent second growth, and shaded plantations. Usually in pairs or small groups following mixed flocks. Forages actively. Often clings or hangs while rummaging through clusters of suspended dead leaves and other arboreal litter. Bounds heavily along larger branches and makes short, direct flights. **VOICE** Usually quiet. Infrequently heard song (1) a series of short, hollow notes lasting about two seconds *who-oh-oh-oh-oh-oh*. Compare with song of Scaled Antpitta.

Spot-crowned Barbet *Capito maculicoronatus* 17.5 cm

CA and north SA. Uncommon resident in humid lowlands and foothills (to 900 m) of PA. **ID** Stout and large-headed. Mostly *black above with white spotting or mottling on crown*. Both sexes have heavy blue-gray bill with dark tip, red (or orange) on flanks, and *bold black-and-white streaking or spotting on lower underparts*. Male has white throat and yellow breast. Female has black throat and breast. **GV** Birds from east PA have red on flanks and bolder whitish spotting on crown. **HABITS** Upper midstory to canopy and edge of humid broadleaf forest, tall second growth, and adjacent shaded plantations. Pairs or small groups sometimes follow mixed flocks. **VOICE** Usually quiet. Call (1) a series of short, harsh, slightly hoarse cries *aaak* or *errrk*.

BARBET Semnornithidae

Prong-billed Barbet *Semnornis frantzii* 18 cm

CA endemic. Uncommon to locally fairly common resident in highlands (mainly 750 to 2450, rarely or locally as low as 500 m) of CR and west PA. May undertake local or altitudinal movements (92). **ID** Stout and large-headed. *Heavy gray bill* and narrow, short tail. Pale gray base of bill contrasts with restricted *black mask* and chin. Head and breast mostly tawny ochre. Male has inconspicuous long black feathers on nape. **HABITS** Midstory to subcanopy and edge of very humid broadleaf (cloud) forest, adjacent second growth, and plantations. Pairs or groups hop heavily through vegetation or loiter at fruiting trees. Often sluggish and unsuspicious. Flight heavy and labored. Groups fly single file, like toucans, between trees. **VOICE** Call (1) a long series of hollow, resonant, low-pitched cries *cwa-cwa-cwa-cwa* . . . Pairs call in duet and groups may vocalize in chorus. Sometimes gives (2) a low-pitched, dry, nasal *kwaaah*.

40%

widespread

east PA

White-fronted Nunbird

east PA ♂

widespread ♀

widespread ♂

Red-headed Barbet

Spot-crowned Barbet

central PA ♀

central PA ♂

east PA ♂

♀

♂

Prong-billed Barbet

TOUCANETS AND ARACARIS Ramphastidae

Smaller toucans found mainly in humid broadleaf forest. All have loud, often repeated calls, and most are detected by voice. Collared Aracari is the most common and widespread.

Emerald Toucanet[16] *Aulacorhynchus prasinus*   32 cm

MX and CA. Uncommon resident in foothills and highlands (mainly 800 to 3000 m, seasonally or locally as low as SL in Caribbean lowlands). Also volcanic highlands of SV (San Miguel, San Vicente, 183, 341). May move to lower elevations outside breeding season. **ID** *Maxilla mostly yellow*. White face and throat. Mostly *plain green* with cinnamon crissum and cinnamon tips of rectrices. **HABITS** Midstory to canopy and edge of semihumid to humid broadleaf forest, shaded plantations, and pastures with scattered trees. **VOICE** Call (1) a loud, slightly hoarse *raak raak raak raak* or *ak ak ak ak* . . . often continued for several minutes. Less frequently heard (2) a soft *eeaaah*.

Blue-throated Toucanet[16] *Aulacorhynchus caeruleogularis*   32 cm

CA and SA. Uncommon to locally common resident in south foothills and highlands (600 to 2400 m). Rare and local in central PA. **ID** *Maxilla mostly yellow*. Face and throat blue. Mostly *plain green* with cinnamon crissum and cinnamon tips of rectrices. **GV** Birds from central and east PA have blackish (not chestnut) spot on base of culmen. **HABITS** Midstory to canopy and edge of semihumid to humid broadleaf forest and shaded plantations and pastures with scattered trees. **VOICE** Call (1) a loud, slightly hoarse *raak raak raak raak* or *ak ak ak ak* . . . like Emerald Toucanet. Compare with coarser, lower-pitched call of Yellow-eared Toucanet.

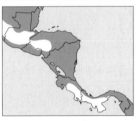

Yellow-eared Toucanet *Selenidera spectabilis*   38 cm

CA and north SA. Uncommon resident in humid lowlands and foothills (breeds 300 to 1200 m, may descend to lower elevations outside breeding season). Rare and poorly known in HN (Atlántida, Gracias a Dios, 442) and NI (Jinotega, RAAN, Matagalpa, 332, 358). Historically reported from central NI (Chontales, 537). **ID** *Green bare facial skin* and *mostly black head and underparts*. Crissum red. Male has *yellow tufts extending from auriculars*. Female has chestnut crown and nape. **HABITS** Midstory to canopy and edge of humid broadleaf forest and adjacent tall second growth. Inconspicuous when not vocalizing. Often in pairs or small groups. Vocalizing male throws head back and flips tail up with each croak. **VOICE** Typical call (1) a repeated, hoarse rattle *k'krrruk k'krrruk k'kruuuk* . . . or *k'rrrak k'rrrak* . . . with clicking introductory note. Compare with higher-pitched, smoother croaking of Keel-billed Toucan. Also compare with call of Emerald Toucanet.

Collared Aracari *Pteroglossus torquatus*   45 cm

South MX to north SA. Fairly common resident in Caribbean lowlands and foothills (to 1200, rarely or locally to 1650 m in north). Uncommon and local in north Pacific. **ID** Slender with long, narrow tail. Head mostly black with bare red facial skin. Eyes yellow. *Dark belly-band and central spot* divide *mostly yellow lower underparts*. Maxilla mostly ivory. Fiery-billed Aracari allopatric. **GV** Birds from east PA have dark stripe on maxilla and often lack rufous collar. **HABITS** Upper midstory to canopy and edge of semihumid to humid broadleaf forest, tall second growth, and shaded plantations. In pairs or groups that fly single file across gaps or through subcanopy. Call (1) a loud, emphatic, metallic *pseek* or *pisseek* or *pink* repeated in short series or given in chorus by several birds. In interactions (2) a rasping *grahhrr*. Also (3) a high-pitched, squealing *eeeyeeek* and (4) rapidly repeated, sharp *pitit*.

Fiery-billed Aracari *Pteroglossus frantzii*   45 cm

CA endemic. Uncommon resident in humid Pacific lowlands and foothills (to 1500 m) of east CR (Puntarenas) and west PA (Chiriquí). **ID** Slender with long, narrow tail. Head mostly black with bare red facial skin. Eyes yellow. Dark belly-band and central spot divide mostly yellow lower underparts. *Maxilla mostly yellow grading distally to orange-red*. Collared Aracari allopatric. **HABITS** Upper midstory to canopy and edge of humid broadleaf forest, tall second growth, and shaded plantations. In pairs or groups. Flies single-file across gaps or through subcanopy. **VOICE** Call (1) a loud, sharp, metallic *k-leek* or *ka-seek*. Very similar to Collared Aracari but perhaps more distinctly two-syllabled.

Emerald Toucanet

Blue-throated Toucanet

CR and
west PA

central and
east PA

♀

♂

Yellow-eared Toucanet

widespread

Collared Aracari

east PA
♂

Fiery-billed Aracari

TOUCANS Ramphastidae

Large toucans found in canopy of humid broadleaf forest. Keel-billed Toucan is the most common and widespread.

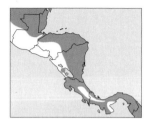

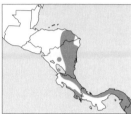

Keel-billed Toucan *Ramphastos sulfuratus*   50 cm

South MX to north SA. Widespread and fairly common resident in lowlands and foothills (to 1400 m). Local Pacific NI at Volcán Mombacho (Granada, 413). **ID** Large. *Mostly green bill with red tip.* Throat and breast yellow. In south compare with Yellow-throated Toucan. Note different bill pattern and voice. **GV** Some birds from north GT and BZ lack red border of breast and have more extensive red on bill. **HABITS** Subcanopy to canopy and edge of semihumid to humid broadleaf forest, tall second growth, and adjacent shaded plantations. Usually in pairs or small groups. Often perches conspicuously on high, bare limb while vocalizing. **VOICE** Call (1) a harsh, croaking *crrrik crrrik crrrik . . .* or *crrruk crrruk crrruk . . .* with resonant, wooden or mechanical quality. Often repeated in long, monotonous series in early morning and late afternoon. In south compare with coarser, more rattlelike call of Yellow-eared Toucanet.

Yellow-throated Toucan *Ramphastos ambiguus*   54 cm

CA and north SA. Fairly common resident in lowlands and foothills (to 1200, locally to 1850 m in Pacific CR). **ID** Large. Bicolored *chestnut and yellow bill.* Throat and breast yellow. Compare with Keel-billed Toucan. Note different bill pattern and voice. **HABITS** Subcanopy to canopy and edge of humid broadleaf forest, tall second growth, and adjacent shaded plantations with tall trees. Groups gather in late afternoon or evening in crowns of emergent tree or on high snag where they vocalize in chorus. **VOICE** Call (1) a shrill, yelping, resonant *eey-yaya, yaya, eeyaya yup ya* or *yo-yip a-yip, a-yip.* Often repeated persistently. Also (2) a loud, mechanical rattle that is lower-pitched than call of Keel-billed Toucan.

Choco Toucan *Ramphastos brevis*   48 cm

Mainly north Pacific SA. Rare, local and poorly known in lowlands and foothills (to 500 m) of east PA (Darién, 512, 48). **ID** Large. Note *black (not chestnut) mandible.* Very similar to larger Yellow-throated Toucan. Note different bill pattern and voice. **HABITS** Like Yellow-throated Toucan. **VOICE** Call (1) a low-pitched, croaking *crrruk crrruk crrruk . . .* Much like Keel-billed Toucan.

Keel-billed Toucan

GT and BZ

widespread

Yellow-throated Toucan

Choco Toucan

PICULET AND WOODPECKERS Picidae
Small woodpeckers found in forest and woodland. Smoky-brown Woodpecker is the most common and widespread.

Olivaceous Piculet *Picumnus olivaceus* 10 cm
CA and north SA. Rare and local resident in Caribbean lowlands and foothills (to 750 m) of GT (Izabal, Alta Verapaz, 380), HN (Cortés, Colón, Yoro, Olancho, Atlántida, Gracias a Dios, 63, 442, 262), and NI (RAAN, 358). Also rare and local in south NI (Río San Juan, 324, 413) and adjacent CR (Alajuela, 600). Uncommon and local in Pacific east CR (Puntarenas, 126) and PA (to 1400, locally to 1600 m). **ID** *Very small* and short-tailed with short bill. Note *black-and-white striped tail*. Male of widespread form has orange spots on crown. Compare with Plain Xenops. **GV** Males from GT and HN (not shown) have red spots on crown. **HABITS** Midstory to canopy and edge of humid broadleaf forest, second growth, mangroves, plantations, and gardens. Pairs or solitary birds may follow mixed flocks but also forage independently. Taps rapidly on small (often bare) twig or bamboo stem. Clings to perch with tail depressed. **VOICE** Calls (1) a high-pitched trill that drops in pitch and may slow slightly at end and (2) a sharp, sibilant *ssit* or *pst*. Sometimes repeated.

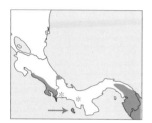

Red-rumped Woodpecker *Veniliornis kirkii* 16.5 cm
CA and north SA. Uncommon and local resident in lowlands and foothills (to 1000 m) of Pacific CR (Puntarenas, 126, 600) and west PA. Formerly perhaps more widespread in west PA (Chiriquí, Veraguas, 657, 512). Rare in Caribbean foothills of east CR (Limón, 570). Disjunctly in east PA (Darién, 657) where fairly common. Also Isla Coiba (Veraguas, 657). **ID** Small and dark. *Barred underparts* and *red rump*. Note yellow on nape. Upperparts mostly plain olive. Male has red crown spotted with black. Female has brown crown. Compare with Smoky-brown Woodpecker. Note different underparts. **GV** Birds from east PA have broader pale bars on underparts and show some red on mantle. **HABITS** Midstory to subcanopy of semihumid to humid broadleaf forest. Creeps and probes along smaller limbs and branches. Pairs or solitary birds follow mixed flocks. **VOICE** Calls (1) a nasal, squeaky *k'wink k'wink* or *kweuu kweuu* or *kew kew kew* with two to four notes and (2) short, nasal *keer*. Compare with harsher, more attenuated call of Rufous-winged Woodpecker.

Smoky-brown Woodpecker *Picoides fumigatus* 16 cm
MX to SA. Common resident in north Caribbean lowlands and foothills (to 1200 m). Uncommon to rare on north Pacific slope in GT, SV (La Paz, Usulután, 183), and NI (Managua, 346). Uncommon to rare in south foothills and highlands (400 to 1900 m). **ID** Small and dark. Mostly *plain grayish-brown including underparts*. Pale sides of head with dusky malar. Male has red crown. Female has brown crown. Compare with Red-rumped Woodpecker. Note different underparts. **HABITS** Understory to subcanopy and edge of semihumid to humid broadleaf forest, second growth and plantations. Locally in mangroves. Forages mainly on slender twigs and vines. Sometimes in foliage. Retiring and inconspicuous. Pairs or solitary birds follow mixed flocks. **VOICE** Call (1) a sharp, metallic *wick* or *pwik*. Softer and more slurred than call of Hairy Woodpecker. Also (2) a low-pitched, rolling, gravelly *jer-jer-jer-jer . . .* or *krr-krr-krr . . .*

Ladder-backed Woodpecker *Picoides scalaris* 15 cm
South USA to CA. Uncommon and local resident in Caribbean north GT (Petén, 229), BZ (529, 343), HN (Gracias a Dios, 442), and NI (RAAN, 327). Locally fairly common in highlands of HN (442). Local in Pacific coastal SV (La Unión, 360), HN (Valle, 442, 336), and NI (León, 413, 134). A report from GT highlands (Sacatepéquez, 317) is dubious. **ID** Short bill. *Black-outlined auriculars* and narrow black malar. Note *speckled breast* and dark barring on flanks. Male has red hindcrown and nape. Female has black crown. Imm male has reduced red. Golden-fronted and Yucatan woodpeckers have different head and underparts pattern. **HABITS** Midstory to subcanopy of arid to semihumid pine and pine-oak woodland, savannas and mangroves. **VOICE** Calls (1) a rapid, harsh rattle that slows abruptly and drops in pitch *chechechejujuju* and (2) a very sharp *ick!* or *chik!*

Hairy Woodpecker *Picoides villosus* 18 cm
NA to CA. Fairly common resident in highlands (1000 to 3700 in north, above 1500 m in CR and PA). **ID** Blackish above with *white central mantle* and *white spots on flight feathers*. Underparts variably light to medium brown. Male has red band on nape. Imm male may show variable extent of red extending to crown. Female lacks red. Black-cheeked Woodpecker (lower elevations) has barred flanks and white rump. **HABITS** Midstory and edge of humid broadleaf and mixed broadleaf-coniferous forest, plantations, and gardens. Creeps on trunks and larger branches. Clings to twigs and vines. Solitary or in pairs. Does not follow mixed flocks. **VOICE** Calls (1) a short, sharp, hard rattle *brr-r-r-r-r* or *t-r-r-r-r-r*, (2) high-pitched, clear, rapid *bic-bic-bic-bic-bic*, and (3) very sharp, hard *pick!* or *eek!*

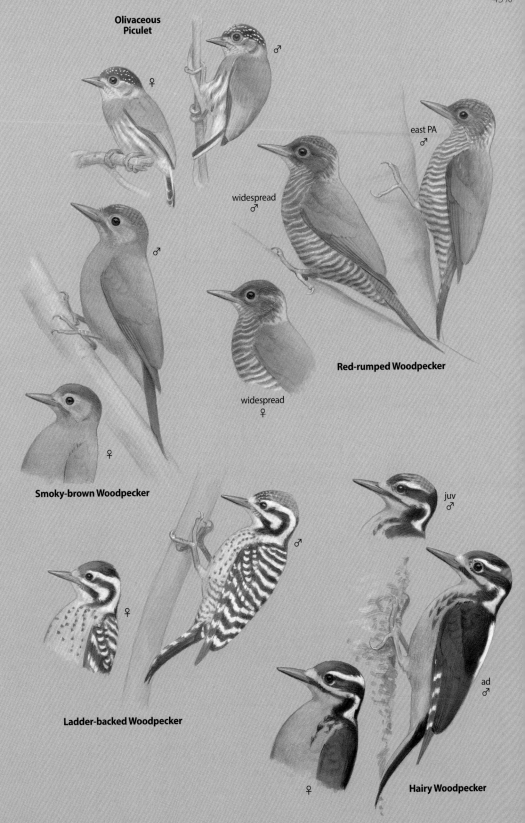

Olivaceous Piculet

♀

♂

east PA ♂

widespread ♂

Red-rumped Woodpecker

widespread ♀

♂

♀

Smoky-brown Woodpecker

juv ♂

Ladder-backed Woodpecker

♂

♀

ad ♂

♀

Hairy Woodpecker

WOODPECKERS Picidae

A complex group of very similar *Melanerpes* woodpeckers that include several geographically variable species. Most are parapatric replacements, but Yucatan and Golden-fronted woodpeckers are locally syntopic in north Caribbean Central America. These species favor arid to semihumid nonforest habitats and are generally common. Observers should note details of head pattern and bill structure as well as geographic range.

Yucatan Woodpecker *Melanerpes pygmaeus*   17.5 cm

South MX and CA. Uncommon to locally fairly common resident in north Caribbean lowlands of BZ and BZ Cays including Ambergris Cay and Cay Caulker (Corozal, Orange Walk, Belize, 528, 529, 343) and north GT (Petén, 229). Also Isla Guanaja and Isla Roatán in Bay Islands (539, 94, 442, 346). **ID** Small with *short bill*. Note *yellow on nasal tufts* (often extending to chin and forecheek). Belly usually red (sometimes orange). Male has red crown and nape. Female has red confined to nape. Compare with locally syntopic Golden-fronted Woodpecker. Note Yucatan's different voice, shorter bill, smaller size, and yellow nasal tufts. Also note Yucatan's broad whitish band on forehead. Hoffman's and Red-crowned woodpeckers allopatric. **GV** Birds from Isla Guanaja in Bay Islands are darker below and on head, and have extensive white on central rectrices. **HABITS** Uses a variety of arboreal habitats including semihumid (deciduous) forest, littoral scrub, gallery forest, second growth, plantations, gardens, savannas, and mangroves. **VOICE** Calls (1) a short, nasal *whehehe* and (2) shorter *jehr*. Compare with call of Golden-fronted Woodpecker.

Golden-fronted Woodpecker *Melanerpes aurifrons*   21 cm

South USA to north CA. Common resident in lowlands and foothills (to 1500, locally to 3000 m). Also Turneffe Island, Cay Caulker, Ambergris Cay, and Moho Cay in BZ Cays (528, 529, 343) and Isla Roatán and Isla Útila in Bay Islands (513, 94, 442). **ID** Male has red crown and nape. Female has red confined to nape. Widespread form has *yellow nasal tufts and central belly*. In BZ and north GT compare with Yucatan Woodpecker. Note Golden-fronted's red nasal tufts and larger size. Golden-fronted typically has *proportionally larger bill* but bill size is variable in both species with males having longer bills. **GV** Birds from mainland Caribbean slope and Isla Roatán have *red nasal tufts* and belly. Birds from BZ Cays have broader white bars on mantle. Widespread mainland and Isla Útila forms have yellow nasal tufts and belly. Birds from Caribbean valleys of GT (not shown) have broader white bars on mantle, yellow nasal tufts, and yellow or orange belly. Some have orange nape. **HABITS** Uses all levels of vegetation in a wide variety of nonforest arboreal habitats including humid broadleaf forest edge, second growth, plantations, gardens, and mangroves. Solitary or in pairs. Does not follow mixed flocks. **VOICE** Calls (1) a quavering rattle *whe-he-heh-heh-heh-he*. Compare with shorter, faster call of Yucatan Woodpecker. Also a short, hoarse *ehk*. Often repeated.

Hoffman's Woodpecker *Melanerpes hoffmannii*   20 cm

CA endemic. Common resident in Pacific lowlands and foothills (to 200, locally to 2000 m). Recently reported from east SV where may be locally syntopic with Golden-fronted Woodpecker (La Unión, 301). Hybrids with Golden-fronted are reported from that area and adjacent Pacific HN (Choluteca, 442). **ID** In all plumages note *yellow nape and belly*. Male has red crown. Hybridizes with Red-crowned Woodpecker in central Pacific lowlands of CR (Puntarenas). Orange-naped birds and mixed pairs occur in that area. **HABITS** Midstory to subcanopy and edge in a wide variety of arboreal habitats including semihumid to humid broadleaf forest, second growth, plantations, gardens, and mangroves. Usually in pairs. **VOICE** Call (1) a metallic rattle *whe-he-heh-heh-hehheh . . .* or *ch-ch-ch-ch-ch-che . . .* May be repeated or extended in short bursts.

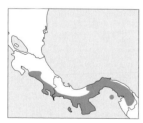

Red-crowned Woodpecker *Melanerpes rubricapillus*   18 cm

CA and north SA. Common resident in Pacific lowlands and foothills (to 1500 m) of east CR (Puntarenas) and PA. Reaches Caribbean slope locally in central CR and central and east PA. Also Isla Coiba and Pearl Islands (Veraguas, Panamá, 58, 455, 653, 470). **ID** Both sexes have pale forehead and *red nape and belly*. Male also has red crown. Golden-fronted Woodpecker allopatric. **GV** Birds from Isla Coiba and Pearl Islands are variably darker. Red-crowned Woodpecker hybridizes with Hoffman's Woodpecker in central Pacific CR and orange-naped birds are sometimes seen there. **HABITS** Midstory to canopy and edge in wide variety of arboreal habitats, including humid broadleaf forest, second growth, plantations, gardens, and mangroves. Usually in pairs. **VOICE** Calls (1) a short, metallic rattle *krr-r-r-r* and (2) nasal *wicka-wicka . . .* Other calls like Hoffman's Woodpecker.

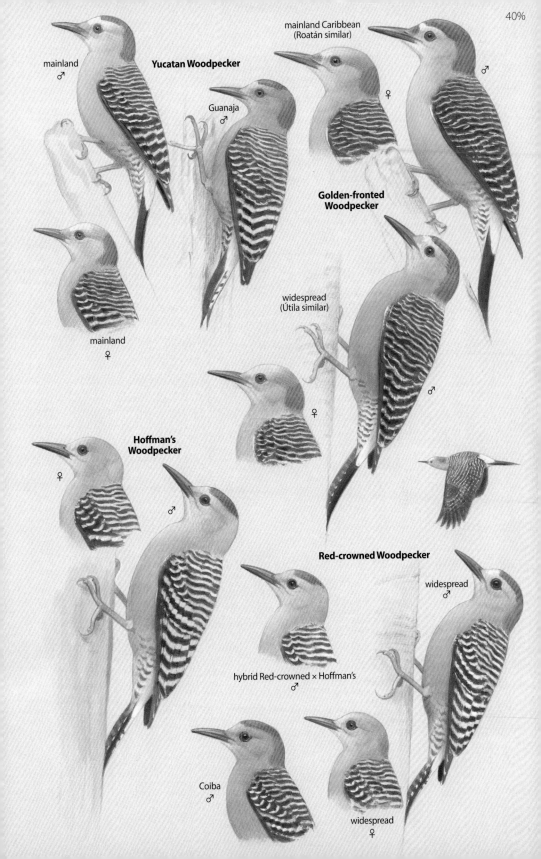

40%

mainland
♂

Yucatan Woodpecker

Guanaja
♂

mainland Caribbean
(Roatán similar)

♀

♂

Golden-fronted
Woodpecker

mainland
♀

widespread
(Útila similar)

♂

♀

Hoffman's
Woodpecker

♀

♂

Red-crowned Woodpecker

widespread
♂

hybrid Red-crowned × Hoffman's
♂

Coiba
♂

widespread
♀

WOODPECKERS Picidae

Black-cheeked Woodpecker *Melanerpes pucherani* 19.5 cm

CA and north SA. Fairly common resident in lowlands and foothills (to 900, locally to 1300 m in north). Rare and local in Azuero Peninsula (Los Santos, 512). **ID** *Black auriculars with white postocular spot* and black sides of neck. Mantle barred with black and white. Wings black with fine white barring and spotting. Male has red crown and nape. Female has red confined to nape. Golden-naped Woodpecker allopatric. **HABITS** Midstory to canopy and edge of semihumid to humid broadleaf forest, tall second growth, plantations, and gardens. Solitary or in pairs. Sometimes clings upside down to feed on fruit. Takes nectar at canopy flowers. **VOICE** Calls (1) a short series of five to seven notes on same pitch forming slightly quavering rattle *we-e-e-e-e-h*. Compare with call of Golden-fronted Woodpecker. Also (2) a short, dry rattle on steady pitch.

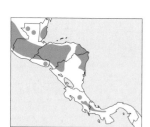

Golden-naped Woodpecker *Melanerpes chrysauchen* 19.5 cm

CA endemic. Confined to Pacific lowlands and foothills (to 1200, rarely or locally to 1500 m) of east CR and west PA. Locally fairly common resident in Pacific CR. Rare in west PA where now confined to Burica Peninsula (Chiriquí, 512). Formerly ranged east to south Veraguas (657). **ID** *Yellow nape* and forehead. Note black auriculars and sides of neck and barred lower underparts. Upperparts black with white barring confined to tertials. Central mantle mostly white. Male has red crown. Black-cheeked Woodpecker allopatric. **HABITS** Midstory to subcanopy and edge of humid broadleaf forest and second growth. Similar to Black-cheeked Woodpecker. **VOICE** Calls (1) a short, nasal rattle or trill *wha-ah-ah* that may be repeated rapidly three to eight times and (2) longer, faster, higher-pitched rattle *re-he-he-he-he-he*. Similar to Black-cheeked Woodpecker.

Acorn Woodpecker *Melanerpes formicivorus* 23 cm

USA to north SA. Common resident in highlands (to 2850 m) and in Caribbean lowlands of BZ, GT, HN, and NI. Also volcanic highlands of SV (San Miguel, 341). **ID** Mostly black above with *whitish eyes* and red crown. White forehead and throat contrast with black chin and auriculars. In flight, shows white on wing and rump. *White underparts variably streaked with black.* **HABITS** Oak-dominated forest or woodland and adjacent semi-open areas. Conspicuous and noisy. Small groups or pairs forage at middle levels. Feeds on acorns. May sally to seize flying insects from an open perch. **VOICE** Call (1) a series of loud, coarse, nasal phrases *rack-up, rack-up* or *whaaka-whaaka* that may be varied to a rolling *r-r-r-rack-up* or more strident *rraaa-har-har, reep-hi-hur-hurr*.

Yellow-bellied Sapsucker *Sphyrapicus varius* 20 cm

Breeds Nearctic. Winters south USA and WI to CA. Uncommon transient and winter resident (mainly Nov to Apr). Most common in highlands (to 3200 m). Very rare in central and east PA (Darién, 117, 425). **ID** Slightly tufted or crested. In all plumages note *bold white wing patch* (conspicuous in flight). Also note white lores, facial stripe and supercilium extending behind eye. Ad male (rare in CA) has red crown and throat. Brownish imm has *extensive blackish barring on wings, tail, and mantle*. Compare with Black-cheeked Woodpecker. Note different head and wing pattern. **HABITS** Midstory to subcanopy and edge in a wide variety of arboreal habitats, including arid to humid broadleaf forest, second growth, savannas, plantations, and gardens. Inconspicuous. Usually solitary. **VOICE** Usually silent in winter. May give (1) a whining, nasal *naaah* or *eyyahhhh*.

Red-naped Sapsucker *Sphyrapicus nuchalis* 20 cm

Breeds west Nearctic. Winters mainly south USA and MX. Historical records from GT highlands (Sololá, 229, 539) and west HN (Santa Bárbara, 442). **ID** Resembles widespread Yellow-bellied Sapsucker. Red-naped Sapsucker distinguished by *red on nape* and narrower (often broken) black border of throat. Female has red throat with restricted white chin. **HABITS** Similar to Yellow-bellied Sapsucker. **VOICE** Similar to Yellow-bellied Sapsucker.

40%

Black-cheeked Woodpecker

♂

♂

♀

Golden-naped Woodpecker

♀

Acorn Woodpecker ♂

♀

imm
♀

Yellow-bellied Sapsucker

ad
♂

ad
♀

imm
♀

Red-naped Sapsucker

ad
♂

WOODPECKERS Picidae

Medium-sized woodpeckers found mainly in humid broadleaf forest. Often in pairs following mixed flocks. Golden-olive Woodpecker is widespread in north Central America but is confined mainly to foothills and highlands in Costa Rica and Panama.

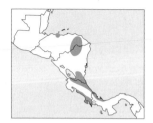

Rufous-winged Woodpecker *Piculus simplex*   19 cm

CA endemic. Uncommon resident in humid lowlands and foothills (to 750, locally to 900 m). Rare in Pacific CR (600) and west PA (Chiriquí, Veraguas, 657, 512) where formerly perhaps more widespread. Very rare in west Caribbean HN (Atlántida). **ID** *Olive upperparts* and rufous primaries barred with blackish (usually visible in folded wing). Note *olive breast spotted with whitish*, and *dusky and whitish barring on flanks and belly*. At close range note pale blue-gray eyes. Male has red malar and mostly red crown and nape. Female has olive crown and auriculars with red confined to nape. Stripe-cheeked Woodpecker allopatric. Compare with Golden-olive Woodpecker. **HABITS** Midstory to subcanopy and edge of humid broadleaf forest and adjacent tall second growth. Pairs or solitary birds may follow mixed flocks that include caciques or nunbirds. **VOICE** Call (1) a loud, emphatic series of four to twelve downslurred, slightly nasal notes *keeeah keeeah keeah* or *heew heew heew heew*. Also (2) a loud, sharp, nasal *deeeeh*. Compare with lower-pitched call of Golden-olive Woodpecker and more nasal call of Slate-colored Grosbeak.

Stripe-cheeked Woodpecker *Piculus callopterus*   19 cm

CA and SA. Uncommon to rare and local resident in foothills (300 to 1000 m, locally to near SL) of east PA. **ID** Mostly olive (including auriculars) with *pale moustache*. Eyes blue-gray. Note olive breast spotted with whitish, and dusky and whitish barring on flanks and belly. Male has broad red malar stripe and red crown and nape. Female has red restricted to nape. Female's crown dark gray. Rufous-winged Woodpecker allopatric. Compare with Golden-olive Woodpecker. Note different head pattern. **HABITS** Interior midstory to subcanopy of humid broadleaf forest. Usually inconspicuous. Solitary or in pairs. **VOICE** Calls (1) a rapid, rhythmic *eeyuk-eeyuk-eeyuk . . .* or *eweek-eweek-eweek . . .*, (2) longer, downslurred, nasal, whining *kweeeeeuu*, and (3) rapid series of short, squeaky cries *kweet-kweet-kweet . . .*

Golden-green Woodpecker *Piculus chrysochloros*   22 cm

CA and SA. Poorly known. Uncommon to rare and local resident in lowlands and foothills (to 450, rarely or locally to 800 m) of east PA (Panamá, Darién, Kuna Yala, 657, 512, 42). **ID** Short crest. Both sexes have *olive-and-yellow barring on underparts* (no spotting on upper breast) and *long, yellow moustache*. Upperparts mostly olive-green. Note yellow throat and pale gray eyes. Ad male has red crown, nape, and malar stripe. Female's crown mostly deep yellow with contrasting olive auriculars and malar stripe. Imm male has drab buff throat and lacks red moustachial stripe. Compare with Stripe-cheeked Woodpecker. Note different head pattern. Rufous-winged Woodpecker allopatric. **HABITS** Poorly known in region. Midstory to subcanopy and edge of broadleaf (semi-deciduous) and swamp forest. Pairs or solitary birds follow mixed flocks. **VOICE** Call (1) a harsh, hoarse, downslurred scream *whaaaaah*.

Golden-olive Woodpecker *Colaptes rubiginosus*   21 cm

MX to SA. Uncommon to fairly common resident in north lowlands and foothills (to 1500, rarely to 2500 m) of north. Uncommon and local in south foothills and highlands (750 to 2000 m). Also Pacific volcanic range in NI (Granada, Chinandega, 413). **ID** Gray crown. *Pale grayish-white face* and auriculars contrast with dark crown and throat. *Eyes dark*. Underparts and neck variably dusky to dark olive with fine whitish or yellowish barring. Male has red malar, supercilium, and nape. Female lacks red malar. Spot-breasted Woodpecker (east PA) allopatric. **HABITS** Midstory to subcanopy and edge of arid to humid broadleaf forest, tall second growth, plantations, gardens, and pine savanna. Pairs or solitary birds sometimes follow mixed flocks. Forages mainly along outer limbs and branches, often probing into epiphytes or vine tangles. **VOICE** Calls (1) a loud, clear, abrupt *jeeeah!* and (2) long, steady rattle or trill. Higher-pitched and more rapid than calls of *Melanerpes* woodpeckers.

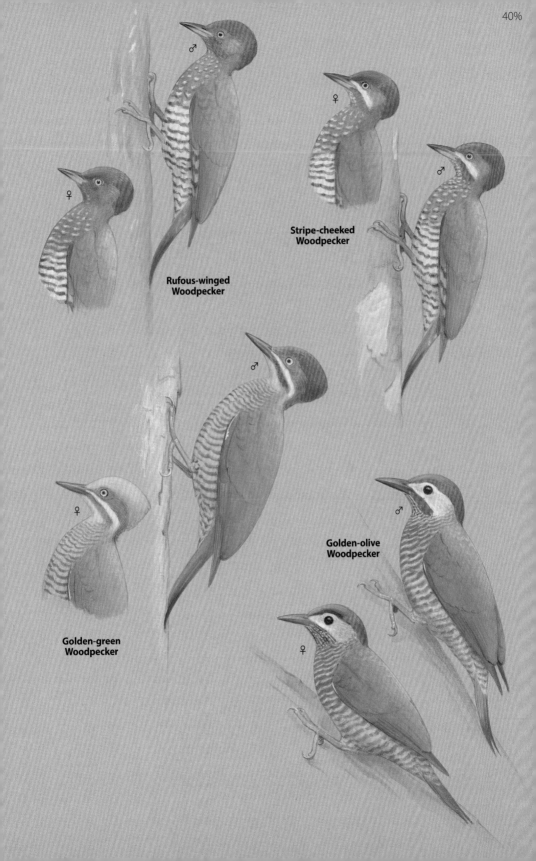

40%

Rufous-winged
Woodpecker

Stripe-cheeked
Woodpecker

Golden-olive
Woodpecker

Golden-green
Woodpecker

WOODPECKERS Picidae

Medium-sized woodpeckers. Northern Flicker and Spot-breasted Woodpecker are found in semi-open areas. *Celeus* woodpeckers are found in tall humid broadleaf forest where they are often detected by their loud, distinctive calls.

Spot-breasted Woodpecker *Colaptes punctigula* 20 cm

CA and SA. Common resident in Pacific lowlands of east PA. **ID** *White auriculars* contrast with black and red crown. Note yellow rump and *pale yellow lower underparts with dark spotting*. Olive upperparts barred and spotted with blackish. Male has broad red malar. Golden-olive Woodpecker allopatric. **HABITS** Midstory to subcanopy of mangroves, littoral scrub, open woodland, plantations, and semi-open areas with scattered trees. Sometimes forages on ground. **VOICE** Call (1) an even-pitched series of hoarse, high-pitched cries *whee-whee-whee-whee . . .* or *ih-ihih-ih-ih-ih-ih . . .*

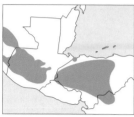

Northern Flicker *Colaptes auratus* 30 cm

NA and CA. Common resident in north highlands (1000 to 4000 m). **ID** Fairly large and boldly patterned. *Black pectoral band* and *cinnamon-brown crown*. Upperparts densely barred with black and light brown. Underparts mostly whitish with *extensive black spotting*. Male has broad red malar. Female has cinnamon malar. In flight, note *pink underwing surface*. **HABITS** Understory to midstory of pine and pine-oak woodland, semi-open areas, scrub, plantations, and gardens. Solitary or in pairs. Often forages on ground. **VOICE** Calls (1) a long series of nasal notes *wh-heh-eh-ehehehehehh* and (2) whining, nasal *wheck-a wheck-a wheck-a.*

Cinnamon Woodpecker *Celeus loricatus* 21 cm

CA and SA. Uncommon resident in humid lowlands and foothills (to 750 m). Local in north NI (RAAN, 332, 413, 626). **ID** *Rufous head* and mantle and bushy crest. Upperparts sparsely spotted and barred with blackish. Bill olive and gray. *Underparts buffy cinnamon* with coarse blackish barring and scaling. Tail barred with black and buff. Male has red throat and moustachial streak. Compare with Chestnut-colored Woodpecker (sympatric in south). **GV** Birds from east PA have sparse dark barring. **HABITS** Lower midstory to subcanopy of humid broadleaf forest. Solitary or in pairs. May follow mixed flocks. **VOICE** Calls (1) a loud, ringing three- to five-note phrase that drops in pitch *peee peew-peu-peu* and (2) short, quavering rattle *waaaah*. Drum (3) a short series of soft taps.

Chestnut-colored Woodpecker *Celeus castaneus* 24 cm

South MX and CA. Uncommon resident in humid lowlands and foothills (to 1100 m). **ID** Both sexes typically have *buff-yellow head* contrasting with *darker chestnut* body and prominent, bushy crest. Note coarse scaled or checkered pattern on *chestnut underparts*. Tail black. Male has red face and moustachial streak. Female has plain *buff-yellow head*. Cinnamon Woodpecker has head concolorous with upperparts (but note that some Chestnut-colored Woodpeckers from north CA have head nearly same color as mantle). Also note different voice. **HABITS** Midstory to canopy and edge of humid broadleaf forest and adjacent tall second growth. Pairs or solitary birds sometimes follow mixed flocks. May feed at flowers in canopy. **VOICE** Call (1) an abrupt, slightly nasal *kyeeeow!* or *kheeeu!* repeated in short series or followed by two to four nasal notes as *kheeeu, eht-eht-eht*. Also (2) a series of sharp, two-syllable phrases *wik-kew wik-kew, wik-kew*. Drum (3) a short, rapid series.

38%

Northern Flicker

♂

♀

Spot-breasted Woodpecker

♂

♀

widespread ♂

east PA ♂

Cinnamon Woodpecker

widespread ♀

♂

♀

Chestnut-colored Woodpecker

WOODPECKERS Picidae

Very large woodpeckers with prominent crest. Details of head and underparts pattern are useful in separating these. *Campephilus* woodpeckers give distinctive double or triple knocks. Lineated is the most common and widespread.

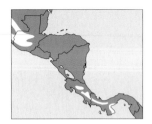

Lineated Woodpecker *Dryocopus lineatus* 33 cm

MX to SA. Common resident in lowlands and foothills (to 1700 m). **ID** Sharply pointed crest. Note *black-and-white striped head* and *widely separated white dorsal stripes*. Female has black forehead and lacks red malar. In flight, shows white underwings. Compare with Pale-billed and Crimson-crested woodpeckers. Note different head and upperparts pattern. **GV** Birds from north CA have pale bill. **HABITS** Midstory to canopy in a wide variety of arboreal habitats including broadleaf forest edge, clearings with scattered trees, plantations, tall second growth, and gardens. Locally inside dry forest but in general less closely associated with forest interior than other large woodpeckers and more often in semi-open or disturbed habitats. Often in pairs. Sometimes perches on high, exposed snag. **VOICE** Calls (1) a long, loud, nearly even-pitched series *wicwicwicwicwicwicwic* . . . or *wheep weep weep weep eep eep ee* . . . and (2) loud, sharp *pik!* or *ick!* sometimes followed by rolling note *pik!-error-r-r*. Drum (3) is several slow taps followed by an accelerating series.

Pale-billed Woodpecker *Campephilus guatemalensis* 36 cm

South MX and CA. Widespread and common resident in lowlands and foothills (to 2000, mainly below 1500 m). **ID** Both sexes have *solid red sides of head* and *pale bill*. Female has black throat and center of crown. Crimson-crested Woodpecker parapatric. Compare with Lineated Woodpecker. Note different mantle and head pattern. **HABITS** Midstory to canopy and edge of broadleaf forest and adjacent shaded plantations and clearings with scattered trees and gardens. Occasionally in humid pine-oak forest. Pairs or solitary birds often perch conspicuously or forage on high, exposed snags. **VOICE** Calls (1) a loud, slightly squeaky, stuttering *k' k'kwidik k'widick* . . . sometimes delivered as a steady rattle *ickickickickickickickick*, (2) whining or moaning cries, and (3) low-pitched *keeu keeu keeu keeu*. Distinctive drum (4) is two loud knocks in quick succession.

Crimson-crested Woodpecker *Campephilus melanoleucos* 35 cm

CA and SA. Fairly common resident lowlands and foothills (to 900 m) of PA. **ID** Male has *bicolored spot on red sides of head*. Female has broad white malar stripe extending to lores and *black crown*. Pale-billed Woodpecker parapatric. Compare with Lineated Woodpecker. Note different head and mantle pattern. **HABITS** Midstory to canopy of humid broadleaf forest, adjacent tall second growth and edges. Forages mainly in canopy and subcanopy. **VOICE** Calls (1) a loud *chiz-ik* and (2) rasping *kiarhh* often followed by snarling *rai-ai-ai-ai*. Typical drum (3) a rapid series of three to five progressively softer knocks. Very different from two-knock drum of Pale-billed and Crimson-bellied woodpeckers.

Crimson-bellied Woodpecker *Campephilus haematogaster* 34 cm

CA and north SA. Uncommon to rare and local resident in lowlands and foothills (to 1600 m) of PA (Colón, Panamá, Kuna Yala, Darién, 657, 512, 426). Rare and poorly known in Caribbean foothills of west PA (Bocas del Toro, Ngöbe-Buglé, 657, 512). **ID** Red crown and hindneck. Note *buff lores and moustache* and red rump. *Upperparts plain black* (no white stripes). At close range note dark red eyes. In flight, shows bands of buff spotting on remiges. Female has black foreneck. Imm male similar to female. Compare with Crimson-crested Woodpecker. Note different head and underparts pattern. Pale-billed Woodpecker mainly allopatric. **HABITS** Midstory of humid broadleaf forest. May forage at lower levels than other large woodpeckers and often found clinging to lower trunks of large trees. Usually in pairs. **VOICE** Calls (1) a high-pitched, squeaky *pink* or *eenk* and (2) nasal *ehk-ehk-ehk, ehk*. Gives a two-knock drum with first knock stronger. Compare with longer drum of Crimson-crested Woodpecker.

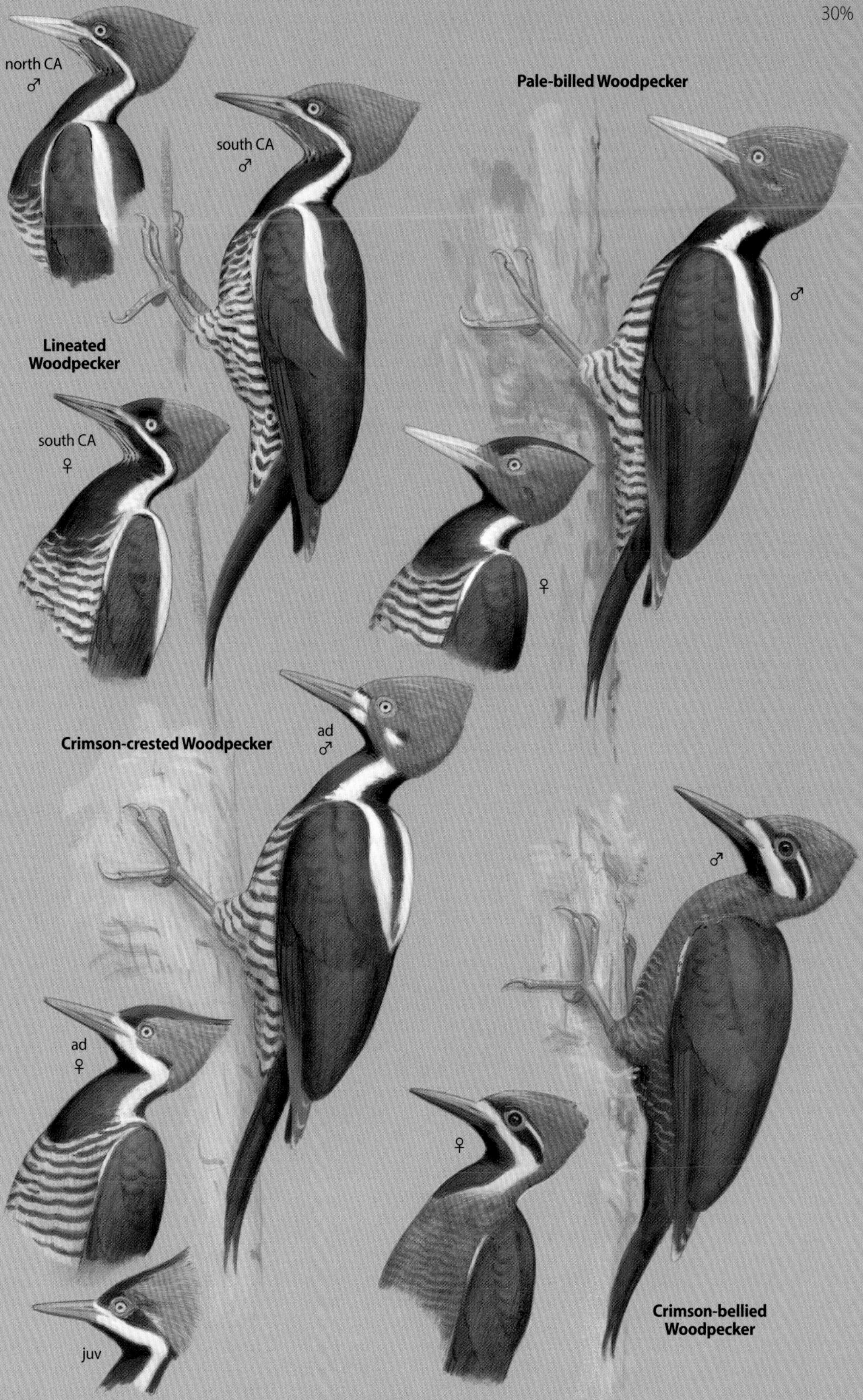

north CA
♂

south CA
♂

Pale-billed Woodpecker

Lineated Woodpecker

south CA
♀

♂

♀

Crimson-crested Woodpecker

ad
♂

♂

ad
♀

♀

juv

Crimson-bellied Woodpecker

FOREST-FALCONS Falconidae

Secretive raptors of broadleaf forest and woodland. Forest-falcons rarely perch in the open but often vocalize persistently in early morning and evening. Collared Forest-Falcon is the most common and widespread.

Barred Forest-Falcon *Micrastur ruficollis* female 36, male 32 cm

MX to SA. Uncommon resident in lowlands and foothills (to 1850, rarely to 2300 m). Rare on Pacific slope in GT (Suchitepéquez Sacatepéquez Quetzaltenango, San Marcos, Escuintla, 154, 229) and SV (Morazán, Ahuachapán, 619). **ID** Small. Short, rounded wings and long, graduated tail. Cere, orbital area, lores, and legs variably orange to yellow. Ad gray above. *Underparts whitish with fine, even, gray barring.* Tail black with narrow white bands and narrow white tip. Imm variable but usually dark brown above with *narrow buff collar* (sometimes concealed). Imm's underparts variably buff or whitish and usually has irregular dusky barring. Compare ad with Tiny Hawk in south. Collared Forest-Falcon is larger and has more strongly graduated tail. Imm Bicolored Hawk lacks barring below and has shorter legs and shorter, less graduated tail. See also Slaty-backed Forest-Falcon. **HABITS** Midstory of semihumid to humid broadleaf forest. Secretive. Usually remains hidden in foliage even when hunting actively. Most often detected by voice. Twitches tail slightly while vocalizing. Attends ant swarms where it may perch very low. **VOICE** Call (1) a long series of short, abrupt cries *our!* or *oow!* May suggest bark of small dog. Compare with more attenuated notes of Collared Forest-Falcon. Also (2) a more rapid, accelerating series that drops in pitch *keo, keo, keo-keo-keo-keo . . .*

Slaty-backed Forest-Falcon *Micrastur mirandollei* 43 cm

CA and SA. Rare resident in lowlands and foothills (to 450 m). Poorly known in north NI (RAAN, 346) and east HN (Gracias a Dios, 626). **ID** Tail proportionally shorter and less graduated. *Base of bill, cere, and legs yellow.* Plain slaty gray above and on sides of neck. *Underparts variably plain white to pale buff* sometimes with very fine, dark shaft-streaks. Imm has dull rufous scalloping on breast. Compare with imm Barred Forest-Falcon. Slaty-backed also resembles imm Bicolored Hawk. Note different structure and lack of pale collar. Semiplumbeous Hawk also has different structure, cere, and tail pattern. **HABITS** Midstory to subcanopy and edge of humid broadleaf forest and adjacent tall second growth. Poorly known. Secretive. Usually detected by voice. **VOICE** Call (1) a steady series of short, mournful cries on steady pitch *ow, ow, ow, ow, ow . . .* Compare with more attenuated phrases of Collared Forest-Falcon. Also (2) a series of ten to fourteen abrupt, short, nasal, barking cries *aah! aah! ahh! ahh! ahh! . . .* and (3) series of two-syllable, nasal phrases *ow-uah, ow-uah, ow-uah, ow-uah . . .* Compare with call of Barred Forest-Falcon.

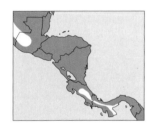

Collared Forest-Falcon *Micrastur semitorquatus* female 58, male 52 cm

MX to SA. Uncommon resident in lowlands and foothills (to 1800, rarely to 2500 m). **ID** Long legs, short, broad wings, and *long, graduated tail.* Cere and bare facial skin *dull greenish.* Ad variable. Buff morph has *buff or tawny underparts and collar.* Dark crown extends behind auriculars in crescent. Tail black with narrow white bands. Light morph *plain whitish below.* Rare dark morph sooty black with white bands on tail and sparse white barring. Imm has greenish bill. Imm has dark brown upperparts banded and edged with tawny and variably whitish to rufous hindcollar. Imm has variably whitish to rufous underparts, richest on chest and coarsely barred with dark brown. Compare with imm Bicolored Hawk. Note different structure and head pattern. **HABITS** Midstory and edge of broadleaf and gallery forest, tall second growth, and adjacent plantations. Less tied to interior of tall forest than Barred Forest-Falcon. Very secretive. Usually remains hidden in dense, shaded cover even when vocalizing persistently. Flies rapidly through tangled vegetation. May drop to ground. Attends ant swarms. **VOICE** Call (1) a long, slow series of hollow, resonant cries *oow . . . oow . . . oow . . . oow . . . oow.* Typically slow markedly toward end of series. Slower and steadier than Laughing Falcon. Compare with more clipped, barklike cries of Barred Forest-Falcon.

20%

Barred Forest-Falcon

plain morph
imm

barred morph
imm

ad

**Slaty-backed
Forest-Falcon**

imm

ad

Collared Forest-Falcon

buff morph
ad

typical imm

dark morph
imm

black morph
ad

white morph
ad

LAUGHING FALCON AND CARACARAS Falconidae

Diurnal raptors. Most with buff or white patches on rounded wings. Red-throated Caracara is rare, local, and declining in Central America. Crested and Yellow-headed caracaras are widespread and often common scavengers found mainly in arid or open areas.

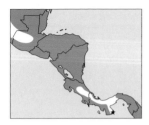

Laughing Falcon *Herpetotheres cachinnans* 46 cm

MX to SA. Uncommon to fairly common resident in lowlands and foothills (to 1000, rarely or locally to 2000 m). Uncommon in PA. **ID** Large-headed with short wings and long tail. *Broad dark mask.* Upperparts mostly plain dark brown. *Head, neck, and underparts plain buffy white to buff.* Tail black with buffy white bands. Note buff on primaries. Yellow-headed Caracara has different head pattern and habits. **HABITS** Canopy of forest edge, open woodland, gallery forest, plantations, and savanna. Pairs or solitary birds perch for long periods on high, exposed branch or utility pole. Flies with stiff, rapid wingbeats and short glides. Does not soar. Solitary or in pairs. **VOICE** Call (1) a loud *gua-co, gua-co, gua-co . . .* or *gua-cow, gua-cow, gua-cow . . .* Often continues for several minutes. May begin with single note repeated at long intervals then gradually increase in tempo and volume. Slow first part may suggest Collared Forest-Falcon. Less often (2) a laughlike *heh hah, hah-hah-hah-hahhahha-hah.*

Red-throated Caracara *Ibycter americanus* 56 cm

South MX to SA. Rare and local resident in lowlands and foothills (to 1000 m) of east HN (Olancho, 457, 346, 80) and north NI (RAAN, 358). Formerly more widespread in Pacific GT (Retalhuleu, Suchitepéquez, 539, 279) and west HN (Cortés, Yoro, Francisco Morazán, 554, 603, 442). Uncommon to rare in humid lowlands of south NI (Río San Juan, 413, 358), Osa Peninsula (Puntarenas, 570, 600) and Caribbean lowlands of CR (Limón, Alajuela, 506, 341, 346), and PA (Bocas del Toro, Ngäbe-Buglé, Panamá, Kuna Yala, Darién, 657, 512). Historical records and perhaps Central Valley in CR (Guanacaste, 257). **ID** Large. Glossy black with *white belly and crissum.* Bill dull yellow with gray base. Note *red bare facial skin, eyes, throat, and legs.* Imm has dark eyes and yellow and gray bare skin. **HABITS** Midstory to canopy of humid broadleaf and mixed broadleaf and pine-oak forest. In pairs or small groups. May descend briefly to midstory or to ground to forage. Feeds mainly on larvae of social hymenoptera. May take fruit. Flight appears weak and labored. **VOICE** Very loud, harsh calls. Pairs or groups may call in chorus creating an impressive cacophony. Calls (1) a rhythmic, coarse phrase of four or more syllables *ca-ca-ca-cao* or *cowh cah-cowh* or *ka-ow ka-ow* and (2) low-pitched, guttural, throaty *rrah!* or *rrak!* Compare with calls of *Ara* macaws.

Yellow-headed Caracara *Milvago chimachima* 43 cm

CA and SA. Fairly common to common resident in south Pacific slope lowlands and foothills. Perhaps expanding with deforestation (55, 353, 602, 426). Recent reports from Caribbean CR (Limón, 346), NI (Rivas, Matagalpa, RAAN, 346, 412, 421), HN (Atlántida, Francisco Morazán, 346), and Caribbean east PA (Kuna Yala, 346). Also Pearl Islands (Panamá, 611, 455, 657). **ID** Ad's *head, neck, and underparts buff.* Narrow dark brown streak extending behind eye. Note *pink bare facial skin.* Mantle and wings brown with fine pale scaling. Tail has blackish and buff bands. In flight, shows dark wings with *buff on base of primaries.* Imm streaked and mottled with dark brown and buff on head, neck, and underparts. Compare with Crested Caracara and Laughing Falcon. Note different head pattern and structure. **HABITS** Grassy or scrubby areas including agricultural fields. Often in small groups. Forages for carrion and other refuse on ground. Often loiters along roadsides. May soar briefly. **VOICE** Usual call (1) a harsh *krrrr-krrrr-krrr.* Also (2) a harsh, hissing *ksyeeeh.*

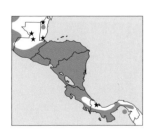

Crested Caracara *Caracara cheriway* 52 cm

South USA to SA. Fairly common to common resident in open (especially arid) regions of lowlands and foothills (to 750, occasionally or locally to 2000 m). Perhaps expanding. Recently found breeding in BZ where previously a rare vagrant (Cayo, Toledo, 345, 492, 346). Also reported recently from Caribbean north GT (Petén, 346). Poorly documented in Caribbean NI where perhaps widespread. Also Pearl Islands (Panamá, 611). **ID** Large with long legs and *short crest.* Note *red bare facial skin and base of bill.* Crown black. Sides of face, neck, and throat whitish. Otherwise mostly blackish above. Breast barred with whitish and dusky, becoming solid dusky on belly. Rump and most of tail white with narrow dusky barring and black subterminal band. In flight, shows white on primaries. Juv streaked with buff and brown on neck and breast. **HABITS** Open grassy, scrubby, or barren areas including roadsides, beaches, agricultural areas, and savannas. Often in pairs or small groups. Perches low. Walks or loiters on ground. Flies strongly with occasional short glides. Rarely soars. **VOICE** Usually quiet. May give (1) harsh, squealing cries *wheee-ah.* May be repeated or combined with low-pitched, throaty rattles.

Laughing Falcon

Red-throated Caracara

Yellow-headed Caracara

juv

ad

Crested Caracara

juv

ad

ad

FALCONS Falconidae

Nearctic migrant falcons. Females are larger than males.

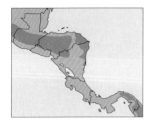

American Kestrel *Falco sparverius*   23–27 cm

NA to SA. Nearctic breeding and resident birds occur. Breeds in north highlands and in north Caribbean slope lowlands. Also breeds very locally in east PA (Panamá, Darién, 42). Nearctic birds occur as uncommon transients and winter residents (mainly Sep to Mar). **ID** Small, slender and long-tailed. Male mostly *rufous above* with *bluish-gray crown and wings*. Note blackish marks on auriculars and below eye. Underparts variably buff spotted with blackish on breast and sides. Long tail with black subterminal band and white tip. Imm male's breast white, heavily spotted with black. Female has *entirely rufous upperparts* (including wings) and mostly rufous tail with narrow black bands. **GV** Birds from north CA breeding population are smaller than NA breeding migrants and have rufous on crown reduced or absent. Breeding male from north CA is whiter below and has extensive black markings (similar to imm male Nearctic migrant). PA breeding bird also lacks rufous crown patch. PA breeding male is richly colored with sparse black markings. **HABITS** Open areas including savannas, agricultural fields, plantations, beaches, and pastures. Resident birds in north found in pine woodland and savanna. Solitary or in pairs. Perches conspicuously on utility pole, wire, or high open branch. Flips tail upon alighting. Hovers while foraging. Occasionally soars. **VOICE** Wintering birds usually quiet. Call (1) a loud, shrill, emphatic *kleekleekleeklee . . .* Similar to call of Bat Falcon.

Merlin *Falco columbarius*   female 30, male 27 cm

Breeds Holarctic. Nearctic birds winter USA to SA. Uncommon to rare transient and winter resident (mainly Oct to Mar). Most common in coastal lowlands. **ID** Typical *Falco* structure. Heavily streaked with brown on sides of head and nape. Underparts buff to whitish streaked with brown. Ad male (variably) dark bluish-gray above. Female and imm browner above. Very pale birds, perhaps from populations breeding in central NA, have (rarely) been reported in north CA. American Kestrel has rufous back and tail and different structure. Peregrine Falcon is larger. Note different head pattern. Also compare with Bat Falcon. **HABITS** Open areas including marshes, agricultural areas, and beaches. Transients may occur in a wide variety of habitats but most frequent in coastal areas. Usually seen in fast flight low over ground or resting on high, exposed perch. Solitary. **VOICE** Usually quiet.

Peregrine Falcon *Falco peregrinus*   female 48, male 40 cm

Cosmopolitan. Nearctic breeding birds winter NA to SA. Uncommon transient and winter resident (mainly Sep to Apr). Primarily in coastal lowlands. Rare in summer. Recently reported breeding in GT (Guatemala, 229). **ID** Large and robust with long, pointed wings and tapered tail. Ad mostly slaty gray above becoming black on head with *broad black mark below eye*. Ad's underparts mostly whitish washed with buff and irregularly barred with black. Imm mostly dark brown above and buffy whitish below with brown streaking. **HABITS** Uses a wide variety of habitats but most common in coastal regions with concentrations of migrant shorebirds or waterfowl. Solitary. Rests on high, exposed perch. Sometimes soars and may circle slowly on thermals. **VOICE** Usually quiet away from breeding sites.

N A breeding ads

♀

American Kestrel

♂

♂

north CA
breeding ad
♂

PA
breeding ad
♂

Merlin

♀

♂

Peregrine Falcon

imm
♀

ad
♂

FALCONS Falconidae

Resident *Falco* falcons. Bat and Orange-breasted falcons are very similar in plumage and can present identification problems when size is difficult to judge. Orange-breasted Falcon is very rare and local in Central America. Any observations of this species away from known breeding areas should be carefully documented.

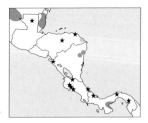

Aplomado Falcon *Falco femoralis*   female 43, male 39 cm

MX to SA. Uncommon to rare and local resident in lowlands and foothills (to 1100 m). Recorded from BZ (529, 630, 343), GT (Petén, 229), SV (Chalatenango), HN (Gracias a Dios, 401), NI (Chinandega, RAAN, 327), CR (Guanacaste, Puntarenas, Alajuela, Limón, 600, 346), and PA (Coclé, Herrera, Los Santos, Panamá, 657, 512). **ID** Slender with *long tail*. Ad's upperparts mostly gray with *long white supercilium* and black mark extending below eye. Sides of neck, throat, and chest whitish to pale buff contrasting with black sides and mid-breast. Belly plain cinnamon. Tail blackish with narrow white bars. Imm brownish above with coarse brown streaking on breast. Compare with Peregrine Falcon. Note different pattern and structure. Also compare with smaller American Kestrel. **HABITS** Savannas, marshes, and open agricultural areas. Perches low on shrub or fence post. Flies rapidly, often low. Occasionally hovers. Solitary or in pairs. May follow grass fires or farm machinery. **VOICE** Calls (1) a barking, two-syllable *keeh-up* or *keeh-ah* and (2) sharp *keeh* or *kiih* or *keep*. May be doubled or repeated in long series.

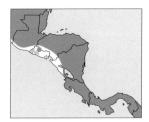

Bat Falcon *Falco rufigularis*   female 28, male 25 cm

MX to SA. Uncommon to fairly common resident in lowlands and foothills (to 1600 m). Occasionally wanders to highlands. Rare in Pacific GT (Retalhuleu, Suchitepéquez, Quetzaltenango, 633) and SV (Ahuachapán, Sonsonate, San Miguel, Usulután, 183, 346). **ID** Typical *Falco* structure with long, narrow, pointed wings. White throat contrasts with otherwise dark head. Mostly dark bluish-slate above and on sides of head. Throat, upper chest, and sides of neck white, sometimes tinged with tawny. Lower chest, breast, and upper belly black, narrowly barred with white. Belly rufous. In soaring flight may recall White-collared Swift. Also compare with Merlin. Note different underparts. **HABITS** Canopy and edge of forest and adjacent open areas. Usually seen perched on high, exposed branch or tall structure. Often in pairs. Seems to forage mainly in early morning and late afternoon. Takes prey in very fast flight, sometimes low over ground. Nests in tree cavities. **VOICE** Calls (1) a rapid series of shrill, high-pitched cries *kree-kree-kree . . .* or *hew hew hew . . .* and (2) single *kik* or *kiik*. Compare with American Kestrel.

Orange-breasted Falcon *Falco deiroleucus*   female 40, male 32 cm

South MX to SA. Very rare and local resident in lowlands and foothills (to 1000 m) of BZ (Cayo, 291, 313, 348, 81) and GT at Tikal and perhaps formerly elsewhere on Caribbean slope (Petén, Izabal, Alta Verapaz, 533, 377, 581, 579, 341, 227). Historical records from HN (Francisco Morazán, 442), NI (Matagalpa, RAAN, 539, 327), and CR (San José, 126, 570, 600). Rare in PA (Darién, Coclé, Veraguas, 614, 48, 346). **ID** Large. Closely resembles more common Bat Falcon. Orange-breasted has proportionally larger feet and *coarser, more rufescent barring on black breast-band and belly*. Bat Falcon sometimes shows some orange-rufous on breast, especially just above black breast-band. Orange-breasted typically has *orange extending well into pale areas at sides of neck*. Also note blacker upperparts of Orange-breasted Falcon. **HABITS** Canopy and edge of humid broadleaf forest. Favors foothill areas with cliffs overlooking extensive areas of humid broadleaf forest. Pairs or solitary birds perch prominently on high, bare limb. Preys mainly on birds overtaken in flight. Solitary or in pairs. **VOICE** Calls (1) a series of low-pitched, nasal cries *kyow-kyow-kyow . . .* or *kyah-kyah-kyah . . .* and (2) a single, slightly hollow *kyowh* or *kyoh-weh*.

Aplomado Falcon

imm
♀

ad
♂

ad

ad

Bat Falcon

imm
♀

ad
♂

ad

imm
♂

ad
♀

ad

Orange-breasted Falcon

MACAWS Psittacidae

Spectacular, large, long-tailed parrots found mainly in humid forested regions. All have bare facial skin and very heavy bill. Scarlet Macaw, though uncommon and local, is the most widespread species. Three of these species are confined mainly to remote areas of eastern Panama.

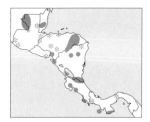

Scarlet Macaw *Ara macao* 95 cm

MX to SA. Uncommon and local resident in lowlands and foothills (to 800 m). Small numbers persist in south BZ (Cayo, Stann Creek, 433, 343, 422). In GT formerly widespread including Pacific slope (Suchitepéquez, San Marcos, Izabal, Alta Verapaz, 539, 279, 378) but now confined to north Caribbean (Petén, 164, 227). Locally fairly common in east HN (Colón, Gracias a Dios, 629) and recently reported from Pacific HN (Valle). Formerly ranged to west Caribbean HN (Atlántida, 35, 629, 346). Formerly resident in southeast SV where now extirpated (La Unión, San Miguel, 183, 619). Small numbers persist in east NI (RAAN, 327, 413, 626) and recently reported from Volcán Cosigüina in Pacific (Chinandega, 346). Formerly more widespread in NI (466). Local, but perhaps increasing in Pacific lowlands of CR (Guanacaste, Puntarenas, 474, 456). Fairly common on Isla Coiba off PA (Veraguas, 653, 470). Formerly more widespread in PA (Colón, Chiriquí, 61, 653). **ID** Large. Mostly red with blue flight feathers. *Wing coverts mostly yellow.* **GV** Some birds from CR and PA (not shown) have green dividing blue and yellow areas of wing coverts. **HABITS** Canopy of semihumid to humid broadleaf forest, pine savannas, and adjacent semi-open areas. Often in pairs, sometimes in small groups. **VOICE** Call (1) a very loud, low-pitched, hoarse *raaaak* or *rowwka.*

Red-and-green Macaw *Ara chloropterus* 86 cm

CA and SA. Uncommon and local resident in lowlands and foothills (to 900 m) of east PA (Darién, 657, 48). Historical records from central PA (Panamá, Colón, 554). **ID** Large. *Mostly red* with blue flight feathers and outer rectrices. *Wing coverts green.* Compare with more widespread Scarlet Macaw. Note different wing and head pattern. **HABITS** Subcanopy to canopy and edge of humid broadleaf forest and adjacent clearings with tall trees. Often in pairs. Occasionally in small groups. **VOICE** In flight, gives (1) harsh cries like Scarlet Macaw but slightly higher-pitched and often including higher-pitched note in middle or with last two or three notes high-pitched and slurred *kaarrrrr ul-a.*

Blue-and-yellow Macaw *Ara ararauna* 83 cm

CA and SA. Uncommon and local resident in lowlands and foothills (to 600 m) of east PA (Darién, 512). Historical records from central PA (Panamá, 657). Small numbers released and perhaps now reestablished in Canal Area (Panamá, Colón, 48). **ID** Large. Mostly *blue above* and *yellow below.* Undersurface of wing yellow. **HABITS** Subcanopy to canopy and edge of semihumid to humid broadleaf forest and adjacent clearings with tall trees. Often in pairs. Occasionally in small groups. **VOICE** Call (1) a coarse, upslurred *raaak.* Less harsh than other macaws. Also gives (2) semimusical calls that are weaker, more nasal, and mellower than other macaws.

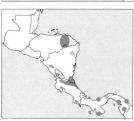

Great Green Macaw *Ara ambiguus* 75 cm

CA and SA. Rare and local resident in lowlands and foothills (to 600 m) of east HN (Colón, Gracias a Dios, 401, 402, 35, 629), NI (RAAN, Río San Juan, Rivas, 438, 439), and Caribbean CR (Limón, Heredia, Alajuela, 600, 438). Persists locally in central and east PA (Veraguas, Los Santos, Darién, 48, 519, 512 426, 425). Historical records from Canal Area and west Caribbean slope of PA (Colón, Bocas del Toro, 535, 657). **ID** Very large. Heavy bill and large head. *Mostly green* with red forehead and blue flight feathers. **HABITS** Subcanopy to canopy and edge of humid broadleaf forest and adjacent clearings with tall trees including savannas. Usually in pairs or small groups. **VOICE** Gives (1) very loud, hoarse, raucous shouts, squawks, and growls *aaaahrk* or *aowrk.* Lower-pitched and more resonant than Scarlet Macaw.

Chestnut-fronted Macaw *Ara severus* 45 cm

CA and SA. Uncommon to locally fairly common resident in lowlands and foothills (to 600 m) of east PA (Darién, 657, 519). Formerly more widespread and historically ranged west at least to Canal Area (Colón, 383, 657). **ID** Smallest CA macaw. *Mostly green* with chestnut forehead. In flight, *red undersurface of wings* and tail contrast with green underparts. Compare with larger Great Green Macaw. **HABITS** Subcanopy to canopy and edge of humid broadleaf forest and adjacent clearings. Pairs or groups gather on high, bare limbs before roosting. **VOICE** Song (1) a long series of gurgling phrases, slurred notes, and occasional harsher notes. Flight call (2) a scratchy, shrill *raiiit* or *jaiiit.* Higher-pitched than large macaws. While perched gives (3) a liquid or gurgling *kurrit.*

20%

Scarlet
Macaw

Red-and-green
Macaw

Blue-and-yellow
Macaw

Great Green
Macaw

Chestnut-fronted
Macaw

PARAKEETS Psittacidae

Long-tailed parakeets found mainly in arid or semihumid regions. All have pale bare eye ring. Observers should note geographic distribution, habitat, and details of head pattern. Flight is rapid. Most of these species are gregarious and often seen in large flocks or at noisy communal roosts.

Pacific Parakeet *Psittacara strenuus*   33 cm

South MX and north CA. Uncommon to locally fairly common resident on Pacific slope (SL, locally to 2500 m). Reaches Caribbean slope locally in GT (229). Vagrant to north Caribbean slope (Alta Verapaz, 229). **ID** Large. *Near-uniform green.* Very heavy pale bill. Variable. Some show scattered orange-red feathers on throat and sides of head. Eye ring brownish-gray. Crimson-fronted Parakeet allopatric. **HABITS** Subcanopy to canopy of arid to semihumid broadleaf forest, pine-oak woodland, and plantations. **VOICE** Calls (1) a coarse, low-pitched *rhekrhek-rhek . . .* or *kreh-kreh-kreh . . .* and (2) higher-pitched, smoother *kriih-kriih . . .*

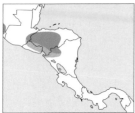

Green Parakeet *Psittacara holochlorus*   29–32 cm

South MX and CA. Uncommon resident in north Pacific foothills and highlands (breeds 600 to 1800 m, wanders seasonally to SL). **ID** Fairly large. Mostly green with *red-orange throat and breast* variably extending to sides of head and neck. Eye ring pale gray. Eyes orange-red. Red on throat and upper breast distinguish ad from other *Psittacara* parakeets. All-green juv may not be separable from slightly larger and longer-tailed Pacific Parakeet. Crimson-fronted Parakeet allopatric. **GV** Birds from west GT (not shown) have plain green throat and breast. **HABITS** Subcanopy to canopy of arid to semihumid broadleaf, pine, and pine-oak woodland. In pairs or small groups. **VOICE** Call (1) a shrill *kreeah-kreeah* or *kri-kri-kri . . .* Higher-pitched than call of Pacific Parakeet.

Crimson-fronted Parakeet *Psittacara finschi*   28 cm

CA endemic. Fairly common but irregular resident in lowlands and foothills (to 1600, mainly below 1200 m). **ID** Fairly large. In flight, shows *red and yellow on underwing.* Otherwise near-uniform green with *red forecrown* and irregular red flecking on nape, neck, and wing coverts. Compare with Olive-throated and Orange-fronted parakeets. Note different head and underparts. Green and Pacific parakeets allopatric. **HABITS** Midstory to canopy in open areas with scattered trees, plantations, suburban areas and gardens. **VOICE** Call (1) a series of short, slurred, slightly nasal, chattering cries *reh, eh-eh, rhe-rhe* or *kih-kih-kih-keeh-keh . . .*

Olive-throated Parakeet *Eupsittula nana*   25 cm

MX, WI and CA. Fairly common resident in Caribbean lowlands and foothills (to 700, locally to 1200 m). Poorly known in Caribbean west PA (Bocas del Toro, 512, 469) where perhaps expanding. **ID** Green above including sides of head and crown with blue flight feathers. Note *broad gray eye ring.* Throat and breast variably light or dark brown. Smaller Orange-fronted Parakeet has dull yellow eye ring and blue and orange markings on crown. Crimson-fronted Parakeet of south CA has mostly green underparts. **HABITS** Canopy and edge of semihumid to humid broadleaf forest, second growth, and plantations. **VOICE** Typically gives (1) dry, scratchy, screeching cries in flight similar to White-crowned Parrot but higher-pitched. While perched gives (2) a variety of mainly harsh, but sometimes melodious cries that are squeakier and higher-pitched than Brown-hooded Parrot.

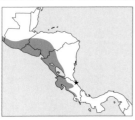

Orange-fronted Parakeet *Eupsittula canicularis*   24 cm

MX and CA. Common resident in Pacific lowlands and foothills (to 1500 m). Perhaps expanding in Caribbean lowlands of CR (Limón, 346). **ID** *Orange forehead* and *blue forecrown.* Otherwise mostly green with brownish breast and blue flight feathers. *Broad dull yellow eye ring.* Other CA parakeets have grayish eye ring. Compare with Brown-throated Parakeet. **HABITS** Upper midstory to canopy and edge of arid to semihumid woodland, second growth, savanna, plantations, and gardens. Flies with fast wingbeats and short glides. **VOICE** Call (1) a repeated, slurred *kleet kleet . . .* or *klleur klleur . . .* Compare with more nasal calls of Crimson-fronted Parakeet. Also (2) various dry, grating chirps and chatters. Compare with lower-pitched calls of White-fronted Parrot.

Brown-throated Parakeet *Eupsittula pertinax*   24 cm

CA and north SA. Uncommon to locally fairly common resident in Pacific lowlands and foothills (to 1200 m) of west PA. Perhaps expanding in Pacific east CR (Puntarenas, 542, 341, 546). **ID** Mostly plain green (including crown). Note *orange mark below eye* and *brown sides of head, throat, and upper breast.* Bill dusky. Olive-throated Parakeet allopatric. **HABITS** Canopy and edge of semihumid forest, second growth, scrub, savanna, agricultural areas, and plantations. **VOICE** Flight call (1) a shrill *crik-crik-crik . . .* or *crak-crak-crak* repeated rapidly. While perched gives (2) a two-syllable *cherr-cheedit* with second note attenuated.

Pacific Parakeet

Green
Parakeet

juv

ad

Crimson-fronted
Parakeet

Olive-throated Parakeet

Orange-fronted
Parakeet

Brown-throated
Parakeet

PARAKEETS AND PARROTLET Psittacidae

Small parrots. Some are uncommon or rare with restricted distributions in south Central America. Orange-chinned Parakeet, often found in disturbed or even urban areas, is the most common and widespread.

Azuero Parakeet[17] *Pyrrhura eisenmanni*   24 cm

CA endemic. Confined to lowlands and foothills (to 1600 m) of south Azuero Peninsula, PA (Los Santos, Veraguas, 167, 512, 425). Considered resident but undertakes local movements. **ID** Slender with long, mostly red tail. *Dark red face* contrasts with gray eye ring and pale auriculars. Note *dark scalloping on gray breast* and sides of neck and *red center of belly*. Sulphur-winged Parakeet allopatric. **HABITS** Canopy and edge of humid broadleaf forest, adjacent second growth, and plantations. In pairs or small flocks. **VOICE** Calls (1) a short, slightly dry, harsh *eeek* given in flight (often repeated), (2) single loud, slightly buzzy *peeea* or *eeeha*, and (3) harsh, guttural *kleekkleek*. Some calls have slightly slurred quality. Compare with calls of Brown-hooded Parrot.

Sulphur-winged Parakeet *Pyrrhura hoffmanni*   25 cm

CA endemic. Uncommon resident in highlands (1200 to 3000 m) of east CR and west PA. **ID** Long, dull-reddish tail and red spot on auriculars. Mostly dark green with variably extensive yellow mottling on crown and nape. Note *broad yellow stripe at base of flight feathers* (conspicuous in flight, but may be difficult to see on folded wing). Barred Parakeet is smaller and has different wing pattern. **HABITS** Canopy and edge of humid broadleaf forest, second growth, plantations, and hedgerows. Usually in groups. Difficult to locate and approach when perched. Most often seen flying rapidly overhead. **VOICE** Calls (1) fairly high-pitched, slightly metallic *ch cheee cheeeah chheeh*. While perched (2) a clear, grating *zeewheet*.

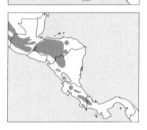

Barred Parakeet *Bolborhynchus lineola*   16.5 cm

South MX to SA. Uncommon to rare and irregular resident in foothills and highlands (750 to 3000, rarely or locally as low as 600 m). May be locally (or briefly) abundant. Rare in SV (Santa Ana, 341) and north NI (411, 346). Perhaps nomadic. **ID** Pointed tail. Mostly green with *fine dusky barring and scalloping*. Orange-chinned Parakeet (mainly lower elevations) is similar in size and structure but has brown wing coverts. In south compare with Sulphur-winged Parakeet. **HABITS** Canopy and edge of humid broadleaf forest. Also pine-oak forest in north. Often seen in small flocks that fly rapidly overhead. Difficult to locate and approach when perched. Attracted to stands of seeding bamboo (*Chusquea*). **VOICE** Often calls in flight. Calls (1) a slightly scratchy, slurred *shreet* or *churree* or *cheer-churr* and (2) nasal chatter *jur-jur-jur-jur*. Compare with harsher calls of Sulphur-winged Parakeet.

Orange-chinned Parakeet *Brotogeris jugularis*   18 cm

South MX to north SA. Common resident in lowlands and foothills (to 900, locally or seasonally to 1400 m). Confined mainly to Pacific in north. Perhaps expanding with deforestation. Also Isla Coiba (Veraguas, 653, 470). **ID** Small with pointed tail. Bill pinkish. Mostly plain green with gray eye ring and *brown wing coverts*. In close view note *orange chin*. Compare with Barred Parakeet (mainly higher elevations). **HABITS** Canopy and edge of semihumid (deciduous) forest, second growth, gardens, plantations, and urban areas. Gregarious. Forms large flocks. **VOICE** Often noisy. Typically (1) alternates dry, scratchy chatters with clear, shrill chirps and slurred *chreek*.

Spectacled Parrotlet *Forpus conspicillatus*   12 cm

North SA and CA. Uncommon resident in lowlands and foothills (to 1600 m) of east PA (Panamá, Darién, 282, 657). **ID** *Tiny* with short, wedge-shaped tail. Male has blue on leading edge of wing and bluish-green underwing coverts. Male otherwise plain green with *blue rump* and broad but inconspicuous *blue eye ring*. Female mostly plain green. Compare with Orange-chinned Parakeet. **HABITS** Midstory to canopy edge of semihumid to humid broadleaf forest, second growth, open woodland, plantations, and hedgerows. Often in flocks. Difficult to locate when perched. Usually detected by voice as flocks pass rapidly overhead. **VOICE** Calls include (1) short, high-pitched, buzzy or chattering *djiit djiit djit* or *tzit, tzit, tzit . . .*

Azuero Parakeet

**Sulphur-winged
Parakeet**

Barred Parakeet

**Orange-chinned
Parakeet**

♀

♂

Spectacled Parrotlet

PARROTLETS AND PARROTS Psittacidae

Small to medium-sized parrots found in humid broadleaf forest. Red-fronted and Blue-fronted parrotlets are closely related geographic replacements. Both are rare and have restricted ranges. Brown-hooded Parrot is the most common and widespread and is often detected by its distinctive calls given in flight.

Red-fronted Parrotlet *Touit costaricensis* 17 cm

CA endemic. Uncommon to rare and local in foothills and highlands (mainly 500 to 1500, locally or seasonally to 3100 m or as low as SL) of CR (570, 602) and west PA (Chiriquí, Bocas del Toro, 657). Considered resident but may undertake local or seasonal movements. **ID** Small. *Short, square tail* with dark terminal band. Otherwise green becoming yellowish on throat. Male has distinctive wing pattern with *red coverts.* Note yellow-green wing linings contrasting with darker primaries. Male has red forehead, forecrown, and small red patch on auriculars. Female has less extensive red on wing and head. Imm has no or little red. Blue-fronted Parrotlet allopatric. **HABITS** Subcanopy to canopy and edge of humid broadleaf forest. Usually seen in pairs or small groups flying overhead. Difficult to locate while perched in foliage. **VOICE** Poorly known. Calls (1) a short *dree durr* or longer series of similar notes and (2) a soft, rolling *chrrik.*

Blue-fronted Parrotlet *Touit dilectissimus* 17 cm

CA and north SA. Uncommon to rare and local resident in foothills (600 to 1600 m) of PA (Panamá, Colón, Kuna Yala, Darién, 657, 48). Poorly known. **ID** Small. *Short, square tail* with dark terminal band. Male has red area on wing coverts and yellow wing linings (like Red-fronted Parrotlet). Note male's *blue forecrown* and small red marks beneath eye and on lores. Female has less extensive red on wing and head. Red-fronted Parrotlet allopatric. Compare with Spectacled Parrotlet. **HABITS** Canopy and edge of humid broadleaf forest. Similar to Red-fronted Parrotlet. **VOICE** Gives (1) short, scratchy *dree chee* or longer, variable series *dree dree deeeah dree, durr . . .* and (2) soft, rolling *chrrik* or *cheeah.*

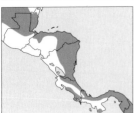

Brown-hooded Parrot *Pyrilia haematotis* 24 cm

South MX to north SA. Widespread and locally fairly common resident in lowlands and foothills (to 1600 m). Poorly documented in Caribbean NI but probably more widespread there than few records suggest (413, 548). **ID** *Mostly brown head with whitish orbital ring* and pale lores. Bill pale. Neck and breast light brown. In flight, blue-green undersurface of wing contrasts with red axillars. Folded wing shows blue flight feathers (no red as in *Amazona* parrots). Compare with Olive-throated Parakeet. Note different structure. **GV** Birds from central and east PA have variable extent of red on breast. **HABITS** Subcanopy to canopy and edge of semihumid to humid broadleaf forest and adjacent tall second growth. More closely associated with forest interior than most other CA parrots. Rarely in disturbed or open areas. Often in pairs or small groups. Flies with deep wingbeats, unlike *Amazona* parrots. **VOICE** Gives a variety of loud, screeching calls, often in flight. Most phrases include (1) clear, upslurred *kleeeee* notes that are higher-pitched and smoother than calls of other parrots.

Saffron-headed Parrot *Pyrilia pyrilia* 22 cm

CA and north SA. Uncommon to rare and local resident in foothills (400 to 1000 m) of east PA. Reported mainly from slopes of Pirre Massif (Darién, 657, 519, 328). **ID** Compact structure with short tail. Note *yellow hood* and wing coverts and *red wing linings* (conspicuous in flight). Folded wing shows blue on secondaries and coverts. Bill and *broad eye ring whitish.* Otherwise mostly green with contrasting dusky primaries and olive breast. Juv has broad grayish eye ring but lacks ad's yellow hood and is mostly green grading to brownish-olive on breast and sides of head (compare with Brown-hooded Parrot). **HABITS** Poorly known. Midstory to canopy of humid broadleaf forest. Most often in pairs or small groups. **VOICE** Calls (1) a buzzy *reeenk* and (2) high-pitched, slurred *kleeek.*

Red-fronted Parrotlet

♀

♂

♀

♂

♂

Blue-fronted Parrotlet

♀

♂

Brown-hooded Parrot

widespread
ads

central and east PA
ad

Saffron-headed Parrot

ad

juv

ad

PARROTS Psittacidae

Large parrots. Often detected by voice while flying overhead. Each species has distinctive and frequent vocalizations and these are often helpful in identification. In close views note details of the head pattern. *Amazona* parrots have direct flight style, rarely veering or making abrupt turns. Wingbeats are shallow and rapid. *Pionus* parrots (like *Pyrilia* parrots) have less direct, more weaving flight style with deeper wingbeats. White-fronted Parrot is the most common and widespread.

White-crowned Parrot *Pionus senilis*   27 cm

South MX and CA. Fairly common resident in lowlands and foothills (to 2000 m). Confined to Caribbean slope in north. Rare in Pacific NI where formerly perhaps more widespread (Managua, 324). **ID** *White forecrown* contrasts with dark blue sides of head and underparts. Note broad, pale orbital ring and white throat. *Bill dull whitish.* Wing coverts brownish-olive with pale speckling. Crissum red. In flight, shows blue undersurface of wing. Juv duller with drab greenish underparts. Compare with Brown-hooded Parrot. Note different underwing and head pattern. No other CA parrot has *white throat.* **HABITS** Canopy and edge of semihumid to humid broadleaf forest, second growth, and plantations. Usually in pairs or small groups. **VOICE** Call (1) often given in flight, a single or series of dry to slightly metallic, raucous, downslurred shrieks *kreeeah* or *keeerh.* Perched birds give (2) a variety of shorter notes.

Blue-headed Parrot *Pionus menstruus*   26 cm

CA and SA. Fairly common resident in lowlands and foothills (to 1800 m) of east CR and PA. Also Isla Coiba (Veraguas, 470) and Pearl Islands (Panamá, 653). **ID** Short tail. *Blue head and breast.* Otherwise mostly green becoming greenish-yellow on wing coverts. Crissum and base of rectrices red. At close range note gray eye ring and dark spot on auriculars. In flight, shows mostly green underwing surface. Bill mostly dusky with reddish base. Juv has dusky olive sides of head. Like Brown-hooded Parrot flies with deep wingbeats (compare with shallow, quivering wingbeats of *Amazona* parrots). **HABITS** Subcanopy to canopy and edge of humid broadleaf forest, tall second growth, mangroves, littoral woodland, clearings with scattered trees, and plantations. In pairs or small groups. **VOICE** Calls (1) a high-pitched, metallic, upslurred *sheeeng* or *shweeeenk* and (2) variety of shorter, rolling notes.

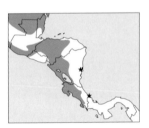

White-fronted Parrot *Amazona albifrons*   27 cm

MX and CA. Common resident in lowlands and foothills (to 1100, seasonally or locally to 1800 m). Uncommon and local on north Pacific slope in GT and SV. Rare in Caribbean CR and NI. **ID** Mostly green with fine dark scaling on nape, mantle, and breast. *Auriculars plain green.* Red eye ring and lores contrast with *white forehead* and blue crown. Bill dull yellow. In flight, both sexes show mostly blue secondaries (compare with wing pattern of larger *Amazona* parrots). Male has red on primary coverts. Some imms have yellow forehead and reduced blue on crown. **HABITS** Subcanopy to canopy and edge in a wide variety of arboreal habitats, including arid to semihumid broadleaf forest, second growth, gallery forest, plantations, and pine savannas. Solitary, in pairs or in groups that form tight flocks. Flight rapid with shallow, quivering wingbeats. **VOICE** Call (1) a rapid series of short, high-pitched, harsh notes with last note separated by pause *ka-ka-ka-ka, ka* or *k-kak-k-kak-k, kack.* Also (2) a variety of harsh, squealing cries. May suggest a parakeet.

Yellow-lored Parrot *Amazona xantholora*   26 cm

South MX and CA. Uncommon and local resident in lowlands of north BZ and (rarely) adjacent GT (Petén). Also Isla Roatán in Bay Islands (442, 346). **ID** Resembles White-fronted Parrot, but note *yellow lores* and *dark mark on auriculars.* Mostly green with dark scaling on nape, mantle, breast, and wing coverts. Red on face contrasts with white forecrown and blue crown. Bill dull yellow. In flight, both sexes show blue secondaries and red primary coverts. Ad male also has red on leading edge of wing. Compare with more widespread White-fronted Parrot. Note different head and wing pattern. **HABITS** Canopy of arid to semihumid forest, second growth, gallery forest, mangroves, plantations, arid scrub, and pine savannas. Uses mangroves on Isla Roatán. In pairs or groups. Flight rapid in tight flocks. **VOICE** Similar to White-fronted Parrot.

30%

White-crowned Parrot

juv

ad

Blue-headed Parrot

ad

juv

White-fronted Parrot

ad ♀

♀

♂

imm

ad ♂

Yellow-lored Parrot

♀

♀

♂

♂

PARROTS Psittacidae

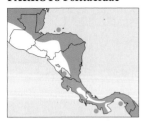

Red-lored Parrot *Amazona autumnalis* 34 cm

MX to SA. Locally fairly common resident in lowlands and foothills (to 1000 m). Confined to Caribbean slope in north. Also Bay Islands off HN (442) and Isla Coiba and Pearl Islands off PA (Veraguas, Panamá, 657). **ID** Mostly green with fine dark scaling on nape. Ad has *red forehead and lores* and (in north CA) yellow patch below eye. Note narrow grayish eye ring and diffuse, bluish crown. Tail has relatively narrow yellowish terminal band. Like other large *Amazona* parrots, has red on secondaries (conspicuous in flight). Mealy Parrot larger with broader eye ring. **HABITS** Subcanopy to canopy and edge of broadleaf forest, tall second growth, and plantations. Often in pairs or small groups. **VOICE** While perched or in flight, gives wide variety of loud, shrill squawks, shrieks, and rolling phrases. Among most frequent (1) an abrupt, metallic, two-syllable *yo-reek yo-reek yo-reek* or *ka-link ka-link* or *k'leek k'leek*.

Yellow-crowned Parrot[18] *Amazona ochrocephala* 32–37 cm

MX to SA. Uncommon to rare and local resident in Caribbean lowlands of BZ (Orange Walk, Belize, 529, 630, 240, 343) and east GT (Izabal, 396, 219). Vagrant to north GT (Petén, 144). Also Caribbean lowlands and foothills (to 750 m) of HN (Atlántida, Cortés, Yoro, Gracias a Dios, 483, 603, 443 442, 396). Also Roatán, Barbareta, and Guanaja in Bay Islands (538, 94, 442, 622, 395). More continuously distributed in Pacific lowlands and foothills of GT, HN (Choluteca, 443, 442), south to west CR (Guanacaste, Puntarenas, 570, 600). Disjunctly in PA including Pearl Islands (Panamá, 657, 512). Perhaps most common in Pacific PA. Formerly perhaps more widespread. **ID** Mostly plain green with variable extent of *yellow on forehead, sides of head, crown, and nape*. Imm has variable extent of fine dusky barring on head and underparts and is thought to show less yellow and have darker reddish eyes. In flight, note pale yellowish-green terminal band on tail. **GV** Individually and geographically variable. Birds from BZ have yellow crown and sides of head and pale bill. Birds from Caribbean GT similar, but may show some yellow on nape. Birds from Caribbean west HN (Sula Valley) and Bay Islands usually have yellow forecrown and nape. Some birds from Sula Valley (HN) have yellow restricted to forecrown. Birds from east Caribbean HN and Caribbean NI have yellow nape (and sometimes yellow forecrown). Birds from north Pacific typically have yellow confined to nape (some have variable extent of yellow on forecrown). Birds from PA are smaller than birds from north CA and have yellow crown and forehead. **HABITS** Midstory to canopy in pine savanna, palm savanna, mangroves, semihumid woodland, and gallery forest. Often in pairs. **VOICE** Call (1) a very low-pitched, hollow, rolling *raaaaaaah*. Calls variable but generally deeper, hollower, and less harsh than other CA *Amazona* parrots.

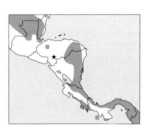

Mealy Parrot *Amazona farinosa* 38 cm

South MX to SA. Uncommon resident in lowlands and foothills (to 1200, rarely or locally to 1500 m). Formerly perhaps more widespread on west Pacific slope of PA (Chiriquí, 657, 512). Persists in south Azuero Peninsula (Veraguas, Los Santos, 46). Also Isla Coiba (Veraguas, 657, 470). **ID** Largest CA *Amazona* parrot. Note *broad pale grayish or whitish eye ring*. Bill dusky. Tail has broad yellow-green terminal band. Like other large CA *Amazona* parrots, has red speculum on secondaries (conspicuous in flight). Geographic variation is clinal and there is also considerable individual variation. Compare with smaller Red-lored Parrot. Note Mealy's relatively plain head with broad pale orbital ring. **GV** Birds from north CA have blue crown. Birds from HN to west PA have pale blue-green crown. Birds from most of PA have deep green sides of head and crown and red margin on forewing. **HABITS** Canopy and edge of semihumid to humid broadleaf forest. May visit areas of tall second growth or isolated trees adjacent to forest but more closely associated with intact forest than other CA *Amazona* parrots. Usually in pairs or groups. **VOICE** Gives a variety of loud squawks and low-pitched, rolling calls. Most distinctive and frequent (1) an abrupt, explosive *por-cheeeer!*

28%

north
CA

south
CA

Red-lored Parrot

BZ
ad

north Pacific
ad

imm

Caribbean
GT to NI
typical ad

**Yellow-crowned
Parrot**

PA
ad

Mealy Parrot

north CA

HN to west PA

PA

ANTSHRIKES Thamnophilidae

Large, heavy-billed antbirds found mainly in understory of broadleaf forest and second growth. Russet Antshrike is found with mixed flocks in forest canopy and is also distinctive in being sexually monomorphic.

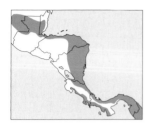

Great Antshrike *Taraba major* 21 cm

South MX to SA. Fairly common resident in humid lowlands and foothills (to 750, locally to 1500 m in south). Uncommon and local in Pacific west CR (Guanacaste, 574). Rare, and local in north GT (Petén, 346) and north BZ (Orange Walk). **ID** Large and bulky with heavy, strongly hooked bill. May raise shaggy crest. *Eyes red*. Male *black above* with white wingbars and mostly *plain white below*. Female rufous-chestnut above and mostly plain white below. Compare female with Bicolored Antbird. Note different structure and habits. **HABITS** Understory to lower midstory at edge of humid broadleaf forest and tangled second growth, especially in riparian or poorly drained areas and overgrown plantations. Pairs or solitary birds hop heavily through interior of dense, low cover. Skulking and secretive. Usually detected by voice. Does not follow mixed flocks and rarely emerges from deep shade. Pounds tail when vocalizing. **VOICE** Song (1) a series of hollow, nasal notes that accelerate and end with a harsh, nasal note *tok, tok, tok too too too to-to-to trrr-waaanh*. Compare with song of Black-headed Trogon. Also compare with song of Barred Antshrike. Calls (2) a low-pitched, throaty rattle *rahahahahaha-ha-ha* that slows slightly at end and (3) a low-pitched *churrr*.

Fasciated Antshrike *Cymbilaimus lineatus* 18 cm

CA and SA. Uncommon to locally fairly common resident in humid lowlands and foothills (to 600, locally to 1240 m in east PA). **ID** Fairly large. Heavy, hooked and swollen bill (mandible gray). *Eyes red*. Male mostly blackish with *extensive fine white barring*. Female pale brownish-buff with fine dark barring. Note female's *rufous crown*. Vaguely recalls smaller Barred Antshrike. Note different pattern and habits. **HABITS** Upper understory to midstory and edge of humid broadleaf forest and adjacent tall second growth. Pairs or solitary birds skulk in tangled, shaded vegetation at gaps or edges. Moves deliberately and may appear sluggish. May ascend to midstory to forage in vine tangles. Usually reclusive. **VOICE** Song (1) a series of clear, mournful, upslurred whistles *uwhoo-uwhoo-whoo-whoo-whoo* or *whap whap whap whap whap*. Calls include (2) a whining *errr-ah*. Often repeated. Also (3) a descending, nasal, querulous *chew* or *chu*.

Russet Antshrike *Thamnistes anabatinus* 14 cm

CA and SA. Fairly common resident in humid lowlands and foothills (to 1500, mainly below 500 m in north). Most common in foothills. **ID** Large-headed and short-tailed. Fairly heavy bill with hooked tip and slightly swollen mandible. Sexes similar. *Plain rufescent-brown above* (becoming brighter on wings and tail) and dull, pale olivaceous-buff below with *dusky eyeline* and *broad, ochraceous supercilium*. Orange interscapular patch usually concealed. Rufous tail may suggest a foliage gleaner. Note different structure and habits. **GV** Birds from central and east PA are slightly darker and have ochre breast. **HABITS** Upper midstory to subcanopy of humid broadleaf forest. Pairs or small groups follow mixed flocks. Forages in deliberate, vireo-like fashion by reaching to glean prey from live foliage or from hanging clusters of dead leaves. **VOICE** Song (1) a rapid series of high-pitched, plaintive notes that become louder, then softer *cheep cheep cheep cheep cheep*. Calls (2) a squeaky, upslurred *sweek* and (3) two-syllable *sweesik* or *sweechip*.

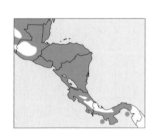

Barred Antshrike *Thamnophilus doliatus* 15.5 cm

MX to SA. Uncommon to common resident in lowlands and foothills (to 1500, rarely or locally to 2000 m). Also Isla Coiba (Veraguas, 653, 657, 470) and Pearl Islands off PA (Panamá, 611, 649, 657). **ID** Fairly heavy, hooked bill. *Loose, shaggy crest* and pale gray eyes. Ad male *boldly barred with black and white*. Female plain rufous above and buff below with *black-and-white–streaked auriculars* and nape. **GV** Male from Pacific slope (HN to west PA) has more white on crown. Female from Isla Coiba is darker than mainland PA female. Male in most of PA has mostly black crest and white central belly. **HABITS** Understory to lower midstory and edge of deciduous forest, second growth, riparian thickets, and scrub. Pairs or solitary birds skulk in dense, low vegetation or suspended vine tangles. Sings from concealed perch while pounding tail. **VOICE** Song (1) an accelerating series of loud wooden or nasal notes that first rise in pitch then drop *eh-eh eh-eh-eh-ehehehehehe-wahnk*. Usually ends with emphatic, upslurred *wahnk*. Song higher-pitched and more nasal than song of Great Antshrike. Also compare with song of Plain Antvireo, which is descending and lacks emphatic last note. Calls include (2) upslurred, nasal, whistle *wuuui* and (3) nasal *naah* or *charrr*.

45%

Great Antshrike

♀

♂

Fasciated Antshrike

♀

♂

Russet Antshrike

widespread

central
and east PA

Barred Antshrike

widespread
♂

Coiba
♀

widespread
♀

Pacific slope
HN to PA
♂

PA
♂

ANTSHRIKES Thamnophilidae

Antbirds found in lower and middle levels of humid broadleaf forest. All are distinctively patterned, but some can be difficult to glimpse in dense vegetation. Voice is often helpful in locating and identifying these. Black-crowned Antshrike is the most common and widespread.

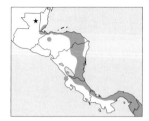

Black-crowned Antshrike *Thamnophilus atrinucha* 15 cm
CA and north SA. Common resident in humid lowlands and foothills (to 1000 m). Uncommon and local in south BZ (Toledo, 343). Rare in north GT (Petén, 78) and Pacific west CR (Guanacaste, 388, 341). **ID** Note grizzled sides of head, wings spotted and edged with white, and *white tips on rectrices*. Male mostly gray with *black crown*. Female mostly brownish with rufous crown. **HABITS** Midstory of humid broadleaf forest, adjacent tall second growth, mangroves, and shaded plantations. Not skulking. Perches motionless in open. Hops heavily through foliage and vine tangles. Pauses to twist neck slowly and peer at vegetation. Pairs or solitary birds follow mixed flocks but also forage independently. Quivers tail as it sings. **VOICE** Song (1) a low-pitched, accelerating series of wooden notes. Ends with abrupt, loud, upslurred bark *ri-ri-ri-r-r-r-r-r wank*. Compare with higher-pitched songs of Barred Antshrike and Plain Antvireo. Calls include (2) a barking note with downslurred inflection sometimes followed by an ascending rattle *urh-rrrrrrrrrr*. Compare with Chestnut-colored Woodpecker. Also (3) softer rattles and (4) a short series of hollow, barking *ow* or *owr* notes. Compare with call of Collared Trogon.

Black-hooded Antshrike *Thamnophilus bridgesi* 16.5 cm
CA endemic. Common to locally very common resident in Pacific lowlands and foothills (to 1100 m) of CR (Puntarenas) and west PA. Rare and local in Pacific west CR (Guanacaste, 600). **ID** Typical antshrike with heavy, hooked bill. *Fine white spotting on wing coverts*. Male *slaty black* becoming darkest on head and breast. Female mostly olive-gray with *white streaking on head and underparts*. Note female's white-tipped rectrices. Female superficially resembles smaller *Dysithamnus* antvireos. Black Antshrike allopatric. **HABITS** Understory and edge of humid broadleaf forest, second growth, littoral woodland, and mangroves. Often confiding. Usually in pairs. Quivers tail as it sings. **VOICE** Song (1) a loud, accelerating series of six to ten nasal, wooden, barking notes on mainly even pitch. Ends with an emphatic, downslurred note *cow cow cow co co k'k'k' cow*. Also (2) a far-carrying *cack cack cack*.

Black Antshrike *Thamnophilus nigriceps* 15 cm
CA and SA. Uncommon and local resident in lowlands (to 450 m) of east PA. **ID** Typical antshrike with heavy, hooked bill and short, broad tail. Male *entirely plain black*. Female mostly *plain rufous-brown above*. Female's underparts and head dusky with *whitish streaking*. Black-hooded Antshrike allopatric. **HABITS** Understory and edge of semihumid to humid broadleaf forest and second growth. Usually in pairs. Does not follow mixed flocks. **VOICE** Song (1) a nasal, slightly accelerating *kuok, kuok, kuok kuok-ku-ku-k-k*. Call (2) a hollow *pwow* or *peeow*.

Spiny-faced Antshrike *Xenornis setifrons* 16 cm
CA and SA. Rare and local resident in foothills (120 to 800, mainly above 350 m) of east PA (Panamá, Kuna Yala, Darién, 131, 657, 512, 91, 661, 3, 48). **ID** Heavy, hooked bill. Note *rufous spots and streaks on wing coverts, mantle, and crown*. Male has slaty gray sides of head and underparts. Female has brownish underparts with soft mottling. Female Black Antshrike vaguely similar. Note different wing and upperparts pattern. **HABITS** Understory to midstory of humid broadleaf forest. Favors dark ravines or streamsides in hilly forest. Solitary birds or pairs perched inconspicuously (usually upright) on open limbs or vines. Sallies abruptly to seize prey from foliage then takes another open perch. Follows mixed flocks. Quiet and reclusive. Unlike many antbirds does not pound tail deeply while vocalizing. **VOICE** Song (1) a series of three to nine (usually five) high-pitched, evenly spaced notes that rise steadily in pitch. Female's song rises less rapidly (especially initially) and is shorter and slightly lower-pitched. Compare with song of Ocellated Antbird. Also (2) a loud, fast *chak-chak-chak* (one to five syllables).

45%

Black-crowned Antshrike ♀ ♂

Black-hooded Antshrike ♀ ♂

Black Antshrike ♀ ♂

Spiny-faced Antshrike ♀ ♂

ANTWRENS Thamnophilidae

Small antbirds found in humid broadleaf forests of south Central America. All are distinctively patterned but can be difficult to locate and identify as they forage actively with large mixed flocks. Voice is often helpful in locating these.

Rufous-rumped Antwren *Euchrepomis callinota*　　　10.5 cm
CA and north SA. Rare and local resident in foothills (600 to 1250 m) of CR (Cartago, San José, Heredia, Limón, 589, 600) and PA (Chiriquí, Bocas del Toro, Ngäbe-Buglé, Veraguas, Darién, 657, 519, 512). **ID** Small and slender. Note *pale yellow lower underparts*, bold wingbars, and *rufous rump*. Male has blackish crown and eye stripe. Female has olive crown. Compare with Rufous-winged Antwren. Note different tail pattern. **HABITS** Subcanopy to canopy of humid broadleaf forest. Pairs or solitary birds follow mixed flocks. Forages actively in foliage and outer branches. Often clings or hangs upside down to peer at undersides of branches or leaves. **VOICE** Song (1) a series of very high-pitched *tsi* or *chi* notes that accelerate and rise rapidly in pitch *tsi tsi tsi tsi-tsi-tsitsitititititittttt.*

Rufous-winged Antwren *Herpsilochmus rufimarginatus*　　　11 cm
CA and SA. Locally fairly common resident in humid lowlands and foothills (to 1050 m) of east PA. **ID** Small. White markings on tail and *blackish eyeline*. Underparts mostly plain pale yellow. Note white wingbars and *rufous flight feathers*. Male's crown black. Female's crown rufous. Rare Rufous-rumped Antwren has different tail. **HABITS** Upper midstory to subcanopy and edge of humid broadleaf forest and adjacent tall second growth. Solitary birds or pairs follow mixed flocks. Forages actively in foliage and vine tangles. Quivers tail while singing. **VOICE** Song (1) a rapid accelerating series of high-pitched, nasal notes *eh, eh eh ehehrrrr.* Compare with song of Red-faced Spinetail.

Moustached Antwren *Myrmotherula ignota*　　　8 cm
CA and north SA. Uncommon resident in lowlands and foothills (to 600 m) of central and east PA. **ID** *Tiny* with *very short tail.* Upperparts streaked with black and white. *Underparts mostly plain, pale yellow* becoming whitish on upper breast and throat. Note *black malar*. Both sexes have mostly whitish, unstreaked auriculars. Female has buff-tinged head. Pacific Antwren is larger and has streaked underparts (also note different habits). **HABITS** Midstory to canopy and edge of humid broadleaf forest and tall second growth. Often in vine tangles. May follow mixed flocks but also encountered in pairs. **VOICE** Song (1) an accelerating series of notes that end in a short trill *chree, chree-chre-chre-che-che-che-che-ee-ee-e-e-e.*

Pacific Antwren *Myrmotherula pacifica*　　　9.5 cm
CA and north SA. Uncommon resident in lowlands and foothills (to about 600 m) of PA. **ID** Small with short tail. Male *extensively streaked with black and white including head and breast.* Lower underparts white. Female has rufous crown and *buff underparts.* Compare with Moustached Antwren. **HABITS** Midstory to subcanopy in riparian thickets, humid broadleaf forest edge, shaded plantations, and second growth. Usually in pairs. Does not follow mixed flocks. **VOICE** Song (1) a fast, accelerating series of notes that rise slightly in pitch *chep-che-che-che-chee-chee-chee.* Call (2) a nasal *ee-de-deh.*

White-fringed Antwren *Formicivora grisea*　　　11.5 cm
CA and SA. Fairly common resident on Pearl Islands off Pacific PA including Islas del Rey, San José, Pedro González, and Viveros (62, 611, 649, 658, 512). **ID** Small and fairly *long-tailed.* Bold white spotting on wings and white bands on underside of tail. Male brownish-gray above with white supercilium extending to sides of neck and flanks and contrasting with *black central underparts.* Female has wings and tail like male but has mostly whitish underparts becoming *buff on breast.* Imm male resembles female. Dot-winged Antwren allopatric. **HABITS** Understory to upper midstory and edge of forest, second growth, and plantations. Solitary birds or pairs forage actively in foliage, vine tangles, and along branches. Frequently fans tail and droops wings. **VOICE** Calls (1) a soft, mellow *tu, tr-rr-r* and (2) sharper *tru-ik, tru-ik . . .* or *chu-ik chu-ik . . .* Sometimes combined.

**Rufous-rumped
Antwren** ♀

♂

**Rufous-winged
Antwren** ♀

♂

**Moustached
Antwren** ♀

♂

imm
♂

♀

ad
♂

Pacific Antwren

♀

♂

White-fringed Antwren

ANTWRENS Thamnophilidae

Tiny, very active antbirds found mainly with mixed flocks at middle levels in humid broadleaf forest and edge. Males of these species are distinctively patterned. Females are more similar but each has a distinctive head pattern. Dot-winged Antwren is the most common and widespread.

Checker-throated Antwren *Epinecrophylla fulviventris*　　11 cm
CA and north SA. Uncommon to locally fairly common resident in humid lowlands and foothills (to 700 m). **ID** *Pale eyes* and *buff spotting on wing coverts*. Male has *black-and-white streaked throat*. Female has plain grayish throat. Compare female with females of Slaty and White-flanked antwrens. **HABITS** Midstory of humid broadleaf forest and tall second growth. Forages actively. Probes and gleans from hanging clusters of dead leaves. Pairs or solitary birds follow mixed flocks. **VOICE** Song (1) a steady series of high-pitched, loud, emphatic notes with steady pitch *tseek-tseek-tseek-tseek tseek* or *pseep pseep-seep-seep-seep-seep*. Calls (2) a high-pitched, thin *cheep* and (3) high-pitched, sharp *peeesk* or *tseeet*.

White-flanked Antwren *Myrmotherula axillaris*　　10 cm
CA and SA. Uncommon to fairly common resident in humid lowlands and foothills (to 900 m). **ID** Small and short-tailed. Eyes dark. Ad male mostly black with fluffy white patches on flanks and white spots on wing coverts. Female has *grayish head* and whitish throat. Note female's cinnamon wingbars and *broken whitish eye ring*. Compare male with male Dot-winged Antwren. Note different structure. Female Slaty Antwren (mainly higher elevations) has brown head. Female Checker-throated Antwren has pale eyes. **HABITS** Understory to midstory of humid broadleaf forest. Forages actively, mainly in foliage. Often flicks wings and switches position rapidly on perch. Pairs or solitary birds follow mixed flocks. **VOICE** Song (1) a series of clear, upslurred whistles that gradually drop in pitch *pwee pwee pwee pwee pwee pwee*. Sometimes ends with burry note *pwee pwee pwee pwee pwee pwee breer*. Calls (2) a nasal *eer-uur* or *eer-eruuur* and (3) clear, nasal *chee cheeup*.

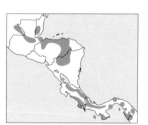

Slaty Antwren *Myrmotherula schisticolor*　　11 cm
MX to SA. Uncommon to locally fairly common resident in foothills (mainly 500 to 1700 m). Also Maya Mountains of BZ (Toledo, 477, 347). **ID** Small and short-tailed. Dark eyes. Ad male *slaty gray with black throat and breast* and white spotting on wing coverts. Ad female *near-uniform buffy brown* with *plain wings*. Female White-flanked Antwren has grayish head and whitish throat. Female Checker-throated Antwren has wing spots. Female Dusky Antbird similarly plain. Note different size and habits. **HABITS** Understory to midstory of humid broadleaf forest. Forages actively by gleaning from live foliage and dead leaf clusters. Pairs or solitary birds follow mixed flocks. **VOICE** Song (1) an accelerating series of soft, low-pitched notes *t'weet t'weet t'weet t'weet weet weet weet weet*. Calls (2) a squeaky, whining, downslurred *cheeur* or *whaaaa* and (3) two-syllable *skee yew* or *cheer-cheeur*. Compare with less nasal calls of White-flanked Antwren.

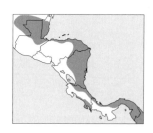

Dot-winged Antwren *Microrhopias quixensis*　　11.5 cm
South MX to SA. Uncommon to fairly common resident in lowlands and foothills (to 1100 m). **ID** *Long tail* often cocked or briefly fanned. Note *white spots on tail*, white wingbar, and white spotting on wing coverts. Male *mostly black*. Female slaty gray above with *rufous underparts*. **GV** Male from east PA is blacker and has more extensive white on rectrices. **HABITS** Midstory of semihumid to humid broadleaf forest and adjacent tall second growth. Favors cluttered areas and tangled light gaps. Forages actively in foliage or vine tangles. Pairs or small groups follow mixed flocks. **VOICE** Song (1) an accelerating series of five to eight notes that rise in pitch and grow louder before becoming a descending trill or rattle *tew tew tew tewtewtewtewttttt*. Calls (2) a mellow, clear, downslurred *peer* or *teeew* and (3) nasal *cheer*. Compare with call of Slaty Antwren.

Checker-throated Antwren

imm ♂

♀

ad ♂

White-flanked Antwren

imm ♂

♀

ad ♂

Slaty Antwren

widespread ♂

widespread ♀

east PA ♂

Dot-winged Antwren

ANTVIREOS AND ANTBIRDS Thamnophilidae

Small antbirds found at lower and middle levels in humid broadleaf forest and edge. Voice is often helpful in locating and identifying these. Dusky Antbird is the most common and widespread.

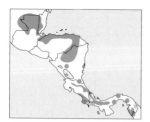

Plain Antvireo *Dysithamnus mentalis*   11.5 cm

MX to SA. Uncommon resident in north lowlands and foothills (to 1500 m) of north. In south, fairly common in foothills and highlands (700 to 2500 m). **ID** Short tail and heavy, hooked bill. *Dark eyes.* Male mostly drab grayish becoming paler below with *plain gray crown* and narrow white wingbars. Note *dusky mask.* Female has *plain rufous crown* and narrow buff wingbars. Note female's pale yellow underparts and whitish eye ring. Female recalls Tawny-crowned Greenlet. Also compare with female Slaty Antwren. **HABITS** Understory to midstory of humid broadleaf forest and adjacent tall second growth. Pairs or solitary birds follow mixed flocks. **VOICE** Song (1) an accelerating and descending series of wooden notes *ow ow ow ow er er-er-er-r.* Like Barred Antshrike but without emphatic ending. Calls (2) a melodious, rising trill and (3) soft, slightly hoarse, slurred *tew-tew* or *ew-it* and (4) a mournful *cher cher cher . . .*

Streak-crowned Antvireo *Dysithamnus striaticeps*   11 cm

CA endemic. Uncommon to locally fairly common resident in Caribbean lowlands and foothills (to 800 m). **ID** Short tail and heavy, hooked bill. *Eyes pale gray.* Closely resembles Spot-crowned Antvireo (sympatric in Río Sixaola region of Caribbean east CR). Note *more distinct streaking on breast* and *streaked crown.* **HABITS** Midstory to subcanopy and edge of humid broadleaf forest. Gleans prey from foliage with slow, deliberate movements. Pairs follow mixed flocks. **VOICE** Song (1) an accelerating series of rich, clear notes that rise in pitch, grow louder, then fall in pitch and end with a roll *oot, oot, oot oot ootootootoot-t-t-t-t-t.* Compare with simpler song of Dusky Antbird. Call (2) a soft, slurred, clear, single or double whistle *wheer* or *wheer-here.*

Spot-crowned Antvireo *Dysithamnus puncticeps*   11 cm

CA and north SA. Uncommon resident in lowlands and foothills (to 800 m) of Caribbean east CR (Río Sixaola region, Limón, 281, 570) and PA. **ID** Short tail and heavy, hooked bill. *Eyes pale gray.* Streaked throat and breast. Male has dark gray *crown with fine whitish spotting* and white spotted wingbars. Female has dull yellowish underparts and narrow, buff-spotted wingbars. Note female's rufous crown with fine black speckling. Plain Antvireo has unmarked crown and dark eyes. Streak-crowned Antvireo may be locally syntopic. Note different crown and underparts pattern. **HABITS** Midstory to subcanopy of humid broadleaf forest. Like Streak-crowned Antvireo. **VOICE** Song (1) like Streak-crowned Antvireo but faster and higher-pitched. Call (2) a short, rolling, descending *prrrr.*

Jet Antbird *Cercomacra nigricans*   15.5 cm

CA and SA. Uncommon to locally fairly common resident in lowlands (to 600 m) of PA. Also Pearl Islands (Panamá, 657). **ID** Long tail with white-tipped rectrices forming *black-and-white bands on underside of tail.* Male near-uniform black with white edging on wing coverts and concealed white dorsal patch. Female gray with variable *whitish streaking on underparts.* Imm male resembles female. Compare male with male Black Antshrike. Note different structure and tail pattern. **HABITS** Understory of humid second growth, forest edge, plantations, gardens, and shrubby clearings. Pairs haunt dark interior of dense vegetation. Reclusive and usually detected by voice. Does not follow mixed flocks. **VOICE** Call (1) a repeated, two-syllable, very nasal *ehh-oo, ehh-oo, eh-oo . . .*

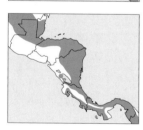

Dusky Antbird *Cercomacroides tyrannina*   15 cm

South MX to SA. Common resident in lowlands and foothills (to 1200 m). Mainly Caribbean slope in north, but reported from Volcán Mombacho, NI (Granada, 413). **ID** Male *near-uniform gray* with *narrow white wingbars.* Female olive-brown above and rufous below with *plain wings.* Imm resembles female. Compare with smaller Slaty Antwren. Note different structure and habits. **GV** Male from east PA is paler. **HABITS** Midstory and edge of semihumid to humid broadleaf forest, second growth, and riparian thickets. Pairs or solitary birds creep and hop through dense, tangled growth. Often in tree-fall gaps. Does not follow mixed flocks but may become more active as they pass nearby. **VOICE** Song (1) a series of short, rich notes that rise slightly in pitch *chew, chew-chew-chew-chi-chi-chichi.* Female's song shorter and rises steeply in pitch. Call (2) a soft, slightly nasal *kick* or *kip.* Often repeated.

48%

Plain Antvireo

♀

♂

Streak-crowned
Antvireo

♀

♂

♀

♂

Spot-crowned Antvireo

Jet Antbird

♀

♂

Dusky Antbird

widespread
♂

east PA
♂

♀

ANTBIRDS Thamnophilidae

Reclusive antbirds found in lower levels of humid broadleaf forest and edge. Voice is helpful in locating and identifying these species. Chestnut-backed Antbird is widespread and displays complex geographic variation in Central America.

Dull-mantled Antbird *Myrmeciza laemosticta*   14 cm

CA and north SA. Uncommon and local resident in south humid lowlands and foothills (to 750 m). **ID** *Red eyes* and *fine white spotting on wing coverts.* Note dark gray head and blackish breast. Female has *whitish scaling on black throat.* When agitated, displays white interscapular patch. Resembles Chestnut-backed Antbird but note Dull-mantled's different eye color and plain gray sides of head (no bare blue skin). Note that Chestnut-backed Antbird from east PA (mainly lower elevations) has white spotting on wings like Dull-mantled Antbird. **HABITS** Understory of humid broadleaf forest. Prefers streamside undergrowth and shaded ravines in very humid, hilly areas. Usually in pairs. Secretive and tends to remain concealed in dense cover. Does not follow mixed flocks. Attends ant swarms but not an obligate ant-follower. Best located by voice. **VOICE** Song (1) a series of three to four clear, high-pitched whistles followed by three to five notes on (usually) lower pitch *tsee tsee tsee, tyew-tyew-tyew-tyew.* Calls (2) a rolling, grating, downslurred *dzhrw* or *jeew* sometimes repeated and (3) harsh, explosive *sput.*

Chestnut-backed Antbird *Myrmeciza exsul*   15 cm

CA and north SA. Fairly common resident in humid lowlands and foothills (to 1200, mainly below 250 m in north). **ID** Compact with fairly short tail. Mostly plain chestnut-brown with dark gray head and breast and *bare blue facial skin.* Eyes dark. Female has brown underparts. Compare with Dull-mantled Antbird (mainly higher elevations). Note different wing pattern (in most populations), head pattern, eye color, and habits. **GV** Birds from east PA have white spotting on wing coverts like Dull-mantled Antbird. Female from Pacific east CR and west PA have tawny underparts. **HABITS** Understory of humid broadleaf forest and tall second growth. Prefers damp, shaded understory. Reclusive. Perches on low, vertical stems. May attend ant swarms but not an obligate ant-follower. Usually in pairs. Does not follow mixed flocks. **VOICE** Song (1) a series of two to three emphatic whistles *peeh, peeh, peeea* or *peh, peeeah.* Compare with song of Black-faced Antthrush. Call (2) a harsh, rolling *reahhh* or *dzeeer.*

Zeledon's Antbird[19] *Myrmeciza zeledoni*   19 cm

CA and north SA. Fairly common resident in south foothills and highlands (300 to 1700 m). Rare and poorly known in east PA (Darién, 657). **ID** Fairly long, rounded tail. Bare blue skin surrounding eyes. Plain wings. Male *uniform black* with (usually) concealed white patch at bend of wing. Female *uniform brown* with dusky auriculars and throat. Compare with Bare-crowned and Chestnut-backed antbirds (mainly lower elevations). **HABITS** Understory and floor of humid broadleaf forest. Pairs or solitary birds haunt damp, shaded vegetation in ravines or along small streams in hilly terrain. Usually reclusive. Hops heavily through dense vegetation. Habitually pounds tail. Attends ant swarms where it forages boldly but not an obligate ant-follower. Does not follow mixed flocks. **VOICE** Song (1) a rapid series of clear, loud notes *peer peer peer peer peer peer peer peer.* Series may drop slightly in pitch and slow very slightly at end. Also (2) a rapid, thin, harsh chatter *ch-t-t-t-t-t.* Compare with song of Bare-crowned Antbird.

Bare-crowned Antbird *Gymnocichla nudiceps*   17 cm

CA and north SA. Uncommon and local resident in lowlands and foothills (to 1200, but mainly below 250 m in north). Rare and local in BZ (Cayo, Stann Creek, Toledo, 313, 343). Historical records from Caribbean GT (Izabal, Petén, 164, 607) and west HN (Cortes, 516, 442). Reported in MX near border of west Petén, GT (500). Formerly perhaps more widespread in Pacific west PA (Chiriquí, 657). **ID** Male black with white wingbars and *bare blue skin around eyes and extending across forehead and crown.* Female warm brown above with *cinnamon wingbars* and blue bare skin around eye. Female's underparts rufous. Imm male has reduced extent of bare blue skin. Compare with Zeledon's Antbird (mainly higher elevations). Note different head and wing pattern. **GV** Females from Pacific east CR and west PA, as well as those from central and east PA, have less contrasting wingbars. **HABITS** Understory of humid broadleaf forest and adjacent second growth. Prefers shaded, dense, damp vegetation in poorly drained areas. Reclusive. Usually in pairs. Habitually pounds tail. Attends ant swarms but not an obligate ant-follower. Does not follow mixed flocks. **VOICE** Song (1) a series of eight to twelve loud, sharp *cheer* or *cheep* notes on steady pitch and accelerating slightly at end. Calls (2) a softer *tseeuw*, often repeated with rising and falling cadence *tsee tseeuw tsuu* and (3) shrill, downslurred *cheeah.*

45%

Dull-mantled Antbird

♀

♂

widespread
♀

widespread
♂

Chestnut-backed Antbird

Pacific east CR
and west PA
♀

east
Pacific PA
♀

east
Pacific PA
♂

Zeledon's Antbird

♀

♂

Bare-crowned Antbird

imm
♂

ad
♂

GT to
Caribbean
west PA
♀

Pacific east CR and west PA,
and central and east PA
♀

ANTBIRDS Thamnophilidae

Antbirds found in lower levels in humid broadleaf forest. Bicolored and Ocellated antbirds are most often seen at swarms of army ants where they feed on invertebrates and other small prey fleeing from the advancing ants. Spotted Antbird also forages at ant swarms, but is often seen singly or in pairs away from swarms.

White-bellied Antbird *Myrmeciza longipes*　　　　14 cm
CA and north SA. Fairly common resident in lowlands and foothills (to 600 m) of central and east PA. **ID** Ochre lower underparts and pink legs. Male *rufous-brown above* with black sides of head, throat, and breast. Supercilium, forehead, and neck gray. Female has ochre breast. **HABITS** Floor and understory of semihumid broadleaf forest edge, dense second growth, and scrub. Favors less humid and more disturbed areas than other CA antbirds. Forages mainly on or near ground beneath dense vegetation. Usually in pairs. Does not follow mixed flocks. Vocalizes from slightly elevated perch. **VOICE** Song (1) a rapid, loud series of rich whistles that gradually slow and drop slightly in pitch *cheercheer-cheer-cheer-cheercheercheer-cheer, chew, chew, chew.*

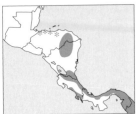

Bicolored Antbird *Gymnopithys bicolor*　　　　14.5 cm
CA and SA. Uncommon to fairly common resident in humid lowlands and foothills (to 1700, mainly below 1500 m). Historical records from west HN (Cortés, Atlántida, 167, 442). **ID** Short tail and rounded shape. Brown above and on flanks. *White median underparts* and *bare bluish-gray skin around eye* contrast with dusky auriculars. **GV** Birds from central and east PA have gray forecrown and supercilium. **HABITS** Understory of humid broadleaf forest and adjacent tall second growth. An obligate ant-follower. Rarely seen away from ant swarms. Usually in pairs or small groups. Perches on low, vertical stems. Makes short, rapid flights to seize fleeing invertebrates from ground or other surfaces. Persistent calls betray presence of an ant swarm. **VOICE** Song (1) a series of clear, thin, high-pitched whistles that accelerate and rise in pitch. Series may end with high-pitched note or become lower-pitched and slower and end with one or more harsh, nasal notes. Compare with song of Ocellated Antbird. Calls (2) a nasal *per-r-r-r-r* or *cheeurr* and (3) low-pitched *churr*.

Ocellated Antbird *Phaenostictus mcleannani*　　　　21 cm
CA and north SA. Uncommon resident in humid lowlands and foothills (to 1200 m). Historical record from central NI (Chontales, 539). **ID** Large and boldly patterned with long tail. Black throat, *blue bare skin around eye*, and *scaled upperparts and breast*. Legs and feet pink. **GV** Birds from PA (not shown) are less rufous and have paler, more contrasting scaling. **HABITS** Understory of humid broadleaf forest. An obligate ant-follower. In pairs or small groups. Forages actively from low, vertical stems above advancing ants. Rarely seen away from ant swarms. **VOICE** Song (1) a series of ten to twelve clear whistles that rise in pitch and accelerate slightly, then slow and drop in pitch. Song of Bicolored Antbird shorter, mellower and less penetrating. Call (2) a penetrating, rolling *cheeer* sharper than call of Bicolored Antbird.

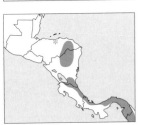

Spotted Antbird *Hylophylax naevioides*　　　　12 cm
CA and north SA. Uncommon to locally fairly common resident in humid lowlands and foothills (to 1000 m). **ID** Small. Short tail with buff-tipped rectrices. Note *cinnamon-rufous wingbars and edging on tertials.* Mantle deep rufous. Male has mostly dark gray head and black throat. Note male's *bold black spotting* on white underparts. **GV** Females from east PA (not shown) are slightly more buff below. **HABITS** Understory of humid broadleaf forest and adjacent second growth. Forages low or on ground. Follows mixed flocks and also attends ant swarms. **VOICE** Song (1) a thin, soft, burry *peede weede weede weede weede weede* or *peede peede peede sip sip sip.* Calls (2) a sharp *skeeip* or *psiip* sometimes repeated rapidly, (3) low-pitched, rolling *churrr*, and (4) softer *cheep.*

Wing-banded Antbird *Myrmornis torquata*　　　　15 cm
CA and SA. Rare and local resident in humid lowlands and foothills (to 600 m) of east HN (Gracias a Dios, 629) and east NI (Río San Juan, RAAN, Jinotega, Matagalpa, 147, 452, 413, 137, 138, 626). Also PA (Colón, Panamá, Darién, 350, 657, 512). **ID** Plump with very short tail and *long bill.* Blackish wings with *buff wingbars.* Note *fine whitish vermiculations on sides of head and neck.* Male has black face, throat, and breast. Female has rufous throat and bib. Juv mostly plain brown. Compare with Spotted Antbird. **HABITS** Floor and understory of humid broadleaf forest. Prefers steep slopes in hilly areas with open, shaded understory. Hops on ground. Flips fallen leaves like a *Sclerurus* leaftosser. Takes an elevated perch when disturbed or vocalizing. Solitary or in pairs. Does not follow mixed flocks. Rarely attends ant swarms. **VOICE** Song (1) a long series of emphatic whistles that rise gradually in pitch and increase in intensity *tueee, tueee-tueee-tueee-tueee . . .* or *tweetweetweetweetwee* or *prea prea prea prea prea.* Call (2) a coarse, low-pitched *churrr* or *chirrr* or *wrrr.*

45%

White-bellied Antbird ♀

♂

widespread

Bicolored Antbird

central and
east PA

Ocellated Antbird

Spotted Antbird ♀

♂

Wing-banded Antbird ♀

♂

BLACK-CROWNED ANTPITTA Conopophagidae

A distinctive species with no close relatives in the region.

Black-crowned Antpitta *Pittasoma michleri*   19 cm

CA and SA. Uncommon and local resident in south foothills (mainly 300 to 1200 m, locally near SL in east PA). **ID** Large and robust with very short tail, long legs, and heavy gray bill. *Bold black-and-white scaling on underparts.* Note *white spots on wing coverts.* Male has black throat. **GV** Birds from CR and west PA have black auriculars and less white on face. **HABITS** Floor and understory of humid broadleaf forest. Pairs or solitary birds bound rapidly over forest floor pausing briefly to stand on fallen log or other low perch. Generally reclusive but attends ant swarms where it forages boldly. Habitually flicks wings and tail. **VOICE** Song (1) a very long series of loud, sharp notes *wi-i-i-i-ii-i-i-i . . .* that gradually slow and drop in pitch. May continue for almost one minute. Also (2) an abrupt, low-pitched, guttural three- to ten-note rattle *kuk kuk kuk . . .* or *wucwuc-wuc-wuc . . .*

ANTTHRUSHES Formicariidae

Reclusive birds usually found walking on floor of humid broadleaf forest. The three *Formicarius* antthrushes are segregated mostly by elevation. All have distinctive vocalizations and are most often detected by voice.

Black-faced Antthrush[20] *Formicarius analis*   18 cm

South MX to SA. Fairly common resident in humid lowlands and foothills (to 1500 m). Confined mainly to Caribbean in north. **ID** Short tail held cocked. Plain brown above and plain gray below. Rufous neck contrasts with black throat and auriculars. Blue-gray eye ring flared behind eye. Black-headed and Rufous-breasted antthrushes (higher elevations) have different head pattern and underparts color. **GV** Birds from BZ and GT to east HN (Gracias a Dios) have rufous forecollar. **HABITS** Floor and understory of semihumid to humid broadleaf forest. Walks over shaded leaf litter. Habitually jerks tail. Solitary. **VOICE** Song (1) in north a sharp introductory note followed by a descending series of short notes *keep, too too too too too.* In south (east HN to PA), song a shorter *keep too too.* Alarm note (2) a sharp *kwip* or *twip.* Compare with songs of Chestnut-backed Antbird and Streak-chested Antpitta.

Rufous-breasted Antthrush *Formicarius rufipectus*   18 cm

CA and SA. Uncommon to rare resident in south foothills and highlands (750 to 1850, mainly above 1200 m). **ID** *Rufous crown, nape, and breast.* Black-headed Antthrush (lower elevations) has entire head and breast black. **HABITS** Floor and understory of humid broadleaf forest. Partial to steep, forested slopes. Walks deliberately over shaded forest floor. Habitually jerks tail. Notably secretive and difficult to observe. Attends ant swarms. Solitary or in pairs. **VOICE** Song (1) a pair of short, clear whistled notes *toot-toot.* Second note on same or slightly higher pitch. Call (2) an abrupt *chirip-irup-irup.*

Black-headed Antthrush *Formicarius nigricapillus*   17 cm

CA and north SA. Uncommon to locally fairly common resident in south humid foothills (400 to 1200, mainly above 600 m). **ID** *Black head and breast.* Note pale blue-gray skin around eye. Black-faced Antthrush (lower elevations) has gray breast and rufous nape. Rufous-breasted Antthrush (mainly higher elevations) has rufous breast. **HABITS** Floor and understory of humid broadleaf forest. Walks over shaded forest floor in ravines or dark streamsides. Habitually jerks tail. Tosses leaves aside with bill. Usually solitary. **VOICE** Song (1) a rapid series of about twenty short whistles that accelerate slightly and may rise slightly in pitch *tu-tu-tu-tu-tu-tutututututu.* Compare with shorter, rising song of Thicket Antpitta. Call (2) a sharp, abrupt *chirip* or *chwip.*

ANTPITTAS Grallariidae

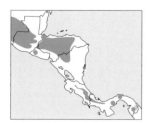

Scaled Antpitta *Grallaria guatimalensis*   17 cm

MX to SA. Uncommon to rare and local resident in foothills and highlands (100 to 2850 m in north, 450 to 1650 m in south). Also volcanic highlands of SV (Santa Ana, 183, 619). Recently reported from Cerro Musún in central NI (Matagalpa, 137). **ID** Plump and short-tailed. Note *gray crown scaled with black and pale malar and lores.* Underparts mostly cinnamon with variable, narrow, pale crescent dividing throat and breast. Rump and wings rufous-brown. Juv mostly dusky with fine whitish and buff streaking on crown, nape, mantle, and breast. **GV** Ads from north CA (not shown) are less richly colored below. **HABITS** Floor and understory of humid broadleaf forest and second growth. Hops rapidly over ground. Secretive, but may forage in open on muddy forest trails or in shaded clearings. May attend ant swarms. Usually solitary. Sings briefly at daybreak. **VOICE** Song (1) a series of low-pitched, resonant notes that start as a trill, rise in pitch and volume, then slow to form distinct, hollow, individual notes before stopping abruptly *huhuhuhHUHUuhuhu hu hu hu.* Compare with song of Black-headed Antthrush. Calls include (2) a low-pitched grunt or croak.

Black-crowned Antpitta

CR and west PA
♂

central and
east PA
♀

central and
east PA
♂

north CA
ad

south CA
ad

**Rufous-breasted
Antthrush**

juv

**Black-faced
Antthrush**

**Black-headed
Antthrush**

juv

ad

Scaled Antpitta

Scaled Antpitta with Streak-
chested Antpitta.

ANTPITTAS Grallariidae

Thicket and Streak-chested antpittas are retiring birds found in lower levels of humid broadleaf forest and edge. Most are detected by voice.

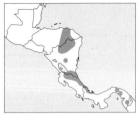

Thicket Antpitta *Hylopezus dives*   13.5 cm

CA and north SA. Uncommon resident in humid lowlands and foothills (to 900, locally to 1200 m). Recently found in east HN (Gracias a Dios, 34, 629). **ID** Rounded with very short tail. Resembles Streak-chested Antpitta but has narrower, more diffuse eye ring, relatively *plain wings*, and softer streaking below. **HABITS** Floor and understory of dense, humid second growth, tangled forest gaps, and humid broadleaf forest edge. Often detected by voice but difficult to glimpse. Sings from elevated, concealed perch. Solitary. **VOICE** Song (1) a rapid, rising series of short, hollow, whistled notes. Grow louder and slightly faster toward end. Compare with songs of Black-headed Antthrush and Scaled Antpitta. Call (2) a rapid, tapaculo-like rattle *tr-r-rrrrr* with steady pitch.

Streak-chested Antpitta *Hylopezus perspicillatus*   13.5 cm

CA and north SA. Uncommon resident in humid lowlands and foothills (to 1200 m). **ID** Broad *buff eye ring* and loral spot. Note black malar, *black streaking on breast*, and *cinnamon spots on wing coverts*. Compare with Thicket Antpitta. Note different wing pattern, habits, and voice. **GV** Birds from Pacific CR and most of PA have white lower underparts. **HABITS** Floor and understory of humid broadleaf forest and adjacent tall second growth. Hops rapidly over shaded forest floor. Sings from elevated perch on log or tree buttress. Sidles body from side to side with head stationary. Solitary. **VOICE** Song (1) a series of six to nine mellow whistles that accelerate then slow at end *cow-cow-cow cow cow cow-cow-cow* or *pee pee peepeepeepee pew pew pew*. Compare with simpler song of Black-faced Antthrush. Female's song a higher-pitched *cowee cowee cowee*. Also (2) an explosive *teew* and (3) loud rattle.

Ochre-breasted Antpitta *Grallaricula flavirostris*   10 cm

CA and north SA. Rare and local resident in foothills of CR (Alajuela, Cartago, 570, 600, 670) and west PA (Bocas del Toro, Chiriquí, Ngäbe-Buglé, Veraguas, 512). Mainly Caribbean slope (750 to 1300 m). Local on Pacific slope in east CR (750 to 1850 m Puntarenas, 570, 600, 305) and in east PA (Darién, 512). **ID** *Tiny* with very short tail. Note *broad ochre eye ring, face, and breast*. White lower underparts and *yellow bill* with dusky culmen. **HABITS** Understory and edge of humid broadleaf forest and tall second growth. Hops among tangled stems in rank, shaded growth, usually at one to two meters above ground. Sidles thorax from side to side. Solitary. **VOICE** Song (1) a long, high-pitched trill that first drops then rises in pitch. Compare with more liquid trill of Long-billed Gnatwren. Calls (2) a harsh, vireo-like *reeeah* and (3) soft, slurred *peeuhh* or *pee-ip* that may be repeated.

TAPACULOS Rhinocryptidae

Scytalopus tapaculos are small, secretive birds found on the floor of humid broadleaf forest in highlands. The three Central American species are allopatric.

Silvery-fronted Tapaculo *Scytalopus argentifrons*   10.5 cm

CA endemic. Common resident in highlands (mainly above 1500 m) of CR and west PA. **ID** Ad male slaty gray with *pale gray forehead and supercilium*. Female and imm browner with extensive, fine, dusky barring. Other tapaculos allopatric. Compare female and juv with various wrens. **GV** Male from east Chiriquí to Coclé, PA, is darker with faint pale brow and supercilium. **HABITS** Floor and understory of humid broadleaf (cloud and elfin) forest. Pairs or solitary birds creep over shaded, mossy forest floor. Often disappears beneath dense vegetation or litter. Secretive and usually detected by voice. **VOICE** Song (1) a long, rapid, steady series of sharp, high-pitched notes with resonant, wooden quality *kewkewkewkewkew . . .* Call (2) a shorter series of sharp, metallic notes *chi-chi-chi-chi*.

Tacarcuna Tapaculo *Scytalopus panamensis*   11.5 cm

CA and north SA. Poorly known resident in Tacarcuna Massif (1000 to 1500 m) of east PA (Darién, 512, 642, 48). **ID** Mostly dark gray with whitish supercilium. Imm browner with extensive, dusky barring. Choco and Silvery-fronted tapaculos allopatric. **HABITS** Like Silvery-fronted Tapaculo. **VOICE** Song (1) a very long, steady series of short, harsh notes *chi, chi, chi, chi, chi, chi, chi . . .* Call (2) a harsh, nasal, five-note *chichichichichew*.

Choco Tapaculo *Scytalopus chocoensis*   11.5 cm

CA and north SA. Uncommon and local resident in foothills and highlands (750 to 1500 m) of Pirre Massif and Serranía de Jungurudó in east PA (Darién, 512, 45). **ID** Male mostly dark gray. Ad female browner. Imm browner with extensive, dusky barring. Silvery-fronted and Tacarcuna tapaculos allopatric. **HABITS** Like Silvery-fronted Tapaculo. **VOICE** Song (1) a fairly slow series of sharp, slightly nasal notes *eh, eh, eh, eh, eh, eh, eh, eh, eh . . .* May rise slightly in pitch at start. Call (2) a squeaky, four-note phrase *chew-chew-chewchew*.

50%

Pacific CR
and most of PA

Thicket Antpitta

Streak-chested Antpitta

Caribbean
HN to
west PA

**Ochre-breasted
Antpitta**

CR and west Chiriquí
ad ♀

CR and west Chiriquí
ad ♂

juv

east Chiriquí to Coclé
ad ♂

Silvery-fronted Tapaculo

ad

ad

Tacarcuna Tapaculo

Choco Tapaculo

WOODCREEPERS Furnariidae

Woodcreepers with mostly plain (unstreaked) plumage. Olivaceous and Wedge-billed woodcreepers are widespread, small woodcreepers each with a distinctive bill shape. *Dendrocincla* woodcreepers sometimes raise their crown and throat feathers to appear shaggy. They are often found at army ant swarms, particularly in north Central American lowlands.

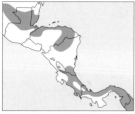

Wedge-billed Woodcreeper *Glyphorynchus spirurus*　　　15 cm

MX to SA. Uncommon to common resident in lowlands and foothills (to 1500, locally to 1700 m). Confined to Caribbean slope in north. A report from SV is dubious (Ahuachapán, 301). **ID** Small. *Short, slightly upturned bill* and long tail spines. Note buff throat and supercilium and fine, pale streaking on breast. Mantle plain rufous-brown. **HABITS** Midstory to subcanopy of humid broadleaf forest, tall second growth, and shaded plantations. Hitches rapidly along trunks and larger branches of trees. Flicks wings rapidly. Follows mixed flocks but also found alone or in pairs. **VOICE** Song (1) a rapid series of four or five high-pitched notes *wichichichichi* that become loudest in middle then taper off sharply. Call (2) an abrupt, *schip* or *sfik* sometimes repeated. Compare with call of Orange-billed Woodcreeper.

Olivaceous Woodcreeper *Sittasomus griseicapillus*　　　14.5–15.5 cm

MX to SA. Common resident in north Caribbean lowlands and foothills (to 1200 m). Very rare and local in Pacific GT (Esquintla, Sololá, 539) and SV (Santa Ana, 183, 619, 346). Uncommon in south foothills and highlands (500 to 1500 m). Local near SL on Nicoya Peninsula, CR. **ID** Small with *plain, unstreaked plumage*. Note *fine, near-straight bill*. Gray head, neck, and breast contrast with brighter rufous wings and tail. In flight (or in hand) shows tawny wing stripe. Wedge-billed Woodcreeper has different underparts and bill shape. **HABITS** Midstory to canopy and edge of semihumid to humid broadleaf forest, shaded plantations, and tall second growth. Follows mixed flocks. Solitary or in pairs. Hitches along open bark of tree trunks and larger branches. **VOICE** Song (1) a fine, rapid trill that rises and falls in pitch *preeeew*. Song of Plain Xenops similar but sharper and usually with stuttering introductory notes.

Plain-brown Woodcreeper *Dendrocincla fuliginosa*　　　22 cm

CA and SA. Uncommon resident in lowlands and foothills (to 800 m). Rare in east HN and south Pacific slope highlands. **ID** Straight bill. Mostly dull brown (slightly more rufous on wings and tail). *Gray face and auriculars* contrast with *dark malar*. Eyes gray. Compare with Ruddy Woodcreeper. Note different head pattern. **HABITS** Understory to midstory of humid broadleaf forest and tall second growth. Usually solitary but ant swarms may attract groups. Clings to low, vertical perch over advancing ants. **VOICE** Song (1) a very long trill or rattle that gradually slows and drops slightly in pitch. Call (2) a slightly hoarse, sharp *psick* or *pseeuk*. Sometimes repeated.

Tawny-winged Woodcreeper *Dendrocincla anabatina*　　　19 cm

South MX and CA. Uncommon to fairly common resident in lowlands and foothills (to 1500 m). Rare and local on Pacific slope in CR and west PA. **ID** Plain brown with *contrasting rufous remiges* and *pale supercilium*. Whitish throat contrasts with *dark malar*. Ruddy and Plain-brown woodcreepers have similar structure but both have uniform wings and different head pattern. **HABITS** Understory to midstory of semihumid to humid broadleaf forest, tall second growth, shaded plantations, and mangroves. Forages at ant swarms in small groups. Usually solitary. Flicks wings rapidly. **VOICE** Song (1) a very long, rapid, high-pitched series *whehehehehehehehe . . .* or *chchchchchchch . . .* Mostly even in pitch and speed. Call (2) a sharp, querulous, whining *tyew* or *deew* or *deyeew*.

Ruddy Woodcreeper *Dendrocincla homochroa*　　　20 cm

CA and north SA. Fairly common resident in north Caribbean lowlands. Rare and local in Pacific foothills and highlands of GT (Escuintla, Suchitepéquez, 539), SV (Ahuachapán, 619), and NI (Granada, Chinandega, 413). Uncommon to rare, mainly at middle elevations (600 to 1000, rarely to 1600 m) in CR and PA (Chiriquí, 89, 346). **ID** Straight bill often light pinkish-gray. *Near-uniform rufous-brown* (brightest on crown). Note *gray eye ring and lores*. Structure and behavior like other *Dendrocincla* woodcreepers but plain pattern and reddish color are distinctive. Compare with Plain-brown Woodcreeper. Note different head pattern. **HABITS** Understory to midstory of semihumid to humid broadleaf forest and tall second growth. Solitary or in pairs. Rarely with mixed flocks. Attends ant swarms. Perches low on vertical stem or trunk. Flicks wings rapidly. **VOICE** Song (1) a very long, high-pitched, excited-sounding series *whehehehehehehehehe . . .* or *chchchchchchch . . .* First drops then continues at steady pitch before slowing and trailing off. Call (2) a downslurred, nasal *deeeeah* or *squeeirrr*.

Wedge-billed Woodcreeper

Olivaceous Woodcreeper

Tawny-winged Woodcreeper

Plain-brown Woodcreeper

Tawny-winged Woodcreeper raising bushy crest.

Ruddy Woodcreeper

45%

WOODCREEPERS Furnariidae

Large woodcreepers. Northern Barred, Black-banded, and Strong-billed woodcreepers are usually solitary or in pairs (not often with mixed flocks). Northern Barred-Woodcreeper is the most common and widespread.

Strong-billed Woodcreeper *Xiphocolaptes promeropirhynchus*   31 cm
MX to SA. Uncommon in north foothills and highlands (SL to 3000 m) of GT and HN. Rare and local near SL on Caribbean slope in BZ (Orange Walk, Cayo, Stann Creek, Toledo, 529, 433, 343) and north GT (Petén, 579). Rare in SV (Ahuachapán, Morazán, Chalatenango, 183, 619). Very rare in foothills (500 to 1700 m) of both slopes in CR (Puntarenas, Alajuela, Limón, 126, 570, 600, 523) and west PA (Chiriquí, Veraguas, Coclé, 274, 657). **ID** Largest CA woodcreeper. *Long, heavy gray bill* with curved culmen. Note plain whitish or buff throat, *fine pale streaking on head and upper breast*, and *dark malar*. Northern Barred and Black-banded woodcreepers have different underparts. **HABITS** Understory to subcanopy of semihumid to humid broadleaf forest. Also humid pine-oak forest in north. Most common in foothill areas with abundant epiphytes. Solitary or in pairs. Does not follow mixed flocks. **VOICE** Song (1) a series of loud, whining, two-syllable phrases *oow-wheet oowwheet oow-wheet*. First note of each phrase thin, rising, and querulous. Second is loud and full. Sometimes varied to three notes as *coo-wheee-wheew*. Compare with songs of Spotted and Northern Barred woodcreepers.

Black-banded Woodcreeper *Dendrocolaptes picumnus*   27 cm
MX to SA. Rare and local resident in foothills and highlands (7500 to 2900 m) of GT (Alta Verapaz, Zacapa, 555, 279, 375), HN (Lempira, Copán), SV (Santa Ana, 346), NI (Madriz, Jinotega, 419, 346), CR (Limón, Cartago, Alajuela, 516, 126, 570, 600, 253), and west PA (Chiriquí, Veraguas, 657, 512, 346). **ID** Large and fairly heavy, dark bill. Note *streaked throat and chest* and *barred lower underparts*. Compare with more widespread Northern Barred-Woodcreeper and with Strong-billed Woodcreeper. Note different bill shape and underparts pattern. **GV** Birds from CR and PA have less streaking and more extensive barring below. **HABITS** Poorly known. Midstory to subcanopy of semihumid to humid broadleaf forest. Forages mainly along trunks or larger branches of trees. Inconspicuous. Often perches quietly at lower levels. Attends ant swarms. Solitary or in pairs. Does not follow mixed flocks. **VOICE** Poorly known. Song (1) a descending, laughlike series of short, whistled notes *wihihihihihee*. Compare with song of Ivory-billed Woodcreeper.

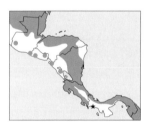

Northern Barred-Woodcreeper *Dendrocolaptes sanctithomae*   28 cm
South MX to north SA. Uncommon resident in lowlands and foothills (to 1300, locally to 1800 m in north). Rare and local in Pacific foothills (70 to 1100 m) of GT (San Marcos, 154), SV (Ahuachapán, Morazán, San Miguel, Libertad, 183, 341) and NI (Chinandega). **ID** Large and dark. Mostly dull brownish (more rufous on wings and tail) with *blackish barring on mantle, head, and entire underparts*. Heavy, dark bill and dark gray eyes. **HABITS** Understory to midstory of semihumid to humid broadleaf forest and shaded plantations. Rarely at forest edge. Pairs or small groups attend ant swarms where they perch on vertical stems and make abrupt sallies to seize prey from vegetation or from ground. Does not follow mixed flocks. **VOICE** Loud song (1) often given in predawn darkness, a long series of two-syllable whistles *toooit-toooit-toooit-tooo* or longer *tewy-tewy-tewy-tooey-toooey-toooey-toooit-tew-tew-tew*. Song rises in pitch and volume before trailing off with several squeaky notes.

Black-striped Woodcreeper *Xiphorhynchus lachrymosus*   female 24, male 27 cm
CA and north SA. Uncommon to fairly common resident in humid lowlands and foothills (to 1200 m). Very local in Pacific foothills of west CR (Puntarenas, Guanacaste, 523). Rare and poorly known in NI (RAAN, Chontales, Río San Juan, 413, 358). **ID** Fairly large. Blackish crown and mantle with *bold whitish or pale buff spotting* contrast with rufous wings and tail. Long bill grayish with dull flesh or orange mandible. **HABITS** Midstory to subcanopy of humid broadleaf forest and tall second growth. Pairs or solitary birds follow mixed flocks, especially those with large insectivores such as caciques, nunbirds, and *Celeus* woodpeckers. **VOICE** Song (1) a long, high-pitched trill or rattle that drops gradually in pitch. Calls (2) a loud, rolling, downslurred *cheer* or *chirrr* or *wheer! here-here* (compare with Cocoa Woodcreeper) and (3) loud, clear, upslurred *doweeet* more emphatic than Northern Barred-Woodcreeper.

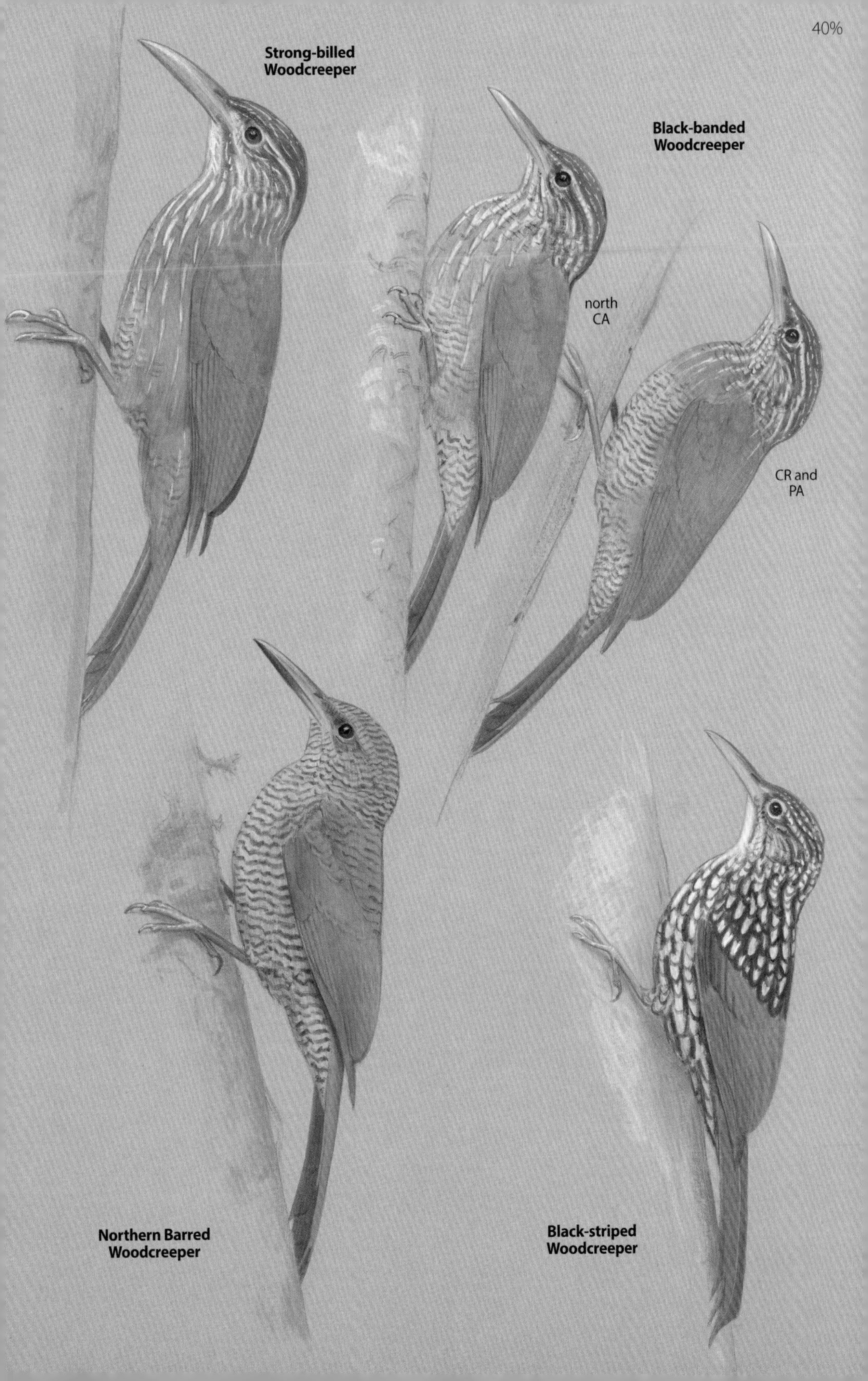

40%

Strong-billed Woodcreeper

Black-banded Woodcreeper

north CA

CR and PA

Northern Barred Woodcreeper

Black-striped Woodcreeper

WOODCREEPERS Furnariidae

Medium-sized to large woodcreepers often found with mixed flocks.

Straight-billed Woodcreeper *Dendroplex picus*   20 cm
CA and SA. Locally fairly common resident in Pacific coastal lowlands of PA. On
Caribbean slope locally in Canal Area (Colón). **ID** *Bold white spotting on breast* and
straight, pale bill. Mantle mostly plain rufous-brown. Compare with Black-striped
Woodcreeper. Note different bill shape and habits. **HABITS** Understory to subcanopy of
mangroves and adjacent woodland or littoral scrub. Hitches along branches or trunks.
Solitary birds or pairs may follow mixed flocks. Vocalizes throughout day. **VOICE** Song
(1) a descending series that slows at the end *chee-hee-hee-hee-hee-hu-hu-hu, hu.*

Ivory-billed Woodcreeper *Xiphorhynchus flavigaster*   female 22, male 24 cm
South MX and north CA. Fairly common resident in north lowlands and foothills (to
1500, locally to 1800 m). Uncommon in Pacific lowlands and foothills (mainly 400 to
900 m, locally to near SL) of west CR. **ID** Fairly large with *fairly heavy, near-straight,
pale pinkish-gray bill* and buff throat. Note extensive streaking on mantle. Streak-
headed Woodcreeper (may be locally syntopic) has similar pattern. Note different
bill, structure, and habits. Resembles (mainly allopatric) Cocoa Woodcreeper but
Ivory-billed's pale bill is distinctive. **HABITS** Midstory and edge of semihumid to
humid forest, tall second growth, gallery forest, shaded plantations, and mangroves.
VOICE Song (1) a variable, laughlike series of five to twenty thin, high-pitched notes
that slow, drop in pitch, and become louder *wihihihihihihewhewhewh.* Call (2) a sharp,
squeaky, downslurred *cheeo* or *chu.*

Cocoa Woodcreeper *Xiphorhynchus susurrans*   23 cm
CA and north SA. Uncommon to fairly common resident in humid lowlands and
foothills (to 600, locally to 1200 m). Uncommon in north. A report from Pacific SV
(Santa Ana, 346) is dubious. **ID** Fairly large. Near-straight, *dark bill*. Note heavily
streaked breast and buff throat. Upperparts mostly rufous-brown with extensive
fine buff streaking on mantle. Streak-headed Woodcreeper has similar pattern. Note
different bill, structure, and habits. Also compare with Ivory-billed Woodcreeper
(sympatric in Caribbean GT and HN). Note different bill color and mantle pattern.
GV Birds from Caribbean GT and HN (not shown) have more whitish throat.
HABITS Midstory to subcanopy of humid broadleaf forest and adjacent second
growth. Pairs or solitary birds often follow mixed flocks. May forage at ant swarms.
VOICE Song (1) a series of about seven to twenty clear, upslurred *wic* or *doy* notes
wicwicwicwicwicwicwic. First rise then drop in pitch. May slow slightly at end. Calls (2)
a loud, clear, rolling *cheer* and (3) repeated *chu* or *dew.*

Spotted Woodcreeper *Xiphorhynchus erythropygius*   female 22, male 24 cm
CA and north SA. Fairly common resident in north foothills and highlands (mainly
700 to 1700, locally to 2500 m). Rare and local in foothills of east GT (Izabal, 227) and
Maya Mountains (above 700 m) of BZ (Cayo, Toledo, 433). Common in south lowlands
and foothills (mainly 300 to 1350, locally to 1700 m). **ID** Near-straight bill with light
gray mandible. Mostly *dark olive-brown* with *pale grayish-buff eye ring*, supercilium,
and throat, and *buff spotting on underparts, neck, and mantle.* Note bluish-gray feet.
Dull coloration and spotted (not streaked) pattern are distinctive. **GV** Birds from CR
and PA have less extensive pale spotting. **HABITS** Midstory to subcanopy of humid
broadleaf forest, tall second growth, and edge. Hitches inconspicuously along larger
trunks or branches while inspecting crevices and epiphytes. Pairs or small groups
follow mixed flocks. **VOICE** Song (1) a descending series of one to six clear, mournful
whistles *pweeeer pweeeer pweeeer eeeeer . . .* Call (2) a downslurred *diiu* less emphatic
than individual song notes. Rarely (3) a buzzy trill.

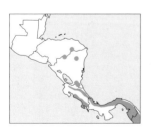

Long-tailed Woodcreeper *Deconychura longicauda*   female 19, male 21 cm
CA and SA. Uncommon to rare and local resident in humid lowlands and foothills (to
1300 m). Poorly known in north Caribbean NI (RAAN, Río San Juan, 412, 413, 548)
and HN near NI border at Arenal (El Paraíso, Gracias a Dios, 321, 346). **ID** Small with
fairly short, near-straight bill. Long tail spines. Note buff eye ring and supercilium and
plain mantle. Resembles more common Wedge-billed Woodcreeper. Note different bill.
HABITS Understory to midstory of tall humid broadleaf forest and adjacent tall second
growth. Pairs or solitary birds often follow mixed flocks that include antwrens.
VOICE Song (1) a series of loud, clear, downslurred whistles that drop in pitch *chear,
chee-chee-chew chew chu.*

40%

Straight-billed
Woodcreeper

Ivory-billed
Woodcreeper

Cocoa
Woodcreeper

north
CA

south
CA

Spotted
Woodcreeper

Long-tailed
Woodcreeper

SCYTHEBILLS AND WOODCREEPERS Furnariidae

Streak-headed Woodcreeper is found mainly at edge or in nonforest habitats including shade trees in pastures, plantations, and savanna woodland. The similar Spot-crowned Woodcreeper is found at higher elevations. *Campylorhamphus* scythebills have very long decurved bills that can be surprisingly difficult to see as the birds forage among dense epiphytes.

Brown-billed Scythebill *Campylorhamphus pusillus*   24 cm

CA and SA. Uncommon resident in south foothills and highlands (300 to 1700 m). **ID** *Very long, dark, deeply decurved bill.* Mostly brownish with buff throat and fine buff streaking on mantle, crown, auriculars, and breast. Imm has shorter bill. Red-billed Scythebill (lower elevations) has longer, redder bill, and paler crown with finer streaking. **HABITS** Midstory to subcanopy of very humid, epiphyte-laden broadleaf forest and adjacent tall second growth. Pairs or small groups follow mixed flocks. Probes in rotted wood or epiphytes. Wary and usually difficult to observe as it forages in dense vegetation. **VOICE** Song (1) a variable series of fine, clear, slurred whistles and rapid trills *tewe tewew twee tewe tewe we we we we* that drop in pitch or (2) shorter *teww, teww, tewtewtew* that begin with one to three clear, slurred notes. Compare with song of Spotted Woodcreeper.

Red-billed Scythebill *Campylorhamphus trochilirostris*   25 cm

CA and SA. Uncommon and local resident in lowlands and foothills (to 1000 m) of east PA (Coclé, Panamá, Colón, Darién, 657, 512). **ID** *Very long, deeply decurved, reddish bill.* Mostly brownish with fine buff streaking on head, mantle, and underparts. Juv has shorter, pale bill and somewhat darker plumage. More widespread Brown-billed Scythebill (mainly higher elevations) has darker crown and duller bill. **HABITS** Midstory to subcanopy and edge of humid broadleaf forest and tall second growth. Hitches along branches or tree trunks. Probes in epiphytes or bark. Pairs may follow mixed flocks but often solitary. **VOICE** Song (1) a series of loud whistles *kuuheeheeheeheeheeheeheeheehee-hu-hu-hu* that rise then drop in pitch.

Spot-crowned Woodcreeper *Lepidocolaptes affinis*   21 cm

South MX and CA. Fairly common resident in foothills and highlands (mainly above 1000, locally as low as 400 m). Also volcanic highlands of SV (San Vicente, San Salvador, Santa Ana). **ID** *Slender, pale, slightly decurved bill* and fine whitish *spotting on crown.* Similar Streak-headed Woodcreeper (lower elevations) has different crown pattern and voice. Also compare with Spotted Woodcreeper. Note different bill shape. **HABITS** Midstory to subcanopy of very humid, epiphyte-burdened broadleaf forest, adjacent plantations, and clearings with scattered trees. Also humid pine-oak forest in north highlands. Pairs follow mixed flocks. **VOICE** Song in north CA (1) a thin, nasal note usually followed by a trill *deeeeeah, hihihihihi.* In south CA, song (2) a thin, nasal, upslurred note followed by two to several shorter notes that fall in pitch *deeeeeah deu deu deu.* Call (3) a squeaky *deeeik.* Sometimes doubled. Compare with call of Rose-throated Becard.

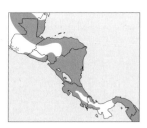

Streak-headed Woodcreeper *Lepidocolaptes souleyetii*   22 cm

South MX to SA. Common resident in lowlands and foothills (to 1500, locally to 1850 m). **ID** Pale, slender, slightly decurved bill. Note fine whitish *streaking on crown,* mantle, and underparts. Spot-crowned Woodcreeper mainly at higher elevations. Note different voice. Cocoa and Ivory-billed woodcreepers have similar patterns but are larger with proportionally heavier bills. **HABITS** Midstory to subcanopy and edge in semi-open habitats including broadleaf forest, second growth woodland, pine savanna, plantations, gardens, and mangroves. Most widespread CA woodcreeper in nonforest habitats. Pairs or solitary birds follow mixed flocks. **VOICE** Song (1) a clear, descending trill. Compare with song of Long-billed Gnatwren. Call (2) a shorter, downslurred *preeuu.*

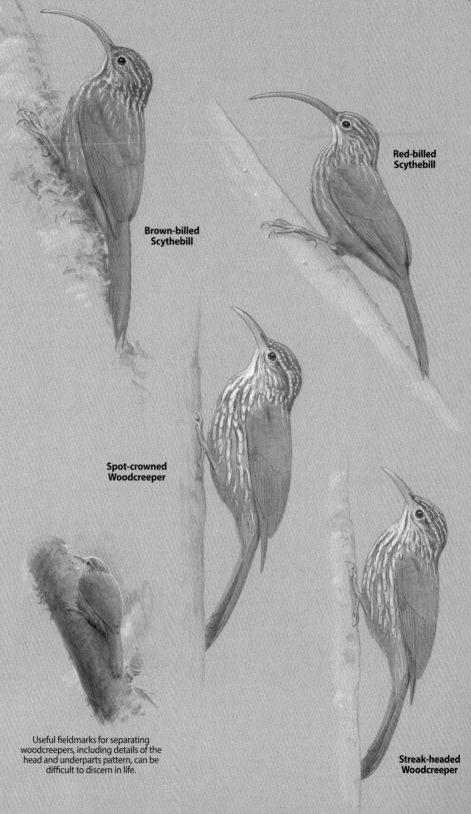

Brown-billed Scythebill

Red-billed Scythebill

Spot-crowned Woodcreeper

Useful fieldmarks for separating woodcreepers, including details of the head and underparts pattern, can be difficult to discern in life.

Streak-headed Woodcreeper

TREERUNNERS, BARBTAIL, XENOPS, AND GRAYTAIL Furnariidae

Small birds found in middle and upper levels of broadleaf forest. Often with mixed flocks. Treerunners and Spotted Barbtail are found in humid foothill and highland forest with abundant moss or epiphytes. Xenops are found mainly in lowlands and foothills. Plain Xenops is the most common and widespread.

Ruddy Treerunner *Margarornis rubiginosus*   15 cm
CA endemic. Common resident in highlands (above 1200 m) of CR and west PA.
ID Long, notched tail with pointed rectrices. Mostly *bright cinnamon-rufous* becoming paler below. Note *whitish throat*, pale supercilium, and faintly scaled or spotted breast. Short bill pinkish. Compare with Spotted Barbtail. Beautiful Treerunner allopatric. **HABITS** Midstory to subcanopy of very humid broadleaf (cloud) forest. Creeps along mossy branches inspecting crevices and undersides of limbs. Pairs or groups follow mixed flocks. **VOICE** Usually quiet. Song (1) a very high-pitched, fine trill. Call (2) a very high-pitched, single *tsit* or *tseet*.

Beautiful Treerunner *Margarornis bellulus*   15 cm
CA and north SA. Locally fairly common in highlands (mainly above 1350, locally as low as 900 m) of east PA including Serranía de Majé (Panamá, Darién, 519, 643, 44, 45). **ID** Long, notched tail with pointed rectrices. Whitish supercilium and streaking on neck. *Throat white.* Remaining underparts brown with *white spots edged with black.* Compare with Spotted Barbtail. Note different structure and habits. Ruddy Treerunner allopatric. **HABITS** Midstory to subcanopy of very humid broadleaf (cloud) forest. Like Ruddy Treerunner. **VOICE** Usually quiet. Song (1) a high-pitched trill (much like Ruddy Treerunner). Call (2) a high-pitched, thin *tik* or *tsit.*

Spotted Barbtail *Premnoplex brunnescens*   14 cm
CA and SA. Uncommon resident in south foothills and highlands (600 to 2500 m). **ID** Small and dark with fine, slightly decurved bill. Note blackish-brown notched tail with pointed rectrices. Mostly dark brown with buff throat and supercilium. *Buff or whitish spotting on nape, sides of head, and underparts.* Compare with Spotted Woodcreeper. **HABITS** Understory to midstory of very humid broadleaf forest. In pairs or small groups. May follow mixed flocks. Quiet and unobtrusive. Creeps on mossy branches and trunks inspecting crevices and accumulations of arboreal litter. **VOICE** Song (1) a rapid series of high-pitched notes that form a dry rattle or trill. Call (2) a sharp, thin, high-pitched *tseep* or *peek.*

Streaked Xenops *Xenops rutilans*   12 cm
CA and SA. Uncommon to rare and very local resident mainly in south foothills and highlands (400 to 2450 m). Local near SL in Bayano drainage (Panamá, 346). **ID** Small with upturned bill and white malar. Note *pale streaking on crown, mantle, and underparts* and mostly plain rufous tail. Plain Xenops has plain mantle and underparts. **HABITS** Midstory to subcanopy and edge of humid broadleaf forest, tall second growth, and clearings with scattered trees. **VOICE** Song (1) a series of harsh, high-pitched notes that become gradually louder then trail off. Call (2) a high-pitched, thin, sibilant *tsip* or *zis.* Sometimes repeated several times with steady pitch.

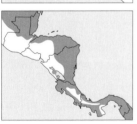

Plain Xenops *Xenops minutus*   12 cm
South MX to SA. Fairly common resident in lowlands and foothills (to 1500, but mainly below 1200 m). Confined to Caribbean slope in north but reported from Volcán Mombacho in Pacific NI (Granada, 413). **ID** Small with *upturned bill* and *white malar.* Note *black-and-rufous patterned tail* and wings and plain (unstreaked) mantle and underparts. **GV** Birds from north CA (not shown) are slightly more rufous above. **HABITS** Understory to subcanopy and edge of semihumid to humid broadleaf forest, shaded plantations, and second growth. Clambers actively in fine twigs and foliage. Hangs with tail depressed. Taps quietly on woody substrates. Pairs or solitary birds follow mixed flocks. **VOICE** Song (1) a high-pitched, rapid trill. Often with one or two introductory notes. Accelerates slightly at end *t-trrrrrrrr.* Compare with call of Olivaceous Woodcreeper. Call (2) a high-pitched, sharp *peep.* Often doubled.

Double-banded Graytail *Xenerpestes minlosi*   10.5 cm
CA and north SA. Uncommon and local resident in lowlands and foothills (to 400 m) of east PA (Darién, 274, 519, 512). **ID** Small and slender. Narrow, graduated tail and pinkish mandible. Gray above becoming darker on crown. Note *white supercilium* and wingbars. Underparts whitish with faint, dusky speckling on sides of breast. **HABITS** Midstory to subcanopy and edge of humid broadleaf forest and tall second growth. Forages in suspended vine tangles. Forages actively by inspecting twigs, foliage, and especially clusters of dead leaves. Clings with tail depressed like a *Xenops.* Solitary birds or pairs follow mixed flocks. **VOICE** Song (1) a long, high-pitched, dry or mechanical trill or rattle on even pitch. Call (2) a sharp, high-pitched *tseep* or *tcheep.*

Ruddy Treerunner

Beautiful Treerunner

Streaked
Xenops

Spotted
Barbtail

Plain Xenops

Double-banded Graytail

SPINETAILS Furnariidae

Small birds with long, ragged or pointed tail. *Synallaxis* spinetails favor dense understory at broadleaf forest edge. They are often difficult to glimpse but may call persistently. *Cranioleuca* spinetails are found at middle levels in humid broadleaf forest. Often with mixed flocks. Voice is often helpful in locating these.

Pale-breasted Spinetail *Synallaxis albescens*   14 cm
CA and SA. Fairly common resident in lowlands and foothills (to 1250 m) of Pacific east CR (Puntarenas, 172, 600) and PA. Perhaps expanding with deforestation in CR. **ID** Long tail. Note *whitish underparts* and rufous on wings and hindcrown. Slaty Spinetail is darker below. Also note different habits. **HABITS** Understory of dense, damp scrub, humid broadleaf forest edge, and riparian thickets. Usually remains concealed inside dense, low cover. Solitary or in pairs. Does not follow mixed flocks. **VOICE** Song (1) a harsh, slightly buzzy, emphatic, two-syllable phrase *bhet-chuw* or *guit-tcheeo*. Often repeated persistently. Also (2) a sharp, staccato *bip* or *tyip*. May be repeated rapidly.

Slaty Spinetail *Synallaxis brachyura*   16 cm
CA and SA. Fairly common resident in humid lowlands and foothills (to 1500 m). Historical records from west HN (Cortés, Atlántida, 442). Uncommon and local in foothills of east PA (Darién). **ID** Long tail. Mostly *dark slaty gray* with contrasting *rufous hindcrown and wings*. **HABITS** Understory of low, humid second growth, broadleaf forest edge, and riparian thickets. Pairs or solitary birds skulk in shade of dense tangles. Rarely emerges into view. Does not follow mixed flocks. **VOICE** Song (1) a very rapid, short, downslurred trill or rattle *ch-ch-churrr* or *chu-chu-chrrrr*. Sometimes given persistently. Calls include (2) a sharp, dry *chip* or *kyip*.

Rufous-breasted Spinetail *Synallaxis erythrothorax*   15 cm
South MX and CA. Uncommon to locally fairly common resident in north lowlands and foothills (to 900, locally to 1500 m). **ID** Distinctive in range. Long tail. *Rufous wings and breast* and gray head, mantle, and lower underparts. Compare with Slaty Spinetail in HN (mainly allopatric). **GV** Birds from Pacific slope are paler and have less extensive blackish bib. **HABITS** Understory of semihumid to humid forest edge, overgrown borders, tangled second growth, scrub, and plantations. Pairs or solitary birds lurk in dense vegetation. Does not follow mixed flocks. Reclusive. Usually detected by voice. **VOICE** May call persistently. Call (1) a short, ascending phrase of three or four harsh notes followed by a lower-pitched note *je je-jeje-ssuu*.

Red-faced Spinetail *Cranioleuca erythrops*   15.5 cm
CA and north SA. Uncommon resident in south foothills and highlands (mainly 700 to 2300 m). Local in east PA with records from Pirre Massif and Tacarcuna Massif (Darién, 657). **ID** Long, notched tail with pointed rectrices. *Rufous-red crown and auriculars* and dull whitish throat. Juv has buff supercilium and underparts. **HABITS** Midstory to subcanopy of humid broadleaf forest and adjacent tall second growth. Forages actively. Investigates arboreal litter and hanging dead leaf clusters while clambering and hitching along tree limbs. Frequently hangs upside down or clings to undersides of branches. Pairs or small groups follow mixed flocks. **VOICE** Song (1) an accelerating series of squeaky, high-pitched notes *tchi tchi tsisisisisisisi*. Usually drop in pitch but sometimes upslurred. Calls (2) a short, rolling, high-pitched *prrreep* and (3) squeaky *chew-seep*.

Coiba Spinetail *Cranioleuca dissita*   13 cm
CA endemic. Fairly common resident on Isla Coiba off Pacific west PA (Veraguas, 653, 657, 512, 470). **ID** Distinctive in limited range. Long tail. *Dull buff below* with plain rufous upperparts and *whitish supercilium*. **HABITS** Understory to midstory and edge of broadleaf forest. Creeps through dense foliage and vine tangles. Sometimes hitches briefly along tree trunks. Solitary or in pairs. May follow mixed flocks. **VOICE** Song (1) a series of short, slightly hoarse or squeaky notes that gradually slow and drop in pitch *che chee chee chee chu chu cheew*. Call (2) a rapid series of three high-pitched notes *tsst-tsst tsst*.

50%

Pale-breasted Spinetail

juv

ad

Slaty Spinetail

juv

ad

juv

Pacific slope
ad

Caribbean slope
ad

Rufous-breasted Spinetail

Red-faced Spinetail

juv

ad

Coiba Spinetail

FURNARIDS Furnariidae

Medium-sized birds of humid broadleaf forest. Most follow mixed flocks. Lineated Foliage-gleaner and Striped Woodhaunter are very similar in plumage pattern. Voice is often helpful in locating these.

Buffy Tuftedcheek *Pseudocolaptes lawrencii*   21 cm
CA endemic. Uncommon resident in highlands (mainly above 1600 m) of CR and west PA. **ID** Large. Rufous tail with pointed rectrices. Dark auriculars contrast with narrow, pale supercilium and *buff neck tuft*. Note blackish wings with *narrow cinnamon wingbars*. **HABITS** Midstory to subcanopy of humid, epiphyte-laden broadleaf (cloud) forest. Creeps and hops along larger branches probing and rummaging (sometimes vigorously) in epiphytes (especially bromeliads). Pairs or solitary birds follow mixed flocks. **VOICE** Song (1) one to four sharp, clear notes followed by a trill that first rises in pitch then slows and drops *peenk peenk peenk priiiieeeee*. Call (2) a sharp, metallic *jeenk* or *pweenk*. Compare with call of Hairy Woodpecker.

Streak-breasted Treehunter *Thripadectes rufobrunneus*   21 cm
CA endemic. Uncommon resident in foothills and highlands (mainly 700 to 2500 m) of CR and west PA. Also volcanic highlands of west CR (Guanacaste, 600). **ID** *Large* and robust with heavy bill. Note tawny throat and *tawny streaking on breast*. Compare with smaller Lineated Foliage-gleaner. Note different underparts. **HABITS** Understory to lower midstory and edge of humid broadleaf forest. Favors damp, shaded ravines or streamsides in steep terrain. Forages actively by rummaging and probing in arboreal litter. Solitary or in pairs. **VOICE** Song (1) a harsh, burry, two-syllable phrase repeated in a long series *chi-wawr, chi-wawr, chi-wawr . . .* or *ti-chr, ti-chr, ti-chr, ti-chr . . .* Call (2) a loud, harsh *zeck zeck* or *cheyt cheyt*.

Scaly-throated Foliage-gleaner *Anabacerthia variegaticeps*   16.5 cm
South MX to north SA. Uncommon resident in humid highlands and foothills (mainly 1200 to 2500, locally as low as 800 m). Also upper slopes (above 600 m) of Maya Mountains in BZ (Cayo, Toledo, 433, 313). Rare in NI (Nueva Segovia, Matagalpa, Jinotega, 412). **ID** *Broad buff eye ring* and *supercilium*. Note pale throat with *variable dusky scaling* and dark moustache. Upperparts plain rufous-brown becoming brightest on tail. Lower underparts plain brown. Compare with larger Buff-throated Foliage-gleaner (mainly lower elevations). Note different head pattern and habits. **HABITS** Midstory to subcanopy of humid broadleaf forest and adjacent tall second growth. Probes in arboreal litter or epiphytes. Often clings or hangs while inspecting mossy undersides of limbs. Solitary or pairs follow mixed flocks. **VOICE** Song (1) a long series of squeaky, emphatic notes *skew, skew, skew, skew . . .* sometimes increasing in volume or rising or falling in pitch. Calls (2) an abrupt, sibilant *squick* or *squeew* and (3) scratchy, squeaky *kweeeah*.

Lineated Foliage-gleaner *Syndactyla subalaris*   19 cm
CA and SA. Uncommon resident in south foothills and highlands (600 to 2300 m). Perhaps also in volcanic highlands of west CR (Guanacaste, 570). Rare in highlands (1220 to 1580 m) of east PA at Pirre Massif and Tacarcuna Massif (Darién, 657). **ID** Wings concolorous with mantle. Contrasting buff throat sometimes distended. *Sharply streaked with buff below*. Note distinct supercilium. Compare with similar Striped Woodhaunter (mainly lower elevations). Note different underparts. **HABITS** Understory to lower midstory and edge of humid broadleaf forest. Favors vine tangles and cluttered vegetation in gaps. Probes in dead leaves and arboreal litter. Pairs or solitary birds may follow mixed flocks. **VOICE** Loud, harsh vocalizations. Song (1) a long series of sharp, dry, harsh notes. Speed up then slow toward end *ehk, ehk ehk-ehk-ehkehkehkehkehkehk*. Call (2) a dry, harsh *tzuk* or *tzzek*.

Striped Woodhaunter *Automolus subulatus*   18.5 cm
CA and SA. Uncommon to rare and local resident in humid lowlands and foothills (to 1000, rarely or locally to 1200 m). Rare, local and poorly known in east HN (Gracias a Dios, 629) and north NI (Matagalpa, Jinotega, RAAN, 413, 429). **ID** Buff throat, weak supercilium, and *soft buff streaking* on underparts. *Rufous wings contrast with dull brown mantle*. Resembles Lineated Foliage-gleaner (especially widespread form). Note more contrasting rufous wings and less crisply streaked underparts. Also compare with Buff-throated Foliage-gleaner. Note different head pattern. **GV** Birds from east PA have plain (unstreaked) mantle and softer streaking below. **HABITS** Understory to midstory of humid broadleaf forest and tall second growth. Pairs or solitary birds follow mixed flocks. Favors vine tangles and accumulations of arboreal litter. **VOICE** Often noisy. Song (1) a series of eight to ten loud, wooden notes *kick kick kick . . .* or *ehk ehk ehk . . .* Call (2) a loud, harsh *chook* or *churk*. Sometimes repeated.

Buffy Tuftedcheek

Streak-breasted Treehunter

Scaly-throated Foliage-gleaner

Lineated Foliage-gleaner

juv

ad

widespread

east PA

Striped Woodhaunter

45%

FOLIAGE-GLEANERS Furnariidae

Secretive birds found in lower levels of humid broadleaf forest. These species typically remain hidden in dense vegetation even when foraging actively. Details of head and underparts pattern are useful for identification. Range, habitat, and especially voice are also helpful. Buff-throated Foliage-gleaner is the most common and widespread.

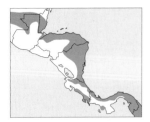

Buff-throated Foliage-gleaner *Automolus ochrolaemus*   19 cm

South MX to SA. Fairly common resident in lowlands and foothills (to 1300 m). **ID** Rufous tail. Note *pale buff or whitish throat, eye ring, and supercilium.* Otherwise plain dull brown. Compare with Scaly-throated Foliage-gleaner (mainly higher elevations). Note different habits and voice. **GV** Birds from central and east PA have white throat, less scaling on breast, and indistinct supercilium. Birds from Pacific CR and west PA similar. **HABITS** Understory and edge of humid broadleaf forest. Pairs or solitary birds haunt dense vegetation in gaps or shaded vine tangles at forest edge. Forages actively by rummaging in arboreal litter but often secretive. Does not follow mixed flocks but may become more active as they pass nearby. Usually detected by voice. Pounds tail while singing. **VOICE** Song (1) a harsh, one-second rattle that gradually slows and drops in pitch (sometimes first ascending and then falling) *eheheheheh-eh-eh eh eh.* In Pacific CR and west PA, song a loud, harsh rattle lasting two to five seconds. In south Caribbean lowlands, song sharper, higher-pitched, more rapid and whinnying, usually falling and slowing toward end with peculiar nasal twang or metallic ring. Call (2) a nasal, burry *rack* or *ahk.*

Ruddy Foliage-gleaner *Clibanornis rubiginosus*   18–20 cm

South MX to SA. Uncommon resident in north foothills and highlands (500 to 2500 m). Local in Pacific highlands of NI at Volcán Mombacho and Volcán San Cristóbal (Rivas, Chinandega, Grenada, 324, 413). Rare and local in foothills and highlands (450 to 1350 m) of east CR (Puntarenas, 126, 602, 600) and west PA (Chiriquí, 657). Rare and local in east PA (Panamá, Darién, 657, 45). **ID** *Near-uniform, dull chestnut brown* becoming brighter rufous on throat and breast. *Plain, dark head pattern.* In close view note *bluish-gray bare skin around eye.* Ruddy Woodcreeper has different structure, head pattern, and habits. Tawny-throated Leaftosser has different habits and tail shape. **GV** Birds from east PA are duskier, with rufous confined to throat and breast, and have black tail. Birds from east CR and west PA (not shown) resemble the north CA form but are slightly more olivaceous. **HABITS** Understory of humid broadleaf, pine-oak, and pine forest and tall second growth. Favors shaded interior of tangled vegetation. Secretive and retiring. Solitary or in pairs. Does not follow mixed flocks. **VOICE** Song (1) a two-syllable phrase *yeh-nek yeh-nek yehnek* . . . usually repeated two or three times. Calls (2) a harsh, dry chatter and (3) slow series of nasal *chaak* cries.

Buff-fronted Foliage-gleaner *Philydor rufum*   20 cm

CA and SA. Rare and local resident in foothills and highlands (800 to 2300 m) of east CR (Cartago, Puntarenas, 126, 570, 600) and west PA (Chiriquí, Bocas del Toro, 61, 657, 346). **ID** Rufous wings and tail with pointed rectrices. *Bright buff throat and supercilium* contrast with *gray eye stripe and crown.* Might be confused with various other furnarids but note solid (unstreaked) pattern and *plain buff underparts.* Compare with Buff-throated Foliage-gleaner. Note different head and underparts pattern. **HABITS** Midstory to subcanopy of humid broadleaf forest. Forages actively on mossy branches and in foliage. Hops along limbs swinging body from side to side. May cling or hang upside down. Solitary birds or pairs follow mixed flocks. **VOICE** Poorly known in CA. In SA, song (1) a metallic rattle that drops slightly in pitch. Calls (2) a squeaky *wikikikik* and (3) sharp, metallic *chik* or *tzik.*

Slaty-winged Foliage-gleaner *Philydor fuscipenne*   16 cm

CA and north Pacific SA. Fairly common resident in lowlands and foothills (to 1200 m) of central and east PA. **ID** Plain chestnut-brown mantle contrasts with *gray wings.* Note tawny eye ring and long supercilium extending behind eye. *Throat and underparts plain tawny buff.* No other CA foliage-gleaner has gray wings. **GV** Birds from east PA (Darién, not shown) are slightly paler. **HABITS** Upper understory to midstory of humid broadleaf forest and edge. Solitary birds or pairs follow mixed flocks. Forages actively by rummaging in arboreal litter and epiphytes. Often clings or hangs upside down. **VOICE** Calls (1) a short, trilled or rolled *bree-e-e-et* and (2) sharp, high-pitched *chif* or *chit.*

45%

Caribbean north CA
to west PA

**Buff-throated
Foliage-gleaner**

central and
east PA

widespread
ad

east PA
ad

Ruddy Foliage-gleaner

widespread
juv

east PA
juv

Buff-fronted Foliage-gleaner

Slaty-winged Foliage-gleaner

STREAMCREEPER AND LEAFTOSSERS Furnariidae

Retiring birds found on floor of humid broadleaf forest. All have compact structure with blackish, rounded tail. Usually solitary or in pairs. Not with mixed flocks. Scaly-throated Leaftosser is the most common and widespread.

Sharp-tailed Streamcreeper *Lochmias nematura*   14 cm

CA and SA. Rare and local resident in foothills and highlands (725 to 1550 m) of east PA at Cerro Malí, Cerro Quia, Serranía de Jungurudó, and Pirre Massif (Darién, 9, 657, 45, 346). **ID** Dark brown with *white spotting on underparts*. Structure and behavior like a *Sclerurus* leaftosser. Imm has reduced white spotting on underparts. Compare with Spotted Barbtail. Note different habits. **HABITS** Floor and understory of humid broadleaf forest in vicinity of streams. Forages by probing or flipping fallen leaves with bill. Favors mossy rocks and damp, low vegetation in dim canyons. Secretive. **VOICE** Song (1) a very rapid series of sharp *chip* notes that accelerate to become a trill. Call (2) a dry, flat *t-t-chk, t-t-chk, t-t-chk*. Sometimes repeated persistently.

Tawny-throated Leaftosser *Sclerurus mexicanus*   15.5 cm

MX to SA. Uncommon resident in foothills and highlands (mainly 1000 to 1850, locally to 2300 or as low as 400 m). Also Maya Mountains in BZ (Cayo, Toledo, 347) and slopes of Cordillera de Guanacaste in CR (Guanacaste, 570). Recently reported from north SV (Santa Ana, 364, 301). **ID** Slender, fairly long, near-straight bill and broad, rounded black tail. *Near-uniform chestnut brown becoming brighter rufous on throat and rump*. **GV** Birds from CR and PA are darker. **HABITS** Floor and understory of humid broadleaf forest and adjacent tall second growth. Forages on ground in damp leaf litter. Takes elevated perch when disturbed or vocalizing. Solitary or in pairs. May attend ant swarms. **VOICE** Song (1) a series of four to seven high-pitched, slurred notes becoming progressively shorter and lower in pitch *pseeer-pseeer-psee-pse*. Call (2) a sharp, squeaky *sweek*.

Gray-throated Leaftosser *Sclerurus albigularis*   17.5 cm

CA and SA. Uncommon to rare resident in foothills and highlands (1200 to 1800 m) of CR, including west volcanic highlands (Guanacaste, 126, 570, 600). Very rare in west PA (Chiriquí, 657). **ID** Slender near-straight bill. Broad, rounded black tail. Note *pale gray throat* and plain rufous breast. Warm brown above becoming rufous on rump. Scaly-throated Leaftosser found at lower elevations. Compare with Tawny-throated Leaftosser. Note different head pattern and bill shape. **HABITS** Floor and understory of humid broadleaf forest and adjacent tall second growth. Terrestrial. Forages on ground on leaf-strewn slopes. Solitary or in pairs. **VOICE** Song (1) a series of five or six high-pitched, squeaky notes *che-che-che chu chu chew* or *cheche-che chu chu chew . . .* often repeated persistently. Call (2) a squeaky *swick*. Compare with sharper call note of Tawny-throated Leaftosser.

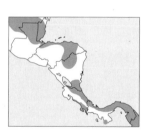

Scaly-throated Leaftosser *Sclerurus guatemalensis*   17.5 cm

South MX and CA. Fairly common resident in lowlands and foothills (to 1000 m). Rare and poorly known on Azuero Peninsula at Cerro Hoya in PA (Los Santos, 657). **ID** *Plain dull brown including rump* with broad, rounded, blackish tail. In close view note brown and buff scaling on throat and breast. Duller and more uniform than other CA leaftossers and mainly at lower elevations. **HABITS** Floor and understory of humid broadleaf forest. Forages on ground in damp leaf litter. Furtive and retiring. May take an elevated perch when disturbed or while vocalizing. Solitary or in pairs. **VOICE** Song (1) a rapid series of ten to fifteen sharp, clear notes. First four to six notes gradually drop in pitch. Last notes gradually rise. Series ends with short trill. Sometimes gives longer series lasting five to six seconds that rises gradually in pitch and may be repeated persistently. Call (2) a sharp, sometimes metallic *pick* or *zick*.

Sharp-tailed Streamcreeper

Though usually seen on the
ground, leaftossers may take an
elevated perch when disturbed.

north CA

Tawny-throated Leaftosser

CR and PA

Gray-throated Leaftosser

Scaly-throated Leaftosser

SAPAYOA Sapayoidae

Sapayoa is a highly distinctive species with no close relatives in the region.

Sapayoa *Sapayoa aenigma* 15 cm

CA and north SA. Uncommon to rare and local resident in lowlands and foothills (to 600 m) of east PA (Colón, Panamá, Kuna Yala, Darién, 67, 350, 91, 522, 426). **ID** *Broad bill.* Mostly plain olive-green. Eyes red. Male has semiconcealed yellow crown stripe. Compare with Olivaceous Flatbill. Note Sapayoa's plain breast and wings. Schiffornis have different bill shape and habits, etc. Compare with Carmiol's Tanager. Note different posture. **HABITS** Midstory of humid broadleaf forest. Favors damp ravines or shaded streams with closed canopy in hilly terrain. Perches in open on looping vine or horizontal branch. Often solitary, but up to three birds may follow mixed flocks (often with Carmiol's Tanagers). **VOICE** Song (1) a short, liquid trill or rattle *trrrrrr* or *preeeeeer*. May drop steeply or only slightly in pitch. Compare with call of Blue-crowned Manakin. Calls (2) a loud *pick* or *pyuk* and (3) squeaky *chee-chew*.

SPADEBILLS, PIPRITES, and TWISTWING Tyrannidae

Platyrinchus spadebills are small, short-tailed birds with very broad bill found in lower levels of broadleaf forest. Spadebills make abrupt, upward sallies to seize prey from undersides of foliage or twigs. Most are detected by voice. The enigmatic Gray-headed Piprites is a distinctive species of uncertain affinities and is classified *incertae sedis*.

Golden-crowned Spadebill *Platyrinchus coronatus* 9 cm

CA and SA. Uncommon resident in humid lowlands and foothills (to 1200 m). **ID** Tiny with very short tail and very broad bill. Two dark marks on side of head. Olive above with *orange and rufous crown.* Underparts pale olive-yellow. Compare with White-throated Spadebill (mainly higher elevations). Note different crown pattern. **HABITS** Understory to midstory of humid broadleaf forest and adjacent tall second growth. Solitary or in pairs. Does not follow mixed flocks. Inconspicuous. **VOICE** Song (1) a long, high-pitched, insect-like trill that drops then rises in pitch. Call (2) a soft *chiirp.* May be repeated two or three times.

Stub-tailed Spadebill *Platyrinchus cancrominus* 10 cm

South MX and CA. Fairly common resident in Caribbean lowlands and foothills (to 1500 m). Uncommon to rare and local in north Pacific with records from GT (Suchitepéquez, 229), SV (Ahuachapán, 619), and CR (Guanacaste, Puntarenas, 600). Also islands off west PA (Bocas del Toro, 469). **ID** Small with very short tail and very broad bill. Two dark marks on side of head. *Crown brown.* White-throated Spadebill mainly allopatric. Note different voice. **HABITS** Understory of semihumid to humid broadleaf forest and adjacent tall second growth. Solitary or in pairs. Does not follow mixed flocks. Inconspicuous. **VOICE** Call (1) a soft, but emphatic *didi-dunk* or *d-dunk*. Compare with short call of Bright-rumped Attila.

White-throated Spadebill *Platyrinchus mystaceus* 10 cm

CA and SA. Fairly common resident in south foothills and highlands (700 to 2150 m). **ID** Small with very short tail and very broad bill. Two dark marks on side of head. *Crown grayish-brown.* Male has semiconcealed yellow crown stripe. Stub-tailed Spadebill mainly allopatric. Note different voice. **HABITS** Understory of humid broadleaf forest and adjacent second growth. Like Stub-tailed Spadebill. **VOICE** Song (1) a short, squeaky rattle or trill that rises slightly in pitch. Call (2) a sharp, loud *pwick* or *pwiik.* May be doubled or repeated. Compare with call of Hairy Woodpecker.

Gray-headed Piprites *Piprites griseiceps* 11.5 cm

CA endemic. Very rare and local resident in Caribbean foothills (SL to 1000, but mainly 100 to 750 m) of GT (Izabal, 380, 377, 227), HN (Atlántida, Olancho, Gracias a Dios, 35, 346), NI (RAAN, Río San Juan, 332, 413, 357, 626), CR (Guanacaste, Heredia, Cartago, Limón, 66, 126, 570, 600, 92, 564), and west PA (Bocas del Toro, 42, 346). **ID** Rounded crown. *Gray head with white eye ring.* Mostly olive-green above and greenish-yellow below. Note pale edging on tertials. Juv has olive head. Compare with Lesser Greenlet. **HABITS** Midstory to subcanopy of humid broadleaf forest. Solitary birds or pairs follow mixed flocks. **VOICE** Song (1) a short, staccato phrase *pik pik prrrity pree-kit prrrity peer* or *wip-pip preeer*. May be repeated persistently. Compare with song of Tawny-chested Flycatcher. Call (2) a soft, rolling *purrr* or *wurr* less nasal than Northern Bentbill. Also (3) a series of soft chip notes. Flicks tail with each note.

Brownish Twistwing *Cnipodectes subbrunneus* female 16, male 19 cm

CA and SA. Uncommon resident in lowlands and foothills of PA. Recently reported from Caribbean west PA (Bocas del Toro, 469). **ID** Fairly long tail. Long, fine facial feathers create shaggy appearance. Mostly dull brown with *rufous-brown rump and tail.* Note pale edgings on tertials and *pale brown eyes.* Female smaller. Compare with Russet-winged Schiffornis. Note different eye color and wing pattern. **HABITS** Understory to midstory of humid broadleaf forest. Perches in open. Deliberately lifts or stretches individual wings. Solitary or in pairs. Does not follow mixed flocks. **VOICE** Calls (1) an abrupt *kwee-oo* often doubled, and (2) short, squeaky, upslurred *keeyuk.* May be repeated. Produces (3) squeaky, rattling sonation with wings.

Sapayoa

imm

ad

**Golden-crowned
Spadebill**

♂

♀

Stub-tailed Spadebill

♂

♀

**White-throated
Spadebill**

Gray-headed Piprites

Brownish Twistwing

♂

FLATBILLS AND FLYCATCHERS Tyrannidae

Rhynchocyclus flatbills are found in lower and middle levels of humid broadleaf forest. *Tolmomyias* flatbills are found mainly in forest canopy, edge, and second growth. Most are detected by voice. Yellow-olive Flycatcher is the most common and widespread *Tolmomyias*.

Eye-ringed Flatbill *Rhynchocyclus brevirostris*   16 cm

South MX to north SA. Locally common resident in north lowlands and foothills (to 1500, locally to 1800 m). Uncommon in north Pacific. Fairly common in south foothills and highlands (to 2100 m). **ID** Rounded head and *very broad bill*. Mostly olive-green becoming slightly paler below with *broad whitish eye ring*. Note faint, diffuse streaking on breast. Olivaceous Flatbill has brighter wing edgings and paler underparts. **HABITS** Midstory of semihumid to humid broadleaf forest and adjacent tall second growth. Pairs or solitary birds follow mixed flocks. Flits deliberately between perches pausing frequently to crane neck and peer at surrounding vegetation. **VOICE** Call (1) a high-pitched, scratchy, harsh *siiiiiiiiiip* or *sweeeeeip* that rises steeply in pitch. Given singly or in series of three to four with phrases becoming shorter toward end of series. Compare with call of Yellow-olive Flycatcher. Also (2) a short, bright *tsiit* that may be repeated.

Olivaceous Flatbill *Rhynchocyclus olivaceus*   15 cm

CA and SA. Uncommon resident in humid lowlands and foothills (to 600 m) of PA. **ID** *Very broad bill*. Resembles Eye-ringed Flatbill, but has *paler yellow lower underparts* with more distinct streaking and *brighter yellow edging on wing*. **HABITS** Understory to midstory of humid broadleaf forest and adjacent tall second growth. Pairs or solitary birds sometimes follow mixed flocks. **VOICE** Infrequently heard song (1) a very thin, high-pitched *tee-tee-tee-tee*. Call (2) a loud, harsh *tsheet* or *breeyt*.

Yellow-olive Flycatcher *Tolmomyias sulphurescens*   13.5 cm

MX to SA. Common and widespread resident in lowlands and foothills (to 1500 m). **ID** *Very broad bill*. Mostly horizontal posture with tail sometimes slightly cocked. Note gray crown, whitish spectacles, and (usually) *pale gray eyes*. Lower underparts clear, pale yellow. Pale yellow edging on wing coverts and flight feathers. In south compare with Yellow-margined Flycatcher. Note different head pattern and habits. Also compare with Greenish Elaenia and Paltry Tyrannulet. Note different bill shape. **GV** Birds from PA are more olive on crown, more extensively yellow below, and have faint dark mark on auriculars. **HABITS** Midstory to canopy and edge in wide variety of arboreal habitats including semihumid broadleaf forest, gallery forest, second growth, gardens, and plantations. Forages deliberately in foliage. Usually solitary. Inconspicuous, but vocalizes persistently throughout day and readily detected by voice. **VOICE** Call (1) a high-pitched, thin, hissing or slightly scratchy *psssssssst* or *bzeeeeeek*. Sometimes repeated three or four times. Compare with more emphatic call of Eye-ringed Flatbill.

Yellow-margined Flycatcher *Tolmomyias assimilis*   13 cm

CA and SA. Fairly common resident in Caribbean humid lowlands and foothills (to 1000 m). Rare in Pacific east CR (Puntarenas) and west PA (Chiriquí). Recently reported from NI (Río San Juan, RAAS, Rivas, 148, 452, 413, 548) and east HN (Gracias a Dios, 263). **ID** Tail often slightly cocked. *Very broad bill*, brown eyes, and broken whitish eye ring. *Crown dark gray*. Shows pale speculum at base of primaries and *broad, deep yellow edging on greater wing coverts*. Underparts clear, pale yellow. Legs gray. Resembles Yellow-olive Flycatcher. Note Yellow-margined's darker crown and different wing pattern. Habits and voice also distinctive. **HABITS** Upper midstory to canopy of humid broadleaf forest and adjacent tall second growth. Solitary birds or pairs follow mixed flocks. Makes abrupt, upward sallies to seize prey from foliage. **VOICE** Call (1) a series of three to five short, high-pitched, sibilant notes *tseep tseep tsee-uu tseep* that rise in pitch.

Yellow-breasted Flycatcher *Tolmomyias flaviventris*   12 cm

CA and SA. Fairly common resident in Pacific lowlands of east PA (Darién, 42, 346, 424). **ID** Very broad bill. Note dark eyes and olive upperparts. *Mostly yellow below and on sides of head* becoming brightest on auriculars and supercilium. Note yellow edging on wing. Structure and behavior much like other CA *Tolmomyias*. Yellow-breasted is distinctive in having *no gray on crown*. Compare with Yellow Tyrannulet. Note different bill shape and habits. **HABITS** Midstory to subcanopy and edge in semi-open areas including forest clearings, plantations, second growth, and scrub. Often near water. Makes short, deliberate flights or hops through vegetation. Usually solitary. **VOICE** Call (1) a high-pitched *tsueet* or *weeip*.

Eye-ringed Flatbill

Olivaceous Flatbill

Yellow-olive Flycatcher

widespread
ad

juv

PA
ad

Yellow-margined Flycatcher

Yellow-breasted Flycatcher

TODY-FLYCATCHERS, PYGMY-TYRANT, AND BENTBILLS Tyrannidae

Tiny and often inconspicuous birds of broadleaf forest and edge. Most are detected by voice. Note their distinctive bill shapes. Common Tody-Flycatcher is the most common and widespread.

Black-headed Tody-Flycatcher *Todirostrum nigriceps*   8 cm

CA and north SA. Uncommon resident in humid lowlands and foothills (to 1000 m). Rare and poorly known in north NI (RAAN, 626) and HN (Colón, El Paraíso, 263). **ID** Tiny and short-tailed. Blackish head contrasts with *white throat* and yellow-olive mantle. *Eyes dark.* Compare with larger-billed Common Tody-Flycatcher. Note different underparts and habits. **HABITS.** Subcanopy to canopy and edge of humid broadleaf forest and adjacent tall second growth. Pairs or solitary birds follow mixed flocks. Forages actively in foliage. Difficult to observe. Often remains high in canopy foliage. **VOICE** Call (1) a steady series of five to eight sharp *chip* or *tsip* notes.

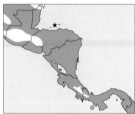

Common Tody-Flycatcher *Todirostrum cinereum*   9.5 cm

MX to SA. Common resident in lowlands and foothills (to 1600 m). Also Isla Coiba off PA (470). One report from Isla Roatán (119). **ID** *Long, broad bill.* Long, narrow tail often cocked or wagged from side to side displaying white-tipped rectrices. *Pale eyes* set in blackish sides of head. Mostly dark gray above and *yellow below, including throat.* **HABITS** Understory to canopy in wide variety of nonforest habitats including second growth, forest edge, plantations, gardens, and mangroves. Solitary or in pairs. Does not follow mixed flocks. Forages actively by hopping through dense vegetation. Typically remains inside cover. **VOICE** Song (1) a short trill of four notes recalling Tropical Kingbird, but shorter and weaker. Also (2) short, rapid, insect-like trills *t-trrrc t-trrrc . . .* and (3) sharp, high-pitched *tic* notes delivered at varied intervals.

Slate-headed Tody-Flycatcher *Poecilotriccus sylvia*   9.5 cm

MX to SA. Uncommon resident in lowlands and foothills (to 1100 m). **ID** Small with broad bill. Mostly *gray head and pale gray breast.* Note *whitish spectacles.* Eyes usually pale in ad. Compare with Northern Bentbill. Note different bill shape and habits. **HABITS** Understory to midstory and edge of arid (deciduous) to humid broadleaf forest, second growth, scrub and riparian thickets. Favors gallery forest in drier regions. Pairs or solitary birds skulk in dense, tangled vegetation. Inconspicuous. Does not follow mixed flocks. Usually detected by voice. May vocalize persistently. **VOICE** Song (1) a low-pitched, emphatic introductory note followed by short, downslurred trill *tip, turrr* or *tic, trrr.* Sometimes with stuttering introductory note *tip, tip-trrr* or followed by shorter, higher-pitched trill *tip trrr-trri.*

Black-capped Pygmy-Tyrant *Myiornis atricapillus*   7 cm

CA and north SA. Uncommon to fairly common resident in humid lowlands and foothills (to 600 m). Recently reported from NI (Río San Juan, RAAN, RAAS, 452, 548, 346). **ID** *Tiny* with *very short tail.* Male has blackish crown and *bold white spectacles.* Female has grayer crown. Compare with Black-headed Tody-Flycatcher. **HABITS** Upper midstory to canopy and edge of humid broadleaf forest, tall second growth, and clearings with tall trees. May descend to lower levels in vegetation at gaps or edges. In pairs or small groups. Does not follow mixed flocks. Forages actively. Makes short, fluttering sallies to seize prey from foliage or terminal twigs. Inconspicuous but often vocal throughout the day. **VOICE** Song (1) a short, very hard, insect-like trill *tree treet-treet-treet-treet.* Call (2) an inconspicuous, insect-like, sharp *tseep* or *keep* repeated at regular intervals.

Northern Bentbill *Oncostoma cinereigulare*   10 cm

South MX and CA. Common resident in lowlands and foothills (to 750, locally to 1500 m in north). Uncommon to rare in north Pacific. **ID** Small with upright posture. Pale eyes and *heavy, decurved bill.* Note grayish throat and soft streaking on breast. Lower underparts pale yellowish. Juv has light brown eyes. Compare with Slate-headed Tody-Flycatcher. Note different head pattern and bill shape. Southern Bentbill (mainly allopatric) has yellowish-olive throat and chest. **HABITS** Understory and edge of semihumid to humid broadleaf forest, shaded plantations, and second growth. Favors shaded interior of tangled vegetation. May remain motionless on low perch for long periods. Makes abrupt, short sallies to seize prey from undersides of leaves. Solitary. Does not follow mixed flocks. **VOICE** Song (1) a short (0.5 s) usually flat, buzzy trill *naaaaaahrr* sometimes preceded by short introductory *kip* note. Compare with calls of Sepia-capped Flycatcher and Slate-headed Tody-Flycatcher.

Southern Bentbill *Oncostoma olivaceum*   9 cm

CA and north SA. Fairly common resident in lowlands and foothills (to 400 m) of PA. **ID** Pale eyes and *heavy, decurved bill.* Note faintly streaked, *yellowish-olive throat and breast.* **HABITS** Like Northern Bentbill. **VOICE** Song (1) a short buzzy, trill *jrrrrrrrrrrrrr* or *praaaaaahrr* that drops slightly in pitch. Compare with calls of Sepia-capped Flycatcher and Slate-headed Tody-Flycatcher. Also (2) a short *krip* or *prip.*

Black-headed Tody-Flycatcher

Common Tody-Flycatcher

Slate-headed Tody-Flycatcher

juv

ad

Black-capped Pygmy-Tyrant

Northern Bentbill

Southern Bentbill

PYGMY-TYRANTS AND FLYCATCHERS Tyrannidae

Small or tiny birds. Most are found in humid broadleaf forest and second growth. Often detected by voice. Several habitually flick individual wings. Ochre-bellied Flycatcher is the most common and widespread.

Scale-crested Pygmy-Tyrant *Lophotriccus pileatus*　　　　　　10 cm
CA and SA. Fairly common resident in south foothills and highlands (300 to 1700 m). Locally near SL on Osa Peninsula, CR. Rare and local in HN (Olancho, 401) and NI (Jinotega, RAAN, 135, 626). **ID** Small. *Black and rufous crest* usually flat against nape. Note *pale orange eyes* and pale lores. Compare with Southern Bentbill. **HABITS** Understory and edge of humid broadleaf forest, shaded plantations and second growth. Often in bamboo. Inconspicuous when quiet. May remain motionless on hidden perch for long periods. Makes abrupt, short sallies to take prey. Usually solitary. Does not follow mixed flocks. **VOICE** Song (1) a long series of loud, sharp, variably wooden or metallic notes *tuc tuc tuctuctuctuctuc tuc*. May be steady or may rise in pitch and drop steeply at end. Call (2) a sharp, trilled *preet*.

Pale-eyed Pygmy-Tyrant *Lophotriccus pilaris*　　　　　　9 cm
CA and SA. Uncommon resident in Pacific lowlands of PA (to 900 m). **ID** *Tiny* with straight bill. Note *pale yellowish eyes* and *pale buff lores and face*. Breast whitish with faint streaking. Olive above with narrow buff wingbars. Compare with Southern Bentbill. Note different bill. **HABITS** Understory of dense second growth, scrub, mangroves, and gaps in semihumid broadleaf forest. Inconspicuous and usually stays hidden in shaded vegetation. Makes short, abrupt upward sallies to seize prey. May hover briefly. Often in pairs. Does not follow mixed flocks. **VOICE** Call (1) a short, burry, trilled phrase that rises then drops in pitch *breeeeuur*. Compare with steady trill of Southern Bentbill.

Slaty-capped Flycatcher *Leptopogon superciliaris*　　　　　　13 cm
CA and SA. Uncommon to fairly common resident in south foothills (600 to 1600 m). **ID** *Slate-gray crown*, gray and whitish grizzled sides of head, and *dark mark on auriculars*. Bold wingbars and wing edging variably yellowish or cinnamon. Compare with Sepia-capped Flycatcher (lower elevations). **HABITS** Midstory of humid broadleaf forest and adjacent tall second growth. Pairs or solitary birds follow mixed flocks. Forages from open perch. Flicks individual wings open and shut. **VOICE** Call (1) a sharp, emphatic *wsst* or *swick*. May be followed by a variable, hard rattle *wsst-trrrrrrrrru* that drops in pitch. Also (2) a repeated *chu-hit chu-hit chu-hit* with second syllable thin and attenuated.

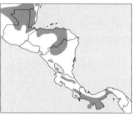

Sepia-capped Flycatcher *Leptopogon amaurocephalus*　　　　　　13 cm
South MX to SA. Uncommon resident in north Caribbean lowlands and foothills (to 1300 m). Uncommon to rare and local in lowlands and foothills of east CR and PA (600, 341). Also Isla Coiba (653, 470). **ID** *Brown crown*, pale grayish lores, and *dark mark on auriculars*. Slaty-capped Flycatcher (higher elevations) has gray crown. **HABITS** Midstory of semihumid broadleaf forest, tall second growth, and shaded plantations. May follow mixed flocks. Solitary or in pairs. Forages from open perch. Flicks individual wings. **VOICE** Song (1) a hard trill or rattle that accelerates very slightly. Sometimes with one or two short introductory notes *wic, wic purrrrrrrrrru*. Compare with Northern Bentbill. Also (2) a short *vhit*.

Olive-striped Flycatcher *Mionectes olivaceus*　　　　　　13 cm
CA and SA. Fairly common resident in south foothills and highlands (mainly 600 to 2150 m, locally near SL in east PA, 426). May undertake altitudinal movements (593, 92). **ID** *White postocular spot*. Drab olive with grayish crown and nape and *yellowish streaking on underparts*. Note pale pinkish base of mandible and faint wingbars. **GV** Birds from central and east PA are darker than widespread form. **HABITS** Midstory of humid broadleaf (cloud) forest. Solitary. May follow mixed flocks. Often hover-gleans. **VOICE** Usually quiet. Song (1) a series of very high-pitched, long, slurred, hissing notes *pseeuuueeeuuueeeuuueee . . .* Sings with bill open and head swaying from side to side.

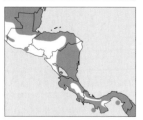

Ochre-bellied Flycatcher *Mionectes oleagineus*　　　　　　11.5–12.5 cm
MX to SA. Common resident in lowlands and foothills (to 1200, locally to 1800 m). May undertake altitudinal movements (92, 394). Rare in north Pacific slope (183). Also Isla Coiba and Pearl Islands (Veraguas, Panamá 60, 611, 649, 470). **ID** *Orange or pinkish base of mandible* and plain olive head. *Lower underparts deep ochre*. **GV** Birds from central and east PA are more richly colored below and have cinnamon wingbars. **HABITS** Understory to subcanopy and edge of semihumid to humid broadleaf forest, shaded plantations, and tall second growth. Locally in pine-oak woodland. Solitary or in pairs. Forages actively. Often hover-gleans. Habitually flicks wings. May follow mixed flocks. **VOICE** Often quiet. Song (1) a long, staccato series of squeaky notes. Alternates lower-pitched *plic* and higher-pitched *wit* notes *plic, plic, plic, plic, plic, plit, wit-whit-whit-whit . . .*

55%

Scale-crested Pygmy-Tyrant

Pale-eyed Pygmy-Tyrant

Slaty-capped Flycatcher

Sepia-capped Flycatcher

CR and
west PA

central and
east PA

Olive-striped Flycatcher

widespread

central and
east PA

Ochre-bellied Flycatcher

TYRANNULETS Tyrannidae

Tiny or small birds found locally in humid broadleaf forest and edge. Most of these species are confined to south Central America.

Bronze-olive Pygmy-Tyrant *Pseudotriccus pelzelni*   11 cm
CA and SA. Uncommon and local resident in foothills and highlands (1200 to 1500 m) of east PA (Darién, 463, 512, 657, 45). **ID** *Mostly dark olive-brown* becoming paler below. *Eyes dark red.* Compare with various female manakins. **HABITS** Understory and edge of very humid broadleaf (cloud) forest. Favors tangled edges at light gaps and tree falls. Inconspicuous. May remain motionless for long periods on low perch. Makes abrupt, short sallies to take prey from undersides of leaves. Usually solitary. May follow mixed flocks briefly or may become more active as they pass. **VOICE** Wings whir audibly in flight. Produces (1) a rapid, snapping or ticking sonation with wings.

Yellow-green Tyrannulet *Phylloscartes flavovirens*   11.5 cm
CA endemic. Uncommon resident in lowlands and lower foothills (to 500 m) of east PA (Panamá, Colón, Darién, 657, 512). **ID** Small and long-tailed. Mostly horizontal posture with tail slightly cocked. Olive-green above with *yellow eye ring.* Note bright yellow wingbars and yellow edging on flight feathers. Underparts uniform pale yellow. Compare with female Gray Elaenia. Note different head pattern. **HABITS** Subcanopy to canopy and edge of semihumid to humid broadleaf forest and tall second growth. Pairs or solitary birds forage actively in foliage. Follows mixed flocks. Droops wings or flicks each wing separately. **VOICE** Calls (1) a very rapid *dree-di-didit* and (2) short, high-pitched, upslurred *pweet* or *pwit* that may be followed by short series of thin, high-pitched notes.

Rufous-browed Tyrannulet *Phylloscartes superciliaris*   11–12 cm
CA and north SA. Uncommon to rare and local in south foothills (600 to 1200 m). Poorly known in east PA where recorded from Tacarcuna Massif and Pirre Massif (Darién, 282, 657). **ID** Slender, with long, notched tail sometimes slightly cocked. Gray crown and nape contrast with short rufous supercilium. Note *white at base of maxilla* and *whitish auriculars outlined with black.* **GV** Birds from east PA are larger, whiter below, and have darker mantle. **HABITS** Subcanopy to canopy and edge of humid broadleaf forest. Forages actively in terminal foliage, hopping and sallying to seize prey. Flicks wings individually. In pairs or small groups. Follows mixed flocks. **VOICE** Calls (1) a sharp, squeaky *swick* or *squeet,* (2) a breathy, emphatic *pisseeet,* and (3) sharp *swee-swee* or *sweet-sweet.*

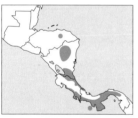

Yellow Tyrannulet *Capsiempis flaveola*   11.5 cm
CA and SA. Fairly common resident in humid lowlands and foothills (to 1200 m). Recently reported from east HN (Olancho). Also Isla Coiba off PA (653, 470). **ID** Long tail. Olive-brown above with *completely yellow underparts, yellow wingbars,* and *yellow supercilium.* **HABITS** Understory to midstory and edge in humid semi-open areas, including low second growth, scrub, hedgerows, and riparian thickets. Forages actively in foliage. Usually inside shaded, rank vegetation. Often noisy and easily located by voice. Solitary, in pairs, or in small groups. Does not follow mixed flocks. **VOICE** Calls (1) a short, slightly upslurred, liquid trill or rattle *prrrrreep.* Compare with calls of Southern Bentbill and Slate-headed Tody-Flycatcher. Also (2) a long series of alternating upslurred *wick* or *pick* notes and short, rolling or sputtering phrases *wick wick wick preeeep wick . . .* or *tu wick wick-week brrree wick wick burrr . . .*

Rough-legged Tyrannulet[21] *Phyllomyias burmeisteri*   11 cm
CA and SA. Uncommon to rare and local resident in highlands (900 to 1850 m) of CR and west PA (Chiriquí, Ngäbe-Buglé, 657, 512). **ID** Small bill with *orange base of mandible.* Note gray crown, *grizzled gray and whitish sides of head,* whitish supercilium, and pale yellow wingbars. Eyes red. Breast yellowish-olive with faint streaking. Compare with Paltry Tyrannulet. Note different head and wing pattern. **HABITS** Midstory to subcanopy of humid broadleaf forest. Pairs or small groups forage actively in foliage. May follow mixed flocks. Habitually flicks wings. Posture fairly upright and does not cock tail. **VOICE** Song (1) a series of three to six piercing, emphatic notes *tsseeeup, tsseeeup tsseeeup . . .* Calls (2) a sharp, sibilant *tsip* or *tseeet.*

Sooty-headed Tyrannulet *Phyllomyias griseiceps*   10.5 cm
CA and SA. Uncommon resident in humid lowlands and lower foothills of east PA (Darién, SL to 550 m). **ID** Note short, dark bill and dark eye stripe. *Sooty-brown crown* contrasts with *pale supercilium.* Wings rather plain. Lower underparts pale yellow. Compare with Greenish and Forest elaenias. **HABITS** Subcanopy to canopy and edge of humid broadleaf forest, tall second growth, and clearings with isolated trees. Forages and vocalizes in open but difficult to observe high in canopy. May descend to lower levels at forest edge. Solitary or in pairs. Does not follow mixed flocks. **VOICE** Pairs duet. Song (1) a loud, rapid, rhythmic *wheep, whip-whip-weedeedeet* or *whit, whitwheeu-deedee . . .*

Bronze-olive Pygmy-Tyrant

Yellow-green Tyrannulet

Rufous-browed Tyrannulet

CR and
west PA

east PA

Yellow Tyrannulet

Rough-legged Tyrannulet

Sooty-headed Tyrannulet

TYRANNULETS Tyrannidae

Tiny or small birds found in middle and upper levels of broadleaf forest and woodland.

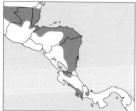

Yellow-bellied Tyrannulet *Ornithion semiflavum* 9 cm

South MX and CA. Fairly common resident in lowlands and foothills (to 1500 m). Recently reported from Pacific west PA (Chiriquí, 42). **ID** Small and *short-tailed* with short bill. Note *gray crown* and *white supercilium*. Underparts completely yellow. Brown-capped Tyrannulet mainly allopatric. **HABITS** Subcanopy to canopy of semihumid to humid broadleaf forest. May descend to lower levels at edges or gaps. Often in pairs. Follows mixed flocks. Forages actively in foliage. **VOICE** Song (1) a loud, emphatic *bee!* followed by long series of short, clear *bee* or *beer* notes that accelerate and drop in pitch *bee! bee bee bee beebeebeebee*. In north CR and south NI compare with more nasal song of Brown-capped Tyrannulet and with slower song of Northern Beardless Tyrannulet. Call (2) a single or short series of *bee* notes.

Brown-capped Tyrannulet *Ornithion brunneicapillus* 8.5 cm

CA and north SA. Uncommon to common resident in south lowlands and foothills (to 900 m). Poorly known in southeast NI (Río San Juan, 548). **ID** Very small and *short-tailed* with short bill. Note *brown crown* and *white supercilium*. Underparts completely yellow. Yellow-bellied Tyrannulet has gray crown. **HABITS** Like Yellow-bellied Tyrannulet but prefers more humid forest where ranges overlap. **VOICE** Song (1) a series of loud, high-pitched, slightly nasal notes with first one or two notes emphatic and upslurred. Remaining four to six successively lower-pitched and shorter *peek!, peek pi pipi-pee-pee-pee*. Variations include (2) a simple descending series *pi pi-pi-pee-pee-pee*. Very similar to Yellow-bellied Tyrannulet.

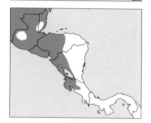

Northern Beardless-Tyrannulet *Camptostoma imberbe* 10 cm

South USA to CA. Fairly common resident in lowlands and foothills (to 800, locally to 1500 m). **ID** Tail often slightly cocked. Note *bushy crest*. Plain, with mostly gray plumage. Underparts whitish with faint yellow tinge on belly. Shows pale supercilium and *dull buff wingbars*. Base of mandible orange. In CR compare with Southern Beardless-Tyrannulet (mainly allopatric). **HABITS** Midstory to canopy of semihumid (deciduous) forest, pine-oak woodland, scrub, and tall vegetation in savannas. Flicks tail and wings between foraging sallies. Solitary or in pairs. Does not follow mixed flocks. **VOICE** Song (1) a slightly descending series of four to five loud whistles *peee-peeew-peeew-peeeuu*. Compare with call of Scrub Euphonia and with more rapid song of Yellow-bellied Tyrannulet. Calls (2) a loud, piercing, jacamar-like *fleeet* or *peeeeuk* and (3) two-syllable, whistled *deee-weep*. Compare with song of Yucatan Flycatcher.

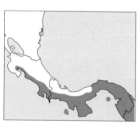

Southern Beardless-Tyrannulet *Camptostoma obsoletum* 9.5 cm

CA and SA. Fairly common resident in south lowlands and foothills (to 750 m). Also Isla Coiba (653, 470) and Pearl Islands (611, 649). **ID** Tail usually slightly cocked. *Slightly raised or bushy crest*. Very plain. Note pale supercilium and *whitish wingbars*. Very similar to Northern Beardless-Tyrannulet. Note Southern's *brighter yellow lower underparts* and lighter, more contrasting wingbars. **GV** Birds from Isla Coiba (not shown) have slightly darker crown. **HABITS** Midstory to canopy and edge of open woodland, semihumid forest, second growth, and plantations. Similar to Northern Beardless-Tyrannulet. **VOICE** Dawn song (1) a repeated *tee be be be*. Usual call (2) a short, descending series of clear, high-pitched notes that become progressively softer and shorter *wheew weew weu*.

Mouse-colored Tyrannulet *Phaeomyias murina* 11.5 cm

CA and SA. Uncommon to locally fairly common resident in Pacific lowlands and foothills (to 650 m) of PA. Rare and local in east CR (San José, Puntarenas, 542, 546). **ID** Drab brown above. Rounded crown and short, fairly heavy bill with dull pinkish base of mandible. Note *diffuse whitish supercilium* and *buff wingbars*. Compare with Southern Beardless-Tyrannulet. Note different structure and wing pattern. **HABITS** Midstory and edge of open woodland, semihumid forest, scrub, second growth, plantations, mangroves, littoral scrub, and gardens. Solitary. **VOICE** Call (1) a short, dry, coarse rattle *jew-jew-jew-je-je-je-jew* that first rises in pitch then drops on last note.

Cocos Flycatcher *Nesotriccus ridgwayi* 13 cm

CA endemic. Confined to Isla del Coco off Pacific CR (571, 600). Common resident. **ID** Brownish overall with *long bill* and *drab brownish-buff wingbars*. No other flycatcher occurs regularly on Isla del Coco. **HABITS** Understory to subcanopy and edge of broadleaf forest, second growth and scrub. Sallies to seize prey from vegetation or ground. Solitary or in pairs. **VOICE** Call (1) a short, harsh, downslurred trill, sometimes followed by single harsh *jeer* notes.

Yellow-bellied Tyrannulet

Brown-capped Tyrannulet

Northern Beardless-Tyrannulet

Southern Beardless-Tyrannulet

Mouse-colored Tyrannulet

Cocos Flycatcher

TYRANNULETS AND ELAENIAS Tyrannidae

Tiny or small birds found in middle and upper levels of humid broadleaf forest, second growth, and woodland. Paltry Tyrannulet is the most common and widespread.

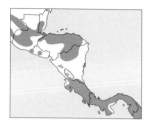

Paltry Tyrannulet[22] *Zimmerius vilissimus* 10.5–11.5 cm
South MX to SA. Common resident in north foothills and highlands (500 to 3000 m, locally near SL). Uncommon in Maya Mountains of BZ (347). Also volcanic highlands of SV (Ahuachapán, La Libertad, San Vicente, 183, 341). Widespread and common (SL to 3000 m) in CR and PA. May undertake local or elevational movements in some regions (593, 670). **ID** Small with short bill. Tail often cocked. Note *yellow edging on wing*, plain gray crown, and whitish supercilium. Underparts pale grayish with very indistinct streaking. Compare with Greenish Elaenia. In south compare with Yellow-crowned Tyrannulet. Note different head and wing pattern. **GV** Birds from CR and PA are smaller and have brighter yellow edging on wings. **HABITS** Midstory to canopy of broadleaf forest, second growth, plantations, hedgerows, and gardens. Forages actively in foliage. Often perches with legs fully extended. Solitary or in pairs. Does not follow mixed flocks, but may become more active as they pass nearby. **VOICE** Dawn song (1) a plaintive *yer-de-dee, yer-de-dee, pe-pe-pe* or *deeu deeu dee tee-a-weedy*. Call (2) in north a loud, clear, plaintive *peeeu* or *peeyup*. In south (HN to PA) gives a longer, more clearly two-syllable *bee-yip* singly or at long intervals. Also (3) a short trill.

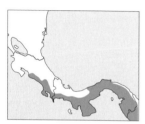

Yellow-crowned Tyrannulet *Tyrannulus elatus* 10 cm
CA and SA. Fairly common resident in Pacific lowlands of east CR and PA (to 400 m). **ID** Small with short black bill. Mostly upright posture. Tail sometimes slightly cocked. Note gray sides of head and *black crown with (semiconcealed) yellow coronal patch*. Wingbars white. Compare with Paltry Tyrannulet. Note different head and wing pattern. Also compare with Forest Elaenia. Note different wing pattern and habits. **HABITS** Midstory to canopy of open areas with scattered trees, hedgerows, gardens, scrub, and humid forest edge. Often conspicuous. Forages actively. Frequently perches in the open. Solitary or in pairs. **VOICE** Calls throughout the day. Call (1) a two-syllable *whiiiideeer* or *wheee-peer*.

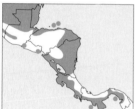

Greenish Elaenia *Myiopagis viridicata* 14 cm
MX to SA. Uncommon to locally common resident in lowlands and foothills (to 1500, locally to 1800 m in north). Most common and widespread in Caribbean lowlands of GT and BZ. Also Bay Islands (317), Isla Coiba (Veraguas, 653, 470), and Pearl Islands (Panamá, 649). **ID** *Whitish supercilium* and eye ring. Yellow on crown usually concealed. Olive above with inconspicuous olive wingbars. *Breast pale grayish-olive with faint streaking.* Lower underparts pale yellow. In PA compare with Forest Elaenia. Note different wing pattern and habits. Also compare with Yellow-olive Flycatcher. Note different head pattern, bill shape, and habits. **HABITS** Midstory of arid (deciduous) to semihumid broadleaf forest, second growth, shaded plantations, mangroves, and gallery forest. Pairs or solitary birds follow mixed flocks. **VOICE** Dawn song (1) a repeated, whistled *see-ah seer seer see-ah . . .* Call (2) a single downslurred, nasal or slightly trilled *pweeeeu or seeeyuu*. Compare with more emphatic call of Rose-throated Becard.

Forest Elaenia *Myiopagis gaimardii* 13 cm
CA and SA. Uncommon resident in lowlands and foothills (to 500 m) of east PA. **ID** Fairly upright posture. Sometimes cocks tail slightly. Bill small. *Dark gray crown* contrasts with whitish supercilium and eye ring. Yellow on crown usually concealed. Breast olive with faint, soft streaking. Lower underparts yellow. Note *yellow wingbars* and wing edging. Very similar to Greenish Elaenia but note *bolder wing markings*, darker crown, and different habits. Also compare with female Gray Elaenia. **HABITS** Midstory to canopy and edge of humid broadleaf forest and tall second growth. Locally in mangroves. Often with mixed flocks. **VOICE** Call (1) a sharp, upslurred, emphatic *pitchweet* or *pitchew*.

Gray Elaenia *Myiopagis caniceps* 11 cm
CA and SA. Uncommon and local resident in lowlands and foothills (to 600 m) of east PA (Panamá, Colón, Darién, 512). **ID** Male mostly *cool gray above* and whitish below with *white wingbars and white edging on tertials*. Female has similar pattern but is mostly greenish-olive above (thus resembles Forest Elaenia). Female's *olive-green mantle contrasts with gray nape*. Note short supercilium. Both sexes have (usually) concealed white on crown. **HABITS** Subcanopy to canopy and edge of humid broadleaf forest and adjacent tall second growth. Pairs sometimes follow mixed flocks. **VOICE** Calls (1) a series of high-pitched notes that accelerate to become a slightly descending trill *pseep pseep psee-ee-ee-eee*. Compare with simpler song of Tropical Gnatcatcher. Also (2) a high-pitched single or double *wheep* and (3) excited *e-e-e-e-pitchew-peechew*.

Paltry Tyrannulet

north CR

CR and PA

Yellow-crowned Tyrannulet

Greenish Elaenia

Forest Elaenia

♀

♂

Gray Elaenia

ELAENIAS AND FLYCATCHER Tyrannidae

Small, drab birds found at middle levels in woodland and semi-open areas. *Elaenia* elaenias may be slightly to strongly crested and all have small bill. Head pattern, structure, and voice are useful in separating these. Yellow-bellied Elaenia is the most common and widespread.

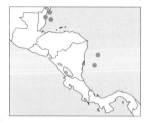

Caribbean Elaenia *Elaenia martinica*   15.5 cm
WI and CA. Confined mainly to BZ Cays (529, 481, 313, 343). Poorly known in mainland BZ (Belize, 343). **ID** Slight crest. Drab with plain grayish underparts. Note relatively *plain head pattern* (no eye ring) and whitish edging on tertials. Bill has pinkish-orange base of mandible. White crown stripe usually concealed. Upperparts dull olive with two whitish wingbars. Yellow-bellied Elaenia has stronger eye ring, yellow lower underparts, and more prominent crest. Mountain Elaenia allopatric. Also compare with Greenish Elaenia. **HABITS** Midstory of littoral scrub, mangroves, and gardens. Solitary or in pairs. Does not follow mixed flocks. **VOICE** Call (1) a clear *wheeur* or *peeur*. Compare with harsher, hoarser or more nasal call of Yellow-bellied Elaenia.

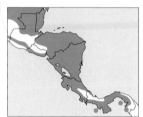

Yellow-bellied Elaenia *Elaenia flavogaster*   16.5 cm
South MX to SA. Common resident in lowlands and foothills (to 1850, rarely or locally to 2200 m). Mainly below 1500 m in north. Also Isla Coiba and Pearl Islands off PA (Veraguas, Panamá, 649, 470). **ID** Large and long-tailed. Note small bill (with pinkish base of mandible) and *whitish eye ring*. Shaggy crest sometimes parted to reveal white on crown. Grayish-olive above with two whitish wingbars. Underparts grayish-white with *pale yellowish belly*. In south compare with Lesser Elaenia. Mountain Elaenia (mainly higher elevations) has rounded crown. Also compare with *Myiarchus* flycatchers. **HABITS** Midstory of open areas with scattered shrubs, trees, or hedgerows including savannas, plantations, scrub, and gardens. Solitary or in pairs. Perches prominently in open. Often noisy and conspicuous. Does not follow mixed flocks. **VOICE** Dawn song (1) a harsh *pitiweer pitiweer brriii weu* or *chebeer* or *jur-jeer* repeated rapidly and persistently. Call (2) a loud, harsh *breeeer*. Compare with calls of Dusky-capped Flycatcher and Couch's Kingbird. Also (3) a two-syllable *wheer-chup* or *well-chip* with second syllable clipped.

Lesser Elaenia *Elaenia chiriquensis*   15 cm
CA and SA. Fairly common breeding resident (or visitor Jan to Sep?) in lowlands and foothills (to 1500, rarely to 1900 m) of Pacific east CR (Puntarenas, 65, 600) and PA. Perhaps withdraws to SA outside breeding season. Also Isla Coiba and Pearl Islands off PA (Veraguas, Panamá, 58, 649, 657, 470). **ID** Resembles Yellow-bellied Elaenia but has *shorter crest* and *dingy, less contrasting yellow belly*. Mandible pinkish. **HABITS** Midstory in open areas with scattered trees or shrubs including hedgerows, plantations, and pastures. Similar to Yellow-bellied Elaenia. **VOICE** Calls (1) a burry *chibur* or *jwebu* and (2) longer *freeeeeuu* or *wheeeeuuu*. Compare with similar call of Yellow-bellied Elaenia. Also (3) a softer *weeb* or *beezb*. Sometimes repeated.

Mountain Elaenia *Elaenia frantzii*   16 cm
South MX to north SA. Uncommon to locally fairly common resident in highlands (mainly above 1200 m). May move to lower elevations outside breeding season. **ID** *Rounded crown* (may appear bushy but never sharply crested). Drab brownish-olive becoming whitish below. Plain head with faint whitish eye ring. Note *broad pale edging on tertials*. Mandible orange. Drab plumage like other CA *Elaenia*. Note Mountain's different structure and highland distribution. Also compare with *Contopus* pewees. **HABITS** Midstory to canopy of semi-open areas such as gardens, hedgerows, plantations, and pastures with scattered trees. Perches prominently in open. Solitary or in pairs. **VOICE** Dawn song (1) a buzzy *d'weet d'weet . . .* or *ch'weet ch'weet . . .* Calls (2) an emphatic, clear *peeeuu* and (3) trilled *briiiuuu*. Compare with less emphatic call of Paltry Tyrannulet. Also (4) trilled, downslurred whistles *dededededededede*.

Northern Scrub-Flycatcher *Sublegatus arenarum*   15 cm
CA and north SA. Uncommon and local resident in Pacific lowlands of CR (Guanacaste, Puntarenas) and PA. Also Isla Coiba and Pearl Islands off PA (Panamá, Veraguas, 611, 455, 649, 470). **ID** Short *black bill* and bushy crown. Drab grayish-brown above including crown. Note *faint whitish supraloral* and *dull whitish or tan wingbars*. Breast plain, dull grayish. Lower underparts pale yellow. Compare with various elaenias (especially Yellow-bellied). Note different bill color and head pattern. Also compare with Southern Beardless-Tyrannulet and with *Myiarchus* flycatchers. **HABITS** Midstory of mangroves, scrub, and littoral woodland. Inconspicuous. Usually remains inside vegetation. Often in pairs. Does not follow mixed flocks. **VOICE** Call (1) a soft, clear *peep* or *peeip* or *wheeip* sometimes doubled as *bee-ip* or *bee-hip*.

50%

Caribbean Elaenia

Yellow-bellied Elaenia

juv

ad

Lesser Elaenia

Northern
Scrub-Flycatcher

Mountain Elaenia

TYRANT, WATER-TYRANT, TYRANNULET, PHOEBE, AND FLYCATCHER Tyrannidae

A diverse group of distinctive birds found mainly in nonforest habitats. Most are found near water. Black Phoebe is the most common and widespread.

Long-tailed Tyrant *Colonia colonus*　　　　　　　　　　　　　female 20, male 26 cm
CA and SA. Uncommon resident in lowlands and foothills (to 600 m). **ID** *Very long, narrow central rectrices. Mostly black*. Gray crown bordered by *white supercilium.* **HABITS** Subcanopy to canopy at edge of humid forest, adjacent plantations, riparian woodland, and clearings with tall trees. Often conspicuous. Pairs or solitary birds perch prominently in open on high, exposed branch or snag and sally for flying insects. **VOICE** Song (1) a high-pitched, plaintive *weeee we we we* or *bee wee we wee.* Longer notes have slightly quavering quality. Call (2) a repeated, high-pitched, strongly upslurred *pweet* or *sweet.*

Pied Water-Tyrant *Fluvicola pica*　　　　　　　　　　　　　　　　12.5 cm
CA and SA. Locally fairly common resident in lowlands of east PA (Panamá, Darién, 50, 657, 512). **ID** Mostly horizontal posture with tail sometimes slightly cocked. *Mostly white* with contrasting *black wings, tail, and nape.* **HABITS** Wetlands with emergent or floating vegetation and adjacent open grassy areas. Forages actively on ground or on floating vegetation by flitting or hopping over flooded grass and tangled edges. Solitary or in pairs. **VOICE** Calls (1) a nasal, slightly buzzy *zhweeoo* or *pzweeu* and (2) repeated, dry *twec* or *twic.*

Torrent Tyrannulet *Serpophaga cinerea*　　　　　　　　　　　　　　10 cm
CA and SA. Uncommon resident in south foothills and highlands (mainly 1000 to 2200, locally as low as 600 m on Caribbean slope). **ID** Small with horizontal posture. Mostly plain gray with blackish crown, sides of head, and wings. Tail mostly blackish with fine whitish tips on rectrices. Compare with larger Black Phoebe (often in same streamside habitat). **HABITS** Riparian edges. Perches on and flits over boulders or other low perches in or near fast-flowing streams or rivers in hilly terrain. Makes short sallies to capture insects. Often flies low over water. Wags tail. Solitary or in pairs. **VOICE** Call (1) a loud, sharp, piercing *chip* or *tseep.* May be repeated rapidly.

Black Phoebe *Sayornis nigricans*　　　　　　　　　　　　　　　　16.5 cm
West USA to SA. Fairly common resident in foothills and highlands (mainly 500 to 2500 m, locally near SL). Local in SV (Ahuachapán, La Libertad, 635, 619) and east PA (Panamá, Darién, 346). **ID** *Slaty black with white belly*, white outer rectrices and whitish wingbars. Juv has pale cinnamon edging on wings and upperparts. In south compare with smaller Torrent Tyrannulet. **GV** Birds from east PA have more white on wings. **HABITS** Riparian edges. Closely tied to vicinity of water. Favors rocky streams or pools. Often bold and confiding. Perches upright on ground or at low levels on submerged snag, boulder, or streamside vegetation. Wags tail. Often in pairs. Does not follow mixed flocks. **VOICE** Song (1) given mainly at daybreak, a dry *fee-bee* often repeated persistently. Call (2) a sharp *chip.*

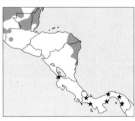

Vermilion Flycatcher *Pyrocephalus rubinus*　　　　　　　　　　　13.5 cm
MX, CA and SA. Locally common resident in BZ, and north GT (Petén, 229). Local on Pacific slope and interior (to 2400 m) of GT (Huehuetenango, Quetzaltenango, 229). Also Mosquitia region of east HN (Gracias a Dios) and north NI (RAAN). Rare in CR (Guanacaste, 265) and PA (Panamá, Chiriquí, 199, 512, 46, 346) where records may involve migratory SA populations. **ID** Ad male has *brilliant red crown and underparts* and blackish-brown mask. Brownish ad female has pale supercilium, *dusky streaked chest*, and unique *pinkish lower underparts.* Imm has yellowish lower underparts. **HABITS** Midstory in savanna, coastal scrub, agricultural areas, and gardens. Perches prominently on exposed branch or structure. Often near water. Sallies to seize prey from ground or air. In display flight, males flutter upward and hover briefly with exaggerated, slow wingbeats then drop back to perch. Usually solitary. **VOICE** Song (1) one or two introductory notes followed by rapidly accelerating trill *pi-pi-trrrrrreee* or *ti ti-li-li-li-liu.* Repeated rapidly in display. Compare with song of Tropical Kingbird. Call (2) a sharp, thin *pseeup* or *pseep.*

50%

Long-tailed Tyrant

juv

juv

ad

ad

Pied Water-Tyrant

Torrent Tyrannulet

widespread

east PA

Black Phoebe

ad
♂

imm
♀

juv

ad
♀

Vermilion Flycatcher

FLYCATCHERS Tyrannidae

Distinctive flycatchers of uncertain relationships found in lower and middle levels of humid broadleaf forest. Sulphur-rumped Flycatcher is the most common and widespread of the three Central American *Myiobius* flycatchers.

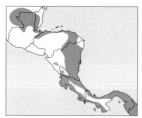

Ruddy-tailed Flycatcher *Terenotriccus erythrurus* 10 cm

South MX to SA. Fairly common resident in lowlands and foothills (to 800, locally to 1200 m). **ID** Small and large-headed. Large eyes and short, broad bill surrounded by long rictal bristles. Crown, mantle, and plain sides of head mostly olive-gray. *Underparts plain cinnamon.* Note rufous tail and rump and *broad rufous edgings on wings.* **HABITS** Understory to lower midstory of broadleaf forest and adjacent tall second growth. Solitary. Twitches both wings and habitually raises them over mantle. Usually solitary. Does not follow mixed flocks. Inconspicuous and best located by voice. **VOICE** Call (1) a soft, two-syllable, upslurred *peeer-ti.*

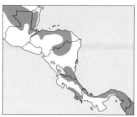

Sulphur-rumped Flycatcher *Myiobius sulphureipygius* 12.5 cm

South MX to north SA. Fairly common resident in lowlands and foothills (to 1200 m). **ID** Mostly horizontal posture. Wings often drooped. Long tail sometimes slightly cocked or spread. *Pale yellow rump* contrasts with black tail and dark olive-brown mantle. Male has lemon-yellow crown patch. Underparts pale tawny on breast grading to pale yellow on belly and flanks. Long rictal bristles extend nearly to tip of bill. In south compare with Black-tailed Flycatcher. Note different breast color, tail color, and habits. **HABITS** Understory to midstory of semihumid to humid broadleaf forest. Pairs or solitary birds forage actively in foliage and along twigs or vines making short sallies to seize prey from air or foliage. Usually in pairs. Follows mixed flocks. **VOICE** Infrequently heard song (1) a variable, clear, high-pitched *tseuu tseuu tseuu tseer tseer.* Frequently given call (2) a sharp, dry *spiu.*

Black-tailed Flycatcher *Myiobius atricaudus* 12.5 cm

CA and SA. Uncommon resident in south lowlands and foothills (to 900, rarely or locally to 1200 m). Rare in Pacific west CR (Puntarenas, Guanacaste, 474). **ID** Mostly horizontal posture. Long tail frequently spread and/or slightly raised. Pale yellow rump contrasts with broad, rounded *black tail* and dark mantle. Both sexes have lemon-yellow crown patch. Closely resembles widespread Sulphur-rumped Flycatcher. Note different underparts with paler breast and *blackish tail contrasting with olive wings.* **HABITS** Understory to midstory and edge of semihumid woodland, scrub, second growth, borders of mangroves, and gallery forest. Often near streams. **VOICE** Song (1) a short, slightly nasal phrase *cheeer-cheer-cheer.* Call (2) a very sharp, ringing *tsiit* or *tseep.* Compare with call of Sulphur-rumped Flycatcher.

Tawny-breasted Flycatcher *Myiobius villosus* 13 cm

CA and SA. Poorly known resident in highlands (1000 to 1800 m in SA) of east PA at Tacarcuna Massif (Darién, 512). **ID** Mostly horizontal posture. Long black tail frequently spread and slightly raised. Pale yellow rump contrasts with olive mantle. Male has lemon-yellow crown patch. Female has *cinnamon crown patch.* In both sexes *underparts deep tawny* including flanks and crissum with yellow confined to central belly. Resembles smaller Black-tailed and Sulphur-rumped flycatchers. Note different underparts and crown pattern. **HABITS** Understory to upper midstory of humid broadleaf forest and edge. **VOICE** Song (1) a very sharp, piercing phrase *chip chew checheechee.*

Royal Flycatcher *Onychorhynchus coronatus* 17 cm

MX to SA. Uncommon resident in lowlands and foothills (to 1200 m). Historical records from Pacific GT (Suchitepéquez, 164) and SV (Ahuachapán, Usulután, San Miguel, 183). Rare in Caribbean CR (575, 600). **ID** Fairly long, rufous tail. *Long, folded crest* and *long, broad bill* create hammer-headed silhouette. Spectacular crest rarely displayed and usually held folded against nape. Female's crest pale orange. Male's crest red. Note bright tawny rump and fine pale spotting on wing coverts and tertials. Tawny breast with indistinct dusky scaling. **HABITS** Midstory and edge of semihumid to humid broadleaf forest, gallery forest, and riparian woodland. Prefers vine-tangled edges overhanging forest pools or streams. Often in pairs. Does not follow mixed flocks. **VOICE** Song (1) a long series of squeaky notes *duh whee-ah whee-ah whee-ah whee-ah whee-ah.* Call (2) a mellow, two-syllable *bee-uk* or *ee-yuk.* Compare with louder, more strident call of Rufous-tailed Jacamar and call of Great Crested Flycatcher.

50%

Sulphur-rumped Flycatcher

♀

♂

Ruddy-tailed Flycatcher

Black-tailed Flycatcher

♂

Tawny-breasted Flycatcher

♀

displaying
♂

♀

♂

Royal Flycatcher

FLYCATCHERS Tyrannidae

Small flycatchers. Voice is often helpful in locating these. Some are rare and range-restricted. Tufted Flycatcher is common and widespread in highlands.

Bran-colored Flycatcher *Myiophobus fasciatus*   11.5 cm

CA and SA. Uncommon and local resident in Pacific lowlands and foothills (to 1300 m) of east CR (Puntarenas) and PA. Also Pearl Islands and Isla Coiba (Veraguas, Panamá, 455, 649, 470). Local on Caribbean slope in Canal Area (Colón). **ID** Brown above and whitish below with *streaked breast and flanks* and *buff wingbars*. Yellow on crown usually concealed. Imm rufous above and on wingbars. Compare with female Vermilion Flycatcher. Note different habits. Also compare with White-throated Flycatcher. Note different head and underparts. **HABITS** Understory to lower midstory of shrubby edges, savannas, hedgerows, gardens, plantations, marshes, and low second growth. Perches inconspicuously inside vegetation. Makes short sallies to seize insects or fruit. Habitually quivers tail. Solitary or in pairs. Does not follow mixed flocks. **VOICE** Dawn song (1) a simple, soft, rich *chite* or *chuweet* repeated persistently. Calls (2) a mellow whistle repeated rapidly *whee he he he he* or *wee, wee, wee* and (3) short trill or rattle *tree-te-te-te-te-te.*

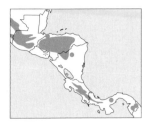

Tufted Flycatcher *Mitrephanes phaeocercus*   12.5–13.5 cm

MX to north SA. Common resident in upper foothills and highlands (mainly 700 to 3000 m). Historical records from SV (Morazán, 183). **ID** *Pointed crest. Mostly cinnamon head and breast.* Mandible orange. Juv has cinnamon edging on mantle and cinnamon wingbars. *Contopus* pewees also crested and in same habitat but none has similar cinnamon color. **GV** Birds from north CA have mostly deep cinnamon head and underparts. Birds from CR and PA have yellowish lower underparts. Birds from central and east PA have ochre breast, extensive yellow on lower underparts, and olive mantle. **HABITS** Midstory and edge of humid broadleaf and pine-oak forest. Pairs or solitary birds perch in open in gaps or small clearings. Sallies to capture prey in flight and returns to same perch. Shakes tail and often calls upon alighting. Does not follow mixed flocks but may become more active as they pass nearby. **VOICE** Song (1) a long series *bip-bip-bip seew bip bip diu*. In north CA, calls include (2) a short *chwee-chwee*. In south CA, gives (3) a short, rapid series of slurred notes *beep beep beep . . .* or *weet weet weet weet*, (4) two-syllable *beepseew*, and (5) single, downslurred *seeew.*

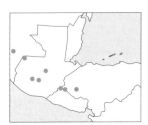

Belted Flycatcher *Xenotriccus callizonus*   13 cm

South MX and CA. Rare and local resident in highlands (1200 to 2000 m) of GT (Huehuetenango, Sacatepéquez, Sololá, Baja Verapaz, 196, 279, 380, 229), north SV (Santa Ana, 296, 364), and west HN (Intibucá, 289). **ID** Pointed crest and *flared, whitish eye ring*. Upperparts mostly gray. *Cinnamon breast contrasts* with *whitish throat* and *yellow lower underparts*. Note cinnamon wingbars and edging on secondaries. Compare with Tufted Flycatcher. Note different underparts and habits. **HABITS** Understory to midstory of arid to semihumid pine-oak woodland and brushy second growth with grassy understory. Reclusive. Usually remains hidden in dense vegetation. Nervous and restless. Habitually flicks wings. Solitary or in pairs. Does not follow mixed flocks. **VOICE** Song (1) a short, accelerating, slightly nasal *pic pi-pi-pi-pi breeeer* or *chi-chi-chi-chi-iiiiiir*. May recall Cabanis's Wren. Calls (2) an abrupt, buzzy, nasal *rreeeah* or sharper *cheeuh* and (3) burry *picweehr.*

Tawny-chested Flycatcher *Aphanotriccus capitalis*   13 cm

CA endemic. Rare and local in Caribbean lowlands and foothills (to 1000 m) of east HN (Olancho, Gracias a Dios, 346), NI (RAAN, Río San Juan, 358, 413), and CR (Cartago, Limón, Alajuela, 126, 570, 600). **ID** Upright, *Empidonax*-like posture. *Breast tawny.* White throat, *whitish supraloral streak*, and *broken whitish eye ring* contrast with gray head. Note cinnamon wingbars and edging. Compare with *Myiopagis* elaenias. Note different underparts and habits. **HABITS** Understory to lower midstory of humid broadleaf forest and adjacent tall second growth. Favors forest edge and gaps. Solitary or in pairs. Makes sudden, upward sallies to seize prey. Rarely follows mixed flocks but may become more active as flocks pass nearby. **VOICE** Song (1) a staccato series of loud phrases that end with slightly buzzy trill *choot choot choot ch-ch-chchttttttree ih*. Compare with song of Gray-headed Piprites. More often gives (2) a short, slightly buzzy *pew* or *cheeu.*

Black-billed Flycatcher *Aphanotriccus audax*   13 cm

CA and SA. Uncommon to rare and local resident in lowlands and foothills (to 600 m) of east PA (Panamá, Darién, 276, 519, 657). **ID** Bill black. Upperparts olive becoming gray on head. *Whitish supraloral* and *narrow, broken eye ring*. Shows two pale buff wingbars. *Throat whitish. Olive breast grades to yellow on lower underparts.* Compare with *Myiopagis* elaenias. Note different underparts and habits. **HABITS** Understory to lower midstory of humid broadleaf forest and adjacent tall second growth. Often near small streams or in wet areas. Usually remains inside dense vegetation. Perches quietly for long periods. Makes abrupt sallies to seize prey (usually from foliage) then continues to new perch. Solitary or in pairs. Does not follow mixed flocks. **VOICE** Call (1) a short, emphatic, burry *jee-jee-jew* or *bree-juju.*

Bran-colored Flycatcher

juv

ad

Tufted Flycatcher

north CA
ad

CR and west PA
ad

central east PA
ad

Belted Flycatcher

juv

Tawny-chested Flycatcher

Black-billed Flycatcher

PEWEES Tyrannidae

Larger *Contopus* pewees. Most have pointed crest. Pewees sally for insects from an open perch in forest canopy or edge and return to the same perch after each flight. Voice is often helpful in locating these.

Ochraceous Pewee *Contopus ochraceus* 16 cm

CA endemic. Uncommon to rare and local resident in upper foothills and highlands (1200 to 3000 m) of CR (Cartago, 600, 667) and west PA (Chiriquí, 657, 512). **ID** *Ochre below* becoming yellowish on belly and crissum. Mandible orange. Compare with smaller and more common Tufted Flycatcher (often in same habitat). Note different underparts. **HABITS** Midstory to subcanopy of humid, oak-dominated (cloud) forest. Like other *Contopus* pewees. Solitary. Does not follow mixed flocks. **VOICE** Song (1) a high-pitched, thin, piercing *peeeeyit* or *peeeeeyeeet* with first syllable accented. Call (2) a sharp, piercing *pwi*. Often repeated two or three times. Compare with lower-pitched, softer call of Black-capped Flycatcher.

Dark Pewee *Contopus lugubris* 17.5 cm

CA endemic. Uncommon to rare and local resident in foothills and highlands (1200 to 2200 m) of CR and west PA (Chiriquí, Ngäbe-Buglé, Veraguas). **ID** Sharply pointed crest. Darkest CA *Contopus* pewee. Mandible mostly orange. *Near-uniform dark gray* becoming paler on lower underparts. Faint pale wingbars. Juv has pale cinnamon wingbars. Compare with Olive-sided Flycatcher. Note different structure and underparts. **HABITS** Midstory to subcanopy and edge of humid broadleaf forest and adjacent clearings or shaded plantations. Much like other *Contopus* pewees. Hawks insects from exposed perch. Typically returns to same perch after each sally. Solitary. Does not follow mixed flocks. **VOICE** Dawn song (1) a repeated *fred-rick-fear*. Second note rises in pitch. Last note drops. Most frequent call (2) a staccato series of loud, bright *wic* or *whip* notes. Less often (3) a lower-pitched, loud, clear to throaty *weer*.

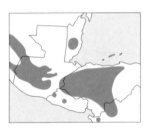

Greater Pewee *Contopus pertinax* 18–19 cm

USA to CA. Uncommon to fairly common resident in north foothills and highlands (mainly above 800 m). May move to lower elevations outside breeding season. Uncommon in Mountain Pine Ridge region of BZ (near 450 m, Cayo, 343). Reported from Pacific NI at Volcán San Cristóbal (Chinandega, 413). **ID** Long tail and *pointed crest*. Mandible mostly orange. Olive-brown becoming slightly paler below. Juv has pale cinnamon wingbars. Olive-sided Flycatcher lacks pointed crest, has bulkier structure with shorter tail and different underparts. Compare with smaller Tropical, Eastern, and Western wood-pewees. Note different structure and voice. Dark Pewee allopatric. **HABITS** Upper midstory to canopy and edge of pine and pine-oak woodland. Sallies for flying insects from high, open perch in clearing or gap. Solitary or in pairs. Does not follow mixed flocks. **VOICE** Dawn song (1) a repeated *weedidi, wheeer*. Song (2) a clear, or slightly nasal, downslurred *wheeer wit wit* or *wheeer-ti-ti* or simple *wheeer*. Call (3) a sharp to mellow *beeek* or *eeek*. Sometimes repeated steadily.

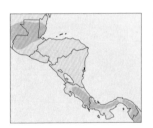

Olive-sided Flycatcher *Contopus cooperi* 18 cm

Breeds Nearctic. Winters mainly SA. Reaches CA mainly as a transient (mainly Mar to May and Aug to Oct). May be briefly or locally common in migration. Rare and local winter resident in lowlands and foothills of BZ (343), north GT (Petén, 346), GT Pacific slope (346), and south highlands. **ID** Large. Short-tailed and large-headed. Crest rounded. *Upperparts and flanks olive-gray contrasting with whitish throat and center of breast and belly.* White tufts of flank feathers sometimes visible behind folded wing. Compare with Greater and Dark pewees. Note different structure and underparts. **HABITS** Subcanopy to canopy at edge of semihumid to humid broadleaf forest. Sallies to capture prey from high, open perch. Solitary. **VOICE** Call (1) a series of loud, bright *wic* or *whip* notes *wic wic wic wic whip whip whip . . .*

Ochraceous Pewee

Dark Pewee

Greater Pewee

ad

juv

Olive-sided Flycatcher

Olive-sided Flycatcher
often shows tufts of
white flank feathers
behind each folded wing.

PEWEES AND FLYCATCHERS Tyrannidae

Smaller *Contopus* pewees including two very similar Nearctic migrant species. Voice is often helpful in locating and separating these. Alder and Willow flycatchers are closely similar Nearctic migrants.

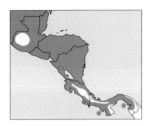

Tropical Pewee *Contopus cinereus*   13.5 cm

MX to SA. Uncommon to fairly common resident in lowlands and foothills (to 1500 m). Also Isla Coiba (Veraguas, 653, 470) and Pearl Islands off PA (Panamá, 649). **ID** Very similar to Western and Eastern wood-pewees. Note *pale lores*, mostly orange mandible, short primary projection and *dark crown*. Juv scaled with whitish. **GV** Birds from Isla Coiba (not shown) are darker. **HABITS** Understory to midstory of arid (deciduous) to semihumid forest and woodland, pine savanna, plantations, gardens, and mangroves. Similar to other *Contopus* pewees but tends to perch lower. Solitary or in pairs. Does not follow mixed flocks. **VOICE** Dawn song (1) a series of high-pitched, sharp notes *weet weet weet* alternating with lower-pitched *we-yee* phrases. Song (2) a short, upslurred, liquid trill *bree-e-e* or *preee-e-e* sometimes repeated. Call (3) a sharp *peet* or *fweet* often repeated or combined with previous as *peet breee-e-e*.

Western Wood-Pewee *Contopus sordidulus*   14.5 cm

Breeds west USA and MX. Winters SA. Briefly or locally common transient (mainly Mar to May and Aug to Nov). Breeding confirmed in highlands of GT (Huehuetenango, 229, 375). Perhaps also breeds in highlands of HN (442) and CR (600). Rare in BZ (Cayo, 311, 347). **ID** Ad grayish-olive with dull whitish wingbars and whitish throat, belly, and crissum. Note dusky smudged crissum. Imm may have dull buff wingbars. Resembles Eastern Wood-Pewee and usually not distinguishable except by voice. Subtle differences include Western's more extensively dark underparts and typically less contrasting wingbars, especially upper. Also note Western's mostly dark mandible. **HABITS** Similar to Eastern Wood-Pewee. Solitary. Does not follow mixed flocks. **VOICE** Song (1) a burry, nasal whistle *dree-yurr* or *breeer* or *brreeee* with rough quality. Compare with call of Mountain Elaenia. Also a variety of clear, whistled phrases like Eastern Wood-Pewee including (2) a thin, clear *peee-didip* or *pee-ee* or *peeaa*. Call (3) a flat, buzzy *brrt* or *dup*.

Eastern Wood-Pewee *Contopus virens*   14.5 cm

Breeds east Nearctic. Winters mainly SA. Widespread and locally (or briefly) very common transient (mainly Mar to May and Aug to Nov) mainly on Caribbean slope. Rare winter resident in lowlands and foothills. **ID** Ad mostly grayish-olive with whitish wingbars and whitish throat, belly, and crissum. Mandible typically orange with dark tip. Juv (Jun to Oct) has buff to whitish wingbars and may have mostly black mandible. Compare with Tropical Pewee. Note longer primary projection and different mandible. Closely resembles Western Wood-Pewee and best separated by voice. **HABITS** Midstory to canopy of forest, second growth, and plantations. Forages from high, exposed perch in typical *Contopus* fashion. Solitary. Does not follow mixed flocks. **VOICE** Call (1) a high-pitched, clear, whistled *puueee* or *pee-wee* or *pee-a-wee*. Compare with burry, lower-pitched call of Western Wood-Pewee.

Alder Flycatcher *Empidonax alnorum*   13 cm

Breeds Nearctic. Winters mainly SA. Widespread transient (Apr to May and Sep to Oct). **ID** Virtually identical to Willow Flycatcher and usually not separable in field except by voice. Relatively large and long-winged in comparison with other *Empidonax*. Upperparts brownish becoming dusky on crown. Whitish eye ring inconspicuous. Whitish throat usually contrasts with darker sides of head. Juv has buff wingbars. Like Willow Flycatcher, but Alder has slightly more prominent eye ring, is slightly longer-winged and longer-tailed, slightly shorter-billed, and perhaps has more rounded head. Alder also tends to be more olivaceous above (less brownish) and slightly darker on head. **HABITS** Upper understory to midstory of forest edge, second growth, plantations, and scrub. Solitary. Transients may occur in a wide variety of terrestrial habitats. **VOICE** Song, sometimes given by spring transients (1) a burry *phee-be-ah*. Call (2) a sharp *pip* or *peep*.

Willow Flycatcher *Empidonax traillii*   13 cm

Breeds Nearctic. Winters MX and CA. Uncommon transient and winter resident (Aug to Oct), mainly in Pacific lowlands and foothills (600, 413). Status poorly known. Peak fall passage late Sep to early Oct (271). **ID** Virtually identical to Alder Flycatcher. See under that species for subtle differences. Juv has buff wingbars. White-throated Flycatcher is shorter-billed, shorter-winged, warmer brown above, and has darker wingbars. Also note different voice. **GV** Birds from breeding population in southwest NA are browner and plainer. **HABITS** Understory to midstory of forest edge, second growth, plantations, and littoral scrub. Transients may occur in a wide variety of terrestrial habitats. Solitary. **VOICE** Song (1) a burry *fitz-beuw*. Call (2) an emphatic *whit*.

50%

Tropical Pewee

juv

ad

Western Wood-Pewee

Eastern Wood-Pewee

ad

juv

Alder Flycatcher

Willow Flycatcher

juv

southwest NA
breeding ad

east NA
breeding ad

FLYCATCHERS Tyrannidae

Nearctic migrant *Empidonax* flycatchers. Voice is often helpful in locating and separating these closely similar species. Yellow-bellied Flycatcher is the most common and widespread.

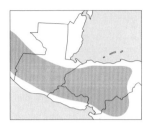

Hammond's Flycatcher *Empidonax hammondii* 13 cm

Breeds west Nearctic. Winters MX and CA. Fairly common transient and winter resident (mainly Sep to Apr) in north highlands (mainly 1500 to 3500 m). Vagrant to west PA (Chiriquí, 512). **ID** Long-winged. Short, narrow bill blackish with light base of mandible. *Grayish-olive overall.* Complete, flared *whitish eye ring.* Sides of head do not contrast strongly with throat. Dusky breast separates whitish throat and yellowish belly. Like Least Flycatcher, grayish head contrasts with olive-brown mantle. Compare with Pine Flycatcher. Note Hammond's shorter bill and tail and different bill pattern. Also compare with Least Flycatcher. Note longer primary projection and different bill and throat pattern. **HABITS** Midstory to canopy and edge of pine and mixed pine-broadleaf forest and plantations. Locally or occasionally in humid broadleaf forest. Solitary. Follows mixed flocks. Habitually flicks wings and tail. **VOICE** Song (1) rarely heard in winter, typically a burry *chi-pit . . . brrrk . . . grrip.* Call (2) a high-pitched, sharp *peek* or *peep* or *pic.* Compare with call of Least Flycatcher.

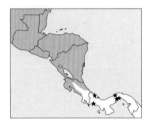

Least Flycatcher *Empidonax minimus* 12 cm

Breeds Nearctic. Winters MX and CA. Transient and winter resident (mainly Sep to May) in lowlands and foothills (to 1200 m). Fairly common in north Caribbean. Rare in central PA. **ID** Small with rounded head and short bill. *Bold, rounded, whitish eye ring.* Brownish-gray overall with whitish wingbars (narrow when worn). Broken dusky breast-band contrasts with dull whitish throat. Underside of bill mostly pale orange-yellow (may have indistinct dark tip). Imm has buffy wingbars. Acadian Flycatcher larger with more olive upperparts and longer primary projection. Yellow-bellied Flycatcher is also more olive above and has yellow-tinged eye ring and underparts. Note different voice. In north compare with Hammond's Flycatcher. Note different bill and underparts pattern. Larger Alder and Willow flycatchers have longer wings and less prominent eye ring. **HABITS** Upper understory to midstory of forest edge, second growth, plantations, gardens, and scrub. Transients may occur in a wide variety of terrestrial habitats. Forages actively. Frequently changes perch. Solitary. **VOICE** Song (1) occasionally heard in spring migration, a sharp, dry *che-bek.* Call (2) a sharp *whit* or *pwit* or *schwic* similar to call of Willow Flycatcher.

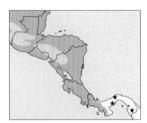

Yellow-bellied Flycatcher *Empidonax flaviventris* 12 cm

Breeds Nearctic. Winters MX and CA. Widespread transient and fairly common winter resident (mainly Aug to May). Most common in north Caribbean lowlands and foothills (to 1500, transients may occur to 2500 m). **ID** Relatively short-tailed with large, broad bill. Greenish-olive overall with *yellowish underparts including throat* and rounded *yellowish eye ring.* Imm may be less yellowish. Compare with Yellowish Flycatcher (resident in highlands); note different eye ring shape and habits. Larger Acadian Flycatcher has longer primary projection. Also note different voice and throat color. **HABITS** Midstory and edge of broadleaf forest, tall second growth, and shaded plantations. Solitary. **VOICE** Song (1) rarely given in CA, a dry *che-bunk* or *je-burk.* Harsher than song of Least Flycatcher. Call (2) a soft, high-pitched *beeyip.*

Acadian Flycatcher *Empidonax virescens* 13.5 cm

Breeds east Nearctic. Winters south CA to north SA. Fairly common winter resident (mainly Sep to May) in south humid lowlands. Common in east PA. Elsewhere widespread but uncommon to rare transient in lowlands and foothills (to 1200 m). **ID** Large-billed and long-winged. Head and upperparts olive. Paler-breasted than other *Empidonax.* Narrow whitish eye ring. Throat typically white or sometimes yellowish. Wingbars pale buff. Imm has pale cinnamon wingbars. Willow and Alder flycatchers have similar structure but are more brownish above and have less distinct eye ring. Note different habits and voice. Least Flycatcher has smaller bill and is more brownish above. Also note shorter primary projection and different voice. Compare with smaller Yellow-bellied Flycatcher. Note different structure and voice. **HABITS** Midstory and edge of broadleaf forest and tall second growth. Solitary. Does not follow mixed flocks. Sometimes holds wings slightly drooped. **VOICE** Wintering birds give (1) a fairly loud *vhiit* or *peep* usually at long intervals, but sometimes repeated persistently. Compare with call of Yellow-bellied Flycatcher.

Hammond's Flycatcher

Least Flycatcher

juv

ad

Yellow-bellied Flycatcher

juv

ad

Acadian Flycatcher

juv

ad

FLYCATCHERS Tyrannidae

Resident, breeding *Empidonax* flycatchers. Most are range-restricted and found in highlands. Yellowish Flycatcher, found in both north and south Central American highlands, is the most common and widespread.

Black-capped Flycatcher *Empidonax atriceps* 11.5 cm
CA endemic. Fairly common resident in highlands (mainly 2400 to 3300 m) of CR and west PA. **ID** Small and dark. *Blackish crown*, and *whitish eye ring flared behind eye*. In fresh plumage shows narrow white wingbars. **HABITS** Understory to canopy and edge of very humid broadleaf (cloud) forest, second growth, and clearings with scattered trees. Sallies for insects from exposed perch. Quivers tail upon landing. Usually solitary. Often confiding. **VOICE** Dawn song (1) a loud, repeated *keep-keep-kreer, keep-keep kreeer* . . . Calls (2) a simple *peek* or *piit* and (3) loud *keep-keer*.

White-throated Flycatcher *Empidonax albigularis* 12.5 cm
MX and CA. Breeds (Apr to Jul) in foothills and highlands (above 600 m). Winters locally in lowlands in north. Records from BZ (Orange Walk, Belize, Cayo, 529, 667, 630, 493), GT (Petén, Alta Verapaz, Zacapa, Sololá, 229, 279, 637, 375, 377), SV (Santa Ana, 408, 619), and HN (Cortés, Atlántida, Ocotepeque, 603, 442). Rare in NI (Jinotega, Matagalpa, 413, 429). Reported mainly from foothills and highlands (500 to 1500 m) in CR (Cartago, Heredia, 385, 512) and PA (Chiriquí, 89, 385, 512). **ID** Large bill. Brownish above. Note *buff or pale brown wingbars, white throat*, indistinct eye ring and *short primary projection*. Compare with Willow Flycatcher. **HABITS** Understory to lower midstory of low second growth, scrub, marshes, damp pastures, and hedgerows. Forages from shaded perch inside vegetation. Makes short sallies to seize prey. Shivers wings and tail upon alighting. Solitary or in pairs. **VOICE** Call (1) a burry, upslurred *neeee-ark* or *reeee-eh*. Sometimes repeated persistently.

Buff-breasted Flycatcher *Empidonax fulvifrons* 11.5 cm
South USA to CA. Uncommon and local resident in north highlands (1400 to 3300 m). Rare in NI (Nueva Segovia, 346). **ID** Small and large-headed. Note small bill and narrow, notched tail. Brownish-olive above with *cinnamon breast and flanks* (worn birds may be paler). Mandible orange-yellow. Whitish eye ring is slightly flared behind eye. **HABITS** Upper understory to midstory and edge of open pine or pine-oak woodland, adjacent pastures with scattered trees and hedgerows. Sallies from open perch. Often near water or wetlands. Solitary or in pairs. May follow mixed flocks. **VOICE** Song (1) a series of two-syllable, short, sharp phrases *p-teek!, pit p-teek! pi-tik, peek pi-chu* . . . or *bjeep-wheer!* or shorter phrases *sipit siu, sipit piu*. May be repeated persistently at dawn. Call (2) a sharp to mellow *pic* or *pit* or *whic*. Compare with call of Least Flycatcher.

Yellowish Flycatcher *Empidonax flavescens* 13 cm
South MX and CA. Common resident in humid highlands (mainly 800 to 2500, locally to 3000 m in north). Local in volcanic highlands of SV (San Vicente, 341) and Cordillera de Guanacaste, CR. **ID** Peaked crown. Dull yellowish-ochre below. *Whitish eye ring flared behind eye*. Juv brownish-olive with cinnamon wingbars and whitish belly. Superficially resembles Yellow-bellied Flycatcher (mostly lowlands). Note different eye ring shape and wingbar color. **GV** Birds from north CA are duller and more olivaceous. **HABITS** Midstory of humid broadleaf (cloud) forest and pine-oak forest in north. Often near gaps or tree falls. Solitary. Makes short sallies from exposed perch. Occasionally flicks tail. Does not follow mixed flocks. **VOICE** Dawn song (1) a high-pitched, thin *see seee chit*. Often repeated. Call (2) a high-pitched, thin *seee* or *tseeep*. Sometimes shortened to stronger *tsick* or *tseet*.

Pine Flycatcher *Empidonax affinis* 13.5 cm
MX and CA. Uncommon and local resident in highlands (1600 to 3500 m) of GT. **ID** Distinct crest and fairly long tail. Bill fairly long and narrow with orange mandible. *Whitish eye ring flared behind eye*. Crissum and belly pale yellow. Mostly greenish-olive upperparts and head. Hammond's Flycatcher is grayer overall with longer primary projection and smaller bill. Also compare with Yellowish and Yellow-bellied flycatchers. Note different habits. **HABITS** Understory to midstory and edge of pine-oak, pine, and fir forest and adjacent clearings or scrub with scattered trees. **VOICE** Song (1) a slow, deliberate series of slurred and burry whistles and shorter, harder notes *chrip whee-u, chik-wheeer* . . . or *cheenk, cheenk t-weeree* . . . or *chkwheeu chik*. The *wheeu* notes may suggest Hutton's Vireo. Call (2) a bright, clear, liquid *whik* or *pwic*.

Black-capped Flycatcher

White-throated Flycatcher

Buff-breasted Flycatcher

juv

ad

Yellowish Flycatcher

north CA
ad

CR and PA
ad

juv

ad

Pine Flycatcher

FLYCATCHERS Tyrannidae

Flycatchers with streaked yellow or yellowish underparts. Some withdraw from the region after breeding. All forage from high, open perch. Piratic Flycatcher is the most common and widespread.

White-ringed Flycatcher *Conopias albovittatus*   15 cm
CA and north SA. Uncommon resident in humid lowlands and foothills (to 600 m). **ID** Long bill. *White supercilium extends to nape.* White throat contrasts with blackish mask and crown. Yellow on crown usually concealed. Compare with *Myiozetetes* flycatchers. Note different habits, head pattern, and bill shape. **HABITS** Subcanopy to canopy and edge of humid broadleaf forest and tall second growth. Solitary birds or small groups take exposed perches or move through crowns of trees with mixed flocks. Makes abrupt (often downward) sallies to seize prey. **VOICE** Call (1) an emphatic, nasal note followed by a rapid trill *tree-r-r-r-r* or *chee t-t-t-t-t-t*. May be repeated.

Piratic Flycatcher *Legatus leucophaius*   15.5 cm
MX to SA. Winters SA. Fairly common transient and breeding visitor (Mar to Jul in north, Jan to Oct in south) in lowlands and foothills (to 1500, rarely or locally to 1850 m). **ID** Small with small bill. Pale yellow below with *soft olive streaking on breast and flanks.* Upperparts mostly dull olive-brown becoming darker on crown. Note whitish edging on dusky brownish wings. *Dusky mask* contrasts with whitish supercilium and malar. Pattern suggests larger *Myiodynastes* flycatchers. Note Piratic's smaller bill. **HABITS** Canopy and edge of humid broadleaf forest, tall second growth, plantations, gardens, and isolated trees in open areas. Perches prominently in crown of tall tree. Usually solitary. **VOICE** Calls persistently. Gives (1) a high-pitched, *weeu dididi* and (2) a monotonous series *wid wid wid wid . . .* suggesting a euphonia.

Golden-bellied Flycatcher *Myiodynastes hemichrysus*   20 cm
CA endemic. Uncommon to locally fairly common resident in highlands (700 to 2300 m) of CR and west PA. **ID** *Plain yellow underparts.* Note *blackish malar* and mask. Mostly olive above with rufous edging on secondaries. Resembles Streaked and Sulphur-bellied flycatchers in structure. Note different underparts and habits. Golden-crowned Flycatcher allopatric. **HABITS** Canopy of humid broadleaf (cloud) forest and adjacent clearings and plantations. Pairs or solitary birds forage from exposed perch on bare snag. **VOICE** Dawn song (1) a clear *tree-le-loo* repeated persistently. Call (2) a thin, squeaky *speeyuk* or *seeik* or *seek-a-skeeir*. Compare with calls of Sulphur-bellied Flycatcher. Also, (3) plaintive *pee-ah* or *peeeir* like Social Flycatcher.

Golden-crowned Flycatcher *Myiodynastes chrysocephalus*   20 cm
CA and SA. Uncommon and local resident in highlands (above 1200 m) of east PA (Darién). **ID** Fairly heavy bill. Yellow lower underparts and *soft olive streaking on breast.* Note dusky malar and mask. Mantle and crown plain olive. Yellow on crown usually concealed. Dusky wings and tail show extensive rufous edging. Compare with Streaked and Sulphur-bellied flycatchers (mainly lower elevations). Note plain upperparts. Golden-bellied Flycatcher allopatric. **HABITS** Subcanopy to canopy at edge or in gaps in humid broadleaf (cloud) forest. Takes high, exposed perch. Sallies to seize prey. Usually solitary. **VOICE** Often noisy. Call (1) an emphatic, squeaky *pssee-yu*. Often repeated.

Sulphur-bellied Flycatcher *Myiodynastes luteiventris*   19 cm
South USA to SA. Uncommon breeding visitor (mainly Mar to Oct) in north lowlands and foothills (to 1800, mainly below 1000 m). Widespread transient. Winters SA. **ID** Fairly heavy black bill and mostly rufous tail. Note *nearly plain crissum, broad dark malar,* and dark chin. Underparts pale yellow with blackish streaking on breast. Juv (not shown) has faint cinnamon edging on wing. Compare with Streaked Flycatcher. **HABITS** Midstory to subcanopy and edge of broadleaf forest, second growth, plantations, and isolated trees in open areas. Usually solitary. Perches in open. Often noisy and conspicuous. **VOICE** Dawn song (1) a persistently repeated, whistled, warbled phrase *dwee-dludlu.* Call (2) a high-pitched, squeaky, whistled phrase *squeeeuh* or *pyeeeeuh* sometimes with stuttering start *p'p'p'peeeeuh.*

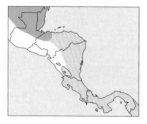

Streaked Flycatcher *Myiodynastes maculatus*   20 cm
MX to SA. Uncommon breeding visitor (Mar to Sep) in north Caribbean lowlands and foothills (to 1500 m). Winters SA. Widespread transient. Status and movements poorly known. Also Isla Coiba (Veraguas, 470) and Pearl Islands (649). **ID** Heavy bill with *pink base of mandible.* Note *rufous edging on primaries* and *streaked crissum.* Dark malar indistinct. Supercilium and moustachial stripe pale buff (whitish in Sulphur-bellied Flycatcher). Also note different wing pattern. **HABITS** Canopy and edge of humid broadleaf forest, second growth, plantations, pastures with scattered trees, and gardens. Solitary. Forages from open perch. **VOICE** Dawn song (1) a repeated, squeaky *whee-weeda-dweet.* Calls (2) a sharp, dry *dik* or *iik* sometimes repeated persistently and (3) dry, nasal *chuk-yi chuck-yi* often repeated.

40%

White-ringed Flycatcher

Piratic Flycatcher

Golden-bellied Flycatcher

Golden-crowned Flycatcher

Sulphur-bellied Flycatcher

Streaked Flycatcher

FLYCATCHERS AND KISKADEES Tyrannidae

Medium-sized to large flycatchers with plain yellow underparts. Most have white supercilium. Head pattern, bill shape, and voice are helpful in separating these. Social Flycatcher is the most common and widespread *Myiozetetes*.

Rusty-margined Flycatcher *Myiozetetes cayanensis* 17 cm

CA and SA. Fairly common resident in lowlands of PA (to 450 m). Local in Pacific east CR (Puntarenas, 341, 546). **ID** Short bill. *Black crown and auriculars* and long white supercilium. Note *rufous edging on primaries*. Yellow on crown usually concealed. Social Flycatcher has more olivaceous upperparts. **HABITS** Midstory to canopy of forest edge, clearings with scattered trees, riparian woodland, and gardens. Perches prominently in open. **VOICE** Calls include (1) a long, high-pitched, thin *fweeeeee* or *wheeeeee*. May be repeated. Compare with call of Dusky-capped Flycatcher and harsher call of Yellow-bellied Elaenia. Also (2) a squeaky *chuwee-chuwee chuweee*. Other calls like Social Flycatcher including (3) a squeaky, stuttering *cheepcheeree-chew* and (4) short, repeated *keewit*.

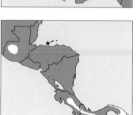

Social Flycatcher *Myiozetetes similis* 16.5–18 cm

MX to SA. Very common resident in lowlands and foothills (to 1700, locally to 2000 m). **ID** Short bill. Dark gray mask and crown contrast with white supercilium. Orange-red on crown usually concealed. Note ad's *olive upperparts* including wings. Juv has rufous edgings on wing. Compare with Gray-capped Flycatcher. In south compare with Rusty-margined Flycatcher. Note different head and upperparts. **GV** Ads from Pacific east CR and west PA, as well as those from central and east PA, are smaller and have more extensive pale edging on wing. **HABITS** Midstory to subcanopy of forest edge, gardens, plantations, and urban areas. Perches prominently in open. Often near water. In small groups or pairs. Noisy and conspicuous. **VOICE** Calls (1) a loud, squeaky *cheeeoo* repeated rapidly and sometimes with stuttering introduction *chee-cheeoo ch-cheeo . . .* (2) a harsh, sharp *teeer* or *peeeeur* sometimes softened to plaintive *pe-ah* or *chee*, (3) harsh *wheer* or *whaaa* repeated, (4) short *wit*, and (5) series of *chu* notes.

Gray-capped Flycatcher *Myiozetetes granadensis* 17.5 cm

CA and SA. Common resident in lowlands and foothills (to 1650 m). **ID** Short bill. *Gray crown and nape* and *short, whitish supraloral*. Note *olive mantle*. Orange-red on crown usually concealed. Eyes pale grayish-brown. Compare with Social and Rusty-margined flycatchers. Note different head and wing pattern. **HABITS** Midstory to canopy at edge of humid broadleaf forest, second growth, plantations, riparian woodland, and gardens. Often near water. Sallies from open perch. In pairs or small groups. **VOICE** Dawn song (1) a loud, hoarse *kip kip kip k'beer* or *kip-kip whee-heer*. May be repeated persistently. Calls (2) a dry, sharp *bip* or *wic* and (3) variety of harsh, strident, staccato and burry notes *kurr keer ch'beer, k'keer keer jeer k'beer . . .* Compare with Social Flycatcher.

Lesser Kiskadee *Pitangus lictor* 17 cm

CA and SA. Locally fairly common resident in lowlands and foothills (to 450 m) of PA. **ID** *Long, slender bill* and narrow rufous edging on wings and tail. Great Kiskadee larger with different bill. Rusty-margined Flycatcher has different bill and voice. **HABITS** Understory to midstory of riparian woodland and borders of ponds and lakes. Solitary or in pairs. Perches in open on vegetation over water or partly submerged branch. **VOICE** Calls (1) a harsh, nasal, upslurred *dzraaai* or *dzraaai-du*. Sometimes only first note is given.

Great Kiskadee *Pitangus sulphuratus* 23 cm

MX to SA. Common resident in lowlands and foothills (to 1500 m). Also islands including Belize Cays and Isla Coiba. **ID** *Large* with *heavy bill*. Brownish mantle and *extensive rufous on wings*. Yellow on crown usually concealed. Boat-billed Flycatcher has dull wings and different bill. *Myiozetetes* flycatchers have smaller bill. **HABITS** Midstory to edge of riparian woodland, semihumid and deciduous forest, plantations, gardens, littoral scrub, mangroves, and urban areas. May forage on or near ground. Solitary or in pairs. Noisy and conspicuous. **VOICE** Call (1) a loud, strident *kis ka dee* or *kick a deer*. First note sometimes repeated in stuttering introduction *kik-kik-kik a deer*. Also (2) a nasal *ki-yaa* or attenuated *hiyaa* like Golden-olive Woodpecker and (3) a rolling trill.

Boat-billed Flycatcher *Megarynchus pitangua* 23 cm

MX to SA. Fairly common resident in lowlands and foothills (to 1850, rarely or locally to 2100 m). Also Isla Coiba off PA (470). **ID** Large. *Broad, very heavy bill* with curved culmen. *Dull olive above including wings*. Red on crown usually concealed. Great Kiskadee has more rufous on wings and different bill. Social and Rusty-margined flycatchers smaller with smaller bill. **HABITS** Subcanopy to canopy and edge of arid to humid forest, second growth, plantations, scrub, and gardens. Often perches in crown of isolated or emergent tree. Solitary. **VOICE** Dawn song (1) a repeated *chire-chi chire-chi chire-chi . . .* Calls (2) an attenuated, loud, nasal *neeeeeeah* or *raaaaaaah*, (3) short, clear, rolling *cheeeur*, and (4) loud, rapidly repeated *choip choip . . .*

40%

Social Flycatcher

widespread
ad

juv

PA and
Pacific east CR
ad

Rusty-margined
Flycatcher

Gray-capped Flycatcher

juv

ad

Lesser Kiskadee

Great Kiskadee

Boat-billed Flycatcher

CATTLE TYRANT AND KINGBIRDS Tyrannidae

Kingbirds are large tyrants found mainly in open areas where they typically take high, prominent perch. Western and Cassin's kingbirds are Nearctic breeding migrants. Details of head, underparts, and tail pattern as well as voice are useful in separating these. Tropical Kingbird is the most common and widespread.

Cattle Tyrant *Machetornis rixosa* 19 cm

CA and SA. Uncommon and local resident in lowlands of central and east PA. Recently established in region (659, 512, 42). Also Pearl Islands (Panamá, 346). **ID** Long legs. *Eyes red.* Yellow below with faint dusky eyeline. Upperparts and tail plain olive-brown. Orange-red on crown usually concealed. Compare with *Tyrannus* kingbirds. Note different eye color and habits. **HABITS** Savannas, agricultural areas, plantations, pastures, and open roadsides. Forages on ground. Often with domestic animals and may loiter on backs of cattle or horses. Also perches low in trees. Solitary or in pairs. **VOICE** Call (1) an ascending series of short, squeaky phrases. Compare with call of Tropical Kingbird.

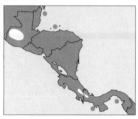

Tropical Kingbird *Tyrannus melancholicus* 21 cm

MX to SA. Common resident in lowlands and foothills (to 2400, mainly below 1800 m). Also larger BZ Cays (343), Bay Islands, and Isla Coiba and Pearl Islands off PA (Panamá, Veraguas, 649, 470). **ID** Relatively long-billed. Note *all-dark (brownish), notched tail* and olive breast. Distinct *dusky mask* (note plain gray sides of head in Western Kingbird). Yellow-orange on crown usually concealed. Juv has cinnamon edging on wing coverts. Best distinguished from Couch's Kingbird (sympatric in BZ and north GT) by voice. **HABITS** Midstory to canopy in wide variety of nonforest habitats including savannas, agricultural areas, plantations, pastures, roadsides, littoral scrub, mangroves, urban and suburban areas. Usually solitary. Perches conspicuously in tree crown, on fence post, or on utility wire. Sallies to take flying insects. **VOICE** Song (1) a repeated *pic-pic-pic, prrrrr* or *wic-wic-wic-wic-wic-wic-prrrrii*. Call (2) a sharp *pic* given at varied intervals. Sometimes repeated to form a short trill that rises or drops in pitch. Compare with Common Tody-Flycatcher.

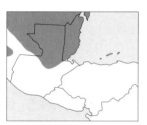

Couch's Kingbird *Tyrannus couchii* 22 cm

South USA to CA. Uncommon to fairly common resident in Caribbean lowlands and foothills (to 1400 m) of BZ (669) and north GT. **ID** Very similar to (and often occurs with) more widespread Tropical Kingbird. Subtle differences include Couch's more olive mantle, less notched tail, and larger bill. *Best separated by voice.* **ABITS** Midstory to canopy in open or semi-open areas including savannas, agricultural areas, plantations, pastures, roadsides, and littoral scrub. Behavior much like Tropical Kingbird. **VOICE** Dawn song (1) a rising series of slightly buzzy notes. Ends abruptly with an emphatic, downslurred note *weedu weedu weedu swee-chu* or *k-leep k-leep k-leep k-leep k-lee-i-chu*. Calls (2) an emphatic, burry *br-eeeeeu*. Compare with call of Yellow-bellied Elaenia. Also (3) a nasal *kip* or *pik* or with previous as *pik pik pik brreeu*.

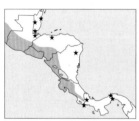

Western Kingbird *Tyrannus verticalis* 21 cm

Breeds west Nearctic. Winters mainly MX and CA. Uncommon to very common transient and winter resident (Sep to May) in north Pacific lowlands and foothills (to 1200 m) south to Pacific slope and Central Valley of CR (Guanacaste, Puntarenas, San José, 570, 567, 600). Rare in PA (Chiriquí, Panamá, 512, 48) and on Caribbean slope in BZ (341, 346) and GT (Izabal, 341). **ID** Blackish, near-square tail with *white on outer rectrices.* Sides of head mostly gray (lacks distinct dark mask of Tropical Kingbird). Note *pale gray breast* and pale yellow lower underparts. Mantle grayish. Orange coronal patch usually concealed. Tropical Kingbird has plain, dark tail with notched tip and longer, heavier bill. Note different head pattern and breast color. **HABITS** Midstory to canopy in open or semi-open areas including savannas, agricultural fields, and beaches. Perches prominently on shrub, utility wire, or fence post. Transients may associate with migrating Scissor-tailed Flycatchers. **VOICE** Usually quiet. Call (1) a sharp *pic.*

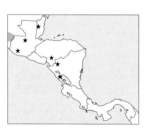

Cassin's Kingbird *Tyrannus vociferans* 21 cm

South USA and MX. Winters mainly MX. Rare winter visitor (Nov to Mar) to BZ (Orange Walk, 382), GT (Baja Verapaz, Huehuetenango, Suchitepéquez, 229, 539), HN (Francisco Morazán, Gracias a Dios, 35, 346), and NI (Carazo, Estelí, 135). **ID** Resembles Western Kingbird but *dark gray breast and sides of head* contrast with *whitish malar and throat.* Mantle olive. Note dark outer rectrices and pale terminal band on tail. **HABITS** Much like Western Kingbird. Solitary. **VOICE** Song (1) a rapidly repeated phrase of burry notes *hi-wheeer* or *chi-chu-chwheer.* Calls include (2) a harsh, burry, downslurred *reeeahr* or *pic-reeehr.*

Cattle Tyrant

Tropical Kingbird

Couch's Kingbird

Western Kingbird

Cassin's Kingbird

KINGBIRDS AND FLYCATCHERS Tyrannidae

Eastern Kingbird and Scissor-tailed Flycatcher can be briefly or locally abundant in migration.

Gray Kingbird *Tyrannus dominicensis*   21 cm

Breeds southeast USA and WI. Winters mainly WI and North SA. Uncommon to rare transient and winter resident (mainly Sep to Oct and Mar to Apr) on Caribbean coast and islands off BZ (313, 311, 347, 343), HN (95), and CR (602). Also Pacific coast in PA (512). Vagrant to Pacific CR (Guanacaste, 341). **ID** *Heavy bill*. Plain dusky tail slightly forked. Drab grayish overall and mostly whitish below with *blackish mask*. Orange on crown usually concealed. Eastern Kingbird has darker mantle, smaller bill, and white on tail. **HABITS** Perches at medium heights in open or semi-open areas including roadsides, gardens, and littoral scrub. Usually solitary. Transients may associate with flocks of Eastern Kingbirds. **VOICE** Usually quiet. Call (1) a short, rapid, buzzy *tee-tre-e-e-e*. Compare with lower-pitched call of Tropical Kingbird.

Eastern Kingbird *Tyrannus tyrannus*   20 cm

Breeds east Nearctic. Winters SA. Fairly common transient (Mar to May and Aug to Oct). May be briefly or locally abundant on Caribbean slope (to 1700, rarely to 2500 m). Vagrant to Isla del Coco (163, 654). **ID** *Dark slaty gray above* with whitish edgings on wings and white below with *white terminal band on tail*. Red or orange on crown usually concealed. **HABITS** Mostly canopy and edge of humid broadleaf forest and tall second growth, but transients can occur in a wide variety of arboreal habitats. Favors outer canopy. Migrants often form flocks. **VOICE** Usually quiet but may give (1) high-pitched, slightly burry *beep* or *breep*. Sometimes given in chorus by flocks.

Scissor-tailed Flycatcher *Tyrannus forficatus*   female 30, male 35 cm

Breeds Nearctic. Winters mainly Pacific MX and CA. Transient and winter resident (mainly Oct to Apr). May be briefly or locally abundant (Apr and Oct) in coastal lowlands. Most numerous in Pacific lowlands and foothills (SL to 2000 m) but also reported regularly from Caribbean slope in BZ (347) and GT (218, 227). Rare in PA (Coclé, 346). **ID** Very long outer rectrices. *Pale gray crown and mantle* and darker tail and wings. Note *pink flanks and axillars* (conspicuous in flight). Red on crown usually concealed. Juv has more orange flanks and shorter tail. Fork-tailed Flycatcher has different head and underparts pattern. **HABITS** Savannas, agricultural areas, plantations, pastures, and roadsides. Perches conspicuously on exposed branch or utility wire. Diurnal migrant. Transients may form large flocks. **VOICE** Call (1) a sharp, bright *kip* or *pic* sometimes repeated.

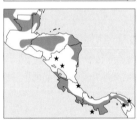

Fork-tailed Flycatcher *Tyrannus savana*   female 30, male 37 cm

CA and SA. Local and somewhat irregular resident in lowlands and foothills (to 1500 m). Most common in north Caribbean savannas. Seasonal movements poorly understood. Perhaps nomadic. Birds from migratory SA populations perhaps occur but this has not been documented. Confined mainly to Pacific in south. **ID** Very long outer rectrices. *Black hood* contrasts with white throat and gray mantle. Yellow on crown usually concealed. Juv has brownish-gray crown and shorter tail. Eastern Kingbird has shorter tail and darker mantle. Compare with Scissor-tailed Flycatcher. Note different head pattern. **HABITS** Prefers extensive open areas such as savannas, agricultural fields, pastures, and marshes. Transients possible in wide variety of terrestrial habitats. Often perches conspicuously on exposed branch or utility wire. May descend to ground while foraging. **VOICE** Calls (1) a low-pitched, weak *jek* or *jiit* sometimes repeated rapidly, (2) lower-pitched, more bleating *ek-ek-ek-ek* . . . and (3) a rapid clicking. In display, male produces (4) a dry, rattling sonation with wings.

Gray Kingbird

Eastern Kingbird

juv

Scissor-tailed Flycatcher

ad

ad

Fork-tailed Flycatcher

juv

ad

SIRYSTES AND FLYCATCHERS Tyrannidae

Choco Sirystes belongs to a mainly South American genus. *Myiarchus* flycatchers are medium- to large-sized tyrants found in middle levels of broadleaf forest and woodland. Details of the head, undertail, and underparts pattern and especially voice are important in separating these. Some are range-restricted. Dusky-capped Flycatcher is the most common and widespread and shows complex geographic variation in Central America.

Choco Sirystes *Sirystes albogriseus*   19 cm
CA and north SA. Uncommon resident in lowlands and foothills (to 1050 m) of east PA. At least formerly ranged west to central PA (Colón, Panamá, 657, 512). **ID** Bushy crest. Pale gray underparts and *black cap*. Note *white rump* and white terminal band on black tail. Structure and posture may suggest a *Myiarchus* flycatcher. Could also be confused with various becards. Note different structure and voice. Also compare with Eastern Kingbird. **HABITS** Canopy and edge of humid broadleaf forest. Often takes prominent perch in outer canopy. Solitary or in pairs. Follows mixed flocks. **VOICE** Call (1) a loud *puc, puc, puc . . .* or *chup-chup-chup . . .*

Yucatan Flycatcher *Myiarchus yucatanensis*   18 cm
South MX and CA. Uncommon to locally fairly common resident in lowlands of north GT (Petén) and north BZ. **ID** Small and pale. Resembles Dusky-capped Flycatcher but has *grayish wingbars*, grayish edgings in tertials and secondaries, and grayer sides of head with *pale lores* (often shows broad, pale eye ring). Note slightly less crested head shape. Ash-throated and Nutting's flycatchers allopatric. **HABITS** Midstory to subcanopy and edge of arid to semihumid broadleaf forest, second growth, pine savanna, and scrub. Solitary. **VOICE** Song (1) a long, plaintive, two-syllable whistled phrase *oooooo-wheeeeeep* or *hoooooo-eu* or *wheeeer hweep*. First note upslurred. Second drops in pitch. Excited birds may give (2) a rapid *ooo-weeeehehehehehee.*

Dusky-capped Flycatcher *Myiarchus tuberculifer*   16–18 cm
Southwest USA to SA. Common and widespread resident (to 1800, locally to 2800 m). **ID** Small with *dark, bushy crown*. Note bright yellow lower underparts. Widespread form has rufous edgings on secondaries, rufous wingbars, and rufous edging on tail. Yucatan Flycatcher (note limited range) is paler, especially on crown and shows less rufous on wing. Great Crested Flycatcher is larger and has paler wingbars (contrasting with rufous primary edges). **GV** Birds from north CA are browner and have rufous edging on wings and tail. Birds from highlands of GT (not shown) are larger and proportionally longer-winged. Birds from south CA have more olive mantle. Birds from east PA lack rufous on wings and tail (but all imms show some cinnamon on wings). **HABITS** Midstory to subcanopy in a wide variety of arboreal habitats including semihumid to humid forest and edge, open woodland, gardens, plantations, and mangroves. May descend to near ground while foraging in open areas. Solitary. **VOICE** Dawn song (1) a long series of notes *whedu wheeeeu whedu wheeeeeeu whedu brrrrrrrrr*. Call, given throughout day (2) a plaintive, clear, whistle *weeeer* or *wheeeu* that drops in pitch. Compare with calls of Yellow-bellied Elaenia and Greater Pewee. Also gives (3) shorter, downslurred note followed by short roll or trill *whuu prrrrrr-rr*, (4) a short *whedu* sometimes followed by rising and falling trill *whedu brrrrrrrrr*, and (5) short *whit* or *pip* notes.

Panama Flycatcher *Myiarchus panamensis*   19 cm
CA and north SA. Fairly common resident in south lowlands and foothills (to 1350, mainly below 500 m). Uncommon and local in Pacific CR. Fairly common in PA. Also Isla Coiba and Pearl Islands off PA (Veraguas, Panamá, 455, 649, 470). **ID** Large *Myiarchus* with relatively long bill and rounded crown. Drab. Crown and nape grayish-olive. Note *grayish edging on wings and tail*. Other *Myiarchus* show rufous in folded wing. **HABITS** Understory to subcanopy and edge of semihumid forest, second growth, mangroves, gardens, and scrub in PA. Confined mainly to mangroves in CR. Sallies to seize prey from open perch. Sometimes descends to ground to forage among mangrove roots. Solitary or in pairs. **VOICE** Dawn song (1) a fast *tseeedewdewdewdew . . .* that drops slightly in pitch. Call (2) a scratchy *gwee heer* or *ku-wiheer.*

Choco Sirystes

Yucatan Flycatcher

Dusky-capped Flycatcher

north CA

south CA

central and
east PA

Panama Flycatcher

FLYCATCHERS Tyrannidae

Flycatchers found in middle and upper levels of woodland and broadleaf forest. Brown-crested Flycatcher and the Nearctic migrant Great Crested Flycatcher are the most common and widespread.

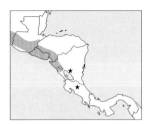

Ash-throated Flycatcher *Myiarchus cinerascens*   20 cm

Breeds west Nearctic. Winters MX and CA. Uncommon winter resident in north Pacific lowlands and foothills (to 1700 m). Very local in arid Caribbean valleys of GT. Vagrant to Caribbean NI (Chontales, 413) and CR (Alajuela, 570). **ID** *Pale grayish sides of head* and slightly peaked crown. Folded wing shows *rufous edgings on primaries contrasting with whitish edgings on secondaries.* In close view note extensive rufous on outer rectrices with dusky extending across tip. Compare with Nutting's Flycatcher. Note different voice, tail pattern, and wing pattern. Also note Ash-throated's more peaked crown, slightly larger bill, and *gray throat extending to sides of head.* Yucatan Flycatcher allopatric. Separated from larger and darker Brown-crested Flycatcher by voice, tail pattern, and proportionally smaller bill. **HABITS** Midstory to subcanopy of arid to semihumid forest or woodland, second growth, and scrub. Wintering birds solitary and inconspicuous. **VOICE** Diagnostic call (1) a short *pip* or *pic.* Also (2) a rolling *prreeer* sometimes combined with previous as *pic breeeer* and repeated, and (3) rapid, abrupt *p-reer* or *kabrick* or *habrick.* Softer than calls of Brown-crested Flycatcher.

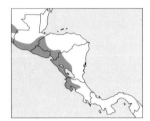

Nutting's Flycatcher *Myiarchus nuttingi*   17.5 cm

MX and north CA. Uncommon resident in Pacific lowlands and foothills (to 1800 m). Local on Caribbean slope in Motagua Valley, GT (279) and in HN (Comayagua, 381). Also Nentón Valley in west GT (Huehuetenango, 229). **ID** Small-billed. Resembles Ash-throated Flycatcher. Folded wing shows rufous edgings on primaries grading softly into (not contrasting with) whitish edgings of secondaries. Also note slightly darker (browner) auriculars and more rounded (less peaked) crown. In close view note rufous on outer rectrices extending to tip of each feather. Also compare with Dusky-capped Flycatcher. Note different head pattern and voice. Larger Brown-crested Flycatcher has different head pattern and voice. Yucatan Flycatcher allopatric. **GV** Birds from Pacific slope have more dusky on tail, more intense yellow belly, and less contrasting throat and auriculars. **HABITS** Midstory and edge of arid (deciduous) to semihumid forest, thorn forest, mangroves, and second growth. **VOICE** Dawn song (1) a repeated, slightly hoarse *p-wheeer.* May be combined with scratchy notes or a trilled *preeer.* Higher-pitched and thinner than dawn song of Brown-crested Flycatcher. Distinctive call (2) an attenuated *weeeek.* Also (3) a sharp *whik* or *pik* that is higher-pitched and more strident than *whik* call of Brown-crested Flycatcher.

Brown-crested Flycatcher *Myiarchus tyrannulus*   19–21 cm

South USA to SA. Common resident in lowlands and foothills (to 900, locally to 1500 m). Also Bay Islands (94). Some perhaps withdraw from north Caribbean slope outside breeding season (Mar to Aug, 343). Nearctic breeding birds perhaps occur as winter residents. **ID** *Large and heavy-billed* with peaked crown. Grayish sides of head contrast only slightly with brownish crown. Resembles Great Crested Flycatcher in size and pattern but generally paler and duller. Note whitish throat. Compare with smaller Ash-throated and Nutting's flycatchers. Note different structure and voice. **GV** Birds from Pacific NI and CR are slightly smaller, have less dusky on rectrices, and are slightly paler above. Birds from Bay Islands are darker than mainland birds. **HABITS** Midstory to subcanopy of open, semihumid to humid woodland, forest edge, plantations, littoral scrub, and mangroves. **VOICE** Dawn song (1) a series of sharp, short *wick* notes and burry, rolling trills *which-wirrick, wik-wheer, which-wi wi-wirreeer . . .* Typical call (2) an abrupt, slightly scratchy or burry *whik.* Sometimes repeated persistently.

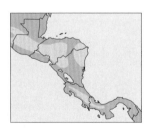

Great Crested Flycatcher *Myiarchus crinitus*   20 cm

Breeds Nearctic. Winters mainly MX and CA. Widespread and fairly common transient and winter resident (mainly Sep to May) in lowlands and foothills (to 1400, rarely or locally to 1800 m). **ID** *Large and heavy-billed.* Most brightly colored *Myiarchus.* Crown and sides of head olive. Gray breast contrasts with *bright yellow lower underparts.* In close view note extensively pinkish base of mandible. Compare with similar-sized Brown-crested Flycatcher. Note different head pattern and darker olive mantle. **HABITS** Upper midstory to subcanopy of semihumid to humid broadleaf forest, tall second growth, shaded plantations, gardens, and mangroves. Solitary. Usually inconspicuous. Often detected by voice. **VOICE** Call (1) a loud, strongly upslurred *wheeeeep* or *wheeeik.* Louder but less emphatic than call of Nutting's Flycatcher.

43%

Ash-throated Flycatcher

Pacific

Nutting's Flycatcher

interior

Brown-crested Flycatcher

widespread

Bay
Islands

north Caribbean

Pacific NI
and CR

Great Crested Flycatcher

ATTILA AND MOURNER Tyrannidae

Mostly brown-plumaged birds found mainly in humid broadleaf forest.

Bright-rumped Attila *Attila spadiceus*   18–20 cm

MX to SA. Fairly common resident in lowlands and foothills (to 1850, locally to 2100 m). Also Isla Coiba off PA (Veraguas, 653, 470). Uncommon to rare in Pacific GT (539, 279, 378, 182) and SV (183, 619). **ID** *Hooked bill.* Note *soft streaking on breast,* variable yellow rump, and red eyes. Imm (not shown) has brown eyes. **GV** Individually and geographically variable. Birds from north CA tend to be larger and more rufous overall and less often show yellow below. Birds from south are typically more olive with more contrasting yellow rump. **HABITS** Midstory and edge of semihumid to humid broadleaf forest, tall second growth, mangroves, and shaded plantations. Solitary or in pairs. Makes abrupt sallies to seize prey. **VOICE** Song (1) a loud, ringing *wip we-eu we-yup we-eyup we-eyup wweeuwip* repeated persistently. Also (2) a shorter, less emphatic *weo-eeo-eeo-eeo-eeo-eeoeeo.* Call (3) a sharp *di-dik* recalling Stub-tailed Spadebill.

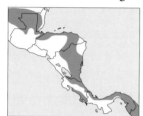

Rufous Mourner *Rhytipterna holerythra*   21 cm

CA and north SA. Fairly common resident in lowlands and foothills (to 1200 m). **ID** Slightly bushy crown. *Uniform cinnamon-rufous* becoming slightly paler on belly. Mandible dull pink with dark tip. Larger Rufous Piha has less pink on mandible. Note different voice. Also compare with Cinnamon Becard. Note different head pattern. **HABITS** Upper midstory to subcanopy of tall semihumid to humid broadleaf forest. Perches in open. May remain motionless for long periods or peer about while slowly craning its neck. Sallies abruptly to seize prey. Solitary or in pairs. May follow mixed flocks that include larger birds such as *Celeus* woodpeckers. **VOICE** Distinctive call (1) two long whistles *wheeee, heeeeeuu.* First note upslurred and second downslurred. Less often (2) a series of two to eight downslurred whistles *weeur-weeur-weeur-weeur . . .*

RUFOUS PIHA Cotingidae   Rufous Piha, a member of the Cotingidae, is shown here for comparison.

Rufous Piha *Lipaugus unirufus*   25 cm

CA and north SA. Uncommon resident in lowlands and foothills (to 600, locally to 1200 m in south). **ID** *Large.* Uniform rufous-brown becoming slightly paler on belly and throat. In close view note restricted pink base of mandible and faint, pale eye ring. Smaller Rufous Mourner has different bill and voice. **HABITS** Upper midstory to subcanopy of humid broadleaf forest. Solitary or in loosely associated pairs. Sits motionless for long periods. **VOICE** Loud calls given abruptly throughout day. Most distinctive (1) a single, explosive *peeeer* or *pee-weeer.* Less often (2) a loud chatter or rattle.

MOURNER AND SCHIFFORNI Tityridae

Speckled Mourner *Laniocera rufescens*   20 cm

CA and north SA. Rare and local resident in lowlands and foothills (to 700 m). Most common in east PA (Darién, 67) and east HN (Olancho, Gracias a Dios, 629). Rare in BZ (Orange Walk, Stann Creek, Toledo, 529, 343), north GT (Petén, Alta Verapaz, Izabal, 229, 279, 317, 556), NI (RAAN, 358), and CR (Guanacaste, Alajuela, Heredia, 624, 600). **ID** Mostly rufous. Usually has *fine dusky scaling on breast* and *pale rufous wingbars or spotting on wing coverts.* Yellow pectoral tufts usually concealed. Some have pale eye ring and slightly dusky crown. Compare with Rufous Mourner and rufous Piha. Note different wing and underparts. **HABITS** Midstory of humid broadleaf forest. Takes open perch above shaded forest stream. Solitary or in pairs. Follows mixed flocks that include caciques, *Celeus* woodpeckers, or nunbirds. **VOICE** Song (1) a high-pitched, squeaky *whii-ti, whii-ti, whii-ti, whii-ti . . .* Also (2) a downslurred *waaaaah* like Dusky-capped or Rusty-margined flycatchers.

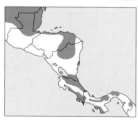

Northern Schiffornis[33] *Schiffornis veraepacis*   17 cm

South MX and CA. Uncommon to locally common resident in north lowlands and foothills (to 800 m). Mainly foothills (above 1000 m?) in PA (297, 657, 512). **ID** Large-headed with rounded crown and large, dark eyes. *Uniform dark brown* becoming slightly more rufous on wings. Compare with Rufous Mourner. Note different habits and color. **HABITS** Understory of semihumid to humid broadleaf forest. Forages deliberately making short flights. Cranes neck and peers about as it perches on slender, vertical stem. Solitary. Does not follow mixed flocks. **VOICE** At long intervals gives (1) a slurred, whistled *wheeee-oo-whee! hee.* Voice of birds from foothills of east PA poorly known but thought to be similar.

Russet-winged Schiffornis[33] *Schiffornis stenorhyncha*   17 cm

CA and north SA. Uncommon in Pacific lowlands and foothills (to 1200 m) of east PA (Colón, Panamá, Darién, 67, 297, 657, 512). **ID** Resembles Northern Schiffornis but is more *rufous-brown* becoming slightly brighter on throat and distinctly grayish below. Northern Schiffornis is found at higher elevations in PA. Compare with Rufous Mourner. Note different habits and color. **HABITS** Like Northern Schiffornis. **VOICE** Call (1) a slurred, whistled *wheee-oo-wee hee hii!* Like Northern Schiffornis but ending with an additional short note that is highest in pitch.

Black-and-white Becard

♀

♂

White-winged Becard

♀

♂

Barred Becard

♀

♂

Black-crowned Tityra

imm

ad ♀

ad ♂

Masked Tityra

♀

♂

SHARPBILL Oxyruncidae

Sharpbill is a highly distinctive species with no close relatives.

Sharpbill *Oxyruncus cristatus* 17 cm

CA and SA. Uncommon and local resident in south foothills (700 to 1400 m). At north limit at Volcán Tenorio, CR (Guanacaste). May move to lower elevations outside breeding season (600). **ID** *Whitish or pale yellow underparts with blackish spotting.* Note fine black-and-white barring on sides of head and pointed bill. Red-orange crest inconspicuous. Spotted underparts may suggest Speckled Tanager (often in same mixed flock). **GV** Birds from east PA are whiter below. **HABITS** Subcanopy of humid broadleaf forest in hilly terrain. Solitary birds or pairs follow mixed flocks. Forages actively by hopping heavily along branches. Probes in epiphytes and dead leaf clusters. **VOICE** Song (1) a long, dry, slightly metallic trill that drops steeply in pitch *eeeeeeuuuuuurrrrrr.*

COTINGAS Cotingidae

The *Cotinga* cotingas are represented by three mainly allopatric species in Central America. They are typically seen perching motionless in the canopy of humid broadleaf forest. They are often solitary but sometimes gather in groups at fruiting trees.

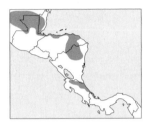

Lovely Cotinga *Cotinga amabilis* 19 cm

South MX and CA. Uncommon to rare and local resident in Caribbean lowlands and foothills (to 1700 m) south to west PA (Bocas del Toro, 48). Very rare on Pacific slope in west CR (Puntarenas, Guanacaste, 523). **ID** Bulky with short tail. Ad male mostly blue with deep violet patches on throat and belly. Note male's *unmarked, blue mantle.* Female mostly whitish or gray with extensive fine scaling and spotting. Turquoise Cotinga (Pacific slope) allopatric. Blue Cotinga mainly allopatric but may be locally syntopic in Caribbean west PA (Bocas del Toro, 48). Male Lovely Cotinga has *plain blue sides of head* (no black eye ring, lores, or forehead) and *long blue uppertail coverts extending nearly to tip of tail.* Male Lovely also has larger purple area on underparts. Female Blue Cotinga is more buff below and less boldly scaled and spotted. **HABITS** Canopy and edge of humid broadleaf forest and adjacent tall second growth. Usually solitary or in pairs but may gather in numbers at fruiting trees. Males perch upright and motionless for long periods in crown of canopy emergent tree, especially during early morning. **VOICE** Usually quiet. Rarely gives (1) a soft *ick.*

Turquoise Cotinga *Cotinga ridgwayi* 18 cm

CA endemic. Uncommon and local resident in Pacific lowlands and foothills (to 1850, but mainly below 900 m) of CR (Puntarenas) and west PA (Chiriquí). **ID** Bulky with short tail. Ad male mostly blue with deep violet patches on throat and central belly. Note male's speckled mantle and wing coverts and black eye ring. Female mostly dull buff with extensive, fine scaling and spotting. Similar Blue and Lovely cotingas are allopatric. **HABITS** Canopy and edge of humid broadleaf forest and adjacent tall second growth. Like Lovely Cotinga. **VOICE** Rarely heard. Call (1) a very high-pitched *siiii.* In flight, gives (2) a doubled *seesee.*

Blue Cotinga *Cotinga nattererii* 19 cm

CA and north SA. Uncommon to locally fairly common resident in lowlands and foothills (to about 900 m) of PA. **ID** Bulky with short tail. Ad male mostly blue with deep violet patches on throat and lower underparts. Note male's *broad black eye ring* and dark spotting on wing coverts. Female dull buff with extensive scaling and spotting and *pale eye ring.* Imm male resembles female. Turquoise Cotinga allopatric. In Caribbean west PA compare with Lovely Cotinga. Note male's different upperparts and head pattern. **HABITS** Canopy of humid broadleaf forest. Usually solitary. May assemble in groups at fruiting trees. **VOICE** Rarely heard call (1) a short *beep.* Male produces (2) fluttering sonation with wings in flight.

Sharpbill

CR and
west PA

east PA

Lovely Cotinga

♂

♀

Turquoise Cotinga

♂

♀

Blue Cotinga

♂

♀

COTINGAS Cotingidae

Striking cotingas found in canopy of humid broadleaf and tall mangroves. All have similar, pigeon-like structure with rounded head and broad wings. All are allopatric. Two are endemic to the region. *Carpodectes* cotingas are usually silent but can be conspicuous owing to their habit of perching high in the canopy where the male's white plumage contrasts starkly with dark foliage.

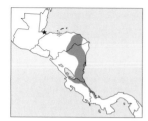

Snowy Cotinga *Carpodectes nitidus*   female 20, male 22 cm
CA endemic. Uncommon to rare and local resident in Caribbean lowlands and foothills (to 750 m). Formerly perhaps more widespread in HN (Atlántida, Gracias a Dios, 63, 629). One record from lowlands of east GT (Izabal, 220). **ID** Bulky, short-tailed, pigeon-like structure. Striking male mostly *white* becoming slightly grayish above with black bill. Female mostly plain gray becoming paler below with white eye ring. Female's wings mostly dusky with whitish edging. Imm male resembles female but is whiter below and has mostly white wing coverts. Black-tipped and Yellow-billed cotingas allopatric. Compare female with female Lovely Cotinga. **HABITS** Canopy of humid broadleaf forest. Pairs or solitary birds perch motionless for long period in crown of emergent tree. Small groups may gather at fruiting trees. Conspicuous as it undertakes long flights across dark, forested landscapes. **VOICE** Usually silent. Rarely gives (1) a dry, scratchy *chih* or *chee*. May be repeated rapidly two to eight times.

Yellow-billed Cotinga *Carpodectes antoniae*   female 20, male 22 cm
CA endemic. Rare and local resident in Pacific coastal lowlands of CR (Puntarenas, 570, 600, 121, 340, 384) and west PA (Chiriquí, Veraguas, 60, 657, 341, 346). An old report from Coclé (512, 340) is regarded as hypothetical. **ID** *Yellow bill*. Mostly white male unmistakable in range. Female mostly plain gray becoming paler below, with white eye ring. Female's wings mostly dusky with whitish edging. Compare female with various becards and tityras. Black-tipped and Snowy cotingas allopatric.
HABITS Canopy of extensive mangroves and adjacent humid broadleaf forest. Poorly known. Males may perch motionless and upright for long periods in crown of emergent tree. Often in pairs or small groups. **VOICE** Usually silent. Rarely gives (1) a dove-like or trogon-like *cah* or *cow*.

Black-tipped Cotinga *Carpodectes hopkei*   female 23, male 25 cm
CA and north SA. Uncommon and local resident in lowlands and foothills (to 900 m) of east PA (Darién). **ID** Male *mostly white* with black bill. At close range note black spots near tips of primaries and red eyes. Imm male similar but also has black tips on rectrices. Female mostly plain gray becoming paler below, with white eye ring. Female's wings mostly dusky or whitish edging. Yellow-billed and Snowy cotingas allopatric. Compare female with female Blue Cotinga. **HABITS** Canopy of humid broadleaf forest and adjacent clearings or second growth. Solitary or in pairs. Males take prominent perches in crown of emergent tree. Larger groups may assemble at fruiting trees. In display males fly slowly between perches with exaggerated, deep wingbeats. **VOICE** Usually silent.

Snowy Cotinga

♀

♂

Yellow-billed Cotinga

♀

♂

Black-tipped Cotinga

♀

♂

COTINGAS Cotingidae

Large, spectacular cotingas found in middle and upper levels of humid broadleaf forest. Bare-necked Umbrellabird and Three-wattled Bellbird are elevational migrants.

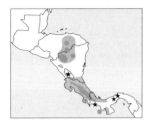

Three-wattled Bellbird *Procnias tricarunculatus*   female 25, male 30 cm
CA endemic. Uncommon and local in lowlands and foothills (SL to 1500 m). CR breeding populations undertake three-part pattern of seasonal movements (497). Distribution, status, and movements of birds in HN and NI are poorly known (34, 629, 626). Recently reported from Cerro Musún and Volcán Maderas in central NI (Matagalpa, Rivas, 137). Also Isla Coiba off PA (Veraguas, 657, 470) and Azuero Peninsula (Los Santos, Veraguas, Herrera, 657, 425). Rare elsewhere on Pacific slope of PA and in Canal Area. **ID** Large. Ad male *plain rufous-brown* with contrasting *white head, breast, and upper mantle*. Male has three long, fleshy wattles hanging from base of bill. Ad female near-uniform olive-green above. Female's *underparts mostly yellowish with olive streaking.* Imm male resembles female but may have irregular patches of rufous plumage and smaller wattles. **HABITS** Subcanopy to canopy of humid and (seasonally) semihumid broadleaf forest and adjacent shaded plantations. Males call persistently from favored perches during breeding season. Calling males often difficult to locate in dense foliage but sometimes vocalize on exposed snags in canopy. May gather in small numbers at fruiting trees. **VOICE** Striking and unmistakable song (1) a very loud, hollow, low-pitched *bong* or *ong* often preceded by a short, high-pitched note.

Purple-throated Fruitcrow *Querula purpurata*   female 26, male 29 cm
CA and north SA. Uncommon and local resident in humid lowlands and foothills (to 600 m). Rare in southeast NI (Río San Juan, 269, 662). **ID** Robust with *broad, gray bill* and broad wings. Ad male black with *broad magenta-purple gorget.* Female *uniform black.* **HABITS** Upper midstory to subcanopy of humid broadleaf forest. Pairs or (more often) small groups travel through subcanopy of tall forest or adjacent second growth. May follow mixed flocks that include caciques, *Celeus* woodpeckers, etc. In display, males extend gorget laterally and shake tail from side to side. Noisy and conspicuous. **VOICE** Calls include a variety of rich, whistled phrases. Most often heard (1) a wavering, slightly hoarse *kweeowee* or *queruwee* repeated two or three times. Also (2) an upslurred *wooooeeep* and (3) various dry, scratchy cries *hwwwwk* or *hwak-hwak* or *hwak-wak-wak.*

Bare-necked Umbrellabird *Cephalopterus glabricollis*   female 36, male 45 cm
CA endemic. Rare and local in Caribbean lowlands and foothills of CR (Alajuela, Guanacaste, Heredia, San José, Limón, 570, 600, 253, 254, 140) and PA (Chiriquí, Ngäbe-Buglé, Veraguas, Coclé, Colón, 657, 512, 357). Breeds in foothills and highlands (mainly 800 to 1650, rarely 2000 m) during Mar to Jun. Outside breeding season moves downslope to adjacent forested Caribbean lowlands and lower foothills. Females migrate to areas mainly below 200 m, males mainly 100 to 500 m. Rare in southeast NI (Río San Juan, 452) where status uncertain. **ID** *Very large, bulky and short-tailed.* Plumage *uniform black.* Note males *forward-swept crest* and *bare scarlet, inflatable skin on throat.* Female has much smaller crest. Compare with Purple-throated Fruitcrow. Note different structure. **HABITS** Midstory to subcanopy of humid broadleaf forest. Males gather at leks during late Mar to May. Usually solitary outside breeding season but may follow mixed flocks that include Purple-throated Fruitcrows and nunbirds. **VOICE** Male's call in display (1) several very low-pitched, flat notes followed by a very different scratchy, upslurred phrase *hoo, hoo, hr-rrrach.* May give (2) short, very low-pitched *hoo* in long series without second part.

Three-wattled Bellbird

♀

♂

Displaying male.

Purple-throated Fruitcrow

♀

♂

Displaying male.

♀

♂

Displaying male.

Bare-necked Umbrellabird

MANAKINS Pipridae

Small birds found at lower levels in broadleaf forest. All these species have red or orange legs. Males perform spectacular display at leks. White-collared Manakin is the most common and widespread.

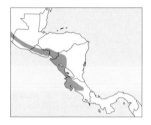

Long-tailed Manakin *Chiroxiphia linearis*　　　　　female 13, male 24 cm

MX and CA. Locally common resident in Pacific lowlands and foothills (to 1500 m). **ID** Red legs. Distinctive tail shape with *long central rectrices*. Ad male mostly black with *red crown* and *blue mantle*. Female has shorter (but still projecting) central rectrices and is mostly plain olive with paler lower underparts. Subad male mostly plain olive but has *red crown*. Lance-tailed Manakin allopatric. **HABITS** Understory to canopy of arid to humid broadleaf forest, gallery forest, and tall second growth. Males perform spectacular display at leks. **VOICE** Varied, loud, and distinctive vocalizations are among most familiar sounds of Pacific dry forest including (1) a short, sharp *weet* or *pwit* that may be repeated, (2) a very nasal, whining *waaaah* that drops slightly in pitch, (3) a clear, resonant *wheer* or *heer* or *heer-ho*. Males at lek give (4) a clear, ringing *to-lay-do* or *toe-lee-doo*. At lek, males repeat (5) a nasal, catlike *miaow-raow* and (6) piercing *pweet*.

Lance-tailed Manakin *Chiroxiphia lanceolata*　　　　　female 12, male 13 cm

CA and SA. Locally fairly common resident in south Pacific lowlands and foothills (to 1500 m). Also Isla Coiba (Veraguas, 653, 470). **ID** Red legs. Distinctive tail shape with *long central rectrices*. Ad male black with *red crown* and *blue mantle*. Subad male mostly plain olive with *red crown*. Female mostly plain olive with paler lower underparts. Long-tailed Manakin allopatric. **HABITS** Understory to midstory of semihumid broadleaf forest and tall second growth. Locally in mangroves. Males display at leks. **VOICE** Song (1) given at lek a clear *to-wit-do*. Varied repertoire also includes (1) a clear, mellow *peeew* or *keer*, (2) a sharp *kip*, (3) a very nasal, descending *waaanh*, (4) a single or short series of whistled *tyooi* notes, and (5) mellow trill or rattle *whatutututu*.

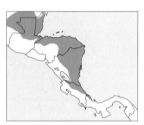

White-collared Manakin[24] *Manacus candei*　　　　　11.5 cm

South MX and CA. Fairly common resident in Caribbean lowlands and foothills (to 700, locally to 1000 m). **ID** Large-headed with flat crown. *Orange legs*. Male has shaggy throat typical of genus. Ad male has *white foreparts* and *black cap*. Female mostly plain olive like several other CA female manakins but note *yellowish lower underparts*. Imm male resembles female. **GV** Hybridizes with Golden-collared Manakin in west PA (Bocas del Toro) where some birds are intermediate in color and pattern. **HABITS** Understory of semihumid to humid broadleaf forest and tall second growth. Males display at leks. **VOICE** At lek males produce (1) loud cracking and (2) short, dry, buzzy rattling sonation with wings. Calls include (3) a sharp, downslurred *weeer* or *weecheeur*.

Golden-collared Manakin[24] *Manacus vitellinus*　　　　　11–13 cm

CA and north SA. Fairly common resident in lowlands and foothills (to 450 m) of PA. Also Isla Escudo (Bocas del Toro, 656). **ID** *Orange legs*. Ad male has bright yellow foreparts and black cap. Like other *Manacus* manakins, male's throat often distended or shaggy. Female near-uniform olive with bright orange legs. Imm male resembles female. Hybridizes with White-collared Manakin in west PA. **GV** Birds from Isla Escudo PA (Bocas del Toro) are larger and proportionally shorter-winged. Females from that population are darker. **HABITS** Understory of humid broadleaf forest and tall second growth. Males are noisy and conspicuous in elaborate display at leks. **VOICE** Like White-collared Manakin.

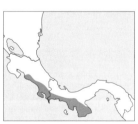

Orange-collared Manakin[24] *Manacus aurantiacus*　　　　　10.5 cm

CA endemic. Locally common resident in Pacific lowlands and foothills (mainly SL to 100, locally to 1100 m) of east CR (Puntarenas) and west PA. **ID** *Orange legs*. Ad male has *orange foreparts* and black cap. Like other *Manacus* manakins, male's throat often shaggy or distended. Female closely resembles female of allopatric White-collared Manakin. Imm male resembles female but is more yellowish on throat and breast. **HABITS** Understory of humid broadleaf forest and tall second growth. Males display at leks. **VOICE** Like White-collared Manakin.

50%

imm
♂

ad
♂

subad
♂

♀

**Long-tailed
Manakin**

imm
♂

♀

**Lance-tailed
Manakin**

ad
♂

**White-collared
Manakin**

♀

**Golden-collared
Manakin**

♂

hybrid
White-collared ×
Golden-collared
♂

♀

♂

♀

♂

Escudo

♂

♀

♀

♂

Orange-collared Manakin

MANAKINS Pipridae

Small birds found at lower and middle levels of humid broadleaf forest. All these species have drab-colored legs. Excepting the rare Green Manakin, males of these sexually dimorphic species perform elaborate displays at leks. Red-capped Manakin is the most common and widespread.

Green Manakin *Cryptopipo holochlora* 12.5 cm

CA and north SA. Uncommon to rare and local resident in lowlands and foothills (to 1250 m) of east PA. **ID** Sexes similar. Mostly uniform olive with *yellowish crissum and center of belly*. Note *diffuse pale eye ring*. Eyes dark. Legs gray. Suggests various female manakins but note larger size and longer tail. **HABITS** Poorly known. Understory to midstory of humid broadleaf forest and adjacent second growth. Solitary. Rarely follows mixed flocks. May visit fruiting trees. **VOICE** Usually quiet. Calls (1) a short trill or rattle and (2) high-pitched, downslurred *sweeeu*.

White-ruffed Manakin *Corapipo altera* 10 cm

CA and north SA. Fairly common resident in foothills and highlands (mainly 400 to 1500 m, rarely or locally as low as SL). Perhaps undertakes local or altitudinal movements (525). **ID** Eyes dark. Male *bluish-black with white throat* extending to sides of neck. Female mostly olive above including crown with pale gray throat and dark grayish legs. Juv male has whitish throat (some females similar). Compare with female White-crowned Manakin. Note different crown and eye color. **HABITS** Understory to midstory and edge of humid broadleaf forest and tall second growth. Makes short sallies to seize invertebrates or fruit. May follow mixed flocks. **GV** Male from Pacific east CR and west PA has less white on throat. **VOICE** Calls (1) a high-pitched, thin, rolling *prreeet* and (2) softer, thin, sharp *seee*. Males produce (3) a dull, snapping sonation with wings followed immediately by vocal *chee waa* or *che-rup*.

Blue-crowned Manakin *Lepidothrix coronata* 10 cm

CA and SA. Uncommon resident in humid lowlands and foothills (to 600, locally to 1350 m) of east CR (Limón, Puntarenas) and PA. **ID** Small. Male black with *blue crown*. Female has *bright green breast and upperparts*. No other CA manakin is bright green above. **HABITS** Understory to midstory of humid broadleaf forest and adjacent tall second growth. Solitary. May follow mixed flocks. **VOICE** Calls (1) a clear rattle or trill *trtrtrtrtreew* or *chk-trtrtrtreew* and (2) thin, strongly upslurred *pweeeep*. Males at lek repeat (3) a guttural, froglike *weechawhuuk* or *weechawook*.

White-crowned Manakin *Dixiphia pipra* 10 cm

CA and SA. Uncommon resident in foothills (800 to 1500 m) of east CR and west PA. Perhaps undertakes local or altitudinal movements (92) descending to lower elevations during wet season. **ID** *Dark red eyes*. Male black with *white crown*. Female mostly plain olive with *gray head*. Compare female with female White-ruffed Manakin. Note different crown and eye color. **HABITS** Understory of humid broadleaf forest and tall second growth. Solitary. **VOICE** Call (1) a scratchy or buzzy, nasal *jeea' eeeh* or *cheeahi*. Sometimes (2) with one or more introductory notes *p'p'p'cheeea'aeeh*.

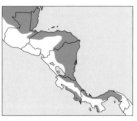

Red-capped Manakin *Ceratopipra mentalis* 10 cm

South MX to north SA. Common resident in lowlands and foothills (to 1050, but mainly below 500 m). May undertake local or altitudinal movements (387, 92). Confined to Caribbean slope in north. Also Azuero Peninsula in PA (Los Santos, Veraguas, 657, 425.) **ID** Ad male mostly black with *scarlet-red head*, yellow tibial tufts, and *white eyes*. Female plain drab olive becoming slightly paler below. *Legs pinkish-gray*. Compare with female White-collared Manakin. Note different leg color. Imm male resembles female but has whitish eyes. Golden-headed Manakin mainly allopatric. **GV** Male from north CA has more orange head and more extensive yellow on chin. **HABITS** Understory to lower midstory of semihumid to humid broadleaf forest and tall second growth. Solitary except at lek. **VOICE** Call (1) a sharp *psip* or *chrip*. Song (2) a series of sharp notes followed by a high-pitched rising and falling whistle and sharp last note *chic chic chic chic pseeeeeu chick*. In display, males produce (3) rattling sonation that is softer than that of White-collared Manakin *tk-tk-tk-tk-tk . . .* and (4) buzzing sounds.

Golden-headed Manakin *Ceratopipra erythrocephala* 9 cm

CA and SA. Uncommon to locally common resident in lowlands and foothills (to 1200 m) of east PA (Panamá, Darién). **ID** Male mostly black with *yellow head* and *pale eyes*. Note red and white tibial tufts. Female has *pinkish legs* and closely resembles female Red-capped Manakin. Imm male resembles female but has whitish eyes. Red-capped Manakin mainly allopatric. **HABITS** Understory to midstory and edge of humid broadleaf forest and tall second growth. Hover-gleans for fruit and arthropods. Males display at leks. **VOICE** Calls (1) a clear note followed by a trill and ending with one or two sharper notes *pu-prrrrrrr-pit-pit* and (2) short, sharp *zit, zit*. In display gives (3) series of *kew* or *pew* notes.

50%

Green Manakin

juv ♂

imm ♂

widespread ♂

Pacific ♂

♀

White-ruffed Manakin

Blue-crowned Manakin ♂

♀

White-crowned Manakin ♂

♀

north CA ♂

♀

south CA ♂

Red-capped Manakin

Golden-headed Manakin

♂

♀

Red-capped Manakins at lek.

PEPPERSHRIKE AND SHRIKE-VIREOS Vireonidae

Larger relatives of the vireos found in middle and upper levels of forest and woodland. All have loud, distinctive vocalizations that are often given persistently throughout the day. Green Shrike-Vireo is widespread but often difficult to glimpse in dense canopy of humid broadleaf forest. Rufous-browed Peppershrike is widespread in Central America and shows complex geographic variation.

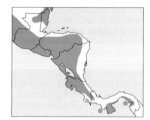

Rufous-browed Peppershrike *Cyclarhis gujanensis*   14.5–16 cm

MX to SA. Uncommon resident (to 2500, but mainly below 2000 m). Complex distribution includes lowlands of north BZ and north GT (Petén), Pacific slope and interior of north CA (south to Pacific west CR) and highlands (700 to 2450 m) of east CR and west PA (Chiriquí). Perhaps absent from Caribbean lowlands of PA but found in Pacific lowlands of PA from Azuero Peninsula east. Poorly known in Caribbean NI (RAAN, Río San Juan, 662, 548). Also Isla Coiba (Veraguas, 653, 470). **ID** Robust and large-headed with heavy, hooked bill. *Rufous forehead and broad supercilium* contrast with gray auriculars and crown. Eyes red. **GV** Birds from BZ have pale supercilium. Birds from north CA have underparts yellow or olive grading clinally south to CR where belly is white. In most of PA underparts are entirely yellow. Birds from Isla Coiba are small and drab. **HABITS** Midstory to subcanopy in semi-open areas including hedgerows, plantations, pastures, savannas, gardens, and mangroves. Typically stays hidden in dense foliage even when vocalizing persistently. Often sings from isolated tree or tall shrub. Solitary. Does not follow mixed flocks. Hops deliberately through vegetation, pausing frequently to scan for prey. **VOICE** Sings throughout day. Song (1) a simple, hoarse, warbled phrase repeated for several minutes before switching suddenly to different phrase. Typical phrases include *chuweechawechawuuu* and *chechachuweeee* and *chipwheeuchuwoo*. Some phrases end with downslurred note. Calls include (2) a descending series of loud *weeeeuh* notes.

Chestnut-sided Shrike-Vireo *Vireolanius melitophrys*   16.5 cm

South MX and GT. Uncommon resident in highlands (800 to 3500 m) of GT. Rare and local on Caribbean slope (Alta Verapaz, Baja Verapaz, Quiché, El Progreso, 229). **ID** Large. Heavy, hooked bill and pale eyes. Complex head pattern with *dark eye stripe* and *narrow dark malar*. Female has gray (not blackish) eye stripe and paler, less distinct cinnamon breast-band and flanks. **HABITS** Midstory to canopy and edge of broadleaf and pine-oak forest, second growth, and plantations. Favors oak-dominated ridgetops in more humid areas. Hops deliberately through foliage. May perch motionless for long periods. Solitary or in pairs. May follow mixed flocks. **VOICE** Calls (1) a downslurred, slightly nasal *reeeeeah* or *reeeeeear* or *wheeeeeeer*. Sometimes given persistently in series or followed by a scolding chatter *reeeeeah cha-cha-cha-cha . . .* Also (2) a hawk-like, burry or squeaky scream *wheeeeeeu* or *wheeeeur*.

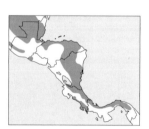

Green Shrike-Vireo *Vireolanius pulchellus*   14 cm

South MX and CA. Fairly common resident in lowlands and foothills (to 1000, locally to 1800 m). Most common in Caribbean lowlands. Uncommon in Pacific GT. Rare and local in SV (Ahuachapán, 619). **ID** Bulky and short-tailed with heavy, hooked bill. *Green with yellow throat.* Imm has broad yellow malar, faint pale supercilium, and is slightly duller overall. **GV** Birds from north CA have entirely blue crown and pale olive underparts. Birds from south (e.g., CR) tend to have less extensive and lighter blue head markings that are restricted to the forehead and nape. Birds from PA have blue confined to nape. **HABITS** Subcanopy to canopy of semihumid to humid broadleaf forest. May forage lower in gaps or vine tangles. Difficult to locate in dense foliage even when vocalizing persistently. Pairs or solitary birds occasionally follow mixed flocks. **VOICE** Song (1) a short (three- to five-note) series of loud, clear, whistled notes *cheer-cheercheer* or *peeter peeter peeter peeter*. Individual notes usually downslurred but some birds in central PA give upslurred notes. Often repeated persistently. Compare with song of Red-crowned Ant-Tanager. Infrequently heard calls include (2) high-pitched, harsh, scolding notes.

Yellow-browed Shrike-Vireo *Vireolanius eximius*   14 cm

CA and north SA. Uncommon in lowlands and foothills (SL to 1000, but mainly above 500 m) of east PA where reported from Pirre Massif and Cerro Quia (Darién, 519). **ID** Green with *yellow supercilium and throat*. Green Shrike-Vireo (thought to be allopatric) lacks yellow supercilium. **HABITS** Subcanopy to canopy of humid broadleaf forest. Like Green Shrike-Vireo. **VOICE** Song (1) a rapid series of four to five loud, upslurred, whistled notes *chwee? chwee? chwee? chwee?* or *wheet wheet wheet weet*. Resembles song of Green Shrike Vireo in tone and rhythm but individual notes upslurred and song phrases with four or five notes (three in Green Shrike-Vireo).

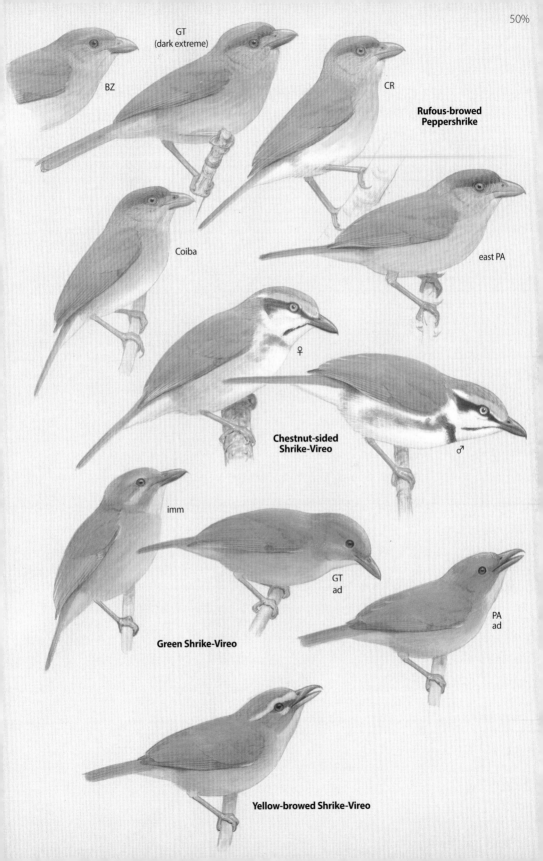

50%

GT
(dark extreme)

BZ

CR

**Rufous-browed
Peppershrike**

Coiba

east PA

♀

**Chestnut-sided
Shrike-Vireo**

♂

imm

GT
ad

Green Shrike-Vireo

PA
ad

Yellow-browed Shrike-Vireo

GREENLETS Vireonidae

Smaller relatives of the vireos. Some are range restricted. Lesser Greenlet is very common and widespread and is often seen with mixed flocks in upper levels of broadleaf forest. It is useful to recognize Lesser Greenlet, which is relatively drab and plain, by structure, size, and voice.

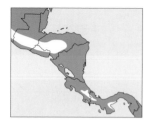

Lesser Greenlet *Pachysylvia decurtata* 9.5–10.5 cm

South MX to north SA. Common to very common resident in lowlands and foothills (to 1500 m). **ID** Small and short-tailed with fine bill and *whitish eye ring*. Note plain, mostly white or light gray underparts including crissum. Widespread form has gray crown and nape contrasting with olive-green mantle. Compare with Tennessee Warbler. Note different structure and head pattern. Also compare with Nashville Warbler. Note different structure and underparts pattern. **GV** Birds from central and east PA have olive crown. **HABITS** Subcanopy to canopy and edge of broadleaf forest, tall second growth, and shaded plantations. Descends to lower levels in vegetation at gaps or in deciduous forest. Forages actively, often in terminal foliage. Sometimes hangs from underside of twigs or clings to clusters of dead leaves. Pairs or solitary birds follow mixed flocks. **VOICE** Sings persistently throughout the day. Song (1) a short, slurred phrase repeated monotonously at two- or three-second intervals *dedjjeep dedjjeep dejjeep . . .* or *chechawee chechawee chechawee . . .* or varied slightly *teecheea teechup teechea . . .* Call (2) a short, rapid series of harsh, nasal, scolding notes *jeh-jehjeh . . .* or *cheer-cheer-cheer . . .*

Golden-fronted Greenlet *Pachysylvia aurantiifrons* 12 cm

North SA and PA. Uncommon to locally fairly common resident in semihumid Pacific lowlands of PA. **ID** Relatively long-tailed. Rounded crown may appear shaggy. Long bill with mostly dull pinkish mandible. Mostly plain dull brownish-olive above and plain dull buff below. Note *yellowish forehead* grading to light brown on crown and *dark eyes*. Vaguely resembles Tawny-crowned Greenlet. Note different eye color and habits. Also compare with Scrub Greenlet. **HABITS** Understory to midstory of scrub and low second growth. Forages actively in foliage. **VOICE** Call (1) a three- to five-note whistled phrase *cheetsacheeyou*. Compare with Lesser Greenlet.

Scrub Greenlet *Hylophilus flavipes* 12.5 cm

CA and north SA. Uncommon to locally fairly common resident in south Pacific lowlands and foothills (to 450, rarely or locally to 1000 m). Poorly known in CR (Puntarenas, 600, 114). Also Isla Coiba off PA (Veraguas, 653, 470). **ID** Relatively long-tailed. *Pale eyes* and *pinkish bill*. Drab with yellow underparts and grayish throat. In PA compare with Golden-fronted Greenlet. **GV** Birds from Isla Coiba are darker below. **HABITS** Midstory of scrub, low second growth, plantations, and brushy areas. Forages by gleaning from foliage. Typically moves more slowly and deliberately than other greenlets. Solitary or in pairs. **VOICE** Loud, distinctive song (1) a simple phrase of slurred or double notes *cheree cheree cheree* or *chi-cheer chi-cheer chi-cheer chi-cheer* or *tuwee tuwee tuwee . . .* repeated rapidly ten to twenty times. Calls include (2) harsh, nasal, buzzy or scratchy notes.

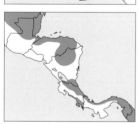

Tawny-crowned Greenlet *Tunchiornis ochraceiceps* 11.5 cm

South MX to SA. Uncommon resident in lowlands and foothills (to 1300 m). **ID** Slightly bushy *rufous crown* and *pale gray eyes*. In south compare with Scrub Greenlet. Note different habits. Also compare with female *Myrmotherula* antwrens, which are similar in size and color and often with same mixed flock. **GV** Birds from central and east PA are more olive. **HABITS** Understory to midstory of semihumid to humid broadleaf forest. Forages actively by gleaning invertebrates from foliage, vine tangles, or dead leaf clusters. Pairs or solitary birds typically follow mixed flocks that may include antwrens and various small tyrannids. **VOICE** Calls (1) a series of harsh, nasal, scolding notes *nya nya nya nya . . .* or *eehn eehn eehn eehn . . .* and (2) single, clear, flat whistle *deeeeee* or *feeeeee*. In east PA compare with call of Stripe-throated Wren.

widespread

Lesser Greenlet

central and
east PA

Golden-fronted Greenlet

Scrub Greenlet

Coiba

mainland

Tawny-crowned Greenlet

widespread

central and
east PA

VIREOS Vireonidae

Small insectivores including Nearctic breeding migrant and breeding resident species. Vireos may vocalize throughout the day and are usually first detected by voice.

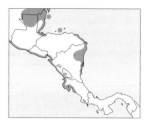

Mangrove Vireo *Vireo pallens*   11.5 cm

South MX and CA. Locally common resident in Caribbean lowlands. Mainly near coasts but ranges inland in BZ, GT (Petén, 229), and Caribbean NI (RAAN, RAAS, 413). Also BZ Cays (529, 343), Bay Islands, and Cayos Cochinos (94, 442, 622, 478). Uncommon and local in Pacific CR (Guanacaste, 478). **ID** Dull *pinkish bill*. Note *broad pale supraloral* and light brown eyes. White-eyed Vireo has different underparts and (usually) pale eyes. **GV** Birds from north Pacific CA are more yellowish. Birds from south Pacific slope in CR are grayer. Caribbean slope birds are more olive. **HABITS** Midstory of arid to semihumid second growth, scrub, gallery forest, littoral woodland, and mangroves. Confined mainly to mangroves in south. Forages actively but often remains hidden in dense foliage. Solitary or in pairs. Does not follow mixed flocks. Sings throughout day. **VOICE** Song (1) a flat, mechanical *jee-jee-jee-jee* or *jew-jew-jew-jew*. Also (2) a dry, flat rattle and (3) dry, nasal, downslurred *waaaaah*.

White-eyed Vireo *Vireo griseus*   12 cm

Breeds Nearctic. Winters south USA to WI and CA. Uncommon transient and winter visitor (Sep to May) in north Caribbean lowlands and foothills (to 1500, mainly below 750 m). Locally fairly common on Caribbean islands including Bay Islands (442). Rare in north Pacific slope and in south CA (229, 302). **ID** *Whitish eyes*, black bill, dusky lores, and *yellow spectacles*. Olive crown and mantle contrast with grayish nape. Underparts whitish with yellow flanks. Juv has dark eyes. Compare with Mangrove Vireo. Note different head pattern and ad's different eye color. **HABITS** Understory to subcanopy and edge of arid to semihumid broadleaf forest, littoral woodland, plantations, gardens, second growth, and mangroves. Forages deliberately in foliage. Solitary. May follow mixed flocks. **VOICE** Sings throughout year. Song (1) a variable, short phrase. Usually begins and ends with sharp *chip* or *tchk* note *tchk iweedle-iwee chik* or *chur di-wer chik*. Compare with call of Yellow-throated Euphonia. Also (2) a nasal scold *sheh-sheh-sheh-sheh . . .* or *jehjehjehjeh . . .*

Bell's Vireo *Vireo bellii*   11.5 cm

Mainly Nearctic. Winters MX and CA. Rare winter resident in lowlands and foothills (to 1500 m) of GT and SV. Vagrant to HN (Valle, Francisco Morazán, Atlántida, 442, 346), NI (Matagalpa, 413), and CR (San José, 346). **ID** Small with relatively long tail (often flicked or cocked). Note *diffuse, broken, whitish eye ring, whitish supraloral*, and dark lores. Usually has two whitish wingbars (upper sometimes indistinct). Mandible usually dull pinkish. Compare with Warbling Vireo. Note different wing pattern. **HABITS** Understory to midstory of semihumid scrub, forest edge, and second growth. Forages actively in foliage. Solitary. May follow mixed flocks. **VOICE** Song (1) a complex, rapid, scratchy or squeaky warbled phrase. Compare with song of White-eyed Vireo (mainly allopatric). Call (2) a very rapid, nasal, scolding *sheh-sheh-sheh-sheh . . .* or *chih-chih-chih-chih . . .*

Plumbeous Vireo *Vireo plumbeus*   12.5 cm

USA to CA. Uncommon to locally fairly common resident in north foothills and highlands (800 to 2500 m). Uncommon to rare in lowlands and foothills of south BZ (Cayo, 636, 529, 343). Rare in SV (Morazán, 346) and NI (Estelí, 419). Nearctic birds perhaps occur as winter visitors. **ID** Rounded crown. Gray crown and auriculars and *white spectacles*. Note *dull olive mantle*. Underparts grayish white with *faint olive wash on flanks*. Blue-headed Vireo more richly colored on head and flanks and has slightly bolder, more contrasting white spectacles and throat. **HABITS** Midstory to canopy of semihumid broadleaf or pine-oak forest, second growth, plantations, and gardens. Forages deliberately in foliage. Solitary or in pairs. Follows mixed flocks. **VOICE** Song (1) a slow series of short warbled phrases. Similar to Blue-headed Vireo. Scolding calls (2) similar to Blue-headed Vireo.

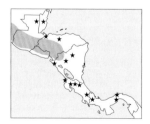

Blue-headed Vireo *Vireo solitarius*   13 cm

Breeds east Nearctic. Winters south USA to CA. Uncommon transient and winter resident (Sep to May) in north Pacific and interior highlands. Rare visitor to north Caribbean and south CA. **ID** Rounded crown. Mostly blue-gray head, white throat, and bright olive mantle. *Bold white spectacles*. Flanks yellow-olive. Compare with Plumbeous Vireo. **HABITS** Midstory to canopy of semihumid to humid forest, second growth, plantations, and gardens. Forages deliberately in foliage. Solitary. Follows mixed flocks. **VOICE** Sings in spring passage. Song (1) a slow, deliberate series of sweet, warbled phrases. Call (2) an accelerating, scolding chatter *sheh, cheh-cheh-cheh-chehcheh . . .* or *shih, ch-chi-ch-chi-ch-chi-ch-chi*. Compare with Yellow-throated Vireo. Also (3) single *shehr* or *sheihr*.

50%

north Pacific

Mangrove Vireo

Pacific HN
to CR

Caribbean

White-eyed Vireo

juv

ad

Bell's Vireo

Plumbeous Vireo

Blue-headed Vireo

VIREOS Vireonidae

Smaller vireos. Some are range-restricted in highlands. Details of the head pattern are useful in separating these. Ruby-crowned Kinglet is shown here for comparison with Hutton's Vireo (see text and map, page 414). Philadelphia Vireo, a Nearctic migrant, is generally the most common and widespread.

Hutton's Vireo *Vireo huttoni*   12 cm

USA to CA. Uncommon resident in highlands (1800 to 3800 m) of GT. Rare in SV (Santa Ana, 346), HN (Ocotepeque, Francisco Morazán, 346), and NI (Estelí, 346, 419) where status uncertain. A report from BZ is erroneous (Cayo, 529, but see 490 and 311). **ID** Small and large-headed. Grayish-olive above and drab whitish-olive below with two bold white wingbars. Note *pale lores and broken whitish eye ring*. May suggest an *Empidonax* flycatcher but note horizontal posture, dark, hooked bill, and rounded head shape. Compare with Ruby-crowned Kinglet. **HABITS** Midstory and edge of broadleaf and pine-oak forest. Forages actively. Solitary or in pairs. Follows mixed flocks. **VOICE** Song (1) a repeated, nasal, two-syllable *siree* or *chur-reee*. Call (2) a scolding *jehr* or *rreah* often followed by a rapid, descending series *rreah heh-heh-heh-heh*.

Yellow-winged Vireo *Vireo carmioli*   12 cm

CA endemic. Fairly common resident in highlands (above 2000 m) of CR and west PA. Reported east to Cerro Santiago (Veraguas, 346). May move to lower elevations outside breeding season (600). **ID** Small. Mostly *yellow below*. Note pale yellowish-white wingbars, broad supercilium, and *mark below eye*. No other CA Vireo is so extensively yellow. **HABITS** Midstory to canopy and edge of humid broadleaf (cloud) forest and paramo shrubbery. Solitary birds or pairs follow mixed flocks. **VOICE** Song (1) a series of short, high-pitched, warbled phrases of two or three notes separated by long pauses. Often with slurred, burry notes *viree chichui chuyee* or *viree viree cheeyu* or *viree witchum viree witchum*. Compare with song of Brown-capped Vireo. Calls include (2) a nasal *psseu*, (3) oriole-like *chwick*, and (4) short, dry chatter.

Brown-capped Vireo *Vireo leucophrys*   11.5 cm

MX to SA. Uncommon to fairly common resident in highlands and foothills (mainly 1200 to 2500, locally as low as 750 m in north). Uncommon to rare in Pacific GT and SV (Santa Ana, 619, 229, 364). Perhaps most widespread in north Caribbean highlands. Poorly known in east PA at Cerro Mali (Darién, 659). **ID** *Brown crown* and diffuse, grayish-white supercilium. Resembles Warbling Vireo. Note different crown color. Also compare with Philadelphia Vireo. Note different head pattern. **HABITS** Midstory to canopy and edge of humid broadleaf (cloud) and pine-oak forest. Pairs or solitary birds follow mixed flocks. Gleans actively from foliage. **VOICE** Song (1) rich or slightly scratchy warbled phrases. Often with upslurred ending. More liquid than song of Warbling Vireo. Compare with song of Golden-crowned Warbler. Call (2) a nasal, upslurred *meiiihk* or *rreeeih* repeated several times. Similar to Warbling Vireo.

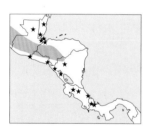

Warbling Vireo *Vireo gilvus*   13 cm

Breeds in Nearctic. Winters MX and CA. Uncommon to fairly common transient and winter resident (Sep to May) in north Pacific and interior. Rare in north Caribbean slope and in south. **ID** May raise shaggy crown. *Gray crown* and diffuse whitish supercilium. Note *pale lores*. Underparts usually whitish but some have pale yellow flanks. Compare with Brown-capped Vireo. Also compare with Philadelphia Vireo. Note different head pattern and underparts. **HABITS** Midstory to canopy of semihumid to humid forest, second growth, plantations, and gardens. Solitary. Follows mixed flocks. **VOICE** Song (1) a series of slightly scratchy or hoarse warbled phrases. Calls (2) a harsh, nasal *rreeeih* or *nyeeah* often repeated and (3) dry, clipped *chif*. May be repeated as a short chatter *ch-ch-ch*. Similar to Brown-capped Vireo.

Philadelphia Vireo *Vireo philadelphicus*   12.5 cm

Breeds Nearctic. Winters mainly CA. Uncommon to fairly common transient and winter resident (mainly Oct to May) in lowlands and foothills (to 1600, rarely to 2300 m). Most common in Pacific foothills (900 to 1500 m) of CR and west PA. Also Isla Coiba (Veraguas, 659). **ID** *Pale yellow breast and crissum*. Note *dark lores* and whitish supercilium. Upperparts olive becoming gray on crown. Red-eyed Vireo has heavier bill, different head pattern, and red eyes. Compare with Tennessee Warbler. Note different bill shape. Also compare with Warbling and Brown-capped vireos. **HABITS** Midstory to canopy and edge of humid broadleaf forest, tall second growth, shaded plantations, and gardens. Gleans from foliage and takes nectar at flowering trees. Forages more actively than larger vireos, sometimes briefly hanging or fluttering. Follows mixed flocks. **VOICE** Usually quiet. May give (1) a soft, downslurred *cheeur* or *ch-ch-cheeur*.

Hutton's Vireo

Yellow-winged Vireo

Ruby-crowned Kinglet
for comparison
(text and map, p. 414)

Brown-capped Vireo

Warbling Vireo

Philadelphia Vireo

VIREOS Vireonidae

Larger vireos. Yellow-green Vireo is generally the most common and widespread, and it is among a handful of Central American breeding species that withdraw to South America in winter. The Nearctic breeding Red-eyed Vireo can be briefly common in migration.

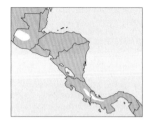

Yellow-throated Vireo *Vireo flavifrons* 13.5 cm

Breeds east Nearctic. Winters MX and CA to SA. Fairly common transient and winter resident (mainly Sep to Apr) in lowlands and foothills (to 1700 m, higher in migration). Most common in north Caribbean. Rare in north Pacific. **ID** *Yellow throat and breast* contrast with white lower underparts and gray wings. Note *yellow spectacles* and white wingbars. **HABITS** Upper midstory to canopy and edge of broadleaf and pine-oak forest, pine woodland, second growth, shaded plantations, and gardens. Forages deliberately in foliage. Solitary. Follows mixed flocks. **VOICE** Song (1) a varied, halting series of rich, or slightly hoarse phrases *ch-i-ree chr-eu, chi-wi, chu-ee-u chi chu-u-ree...* Call (2) a nasal, often accelerating series *shi chi-chi-chi-chi-chi*. Compare with Blue-headed Vireo. Also (3) a buzzy, rasping *kzzchik*.

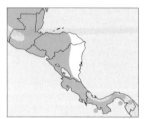

Yellow-green Vireo *Vireo flavoviridis* 14 cm

MX to SA. Winters SA. Fairly common transient and breeding visitor (mainly Feb to Oct, 209, 451, 485) in lowlands and foothills (to 1500 m). Also Isla Coiba and Pearl Islands off PA (Veraguas, Panamá, 649, 470). **ID** Fairly heavy bill. Note gray crown, dark lores, and diffuse whitish supercilium. *Sides of breast, flanks, and crissum yellowish.* Yellowish often extends to neck and auriculars. Eyes red (brown in imm). Resembles Red-eyed Vireo. Note different underparts and less contrasting head pattern. **HABITS** Midstory to canopy and edge in arboreal habitats including broadleaf forest, second growth, plantations and gardens. Hops deliberately through foliage. Solitary or in pairs. Vocalizes throughout day. **VOICE** Song (1) a series of short, clipped, warbled phrases repeated persistently. Higher-pitched and sweeter than Red-eyed Vireo. Call (2) a nasal *whaaaaa* or *eeeeehhh* sometimes repeated.

Red-eyed Vireo *Vireo olivaceus* 14 cm

NA and (disjunctly) SA. Nearctic birds winter SA. Common transient (mainly Mar to May and Aug to Oct). May be briefly or locally abundant in Caribbean lowlands and foothills (to 1500 m, sometimes higher in migration). Fairly common transient in north Pacific. Very rare in winter with records from CR (Guanacaste, 574) and PA (Darién, Panamá, 512). **ID** Fairly heavy bill. Upperparts plain olive. Whitish supercilium contrasts with gray crown and dark eye stripe. Note dark lores and *mostly whitish underparts* (rarely with faint greenish-yellow on crissum). Eyes red (brown in imm). Philadelphia Vireo has shorter bill and less contrasting crown. **HABITS** Midstory to canopy and edge of forest, second growth, plantations, and gardens. Forages deliberately in foliage. May form small flocks or follow mixed flocks. **VOICE** Usually quiet. Spring transients may sing. Song (1) similar to Yellow-green Vireo but phrases longer. Call (2) a nasal, scolding *nyaa*.

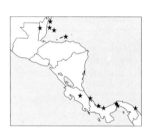

Black-whiskered Vireo *Vireo altiloquus* 14.5 cm

Breeds mainly WI. Winters north SA. Rare transient in Caribbean coastal lowlands and islands of BZ (529, 343, 346, 341), Bay Islands off HN (346), CR (Cartago, Limón, 602, 343, 346), and PA (Ngäbe-Buglé, Panamá, Colón, Kuna Yala, 659, 48). Most records from spring (Mar to May) but also recorded Sep and Oct. Very rare inland. **ID** Fairly long, heavy bill. *Dark streak at sides of throat.* Eyes dark brown. Upperparts brownish-olive. *Underparts drab whitish.* Compare with Red-eyed and Yellow-green vireos. Note different head pattern and underparts. In north compare with Yucatan Vireo. **HABITS** Midstory to subcanopy and edge of mangroves, littoral scrub, and gardens. Forages deliberately in foliage. **VOICE** Song (1) a series of two- or three-syllable phrases *chee-ip chip chuwee feeup, chiip-feeup chillip*. Sharper and less slurred than song of Red-eyed Vireo. Calls (2) a nasal *whaaaaa* like Red-eyed and Yellow-green vireos and (3) a slightly hoarse *vwirr* or *chweer* like Veery. Also (4) a rapid, high-pitched chatter *chi-i-i-i* and (5) short, low-pitched *gwit*.

Yucatan Vireo *Vireo magister* 14.5 cm

South MX, WI, and north CA. Uncommon and local resident in coastal lowlands of BZ and BZ Cays (529). Also Bay Islands and Cayos Cochinos (442, 622, 560). Perhaps undertakes local or seasonal movements. **ID** Large. *Heavy bill. Drab and brownish* with broad whitish supercilium. *Eyes brown.* Compare with Mangrove Vireo (often syntopic). Note different head pattern. Black-whiskered Vireo has similar structure. Note different head pattern. **HABITS** Midstory to subcanopy and edge of mangroves, second growth, littoral forest, scrub, plantations, and gardens. Forages deliberately in foliage. **VOICE** Song (1) a variable, slow, halting series of rich, warbled phrases. Some phrases repeated *chweu-chweu, chwee? che-wee che-wee, chewee? cheuu...* Compare with faster, higher-pitched song of Yellow-green Vireo. Calls (2) a soft, dry chatter *shi tchi-chi-chi-chi...* like Yellow-green Vireo and (3) sharp, slightly nasal *beenk* or *peek*.

Yellow-throated Vireo

Yellow-green Vireo

Red-eyed Vireo

Black-whiskered Vireo

Yucatan Vireo

JAYS Corvidae

Large, sometimes noisy birds found locally in middle or upper levels of humid forests in highlands. Usually seen in groups. Azure-hooded Jay is the most widespread of these species.

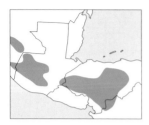

Steller's Jay *Cyanocitta stelleri*   29 cm
NA to CA. Uncommon to locally common resident in north highlands (mainly above 1500 m). Very rare and poorly known in SV (Chalatenango, 634, 408). **ID** *Pointed crest.* Ad mostly deep blue with blackish sides of head, grayish throat, and *dark barring on wing coverts, tertials, and tail.* Note whitish eye crescents. Juv grayer (especially below) with less distinctly barred tail and may lack ad's white facial markings. No other CA jay has pointed crest or barred wings and tail. **HABITS** Midstory to canopy and edge of coniferous and mixed pine-oak forest. May forage on ground in open areas. Usually in pairs or small groups. Sometimes follows mixed flocks that include other corvids. **VOICE** Calls (1) a harsh, repeated *shaaak shaaak shaaak shaaak*, (2) mellow, liquid *klook klook*, and (3) variety of shrill squeaks, squawks, clicks and rattles . . .

Unicolored Jay *Aphelocoma unicolor*   33–35 cm
South MX and north CA. Uncommon to rare local resident in highlands (1200 to 3400, mainly above 1500 m) of GT (Quiché, Quetzaltenango, Totonicapán, Baja Verapaz, Zacapa, 232), HN (Atlántida, Olancho, Lempira, 346), and north SV (Chalatenango, Santa Ana, 635, 183, 619, 364). Rare in north NI (Nueva Segovia, 412). **ID** Ad *uniform, rich blue with darker face.* Eyes reddish-brown. Subad may retain yellow bill. **GV** Birds from SV and HN are more purplish-blue than birds from GT. **HABITS** Midstory to subcanopy of humid broadleaf, coniferous, or mixed pine-oak forest. Hops heavily over larger limbs inspecting epiphytes and foliage. Sometimes follows mixed flocks. May associate with Azure-hooded and Black-throated jays. **VOICE** Loud, ringing calls include (1) an abrupt, two- or three-syllable *zhang-zhangzhang* or *chink-chink*, often repeated, and (2) longer, slightly nasal, one-syllable *eeeeeye.* May be repeated. May suggest Azure-hooded Jay.

Black-throated Jay *Cyanolyca pumilo*   24 cm
South MX and north CA. Uncommon and local resident in highlands (1450 to 3200, but mainly above 1800 m) of GT and HN (Ocotepeque, Copán, Francisco Morazán, La Paz, Olancho). Rare, local and poorly known in north SV (Chalatenango, Santa Ana, 635, 619, 364, 346). **ID** Small. Mostly plain deep blue with *black on forehead, sides of head, and throat.* Note *narrow whitish supercilium* extending across forecrown and contrasting with black forehead. Azure-hooded Jay (often syntopic) has similar structure and pattern. Note different crown and nape color. **HABITS** Midstory to subcanopy of humid broadleaf and coniferous forest. Hops heavily along branches investigating epiphytes. May follow mixed flocks that include Unicolored or Azure-hooded jays. **VOICE** Calls often rapidly repeated including (1) a scratchy, relatively high-pitched *jaajaajaa* or *jaaajaaa*, (2) a squeaky *kirwik-kirwik-kirwik* or *erwik erwik erwik*, and (3) lower-pitched *errrrrrr-eh.*

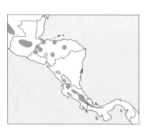

Azure-hooded Jay *Cyanolyca cucullata*   29–32 cm
South MX and CA. Uncommon resident in highlands (800 to 2100 m). **ID** Black sides of head, throat, and breast contrast with white supercilium and *pale blue crown and nape.* In north compare with Black-throated Jay. **GV** Birds from GT are larger and have more extensive white on crown and neck. Birds from HN are bluer (less purple). **HABITS** Midstory to canopy and edge of humid broadleaf and humid mixed pine-oak forest and adjacent tall second growth. Pairs or small groups range through wet, epiphyte-laden forest. Occasionally descends to understory. May attend ant swarms. **VOICE** Calls (1) a loud, abrupt, grating *jeet-jeet* or *djeeek-djeeek-djeeek* and (2) attenuated *errrrrreh* or *errrrrr-eh.* In north compare with call of Unicolored Jay. Other calls (3) a dry, raucous *raaaah* and (4) soft, clear, upslurred *woyt* or *ehrt.*

Silvery-throated Jay *Cyanolyca argentigula*   26 cm
CA endemic. Uncommon to rare and local resident in highlands (2000 to 3200 m) of east CR (Cartago, Limón, 667, 600) and west PA (Chiriquí, 659). **ID** Small. Dark violet-blue becoming *blackish on crown*, sides of head, and breast. Note *pale throat and narrow supercilium.* Juv duller and lacks pale supercilium. Azure-hooded Jay (may be locally syntopic but mainly lower elevations) has similar structure and habits. Note Azure-hooded's black throat. **GV** Birds from east CR and west PA have pale violet throat. Birds from central CR (e.g., Volcán Turrialba and Volcán Irazú) have nearly white throat. **HABITS** Subcanopy of tall, humid broadleaf (oak) forest. Occasionally descends to midstory at forest edge or in openings. Usually in pairs or small groups. Sometimes in flocks of up to thirty. **VOICE** Calls (1) a harsh, nasal, somewhat scratchy *jew-jeah-jeah* or *jeeh-jeeh-jeeh*, (2) single *nyaaaah*, (3) harsher, scolding *zhraaak*, and (4) short series of two to four sharper calls *nyat nyat nyat.*

Steller's Jay

Unicolored Jay

juv

GT
ad

SV and
HN ad

Azure-hooded
Jay

GT

HN

Black-throated Jay

Silvery-throated Jay

CR and PA

central CR

east CR and
west PA

JAYS Corvidae

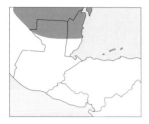

Yucatan Jay *Cyanocorax yucatanicus*   33 cm

South MX and CA. Uncommon to locally fairly common resident in Caribbean lowlands of north GT (Petén) and BZ. **ID** Ad has *black head and underparts* contrasting sharply with *blue upperparts and tail*. Legs yellow-orange. Imm has yellow eye ring and bill. Juv (Jul to Sep) has white head and underparts. Imm and juv have white tips on rectrices. Bushy-crested Jay allopatric. **HABITS** Midstory and edge of arid to semihumid broadleaf and pine-oak woodland, stunted or seasonally flooded woodland, second growth, plantations, and scrub. Often noisy and conspicuous. In pairs or small groups. **VOICE** Calls (1) a harsh, dry, slightly buzzy chatter *eheheheheheheh . . .* often given in chorus by groups, (2) a two- or three-note, dry, hollow *chuduk-chuduk* or *eew-duk*, and (3) mellower *rrauwk*. Reported to mimic predators and may give calls suggesting Collared Forest-Falcon.

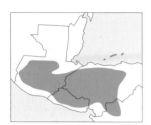

Bushy-crested Jay *Cyanocorax melanocyaneus*   31–33 cm

CA endemic. Common resident in north foothills and highlands (mainly 600 to 2500 m, rarely or locally lower). Also Pacific volcanic highlands of SV (San Miguel, La Libertad, Santa Ana, San Vicente, Santa Ana, 183, 341). **ID** *Black head, neck, and breast* contrast sharply with *blue upperparts and tail*. Note ad's *yellow eyes*. Legs dusky. Juv has yellow bill and dark eyes. Yucatan Jay allopatric. **GV** Birds from east HN and NI are variably darker. **HABITS** Arid to semihumid broadleaf and pine-oak forest and edge, second growth, scrub, and plantations. Forages at all levels in vegetation and sometimes descends to ground along roadsides and in clearings. Often noisy and conspicuous. May follow mixed flocks. **VOICE** Calls, often given by groups in chorus, include (1) a rapid, buzzy, high-pitched *eep-eep-eep-eeep* or *eeh-eeh-eeh-eeh* or *kreep, kreep, kreep* or *kwarrr-kreep, kreep, kreep*. Contact call (2) a liquid *puilik*. Juvs may give (3) a *nyah* call similar to call of Black-vented Oriole.

Green Jay *Cyanocorax yncas*   28 cm

South Texas to CA. Uncommon and local resident in north Caribbean lowlands and foothills (to 1500 m). Most widespread in north GT (Petén) and BZ. Uncommon and local in Pacific and interior lowlands and foothills (to 800 m) of GT (Huehuetenango, Retalhuleu, Suchitepéquez, Escuintla, 539, 164, 229, 279) and north central HN (Atlántida, Yoro, 442, 346). Reports from north NI (RAAN, 412) require verification. **ID** *Green above* with black throat. Note *yellow outer rectrices* and yellow eyes. **GV** Birds from Pacific GT are more greenish below. **HABITS** Midstory to subcanopy and edge of arid to semihumid broadleaf and pine-oak forest, savanna, scrub, and gallery woodland. Locally in mangroves. Usually in groups. Forages actively while hopping heavily through vegetation. May follow mixed flocks that include orioles, saltators, and other large songbirds. **VOICE** Calls, sometimes given in rapid succession, or in chorus by groups include (1) a harsh *cha-cha-cha . . .* or *jeh-eh-eh-eh*, (2) loud, clear, metallic *chenk chenk chenk* or *jink-jink-jink* or *clink-clinkclink*, (3) drier, scolding *cheh-cheh-cheep . . .* (4) buzzier, nasal scolding *jeeeehr jihjihjihjih . . .* and (5) long rattle that drops steeply in pitch *ahrrrrrrrrr* or *eee-ahrrrrrrrr*.

Black-chested Jay *Cyanocorax affinis*   36 cm

CA and north SA. Uncommon to locally fairly common resident in lowlands and foothills (to 1600 m) of east CR (Puntarenas, Limón) and PA. **ID** Large and robust. *Blackish head and chest* contrast with creamy white lower underparts. Note prominent *pale yellow eyes*, blue spot above eye, and *broad white terminal band* on tail. Upperparts plain, dull purplish-blue. Juv (not shown) slightly duller above and lacks blue markings on head. **HABITS** Understory to subcanopy and edge of humid broadleaf forest, second growth, adjacent clearings, shaded plantations, and gardens. Often noisy and conspicuous. Makes swooping flights between trees in semi-open areas. Usually in small groups. **VOICE** Calls (1) a short series of loud, ringing, metallic notes *chowng, chowng chowng* or *kyoo-kyoo-kyoo* or *eyuk-yuk-yuk*, (2) short, sharp, woodpecker-like rattle *ehkehkehkehk*, (3) querulous, nasal, descending *ehhhhha*, and (4) clear, descending *cheeeuw* sometimes doubled as *cheeeuw cheeeuw*.

30%

Yucatan Jay

juv

imm

ad

Bushy-crested Jay

GT
ad

HN and NI
ad

juv

Green Jay

widespread

Pacific GT

Black-chested Jay

JAYS AND RAVEN Corvidae

Large corvids. All have loud, distinctive vocalizations. Brown Jay and White-throated Magpie-Jay are common and widespread.

Brown Jay *Psilorhinus morio*   42 cm

South Texas to CA. Common resident in lowlands and foothills (to 1500, rarely or locally to 2500 m). **ID** Large and long-tailed. Mostly *plain, drab brown* with variably contrasting *plain whitish lower underparts*. Note *whitish tips on outer rectrices*. Bill black in ad and variably yellow in imm. Young birds have yellow eye ring. **HABITS** Uses a wide range of arboreal habitats in mainly semi-open or disturbed areas including forest edge, second growth, scrub, plantations, gardens, and settled areas. Usually at upper and middle levels in vegetation but occasionally descends to forage on ground. Often in groups. Very noisy and conspicuous. **VOICE** Groups call in riotous chorus. Typically repeats (1) a very loud, slightly hollow phrase with abrupt, explosive, popping quality *pwow pwow pwow . . .* or *pam pam pam . . .*

White-throated Magpie-Jay *Calocitta formosa*   48 cm

South MX and CA. Common resident in Pacific lowlands and foothills (to 1400 m). Local on Caribbean slope in north. Expanding to Caribbean slope in west CR. **ID** Large. *Very long, graduated tail* and long, curled crest. Ad mostly pale blue above with plain white lower underparts. White throat and sides of head contrast with *long black crest* and variable *black neck stripe extending to narrow breast-band*. Juv has less distinct head markings. **HABITS** Midstory to canopy and edge of arid to semihumid woodland, pastures with scattered trees or hedgerows, scrub, and gardens. Often in pairs. May form groups. Noisy and conspicuous. **VOICE** Calls (1) a very harsh, grating, upslurred *reeek?* (2) hollow *t'chope,* (3) very harsh, guttural, scolding *raah* or *reeah* often repeated and often given in chorus by several birds, (4) low, rolling *tee-trrrrr tee-trrrrr,* and (5) smooth, whistled *weeeeechup, wheeeechup, chu?*

Common Raven *Corvus corax*   62 cm

Mainly Holarctic. Rare and local resident in north foothills and highlands (SL to 3700, mainly above 1000 m). Few recent records from GT where historically reported to be common and widespread (Huehuetenango, Quiché, Quetzaltenango, Sololá, Sacatepéquez, Chimaltenango, Escuintla, Baja Verapaz, El Progresso, Zacapa, 232, 539, 57, 376, 279, 93). Similarly, few recent reports from HN where also formerly widespread (Choluteca, Francisco Morazán, Intibucá, Santa Bárbara, 603, 442, 346) and from SV where historically considered fairly common (Chalatenango, Morazán, San Miguel, Santa Ana, 183, 408, 364) in NI (San Rafael del Norte, Estelí, Jinotega, Matagalpa, 431, 453, 346) where historically reported south to Juigalpa (Chontales, 413). **ID** *Very large* with uniform, slightly glossy, black plumage. Note *heavy bill* and wedge-shaped tail. **HABITS** Favors steep, rocky terrain. Frequently soars, sometimes for long periods. Solitary or in pairs. Often attracted to carrion and sometimes seen scavenging on ground at roadsides. **VOICE** Often calls in flight. Call (1) a very low-pitched, croaking *rrok* or *rronk* or *rrrahk.* Juv's calls higher-pitched.

Brown Jay

juv

ad

White-throated Magpie-Jay

Common Raven

30%

18%

MARTINS Hirundinidae

Large, broad-winged swallows with forked tail. Found mainly in open areas. Details of the head and underparts pattern are useful in separating these. Gray-breasted Martin is the most common and widespread but Purple Martin can be briefly or locally abundant. Southern and Brown-chested martins are uncommon to very rare in the region.

Purple Martin *Progne subis*
19 cm

Breeds Nearctic. Winters SA. Locally (or briefly) common transient (mainly Feb to Apr and Aug to Oct) in Caribbean lowlands. May be briefly or locally abundant. Less common on Pacific slope. Vagrant to Isla del Coco (600). **ID** Large with broad wings. Tail forked. Ad male *uniform deep violet-blue* including underparts with blackish-brown wings. Ad female has *variably grayish collar, underparts, and forehead* (paler gray in west Nearctic breeding birds). Juv resembles female but has dusky upperparts and whitish crissum and lower underparts with narrow dark streaks. Compare female with Gray-breasted Martin. Note different head pattern. **HABITS** Open areas, especially near water. Transients can occur in a wide variety of open and semi-open habitats including savannas, agricultural fields and pastures, forest clearings, marshes, beaches, and urban areas. **VOICE** Song (1) a series of short, rich, low-pitched whistles with occasional drier, harsh notes *chew, chew-chew chew cheeeuw . . .* Calls (2) a harsh, downslurred *cherr*, sometimes given in series *cheep cherr cherr cherr*, (3) harsh, buzzy *geert* or *cheert*, and (4) dry *skrr*.

Southern Martin *Progne elegans*
20 cm

Breeds austral SA. Migrates to upper Amazonia (Apr to Oct). Perhaps a seasonal (Apr to Jul) visitor to PA. Known from one specimen and several sight records (Panamá, Colón, Kuna Yala, 208, 659). **ID** Large with broad wings. *Tail deeply forked.* Ad male *uniform deep violet-blue* including underparts with blackish-brown wings. Female violet-blue above with brownish flight feathers. Female's *underparts variably uniform brown or mostly brown with whitish scaling on flanks and belly.* Ad male closely resembles ad male Purple Martin (perhaps not separable in field) but has *longer and more deeply forked tail.* Female distinctive as no other female CA *Progne* martin is so uniformly dark below. **HABITS** Open and semi-open habitats including agricultural areas, forest clearings, marshes, and urban areas. May associate with Gray-breasted Martins. **VOICE** Calls (1) a low-pitched, rattling or trilled *drrrr* and (2) chattering *djiik-djiik-djiik . . .*

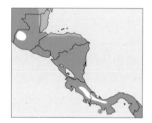

Gray-breasted Martin *Progne chalybea*
17 cm

MX to SA. Common in lowlands and foothills (to 1700 m). Status poorly known (489, 659, 347). In north Caribbean perhaps a breeding visitor (mainly Jan to Oct). On Pacific slope and in south a permanent resident. Also Isla Coiba off PA (Veraguas, 470). **ID** Large with broad wings. Tail forked. Ad male has violet-blue upperparts and blackish wings. *Grayish throat and breast* grade into plain white lower underparts. Female and juv have dull, brownish upperparts. In PA compare with Brown-chested Martin. Note different underparts. Also compare with female Purple Martin. Note different head pattern. **HABITS** Open and semi-open areas including agricultural fields, savannas, forest clearings, marshes, and urban areas. May gather in large numbers outside breeding season and often found resting in groups on utility wires. **VOICE** Song (1) a long series of rich, slightly liquid, gurgling notes *chr-chree chrrup chreee zreee ch-chr . . .* Call (2) a slightly buzzy *cheeup* or *tsee-up*.

Brown-chested Martin *Progne tapera*
17 cm

Breeds SA. Uncommon to rare but regular visitor (mainly Mar to Oct) to PA (201, 202, 659). Rare in CR (Alajuela, Puntarenas, San José, 602, 346). **ID** Large with broad wings. Tail forked. Both sexes mostly drab whitish below with *broad brownish breast-band* and central breast. Lower underparts whitish. Note white throat. Underparts pattern superficially similar to smaller Bank Swallow. Also compare with Gray-breasted Martin. Note different underparts. **HABITS** Open and semi-open areas including agricultural fields, forest clearings, marshes, and urban areas. Sometimes in large flocks. May associate with Gray-breasted Martins but perhaps more likely to perch in trees. Often near water. **VOICE** Song (1) a descending, liquid trill *treeee-uk or teeerrrr.* Calls (2) a dry, buzzy *djzeet* and (3) softer *dureet.*

Purple Martin

juv

subad
♂

typical
♀

dark
♀

♂

Southern Martin

♀

♀

♂

♀

Gray-breasted Martin

♀

♂

Brown-chested Martin

SWALLOWS Hirundinidae

Swallows with glossy or iridescent blue or green upperparts.

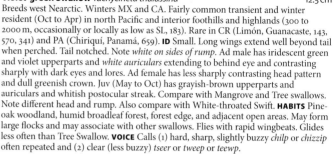

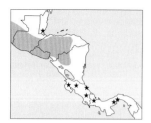

Violet-green Swallow *Tachycineta thalassina*   12.5 cm

Breeds west Nearctic. Winters MX and CA. Fairly common transient and winter resident (Oct to Apr) in north Pacific and interior foothills and highlands (300 to 2000 m, occasionally or locally as low as SL, 183). Rare in CR (Limón, Guanacaste, 143, 570, 341) and PA (Chiriquí, Panamá, 659). **ID** Small. Long wings extend well beyond tail when perched. Tail notched. Note *white on sides of rump*. Ad male has iridescent green and violet upperparts and *white auriculars* extending to behind eye and contrasting sharply with dark eyes and lores. Ad female has less sharply contrasting head pattern and dull greenish crown. Juv (May to Oct) has grayish-brown upperparts and auriculars and whitish postocular streak. Compare with Mangrove and Tree swallows. Note different head and rump. Also compare with White-throated Swift. **HABITS** Pine-oak woodland, humid broadleaf forest, forest edge, and adjacent open areas. May form large flocks and may associate with other swallows. Flies with rapid wingbeats. Glides less often than Tree Swallow. **VOICE** Calls (1) hard, sharp, slightly buzzy *chilp* or *chizzip* often repeated and (2) clear (less buzzy) *tseer* or *tweep* or *teewp*.

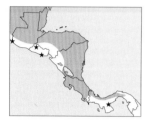

Tree Swallow *Tachycineta bicolor*   14.5 cm

Breeds Nearctic. Winters USA and MX and CA. Irregular transient and winter resident (mainly Sep to Apr) in lowlands and foothills (to 2500 m). Mainly north Caribbean slope, where sometimes briefly or locally common. Rare on north Pacific slope, and in south CA. **ID** Fairly large with broad-based, triangular wings. Tail notched. Ad has iridescent blue (spring) or green (fall) sides of head and upperparts (including rump) and *white underparts including crissum*. Imm drab brownish-gray above (including auriculars) and may show diffuse grayish-brown breast-band. When perched note imm's dark auriculars contrasting with whitish throat. Compare imm with smaller Bank Swallow. Note different underparts. Ad may suggest Blue-and-white Swallow. Note different crissum. Also compare with Violet-green Swallow. Note different head pattern. **HABITS** Open and semi-open habitats. Wintering flocks (sometimes in hundreds) favor flooded savannas or agricultural fields. **VOICE** Call (1) a high-pitched, liquid *chur-lup* or *chu-leep*. Flocks produce (2) a chorus of thin, scratchy *tzeev* notes.

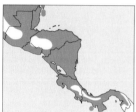

Mangrove Swallow *Tachycineta albilinea*   12 cm

MX and CA. Common resident, mainly in coastal lowlands (locally to 1000 m). Also BZ Cays and Isla Coiba off PA (Veraguas, 470). **ID** Tail notched. Narrow *white supraloral stripe* and *white rump*. Ad mainly iridescent green above with dusky brown wings. Underparts and wing linings entirely plain white. Juv brownish above. Violet-green Swallow vaguely similar. Note different head and rump. Also compare with Tree Swallow. Note different head, upperparts, and habits. **HABITS** Open and semi-open habitats usually in vicinity of water including lakes, marshes, rivers, and lagoons. Pairs or small groups perch low on branches or boulders near water. Flies rapidly, usually low over water. **VOICE** Call (1) a short, scratchy *jeet* or *jrrt*.

Blue-and-white Swallow *Pygochelidon cyanoleuca*   12–13 cm

CA and SA. Common resident in south foothills and highlands (mainly 400 to 3000 m). Rare vagrant to GT (Sacatepéquez, 318, 346) and lowlands of NI (RAAN, Managua, 413, 346). Some records may represent migratory SA breeders (320, 659, 346). **ID** Small, with *forked tail*. Mantle dark glossy blue. Underparts mostly plain white with *dark blue crissum*. Juv brownish-gray above and on crissum with variable extent of buff on throat, breast, and flanks. Larger Tree Swallow superficially similar. Note different underparts. **GV** Birds from migratory South American breeding population have more extensive dusky on crissum and dark underwing. **HABITS** Open and semi-open areas including pastures, agricultural fields, and urban areas. **VOICE** Song (1) a long, thin, weak trill. Often begins with gurgling sputter and rises slightly in pitch *dzzzhreeeee*. In flight, gives (2) hard, bright *chip* or *cheep*.

Violet-green Swallow

imm

♀

♂

♂

Tree Swallow

imm

ad

Mangrove Swallow

CA
ad

Blue-and-white Swallow

juv

ad

SA
ad

SWALLOWS Hirundinidae

Swallows with brown or dusky upperparts. Tail shape and details of the head and rump and underparts pattern are useful in separating these.

Black-capped Swallow *Atticora pileata*   12.5 cm

South MX and north CA. Common resident in GT highlands (1000 to 2500, mainly above 1500 m). Uncommon to rare and local in HN (442) and SV (Santa Ana, Chalatenango, 183, 619). **ID** Small with *long, deeply forked tail*. Mostly *dark brown above* becoming blackish on crown. Throat and breast white. Compare with larger Tree Swallow. Note different tail shape. White-thighed Swallow allopatric. **HABITS** Canopy and edge of humid broadleaf or mixed broadleaf-coniferous forests and adjacent plantations, gardens, and open areas. Usually in small groups or pairs. Nests and roosts in earthen banks along roadsides. **VOICE** Song (1) a series of short, dry notes that accelerate to become a buzzy chatter. Calls (2) an upslurred, nasal *sreet* or *zreeh* and (3) liquid, trilled *tri-i-it*.

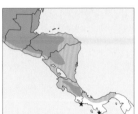

Northern Rough-winged Swallow *Stelgidopteryx serripennis*   13.5 cm

NA to CA. Nearctic migrant and resident breeding birds occur. Breeds in north highlands, locally in Caribbean lowlands of GT and BZ (56, 489, 318), and in highlands (mainly above 1000 m) of CR (585). Nearctic breeding birds reach CA as common transients and winter residents (Sep to Apr) mainly in lowlands and foothills. Rare visitor to Pacific west PA. **ID** Fairly large. *Dull gray-brown including rump* with notched tail. Belly and crissum white. Crown usually concolorous with mantle (no dark cap or crown contrasting very slightly). Ad's throat may be tinged with cinnamon but does not contrast strongly with auriculars. Juv (May to Nov) has rufous wingbars and tertial edges and variably buff or cinnamon throat. Compare with Southern Rough-winged Swallow. Note different throat and rump color. **GV** Birds breeding in Caribbean GT and BZ are darker than northern migrants, and often have pale supraloral spot. Also note blackish terminal feathers on crissum. Birds breeding in foothills and highlands of HN south to CR have more cinnamon throat. **HABITS** Open and semi-open habitats. Usually near water. Gregarious. Transients may form flocks or join mixed associations with other swallow species. Often forages low over water or in clearings. Some breeding populations in north Caribbean are associated with limestone caves or stone structures where they nest. **VOICE** Call (1) a low-pitched, slightly upslurred, coarse *prriit*. Lower and softer than call of Bank Swallow.

Southern Rough-winged Swallow *Stelgidopteryx ruficollis*   13 cm

CA and SA. Fairly common resident in lowlands and foothills (to 1000 m). **ID** Fairly large. Mostly dull brown above with notched tail. Note cinnamon throat and neck and *pale grayish-white rump* (conspicuous in flight). Most have distinctly darker crown. Belly dull yellowish-white. Resembles Northern Rough-winged Swallow. As in breeding Northern Rough-winged Swallows from north CA, terminal feathers of crissum blackish, creating a "squared-off" appearance. **HABITS** Open and semi-open habitats. Usually near water. Forms small flocks outside breeding season and readily associates with Northern Rough-winged Swallows. Often forages low over water or in clearings. **VOICE** Calls (1) similar to Northern Rough-winged Swallow but slightly lower-pitched, mellower, and more liquid.

White-thighed Swallow *Atticora tibialis*   10 cm

CA and SA. Uncommon and local resident in lowlands and foothills (to 900 m) of central and east PA. **ID** *Very small and dark* with *forked tail*. Gray rump slightly paler than dusky mantle. Inconspicuous *white tibial tufts* diagnostic. Black-capped Swallow allopatric. **HABITS** Poorly known. Canopy and edge of humid broadleaf forest and adjacent clearings or plantations. Often near water. May perch on bare limbs at forest edge. In pairs or small groups. Seems not to associate with other swallows. Often flies with erratic, batlike style, sometimes low over ground. Also forages over forest canopy. **VOICE** Usually quiet. Calls (1) a thin, high-pitched *tseet-tit* or *chit-it, chee-dee-dit* and (2) softer *seet-seet* given in flight.

50%

Black-capped Swallow

juv

ad

Caribbean GT
and BZ
ad

juv

ad

**Northern
Rough-winged
Swallow**

interior GT
(Nearctic migrants
similar)

HN to CR
ad

**Southern
Rough-winged
Swallow**

White-thighed Swallow

SWALLOWS Hirundinidae

Swallows with brown or blue upperparts. The square-tailed Cave and Cliff swallows are each geographically variable. Head and rump pattern are useful in separating these. Barn Swallow is the most common and widespread.

Bank Swallow *Riparia riparia*   12 cm

Breeds Holarctic. Nearctic birds winter SA. Widespread transient in lowlands (Mar to May and Aug to Nov). May be locally or briefly common. Uncommon to rare in winter. Vagrant to Isla del Coco (163). **ID** Small with deeply notched tail. Ad brown above and white below with *dark breast-band* widest at center of breast. Dark auriculars contrast with white neck and throat. Note white of throat extending behind auriculars and faint pale supraloral. In flight, brown upperparts contrast with darker wings and tail. Juv (Jun to Dec) and some ads (in fresh plumage) have narrow pale edges on tertials. Compare with larger Northern and Southern Rough-winged swallows. Note different underparts. Juv Tree Swallow may have diffuse dark breast-band but is never as crisply marked as Bank Swallow. **HABITS** Wetlands, agricultural fields, rivers, lagoons, and seacoasts. Joins mixed concentrations with other swallows. Flies with rapid, shallow wingbeats. **VOICE** Usually quiet. Song (1) a repeated *wit wit dree drr drr drr*. Call (2) a short, dry, buzzy *chirr* or *shrrit* often repeated rapidly in long series.

Cave Swallow *Petrochelidon fulva*   12–13.5 cm

Breeds USA, WI, and south MX. Uncommon to locally common winter resident (Nov to Mar) on north Pacific slope in GT (Sacatepéquez, Jutiapa, Sololá, Escuintla, Santa Rosa, 232, 229) and SV (Ahuachapán, Usulután, 361). Rare on Caribbean slope in BZ (Toledo, 347, 341) and GT (Izabal, 229). Uncommon and irregular winter visitor elsewhere on Pacific slope in HN (Copán, Choluteca, La Paz, 346), NI (León, 135), CR (Puntarenas, Guanacaste, 341, 346), and PA (Colón, Panamá, 512, 48, 346). **ID** Small and dark with square tail and broad wings. Dark rump does not contrast with mantle. Dark crown contrasts with *tawny nape, auriculars, and throat*. Ad has *rufous forehead* and blue-black crown. Juv drab with brownish-gray mantle (some have fine pale scaling). Compare with Cliff Swallow. Note different head and underparts. **GV** Birds breeding in north MX and southwest USA have paler cinnamon rump. Birds breeding in Yucatán Peninsula and Chiapas MX, southeast USA, and WI are smaller and darker and have dark rufous rump. **HABITS** Wetlands, agricultural fields, rivers, lagoons, and seacoasts. Transients use a wide variety of open or semi-open habitats. Forms mixed flocks or foraging associations with other swallows. **VOICE** Song (1) a complex, staccato series of short, high-pitched, slurred notes, clicks, and short, nasal, buzzy notes. Calls (2) a soft, upslurred *pwid* or *wiid*, (3) buzzy, hoarse *chep* or *chiip* often repeated in series, and (4) very high-pitched, thin *teeer*.

Cliff Swallow *Petrochelidon pyrrhonota*   13.5 cm

Breeds Nearctic. Winters mainly south SA. May be briefly or locally common transient in coastal lowlands (Mar to May and Aug to Oct). Rare in winter with reports from GT (Petén, 646) and Pacific lowlands of PA (512). Vagrant to Isla del Coco (163). **ID** Small and dark with square tail and broad wings. *Pale buff rump* and *chestnut auriculars and throat*. NA breeding ads have *pale buff forehead*. Also note diffuse blackish on upper breast. Juv mostly brownish-gray with dull buff forehead and rump. Compare with Cave Swallow. Note different head and underparts. **GV** Birds from population breeding in MX have dark rufous forehead suggesting Cave Swallow (but all have pale rump). **HABITS** Wetlands, agricultural fields, rivers, lagoons, and seacoasts. Transients may occur in wide variety of open or semi-open habitats. May form mixed flocks or foraging associations with other swallows. **VOICE** Song (1) a series of thin, slurred, buzzy notes. Compare with more complex song of Barn Swallow. Calls (2) a soft *verr* and (3) lower-pitched *vrrrt*.

Barn Swallow *Hirundo rustica*   female 14, male 17 cm

Breeds Holarctic. Nearctic birds winter MX to SA. Widespread and common transient and winter resident (mainly Aug to May) in lowlands and foothills. May be briefly or locally abundant on coasts. Vagrant to Isla del Coco (163, 268). **ID** Slender. *Long, deeply forked tail* with *white subterminal band*. Note rufous throat and forehead. Lower underparts variably white to cinnamon-buff and usually divided from throat by narrow dark breast-band. Wintering birds can be very pale and drab when worn. Imm paler below with shorter tail. Compare with Cliff Swallow. Note different head pattern and tail shape. **HABITS** Wetlands, agricultural fields, rivers, lagoons, and seacoasts. Transients occur in wide variety of open and semi-open habitats. Joins mixed roosts or foraging concentrations with other swallows. **VOICE** Call (1) an emphatic, slightly buzzy *djeet*. Often repeated.

Bank Swallow

Cave Swallow

ad

juv

northern breeding
ad

Yucatán and Chiapas
breeding ad

Cliff Swallow

ad

juv

northern
ad

MX
ad

juv

pale ad
♀

Barn Swallow

ad
♂

KINGLETS Regulidae, BUSHTIT Aegithalidae, CREEPER Certhiidae

Golden-crowned Kinglet *Regulus satrapa* 9.5 cm

NA to CA. Uncommon and local breeding resident in highlands (above 2500 m) of GT (229). **ID** *Tiny* with short bill, *striped crown* and dark eye stripe. Shows dark bar at base of primaries and yellow edging in folded wing. Male has *orange central crown*. Female's crown yellow. Compare with vireos. **HABITS** Midstory to canopy of coniferous forest. Pairs or small groups forage actively in terminal foliage. May hover briefly. Follows mixed flocks. **VOICE** Call (1) a single or short series of very high-pitched, thin notes *ssi-ssi-ssi*.

Ruby-crowned Kinglet *Regulus calendula* 10 cm

Breeds Nearctic. Winters south USA to MX. Rare winter visitor to highlands (2800 to 3100 m) of GT (Huehuetenango, Totonicapán, Sololá, San Marcos, Sacatepéquez, Chimaltenango, 539, 516, 229). One report from HN (Copan, 263). **ID** Tiny with *very fine bill*. Drab olive, paler below. *Broken whitish eye ring flared behind eye.* Male's red crown patch usually concealed. Compare with Hutton's Vireo. Note different bill shape and wing pattern. **HABITS** Understory to subcanopy and edge of coniferous and pine-oak forest. Habitually flicks wings. Forages actively in terminal foliage. May hover-glean. Solitary birds may follow mixed flocks. **VOICE** Song (1) begins with several high-pitched notes then switches to a short, rich, warbled phrase *tseee-tii-tiii-tii-whee-chu-chu-whiichuchu*. Call (2) a vireo-like, sharp, harsh *ch-chdit, chdit*.

Bushtit *Psaltriparus minimus* 10 cm

USA to CA. Fairly common resident in highlands (1500 to 3500 m) of GT. **ID** *Tiny* with long, narrow tail and *short bill*. Male mostly drab gray brown becoming paler below with *black sides of head*, dark eyes, and white throat. Female has plain brownish sides of head and *pale eyes*. **HABITS** Understory to midstory of arid to semihumid pine-oak forest, second growth, scrub, and edge. Pairs or groups forage actively. Clings or hangs from terminal twigs. May follow mixed flocks. **VOICE** Calls include (1) a high-pitched, slightly buzzy *chiip* or *spik* that is often given in chorus by several birds and (2) thin, harsh, slightly trilled phrase *ssiiir* or *sir-r-rrrrr*.

Brown Creeper *Certhia americana* 12.5 cm

NA to CA. Uncommon resident in north highlands (1500 to 3800, locally as low as 500 m) south to NI (San Rafael del Norte, 430). Recently reported from SV (Santa Ana, Chalatenango, 362, 364, 341, 260) and highlands of north HN (Olancho, Cortés). **ID** Small with *fine, decurved bill*. Long, narrow tail with pointed rectrices. Mostly brown above with fine, pale streaking and spotting. Plain whitish below, with buff on rear underparts. Dusky auriculars contrast with pale supercilium. Note whitish wingbar and *buff bar on flight feathers*. **HABITS** Understory to subcanopy of coniferous forest and woodland. Creeps (usually vertically) on trunks and larger branches of trees. Pairs or small groups follow mixed flocks. **VOICE** Song (1) a series of four to five very high-pitched, slurred notes. Call (2) a very high-pitched, short, repeated note.

WRENS Troglodytidae

Sedge Wren *Cistothorus platensis* 10–11 cm

NA to CA. Uncommon and local resident (SL to 3700 m) in north CA. Rare in CR (Cartago, San José, 126, 600, 373). Historical records from west PA (Chiriquí, 659, 48). **ID** Small. Tail often cocked. *Plain buff below*. Individually and geographically variable. Note *whitish streaks on mantle* and (variable) fine pale speckling on crown. **GV** Birds from BZ have more black on crown and mantle. Birds from lowlands of east HN have less black and nearly plain crown. Birds from west PA have plain crown and blackish mantle. **HABITS** Understory of sedge-dominated wetlands, pastures, and grassy savannas. Secretive but takes low, open perch to sing. **VOICE** Variable song (1) often begins with one or more sharp notes and becomes a long, varied series of chatters and flat, dry trills. Call (2) a sharp, dry *chik* or *chk*.

Rock Wren *Salpinctes obsoletus* 14–15 cm

NA to CA. Uncommon to rare and local resident in foothills and highlands (above 500 m) of GT (Huehuetenango, Sololá, Quiche, Quetzaltenango, Baja Verapaz, 229, 279, 539), SV (San Miguel, Chalatenango, La Unión, 539, 183, 619), HN (Francisco Morazán, El Paraíso, Choluteca, 346, 442), NI (Estelí, Chinandega, 413), and Cordillera de Guanacaste (500 to 1600 m) in CR (Guanacaste, 624, 126, 570, 600). **ID** Long, slightly decurved bill. *Mostly grayish* with *fine pale spotting and dark barring*. Note buff terminal band on tail. Dull whitish below with variable, fine, dark barring or spotting. **GV** Birds from GT are pale and relatively lightly marked below with buff flanks. Birds from north Pacific slope south to CR have less pale spotting above and variably heavy dark barring or spotting below. **HABITS** Open areas with boulders or rock outcroppings including scree slopes, cliffs, and barren lava flows. Pairs or solitary birds creep over rocks or ground investigating crevices. **VOICE** Song (1) a varied, mimid-like series of buzzes, trills, chatters, and whistles *ch-wee ch-wee ch-wee jeer-r-r-r-r, ch-reeoo jeh-jeh-jeh, jirr-rr jirr-rr . . .* Repeats some phrases three or more times. Calls (2) a buzzy, ringing *ch-reer* or *bee-reeehrrr* and (3) higher, clearer *pi-cheeer*.

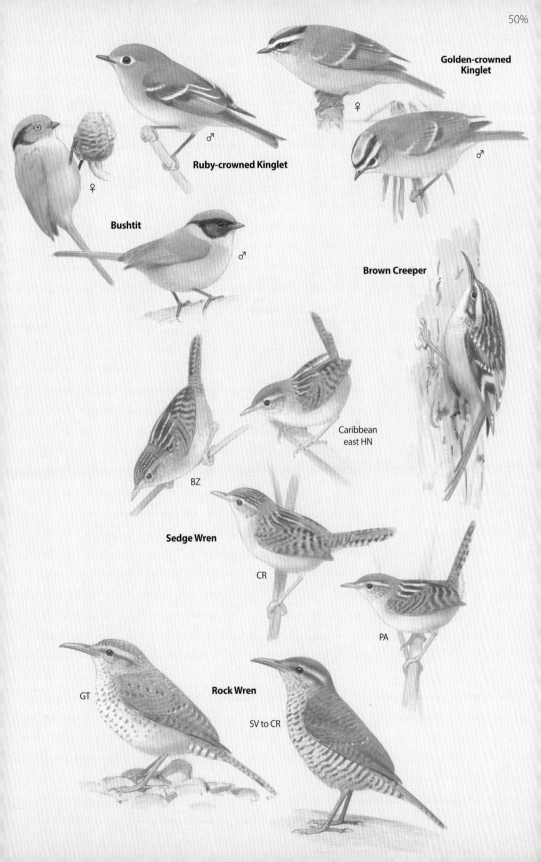

Golden-crowned
Kinglet

♀

♂

Ruby-crowned Kinglet

♂

Bushtit

♀

♂

Brown Creeper

Caribbean
east HN

BZ

Sedge Wren

CR

PA

GT

Rock Wren

SV to CR

WRENS Troglodytidae

Large, noisy wrens. Often found in groups. Giant Wren and Bicolored Wren have only recently been documented from the region. Rufous-naped Wren is the most common and widespread of these species and shows complex geographic variation in Central America.

White-headed Wren *Campylorhynchus albobrunneus* 19 cm
CA and north SA. Uncommon and local resident in lowlands and foothills (to 1200 m) of east PA. **ID** *White head* and underparts. Wings and tail plain dark brown. Imm has grayish head with whitish supercilium. **HABITS** Upper midstory to canopy and edge of humid broadleaf forest, tall second growth, and adjacent clearings with tall trees. Pairs or small groups forage actively in epiphytes, vine tangles, and crowns of palms. Noisy and conspicuous. **VOICE** Song (1) a slightly accelerating series of very harsh, loud, grating notes *ch-ch-ch-ch-chichi chow-kaw*. Calls (2) a harsh, single *churk* and (3) longer *reeeeh*. Two or more birds may call in chorus.

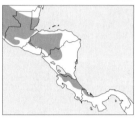

Band-backed Wren *Campylorhynchus zonatus* 17–20 cm
CA and north SA. Uncommon resident in lowlands and foothills (SL to 1500 to 3200 m). Mainly Caribbean slope in south. **ID** *Black-and-white barring on mantle* and whitish breast spotted with black. Lower underparts cinnamon. Compare with Rufous-naped Wren. **GV** Birds from north Caribbean slope often have extensive dark barring on underparts. Birds from interior and Pacific north CA tend to be larger and paler. Birds from south CA tend to be smaller, lack barring on flanks, and have darker upperparts and tail. **HABITS** Upper midstory to canopy and edge of humid broadleaf forest, second growth, gardens, and isolated trees in adjacent clearings in humid areas of south CA. In north uses humid pine woodland, pine-oak woodland, scrub, gardens, and plantations. Pairs or small groups forage actively. Creeps along branches of epiphyte-burdened trees or investigates trash in palm crowns. **VOICE** Often noisy. Pairs sing in duet. Song (1) a varied series of phrases including slurred, rolling notes, dry chatters, and staccato, squeaky sputters. Calls (2) a loud, dry *zrek* or *shreck* often repeated or given in chorus by several birds and (3) shorter, dry *zek* or *zuk*.

Giant Wren *Campylorhynchus chiapensis* 21 cm
South MX and north CA. Uncommon resident in Pacific lowlands of west GT where recently first reported (San Marcos, 229). **ID** Large. Rufous mantle and *long white supercilium*. Note *plain (unbarred) rufous wings*. Resembles Rufous-naped Wren but note different wing pattern. Band-backed Wren allopatric. **HABITS** Understory to canopy of woodland, forest edge, second growth, and gardens. Often in pairs or small groups. May forage on ground. **VOICE** Song (1) like Rufous-naped Wren but lower-pitched, coarser, and hoarser.

Bicolored Wren *Campylorhynchus griseus* 21 cm
CA and north SA. Rare and local resident in lowlands and foothills (to 400 m) of east PA (Darién, 116). **ID** Brown mantle and long white supercilium. Wings and tail plain dark brown. Imm has grayish head with whitish supercilium. **HABITS** Upper midstory to canopy and edge of plantations, tall second growth, gardens, and clearings with tall trees. Pairs or small groups forage actively in foliage, vine tangles, and crowns of palms. Often noisy and conspicuous. **VOICE** Song (1) a series of short, slurred phrases *whee-chup whee-chup*. Calls (2) a repeated *churk* and (3) longer, more drawn-out *reeeeh*. Two or more birds may call in chorus.

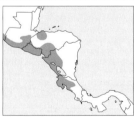

Rufous-naped Wren *Campylorhynchus rufinucha* 18 cm
South MX and north CA. Common resident in Pacific lowlands and foothills (to 800, locally to 1200 m in north). Also Caribbean slope in GT and HN. **ID** *Rufous nape* and *white supercilium*. Complex individual and geographic variation. Band-backed Wren allopatric. **GV** Birds from west Pacific GT have mostly black tail and plain rufous mantle. Birds from east Pacific GT south to CR have banded central rectrices and usually have plain or sparsely mottled brown or rufous mantle. Some birds from that region have narrow, dark malar. Birds from Caribbean HN have plain brown back. Birds from Motagua Valley in GT as well as those from interior NI, and some from west CR, have mantle variably (sometimes boldly) mottled or streaked with rufous, white, and black. Ad males from interior NI often have narrow dark malar. **HABITS** Understory to midstory of arid to semihumid woodland, forest edge, second growth, gardens, plantations, and urban areas. In pairs or small groups. Creeps on branches or virtually any substrate. May forage on ground. Probes in litter or crevices. Bold and confiding. **VOICE** Pairs duet. Song (1) a series of rich, slightly hoarse or hollow whistles alternating with dry chatters and gurgles delivered in three to eight repeated phrases. Whistled phrases may suggest Yellow-tailed Oriole. Calls (2) include short, harsh, scolding notes often given in chorus by two or more birds.

48%

White-headed Wren

ad

juv

juv

Caribbean
north CA
ad

Band-backed Wren

Pacific and
interior north CA
ad

south CA
ad

Giant Wren

Bicolored Wren

west Pacific GT

Rufous-naped Wren

interior NI

WRENS Troglodytidae

Medium-sized wrens found mainly in lower levels of forest edge and second growth. Pairs sing in duet.

Carolina Wren *Thryothorus ludovicianus* 13 cm
USA to north CA. Uncommon resident in lowlands of BZ (Cayo, Orange Walk, 313, 343) and north GT (Petén, 229, 279, 579). Rare and local in foothills (SL to 1000 m) of GT (Quiché, Alta Verapaz, Baja Verapaz, 229, 279), Pacific HN (Choluteca, 346), and NI (Matagalpa, Chinandega, 429, 411, 413). **ID** *Black-and-white streaking on neck.* Grayish-brown above. Note *barred crissum* and dusky barring on grayish tail and primaries. Cabanis's Wren has plain crissum. Rufous-and-white Wren is rufous above. Compare with smaller White-bellied Wren. **GV** Birds from south GT, HN, and NI are more rufescent. **HABITS** Understory of arid to semihumid forest edge, second growth, scrub, and gallery forest. Secretive. **VOICE** Song (1) a rapid series of loud, rich phrases *ch-ree ch-ree ch-ree . . .* Compare with Green Shrike-Vireo. Calls (2) an abrupt, buzzy *bzzeirr*, (3) rapid, buzzy scold *zzhi-zzhi . . .* and (4) harsh *jeh-jeh-jeh.*

Cabanis's Wren[25] *Cantorchilus modestus* 13.5 cm
South MX to CA. Common resident in north (SL to 2000 m). Uncommon in Mountain Pine Ridge, BZ (Cayo, 529, 549). **ID** Plain whitish auriculars. Underparts whitish becoming *cinnamon on flanks and crissum.* Wings and tail brown with faint dusky barring. White-browed Wren smaller. Averages darker and richer than Isthmian Wren but some indistinguishable. Canebrake and Buff-breasted wrens allopatric. **HABITS** Understory at edge of semihumid broadleaf and pine-oak forest, scrub, second growth, and gardens. **VOICE** Variable song (1) a rapid, upslurred phrase *chichi-gwee* or *chinchi-gwee-ee.* Often repeated. Also (2) a longer, more rapid series of high-pitched, slurred phrases *chi-whi-di-chi-wi-di . . .* Calls (3) a dry, rapidly repeated *chutchutchuddit . . .* or *cht cht cht . . .* (4) dry *churr* or *chi-wurp*, and (5) a dry, upslurred rattle.

Canebrake Wren[25] *Cantorchilus zeledoni* 14.5 cm
CA endemic. Uncommon resident in Caribbean lowlands and foothills (to 1000 m) of CR and west PA. **ID** Plain whitish auriculars. Throat and central breast whitish becoming dull buff on sides of breast and lower underparts. *Crissum plain dull buff.* Wings and tail plain grayish-brown (or with variable faint dusky barring). Darker and duller than Isthmian and Cabanis's wrens. **HABITS** Understory at edge of humid broadleaf forest, second growth, and gardens. **VOICE** Song (1) similar to Cabanis's Wren but slower, lower-pitched, and richer. Also (2) a shorter, very high-pitched *cheewhee-tseeu* repeated in short series. Calls include (3) a harsh rattle.

Isthmian Wren[25] *Cantorchilus elutus* 13.5 cm
CA endemic. Common resident in south lowlands and foothills (to 2000 m). **ID** Mostly plain whitish auriculars. *Breast plain whitish* becoming dull buff or cinnamon on sides of breast and lower underparts. *Crissum plain cinnamon.* Wings and tail have indistinct dusky barring. Averages paler and duller than Cabanis's Wren with more distinct barring on tail and wings. Compare with Buff-breasted Wren. **HABITS** Understory at edge of broadleaf forest, scrub, second growth, and gardens. **VOICE** Song (1) a rapid, slurred phrase *chuwhee-chuwee-chu-whah . . .* repeated several times Also (2) a short series of very high-pitched, slurred notes *seewheee-see-ah.* Call (3) a rapid, harsh, scolding *chtchtchtchtchtcht.*

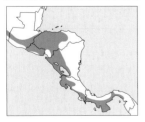

Buff-breasted Wren *Cantorchilus leucotis* 13 cm
CA and SA. Fairly common resident (mainly near SL) in lowlands of central and east PA. Also Pearl Islands (Panamá, 64, 659). **ID** Plain white auriculars and *tawny underparts.* Brown above with *distinct dusky barring on wings and tail.* **GV** Birds from Pearl Islands (not shown) are slightly richer brown above. **HABITS** Understory and edge of semihumid to humid broadleaf forest, second growth, plantations, and scrub. Often near water. **VOICE** Song (1) a loud, rich phrase rapidly repeated several times before switching to another phrase, typically *choreewee, choreewee, choreewee . . . wheeooree-tickwheeoo, wheeooree tickwheeoo . . .* Call (2) a dry, ticking rattle.

Rufous-and-white Wren *Thryophilus rufalbus* 14.5 cm
South MX to north SA. Common resident in semihumid lowlands and foothills (to 1400, locally to 1800 m in north). **ID** *Rufous above.* Auriculars streaked with black and white. Note *black-and-white barring on crissum* and dusky barring on wings and tail. Imm has dusky barring or scaling below. Compare with Banded Wren. Note different underparts. Also compare with Carolina Wren. Note different upperparts and tail pattern. Cabanis's Wren has duller upperparts and plain crissum. **GV** Birds from GT (not shown) have gray flanks. **HABITS** Understory and edge of arid to semihumid forest, brushy second growth, riparian thickets, plantations, and gardens. **VOICE** Song (1) a variable series of hollow, low-pitched, slow trills and clear whistles *hoohoohoohoh-h-h-hoo-eeep* or *weep-hoohoohoohoh-h-h-hoo-hu.* Calls (2) a hard, rapid chatter, (3) short *hoowooo* or *hoo*, and (4) sharp, scratchy *chet* sometimes in rapid series.

50%

Carolina Wren

north GT
and BZ

south GT,
HN and NI

Cabanis's Wren

Canebrake Wren

Isthmian Wren

Buff-breasted Wren

juv

Rufous-and-white Wren

south CA
ad

WRENS Troglodytidae

Medium-sized wrens found in lower and middle levels of broadleaf forest and edge. Usually in pairs. All have loud, distinctive songs. Banded and Spot-breasted wrens are the most widespread and common.

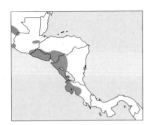

Banded Wren *Thryophilus pleurostictus*   14 cm
MX and north CA. Fairly common resident in Pacific lowlands and foothills (to 800, locally to 1500 m in north). Local on Caribbean slope in Valle de Motagua, GT. **ID** *Black-and-white barred flanks and crissum*, streaked neck, and white supercilium. Upperparts rufous-brown with dusky barring on wings and tail. Head pattern like Rufous-and-white Wren. Note different underparts. **HABITS** Floor and understory of deciduous forest, second growth, and scrub. Hops through dense tangles. May forage on ground by flicking leaves with bill. **VOICE** Complex, variable song (1) usually three to five rich, slurred whistles followed by even trill or rattle *wheeeeet chu chu cheee trrrrrrrr*. May repeat several times then shift to some variation. Calls (2) a staccato tick or sputter and (3) nasal, hard, rattling *cherrrt*. Often (4) alternates a metallic roll with hard rattle *kert rrruk kert rrruk* or (5) alternates slurred whistle with coarse phrase *wheeeeer crrk wheeeeer . . .*

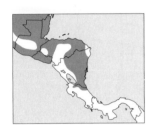

Spot-breasted Wren *Pheugopedius maculipectus*   13.5 cm
South MX and north CA. Common resident in lowlands and foothills (to 1400 m). Rare in CR (Alajuela, 55). **ID** *White breast spotted with black.* Flanks and lower underparts plain cinnamon-rufous. Note black-and-white mottled sides of head and throat and white supercilium. Upperparts brown becoming rufous on crown. Brown tail barred with dusky. Crissum barred with black and white. Compare with Banded Wren. **HABITS** Understory to canopy and edge of semihumid to humid broadleaf forest, second growth, gallery forest, and riparian thickets. Skulks in vine tangles at edges or gaps. May forage actively in open as mixed flocks pass nearby. **VOICE** Pairs duet. Song (1) a complex, melodious phrase of five to seven loud, clear, slurred whistles. Usually drops in pitch. May include a short trill. Often repeated. Compare with song of White-breasted Wood-Wren. Calls (2) a sharp *churr* and (3) upslurred *reeeeeei* like fingers on teeth of a comb.

Rufous-breasted Wren *Pheugopedius rutilus*   13.5 cm
CA and north SA. Locally common resident in south Pacific foothills (300 to 1600 m, locally to near SL). **ID** *Cinnamon-rufous breast* contrasts with black-and-white spotted throat and auriculars and black-and-white barred crissum. Wings brown with only faint dusky barring. Grayish tail shows bold dusky barring. In east PA compare with Stripe-throated Wren. Note different wing pattern. **HABITS** Understory to midstory and edge of semihumid broadleaf forest, tall second growth, plantations, and gardens. Favors cluttered areas such as vine tangles in tree-fall gaps. Does not follow mixed flocks. **VOICE** Pairs duet. Song (1) a repeated phrase of three to seven loud, clear, slurred whistles *whee-cha whee-cha-wheeer* or *whee-chacha-wheer*. Calls (2) a prolonged, questioning *reep* or *ch'reeep* and (3) sharp *churr . . .* and (4) ascending rattle *reeeeeei* like Spot-breasted Wren.

Stripe-breasted Wren *Cantorchilus thoracicus*   12.5 cm
CA endemic. Uncommon to locally fairly common resident in lowlands and foothills (to 1000 m) of northeast HN (Colón, Gracias a Dios, 629, 346) south on Caribbean slope to west PA. **ID** *Black-and-white streaking on sides of head, throat, and breast.* Plain brown lower underparts (including crissum) and barred wings and tail. Compare with *Henicorhina* wood-wrens. Note different underparts. Stripe-throated Wren allopatric. **HABITS** Understory to midstory and edge of humid broadleaf forest, shaded plantations, and tall second growth. Forages actively in foliage, arboreal trash, and vine tangles. May follow mixed flocks or become more active as they pass. **VOICE** Pairs duet. Song (1) a repeated, variable phrase of three to five loud, rich whistles *cha-whee-chacha-weeur cha -whee-cha-cha-weeur . . .* Compare with song of White-breasted Wood-Wren. Also (2) a simple series of clear whistles on even pitch *oot, oot, oot, oot . . .* Call (3) a rolling *cherk* or *chrrik*.

Stripe-throated Wren *Cantorchilus leucopogon*   11.5 cm
CA and north SA. Fairly common resident in lowlands and foothills (to 750 m) of east PA. **ID** *Cinnamon-brown underparts* (including crissum) contrast with *black-and-white streaked sides of head, neck, and throat.* Dusky barring on brown wings and tail. Rufous-breasted Wren has plain tail and only faint dusky barring on wing. Stripe-breasted Wren allopatric. **HABITS** Upper understory to midstory and edge of humid broadleaf forest and tall second growth. Forages actively in vine tangles. May follow mixed flocks. **VOICE** Song (1) a simple, repeated phrase *tee-peee, teeo-peee . . .* or *wurree-tu, wuree-tu . . .* Compare with song of White-breasted Wood-Wren. Call (2) a distinctive *chu, ch-chu* or *chu, ch-chu, ch-chu*.

50%

Banded Wren

juv

ad

Spot-breasted Wren

Rufous-breasted Wren

Stripe-breasted Wren

Stripe-throated Wren

WRENS Troglodytidae

Medium-sized wrens with black-and-white head pattern. All are found at lower levels in humid broadleaf forest and edge in lowlands and foothills. Usually in pairs. Often secretive and difficult to glimpse as they skulk in shaded vegetation. All have loud, distinctive songs. Bay Wren is the most common and widespread and is geographically variable in Central America.

Black-throated Wren *Pheugopedius atrogularis* 14.5 cm

CA endemic. Uncommon and local resident in humid lowlands and foothills (to 1100 m). Poorly known in HN (Colón, Gracias a Dios, 629) and north NI (RAAN, 626). **ID** Plain dark brown (including tail) with *black sides of head, throat, and breast*. Note narrow white supercilium and sparse streaking on auriculars. Sooty-headed Wren allopatric. **HABITS** Understory to midstory and edge of humid broadleaf forest and second growth. **VOICE** Pairs duet. Variable song (1) begins with rich, clear, slurred whistles. Usually ends with steady series of short notes forming a rattle or trill *wu-whee-chu whe-tu-tu-tu-tu-tu . . .* Repeats a phrase several times then shifts to another. Compare with faster song of Bay Wren. Calls (2) a fast, nasal to wooden, rattling *praaaaaht* and (3) guttural, rolling *beewrrr* or *bweeurrrr*.

Sooty-headed Wren *Pheugopedius spadix* 14.5 cm

CA and north SA. Uncommon and local resident in foothills (450 to 1200 m) of east PA (Darién, 519, 45). **ID** *Rufous breast* contrasts with *black throat*. Note restricted white markings on mostly black head. Crown dark sooty brown. Wings plain rufous-brown (no barring). Imm (not shown) has gray head and throat. Compare with Bay Wren (lower elevations). Note different head pattern. **HABITS** Understory to midstory of humid broadleaf forest. Favors vine tangles and dense bamboo stands in gaps. Probes in dead leaves and arboreal litter. **VOICE** Song (1) a loud, rich, whistled phrase that typically ends on lower-pitched note *wee-cha weecheereeuu* or *weecha-weeaweee-chuwooo*. In duet, pairs sing (2) composite phrase of slurred whistles *chee-chaweer-a-chu, chee-chaweer-a-chu* repeated several times. Calls (3) a repeated *cheer-jeja* or *chear-jea* and (4) short, harsh, scolding *cheer-jehr-jehr-jehr*.

Bay Wren *Cantorchilus nigricapillus* 15 cm

CA and north SA. Fairly common resident in lowlands and foothills (to 1000 m). Poorly known in HN (Atlántida, Colón, 263). Also Isla Escudo off PA (Bocas del Toro, 656, 659). **ID** Head mostly black with white supercilium, white eye ring, and *white marks on auriculars*. Wings and tail barred with rufous and black. Compare with Black-bellied Wren. Note different head pattern. Also compare with Black-throated Wren. Note different wing and tail pattern. **GV** Widespread form is mostly rufous below. Birds from central PA have variable extent of rufous on lower underparts and some blackish barring. Birds from east PA have extensive barring. **GV** Birds from Isla Escudo (not shown) are paler and longer-billed than mainland birds. **HABITS** Understory of gaps in humid broadleaf forest, forest edge, riparian thickets, and dense second growth. **VOICE** Pairs duet. Song (1) a fast, loud series of clear, slurred whistles sometimes followed by a fast trill *chewa chewa chee chewa chwa wha wha t-t-t-t-t-t*. Compare with slower song of Black-throated Wren. Calls (2) a repeated *chuweer* or *chuwea* and (3) rolling, low-pitched *jehrrr*.

Riverside Wren *Cantorchilus semibadius* 13.5 cm

CA endemic. Common resident in Pacific lowlands and foothills (to 1200 m) of east CR and west PA. **ID** White supercilium, white eye ring, and black-and-white streaking on auriculars. Extensive *black-and-white barring on underparts*. Wings and tail rufous-brown with dusky and whitish barring. Crown and mantle rufous-brown. Banded and Bay wrens allopatric. **HABITS** Understory and edge of humid broadleaf forest, gaps, riparian thickets, mangrove edge, and second growth. Ascends to midstory to forage in vine tangles or on epiphyte-laden branches. Probes in curled dead leaves. **VOICE** Variable song (1) a repeated, loud, ringing two- or three-syllable phrase *chee-wa-chee-wachee-wa . . .* or *whe-cha-whe-cha-whe-cha . . .* Calls (2) a sharp *ooh-weet*, (3) harsh, rasping *churrr*, and (4) dry, staccato, sputtering scold *jeh-jeh-jeh . . .*

Black-bellied Wren *Pheugopedius fasciatoventris* 15 cm

CA and north SA. Locally fairly common resident in south Pacific lowlands and foothills (to 500 m) of east CR and west PA. Disjunctly in lowlands of east PA. **ID** Broad tail often fanned or depressed. Blackish auriculars contrast with whitish supercilium. *White throat and breast contrast with blackish lower underparts*. Wings rufous-brown with faint dusky barring. Tail barred with blackish. Compare with Bay Wren. Note different underparts. **GV** Birds from central and east PA usually have broader dark bars on tail, more contrasting barring on flanks, and more blackish face and auriculars. **HABITS** Understory to lower midstory and edge of humid broadleaf forest gaps, riparian thickets, and second growth. Favors stands of *Heliconia*. Often near water. **VOICE** Song (1) a repeated phrase of rich, low-pitched, slurred whistles and shorter notes *go wheer go ch'wo go wheer go ch'wo . . .* Compare with faster, harsher song of Bay Wren. Call (2) a low-pitched, rasping chatter or sputter.

Black-throated Wren

Sooty-headed Wren

widespread

central PA

Bay Wren

east PA

Riverside Wren

central and
east PA

Pacific CR
and
west PA

Black-bellied Wren

50%

WRENS Troglodytidae

Small wrens found mainly at lower levels in humid broadleaf forest. Usually in pairs. White-breasted Wood-Wren is the most common and widespread and is geographically variable in Central America.

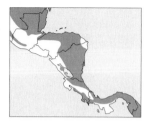

White-breasted Wood-Wren *Henicorhina leucosticta*   10 cm

MX to north SA. Common resident in lowlands and foothills (SL to 1000, locally to 1450 m in north). Mainly middle elevations (300 to 1850 m) in Pacific CR. **ID** Short tail often cocked. Black-and-white striped auriculars. Ad has *white throat and breast*. Juv has gray underparts. Gray-breasted Wood-Wren mainly higher elevations. Note different underparts. **GV** Birds from east PA have blackish crown and sparse streaking on auriculars. **HABITS** Floor and understory of semihumid to humid broadleaf forest. Favors cluttered tree falls and vine tangles. Forages actively. Investigates accumulations of debris or dead wood. Clings to vertical stems like an antbird. Does not follow mixed flocks but may become more active as they pass. **VOICE** Song (1) simple, varied phrases of two to five loud, clear, melodious, whistled notes. Variations include *cheer oweet-oweet* or *cheer-our oweet* or *cheeroo cheer* or *chewychewy-cheee*. May repeat a phrase or pause and switch to different phrase. Another song type (2) composed of several rapid repetitions of a short, ringing phrase *cheery tcheery tcheery tcheery*. Calls (3) a sharp, somewhat burry *cheek* or *bzeet* or *teleet*, (4) a low-pitched, sputtering *churrrr chut-ut-ur*, (5) an explosive *tuck*, and (6) a simple, flutelike whistle. In north gives (7) a loud, bright *blink* or *blink-blink*.

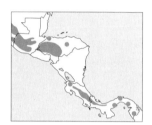

Gray-breasted Wood-Wren *Henicorhina leucophrys*   11 cm

South MX to north SA. Common resident in humid highlands (above 800 m). **ID** Short tail often cocked. Black-and-white streaked auriculars and *gray breast*. White-breasted Wood-Wren has white underparts including throat. **GV** Birds from north CA have unstreaked throat. Birds from Pacific GT also have dull upperparts and pale crown. Birds from east PA (not shown) have unstreaked throat and brownish crown. **HABITS** Understory and floor of humid broadleaf (cloud) forest. Locally in humid pine-oak forest in north. Favors dense, low growth, bamboo thickets, and cluttered tree-fall gaps. Does not follow mixed flocks but may become more active as they pass. **VOICE** Pairs may duet. Song (1) a complex, variable series of clear, rich whistles and warbles. Often includes a dry *chuck* or whistled introductory note *chuck-weeetoodeeweedeewoo*. Calls (2) a dry, staccato ticking or sputtering notes often given in long series *ch-t-t-t-t-t-t-t . . .* (3) harsh, rasping *churrs* (like White-breasted Wood-Wren), and (4) series of *plik* notes.

Timberline Wren *Thryorchilus browni*   10 cm

CA endemic. Locally fairly common resident in highlands (2800 to 3600, locally as low as 2200 m) of CR and west PA at Volcán Barú (Chiriquí, 89, 42). **ID** Short tail held cocked. *Broad white supercilium* and *white spotting on wing coverts*. Note whitish primaries. **HABITS** Floor and understory of humid broadleaf (cloud and elfin) forest, second growth, and paramo. Creeps through bamboo or other dense, low growth. **VOICE** Song (1) a complex, variable series of rapid, high-pitched warbles and short, squeaky notes. Often ends with high-pitched, thin whistle. Calls (2) a sharp, harsh, slightly squeaky *sheee-ip* given singly or repeated, (3) a fast, even-pitched series of scratchy notes *bzee ee-ee-ee-ee-ee*, and (4) high-pitched, thin *bheeee* or *dzeee*.

Rufous-browed Wren *Troglodytes rufociliatus*   9.5–10 cm

South MX and CA. Fairly common resident in north highlands (1700 to 3500, rarely or locally as low as 1200 m). Local in volcanic highlands of SV (Santa Ana, San Vicente, 183, 362). Poorly known in NI (Madriz, Matagalpa, Jinotega, 411, 413). **ID** Small. *Cinnamon supercilium, throat, and chest*. Wings and tail barred with dusky. Note blackish barring on flanks. House Wren duller with longer tail and different habits. Ochraceous Wren allopatric. **GV** Birds from HN and NI are darker and more richly colored. **HABITS** Understory to subcanopy of semihumid to humid broadleaf or pine-broadleaf forest. Often at lower levels but may ascend to subcanopy to forage in epiphytes and arboreal litter. Does not follow mixed flocks but may become more active as they pass. **VOICE** Song (1) a varied, high-pitched warble that accelerates to become a tinkling trill. Calls (2) a loud, scolding, buzzy *zzrrit* or *tzzzup* or (3) longer *jhrrrirr . . .*

Ochraceous Wren *Troglodytes ochraceous*   9.5 cm

CA endemic. Common resident in south highlands (900 to 3000 m). Local in east PA at Serranía de Majé, Tacarcuna Massif, and Pirre Massif (Panamá, Darién, 67, 659, 44). **ID** Small. Tail often cocked. *Long, broad, buff-ochre supercilium* contrasts with dark auriculars. Underparts pale buffy ochre. Wings and tail barred with dusky. Compare with House Wren. Note different head pattern and habits. Rufous-browed Wren allopatric. **HABITS** Midstory to subcanopy of humid broadleaf (cloud) forest and edge. Creeps among epiphytes and in arboreal litter. Follows mixed flocks. **VOICE** Variable song (1) of high-pitched, thin, slurred whistles and liquid trills. Calls (2) a rolling, thin, high-pitched *peeew* or *preeer* and (3) lower-pitched, weak *churr*.

juv

widespread ad

east PA
ad

White-breasted Wood-Wren

Pacific GT

widespread

Gray-breasted Wood-Wren

ad

GT
ad

juv

juv

HN and NI
ad

Timberline Wren

Rufous-browed Wren

ad

Ochraceous Wren

WRENS Troglodytidae

Mostly small wrens. Usually in pairs. House Wren, a familiar bird of disturbed areas, is the most widespread. *Microcerculus* and *Cyphorhinus* wrens are found on the ground and at lower levels in humid broadleaf forest. All have distinctive voices.

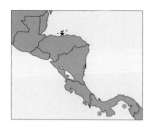

House Wren *Troglodytes aedon*   11 cm

NA to SA. Common resident (SL to 3300 m). Also Isla Coiba and Pearl Islands off PA (Veraguas, Panamá, 64, 653, 470). Reported from Bay Islands and Cayos Cochinos where status uncertain (317, 560). **ID** Small. Dull brown with variable extent of *fine, dusky barring on wings and tail.* Other small wrens have shorter tail and different head pattern and habits. **GV** House Wren from mainland PA is whitish below and has more extensive dusky barring, but there is considerable individual variation. Birds from Isla Coiba are more rufous. **HABITS** Understory of gardens, hedgerows, urban areas, riparian edges with piled debris, and open woodland. Loosely synanthropic. Pairs or solitary birds creep through tangled or cramped spaces investigating crevices and hollows. Makes short, low flights across openings. Uses broadleaf forest on Isla Coiba. **VOICE** Variable song (1) begins with several scratchy notes and becomes a long, liquid warble on lower pitch *tzitzitzi dlidli dliudliudliu.* Alarm call (2) a scratchy series of *rebrebrebrebreb.*

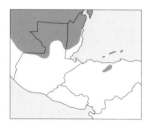

White-bellied Wren *Uropsila leucogastra*   10 cm

South MX and CA. Uncommon to common resident in lowlands (to 500 m) of north GT and BZ. Disjunctly in Aguán Valley of north HN (Yoro, 440). **ID** Small. *Plain whitish underparts* and whitish lores. Mostly plain grayish-brown above with *whitish supercilium* and *dark stripe behind eye.* Compare with larger Carolina Wren. **HABITS** Midstory to subcanopy of semihumid broadleaf forest (GT and BZ) and understory of arid scrub (HN). Favors cluttered vine tangles or thorny woodland. Creeps through epiphytes and hanging detritus. Often disappears from view as it investigates dark crevices. Solitary or in pairs. Does not follow mixed flocks but may forage more actively as they pass. **VOICE** Song (1) a short, simple, tinkling or bubbling phrase *chid-l-er* or *chidl-il-i-chu* or *whi didl-oo* or *toolee-doo* often repeated two or three times. Calls (2) a hard, dry rattle *chidididit . . . iditit . . .* and (3) low-pitched *chek* or *whek.*

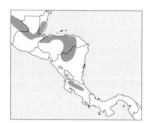

Nightingale Wren *Microcerculus philomela*   10 cm

South MX and CA. Uncommon resident in north Caribbean lowlands and foothills (mainly 200 to 1400, locally at SL or as high as 1800 m in north). Reaches southern limit in Río Reventazón drainage, CR (Limón, 587, 591). **ID** Dark. Fairly *long bill.* Short tail and long legs. Mostly dark brown with *fine dark scaling* including lower underparts. Juv has variably pale grayish throat and extensive gray and dusky scaling on underparts. Scaly-breasted Wren parapatric. **HABITS** Floor and understory of humid broadleaf forest. Pairs or solitary birds hop over damp, shaded ground. Sings from low perch while bobbing tail. Secretive. Detected mostly by voice. **VOICE** Song (1) begins with short, rapid series that rises in pitch and becomes a long series of loud, clear or slightly scratchy whistles, each on different pitch and given deliberately in long, disjointed series. Compare with slower song of Scaly-breasted Wren. Call (2) a short, sharp *tchut* or *chek.*

Scaly-breasted Wren *Microcerculus marginatus*   10 cm

CA and north SA. Uncommon resident in south humid lowlands and foothills (to 1200, locally to 1700 m). **ID** Fairly *long bill.* Short tail and long legs. Brownish above with faint dusky scaling. Lower underparts mostly plain brownish-cinnamon. *Throat and upper breast grayish-white.* Juv variably scaled with dusky and gray on underparts. Nightingale Wren parapatric. **HABITS** Floor and understory of humid broadleaf forest. Like Nightingale Wren. **VOICE** Song (1) begins with brief (three- or four-note), rapid, ascending series of scratchy whistles followed by a very long (two- to four- minute) series of high-pitched, clear whistles, each lasting one second or more and becoming progressively lower-pitched and more widely spaced (up to ten seconds between final notes). Whistles may be doubled. Compare with faster song of Nightingale Wren. Call (2) a sharp *tchip* or *tchik.*

Song Wren *Cyphorhinus phaeocephalus*   12 cm

CA and north SA. Uncommon resident in humid lowlands and foothills (to 1100 m). Poorly known in HN (Colón, Gracias a Dios, 513, 401, 629). **ID** Bill with swollen base. *Rufous auriculars, throat, and breast,* and *bare blue skin around eye.* Wings barred with dusky. May recall an antbird but note barred wings. **HABITS** Lower understory and floor of humid broadleaf forest. Pairs or small groups probe (sometimes noisily) in leaf litter or hop actively through low vegetation. Attends ant swarms. May follow mixed flocks. **VOICE** Song (1) short series of clear, separate whistles alternating with very different, low-pitched, guttural phrases. Call (2) a repeated, low-pitched, guttural *cutta* or *cuttakut.*

50%

north CA

PA

Coiba

House Wren

White-bellied Wren

Nightingale Wren

ad

juv

Scaly-breasted Wren

ad

juv

white-throated
ad

Song Wren

typical ad

GNATWRENS AND GNATCATCHERS Polioptilidae

Tiny birds. Usually in pairs or small groups. Gnatcatchers forage actively in outer foliage and often hover-glean or hang briefly. Also creep along larger limbs. Gnatcatchers are often seen with mixed flocks. Gnatwrens are found at lower levels in broadleaf forest and edge.

Tawny-faced Gnatwren *Microbates cinereiventris*   10.5 cm

CA and north SA. Uncommon resident in south lowlands and foothills (to 1200 m). Poorly known in NI (Río San Juan, 346, 413). **ID** *Short, narrow tail* usually cocked. *Tawny sides of head* and white throat contrast with *black malar* and streaks on breast. Underparts gray. Long-billed Gnatwren has different head pattern and longer tail. **GV** Birds from east PA have dark eye stripe. **HABITS** Understory of humid broadleaf forest. Forages actively. Often perches on slender vertical stems. **VOICE** Song (1) a series of lisping, scratchy, slurred notes alternating with clear whistles and harsh chatters *cher-chwa seee chew cher ch'ch'ch'ch' tweet tsur tsur cher . . .* Calls (2) a nasal, burry *nyaaar* or *meeyaar*, (3) a harsh, dry chatter, and (4) high-pitched whistle *peeee*. Compare with song of Tawny-crowned Greenlet.

Long-billed Gnatwren *Ramphocaenus melanurus*   12.5 cm

MX to SA. Fairly common resident in lowlands and foothills (to 1200, locally to 1700 m in north). Uncommon to rare in Pacific NI (Managua, 413). **ID** *Very long, fine bill.* Long, narrow, white-tipped tail cocked or thrown loosely to side. Head and breast pale cinnamon. **HABITS** Understory to lower midstory of semihumid to humid broadleaf forest and tall second growth. Favors gaps or edges with large, shaded vine tangles. **VOICE** Song (1) a long, slightly hollow trill. Sometimes on steady pitch but more often rises quickly then gradually falls. Varies from clear and melodious to slightly dry and harsh. Compare with song of Streak-headed Woodcreeper. Calls (2) loud, clear whistle, (3) a series of sharp, ticking notes, and (4) low-pitched, dry *chiirr*. May be repeated as a chattering *chiirchiirchiir . . .*

Blue-gray Gnatcatcher *Polioptila caerulea*   11 cm

Resident and Nearctic breeding populations. Locally fairly common breeder in lowlands of BZ (667, 343) and north GT (Petén, Huehuetenango, 229, 378, 637). Uncommon winter resident (to 1500, but transients may range to 2500 m). Rarely reported south to NI (Grenada, 412). **ID** *White eye ring.* Breeding male (Mar to Jul) has short, narrow, black supercilium. Nonbreeding male, female, and imm slightly duller and lack black supercilium. Compare with Tropical and White-lored gnatcatchers. Note different head pattern. **HABITS** Midstory to canopy and edge of humid broadleaf forest, pine-oak woodland, pine savanna, second growth, gardens, and mangroves. **VOICE** Song (1) a nasal, squeaky chatter. Call (2) a nasal *nyear* like Red-legged Honeycreeper.

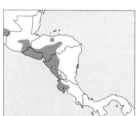

White-lored Gnatcatcher *Polioptila albiloris*   11 cm

South MX and north CA. Common resident in Pacific lowlands and foothills (to 1800, mainly below 750 m). Also arid Caribbean valleys of GT and HN. **ID** Breeding male (Jan to Sep) has black cap and nape contrasting with white auriculars. Nonbreeding male has narrow white supercilium and *blackish eye stripe* extending from lores to behind eye. Female has gray crown and nape. Note female's grayish lores. Female resembles female Tropical Gnatcatcher. Note White-lored's whiter throat and restricted white behind eye. **HABITS** Understory to midstory of deciduous and thorn forest, second growth, scrub, and mangroves. **VOICE** Song (1) a series of downslurred, nasal, squeaky notes. Calls (2) a nasal, downslurred *meeah* or *jehrrr*, (3) longer, downslurred *bzzzzzir*, and (4) harsh, rapid chatter *chtchtcht . . .* Calls harsher than Blue-gray and Tropical gnatcatchers.

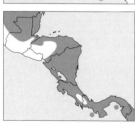

Tropical Gnatcatcher *Polioptila plumbea*   10.5 cm

South MX to north SA. Fairly common resident in lowlands and foothills (to 500, locally to 1500 m). Also Isla Coiba and Pearl Islands off PA (653, 659, 470, 471). **ID** *Dark eyeline* extends from behind eye. In all plumages *lores whitish.* Male has glossy black crown and nape. Female has broad white supercilium and lores. **HABITS** Subcanopy to canopy and edge of semihumid to humid broadleaf forest, tall second growth, and shaded plantations. **VOICE** Song (1) a short, nasal whinny that drops slightly in pitch and slows at end *whi-i-i-i-i-i-i-e-e-e.* Compare with song of Dot-winged Antwren. Call (2) a nasal *whaaaa.* Compare with calls of Blue-gray Gnatcatcher and Red-legged Honeycreeper.

Slate-throated Gnatcatcher *Polioptila schistaceigula*   10 cm

CA and north SA. Uncommon to rare and local resident in foothills (450 to 1000 m) of east PA (Colón, Panamá, Kuna Yala, Darién, 659, 519). **ID** Male's *dark gray throat and chest* contrast with white lower underparts. Note partial white eye ring. Female paler with pale supercilium. **HABITS** Canopy and edge of humid broadleaf forest. **VOICE** Song (1) a short, rising trill *pr-e-e-e-e-e-u-u-u* that slows slightly at end. Compare with faster, higher-pitched song of Tropical Gnatcatcher. Call (2) a high-pitched, sibilant *pyew* or *peeeu*.

Tawny-faced Gnatwren

widespread

east PA

Long-billed Gnatwren

♀

Blue-gray Gnatcatcher

breeding
♂

♀

White-lored Gnatcatcher

nonbreeding
♂

breeding
♂

♀

Tropical Gnatcatcher

♂

Slate-throated Gnatcatcher

♀

♂

DONACOBIUS Donacobidae

Black-capped Donacobius *Donacobius atricapilla* 22 cm
CA and SA. Uncommon to rare and local resident in lowlands and foothills (to 600 m) of east PA (Darién). **ID** *Black head and neck* and *buff underparts*. Note *pale orange eyes* and fine dusky barring on flanks. White on wings and tail conspicuous in flight. Singing birds expose bare orange skin on sides of neck. **HABITS** Understory of marshes and margins of lakes and ponds with floating or emergent vegetation. In pairs or small groups. Often noisy. Sings from low perch while wagging tail. **VOICE** Pairs call in duet. Male's song (1) a series of ringing, upslurred whistles *wheer, wheer, wheer, wheer . . .* or *woit, woit, woit . . .* Female gives lower-pitched, harsh or buzzy phrases. Calls (2) a loud *quoit-quoit-quoit-quoit*, (3) low-pitched *chirru*, and (4) harsh *jeeeya*.

BLUEBIRD AND SOLITAIRES Turdidae

The complex and striking songs of *Myadestes* solitaires are among the characteristic sounds of highland forests in Central America.

Eastern Bluebird *Sialia sialis* 15–17 cm
NA to CA. Uncommon resident in north highlands (to 3700 m). Also Caribbean savannas of HN (Gracias a Dios, 442), NI (RAAN, 325, 413), and Mountain Pine Ridge in BZ (Cayo, 529, 346). **ID** Ad male *blue above* and *orange-rufous below*. Ad female gray above and cinnamon below with whitish eye ring. Ad has buff spotting and blue on wings and tail. **GV** Birds from Mosquitia region (not shown) are smaller and the female is paler. **HABITS** Understory to midstory of open pine and pine-oak woodland, adjacent agricultural lands, pastures, plantations, and gardens. Solitary or in pairs. Sallies to ground from prominent perch above grassy area. **VOICE** Song (1) a short series of hoarse, warbled phrases *whochoo-oo* or *wee-chhoo-oo* or longer *whee-chereer-cha weecha*. Calls (2) a short *chew-ew* sometimes given in flight and (3) rapid, chattering *ch-ch-ch-ch brrrr*.

Brown-backed Solitaire *Myadestes occidentalis* 20 cm
South MX and north CA. Fairly common resident in north highlands (600 to 3500 m). Also volcanic highlands of SV (San Vicente, 341). **ID** Fairly long tail. Mostly gray with *brown mantle* and wings. Note *broken whitish eye ring* and dusky malar. Juv speckled with buff. Slate-colored Solitaire has gray mantle and wings. **HABITS** Midstory to subcanopy of pine, pine-oak and humid broadleaf forest, second growth, and plantations. Reclusive but readily detected by voice. Solitary or in pairs. **VOICE** Song (1) an accelerating series of squeaky, metallic notes that end abruptly. Begins with halting series of *eeenk* notes before accelerating and increasing in volume. Compare with less metallic, more flutelike song of Slate-colored Solitaire. Calls include (2) a metallic, flat *eeenk* or *yeeeh*.

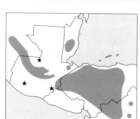

Slate-colored Solitaire *Myadestes unicolor* 19 cm
South MX and north CA. Fairly common resident in foothills and highlands (1000 to 2700, rarely or locally as low as 400 m). Breeds mainly above 1000 m (Mar to Jul). Moves to lower elevations outside breeding season (221). Also Maya Mountains of south BZ (Cayo, 529, 313, 343). Recently reported from Cerro Musún in NI (Matagalpa, 137). **ID** *Mostly plain gray* with *broken whitish eye ring*. Juv speckled with buff and has pale throat. Brown-backed Solitaire has brown mantle and wings. **HABITS** Midstory to subcanopy of humid broadleaf cloud forest. Retiring, but may appear at forest edge or descend to understory to feed at fruiting shrub. Solitary or in pairs. **VOICE** Loud, complex song (1) begins hesitantly with scratchy notes then accelerates and becomes a varied series of clear to quavering, flutelike whistles. Often includes or ends with a liquid trill. Compare with more metallic song of Brown-backed Solitaire. Call (2) a harsh, nasal *rrank* or *rrrah*. May be repeated.

Black-faced Solitaire *Myadestes melanops* 18 cm
CA endemic. Fairly common resident in foothills and highlands (mainly 900 to 2750 m) of CR and west PA. Undertakes altitudinal movements (593, 92). **ID** Mostly gray with black mask, forehead, and chin. *Orange-red bill and legs*. Blackish flight feathers contrast with gray wing coverts. Compare with Slaty-backed Nightingale-Thrush. Other solitaires allopatric. **HABITS** Understory to midstory of humid broadleaf (cloud) forest and second growth. May hover or cling briefly to take fruit. May appear lethargic. Solitary or in pairs. **VOICE** Song (1) a slow series of high-pitched, clear whistles and trills *tooo-leee-do wheeerrrr wiiiiii*. Compare with song of Slaty-backed Nightingale-Thrush. Calls (2) an upslurred, nasal *ghank*, (3) liquid *quirt*, and (4) buzzy *shweee*.

Varied Solitaire *Myadestes coloratus* 18 cm
CA and north SA. Uncommon resident in foothills and highlands (mainly above 1200 m, rarely or briefly lower) of east PA (Panamá, Darién, 519, 44, 45). May move to lower elevations outside breeding season. **ID** Gray head and underparts with *contrasting brown upperparts*. Black forehead, face, and throat. Note black-and-brown wing pattern. Bill and legs yellow-orange. Juv speckled with buff. Other *Myadestes* solitaires allopatric. **HABITS** Midstory of humid broadleaf (cloud) forest. Like Black-faced Solitaire. **VOICE** Song (1) a slow series of rich, liquid or slurred phrases that rise and fall in pitch. Much like Black-faced Solitaire. Call (2) a harsh *reeeeeah*.

Black-capped Donacobius

juv

ad

ad ♀

Eastern Bluebird

juv

ad ♂

Brown-backed Solitaire

juv

ad

Slate-colored Solitaire

juv

ad

Black-faced Solitaire

Varied Solitaire

NIGHTINGALE-THRUSHES Turdidae

Small, resident thrushes found on floor and at lower levels in broadleaf forest. Often secretive but nightingale-thrushes sometimes forage in the open at edges or along trails. Several have striking songs and these are among the characteristic sounds of foothill and highland forests in Central America.

Slaty-backed Nightingale-Thrush *Catharus fuscater*   18 cm
CA and north SA. Fairly common resident in south highlands (800 to 2300 m).
ID Dark slaty gray with *orange-red bill* and red eye ring. Note orange-red legs and *pale eyes*. **GV** Birds from east PA are paler overall and slightly yellowish below.
HABITS Floor and lower understory of humid broadleaf (cloud) forest. Hops over ground. Flicks wings rapidly. Usually solitary. Sometimes in pairs or small groups. Attends ant swarms where it forages boldly in open. **VOICE** Song (1) composed of clear, flutelike whistles. Alternates phrases of two and three notes *peee leee, peee-o-lay* . . . Compare with harsher song of Black-faced Solitaire. Calls (2) nasal, mewing, upslurred *maaaaah* and (3) clear, high-pitched whistle *poeeeee*.

Spotted Nightingale-Thrush *Catharus dryas*   18 cm
CA and (disjunctly) SA. Locally common to rare resident in foothills and highlands (mainly 1200 to 1800, but recorded 750 to 3000 m) of GT, north SV (Santa Ana, 364), HN, and NI (Madriz, 135). **ID** Olive above with black head. Orange-red bill, legs, and eye ring. Underparts mostly *yellow with dark spotting*. **HABITS** Floor and understory of humid broadleaf forest. Sings from elevated perch. Solitary. Secretive. Detected mostly by voice. **VOICE** Song (1) a series of rich, flutelike phrases and clear whistles *clee-oo-leew, clee-oo-low* or *whee-i-lee, wee-i-lou*. Calls (2) a nasal *rrehr* and (3) series of harsh notes *shah-shah-shah*.

Black-headed Nightingale-Thrush *Catharus mexicanus*   16 cm
MX and CA. Fairly common resident in humid foothills (recorded 300 to 1600, but mainly 800 to 1200 m). **ID** Olive above with *blackish face and crown*. Note *orange-red bill, eye ring, and legs*. **HABITS** Floor and understory of humid broadleaf forest. Sings from perch in midstory to subcanopy. May raise bushy crest. Solitary. **VOICE** Song (1) three to eight phrases including clear, thin, high-pitched, slurred whistles and short, trilled, buzzy or harsh notes *chk-ik tsleeeeee deedleeee* . . . Repeats a phrase several times like Orange-billed Nightingale-Thrush but song more melodious. Compare with simpler song of Slaty-backed Nightingale-Thrush. Calls (2) a thin, buzzy, upslurred *dzeeeee* and (3) hard, dry rattle.

Orange-billed Nightingale-Thrush *Catharus aurantiirostris*   17 cm
MX to north SA. Fairly common resident in foothills and highlands (400 to 2500 m). **ID** Rufous-brown above and plain gray below with *orange bill, orbital ring, and legs*. Juv has spotted breast and dusky bill. **GV** Birds from Pacific east CR and PA have mostly gray head. **HABITS** Floor, understory, and edge of semihumid broadleaf or pine-oak forest, second growth, shaded plantations, and scrub. Favors drier habitats than other *Catharus* nightingale-thrushes. Solitary. **VOICE** Song (1) a variable phrase of three to six thin, high-pitched, squeaky or slightly buzzy notes *tss-lllik-a-cheeeu* or *psss-lik-whuuu*. Repeats a phrase several times then switches to another. Often ends with a short trill. Calls (2) a nasal, upslurred *reeeeah* like Gray Catbird that is sometimes repeated or extended to form a nasal chatter and (3) thin, squeaky, downslurred *seeuuuu*.

Ruddy-capped Nightingale-Thrush *Catharus frantzii*   17 cm
MX and CA. Uncommon resident in highlands (1400 to 3500, but mainly above 1800 m). Reported from volcanic highlands in SV (Santa Ana, San Vicente, 183, 619, 341, 610) and at Cerro Musún in NI (Matagalpa, 137). **ID** Dull brown above with *russet crown*. Mostly grayish below with faint brownish breast-band. Mandible orange. Juv has russet crown with pale streaks and pale lores. **HABITS** Floor and understory of arid to humid broadleaf and pine-oak forest and second growth. Sings from low perch in dim light. **VOICE** Variable song (1) includes clear whistles, flutelike trills, and short, high-pitched, warbling phrases. Resembles song of Hermit Thrush. Calls (2) an upslurred whistle *whoeeeet* or *whreeee* and (3) short, nasal chatter *eh-eh, eh-eh-eh* . . .

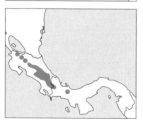

Black-billed Nightingale-Thrush *Catharus gracilirostris*   15 cm
CA endemic. Common resident in highlands (above 2150, rarely as low as 1500 m) of CR and west PA. **ID** Small. *Black bill* and plain gray head. *Gray throat and flanks* contrast with *brown breast-band*. **HABITS** Floor, understory, and edge of humid broadleaf (cloud) forest, second growth, plantations, and gardens. Usually solitary. **VOICE** Song (1) a single, high-pitched introductory note followed by complex, rich, high-pitched phrase *seeee, weechiii-iii-ee*. Calls (2) a high-pitched, thin, descending *pseeeew* and (3) penetrating, upslurred *seeeet* or *wheeeeet*. Compare with calls of Wrenthrush and Timberline Wren. Also (4) an upslurred, nasal note followed by a short chatter *jeet-chchchch*.

38%

juv

widespread
ad

Slaty-backed
Nightingale-Thrush

east PA
ad

Spotted
Nightingale-Thrush

ad
♀

ad
♂

Black-headed Nightingale-Thrush

juv

widespread
ad

Pacific CR
and west PA
ad

Orange-billed
Nightingale-Thrush

Ruddy-capped
Nightingale-Thrush

Black-billed
Nightingale-Thrush

THRUSHES Turdidae

Nearctic breeding migrant thrushes. Upperparts color and details of the head pattern are useful in separating these. Swainson's Thrush is generally the most widespread, but Wood Thrush can be locally common in north Caribbean lowlands.

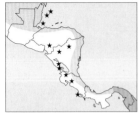

Gray-cheeked Thrush *Catharus minimus*   17 cm

Breeds Nearctic. Winters mainly SA. Uncommon fall transient (Oct to Nov). Rare spring transient (Mar to May). Most records from Caribbean slope. Very rare in winter in lowlands and foothills of NI (135), CR (600), and PA (659, 512). **ID** Grayish-brown above with diffuse but distinctly *gray lores and auriculars and narrow eye ring*. Compare with Swainson's Thrush. Note different head pattern. **HABITS** Floor and understory of forest or woodland. Sometimes ascends to midstory or canopy to feed on fruit. Generally shy and retiring. **VOICE** Call (1) a downslurred *wheeur* or *weeyap*.

Swainson's Thrush *Catharus ustulatus*   17 cm

Breeds Nearctic. Winters Middle America and SA. Widespread transient and winter resident (mainly Sep to May). May be briefly or locally abundant. In north winters mainly on Pacific slope. Irregular in Caribbean lowlands and foothills. Vagrant to Isla del Coco (346). **ID** *Buff eye ring and lores*. Upperparts plain brownish including tail. Gray-cheeked Thrush has different head pattern. **GV** Birds from breeding population in Pacific northwest NA are more rufous-brown above. **HABITS** Floor to subcanopy and edge of forest or woodland. Transients use a wide variety of arboreal habitats. Forages mainly on or near ground. May ascend to midstory or canopy to feed on fruit. **VOICE** Song (1) given mostly by spring transients an ascending warble. Call (2) a low-pitched, liquid *pwip* or *quip* and (3) coarse, nasal chatter usually preceded by a call note *qui-brrrrr*.

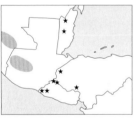

Veery *Catharus fuscescens*   17 cm

Breeds Nearctic. Winters SA. Uncommon to rare fall transient (mainly Sep to Oct). Rare spring transient (Mar to Apr). Reported mainly from Caribbean slope and islands including BZ Cays (343). Very rare on Pacific slope (346). **ID** *Reddish-rufous upperparts* and *sparse reddish spotting on breast*. Resembles other NA migrant *Catharus* but Veery is more softly patterned below and brighter white on lower underparts. Compare with Pacific form of Swainson's Thrush. Also compare with Orange-billed Nightingale-Thrush. **HABITS** Floor and understory of forest or woodland. Forages mainly on ground. May ascend to midstory or canopy to feed on fruit. Usually shy and retiring. **VOICE** Calls (1) a nasal, rough *jerr* and (2) harsh *ho-ch-ch-ch-ch*.

Hermit Thrush *Catharus guttatus*   17 cm

Breeds Nearctic. Winters mainly south USA and MX. Uncommon to rare transient and winter resident (mainly Oct to May) in GT highlands (mainly 1500 to 3000 m). Rare in SV (Santa Ana, Chalatenango, 619, 616, 346), BZ (Cayo, 346), and HN (Copán, La Paz, 346). **ID** Upperparts variably grayish-brown to brown but always has contrasting *rufous tail* and narrow, whitish eye ring. Compare with Swainson's Thrush. Note different upperparts and head pattern. **HABITS** Floor and understory of forest or woodland. Hops over ground, usually beneath cover. Sometimes emerges to forage in open at edges. May ascend to midstory or canopy to feed on fruit. Generally shy and retiring. Solitary, but may join mixed associations at fruiting trees. Habitually raises and slowly lowers tail. **VOICE** Typical call (1) a low-pitched, soft, dry *chup*. Compare with call of Hepatic Tanager. Also (2) a *meeeow* similar to call of Orange-billed Nightingale-Thrush.

Wood Thrush *Hylocichla mustelina*   19 cm

Breeds Nearctic. Winters MX and CA. Widespread transient and winter resident (mainly Oct to Apr) in lowlands and foothills (to 1700 m). Most common in north Caribbean lowlands. Uncommon to rare in north Pacific (183, 408, 619) and in east PA (346). **ID** Robust with relatively short tail and heavy bill. Note rufous crown and nape, *black spotting on white underparts* and black-and-white streaked auriculars. Compare with migrant *Catharus* thrushes. Note different structure, underparts, and head pattern. **HABITS** Floor and understory of semihumid to humid broadleaf forest, tall second growth and shaded plantations. Solitary. **VOICE** Song (1) given by spring transients begins with two or three rich, flutelike notes and ends with complex trill. Call (2) an abrupt *wek wekwekwek wek*.

Gray-cheeked Thrush

Pacific
northwest NA

Swainson's Thrush

widespread

Veery

Hermit Thrush

Wood Thrush

THRUSHES Turdidae

Resident thrushes found in lowlands and foothills. All have striking and complex songs. Clay-colored Thrush is the most common and widespread.

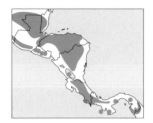

White-throated Thrush *Turdus assimilis* 21–23 cm

MX to north SA. Uncommon to locally common resident in lowlands and foothills (to 1400, rarely to 2000 m). Resident near SL on Isla Coiba (Veraguas, 653, 470). May undertake seasonal movements (593, 512). **ID** *White band on lower throat* contrasts with black-and-white striped throat and variably brown or grayish breast. Note variably *yellow or orange eye ring*. Bill variably yellow or dusky. **GV** Birds from north Caribbean slope tend to be grayer than birds from interior and Pacific slope. However, both gray and brown birds are known from nearby localities in HN. Birds from east PA are smaller, deeper brown, and have dusky tip of bill. Birds from Isla Coiba, are deeper brown, have dusky base of bill, and have dark markings on crissum. **HABITS** Midstory to subcanopy of semihumid to humid broadleaf forest, adjacent tall second growth, and shaded plantations. Often solitary. May gather in numbers at fruiting trees. Attends ant swarms. **VOICE** Song (1) a variable series of contrasting notes and phrases that are frequently doubled (repeated) in mimid-like fashion. Compare with song of Clay-colored Thrush. Calls (2) a short, nasal *ehrt* or *krrt*, (3) a mournful, whistled *peeyuu* or *whuueeet* that suggests Clay-colored Thrush, and (4) peculiar *wheer-chik-a-wheer-chik*.

Pale-vented Thrush *Turdus obsoletus* 23 cm

CA and north SA. Uncommon resident in south foothills (SL to 2500, mainly 750 to 1200 m). Also east PA (Darién, 512). May move to lower elevations outside breeding season (593, 253, 670). **ID** Near-uniform dark brown (becoming slightly paler below) with *blackish bill*. Note *white belly and crissum*. Juv has obscure spotting on breast and narrow cinnamon edging on wing coverts. Clay-colored Thrush has different bill and underparts. Note different habits. **HABITS** Midstory to subcanopy and edge of humid broadleaf forest and adjacent tall second growth. Solitary or in pairs. More arboreal than other *Turdus* thrushes but may descend to ground along trails or openings. Visits fruiting trees in canopy or at forest edge, sometimes in numbers. Somewhat reclusive and usually remains concealed in vegetation. **VOICE** Song (1) a long series of rich, somewhat hoarse, warbled phrases. Compare with slower, sweeter, more varied song of Clay-colored Thrush. Calls (2) a thin, dry, twittering *bzeeek* and (3) throaty *wuk*. At dusk gives (4) a series of two to four querulous whistles that rise in pitch *woeep-woeep-woeep-woeep*.

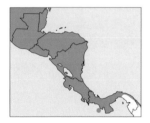

Clay-colored Thrush *Turdus grayi* 24 cm

MX to north SA. Common resident (to 1800, locally to 2400 m). **ID** Near-uniform light brown (becoming slightly paler below) with *greenish-yellow bill*. Throat indistinctly streaked with brown and whitish. Compare with Mountain and Pale-vented thrushes. Note different bill color and habits. **GV** Some birds from north BZ (not shown) are paler below. **HABITS** Uses all levels of vegetation in nonforest habitats including semihumid to humid forest edge, scrub, second growth, plantations, gardens, river margins, and urban areas. In forested regions confined to riparian edges and clearings. Usually solitary. **VOICE** Song (1) a long series of rich, warbled phrases. Often includes long, slurred whistles and short trills. Compare with song of White-throated Thrush. Calls (2) a variable, throaty *tock*, (3) a hoarse, sometimes nasal, *pup pup pup pup . . .* or *toc toc toc toc . . .* typical of *Turdus*, (4) a slightly quavering, upslurred *cheweew* or *chew ew ew* or *eeyuuu-ooo*, and (5) downslurred *keeyoooo* or *chewaa* that may be repeated.

gray
ad

brown
ad

juv

Coiba
ad

east PA
ad

White-throated Thrush

juv

ad

Pale-vented Thrush

juv

ad

Clay-colored Thrush

THRUSHES Turdidae

Resident thrushes found in highlands. Mountain Thrush is the most common and widespread.

Rufous-collared Robin *Turdus rufitorques* 24 cm

South MX and north CA. Resident in north highlands (mainly above 1800 m). Common in GT. Uncommon in HN. Also volcanic highlands of SV (La Libertad, Santa Ana, 183). **ID** Ad male mostly blackish with *broad rufous collar and breast.* Note orange-yellow bill. Female and imm male dull grayish but with similar pattern. Some females near-uniform grayish with *faint suggestion of ad pattern.* Compare with Clay-colored Thrush. Note different head pattern. **HABITS** Semihumid to humid pine-oak and coniferous woodland, forest edge, gardens, and plantations. Forages on ground in semi-open areas. Takes prominent, high perch to sing. Forms flocks outside breeding season. **VOICE** Song (1) a halting, repetitive series of rich or slightly squeaky phrases *cheer chrri-chrri chree-ip chree-ip chee cheer.* Calls (2) a slightly hoarse *kweh-kweh-kweh . . .* typical of *Turdus* thrushes, (3) single, sharper *wheuk,* and (4) high-pitched *ssir.*

Black Thrush *Turdus infuscatus* 24 cm

South MX and CA. Fairly common resident in north highlands (mainly 1500 to 3500 m). Also volcanic highlands of SV (San Vicente, Santa Ana, 183, 341). **ID** *Legs yellow.* Ad male *uniform black* with *yellow bill and eye ring.* Female dark brown becoming slightly paler below with dusky streaking on throat. Compare female with female Mountain Thrush. Note different crissum, throat, and bill color. Female resembles Clay-colored Thrush (mainly lower elevations). Note different leg color and habits. Sooty Thrush allopatric. **HABITS** Midstory to subcanopy and edge of semihumid to humid broadleaf forest, pine-oak woodland, and plantations. Solitary or in pairs. **VOICE** Song (1) a leisurely, varied, repetitive series that includes slurred whistles and trilled notes *wheer cheeri-cheerri toodoodee chree-ip chree-ip cheer dididi cheerwheeeer . . .* Calls (2) a rapid *wehk-wehk-wehk . . .* and (3) high-pitched *psssip.*

Mountain Thrush *Turdus plebejus* 25 cm

South MX and CA. Common resident in highlands (mainly above 1800, locally as low as 1300 m in south). May move to lower elevations outside breeding season. **ID** *Drab.* Ad *near-uniform, dull grayish-brown* with only faint dark streaking on throat. Crissum scalloped with dusky. Note *dark bill, legs, and eyes.* Clay-colored Thrush (lower elevations) is paler and warmer brown with greenish or dull yellow bill. Larger Sooty Thrush (sympatric in south) is darker with pale eyes. Female Black Thrush (sympatric in north) has different leg color and crissum. **GV** Birds from south CA are grayer. **HABITS** Humid broadleaf forest, second growth, plantations, and gardens. Forages at all levels. Solitary or in pairs. Forms flocks outside breeding season. **VOICE** Song (1) a long, monotonous series of short, weak notes with little variation in pitch or quality *chip chip chip cher chip chip cher cher tsur chip . . .* Calls (2) a high-pitched, thin *seee* or *peeent,* (3) rapid *whic-whic-whic-whic . . .* hoarser than Clay-colored Thrush, (4) a lower-pitched *tock tock tock,* and (5) upslurred, hollow *wreeeep* or *oowreeep.*

Sooty Thrush *Turdus nigrescens* 27 cm

CA endemic. Locally very common resident in highlands (mainly above 2500 m) of CR and west PA (Chiriquí). **ID** Large. *Near-uniform brownish-black* becoming darker on wings and tail. Note *yellow bill,* narrow yellow eye ring, and *whitish eyes.* Legs yellow-orange. Juv has fine cinnamon streaking on upperparts and spotting on wing coverts. Compare with Mountain Thrush. Black Thrush allopatric. **HABITS** Open or semi-open areas including paramo, pastures, low scrub, and edge. Forages mainly on ground but uses all levels in vegetation. Usually solitary outside breeding season. **VOICE** Song (1) a series of short, gurgling, buzzy or squeaky phrases repeated three to six times. After pause repeats a different phrase *chuweek chuweek chuweek, seechrrrzit seechrrrzit, tseeur tseeur tseeur tseeur.* Call (2) a low-pitched, harsh *grrrrk* or *grrek* often repeated several times.

Rufous-collared Robin

♀

ad ♂

dull ♀

juv

♀

♂

Black Thrush

north CA

south CA

Mountain Thrush

juv

ad

Sooty Thrush

DIPPER Cinclidae

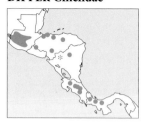

American Dipper *Cinclus mexicanus* 16–18 cm

NA to CA. Uncommon to rare and local resident in foothills and highlands (mainly 1200 to 2500, locally as low as 650 m, vagrant to near SL). Uncommon in GT (229). Rare in SV (Chalatenango, 346) and HN (Francisco Morazán, Intibucá, Yoro, Atlántida, Olancho, 442, 346, 267). Very rare in NI (Jinotega, RAAN, 413, 626). Uncommon and local in CR and PA. **ID** Rounded with long legs. Ad mostly *plain gray* with dull brownish head. Imm whitish below and has whitish tips on wing feathers. **GV** Birds from CR and PA are paler and grayer than birds from north CA. **HABITS** Margins of turbulent mountain streams. Walks over boulders or on gravel bars. Sometimes dives or simply walks below surface. Makes short, rapid flights, often low over water. **VOICE** Song (1) a varied, mimid-like series that includes rich or metallic warbles, trills, and buzzy notes. Compare with song of Tropical Mockingbird. Call (2) a loud, slightly metallic, buzzy *zzeip* or *zzreip* or *rreip* and (3) two- or three-note phrase in flight *zzir-rit* or *kirri-dit-rit* or *rrei-rreirrip*.

WAXWING Bombycillidae

Cedar Waxwing *Bombycilla cedrorum* 17 cm

Breeds Nearctic. Winters USA to CA. Widespread but irregular transient and winter resident (mainly Oct to Apr, rarely to Jun). Mainly in highlands. Uncommon south to central PA (Panamá, 649). **ID** *Black throat and narrow mask* and *pointed crest.* Mostly brown with yellow belly and *orange-yellow to yellow terminal band on tail.* Imm resembles ad but has soft streaking on breast. **HABITS** Midstory to canopy in wide variety of arboreal habitats. Ranges widely. Often in compact flocks of up to 100 birds. **VOICE** Call (1) often given in flight, a high-pitched, hissing *ssseeeep.*

SILKY-FLYCATCHERS Ptiliogonatidae

Gray Silky-flycatcher *Ptiliogonys cinereus* female 20, male 22 cm

MX and north CA. Locally fairly common resident in highlands (1000 to 3500 m) of GT. **ID** *Short, pointed crest, whitish eye ring,* and *long tail wiuth white band.* Male has gray breast. Note olive flanks and yellow crissum. Female has mostly brownish mantle and underparts. Long-tailed Silky-flycatcher allopatric. Compare with Cedar Waxwing. **HABITS** Canopy and edge of semihumid pine oak-forest and adjacent plantations. Pairs or small groups perch prominently in treetops. Forms flocks outside breeding season. **VOICE** Song (1) a fairly soft, warbled series of clucks and quiet, plaintive whistles. Calls (2) variable, short phrases often given in flight *chi-che-rup che-chep* or *chep-chup*, (3) clipped, slightly nasal *k-lik* or *ch-pik* or *k-li-lik*, and (4) clear, fairly sharp *chureet* or *chu-leep* or *chee-tuk.*

Long-tailed Silky-flycatcher *Ptiliogonys caudatus* female 23, male 25 cm

CA endemic. Uncommon to locally fairly common resident in highlands (mainly above 1850 m, rarely as low as 1050 m) of CR and west PA (Chiriquí). **ID** *Pointed crest* and *long tail.* Male has pale gray mantle and breast contrasting with *olive-yellow hood, belly, and crissum.* Female mostly olive-yellow with dark wings and tail. Gray Silky-flycatcher allopatric. **HABITS** Canopy and edge of humid broadleaf forest. Pairs or small groups perch on high, bare branches. Occasionally descends to lower levels in vegetation to feed on fruit. **VOICE** Calls (1) a repeated *che-chip* or *chechip* or *chididit* and in flight (2) a more prolonged, crackling or rattling *che-e-e-e-e.*

Black-and-yellow Silky-flycatcher *Phainoptila melanoxantha* 21–22 cm

CA endemic. Uncommon to fairly common resident in highlands (above 1200 m) of CR and west PA. **ID** Bulky with rounded structure. Male has black head, mantle, and wings contrasting with *yellow rump and flanks.* Female has olive upperparts, *blackish cap,* and gray throat. Compare with Black-faced Solitaire. **GV** Birds from west CR (Cordilleras de Guanacaste and Tilarán) are smaller and ad male has completely yellow belly. Females are pale have faint yellow streaking on breast. **HABITS** Midstory to canopy and edge of very humid broadleaf (cloud) forest and adjacent second growth and shaded plantations. Pairs, small groups, or solitary birds perch quietly. May perch motionless for long periods. Frugivorous. **VOICE** Usually quiet. Call (1) a high-pitched, bright, sharp *psst* or *tsst* or *piik.* May be repeated.

juv

American Dipper

north CA
ad

CR and PA
ad

♀

♂

Gray Silky-flycatcher

Cedar Waxwing

♂

♀

**Long-tailed
Silky-flycatcher**

west CR
♂

west CR
♀

central CR
and PA
♂

central CR
and PA
♀

Black-and-yellow Silky-flycatcher

MOCKINGBIRDS AND CATBIRDS Mimidae

Mockingbirds and catbirds are long-tailed birds with striking and complex songs.

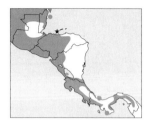

Tropical Mockingbird *Mimus gilvus*   25 cm

MX to SA. Expanding in region (132, 89, 389, 512, 662, 413, 126, 546, 346). Common resident in arid to semihumid regions (SL to 3200 m in north, locally to 1350 m in CR). Also BZ Cays (343). Reported from Útila and Roatán in Bay Islands (317). **ID** Long tail (often raised or fanned). Mostly pale gray (paler below) with *white markings on wings and tail*. Eyes deep yellow. Juv has dark eyes and variable dark spotting on breast. **HABITS** Understory to canopy of savannas, second growth, littoral scrub, agricultural areas, gardens, plantations, and urban areas. Solitary birds or pairs perch conspicuously in crown of shrub or on fence post. May forage on ground. Often spreads or flicks wings. May sing at night. **VOICE** Song (1) a varied series of whistles, trills, and short, warbled phrases often repeated three or four times. Call (2) a short, harsh, abrupt *shaak* or *chak* or *chek*.

Blue-and-white Mockingbird *Melanotis hypoleucus*   28 cm

South MX and CA. Uncommon resident in north highlands (1000 to 3200, mainly above 1500 m). Also volcanic highlands of SV (Santa Ana, San Miguel, San Vicente, La Libertad, 341). Rare in NI (Estelí, 412). **ID** Long tail often partly fanned. Gray-blue above and white below with *black mask*. Eyes deep red. Imm dusky gray with whitish mottling below and dull yellow bill. **HABITS** Understory to midstory of forest edge, plantations, gardens, and scrub. Solitary or in pairs. Often skulking. Forages on ground by noisily disturbing leaf litter with sideways sweeping of bill. Sings from elevated perch. **VOICE** Song (1) a variable series of rich, whistled or trilled phrases and sharp notes. Often squeaky. Some phrases repeated. Calls (2) a loud, rich *tcheeoo pr whee-oo* or (3) *chweet chrr*, (4) a low-pitched, hollow *chuck*, and (5) short growl followed by hollow notes *ahrr took-took-took-took . . .*

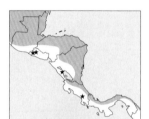

Gray Catbird *Dumetella carolinensis*   21 cm

Breeds Nearctic. Winters MX and CA. Common transient and winter resident (Sep to May) in north Caribbean lowlands and foothills (to 1300, rarely or locally to 2600 m). Rare in east PA (346) and north Pacific (363, 341). **ID** Long tail often elevated or raised and lowered nervously. Plain gray with *black cap* and *chestnut crissum*. **HABITS** Understory to midstory and edge of humid or semihumid broadleaf forest, second growth, plantations, mangroves, and gardens. Solitary and skulking. **VOICE** Calls (1) a nasal, downslurred *yawww* or *owwwr* and (2) shorter *werk*.

Black Catbird *Melanoptila glabrirostris*   20 cm

South MX and CA. Locally fairly common resident in Caribbean coastal lowlands and islands of north BZ (535, 432, 339). Rare in interior of BZ (Orange Walk, 346) and in north GT (Petén, 229, 637, 378, 78). One report from south BZ (Toledo, 341). One old record from west HN (Cortés, 552). Perhaps undertakes seasonal movements. **ID** Rounded tail often fanned. *Uniform glossy black* with *deep red eyes*. Melodious Blackbird has different bill shape and habits. **HABITS** Floor and understory of littoral woodland, mangroves, second growth, gardens, plantations, and scrub. Solitary or in pairs. Skulks in shaded vegetation. Sings from hidden, elevated perch. **VOICE** Song (1) a variably squeaky or sweet to scratchy *klee tu-who-wiik . . .* or *tiche-wee rr cher-wer . . .* often repeated persistently. May include metallic clicks or buzzy notes. Calls (2) a short *toc*, (3) nasal *chehr* or *jeer*, and (4) harsh *reeh* or *rrriah* or *eeyuuu-ooo*, and (5) downslurred *keeyoooo* or *chewaa*.

PIPITS Motacillidae

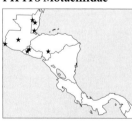

American Pipit *Anthus rubescens*   17 cm

Breeds Nearctic. Winters USA and MX. Rare winter visitor (Nov to May) to BZ (Toledo, Cayo, 343, 346), GT (Santa Rosa, San Marcos, Sacatepéquez, 539, 341, 227), SV (Santa Ana, Cuscatlán, 619, 341), and HN (Francisco Morazán). Vagrant to Isla del Coco (113). **ID** Blackish tail with mostly *white outer rectrices* visible in flight. Fine bill blackish above and pinkish below. Note pale supercilium. Underparts variably whitish to pale buff in nonbreeding ad. Breeding ad (Mar to Aug) tinged pinkish-buff to pale cinnamon below. **HABITS** Walks on ground in open grassy or muddy areas. Often near water. Wags tail. Flight slightly undulating. Often solitary in region but typically forms flocks in winter. **VOICE** Call (1) a clear, high-pitched *tsip* or *sip* or *sip-it* or stuttering series *si-si-si-si-sip*. Often given in flight.

Yellowish Pipit *Anthus lutescens*   11.5 cm

CA and SA. Locally fairly common resident in Pacific lowlands of PA. Rarely reported from Caribbean slope of Canal Area (Colón). **ID** Small and slender with fine bill. Mostly yellowish-ochre with extensive fine brownish streaking above and below. American Pipit is larger, often has a bold dark malar, and has nearly plain mantle. **HABITS** Walks on ground in short grass savannas and agricultural fields. Solitary or in pairs. Male vocalizes in flight display performed high overhead. **VOICE** Song (1) a series of *dzee* notes that rise in pitch followed by a long, downslurred note *dzeeeeeeeeee* and ending with a buzzy *dzip*. Also sings from ground giving (2) a very high-pitched, buzzy *tssiiii-rrit* and shorter, lower-pitched *cheewit* or *tseewit*.

442

juv

ad

ad

Tropical Mockingbird

juv

Blue-and-white Mockingbird

Gray Catbird

Black Catbird

American Pipit

breeding

nonbreeding

Yellowish Pipit

CHLOROPHONIAS AND EUPHONIA Fringillidae

Chlorophonias are closely related to euphonias and, like them, are small frugivores found at upper levels in broadleaf forest and woodland. All have allopatric distributions in highlands. Often detected by voice. Chlorophonias sometimes follow mixed flocks that include various tanagers. May undertake seasonal movements or altitudinal migrations.

Blue-crowned Chlorophonia *Chlorophonia occipitalis*   13 cm

South MX and north CA. Uncommon to fairly common resident in foothills and highlands (1000 to 2500 m). May wander to lower elevations outside breeding season (e.g., regular near SL in north HN). Also Pacific volcanic range in SV (Santa Ana, 183). **ID** Mostly *green* with blue crown. Male has yellow lower underparts separated from green breast by dark band. Female lacks dark breast-band. Other chlorophonias allopatric. Compare with Green Shrike-Vireo. **HABITS** Canopy and edge of humid broadleaf and pine-oak forest and shaded plantations. Usually in pairs or small groups foraging high in trees. May descend to lower level at edge or where fruit is available. **VOICE** Song a series of short, nasal or slurred notes and phrases. Varied calls include (1) a clear, slightly downslurred *yuu* or *hooou* and (2) short, nasal *kyuk* or *eyuk* or *eeuk*.

Golden-browed Chlorophonia *Chlorophonia callophrys*   13 cm

CA endemic. Locally or seasonally fairly common in foothills and highlands (mainly above 900 m) of CR and west PA. Wanders to lower elevations when not breeding. **ID** Mostly *green*. Male has *blue hindcrown and nape* and golden-yellow forecrown and supercilium. Male's yellow lower underparts divided from green breast by dark band. Female lacks supercilium and breast-band. Other chlorophonias allopatric. Compare with Green Shrike-Vireo. **HABITS** Subcanopy to canopy of humid broadleaf forest, second growth, and plantations. Usually in pairs or small groups. Typically forages high in canopy but may descend to lower levels at edges or gaps where fruit is available. **VOICE** Song (1) a series of short, clear whistles. Distinctive call (2) a short, soft, flat *kooow* or *keeeu*. Also (3) gives series of short, nasal, upslurred *jip* or *jup* notes.

Yellow-collared Chlorophonia *Chlorophonia flavirostris*   9.5 cm

CA and SA. Rare resident or seasonal visitor to foothills and highlands of east PA. Reported from Pirre Massif (Darién, 120, 48, 346) and from central PA (Panamá, 346). Thought to undertake seasonal movements in SA. **ID** Small. Mostly green with *pinkish-red bill, white eyes*, and *yellow eye ring*. Male has bright yellow nuchal collar and rump. Female mostly bright green with yellow central underparts. Other chlorophonias allopatric. Compare with Green Shrike-Vireo. **HABITS** Poorly known in CA. Midstory to canopy and edge of very humid broadleaf (cloud) forest. In pairs or small groups. **VOICE** Calls (1) a plaintive, slightly downslurred *peeeeeeee* (often given in flight) and (2) short, harsh *jiip* or *jeet*.

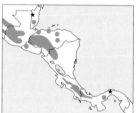

Elegant Euphonia *Euphonia elegantissima*   11.5 cm

MX and CA. Uncommon to locally fairly common resident in highlands (1300 to 3000 m). May wander to lower elevations outside breeding season. Also Maya Mountains of BZ (Cayo, 341, 346) and highlands of SV (Santa Ana, 364). Rare visitor to lowlands in BZ (Orange Walk), coastal north HN (Atlántida), and central PA (Panamá, Colón, 346). **ID** *Azure-blue crown and nape* contrast with dark sides of head and rufous forehead. Male is *ochraceous-orange below*. Female mostly olive with *cinnamon throat*. Some females are very drab and may lack cinnamon throat. **HABITS** Midstory to canopy and edge of humid pine-oak and broadleaf forest (in north), and humid broadleaf (cloud) forest, shaded plantations, and gardens in south. **VOICE** Song (1) a variable, rapid, jumbled sequence of gurgling trills, chips, and buzzy notes. May suggest Barn Swallow. Often includes call notes. Calls (2) a high-pitched, thin *tsee* or *cheezee*, (3) sharply downslurred *schew* or *cheeu*, and (4) lower-pitched, clear *chewp*. Compare with calls of Paltry Tyrannulet and Olive Warbler.

**Blue-crowned
Chlorophonia**

♀

♂

**Golden-browed
Chlorophonia**

♀

♂

**Yellow-collared
Chlorophonia**

♀

♂

juv
♂

♀

♂

Elegant Euphonia

EUPHONIAS Fringillidae

Small birds found in upper levels of woodland or forest. Often in pairs. Most form small flocks of conspecifics outside the breeding season. Forest species such as Olive-backed Euphonia often follow mixed flocks. Although euphonias often perch in the open, adequate views can be difficult to obtain and identification is sometimes challenging. Useful features for identification include the extent of yellow on the crown and the presence or absence of white on the tail in males and underparts pattern and color in females.

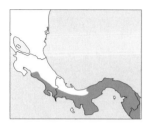

Thick-billed Euphonia *Euphonia laniirostris*   11 cm

CA and SA. Common resident in south lowlands and foothills (to 1100 m). **ID** Heavy bill. Male has yellow throat and *yellow crown extending to behind eye* and white on underside of tail. Female *uniform dull olive-yellow below*. Compare male with male Yellow-throated Euphonia. Compare female with smaller-billed female Yellow-crowned Euphonia. **HABITS** Midstory to subcanopy and edge of humid broadleaf forest and tall second growth. Pairs follow mixed flocks. **VOICE** Song (1) a complex series of chirps, warbles, and staccato notes that often include imitations of other birds. Calls (2) a sweet *chweet* or *wheep*, (3) clear *beem* or *beem-beem*, (4) buzzy *bee-wit*, (5) burry *burrweer*, and (6) clear *peet* or *peet peet*. Shorter and softer than Yellow-crowned Euphonia.

Yellow-throated Euphonia *Euphonia hirundinacea*   11 cm

South MX and north CA. Common resident in lowlands and foothills (to 1500 m). Local in north Pacific. Poorly known in Caribbean NI (548). Perhaps expanding in Pacific west PA (Chiriquí). **ID** Male has *entirely yellow underparts including throat.* Yellow forecrown extends to above eye. Female has *pale grayish throat and center of breast and belly.* Crown concolorous with back. Female similar to female Scrub Euphonia. Note different underparts. **HABITS** Subcanopy to canopy and edge of semihumid to humid broadleaf forest, second growth, plantations, and gardens. **VOICE** Song (1) a long series of short, thin whistles and brief, warbled phrases. Some may suggest White-eyed Vireo. Calls (2) a rapid, slightly buzzy *wee ch-cha weeeu* or *cheek-chereeg* or *t'ch tch weeru*, (3) loud, scratchy *chee-cheet* or *dje jeeet* with second note lower-pitched, and (4) slightly metallic *wee-it*.

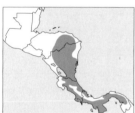

Yellow-crowned Euphonia *Euphonia luteicapilla*   10 cm

CA endemic. Uncommon resident in lowlands and foothills (to 1200 m). Recently confirmed in east HN (Olancho, Gracias a Dios, 100, 629, 346). **ID** Male has *yellow crown patch extending to nape* and dark throat. Note *plain dark tail* (no white spots). Male resembles male Spot-crowned Euphonia but has more extensive, clear yellow crown patch. Female plain olive-green above and uniform dull yellow below, thus very similar to female Thick-billed Euphonia. **HABITS** Midstory to canopy at edge of semihumid forest, plantations, and isolated trees in open areas. Often in pairs. **VOICE** Song (1) a rapid series that begins with high-pitched note *pit ditreea-twiddledee bee bee*. Call (2) a series of two or three short, clear notes *beem-beem-beem*.

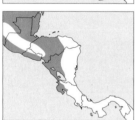

Scrub Euphonia *Euphonia affinis*   10 cm

South MX and CA. Uncommon to fairly common resident in lowlands and foothills (to 1500, locally to 1800 m). **ID** Male bright yellow below (including crissum) with *dark throat.* Yellow forecrown extends to just behind eye. Female mostly grayish-olive with *grayish nape* and yellowish belly and crissum. Compare both sexes with White-vented Euphonia. Female distinguished from female Yellow-throated Euphonia by olive (not grayish) breast and yellow (not whitish) crissum. **HABITS** Midstory to canopy and edge of arid to semihumid (deciduous) broadleaf forest, scrub, second growth, and adjacent plantations. Most common in natural scrub areas with dense, low vegetation. May form mixed flocks with Yellow-throated Euphonias. Sidles along perch while shifting tail from side to side. **VOICE** Song (1) a rapid, accelerating, squeaky *whit-it-it-ititit* or *wheetidy-titity-witity-titity.* Calls (2) a bright, clear *bee-bee* or *bee-bee-bee* or *chwee wee-wee.* Compare with call of Yellow-bellied Tyrannulet. Also (3) a wistful, downslurred *wheeeeu.*

White-vented Euphonia *Euphonia minuta*   9.5 cm

CA and SA. Uncommon and local resident in lowlands and foothills (to 1000 m). May wander to higher elevations. **ID** Small. Male has dark throat, yellow breast, and *white center of belly, crissum, and undertail surface.* Female has *pale gray throat* and *yellowish breast-band.* Center of female's belly, crissum, and *undertail surface white.* Compare with female Yellow-throated Euphonia. Note different underparts. **HABITS** Subcanopy to canopy and edge of humid broadleaf forest, tall second growth, and adjacent plantations and gardens. In pairs or small groups. Usually remains high in trees. May perch on open, bare branch. Sidles along branch while shifting tail from side to side. **VOICE** Song (1) a short, complex series of high-pitched, slurred whistles *weeeseeesweeesee-we-ee-ee.* Very unlike the mechanical or metallic notes of other *Euphonia.* Calls (2) a repeated, sharp, high-pitched *wee-chip-dididi* or *chip-wertily* or *chip-chwee.*

Thick-billed Euphonia ♀ ♂

imm ♂

Yellow-throated Euphonia ♀ ♂

Yellow-crowned Euphonia ♀ ♂

Scrub Euphonia ♀ ♂

White-vented Euphonia ♀ ♂

EUPHONIAS Fringillidae

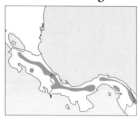

Tawny-capped Euphonia *Euphonia anneae*   11.5 cm
CA and SA. Fairly common resident. May undertake local or altitudinal movements
(92). Mainly Caribbean foothills and highlands (600 to 2000 m, occasionally lower).
Rare and local in Pacific foothills of CR (Puntarenas, San José, 474, 346). **ID** *White
crissum.* Male has rufous crown patch and dark throat. Underparts deep yellow. Female
has *rufous forecrown* and *grayish breast and nape.* Note female's whitish crissum.
GV Males from central and east PA have deep chestnut crown. **HABITS** Midstory to
canopy and edge of humid broadleaf (cloud) forest, adjacent plantations and tall
second growth. Follows mixed flocks. **VOICE** Song (1) a series of piercing or slurred
notes. May include a short, buzzy trill *see see-seep tsew see-seep tsew tsew see chrrrt
see-see tsew . . .* or *cha-bhee-bhee-bhee chew-chew-chew eh-eh-eh.* Calls (2) a scratchy,
downslurred *tsewp* often doubled, (3) a nasal, vireo-like *teer*, (4) a metallic, rolling
chrrrrt like Olive-backed Euphonia, and (5) *ch-ch-tew* suggesting Black-faced
Grosbeak.

Orange-bellied Euphonia *Euphonia xanthogaster*   11.5 cm
CA and SA. Uncommon resident in Pacific foothills (450 to 1500 m) of east PA
(Darién). **ID** Male has deep yellow crown extending to behind eye. Underparts deep
yellow including crissum. Female has dull orange-yellow forehead and gray nape.
Throat and central underparts gray. Compare with female Tawny-capped Euphonia
(no known overlap). **HABITS** Midstory and edge of humid broadleaf forest, tall second
growth, and adjacent shaded plantations. **VOICE** Variable song (1) a short *wheet-wheet*
or *ta-weee taweee* given alone or in combination with call notes. Song phrases may
run together in continuous warble. In dawn song, (2) alternates two types of loud,
clear whistles *wheet wheet wheet* with second two notes lower in pitch and *wheet wheet
wheer* with last note lower-pitched and slurred. Calls (3) a plaintive, buzzy *dee* given
singly or in series of two to four, (4) a buzzy *zhurr-deet*, (5) *chee-chee* and (6) *zhurr-
dit-dit.*

Spot-crowned Euphonia *Euphonia imitans*   female 10, male 10.5 cm
CA endemic. Fairly common resident in Pacific lowlands and foothills (to 1400 m)
of CR. Uncommon to rare and local in PA (Chiriquí, 512). **ID** Male resembles male
Yellow-crowned Euphonia but has less extensive yellow on crown (dark spotting
obscure). Note male's *all-dark tail.* Female mostly olive with *rufous forehead and belly.*
Fulvous-vented and Olive-backed euphonias allopatric. **HABITS** Midstory to canopy in
open areas with scattered trees, humid broadleaf forest edge, clearings, and plantations.
VOICE Song (1) a rapid, complex series of whistles, dry or wheezy notes, and short,
warbled phrases *chip a cher weet, chip tuck tuck, we churee-cha . . .* Calls (2) a rolling,
metallic *chrrrit* often given in series of two to four and sometimes preceded by one or
two downslurred whistles *tewp* and (3) harsh, rolling *jurry-jurry* or *treeah-treeah.*

Fulvous-vented Euphonia *Euphonia fulvicrissa*   9.5 cm
CA and north SA. Fairly common resident in lowlands and foothills (to 900 m) of
central and east PA. **ID** Male has deep yellow underparts. Female mostly greenish-
yellow below with cinnamon center of belly and crissum. Male resembles male
Orange-bellied Euphonia. Note Fulvous-vented's less extensive yellow crown patch
and tawny crissum. Female resembles female of parapatric Olive-backed Euphonia.
HABITS Midstory of humid broadleaf forest (forages lower than other euphonias).
Follows mixed flocks. **VOICE** Song (1) a rapid, complex series of whistles, dry or wheezy
notes, and short, warbled phrases. Repeats a note or phrase two to four times then
switches to different note or phrase. Typical phrases include a whistled *whee whee whee*
or *wheer wheer.* Calls include (2) rolling metallic *chrrrit* and (3) burry *dee-dee-dee.*

Olive-backed Euphonia *Euphonia gouldi*   female 9.5, male 10.5 cm
South MX and CA. Common resident in humid lowlands and foothills (to 600, locally
to 1400 m). **ID** Male is mostly olive with *rufous belly* and crissum and *yellow forecrown.*
Female yellow-olive below with *rufous crissum* and forecrown. Female Fulvous-vented
and Spot-crowned euphonias are similar. Note different underparts. **HABITS** Midstory
to subcanopy of semihumid to humid broadleaf forest, adjacent tall second growth,
and gardens. Follows mixed flocks. **VOICE** Complex and variable song (1) includes
short, squeaky, warbling phrases, sharp *cheet* or *weet* notes, and short, buzzy trills.
Some phrases suggest White-eyed Vireo. Calls (2) a flat, rapid, mechanical *dri-dri-drit*
or *jr-it-it*, (3) buzzy *chii-errr-it-it* that drops in pitch on second phrase, (4) nasal *che-eh-
eht*, and (5) high-pitched, clear *tsii* or *seee.*

Tawny-capped Euphonia

CR and
west PA
♂

central and
east PA
♂

♀

Orange-bellied Euphonia

♀

♂

Spot-crowned Euphonia

♀

♂

Fulvous-vented Euphonia

♀

♂

Olive-backed Euphonia

♀

♂

SISKINS AND GOLDFINCH Fringillidae

Small birds found mainly in highlands. All have fine, conical bills and strongly notched tails. All are gregarious to some degree and some species may form large flocks, especially outside the breeding season. All have deeply undulating flight style.

Pine Siskin *Spinus pinus* · 12 cm

NA to CA. Locally fairly common resident in highlands (2000 to 3800 m) of west GT (Quetzaltenango, Huehuetenango, Totonicapán, 635, 627, 12). **ID** Fine bill. Yellow edging on flight feathers and tail. Highly variable. Gray-breasted morph has olive wingbars and male has blackish cap. Rare streaked morph brownish with beige wingbars. Note soft streaking on breast, crown, and mantle. Some birds are intermediate. Black-capped Siskin mostly olive with longer, pinker bill. Displays poorly understood individual variation in CA. Some birds are mostly gray below with black cap and olive wingbars. Others are brownish overall and have streaked underparts. **HABITS** Uses all levels of vegetation in open or semi-open areas including coniferous woodland, margins of agricultural fields, second growth, pine-oak forest, and plantations. Usually in small groups. May associate with Black-capped Siskins. **VOICE** Like Black-capped Siskin.

Black-capped Siskin *Spinus atriceps* · 12 cm

South MX and north CA. Uncommon to locally common resident in highlands (2000 to 4000 m) of GT. Perhaps wanders to lower elevations outside breeding season. **ID** *Black crown* and *long pinkish bill*. Ad mostly olive with yellow lower underparts and yellow edging on wings and tail. Compare heavily streaked juv with more softly streaked Pine Siskin. **HABITS** Humid to semihumid pine-oak woodland, forest edge, and plantations. Perches upright high in crowns of conifers. Descends to lower levels to feed on thistles at brushy edges. Takes seeds from trees such as alders (*Alnus*). **VOICE** Song (1) a long series of scratchy, warbled phrases. Calls (2) a nasal, downslurred *zweeu*, (3) rapid, dry, staccato *ch-ch-cht* or *cheh-cheh-chet*, and (4) attenuated, buzzy *djeeerrr* or *djeewww*.

Black-headed Siskin *Spinus notatus* · 11.5 cm

South MX and north CA. Uncommon to fairly common resident in highlands (mainly 600 to 3000 m). Near SL on Caribbean slope of east HN (Gracias a Dios) and NI (RAAN). Also Mountain Pine Ridge of BZ (Cayo). **ID** Black-and-yellow wing pattern and fine, conical bill. Ad has *black crown, sides of head, and throat*, greenish-yellow nape, and yellow lower underparts. Imm dull greenish-yellow with pale wingbars and narrow pale edging on tertials. Yellow-bellied Siskin allopatric. **HABITS** Uses all levels of vegetation in arid to semihumid pine-oak forest, forest edge, savannas, gardens, and urban areas. Perches upright high in crowns of conifers. Descends to lower levels to feed at brushy edge. Sometimes in large flocks. **VOICE** Song (1) a long, variable, rapid series of trills, warbled phrases, and short, nasal or buzzy, high-pitched notes. Many phrases repeated two or three times. Calls (2) a nasal *teu* or *cheeuu* or *tseeeu* like Lesser Goldfinch, (3) attenuated *djeein*, (4) dry *jeht-jeht*, and (5) nasal *ti-chii*.

Yellow-bellied Siskin *Spinus xanthogastrus* · 11.5 cm

CA and (disjunctly) SA. Uncommon resident in highlands (mainly 2000 to 3000 m) of CR and west PA. **ID** Fine, conical bill and *yellow wing patches* (conspicuous in flight). Male's *black head and breast* contrast with yellow lower underparts. Lesser Goldfinch has yellow throat and different wing pattern. Other *Spinus* siskins allopatric. **HABITS** Canopy and edge of humid broadleaf (cloud) forest, second growth, and adjacent plantations and gardens. In pairs or small groups. May forage lower at weedy edges or on ground in grassy clearing. **VOICE** Song (1) a rapid series of twittering or chattering notes. Some phrases repeated several times rapidly. Compare with more varied and musical song of Lesser Goldfinch. Calls (2) a high-pitched, piercing *pyeeu* and (3) harsher, scratchy *bziee*.

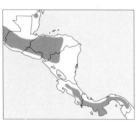

Lesser Goldfinch *Spinus psaltria* · 10.5 cm

USA to SA. Uncommon to fairly common resident (SL to 3000 in north, 800 to 2200 m in CR and PA). Scarce and local in BZ (Orange Walk, 341, 250). **ID** Short, conical bill. Broad white edging on tertials and *white on base of primaries*. Ad male black above and *yellow below including throat*. Siskins similar but have yellow, not white markings on wings and tail. **HABITS** Uses all levels of vegetation in open or disturbed areas including margins of agricultural fields, scrub, arid to semihumid forest edge, savannas, gardens, and plantations. Usually in small flocks (up to ten). May forage at lower levels in grassy or weedy areas and also perches high in trees. **VOICE** Song (1) a long, variable, and complex series that includes clear, slurred notes and buzzy trills. Calls (2) a high-pitched, thin, plaintive *pseee*, (3) clear, descending *tseer*, (4) ascending, slightly burry *chirreee*, and (5) high-pitched, downslurred *peeyooo* or *teeee-uu*.

50%

Pine Siskin

streaked
morph

grayish
streaked
morph

gray morph
♀

gray morph
♂

Black-capped Siskin

juv

ad
♀

ad
♂

Black-headed Siskin

juv

ad

Yellow-bellied Siskin

juv

ad
♀

ad
♂

Lesser Goldfinch

ad
♀

ad
♂

GROSBEAK AND CROSSBILL Fringillidae

Hooded Grosbeak *Coccothraustes abeillei* 17.5 cm

South MX and CA. Uncommon to rare resident in highlands (1000 to 3500 m) of GT. Recently reported from SV (Santa Ana, 619, 364). **ID** *Very heavy, conical, greenish-yellow bill* and short, notched tail. Male has *black hood* and yellow underparts. Yellowish mantle contrasts with black wings. Note white tertials and wing coverts. Female grayer overall with black on head confined mainly to crown and face. Compare with Yellow Grosbeak. **HABITS** Midstory to subcanopy and edge of semihumid to humid broadleaf and pine-oak forest. In pairs or small groups. Inconspicuous when foraging. Most often detected by voice while flying overhead. **VOICE** Song (1) a series of short, clipped, slightly buzzy phrases *bibibidriu drriu diii diiu* sometimes given as (2) shorter version *beenk beenk eihrr-r . . .* or *bee beep wheer-tee . . .* or *beehn beehn bee-beihr . . .* Calls (3) a loud, clear, one- or two-syllable phrase *beehn beehn* or *beenk beenk* or *wheer beenk* and (4) nasal *whew* or *kew*.

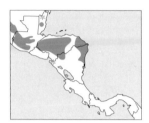

Red Crossbill *Loxia curvirostra* 15 cm

Holarctic including WI. Uncommon to rare and irregular resident, mainly in highlands. Rare in BZ (Cayo, Orange Walk, 529, 343), SV (Chalatenango, Santa Ana, 341, 346), and Caribbean lowlands of east HN (Gracias a Dios, 442) and NI (RAAN, 327). Historical record from Volcán San Cristóbal, NI (Chinandega, 413). **ID** *Crossed bill* and short, deeply notched tail. Ad male mostly *dull red* (brighter on rump) with dusky tail and wings. Ad female and imm variably gray or greenish. Juv streaked. **HABITS** Midstory to canopy of coniferous forest and woodland. Feeds on evergreen cones. Clings or hangs from terminal branches. Forms flocks outside breeding season. Flight deeply undulating. Often calls in flight. **VOICE** Song of CA populations undescribed. Variable call (1) a series of two or three notes *kiip kiip kiip . . .* or lower-pitched *cheh cheh cheh . . .*

HOUSE SPARROW Passeridae

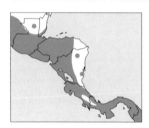

House Sparrow *Passer domesticus* 15 cm

Old World species widely introduced. Most common in arid to semihumid Pacific slope (229, 615, 617). Uncommon and local, but perhaps expanding on Caribbean slope. **ID** Small, stout and large-headed. Ad male has gray crown, dull chestnut nape and *black throat and breast*. Female and imm are very plain but always show *pale, dull buff supercilium* and drab grayish crown and sides of head. Compare female and imm to female and imm Dickcissel. **HABITS** Forages mainly on ground. Most common in urban and suburban areas and near agricultural buildings. Forms flocks outside breeding season. Males call persistently from elevated perch. **VOICE** Call (1) a loud, slightly hoarse *jeet* or *cheet* often repeated persistently.

MUNIA Estrildidae

Tricolored Munia *Lonchura malacca* 10.5 cm

Old World species. Recently introduced and perhaps now locally established in BZ (Corozal, Orange Walk, 341), GT (Petén, Escuintla, 229), SV (Ahuachapán, Usulután, 341, 261, 346), HN (Cortés, Choluteca, 341, 346), CR (Guanacaste, Puntarenas, Alajuela, 346, 546), and PA (Panamá, 48). **ID** Small and stout. *Heavy, deep-based, pale gray bill.* Ad has chestnut tail and upperparts. *Black hood* and lower underparts contrasting sharply with white flanks. Imm mostly plain grayish-brown becoming whitish on lower underparts. Compare with *Sporophila* seedeaters. Note different bill shape. **HABITS** Understory of open grassy areas including roadsides, lawns, agricultural fields, irrigation ditches, and marshes. Gregarious. Forms flocks when not breeding. **VOICE** Calls (1) a high-pitched, thin, slurred *dweet* or *tweeet* and (2) shorter *peep*. Often repeated or given in chorus by several birds.

Hooded Grosbeak

♀

♂

juv

♀

♂

Red Crossbill

♀

♂

House Sparrow

juv

ad
♂

Tricolored Munia

FINCHES AND TOWHEE Passerellidae

Finches found at lower levels in montane forest and woodland. Some of these are endemic to the highlands of south Central America. White-naped Brushfinch is the most common and widespread.

Large-footed Finch *Pezopetes capitalis*   20 cm

CA endemic. Fairly common resident in highlands (above 2150 m) of east CR and west PA (Chiriquí). **ID** Large, heavy-bodied and small-headed. Large feet. Mostly dusky olive. *Gray head* with *black face, crown, and throat*. **HABITS** Floor, understory, and edge of very humid broadleaf (cloud and elfin) forest, second growth, hedgerows, plantations, and gardens. Mainly terrestrial. Pairs or solitary birds forage actively (often noisily) by scratching in leaf litter. Favors bamboo thickets. Occasionally forages in adjacent open areas. **VOICE** Song (1) a halting series of short, rich, whistled or warbled phrases *tchree chreechu chuwee . . .* In duet, pairs give (2) several high-pitched, scratchy notes followed by loud, accelerating series of hard, metallic notes that drop in pitch and end with a short, warbled phrase *cheecheecheecheecheecheechuchuchu chruchreeuu.* Call (3) a thin, high-pitched, soft *psee* or *seet.*

Yellow-green Finch *Pselliophorus luteoviridis*   18 cm

CA endemic. Locally fairly common resident in highlands (1200 to 1800 m) of west PA (east Chiriquí, Ngäbe-Buglé, Veraguas, 273, 659, 512). **ID** Dark gray head, olive mantle, and mostly *yellow-olive underparts* contrast with blackish wings. Note *yellow tibials.* Compare with Sooty-faced Finch. Yellow-thighed Finch is allopatric. **HABITS** Understory to lower midstory and edge of very humid broadleaf (cloud) forest. Like Yellow-thighed Finch. **VOICE** Song (1) a rapid series of buzzy or squeaky, high-pitched phrases that slow slightly toward end. Call (2) a soft, high-pitched *zeeep.*

Yellow-thighed Finch *Pselliophorus tibialis*   18 cm

CA endemic. Common resident in highlands (above 1500 m) of CR and west PA (Chiriquí). **ID** *Dark gray* becoming blackish on face, throat, and forehead. *Note yellow tibials.* Yellow-green Finch allopatric. **HABITS** Understory to midstory and edge of very humid broadleaf (cloud and elfin) forest, second growth, and plantations. Favors dense, mossy, bamboo thickets. In pairs or small groups. Forages actively. Often confiding. Flips tail loosely as it hops through vegetation. Follows mixed flocks. **VOICE** Song (1) a rapid series of short, squeaky, high-pitched phrases *cheedle tweep cheedle cher tweeip tee-dee dee wink wink.* In duet, pairs give (2) a rapid series of high-pitched *tseet* or *tsit* notes. Call (3) a high-pitched, metallic *tchik* or *vick* sometimes repeated or accelerating to become a hard chatter.

White-naped Brushfinch *Atlapetes albinucha*   18 cm

South MX to SA. Uncommon to locally common resident in foothills and highlands (1000 to 3000 m). Local in volcanic highlands of SV (Santa Ana, San Vicente, 183, 341). Also highlands of Azuero Peninsula in PA (Veraguas, 10, 425). **ID** Gray above and plain whitish below with *yellow throat.* Mostly *black head* with *white crown stripe.* Juv has pale crown stripe like ad but is mostly brownish with coarse streaking below. **GV** Birds from Azuero Peninsula, PA are brownish above and have rufous edging on tertials, and brown flanks. **HABITS** In north uses pine-oak forest, second growth, and plantations. In south uses floor, understory, and edge of humid broadleaf forest, second growth, gardens, and plantations. In pairs or small groups. Active and conspicuous. Pumps or wags tail in short flights. Forages mainly on ground but may ascend to midstory in tangled vegetation. **VOICE** Song (1) a series of long, slurred or squeaky whistles and short warbles *pseeeeeu weeesee tseeeuu psweeeuu psweeeu tseeeuu pseweeesee.* Calls (2) a piercing, high-pitched *tsit* or *tseep* and (3) staccato series of *tsit* notes.

Spotted Towhee *Pipilo maculatus*   20 cm

USA to north CA. Fairly common resident in highlands (mainly 2000 to 3500 m) of GT. **ID** Large and long-tailed. *White on outer rectrices* and *prominent white spotting on wings and mantle.* Ad has sooty brown hood (darker in male) extending to upper breast and *rufous flanks* and crissum. Juv has coarse streaking on breast and flanks. **HABITS** Floor and understory of pine-oak forest, semihumid brushy woodland, forest edge, and scrub. Solitary birds, pairs, or small groups forage mainly on ground. Forages noisily in leaf litter by hopping and scratching with both feet. Habitually jerks tail in brief, low flight. Sings from elevated perch. **VOICE** Song (1) a short, metallic trill that starts with lower-pitched introductory note *reh-tiiiiiiiiii.* Calls (2) a buzzy, upslurred *reeeeeh?* and (3) flat, very buzzy *pzeeeet.*

Large-footed Finch

Yellow-green Finch

Yellow-thighed Finch

Azuero
ad

widespread
ad

juv

White-naped Brushfinch

juv

ad

Spotted Towhee

SPARROWS AND BRUSHFINCHES Passerellidae

Finches found on ground and at lower levels in humid broadleaf forest. Often detected by voice. Chestnut-capped Brushfinch and Orange-billed Sparrow are the most common and widespread.

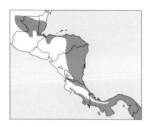

Orange-billed Sparrow *Arremon aurantiirostris*   16 cm

MX to SA. Fairly common resident in humid lowlands and foothills (to 1200, locally to 1400 m). Confined to Caribbean slope in north. Reaches Pacific locally in south NI (Rivas, 548). **ID** Ad has *orange bill* and *black-and-white striped crown*. Black breast contrasts with white throat and lower underparts. Juv dusky olive with dark breast suggesting ad pattern. **HABITS** Floor, understory, and edge of humid broadleaf forest and adjacent tall, shaded second growth. Partial to dark ravines and damp vegetation along forest streams. Usually skulking and shy. Solitary or in pairs. **VOICE** Song (1) a rapid series of very high-pitched, squeaky notes and piercing whistles *cheeeeo tcheeeeo-tcheeeeeeo tchiiiiiiii tcheeeeo* or *tseeeewtseeewtseeew seer* or *tseeeer tseeeew-tsup*. Song (2) on Pacific slope of CR and PA a series of shorter, very high-pitched, thin, metallic or squeaky notes *tseep ti tsep ti tseep see*. Call (3) a very sharp, sibilant *tchip* or *tsuk*.

Sooty-faced Finch *Arremon crassirostris*   16.5 cm

CA endemic. Uncommon and local resident in south humid foothills (600 to 1500, locally to 2400 m). Poorly known in east PA (Darién, 657, 48). **ID** Dark. Note *whitish malar* contrasting with *dark gray sides of head and throat*. Otherwise mostly dark olive with rufous crown and deep yellow central lower underparts. Compare with juv Chestnut-capped Brushfinch. **HABITS** Floor and understory of humid broadleaf forest. Favors wet ravines and streamside vegetation in steep foothills. Skulking and reclusive. Often in pairs. Rarely follows mixed flocks. May attend ant swarms. **VOICE** Song (1) a high-pitched, thin, whistled *see see seeya sue sisi see*. Compare with song of Orange-billed Sparrow. Call (2) a high-pitched, hissing *psee chii*. Compare with call of Chestnut-capped Brushfinch.

Chestnut-capped Brushfinch *Arremon brunneinucha*   18–20 cm

MX to SA. Fairly common resident in foothills and highlands (900 to 3500 m). **ID** *Rufous nape and hindcrown*. Ad's *black pectoral band* contrasts with white throat (often shaggy or distended). Small *white spot above lores* contrasts with black sides of head. Plain olive above. Juv vaguely resembles Sooty-faced Finch. Note pale bill and hint of ad's breast-band. **GV** Birds from east CR and PA have ochre stripe bordering rufous crown and nape. Birds from GT (not shown) are similar. **HABITS** Floor, understory, and edge of humid broadleaf and pine-oak forest, second growth, and shaded plantations. Forages mainly on ground, often by noisily disturbing leaf litter. Sometimes ventures into adjacent open areas during early morning or at dusk. **VOICE** Song (1) a short phrase of high-pitched slurred whistles. Often ends with downslurred note *tsi tsi t'cheeeeeeeo* or *tsit chee-chuuuuuu rrrrrrr*. Compare with song of White-naped Brushfinch. Call (2) a weak, high-pitched *tsii*.

Costa Rican Brushfinch[26] *Arremon costaricensis*   17.5 cm

CA endemic. Uncommon to rare and local resident in foothills and highlands (300 to 1500 m) of Pacific east CR (Puntarenas, 65, 600) and west PA (Chiriquí, 162, 512). **ID** Mostly olive with white throat and breast. Throat often shaggy or distended. *Head mostly black with gray crown stripes*. Compare with Black-striped Sparrow (lower elevations). Black-headed Brushfinch allopatric. **HABITS** Floor, understory, and edge of very humid broadleaf (cloud) forest, adjacent shaded second growth, and shaded plantations. Forages on ground, often by disturbing leaf litter. Skulks beneath dense cover. Solitary or in pairs. **VOICE** Song (1) a series of short, high-pitched notes and rapid trills *tsee-tzu-tzezezeszet-t-t-t-t-t zezeze . . .* Call (2) a thin, piercing *tsst* or *tseet*.

Black-headed Brushfinch[26] *Arremon atricapillus*   18 cm

CA and north SA. Uncommon to rare and local resident in foothills and highlands (600 to 1500 m) of central and east PA including Pirre Massif, Tacarcuna Massif, and Serranía de Jungurudó (Panamá, Darién, 130, 276, 659, 45). **ID** Mostly olive with white throat and breast. Throat often shaggy or distended. Juv has pale mandible and brownish breast. **GV** Birds from east PA have more extensive black on crown. *Head mostly black*. **HABITS** Similar to Costa Rican Brushfinch. **VOICE** Song (1) a short series of high-pitched, slightly buzzy or hissing notes *tseeeeu tsee tsee tseeeu* or *tsee-tsueee tsee-tseeuu*. May be repeated persistently. Call (2) a harsh *jrrt* or *jeert*.

48%

Orange-billed
Sparrow

juv

ad

Sooty-faced Finch

juv

widespread
ad

east CR and PA
ad
(GT similar)

Chestnut-capped
Brushfinch

Costa Rican
Brushfinch

juv

central PA
ad

east PA
ad

Black-headed
Brushfinch

SPARROWS AND GROUND-SPARROWS Passerellidae

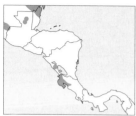

Olive Sparrow *Arremonops rufivirgatus*   14.5 cm
South Texas to CA. Fairly common resident in lowlands of north BZ. Poorly known in north (Petén, 229, 581) and west GT in Nentón Valley (Huehuetenango, 229). Common in Pacific lowlands and foothills (to 800 m) of west CR. Rare in NI (Managua, 413). **ID** *Beige or buff crissum. Crown stripes dark brown.* Upperparts dull olive. Green-backed Sparrow sympatric in BZ. Note different crissum color and habitat. **GV** Birds from CR and NI have shorter tail and buff head and underparts. Birds from west GT (not shown) are similar. **HABITS** Understory, floor, and edge of arid to semihumid scrub, deciduous forest, thorn forest, plantations, and gallery forest. **VOICE** Song (1) a series of sharp, rich notes that accelerate and drop in pitch *cheew cheew cheew chuu chu chu chu.* May start with sharp or buzzy notes *bzzzzzp chip tseeee chip cheew cheew cheew chuu chu chu chu.* Call (2) a thin *tsip* sometimes repeated.

Green-backed Sparrow *Arremonops chloronotus*   14.5 cm
South MX and north CA. Common resident in north Caribbean lowlands and foothills (to 750 m). Local in interior valleys of HN (Yoro, Olancho, 440, 441, 442). **ID** *Crissum olive-yellow.* Mandible gray (often pinkish in Olive Sparrow). Crown stripes blacker and wider than Olive Sparrow. Olive above (brighter than Olive Sparrow) and pale gray below. In hand, note olive underside of tail (gray-brown in Olive Sparrow). **GV** Birds from interior HN are more buff below (including crissum) and have brown crown stripes. In all respects (including voice) these are more similar to Olive Sparrow. **HABITS** Floor, understory, and edge of semihumid to humid broadleaf forest and second growth. Generally favors more humid areas than Olive Sparrow, but in east HN found in arid thorn forest and scrub. **VOICE** Song (1) a long series of short, rich, whistled notes. Usually starts with one or two loud notes *chee, chew, chew-chew-chew-chew-chew-chew* or *eep tcheu chi-chi-chi-chi-chi-chi-chi* or *wheeu wheeu chi-chi-chi-chi-chi-chi.* Does not accelerate like Olive Sparrow. Calls like Olive Sparrow and include (2) a sharp *tsik* or *sik* and (3) thin *sssirr.*

Black-striped Sparrow *Arremonops conirostris*   16.5 cm
CA and north SA. Common resident in lowlands and foothills (to 1500 m). Also Isla Coiba, PA (Veraguas, 653, 470). **ID** Ad has black crown stripes. Upperparts olive. Juv olive with streaked breast and mantle. Green-backed and Olive sparrows allopatric. **HABITS** Understory, floor, and edge of humid broadleaf forest, second growth, and shaded plantations. **VOICE** Song (1) a long series of rich, short, whistled notes. Begins with squeaky notes and accelerates sharply before ending abruptly *weet wuert wooit churt churt churt churt-churt-churt-chuchuchuchu* or *weet ooeet shweee wheeeeit woit-whoit whoit-whoit-whoitwhoitwhoitwoitwoit.* Call (2) a metallic, slightly nasal, upslurred *churk* or *tsook* or *whooit.*

White-faced Ground-Sparrow[27] *Melozone biarcuata*   16 cm
MX and CA. Uncommon resident in north foothills and highlands (mainly 500 to 2100 m). **ID** *White throat* and face and *chestnut nape.* **HABITS** Floor and understory of second growth, forest edge, scrub, and plantations. Pairs or small groups skulk beneath cover. May scratch noisily in leaf litter. **VOICE** Song (1) a high-pitched, thin sputter or buzzy note, followed by three to four clear, loud whistles *tst-t-t-t wheeeeer-peeeeer-peeeer* or *bzeew tow-hewhewhewhewe peeer-peeer-peeer-peer.* Compare with louder, more explosive song of White-eared Ground-Sparrow. Calls (2) a sharp *tchiip,* (3) single *pseeer,* and (4) short, descending series of sibilant notes *psee psee psee.*

Cabanis's Ground-Sparrow[27] *Melozone cabanisi*   15 cm
CA endemic. Uncommon resident in foothills and highlands (mainly 500 to 2100 m) of Valle Central and Pacific slope of Cordillera de Tilarán, CR (Cartago, San José, Puntarenas, 555, 142, 600, 346). **ID** *White throat* and face and *chestnut nape.* White-faced Ground-Sparrow allopatric. **HABITS** Floor and understory of second growth, scrub, and plantations. Like White-faced Ground-Sparrow. **VOICE** Song (1) a series of short, very high-pitched notes followed by three or four slurred whistles on lower pitch *tst-t-t-t wheeeeer-peeeeer-peeeer.* Compare with louder, more explosive song of White-eared Ground-Sparrow. Calls (2) a high-pitched *tchip* and (3) flat buzz or rattle.

White-eared Ground-Sparrow *Melozone leucotis*   16.5–17.5 cm
MX and north CA. Uncommon to locally fairly common resident in Pacific foothills and highlands (500 to 1800, locally to 2000 m) of GT, SV (San Vicente, San Salvador, 183, 341), HN (Olancho, 34), and CR (Puntarenas, Cartago, San José, 126, 570, 600). **ID** Large. *Yellow and white head pattern* and *black throat.* **GV** Birds from HN, NI, and CR have more black on head and breast and lack yellow supercilium. **HABITS** Floor, understory, and edge of semihumid forest, second growth, gardens, and plantations. Scratches noisily in leaf litter. Flicks tail upward when disturbed. **VOICE** Song (1) explosive, short phrases of staccato notes and loud, hoarse, penetrating whistles *chit chit cheuw-cheuw-chew.* Call (2) a high-pitched, piercing *tsip* or *tzip.* In duet, pairs give (3) a buzzy, accelerating and descending *pseeeer-zeeeer-zeeer-zeeer-zur.*

Olive Sparrow

GT and BZ

NI and CR

widespread

interior
HN

Green-backed Sparrow

juv

ad

Black-striped Sparrow

juv

ad

**White-faced
Ground-Sparrow**

**Cabanis's
Ground-Sparrow**

GT and SV
ad

juv

HN, NI
and CR
ad

White-eared Ground-Sparrow

SPARROWS AND JUNCOS Passerellidae

Clay-colored and Lincoln's sparrows are scarce Nearctic migrants. Rufous-collared Sparrow is a widespread and common resident in open areas of highlands. The two Central American juncos are allopatric, range-restricted species found in highlands.

Chipping Sparrow *Spizella passerina*   13 cm

NA and CA. Locally common breeder (SL to 3000 m) of GT (Huehuetenango, Quiché, Totonicapán, Alta Verapaz, 229, 279), SV (Chalatenango, 183, 619), HN (Gracias a Dios, 442), and NI (RAAN, 413). Also Isla Roatán (538, 442). Vagrant to BZ Cays (529, 341) and CR (San José, Cartago, Limón, Puntarenas, Heredia, 600, 546, 346). **ID** Small with fairly long, notched tail. Note dark lores and gray rump (often concealed). Ad has *plain gray underparts*. Breeding ad has *rufous cap* and *white supercilium*. **HABITS** Pine savanna and woodland. Forages mainly on ground. Sings from elevated perch. Usually in pairs or small flocks. **VOICE** Song (1) a flat, fairly dry trill or rattle. Call (2) a simple *tik*.

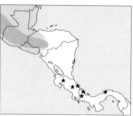

Clay-colored Sparrow *Spizella pallida*   13 cm

Breeds Nearctic. Winters mainly MX. Rare winter visitor (Oct to Mar) to GT (Huehuetenango, Quiché, Petén, 279, 346), BZ (Ambergris Cay, Toledo, 341, 347), CR (Cartago, 4), and PA (Colón). **ID** Structure like Chipping Sparrow. Note *brownish rump* (concolorous with mantle) and *pale lores*. Ad has pale central crown stripe, buff breast, and buff sides of head contrasting with gray nape. Imm Chipping Sparrow has different head pattern and rump color. **HABITS** Floor to lower midstory in open grassy areas including low scrub, agricultural fields, and savannas. Might occur in wide variety of open habitats. Forages on ground. **VOICE** Call (1) a high-pitched, thin *tsi* or *tsip*.

Lincoln's Sparrow *Melospiza lincolnii*   13 cm

Breeds Nearctic. Winters USA to CA. Uncommon transient and winter resident (mainly Oct to Apr) in north foothills and highlands (to 2600 m). Rare in Caribbean lowlands of BZ (Corozal, Cayo, Toledo, 529, 313, 346) and south to CR (Cartago, Limón, Puntarenas, San José, 621, 602, 594, 546, 346) and west PA (Colón, Bocas del Toro, Chiriquí, 512). **ID** *Buff breast with fine dark streaking.* Note narrow whitish eye ring. Gray auriculars and sides of neck contrast with buff malar. Compare with juv Rufous-collared Sparrow. **HABITS** Floor and understory of brushy edges and low second growth. Retiring. Favors damp, shaded areas. Solitary. **VOICE** Call (1) a sharp, light *chip*.

Rufous-collared Sparrow *Zonotrichia capensis*   13.5–14.5 cm

South MX to SA. Very common resident in foothills and highlands (600 to 3800 m). Rare in NI (Jinotega, 412). **ID** *White throat* contrasts with dark malar and *rufous neck*. Ad has *bold head pattern* and *short crest*. Juv has streaked underparts and shows traces of ad's head pattern. **HABITS** Floor and understory in open, semi-open, and disturbed areas including forest edge, pastures, agricultural fields, gardens, urban areas, roadsides, and plantations. Usually in pairs. Forages mainly on ground. Sings from elevated perch. **VOICE** Variable song (1) one or two long, clear, slurred whistles usually followed by high-pitched trill *chee cheeeeuuu t-t-t-t-t* or *seee-seeur te-e-e-e*. May (2) lack trill following song, instead three to six clear whistles that drop in volume and pitch *weeer teuuu too, too, too*. Compare with song of Eastern Meadowlark. Calls (3) a short, warbler-like *chip* or *ch'chip* and (4) high-pitched, thin *tsit*. May be repeated.

Yellow-eyed Junco *Junco phaeonotus*   16 cm

South USA to north CA. Locally common in highlands (2200 to 4000 m) of GT. **ID** *Pale yellow eyes* contrast with dusky face. Note rufous wing coverts and tertials. Ad has bicolored bill with pink mandible. Ad has gray head and nape and *plain brown mantle*. White on outer rectrices conspicuous in flight. Juv has extensive streaking and may have dark eyes. Compare with juv Rufous-collared Sparrow. **HABITS** Floor, understory, and edge of coniferous or pine-oak forest, adjacent clearings, and brushy areas. Forages mainly on ground. May sing from elevated perch. Forms flocks outside breeding season. **VOICE** Song (1) a varied series of clear, short whistles *chiuw ch-ch-ch-ch chiuw*. May include a trill *trrrr chui-chui chichichi*. Call (2) a high-pitched, sharp, slightly metallic *tchik* or *tsik*.

Volcano Junco *Junco vulcani*   16 cm

CA endemic. Uncommon resident in highlands (mainly above 3000 m) of CR (Cartago, 667, 600). In PA known only from Volcán Barú and Cerro Fábrega (Chiriquí, Bocas del Toro, 659, 512). **ID** *Gray head and underparts.* Pinkish bill and *pale orange eyes* contrast with blackish face. **HABITS** Floor and understory of paramo. Solitary or in pairs or small groups. Forages on ground. May perch prominently on low shrub. **VOICE** Song (1) a short series of squeaky or buzzy phrases *cher-we cherwe cher-we . . .* or *tch-ee wee-cha whuu*. Calls (2) a high-pitched, thin, clear *tsee* or *tsee-tsee*, (3) a slightly hoarse *whew* or *jeew*, and (4) repeated *tchup* or *tchip*.

Chipping Sparrow

nonbreeding
ad

breeding
ad

juv

Clay-colored Sparrow

Lincoln's Sparrow

juv

ad

Rufous-collared Sparrow

juv

ad

Yellow-eyed Junco

juv

ad

Volcano Junco

SPARROWS Passerellidae

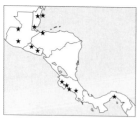

Lark Sparrow *Chondestes grammacus* 16.5 cm

Breeds Nearctic. Winters mainly MX. Vagrant (Oct to Mar) to BZ (Belize, Toledo, 343, 347, 346), SV (Chalatenango, La Paz, 183, 619), GT (Quiché, Sacatepéquez, Baja Verapaz, 229, 279), HN (Cortés, 442), CR (Guanacaste, Puntarenas, San José, 341, 546), and PA (Panamá, 512). **ID** Plain breast with black central spot. *Black malar and rufous auriculars. White on tail conspicuous in flight.* **HABITS** Floor and understory of open, grassy scrub and agricultural margins. Forages mainly on ground. **VOICE** Call (1) a sharp, slightly metallic *tik* or *sik*.

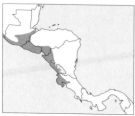

Stripe-headed Sparrow *Peucaea ruficauda* 17 cm

MX and CA. Common resident in Pacific lowlands and foothills (to 800, locally to 1500 m). Local on Caribbean slope in Motagua Valley, GT. **ID** Gray breast. Black auriculars contrast with white throat and *black-and-white striped crown.* **HABITS** Floor to lower midstory of arid to semihumid scrub, hedgerows, plantations, and gardens. Usually remains hidden beneath cover. May sing from elevated perch. Often in small groups. Flies weakly with tail drooped. **VOICE** Song (1) a rapid series of short, squeaky *tchp* or *chep* notes that accelerate to form a flat trill *tchp tchp-t-t-t-t-t-t-t-t.* Call (2) a high-pitched, squeaky *chit* or *psit.*

Rusty Sparrow *Aimophila rufescens* 17 cm

MX and CA. Fairly common resident in north lowlands and foothills (to 1800, locally to 2500 m). Uncommon and local in BZ and in foothills (500 to 1100 m) of west CR (Guanacaste, San José, 600, 675). **ID** *Rufous crown, wings, and tail. White supraloral and blackish malar.* **GV** Birds from Caribbean savannas (not shown) are smaller. **HABITS** Floor and understory of brushy pine or pine-oak forest, pine savanna, scrub, agricultural fields, pastures, plantations, and successional lava flows. Forages mainly on ground. Perches in midstory to sing or when disturbed. Solitary or in pairs. **VOICE** Variable song (1) a series of short, rich phrases *chup-chirup-dididu* or *chirrup chirup chirup si-bur* or *chip chip-chip-seeur* or *chep chepchep weeur.* Calls (2) a dry, rattling *zrrr-zrrr-zrrr . . .* and (3) clear, high-pitched *tsik.*

Botteri's Sparrow *Peucaea botterii* 13–15 cm

South USA to CA. Uncommon and local resident in BZ (Orange Walk, 529), GT (Petén, Baja Verapaz, Sacatepéquez, Guatemala, Sololá, 534, 637), HN (Gracias a Dios, 442), and NI (RAAN, Chinandega, 325, 327, 431). Rare in Pacific foothills (500 to 1100 m) of CR (Guanacaste, 600). **ID** Flat crown. Note *clear, pale brownish-buff underparts,* plain, gray auriculars, and *dark upperparts.* Grasshopper Sparrow has white on tertials, pale crown stripe, and shorter tail. **GV** Birds from north Caribbean CA are smaller and darker above. **HABITS** Grasslands and savannas with scattered shrubs. Forages on ground. Flushes with low, weak flight. Secretive, but may sing from low, exposed perch or in low, fluttering display flight. **VOICE** Variable song (1) several pairs of short, double notes followed by high-pitched trill *chip chip deedee chewchew di-di-di-di-di iiiiii . . .* Call (2) a sharp *tsit* or *swip.*

Grasshopper Sparrow *Ammodramus savannarum* 12 cm

USA to CA. Resident and Nearctic migrants occur. Uncommon and local breeder in BZ (68, 529), HN (Gracias a Dios, 442), NI (RAAN, 327, 54), and foothills (100 to 800 m, locally to near SL, 126, 648) of CR. Rare breeder in Pacific lowlands of PA (Chiriquí, Panamá, Coclé, 9, 468, 48). Nearctic migrants mainly in north. Very rare south to west PA (Bocas del Toro, 468, 512). **ID** Small with flat crown and heavy bill. Short, narrow tail pointed or frayed. *Underparts and auriculars plain buff.* Note *white median crown stripe,* white eye ring, and *white edging on tertials.* Compare with Botteri's Sparrow. **GV** Widespread breeding form in CA is darker than northern migrant and varies individually in extent of black streaking on upperparts and darkness of buff head and breast. Breeding birds from Panama (not shown) are pale like northern migrants. **HABITS** Understory of grasslands and savannas. When flushed drops quickly into cover. Secretive but sings from elevated perch. **VOICE** Song (1) high-pitched, insect-like, buzzy trills on varied pitch and dry, staccato notes *tsk-tsk sweeeeezeeee tik-tik zweeeee tik tiptip sweeee.* Call (2) a piercing *tsee* or *tweet.*

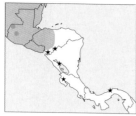

Savannah Sparrow *Passerculus sandwichensis* 13 cm

NA to CA. Winters mainly USA and MX. Breeds locally in highlands (above 2500 m) of west GT (Huehuetenango, Totonicapán, 229, 230, 635). Rare winter visitor (Oct to Apr) to Pacific HN (Choluteca, 346), NI (Nueva Segovia, 419), CR (Guanacaste, Isla del Coco, 265, 571), and PA (Colón, 48). **ID** Pinkish bill and short, notched tail. Short, *yellowish supercilium.* Note streaked breast and pale stripes on mantle. **GV** Some birds from Nearctic breeding populations (not shown) have less prominent yellow supercilium. **HABITS** Grasslands, scrub, agricultural areas, and savannas. Forages on ground. Takes elevated perch when flushed. **VOICE** Song (1) high-pitched, staccato notes followed by buzzy trills *chit chit cheet tzeeeeeeee bzzzzz.* Call (2) a thin, high-pitched *seet.*

Lark Sparrow

Stripe-headed Sparrow

juv

ad

Rusty Sparrow

juv

Botteri's Sparrow

Caribbean
GT and BZ

widespread

juv

Grasshopper Sparrow

northern
migrant ad

resident
breeding ad

Savannah Sparrow

CHLOROSPINGI Passerellidae

Small birds found in middle and upper levels of humid broadleaf forest in foothills and highlands. Head and underparts patterns are useful for identification. Most are allopatric with restricted ranges in south highlands. Common Chlorospingus is the most common and widespread and shows complex geographic variation in Central America.

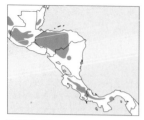

Common Chlorospingus *Chlorospingus flavopectus*   14 cm

MX to SA. Widespread in foothills and highlands (200 to 3000, but mainly 100 to 2500 m). Common to locally very common resident. Also Maya Mountains of BZ (above 700 m, 667, 313). May move to lower elevations outside breeding season. **ID** *White postocular spot.* Juv (not shown) mostly pale olive with whitish belly and throat and small whitish postocular spot. **GV** Shows complex geographic variation in CA (in some regions clinal). All birds from north CA have grayer head. Birds from Caribbean GT have brownish sides of crown and moustache. Birds from central PA have dark head and yellow-orange breast. **HABITS** Understory to canopy and edge of humid broadleaf (cloud) forest, second growth, plantations, and scrub. Forages actively. May drop briefly to ground. Groups follow mixed flocks. **VOICE** Song (1) a long, descending series of high-pitched notes *tseektseektcheep-tststststs*. Calls (2) a thin, sharp *tsip* or *tseep* or *tzzp* or *tseek* sometimes repeated, (3) rattling *tsrrrrr*, and (4) short *cut*.

Tacarcuna Chlorospingus *Chlorospingus tacarcunae*   13 cm

CA endemic. Uncommon resident in foothills and highlands (750 to 1500 m) of central and east PA including Serranía de Majé (44). **ID** *Plain, dusky olive head* and *pale whitish eyes.* Underparts (including throat) mostly dull yellow with grayish central belly. Common and Pirre chlorospingi allopatric. **HABITS** Poorly known. Upper understory to subcanopy and edge of very humid broadleaf (cloud) forest and adjacent second growth. Follows mixed flocks. Forages in moss clumps and epiphytes. **VOICE** Poorly known. Calls (1) a sharp, slightly buzzy *tseeeee* and (2) smoother, downslurred *cheeuuu*.

Pirre Chlorospingus *Chlorospingus inornatus*   14.5 cm

CA endemic. Locally common resident in highlands (above 1400 m) of Pirre Massif, Serranía de Jungurudó, and Cerro Sapo in east PA (Darién, 519, 45). **ID** *Large* and heavy-billed. Note *dusky head* and *pale orange-yellow eyes.* Tacarcuna and Common chlorospingi allopatric. **HABITS** Midstory to subcanopy and edge of humid broadleaf (cloud) forest. Forages actively in clumps of moss, foliage, and epiphytes. Pairs or family groups follow mixed flocks that may include Green-naped Tanagers. **VOICE** Calls (1) a buzzy, thin, high-pitched *speetza*, (2) shorter *tsiip*, and (3) upslurred *chu-weet*.

Ashy-throated Chlorospingus *Chlorospingus canigularis*   13.5 cm

CA and (disjunctly) SA. Rare and local resident in Caribbean foothills (400 to 1200 m) of CR and west PA (Chiriquí, Ngäbe-Buglé, Veraguas, Bocas del Toro, 512, 659, 341, 346). **ID** Olive above including crown. Note *gray malar* and *yellow breast* separating whitish throat and lower underparts. Compare with Yellow-throated Chlorospingus and female White-shouldered Tanager. **HABITS** Upper midstory to subcanopy of humid broadleaf forest. May descend to lower levels in vegetation at edges or gaps. Pairs or small groups follow mixed flocks. **VOICE** Song (1) a high-pitched, thin, sibilant, slightly ascending *tse tse tse tsee*. Call (2) a high-pitched, thin, sharp *zeezit* or *dzee dzit* or *zee zee zit*.

Sooty-capped Chlorospingus *Chlorospingus pileatus*   14 cm

CA endemic. Common resident in highlands (above 1600 m) of CR and west PA. **ID** *Blackish crown and sides of head* and *white supercilium and postocular stripe.* Some birds from central CR (Irazú and Turrialba region) are duller and paler. Compare with Common Chlorospingus. Note different head pattern. **HABITS** Midstory to subcanopy and edge of very humid broadleaf (cloud and elfin) forest. Descends to lower levels at edges or gaps. Forages actively in foliage and epiphytes. Pairs or groups form mixed flocks with Spangle-cheeked Tanagers. **VOICE** Infrequently heard song (1) a rapid, accelerating series of notes that accelerate to become a short, metallic trill *see-chur see-chur see-chur see see see-checheecheechee*. Calls (2) a high-pitched, soft *zit* or *zeet* and (3) variety of high-pitched notes *tsip* or *tseep*.

Yellow-throated Chlorospingus *Chlorospingus flavigularis*   14 cm

CA and (disjunctly) SA. Uncommon and local resident in foothills (mainly 450 to 900 m) of west and central PA. **ID** *Yellow throat* extends to form *partial nuchal collar* and contrasts with *drab, light brown breast.* **HABITS** Midstory and edge of humid broadleaf forest. Pairs or small groups follow mixed flocks. Forages less actively than other *Chlorospingus*. Habitually flicks or stretches individual wings upward. **VOICE** Call (1) a sharp, sibilant *jeet* or *pseet*.

Pacific north
CA

Caribbean
GT

widespread

central PA

Common Chlorospingus

**Tacarcuna
Chlorospingus**

**Pirre
Chlorospingus**

**Ashy-throated
Chlorospingus**

drab
morph

typical
morph

**Sooty-capped
Chlorospingus**

**Yellow-throated
Chlorospingus**

MEADOWLARK, BLACKBIRDS AND BOBOLINK Icteridae

Icterids found mainly in grasslands and marshes.

Eastern Meadowlark *Sturnella magna*   20–22 cm

NA to WI and SA. Locally common resident (SL to 3700 m). Perhaps expanding.
ID Bulky with long, pointed bill. In flight, short tail shows *white outer rectrices*.
Note *yellow breast with black chevron* (less distinct in imm and nonbreeding ad).
GV Shows subtle geographic variation in CA. Birds from PA are smaller and more
rufous-brown above. **HABITS** Grasslands, including open savannas, marshes, pastures,
and agricultural fields. Solitary or in pairs. Forages on the ground. Sings from exposed,
elevated perch on fence post or treetop. Flies with bursts of rapid, shallow wingbeats
and short glides. **VOICE** Song (1) two to six rich, clear, slurred whistles. Last notes
usually drop in pitch *peeealoo, pleuu, peeeu, peealur* or *cheero, cheero, cherio . . .* Calls
(2) a bubbling chatter *ch-ch-ch-ch . . .* (3) harsh, nasal, rolling *dzeerrt*, (4) chattering
chick-che-che-cheer, and (5) shorter *chick*.

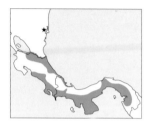

Red-breasted Blackbird *Leistes militaris*   female 16, male 18 cm

CA and SA. Locally fairly common resident in lowlands and foothills (to 900 m).
Expanding. First reported from CR in 1970 (Puntarenas, 353, 602, 600, 341). Recently
reported from Caribbean NI (RAAS, 51). **ID** Pointed bill and fairly short tail. Ad male
mostly dull brownish-black with *red throat and breast*. Red epaulets visible in flight.
Female streaked with dusky on upperparts and flanks. Note female's pale supercilium,
variable red or pink on underparts, and *barred tail*. Juv lacks pink and is more heavily
streaked below. Compare female and juv to female Red-winged Blackbird and
Bobolink. Note different underparts and tail. **HABITS** Damp grassy fields, scrubby
areas, lawns, airports, and agricultural areas such as rice fields. Forages mainly on
ground. Vocalizes from elevated perch on fence post or shrub. Also sings during brief
display flight. Wanders when not breeding, sometimes in flocks with other icterids.
VOICE Song (1) a short, staccato note followed by two buzzing notes on different
pitches *kip-bzzzzz-baaaaa*. Calls (2) a metallic *plik* or *jiink* and (3) dry, sputtering *jrrrt*.
Compare with harsher call of Eastern Meadowlark.

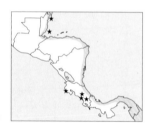

Bobolink *Dolichonyx oryzivorus*   female 16, male 17 cm

Breeds Nearctic. Winters SA. Most passage in WI. Rare and irregular fall transient (Sep
to Oct) on Caribbean coast and islands (600, 96, 659, 343). Very rare in spring (Apr
to Jun) on Pacific slope (111) and at higher elevations. Vagrant to Isla del Coco (571).
ID Female and nonbreeding male *mostly buff* with streaked crown and dorsum. Note
pale lores, dark stripe extending behind eye, and conical pinkish bill. Male gradually
acquires black underparts and contrasting pale nape, scapulars, and rump. Compare
with female Red-winged Blackbird and with smaller Grasshopper Sparrow. Note that
female Red-breasted Blackbird can have very plain underparts. **HABITS** Agricultural
fields, pastures, and grassy marshes. Forages in tall grass or brush. May perch high in
trees. Forms flocks. Flies with undulating style. Often calls in flight. **VOICE** Calls (1) a
sharp, clear *peek* or *plink* and (2) nasal *inhk* or *eenk*.

Yellow-headed Blackbird *Xanthocephalus xanthocephalus*   female 20, male 24 cm

Breeds Nearctic. Winters mainly MX. Rare winter visitor to BZ (Orange Walk, 346),
NI (Jinotega, 412), CR (Guanacaste, 602), and PA (Panamá, Colón, Chiriquí, 604,
512, 346). Vagrant to Isla del Coco (329). **ID** Large. Ad male mostly black with *deep
yellow head* (duller outside breeding season) and dusky lores. *White primary coverts*
conspicuous in flight. Female and imm mostly dusky brown with variable yellow
throat, sides of neck, and supercilium. **HABITS** Agricultural fields and marshes.
May associate with other open-country icterids. **VOICE** In flight gives (1) a low-pitched,
dry *kuduk* or *kek*.

juv

ad

widespread
breeding ad
♂

Pacific west PA
breeding ad
♂

Eastern Meadowlark

juv

♀

♂

Red-breasted Blackbird

♀

breeding
♂

Bobolink

♀

♂

Yellow-headed Blackbird

CACIQUES Icteridae

Scarlet-rumped Cacique *Cacicus uropygialis* 23 cm
CA and north SA. Uncommon resident in humid lowlands and foothills (to 1300 m).
ID Black with *scarlet rump* (often concealed). Note ivory bill. *Eyes pale blue.* Female
tinged gray. Compare with Yellow-billed Cacique. Note different habits. **GV** Birds from
east PA (not shown) have heavier bill and concealed white or gray patch on hindneck.
HABITS Midstory to subcanopy of humid broadleaf forest and tall second growth.
Groups move restlessly through forest. Clings or hangs to seize prey. May form mixed
flocks with oropendolas, jays, tanagers, or nunbirds. **VOICE** Noisy. Call (1) an abrupt,
loud, ringing whistle *pleeeo* or *preeeer.* May be given in series *preeo-preeer-peeeopeeeo-
peo . . .* and (2) single, shrill *eeyah* or *jeeah.* Also (3) a brief, gurgling, wheezy *pu-zeeek-
eew.* May suggest louder songs of oropendolas.

Yellow-rumped Cacique *Cacicus cela* female 23, male 28 cm
CA and SA. Uncommon resident in lowlands and foothills (to 600 m) of east PA.
Local in Pacific west PA (Veraguas, Los Santos, 659, 512). **ID** Male black with blue eyes
and *yellow patches on rump, lower underparts, base of tail, and wing coverts.* Yellow on
wing conspicuous in flight. Female smaller with brownish plumage. Imm resembles
female but may have dark eyes and dusky-tinged bill. **HABITS** Subcanopy to canopy and
edge of humid broadleaf forest, riparian woodland, tall second growth, and adjacent
plantations or shaded clearings. Gregarious, noisy, and often conspicuous. Nests
colonially. **VOICE** Calls (1) a harsh *cheeo chee'cheeo* and (2) short, harsh, emphatic *chow*
and (3) short, nasal bark *eh* or *eh ehh.* Other calls more liquid including (4) a slurred
ssssh sssheweeow. Compare with song of Chestnut-headed Oropendola.

Yellow-winged Cacique *Cassiculus melanicterus* female 27, male 30 cm
MX and north CA. Uncommon and local resident in Pacific slope and interior
lowlands of GT (San Marcos, Escuintla, Santa Rosa, Huehuetenango, 178, 182, 229) and
SV (Sonsonate, 346). **ID** Male black with long, pale, pointed bill and *thin crest.* Eyes
dark. Note *yellow rump, crissum and outer rectrices.* Female browner. Yellow-rumped
Cacique allopatric. **HABITS** Canopy and edge of arid to semihumid forest, second
growth, mangroves, plantations, and gardens. May nest in small colonies. Gathers at
communal roosts. **VOICE** Song (1) a short rattle followed by quiet notes and ending
with discordant, slightly mechanical phrase that is upslurred at end *rrah uh-uu uh-uu
raahn'ee rahn-ee.* Calls (2) a nasal, upslurred *rrhank* or *raaah,* (3) mellow, whistled *tyoo*
or *tiyih,* (4) hollow, slightly plaintive *wheeoo?* (5) clipped *ch-tewk,* (6) ringing *chenk,*
and (7) short, hard, grackle-like rattle followed by clear, slurred notes *ki-errr iik-iik-iik-
iik churweee.*

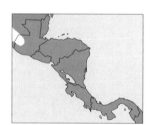

Yellow-billed Cacique *Amblycercus holosericeus* 23 cm
South MX to west SA. Uncommon to locally common resident (SL to 3100 m).
ID Male uniform dull black with *long, straight, pointed ivory bill* and *yellow eyes.* Female
slightly grayer. Imm (not shown) dull brownish with dark eyes. **HABITS** Understory
and edge of semihumid to humid broadleaf forest (particularly stands of large-leaved
herbs or bamboo), second growth, and riparian thickets. Skulks in dark, tangled
vegetation. May ascend to subcanopy in vine tangles. Probes or pries into hollow stems,
arboreal litter, and dead leaf clusters. Solitary or in pairs. Usually detected by voice.
VOICE Pairs duet. Loud song (1) a series of three or four short, rich, slurred, whistled
phrases *cheweea-chewoo, cheweea-chewoo . . .* or *cheer-chew-chew cheer-chew-chew . . .*
Also (2) a long, loud, downslurred whistle followed by a coarse rattle *cheeeeeeeeeu-
chrrrrrrr.* Calls (3) a nasal, two-syllable *rahk rahk* or *erraak erraak* and (4) low-pitched
kwukkwuk-kwuk.

33%

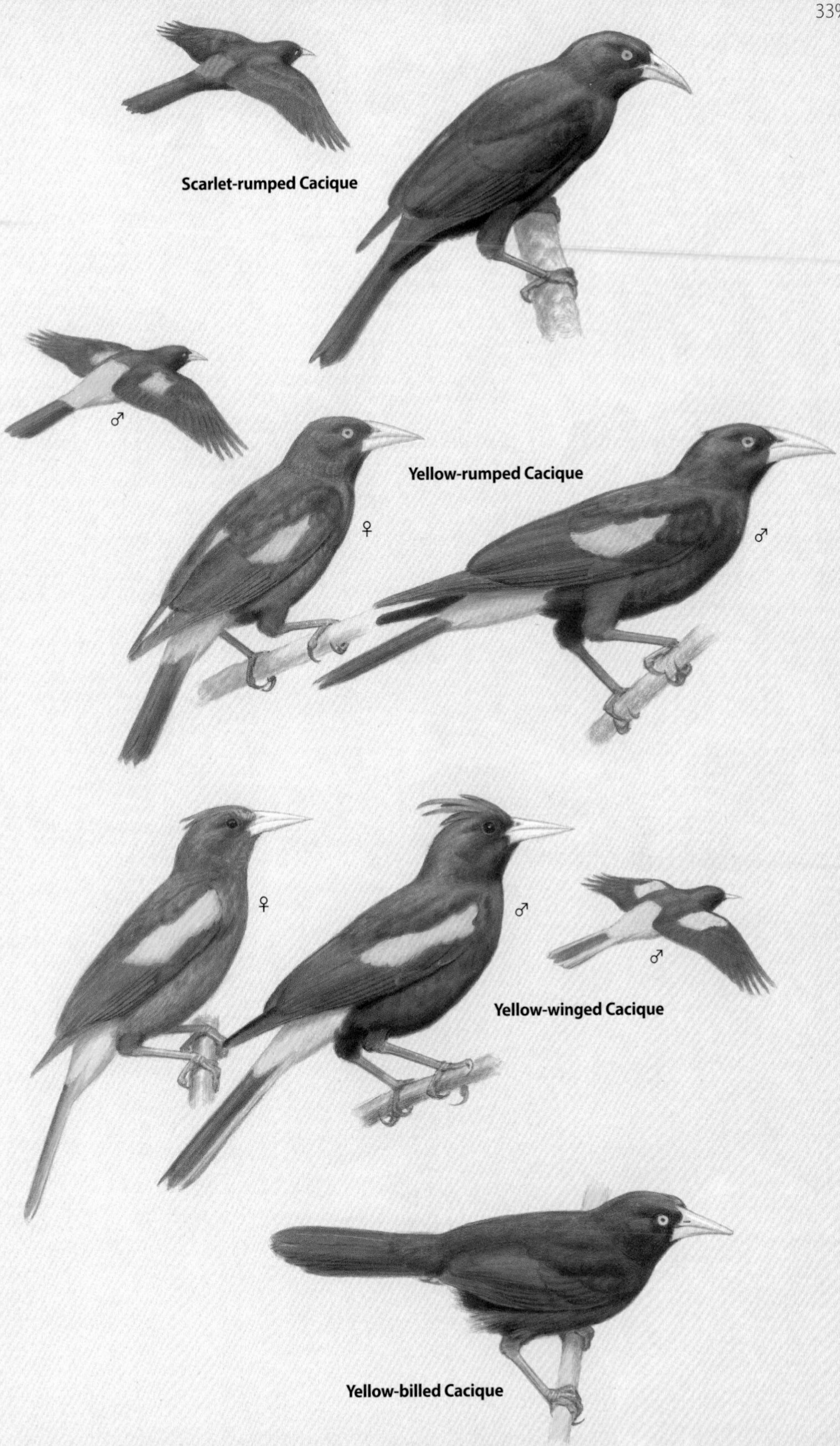
Scarlet-rumped Cacique
♂
Yellow-rumped Cacique
♀
♂
♀
♂
♂
Yellow-winged Cacique
Yellow-billed Cacique

OROPENDOLAS Icteridae

Large icterids. Males are noticeably larger than females. Oropendolas nest colonially, and their long, pendulous nests are a familiar sight in humid Central American lowlands and foothills. All have loud, arresting vocalizations. Identification is straightforward provided good views can be obtained of the bill and head pattern. Montezuma Oropendola is the most common and widespread.

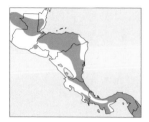

Chestnut-headed Oropendola *Psarocolius wagleri*   female 26, male 36 cm
CA and north SA. Fairly common resident in lowlands and foothills (to 1700, rarely to 2000 m). Mainly Caribbean slope in north but reported from SV (Santa Ana, 341). **ID** Smallest CA oropendola. *Heavy ivory bill* extends to form bulging casque on forehead (more pronounced in male). Eyes pale blue. *Chestnut head and neck* contrast with *blue-black thorax*. In flight, note relatively rapid wingbeats and dark head. Wings narrower and more pointed than Montezuma Oropendola. Crested Oropendola has concolorous blackish-brown head and thorax, lacks bulging casque, and has all-yellow outer rectrices. **HABITS** Subcanopy to canopy and edge of humid broadleaf forest, adjacent tall second growth, and clearings or plantations with scattered trees. Forages actively in pairs or small groups. Nests in colonies in emergent or isolated tree. **VOICE** Song (1) a loud, liquid, downslurred note followed by a short, hollow note *eeeeeeehr hoo*. Calls include (2) a low-pitched, coarse, resonant *kok* or *chek*, (3) various short, liquid notes *poik* or *ploop*, (4) a nasal, whining *heaaaanh*, and (5) abrupt, coarse *cack-cack* or *check-check*.

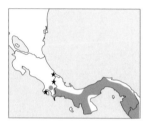

Crested Oropendola *Psarocolius decumanus*   female 36, male 48 cm
CA and SA. Uncommon resident in lowlands and foothills (to 900 m) of PA. Recently found on both slopes in east CR (Puntarenas, Limón, 546, 346). **ID** Long-tailed. Note uniform ivory-yellow bill with straight culmen. *Head, neck, and mantle blackish-brown.* Eyes pale blue. Resembles more widespread Chestnut-headed Oropendola. Note Crested's brown thorax, different bill shape, and tail pattern. **HABITS** Subcanopy to canopy and edge of humid broadleaf forest. Sometimes in small groups. May join mixed associations that include jays and other large birds. Powerful, direct (not undulating) flight. **VOICE** Song (1) a short, loud, downslurred note followed by a short, hollow phrase *eeeeeeehr wha-how*. Calls (2) a short, hoarse, abrupt *cruuk* or *ruuk* and (3) long, wooden rattle that drops steeply in pitch.

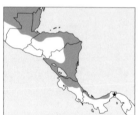

Montezuma Oropendola *Psarocolius montezuma*   female 36, male 48 cm
South MX and CA. Common resident in lowlands and foothills (SL to 1500, mainly below 1000 m in north). **ID** Large. Deep chestnut with black head and breast. *Dark bill with orange tip.* Eyes dark. *Blue bare facial skin* and pink malar wattle contrast with dark head. Female smaller. Chestnut-headed Oropendola has pale bill and lacks bare facial skin of Montezuma Oropendola. Black Oropendola allopatric. **HABITS** Subcanopy to canopy and edge of semihumid to humid broadleaf forest, tall second growth, open areas with scattered trees, plantations, and gallery forest. When breeding, assembles at colonial nest sites in isolated or emergent canopy trees. In flight, wingbeats produce "whooshing" sound. **VOICE** Song (1) a short, loud, upslurred note followed by a liquid gurgle. Calls include (2) a low-pitched, guttural *chuck* or *cluck*, (3) yelping *eeuh*, (4) loud, harsh rattle, and (5) an abrupt *cack*.

Black Oropendola *Psarocolius guatimozinus*   female 38, male 50 cm
CA and north SA. Locally fairly common resident in lowlands and foothills (to 600 m) of east PA (Darién, 512, 659). **ID** *Mostly black* with chestnut wing coverts and mantle. Pink wattle and *bare blue facial skin* contrast with dark head. Note *dark bill with orange tip*. Eyes dark. Female smaller. Montezuma Oropendola allopatric. Crested and Chestnut-headed oropendolas have pale bill and lack blue facial skin. **HABITS** Subcanopy to canopy of humid broadleaf forest, clearings with scattered tall trees, riparian forests, and tall second growth. **VOICE** Song (1) like Montezuma Oropendola but perhaps lower-pitched.

Chestnut-headed
Oropendola

Crested
Oropendola

Montezuma
Oropendola

Nesting colony of
Montezuma Oropendolas.

Black Oropendola

ORIOLES Icteridae

Medium-sized, long-tailed birds found in upper levels of forest or woodland. The Central American orioles include several widespread residents, several range-restricted species, and three Nearctic breeding migrants. While brightly colored and often conspicuous, orioles can present identification problems. Resident species are sexually monomorphic but all show age-related plumage variation. Migrant species have both age- and sex-related plumage variation. Bill shape, wing pattern, and voice are useful in identifying orioles. Black-cowled Oriole is the most common and widespread of the species on this plate.

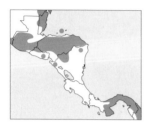

Yellow-backed Oriole *Icterus chrysater*   21–23 cm
South MX and CA. Uncommon to fairly common resident. In north, mainly Caribbean lowlands and interior highlands (SL to 1500, locally to 3000 m). Also Isla Roatán (538, 442). In PA mainly humid lowlands and foothills (SL to 900 m). **ID** *Plain yellow crown and mantle* and *unmarked black wings*. Female and imm duller. Compare with imm Black-cowled Oriole. Note different upperparts. **GV** Birds from PA are more intense yellow-orange. **HABITS** Midstory to subcanopy and edge of open pine and pine-oak forest, pine savanna and scrub in north. In PA uses humid broadleaf forest, tall second growth and scrub. Often in pairs. May follow mixed flocks. **VOICE** Variable song (1) a deliberate, slightly hesitant series of rich whistles *chooooo heehoo wooo heehooo . . .* or *woohooheechoo a woohoochee . . .* often repeated. Calls (2) a plaintive *choo*, (3) nasal, buzzy *chednk* or *yehnk* often repeated, (4) rich *tchew tcheeo cheoo*, and (5) ascending series *wheep wheep wheep wheep*.

Yellow-tailed Oriole *Icterus mesomelas*   22 cm
MX to SA. Uncommon to locally fairly common resident in lowlands (to 500, rarely to 1500 m.) Most common in north Caribbean. Rare in east HN. Uncommon and local in south CA. **ID** *Yellow outer rectrices* and *long yellow wing patch*. Imm duller. Juv lacks black throat and face. **GV** Birds from south CA are larger with larger bill (juv shown). **HABITS** Canopy and edge of semihumid to humid broadleaf forest, pine savanna, riparian woodland, second growth, and shaded plantations. Often near water. Sings from exposed perch. May follow mixed flocks. Habitually jerks tail up and down in flight. **VOICE** Pairs duet. Song (1) a variable, loud, rhythmic series of rich, whistled phrases that gradually increase in volume *tch wee-cheeoweeep, tch wee-choo weeoocheep . . .* or *cheerro-ro-ror chee ro-ror . . .* or *roo chee-roo roo chee-roo*. Compare with songs *Campylorhynchus* wrens. Calls (2) a slightly nasal *cheuk* and (3) harder *chuk* or *chook* often repeated or doubled as *chup-cheet* or *chup-chup*.

Orange-crowned Oriole *Icterus auricapillus*   21 cm
CA and north SA. Uncommon to locally fairly common resident in lowlands and foothills (to 800 m) of east PA. **ID** Mostly *orange head* contrasts with *black face and throat*. Note all-black bill and unmarked black wings and tail. Resembles Yellow-tailed Oriole. Note Orange-crowned's *all-black tail*. **HABITS** Midstory to subcanopy and edge of semihumid to humid broadleaf forest, second growth, plantations, and pastures with scattered trees. Often near water. May forage in canopy of flowering trees. Solitary or in pairs. Sings from exposed perch. **VOICE** Song (1) a long, loud, disjointed, mimid-like series of repeated whistles and short, harsh, scolding notes *werr, cheet-cheet-kurrkurr che che sh-sh-sh ek ek cheche-wurr*.

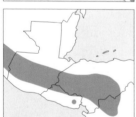

Black-vented Oriole *Icterus wagleri*   22 cm
MX and north CA. Uncommon resident in north foothills and highlands (mainly 500 to 2000, locally to 3000 m). **ID** Long, fine bill. Ad mostly black with yellow rump, belly, lower breast, and epaulets. Ad is only CA oriole with *black crissum*. Imm dull yellow with blackish tail and wings and variable extent of black on face and throat. Mantle may be irregularly mottled with black. Imm resembles imms of Yellow-tailed and Bar-winged orioles. Note imm Black-vented's pale wing edging and mottled back. Black-cowled Oriole allopatric. **HABITS** Midstory to canopy of pine-oak forest, gardens, scrub, and plantations. Often near human dwellings. **VOICE** Song (1) a series of clear whistles *wiiuuu*. Call (2) a flat, nasal *nyeh* or *eehn*. Sometimes repeated.

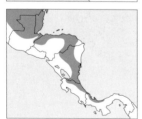

Black-cowled Oriole *Icterus prosthemelas*   20 cm
South MX and CA. Common resident in Caribbean lowlands and foothills (SL to 1000, mainly below 500 m). **ID** Slim, decurved bill. Ad has extensive black hood and black wings with *yellow wing coverts*. Imm and juv always show black bib and blackish greater coverts. Compare imm with brighter ad Yellow-backed Oriole. Black-vented Oriole allopatric. **HABITS** Subcanopy to canopy and edge of semihumid to humid broadleaf forest and tall second growth in north. In south mainly at forest edge and in semi-open areas. Pairs or small groups follow mixed flocks. **VOICE** Song (1) a short, slightly scratchy warbled phrase *choo choo wheechee . . .* Calls (2) an abrupt, nasal *ehh* or *woink*, (3) chattering scold *chuh-chuh . . .* or *cheh-cheh-cheh-chek*, and (4) quiet whistle *wheet*. Sometimes repeated.

Yellow-backed Oriole

juv

♀

north CA
ad ♂

PA
ad ♂

imm
♂

Yellow-tailed Oriole

juv

ad
♂

Orange-crowned Oriole

ad

imm

juv

ad

Black-vented Oriole

juv

♀

♂

Black-cowled Oriole

38%

ORIOLES Icteridae

Baltimore and Orchard orioles are common winter residents in Central America. Hooded Oriole should be compared with the species on the following plate.

Bar-winged Oriole *Icterus maculialatus*   female 20, male 22 cm

South MX and north CA. Uncommon and local resident in Pacific foothills and highlands (mainly 500 to 2300, locally to 3300 m). **ID** Ad male mostly black with yellow lower underparts including crissum. Note *white spots on wing coverts.* Black-bibbed imm male and female resemble several other CA orioles. Note combination of *single wingbar* and relatively plain, *olive dorsum.* **HABITS** Midstory to canopy and edge of broadleaf and pine-oak forest, plantations, and gardens. **VOICE** Song (1) a slow series of short, rich whistles and warbled phrases *whheet weew wee-cheeuu . . .* Calls (2) a short, coarse, downslurred chatter *che-rrr* or *ah-rrr* or *grrrr* and (3) longer *ah-rrrrr* like Baltimore Oriole.

Hooded Oriole *Icterus cucullatus*   female 18, male 20 cm

South USA to north CA. Fairly common resident in lowlands of north BZ. Also BZ Cays. Rare in north GT (Petén, 110, 229). **ID** Slender and long-tailed with *long, slim, decurved bill.* Ad male mostly orange with black face, throat, mantle, and tail. Note bold white upper wingbar and extensive white edging on wing. Compare ad male with larger Altamira Oriole. Note different bill shape and wing pattern. Compare ad female with ad female Orchard Oriole. **HABITS** Midstory to canopy of semi-open areas with scattered tall trees (especially palms), plantations, littoral forest, scrub, urban areas, and gardens. Solitary or in pairs. **VOICE** Song (1) a long series of short whistles, squeaky, warbled phrases, and short, harsh clicking or buzzy notes *whheet weew wee-cheeuuch-t-t . . .* Calls (2) a short, rich, downslurred whistle *whiiiuu* and (3) coarse, rattling *chedik* or *ched-itit* often repeated.

Bullock's Oriole *Icterus bullockii*   19 cm

Breeds west Nearctic. Winters south USA to CA. Rare winter visitor (Oct to Mar) to Pacific slope in GT (San Marcos, Quiché, Sololá, 279, 346), SV (La Libertad, 619), and CR (Guanacaste, Puntarenas, 648, 474, 346). **ID** Ad male has *mostly white wing coverts,* mostly orange head with black crown, eye stripe, and center of throat. Ad female grayish above with yellow sides of head and breast and *pale grayish lower underparts.* Imm male usually has some trace of ad's pattern but has olive back and grayish underparts. Female very similar to imm female Baltimore Oriole (perhaps not separable in field) but tends to be paler and grayer and often has *pale supercilium* lacking in imm female Baltimore Oriole. **HABITS** Might occur in wide variety of arboreal habitats including forest canopy and edge, second growth, open woodland, plantations, and gardens. Similar to Baltimore Oriole. **VOICE** Call (1) a squeaky *juk* or *juk-jink.*

Baltimore Oriole *Icterus galbula*   19 cm

Breeds east Nearctic. Winters mainly MX and WI to north SA. Widespread and common transient and winter resident (Sep to May) mainly in lowlands and foothills (SL to 2500 m). Perhaps most abundant in north Pacific. **ID** Relatively straight culmen. Ad male mostly orange with black hood and mantle. Lesser coverts form orange epaulet. Greater coverts show broad white wingbar. Remiges also edged white. Tail mostly orange with black center and base. Ad female has variable extent of black on head and throat, sometimes approaching "male-like" hood. Some imm females are quite drab. **HABITS** Upper midstory to canopy and edge in a wide variety of arboreal habitats including forest, second growth, open woodland, plantations, pine savanna, and gardens. **VOICE** Wintering birds occasionally sing. Song (1) a series of very rich, whistled notes *cheeuu choo choo choo . . .* Calls (2) a dry, harsh, wrenlike chatter *ch-chch-ch-ch . . .* like Orchard and Bar-winged orioles and (3) a squeaky, metallic *eeet* or *yee.* Sometimes repeated or combined with previous.

Orchard Oriole *Icterus spurius*   17 cm

Breeds Nearctic. Winters mainly CA and north SA. Widespread and fairly common transient and winter resident (Jul to May) in lowlands and foothills (to 1600 m). **ID** Smallest CA oriole. Note fine, slightly decurved bill. Ad male mostly *chestnut-red below.* Ad female and imm resemble several other CA oriole plumages. Compare with female and imm Hooded Oriole. Note Orchard Oriole's *yellow-olive color* and *small size.* **HABITS** Midstory to subcanopy of forest edge, second growth, plantations, and gardens. Gathers at roosts in shrubby or grassy wetlands. Generally insectivorous but also takes nectar at flowering trees. Habitually twitches tail from side to side. **VOICE** Song (1) a short series of slurred, slightly buzzy whistles. Calls (2) a short, harsh *chek* or *chuk-chuk,* (3) guttural *krirk,* and (4) short, harsh chatter, lower-pitched than chatter of Baltimore Oriole.

38%

Bar-winged Oriole
imm ♂
♀
ad ♂

Hooded Oriole
imm ♂
♀
ad ♂

Bullock's Oriole
imm ♂
♀
ad ♂

Baltimore Oriole
imm
♀
ad ♂

Orchard Oriole
imm ♂
♀
ad ♂

ORIOLES Icteridae

Mostly large orioles found in arid to semihumid regions. Useful features for identification include details of the wing pattern, upperparts pattern, and bill shape. Altamira Oriole and Streak-backed Oriole are both geographically variable in Central America.

Orange Oriole *Icterus auratus*   20 cm

South MX and CA. Uncommon and local resident in lowlands of north BZ (Corozal, 313, 343, 417). **ID** Small and slender. Male has black throat and *orange mantle*. Female resembles female of sympatric Hooded Oriole. Note different bill shape and *black scapulars* of female Orange Oriole. Also compare with larger Altamira Oriole. **HABITS** Semihumid forest edge, tall second growth, plantations, and clearings with scattered trees. In pairs or small groups. May follow mixed flocks or form feeding associations with other orioles at flowering trees. **VOICE** Song (1) a varied, slow series of clear, rich, slightly plaintive whistles. Compare with faster song of Altamira Oriole. Also (2) a rapid, fairly mellow, whistled *chuchuchuchu . . .* or *cheechee . . .* Calls (3) slightly nasal, drawn-out *wheet*, (4) fairly hard, nasal *nyehk*, (5) clear *choo*, and (6) low-pitched, dry chatter.

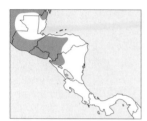

Altamira Oriole *Icterus gularis*   female 23, male 26 cm

South Texas to CA. Fairly common resident in north Pacific (to 1800 m). Also lowlands of north BZ. **ID** Large. Sexes similar. Short, straight, deep-based bill mostly blackish. Compare with Hooded Oriole and note *proportionally deeper-based and larger bill*. Also note Altamira's orange lesser wing coverts (sometimes concealed). Compare with Streak-backed Oriole. **GV** Birds from BZ are smaller and deeper red-orange (thus more similar to locally sympatric Hooded and Orange orioles). **HABITS** Midstory to canopy and edge of arid to semihumid forest, second growth, scrub, plantations, and gardens. Usually in pairs. May form mixed groups with other orioles. **VOICE** Variable song (1) a series of short, rich whistles *chee-choo chee-choo chree-chu-chu-chu-chu-chewee* or *chu chewee chu chocho cho chewee* like song of Spot-breasted Oriole. Calls (2) a simple *che'chu* or *weechu* that may be repeated, (3) short, nasal *oyik* or *yehnk* that may be repeated, (4) bright, slightly ringing *chiu* or *chew*, and (5) a short, harsh rattle.

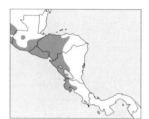

Streak-backed Oriole *Icterus pustulatus*   22 cm

MX and CA. Fairly common resident in Pacific and interior lowlands and foothills (to 1800, mainly below 1000 m). Reaches Caribbean slope locally (277). **ID** Deep, relatively short bill with near-straight culmen and *extensively gray mandible*. Ad usually has extensive white edging on wing including base of primaries, and *streaked mantle*. Imm male resembles female. Compare with Spot-breasted Oriole. Note different bill shape and wing pattern. Compare with Altamira Oriole. Note finer bill with more extensively gray mandible of Streak-backed Oriole. **GV** Male from north CA may have near-uniform black mantle. Some birds from GT have limited spotting on sides of breast. Color also variable, and some males are mostly yellow rather than orange. **HABITS** Midstory to canopy and edge of arid to humid woodland, second growth, thorn forest, mangroves, plantations and gardens. Usually in pairs. May associate with other orioles. **VOICE** Song (1) a variable series of rich whistles *whee'tchi-wee-chi-wee* or *chree chree chree chu chree-chi*. Calls (2) a harsh, nasal *ehk* often repeated, (3) nasal *cheh* or *chehk*, (4) short, slightly liquid *chuwit* or *tuip*, (5) short, clear *chweet* or *chew*, and (6) steady series of clear notes *sweet sweet sweet . . .* or *weet weet weet*. Also (7) a short, dry chatter or rattle.

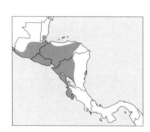

Spot-breasted Oriole *Icterus pectoralis*   22 cm

MX and north CA. Fairly common resident in Pacific and interior lowlands and foothills (to 1500 m). Reaches Caribbean lowlands locally in south BZ (Toledo), GT, and north HN. **ID** Sexes similar. *Long bill with decurved culmen*. Ad has *all-black greater coverts* and *spotted breast*. Imm has white in wing confined to broad white tertial edging (no white on wing coverts). Compare with Streak-backed Oriole. Note different wing pattern. Worn imm may be very similar to Streak-backed Orioles in corresponding plumage. Note different bill shape. **HABITS** Midstory to canopy and edge of arid to humid broadleaf forest, second growth, plantations, and gardens. Usually in pairs. May associate with other orioles. **VOICE** Song (1) a variable, slow, deliberate series of rich, slurred whistles *whi whew hi hew hew . . .* or *whee chu-wee'chu-u . . .* May include a long, repetitive series *chee-hee-oo hee-hee chee-chee-chee-chee-chee-chee . . .* Call (2) a short, nasal *nyeh* or *ehh*. Often repeated in short series.

38%

Orange Oriole

♀

♂

BZ
ad

Altamira Oriole

imm

juv

widespread
ad

Streak-backed Oriole

juv

♀

north
CA
♂

south
CA
♂

Spot-breasted Oriole

imm

juv

ad

BLACKBIRD AND COWBIRDS Icteridae

Mostly black-plumaged icterids found in open or disturbed areas. Bronzed Cowbird is the expected small cowbird species in most of Central America. Shiny Cowbird is thought to be expanding its range northward from South America.

Red-winged Blackbird *Agelaius phoeniceus* 17–23 cm

NA to CA. Locally common resident in lowlands and foothills (to 750 m). **ID** Ad male mostly black with *red on wing coverts* (sometimes concealed). Female mostly brown with variable buff streaking on underparts and dorsum. Compare female with streaked females of other open-country icterids and with various sparrows. **GV** Red-winged Blackbird varies in size and female coloration. Birds from Pacific GT are larger, darker, and less rufous. Birds from north GT are similar but smaller. **HABITS** Freshwater marshes and borders of ponds and lakes. Uses all levels of vegetation. Often forages on ground. Vocalizes from open, elevated perch. Wanders (often to agricultural areas) in flocks. May associate with other open-country icterids when not breeding. **VOICE** Variable song (1) a harsh *ko-leeurlee* or *kurshleeuee* or *zhww-koleeyu*. Last note buzzy or guttural. Calls (2) a dry *chek*, (3) scratchy, wooden *pik*, and (4) nasal *neeah*.

Brown-headed Cowbird *Molothrus ater* female 16.5, male 18 cm

NA and CA. Rare vagrant to GT (Huehuetenango, 346, 229) and BZ (Corozal, Orange Walk, Cayo, 345, 346). **ID** Stout bill. *Eyes dark*. Ad male black with green iridescence and has *brown hood*. Female grayish-brown with *pale throat* and supercilium. Compare with Bronzed Cowbird. Note different eye color. **HABITS** Agricultural fields, pastures, and urban areas. Forages on ground, often near cattle or other livestock. Forms flocks. May associate with other cowbirds or grackles. **VOICE** Song (1) a very high-pitched, slurred phrase *whuu-sleek*. Call (2) a liquid rattle. In flight, a very high-pitched, liquid *p-sleeet*.

Shiny Cowbird *Molothrus bonariensis* female 21, male 24 cm

WI, CA and SA. Locally common resident in PA. Expanding. Reported outside PA in CR (Limón, Heredia, Puntarenas, 341, 410, 346), BZ (Cayo, Toledo, 346), and GT (Chiquimula, El Progresso, 229). Also Isla del Coco (346). **ID** *Dark eyes*. Ad male black with violet iridescence. Female brownish-gray with *pale throat and supercilium*. Juv has soft streaking on breast. Compare with Bronzed Cowbird. Note different eye color. Male lacks neck ruff of Bronzed Cowbird. Female Bronzed Cowbird darker with plain head pattern. **HABITS** Agricultural and urban areas. Forages on ground, often near cattle or other livestock. **VOICE** Male's variable song (1) a series of high-pitched, squeaky, clear, liquid notes and trills. Often ends with one to three liquid *quit* notes *tssssseuuutseetsucheechu trrrr quitquitquit*. Call (2) a high-pitched, liquid or metallic *p-sleeep*. Gives (3) a soft, short rattle in flight.

Bronzed Cowbird *Molothrus aeneus* female 19, male 21 cm

South USA to north SA. Fairly common resident (SL to 3000 m). **ID** *Red eyes*. Male black with *brownish-olive gloss* and blue-black wings. Male has bulky ruff. Female *uniform dark brown* with *plain dark head*. Imm resembles female. Female Shiny Cowbird has dark eyes. Compare male with Melodious Blackbird. Note different eye color and structure. **HABITS** Agricultural and urban areas. Groups forage on ground, often near livestock. In flight, forms tight flocks. **VOICE** Male's song (1) a series of long, high-pitched, slurred, thin notes *see seu seeeeeeeuuu-siiiiiiiii*. Calls (2) a thin, short, buzzy *tsweee* or *zweeep* sometimes repeated and (3) short, rich *chut* or *chuk* repeated rapidly in flight.

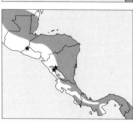

Giant Cowbird *Molothrus oryzivorus* female 30, male 36 cm

MX to SA. Uncommon resident in lowlands and foothills (to 750, rarely or locally to 1200 m). Mainly Caribbean slope in north. Rare in SV (Santa Ana, 341) and Pacific NI (Managua, 413). **ID** *Large* with *heavy bill*. Note long primary projection. Ad male has bulky ruff. Smaller female dull brownish-black and lacks ruff. Most have dark eyes but some birds from east PA have pale eyes. Juv has pale bill. Flies with short glides on long, pointed wings. Compare with Great-tailed Grackle. Note different structure and eye color. **HABITS** Canopy and edge of broadleaf forest, second growth, agricultural areas, plantations, and riparian edges. A brood parasite of oropendolas and caciques. Females loiter on exposed perch near host colonies. May forage on ground, on muddy riverbanks, or in agricultural fields. **VOICE** Usually quiet. Males give (1) an upslurred, screeching *fwreeeeeee* or *schreeeeee-up*. Calls (2) a sharp chatter *chechk chehk* or *chek-chick*, (3) longer *chrrik rrik-rrik-rrik-rrick-rrick-riik*, and (4) low-pitched, nasal *dak* or *kawk* or *ehk*.

Red-winged Blackbird

Pacific GT ♀

widespread ♀

ad ♂

Brown-headed Cowbird

♀

♂

juv

ad ♀

ad ♂

Shiny Cowbird

Bronzed Cowbird

♀

♂

Giant Cowbird

juv

♀

♂

BLACKBIRDS AND GRACKLES Icteridae

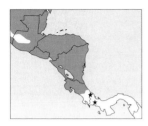

Melodious Blackbird *Dives dives*   26 cm

MX and north CA. Common resident (SL to 2100 m). Formerly confined to north but has expanded. First recorded from Pacific GT in 1970s (182), in SV in 1950s (248, 619). Now widespread in CR where first noted in 1987 (Puntarenas, 594, 542, 341). Recently found in west PA (Bocas del Toro, Chiriquí, 346). **ID** Ad *uniform glossy black* with *near-straight, blackish, conical bill* (culmen slightly arched). *Eyes dark.* Imm duller, less glossy, and faintly tinged brown. Bronzed Cowbird has different bill shape and eye color. Compare with Great-tailed Grackle. Note different tail shape. **HABITS** Forest edge, agricultural areas, pastures, gardens, plantations, pine savanna. Forages mainly on ground. Habitually raises partly spread tail and slowly lowers it. **VOICE** Pairs duet. Song (1) a loud, liquid, downslurred *whi-cheeer* or *wuhr-cheer* or *pit-wheer* sometimes varied to *wur ch'cheer wuhr wuhr ch'cheeer*. First note sometimes repeated *wuhr, wuhr, wuhr, wuhr-cheer*. Calls (2) a variety of slurred, liquid whistles and (3) sharp *peet peet peet . . .*

Yellow-hooded Blackbird *Chrysomus icterocephalus*   female 16.5, male 17.5 cm

CA and SA. Rare and local resident in lowlands of east PA (Darién, 346, 43). **ID** Male *mostly black* with *yellow head, neck, and chest*. Female mostly dusky with dull yellow supercilium, throat, and breast. Imm resembles female and gradually acquires black plumage. Compare with Yellow-headed Blackbird. **HABITS** Freshwater marshes, borders of ponds and lakes, and damp fields. Forages and sings from middle levels in vegetation. May form flocks when not breeding. **VOICE** Song (1) a harsh, squeaky phrase *juuuur-gul-zleee* or *took, too weeeeez*. Compare with song of Red-winged Blackbird. Song sometimes followed by (2) a slurred, musical phrase that drops then rises in pitch *tetiddle-de-de-do-dee* or *cheeee chooo dee di di*. Call (3) a harsh, low-pitched *check*.

Carib Grackle *Quiscalus lugubris*   female 20, male 23 cm

WI, CA, and SA. Recently reported from lowlands of PA where perhaps resident (Panamá, Darién). **ID** *Smaller* than Great-tailed Grackle with *shorter tail*. Ad has yellow eye. Ad male dull purplish-black with blue iridescence on wings (blacker than Great-tailed Grackle). Smaller female *near-uniform dark brown* including underparts (darker than female Great-tailed Grackle). Shining Cowbird has shorter bill, dark eye. Male has different tail shape. **HABITS** Agricultural fields, pastures, and urban areas. Forages mainly on ground. **VOICE** Song (1) a series of thin, upslurred notes followed by a rapid series of harsh notes *kleeeeee klook klook ee-ee-ee-ee* or *cleeee cleeee ek-ek-ek-ek*. Calls (2) a nasal *jet* and (3) dry *chek*.

Nicaraguan Grackle *Quiscalus nicaraguensis*   female 23, male 27 cm

CA endemic. Uncommon and local resident in lowlands of NI (Granada, León, Managua, Masaya, Río San Juan, 324, 413, 548) and north CR (Alajuela, 474, 600). **ID** Smaller than Great-tailed Grackle with shorter primary projection. Ad male black with dull blue-green gloss (blacker than Great-tailed Grackle). Smaller female dull brownish becoming distinctly paler below, with *pale supercilium* (overall paler than female Great-tailed Grackle). **HABITS** Marshes, open scrub, agricultural fields, pastures, and urban areas. Forages mainly on ground. May join mixed gatherings that include cowbirds or Great-tailed Grackles. May associate with livestock. **VOICE** Song (1) a series of thin, upslurred whistles followed by a rattle or staccato series of harsh notes *kleeeeee klookleekleekleekleeee* or *cloooooook cleeeeee ek-ek-ek-ek*. Calls (2) a nasal *jep* and (3) sharp, dry *chik*.

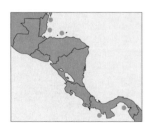

Great-tailed Grackle *Quiscalus mexicanus*   female 34, male 44 cm

USA to SA. Common to locally abundant resident (to 2500 m). Also BZ Cays, Bay Islands, and Pearl Islands. **ID** *Long, graduated tail. Pale eyes.* Male black with blue gloss. Smaller female dull brownish becoming variably paler on sides of head and breast. Juv has soft streaking on underparts. **GV** Female from CR and PA is paler on head and underparts. **HABITS** Marshes, agricultural fields, pastures, urban areas, and gardens. Uses all levels in vegetation but forages mainly on ground. Often near water. May gather in large numbers at roosts. **VOICE** Songs include (1) a staccato series of sharp, loud, squeaky, whistled notes *eet eet eet eet eet . . .* (2) an attenuated, squeaky, upslurred whistle *erh-eeeeeeeet*, (3) a machine gun–like rattle *t-t-t-t-t-t-t*, and (4) higher-pitched, metallic rattle *tre-te-te-te-te-te*. Calls (5) a low-pitched, guttural *chuck* or *check* (often given in flight) and (6) loud, rapid, buzzy *zzik-zzik-zzik . . .*

Melodius Blackbird

Yellow-hooded Blackbird

♀

♂

♀

♂

Carib Grackle

♀

Nicaraguan Grackle

♂

CR and PA
ad ♀

widespread
ad ♀

♂

Great-tailed Grackle

WARBLERS Parulidae

Small insectivorous birds found mainly in middle and upper levels of forest or woodland. In the region, warblers are a diverse group in the region that includes both resident and Nearctic species.

Black-and-white Warbler *Mniotilta varia* 12.5 cm
Breeds east Nearctic. Winters MX to SA and WI. Widespread and common winter resident (Aug to May) in lowlands and foothills (to 1800, rarely or locally to 3200 m). **ID** *Black-and-white streaked plumage.* Note black spots on crissum. Breeding male has black throat and auriculars. Imm female has whitish auriculars and throat and variably buffy underparts. Ad female, imm, and nonbreeding male variably intermediate in pattern. **HABITS** Midstory to subcanopy and edge of semihumid to humid broadleaf forest, second growth, plantations, and mangroves. Creeps along trunks and branches. Solitary. Follows mixed flocks. **VOICE** Usually quiet. May sing after arriving in wintering areas. Song (1) an undulating series of high-pitched phrases *weete-weete-weete-weete*. Call (2) a sharp *stick*.

Prothonotary Warbler *Protonotaria citrea* 13 cm
Breeds east Nearctic. Winters MX to north SA. Uncommon to locally common winter resident (Aug to Apr) in lowlands and foothills (to 2000 m, but mainly near SL). Also BZ Cays and Bay Islands. Rare in north Pacific (341, 336). **ID** Short tail, long bill, and plain blue-gray wings. Belly, crissum, and most of undertail white. Ad male has *orange-yellow head*. Ad female has yellow head and underparts. Compare with Blue-winged Warbler. Note different wing and head pattern. **HABITS** Understory to midstory of wooded swamps, mangroves, littoral forest and scrub, riparian thickets, and damp second growth. Favors foliage or vine tangles overhanging sluggish streams or shaded pools. Solitary. Does not follow mixed flocks. **VOICE** Call (1) a clear, metallic *tsiip*.

Northern Parula *Setophaga americana* 11 cm
Breeds east Nearctic. Winters mainly WI and south MX. Uncommon winter resident (Aug to May) in north Caribbean lowlands and foothills (to 1000 m). Rare but regular in coastal north Pacific. Rare in south (602, 287, 512, 48). **ID** Small with fine bill (mandible orange). Short tail often slightly cocked above drooped wings. Note *broken white eye ring*. Upperparts blue-gray with olive mantle. Ad male has yellow throat and upper breast and variable *rufous and black breast-band*. Ad female has faint or no breast-band. Imm has olive extending to crown and usually shows more diffuse eye crescents and pale lores. Compare with Tropical Parula. Note different head and underparts. **HABITS** Canopy and edge of humid broadleaf forest, mangroves, second growth, plantations, and gardens. Solitary. Follows mixed flocks. **VOICE** Call (1) a loud *chik*.

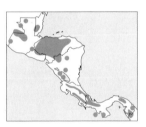

Tropical Parula *Setophaga pitiayumi* 10–10.5 cm
Texas to SA. Uncommon to locally common resident in foothills and highlands (mainly 300 to 1850 m). Locally near SL on Isla Coiba off PA (Veraguas, 653, 470). **ID** Small with fine bill (mandible orange). Underparts mostly yellow. Ad male has *diffuse orange on breast*. Note *dark mask* and variable white wingbars. Ad female has less orange on breast. Resembles Northern Parula. Note different head pattern. **GV** Birds from north CA are paler with two short wingbars. Widespread form (HN to PA) has one wingbar and reduced white spots on tail. Birds from Isla Coiba are larger and darker and have smaller white spots on tail. Birds from east PA are small and have two white wingbars. **HABITS** Canopy and edge of humid broadleaf forest, tall second growth, plantations, and gardens. Pairs or solitary birds forage actively in foliage or epiphytes. Follows mixed flocks. **VOICE** Song (1) a rapid, accelerating trill that begins with a few introductory notes. Song first drops then rises in pitch *si-si-si-si-si sisisisisiiiiiiiii*. Call (2) a sharp *chik*.

Crescent-chested Warbler *Oreothlypis superciliosa* 12 cm
MX and north CA. Fairly common resident in highlands (mainly 1500 to 3500, rarely as low as 900 m). Local in Pacific volcanic highlands of SV (San Vicente, 341). Rare in NI (Jinotega, Nueva Segovia, Matagalpa, 413). **ID** Small. Note *white supercilium* and yellow breast and throat. Gray wings contrast with olive mantle. Ad male has *chestnut breast-band*. Female and imm may lack breast-band. Juv drab grayish with pale tips on wing coverts. **HABITS** Subcanopy to canopy and edge of arid to humid broadleaf and mixed pine-broadleaf forest. Pairs or solitary birds forage actively in terminal foliage or probe in dead leaves or moss. Follows mixed flocks. **VOICE** Song (1) a flat, dry trill or rattle *trrrrrrrrrr*. Call (2) a soft *tik*.

Flame-throated Warbler *Oreothlypis gutturalis* 11.5 cm
CA endemic. Fairly common resident in highlands (mainly above 2000 m) of CR and west PA. May wander to lower elevations outside breeding season. **ID** Gray above with black mantle, blackish mask, and variably *orange throat and upper breast*. **HABITS** Midstory to canopy and edge of very humid, epiphyte-laden broadleaf forest. Pairs or solitary birds forage actively in foliage and epiphytes. Follows mixed flocks. **VOICE** Typical song (1) a dry, insect-like trill that rises slightly then drops in pitch. May begin with several short notes or shorter, lower-pitched trill *pipipipipi ziiiiiiiiiiiiiiiiiiii*. Occasionally only first part is given. Call (2) a high-pitched, sharp, liquid *chit*.

50%

Black-and-white Warbler

nonbreeding ♂

imm ♀

breeding ♂

Prothonotary Warbler

imm ♀

ad ♂

Northern Parula

north CA

imm ♀

ad ♂

widespread

Tropical Parula

east PA

Coiba

Crescent-chested Warbler

juv

dull ad

bright ad

Flame-throated Warbler

WARBLERS Parulidae

Nearctic breeding warblers found in woodland and forest edge. Tennessee Warbler is the most common and widespread.

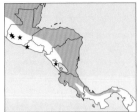

Blue-winged Warbler *Vermivora cyanoptera* 11.5 cm

Breeds east Nearctic. Winters mainly MX and CA. Uncommon transient and winter resident (Sep to Apr) in Caribbean lowlands and foothills (to 1000, rarely to 2500 m). Rare in north Pacific (227, 346) and in CR and PA (334, 659, 346). **ID** *Dark eye stripe* and *white wingbars*. Underparts yellow with white crissum. Ad male has yellow crown. Gray wings contrast with olive mantle. Hybridizes with Golden-winged Warbler. Compare with Prothonotary Warbler. Note different wing and head pattern. The most common hybrid between Golden-winged and Blue-winged warblers, "Brewster's Warbler," has white underparts and yellow wingbars. The scarce "Lawrence's Warbler" has yellow underparts and white wingbars. **HABITS** Midstory and edge of humid broadleaf forest, mangroves, second growth, plantations, and gardens. Solitary. Follows mixed flocks. **VOICE** Call (1) a sharp, dry *tsik* or *tsiit*. Sometimes repeated.

Golden-winged Warbler *Vermivora chrysoptera* 12 cm

Breeds east Nearctic. Winters MX to north SA. Uncommon transient and winter resident (Sep to Apr) in foothills and highlands (mainly SL to 1800, but transients range to 2500 m). Most common in highlands of west CR. Rare in north Pacific. **ID** Mostly gray above and plain white below with *broad yellow wingbars* (or yellow wing patch) and *yellow crown*. Male has *black throat and auriculars*. Female paler with gray head markings. All plumages show some trace of male's head pattern. Hybridizes with Blue-winged Warbler. Most common hybrid, "Brewster's Warbler," has white underparts and yellow wingbars. Less common "Lawrence's Warbler'" has yellow underparts and white wingbars. **HABITS** Midstory and edge of humid broadleaf forest, second growth, plantations, and gardens. Forages actively by probing in clusters of dead leaves. Often hangs or clings. Solitary. Follows mixed flocks. **VOICE** Call (1) a high-pitched, slightly buzzy *tssit* or *tssi*. Much like Blue-winged Warbler.

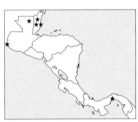

Virginia's Warbler *Oreothlypis virginiae* 11.5 cm

Breeds west Nearctic. Winters Pacific south MX. Very rare winter visitor (Dec to May) to BZ (Belize, Stann Creek, Orange Walk, 313, 347), GT (Petén, San Marcos, 78, 229), and PA (Panamá, 48). **ID** Small. Note *white eye ring*. Ad male *mostly gray* (including wings) with *yellow crissum* and *yellow breast patch*. Female has breast patch reduced (or absent in imm). Resembles imm female Nashville Warbler but Virginia's is grayer and never has olive wings of Nashville. **HABITS** Understory to midstory of scrub, forest edge, second growth, plantations, and gardens. Forages actively in foliage. Follows mixed flocks. **VOICE** Call (1) similar to Nashville Warbler.

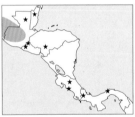

Nashville Warbler *Oreothlypis ruficapilla* 11.5 cm

Breeds Nearctic. Winters mainly MX and CA. Uncommon winter resident (Sep to Apr) in foothills and highlands of GT. Rare in SV (Sonsonate, Ahuachapán, 619, 346), BZ (Belize, Cayo, Orange Walk, 625, 347, 341, 250), CR (Puntarenas, Heredia, Cartago, 664, 346, 546), and PA (Chiriquí, Colón, 659). **ID** Small with white belly and yellow throat. Mostly *gray head with white eye ring*. Imm female has more extensive white below and may show faint pale wingbar. Compare with Lesser Greenlet. Note different structure, underparts color, and habits. **HABITS** Understory to midstory and edge of forest (especially pine-oak), second growth, plantations, and gardens. Forages actively in foliage. Follows mixed flocks. **VOICE** Call (1) a sharp *spink*. Compare with call of Northern Waterthrush.

Orange-crowned Warbler *Oreothlypis celata* 11.5 cm

Breeds Nearctic. Winters mainly south USA to MX. Rare winter visitor (Aug to May) to BZ (Belize, Cayo, 341, 250, 346), GT (Petén, Alta Verapaz, Sololá, 279, 78), SV (La Libertad, Ahuachapán, 619, 346), HN (Francisco Morazán, 346), and CR (Limón, Cartago, 602, 341). **ID** Small with fine bill. Drab and plain. Note *yellow crissum*, short, dark eyeline dividing pale eye crescents, and *faintly streaked underparts*. Tennessee Warbler has white crissum (or very pale yellowish-white crissum in imm). Also compare with imm female Yellow Warbler. Note different tail and head pattern. **HABITS** Understory to midstory and edge of forest, second growth, savannas, plantations, and gardens. Forages actively in foliage. Follows mixed flocks. **VOICE** Call (1) a clear, high-pitched, sharp *chip*.

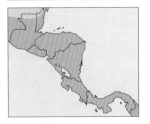

Tennessee Warbler *Oreothlypis peregrina* 11.5 cm

Breeds Nearctic. Winters MX to SA. Fairly common to common transient and winter resident (Sep to May). Most common in Pacific lowlands and foothills (to 3200 m). Uncommon to rare in north Caribbean. **ID** Fine, pointed bill and *long, pale supercilium*. Ad has gray crown and olive upperparts. Note mostly *white underparts including crissum*. Imm variably yellow below and may show two narrow wingbars. Resembles various vireos with gray crowns (particularly Philadelphia Vireo). Note different bill shape. **HABITS** Midstory to canopy and edge of semihumid to humid broadleaf forest, second growth, plantations, and gardens. Forages actively in foliage. Takes nectar at flowering trees. May form small flocks. Also follows mixed flocks. **VOICE** Call (1) a sharp, high-pitched *stik*.

Blue-winged Warbler

Blue-winged ×
Golden-winged
Warbler' hybrids

♀

ad
♂

Golden-winged Warbler

♀

♂

imm

ad

Virginia's Warbler

Nashville Warbler

imm

ad

Orange-crowned Warbler

Tennessee Warbler

imm

ad

50%

Bay-breasted Warbler *Setophaga castanea* 13.5 cm

Breeds Nearctic. Winters CA and SA. Fairly common winter resident in lowlands and foothills of PA. Briefly or locally common transient (Sep to Nov and Apr to May) on north Caribbean slope in spring. Vagrant to Isla del Coco (571). **ID** Bulky. Note dusky feet. Breeding male and female (Apr to Aug) have *rufous flanks*. Nonbreeding female very similar to nonbreeding Blackpoll Warbler but is brighter olive-green above (particularly on nape) and often has *pale rufous wash on flanks* and *buff crissum*. Note plain, pale head pattern (dark eye stripe indistinct). **HABITS** Subcanopy to canopy and edge of humid broadleaf forest, adjacent tall second growth, and plantations. Follows mixed flocks. **VOICE** Call (1) a clear *chip*.

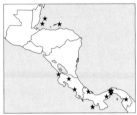

Blackpoll Warbler *Setophaga striata* 13 cm

Breeds Nearctic. Winters SA. Spring passage mainly in WI. Rare transient or vagrant (Oct to Nov and Apr to May) in BZ Cays (347) and south CA (654, 597). Very rare in winter in lowlands of CR (Puntarenas, Guanacaste, 602, 597, 341, 346) and PA (Bocas del Toro, Panamá, Colón, 654, 512, 346). **ID** Bulky. Legs and feet usually yellowish. Breeding male (Apr to Aug) has *black cap*, white auriculars, and white underparts streaked with black. Ad female has olive upperparts streaked with dusky. Imm female differs from corresponding plumage of Bay-breasted Warbler in variable faint streaking on flanks and *whitish crissum and lower underparts*. Also note grayish-olive (not green) nape and neck and distinct dark eye stripe. **HABITS** Subcanopy to canopy and edge of humid broadleaf forest, second growth, and plantations. Transients or vagrants use wide variety of arboreal habitats. Forages actively in foliage. Follows mixed flocks. **VOICE** Call (1) a sharp, clear *chip*.

Cerulean Warbler *Setophaga cerulea* 11.5 cm

Breeds east Nearctic. Winters SA. Uncommon to locally or briefly common transient (mainly Apr and Aug to Oct). Regular in north Caribbean foothills and highlands (477, 476). Vagrant to Pacific slope (600). **ID** Small and short-tailed. Ad male has white underparts with *narrow black band on upper breast*. Upperparts mostly blue. Ad female plain blue above and mostly white below with streaked flanks. Imm female yellowish-white below with white crissum. Note broad, pale supercilium and dark lores. Compare ad male with Crescent-chested Warbler. Compare female with imm female Blackburnian Warbler. **HABITS** Subcanopy to canopy of humid broadleaf forest. Forages actively in foliage. Follows mixed flocks. **VOICE** Call (1) a clear *chip*.

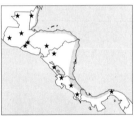

Black-throated Blue Warbler *Setophaga caerulescens* 11.5 cm

Breeds east Nearctic. Winters mainly WI. Rare transient or winter visitor (Oct to Apr) mainly in Caribbean coastal lowlands and islands including BZ Cays. Vagrant to interior and Pacific slope. **ID** *White mark on base of primaries*. Male has plain gray-blue upperparts and *black sides of head, throat, and breast*. Drab imm and female have whitish supercilium and *pale crescent below eye* contrasting with dark sides of head. Compare imm female with other drab-plumaged warblers such as imm Yellow and Orange-crowned warblers. Note different head and wing pattern. **HABITS** Midstory of forest edge, second growth, littoral scrub, plantations, and gardens. Solitary. Follows mixed flocks. **VOICE** Call (1) a high-pitched, sharp *snic*.

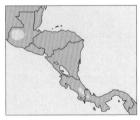

American Redstart *Setophaga ruticilla* 12.5 cm

Breeds east Nearctic. Winters MX, and WI to north SA. Common transient and winter resident (Aug to May) in lowlands and foothills (to 1500 m). Spring passage mainly on Caribbean slope. Winter residents most numerous in north Caribbean. Uncommon in Pacific and south CA. **ID** *Yellow or orange-red markings on wings, flanks, and tail*. Ad male mostly black above with white central lower underparts and orange-red markings on flanks, wings, and tail. Second-year male mostly olive above and white below. Imm male has black lores and orange on flanks. Ad female resembles second-year male but has pale lores and yellow flank patches. **HABITS** Midstory to subcanopy and edge of semihumid to humid broadleaf forest, tall second growth, shaded plantations, and mangroves. Forages actively. Frequently spreads or cocks tail to flash light markings and shifts position restlessly from side to side on perch. Follows mixed flocks. **VOICE** Call (1) a high-pitched, clear *cheep*.

50%

Bay-breasted Warbler

imm

nonbreeding ♂

breeding ♀

breeding ♂

Blackpoll Warbler

imm

nonbreeding ♂

breeding ♀

breeding ♂

Cerulean Warbler

imm ♀

♀

♂

imm ♀

Black-throated Blue Warbler

♂

♂

imm ♀

♀

American Redstart

WARBLERS Parulidae

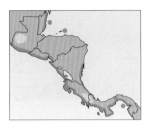

Yellow Warbler *Setophaga petechia*   11.5–12.5 cm

NA to WI and SA. Nearctic migrant and resident breeding birds occur. Breeds in coastal lowlands and islands including BZ Cays, Bay Islands, and Pearl Islands. Nearctic birds are common transients and winter residents (Jul to May) in lowlands and foothills (to 1500, rarely to 2500 m). **ID** *Yellow edging on wings and tail.* Ad male mostly yellow with variable rufous streaking on underparts. Nonbreeding female can be mostly gray but always has yellow edging on tail and wing and yellow crissum. **GV** Ad male from resident breeding population has rufous hood. Ad male from Isla del Coco has rufous crown. Birds from Pacific east PA (Darién) have paler, softer rufous streaking on breast. Nearctic migrants also geographically variable. **HABITS** Wintering birds use wide variety of nonforest arboreal habitats including forest edge, second growth, mangroves, littoral woodland, scrub, plantations, and gardens. Often near water. Resident birds mainly in mangroves, littoral woodland, and scrub. Forages actively in foliage. Often hover-gleans. Usually solitary. **VOICE** Call (1) a variable, clear, loud *chip.*

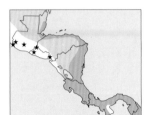

Chestnut-sided Warbler *Setophaga pensylvanica*   12 cm

Breeds east Nearctic. Winters mainly MX and CA. Common transient and winter resident (Aug to May) in lowlands and foothills (to 1850 m). Uncommon in north Caribbean. Rare in north Pacific. **ID** Tail often cocked. *Yellow or greenish-yellow crown* and *yellow wingbars.* Breeding male and female (Mar to Aug) have yellow crown, chestnut stripes on flanks, and *black moustachial stripe.* Nonbreeding ad has gray auriculars and *white eye ring.* Imm female has plain bright olive mantle. Compare with Lesser Greenlet. **HABITS** Understory to canopy and edge of semihumid to humid broadleaf forest, second growth, scrub, plantations, and gardens. Forages actively in foliage. Often hover-gleans. Follows mixed flocks. **VOICE** Call (1) a low-pitched, flat *chidp.*

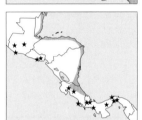

Prairie Warbler *Setophaga discolor*   11 cm

Breeds east Nearctic. Winters mainly WI. Rare transient and winter resident (mainly Sep to Apr). Mainly on Caribbean coast and islands including BZ Cays (529) and Bay Islands (442). Vagrant to Isla del Coco (571). **ID** Dark lores and *dark crescent under eye.* Note streaked flanks (may be faint or indistinct in imm female) and yellow or yellowish wingbars. Ad has rufous streaks on olive mantle and blackish streaking below. Imm female has plain olive mantle and distinctive head pattern with dark eye stripe and broad broken yellow eye ring. Compare with Palm and Yellow warblers. **HABITS** Midstory to subcanopy of littoral scrub, forest edge, second growth, plantations, and gardens. Wags tail. **VOICE** Call (1) a sweet *chip.*

Vitelline Warbler *Setophaga vitellina*   11 cm

Mainly WI. Common resident on Swan Islands off Caribbean HN (251, 513, 480, 442). Poorly known. **ID** Fairly long bill. Mostly plain olive above and yellow below with faint streaking on flanks. Note yellow supercilium, greenish auriculars, and dark lores. Also note pale yellow wingbars and edging on wing. Head pattern suggests Prairie Warbler but is *paler.* **HABITS** Understory to midstory of littoral scrub, forest edge, and second growth. **VOICE** Song (1) a short series of whistles followed by a long, buzzy, descending trill and slurred notes *chewy, chewy chewychewy dzeeeeeeee chweeewhii.* Call (2) a short, clear, metallic *seet.*

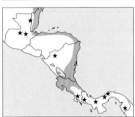

Palm Warbler *Setophaga palmarum*   12.5 cm

Breeds Nearctic. Winters mainly WI. Uncommon to rare transient and irregular winter resident (mainly Oct to Apr) on Caribbean slope and islands including BZ Cays and Bay Islands. Rare on Pacific slope and south to CR (Alajuela, Puntarenas, Limón, 594, 346) and PA (Colón, Darién, 346). Vagrant to Isla del Coco (571). **ID** Long, pale supercilium contrasts with dark eyeline and *diffuse dusky streaking on underparts.* Note *yellow crissum.* Breeding ad (Apr to Aug) gray-brown above with chestnut crown. Throat and supercilium pale yellow. Nonbreeding ad (Aug to Mar) has whitish throat and pale yellow confined to crissum. **GV** Birds from east NA (not shown) are yellower below. **HABITS** Understory to lower midstory and edge of littoral scrub, savannas, open grassy or brushy areas, plantations, and gardens. Forages on ground in open areas. Wags tail. **VOICE** Call (1) a sharp, dry *chik.*

Cape May Warbler *Setophaga tigrina*   11.5 cm

Breeds Nearctic. Winters mainly WI. Uncommon to rare transient or winter visitor (Oct to May) in north Caribbean lowlands and islands. Rare elsewhere (568, 232, 414, 346). **ID** Streaked underparts. Breeding male (Mar to Aug) has *rufous auriculars* and *mostly white wing coverts.* Imm and nonbreeding female have *greenish-yellow rump* contrasting with olive-gray mantle. Note female's greenish-yellow patch on neck contrasting with gray nape. Myrtle Warbler has different head and upperparts. **HABITS** Midstory to subcanopy and edge of littoral scrub, forest, second growth, plantations, and gardens. Solitary. May follow mixed flocks. **VOICE** Call (1) a very high-pitched, hard, short *ti.*

50%

Nearctic migrants

typical NA
♀

Yellow Warbler

gray imm
♀

dark NA
♂

widespread resident

typical NA
♂

imm
♀

♀

♂

Cocos
♂

imm
♂

imm

east Pacific PA
♂

Chestnut-sided Warbler

nonbreeding

breeding
♂

♀

breeding
♂

Vitelline
Warbler

Prairie Warbler

imm

breeding
ad

Palm Warbler

Cape May Warbler

imm
♀

breeding
♂

WARBLERS Parulidae

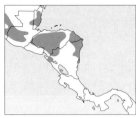

Grace's Warbler *Setophaga graciae*   12 cm

South USA to north CA. Locally common resident in north (SL to 2500, mainly below 1800 m). Also Volcán Casita and Volcán San Cristóbal in northwest NI (Chinandega, 413). **ID** Yellow throat and breast and *short yellow supercilium*. Neck plain gray. Note *yellow spot below eye*. Below mostly white with (variable) blackish streaking on flanks. Imm (not shown) is brownish above. Yellow-throated Warbler has longer bill and white on head and neck. **HABITS** Midstory to canopy of pine-dominated woodland and savanna. Forages actively, typically in terminal foliage of pines. Pairs follow mixed flocks. **VOICE** Song (1) a rapid, usually accelerating series that rises slightly in pitch at end *whi chu-chu-chu-chu-chichichichi-chu* or *chu-chu-chu-chuchichichi*. Call (2) a hard *tsik*.

Yellow-throated Warbler *Setophaga dominica*   12.5 cm

Breeds mainly Nearctic. Winters MX, WI, and CA. Uncommon transient and winter resident (Jul to Apr) in north Caribbean lowlands and islands including BZ Cays and Bay Islands. Uncommon in interior and north Pacific. Rare in CR and PA. **ID** *Long bill* and yellow throat. Note *long white supercilium*, white spot below eye, and *white on neck*. Compare with Grace's Warbler. Note different head pattern, structure, and habits. **HABITS** Midstory to canopy of plantations, forest edge, wooded savannas, littoral woodland, scrub, and gardens. Creeps on branches or through crowns of palms or coniferous trees. Solitary. Not with mixed flocks. **VOICE** Call (1) a clear *chip*. Compare with call of Yellow Warbler.

Myrtle Warbler[28] *Setophaga coronata*   13.5 cm

Breeds Nearctic. Winters mainly USA and MX. Irregular transient or winter visitor (Oct to May). Rare in CR and PA. **ID** *Yellow rump*, *partial whitish eye ring*, and *streaked flanks*. Ad has dark auriculars contrasting with white or whitish throat and *pale supercilium*. Imm female resembles imm female Audubon's Warbler but has more extensive pale throat (extending to neck) and variable pale supercilium contrasting with darker auriculars. **HABITS** Midstory in semi-open areas including plantations, forest edge, savannas, littoral scrub, and gardens. May forage on ground. **VOICE** Call (1) a dry *tchek*.

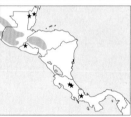

Audubon's Warbler[28] *Setophaga auduboni*   14 cm

Breeds west Nearctic. Winters USA to CA. Common winter resident (Oct to May) in highlands of GT and west HN. Rare in BZ (Orange Walk, Belize, 529, 343), SV (Santa Ana, 341), CR (San Jose, Cartago, 570), and PA (Chiriquí, 512, 346). **ID** *Yellow rump*, partial whitish eye ring, and streaked flanks. Resembles Myrtle Warbler but ad has *yellow throat*. Imm female very similar to imm female Myrtle Warbler but lacks pale supercilium, and pale yellowish throat does not extend to neck. **HABITS** Midstory in semi-open areas including plantations, forest edge, scrub, and gardens. May forage on ground. **VOICE** Like Myrtle Warbler.

Goldman's Warbler[28] *Setophaga goldmani*   15 cm

South MX and CA. Fairly common but local breeding resident in highlands (1800 to 3800 m) of west GT (Huehuetenango, San Marcos, Totonicapán, Quiché, 229, 330, 460). **ID** Ad male has nearly *solid blackish-gray breast, head, and mantle*. Female has mostly sooty-gray mantle with black streaks. In both sexes note white at corners of throat and lack of upper eye crescent. **HABITS** Understory to canopy and edge of pine woodland and adjacent open areas. May forage on ground. **VOICE** Song (1) a rich, loud that rises slightly in pitch. Call (2) a dry *tchek*.

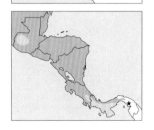

Magnolia Warbler *Setophaga magnolia*   11 cm

Breeds Nearctic. Winters MX, WI, and CA. Common transient and winter resident (Sep to May) in north lowlands and foothills (to 1500 m, higher in migration). Uncommon in CR and PA. **ID** *White base of tail* and crissum. Breeding ad has yellow throat and breast with black streaking. Ad male has *mostly white wing coverts* and black mask. Ad female has narrow white wingbars and olive mantle mottled with blackish. Imm female mostly yellow below with mostly plain, greenish-olive mantle. Note gray crown and auriculars, narrow white wingbars, and narrow white eye ring. **HABITS** Midstory to subcanopy and edge of semihumid to humid broadleaf forest, second growth, plantations, and gardens. Forages actively in foliage. Often fans tail. Solitary. Follows mixed flocks. **VOICE** Call (1) a slightly nasal *eent* or *xeet*.

490

Grace's Warbler

Yellow-throated Warbler

Myrtle Warbler

nonbreeding
♀

breeding
♂

nonbreeding
♀

breeding
♂

Audubon's Warbler

♀

ad
♂

Goldman's Warbler

imm

breeding
♀

breeding
♂

Magnolia Warbler

WARBLERS Parulidae

Nearctic breeding warblers found mainly in upper levels of forest and woodland. Details of the head, underparts, and mantle pattern are useful in separating females. Black-throated Green and Townsend's warblers are the most common and widespread. All these species forage actively in foliage and often follow mixed flocks.

Blackburnian Warbler *Setophaga fusca*   12 cm
Breeds east Nearctic. Winters CA and SA. Fairly common transient. Uncommon winter resident (Aug to Apr) in south foothills and highlands. **ID** Striped mantle, black or dusky auriculars and white wingbars or wing patch. Breeding male (Mar to Aug) has *orange throat, supercilium and neck*. Nonbreeding female duller. Note *dusky auriculars surrounded by yellow throat, supercilium and hindneck*. Drab imm female has *pale stripes on mantle*, pale crown patch and pale spot on neck. Compare with female Cerulean Warbler. Note different upperparts and head pattern. **HABITS** Subcanopy to canopy of humid broadleaf forest, plantations, and gardens. **VOICE** Song (1) a very high-pitched *tsii-tsii-tsii-tsii-sisisisisi*. Call (2) a sharp *tsick*.

Hermit Warbler *Setophaga occidentalis*   12.5 cm
Breeds west Nearctic. Winters west USA to CA. Uncommon to locally fairly common transient and winter resident (Aug to May) in north highlands (1000 to 3500 m). Rare in BZ (Belize, Cayo, 347), CR (Puntarenas, 111, 253), and PA (Chiriquí, 512). **ID** Plain (unstreaked) underparts and gray or grayish-olive mantle. Ad male has *mostly yellow head* contrasting with black throat and upper breast and white underparts. Note *gray mantle streaked with black*. Ad female has diffuse dusky wash on auriculars (not solid olive-green as in Townsend's Warbler). Imm female has plain grayish mantle and plain whitish underparts. Compare with Black-throated Green and Townsend's warblers. Note different underparts and head pattern. **HABITS** Canopy of pine, pine-oak, and mixed broadleaf forest, plantations, and gardens. **VOICE** Song (1) a high-pitched *tsee-tsee-tsee-tsiiiup*. Call (2) a sharp *tsik* or *tek*.

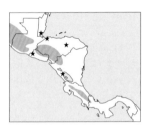

Townsend's Warbler *Setophaga townsendi*   12.5 cm
Breeds west Nearctic. Winters west USA to CA. Common transient and winter resident (Sep to May) in north highlands (1000 to 3000 m). Uncommon to rare in central NI (Granada, 419), CR (Puntarenas, Alajuela, 111, 600, 253, 523), and west PA (Chiriquí, 512, 48, 346). Vagrant to BZ (Toledo, 343). **ID** *Yellow mark below eye* and yellow breast. Breeding male's black throat and auriculars contrast with complex yellow head pattern. Note *olive mantle streaked with black*. Ad female has similar pattern with sharply defined olive-green auriculars and plain olive mantle. Imm female duller and paler. Compare with Black-throated Green Warbler (mainly lower elevations). Note different head and underparts. **HABITS** Canopy of pine, pine-oak, and humid broadleaf (cloud) forest. **VOICE** Song (1) a buzzy *dree-dree-dreeeee-zeeup*. Call (2) a short *tek*, harder than Black-throated Green Warbler.

Golden-cheeked Warbler *Setophaga chrysoparia*   12 cm
Breeds Texas, USA. Winters MX and CA. Rare transient and local winter resident (Aug to Mar) in highlands (1500 to 3000 m) of GT and HN (Intibucá, Francisco Morazán, 442). Very rare in BZ (Cayo, Corozal, 433, 347, 346), NI (Jinotega, Matagalpa, 419, 413), CR (Puntarenas, Alajuela, San José, Cartago, 341, 346, 546), and PA (Chiriquí, 48). **ID** Ad male's black crown, mantle, and throat contrast with yellow auriculars and supercilium. Note *black eyeline*. Ad female has dark olive-gray mantle and crown streaked with blackish. Note female's yellow auriculars, narrow dark eyeline, and whitish lower underparts (never with yellow as in Black-throated Green). Townsend's Warbler has olive mantle and different head pattern. **HABITS** Subcanopy to canopy and edge of pine-oak and mixed broadleaf forests. Occasionally in humid broadleaf (cloud) forest. **VOICE** Call (1) similar to Black-throated Green Warbler.

Black-throated Green Warbler *Setophaga virens*   12.5 cm
Breeds Nearctic. Winters MX and WI to north SA. Widespread and common transient and winter resident (Sep to May) in lowlands and foothills. Most common in north Caribbean slope (SL to 2300, but mainly below 1800 m). In south mainly in foothills and highlands (mainly 300 to 1000 m, rarely to 3000 m). **ID** *Plain olive-green mantle and crown*. Note faint yellow on rear flanks. Olive-tinged auriculars contrast with yellow supercilium and neck. Ad male has black throat and upper breast and black streaks on flanks. Ad male Townsend's Warbler has blackish crown and auriculars. **HABITS** Subcanopy to canopy and edge of broadleaf forest, woodland, plantations, mangroves, and gardens. **VOICE** Song (1) a buzzy *zree-zree-zree-zoo-zee*. Call (2) a sharp *tsik* or *tek*.

50%

Blackburnian Warbler

imm ♀

nonbreeding ♀

breeding ♂

Hermit Warbler

imm ♀

♂

Townsend's Warbler

imm ♀

♀

♂

Golden-cheeked Warbler

imm ♀

♀

♂

imm ♀

♀

Black-throated Green Warbler

♂

YELLOWTHROATS AND WARBLER Parulidae

The *Geothlypis* yellowthroats include three resident species and one widespread Nearctic migrant. All favor lower levels in vegetation in grassy areas or wetlands. Kentucky Warbler is widespread in humid broadleaf forest.

Gray-crowned Yellowthroat *Geothlypis poliocephala* 13.5 cm

South MX and CA. Locally fairly common resident in lowlands and foothills (to 1600, locally to 2300 m). Rare and local in west PA (Chiriquí, 512). **ID** Heavy bill with pink mandible and long tail. Note *gray crown*, yellow throat, and *restricted black mask*. Other *Geothlypis* yellowthroats have finer, all-dark bills. **GV** Birds from north Caribbean CA typically have white eye crescents. **HABITS** Understory of savannas, marshes, pastures, airstrips, and agricultural margins. Forages within grass or other low growth. May perch on shrub or low fence post. Habitually flips tail. Solitary or in pairs. **VOICE** May sing in flight. Song (1) a rich or slightly scratchy warbled phrase *weechu chu weewee chuchu*. Compare with songs of *Passerina* buntings. Also (2) a short series of rich, slightly plaintive whistles *chiu chiu whiu . . .* Call (3) a downslurred, buzzy *cheeed-it* or *chooduit*. Rarely (4) a single *chee*.

Common Yellowthroat *Geothlypis trichas* 11.5 cm

Breeds Nearctic. Winters USA to CA and WI. Fairly common transient and winter resident (Sep to May) in north. Uncommon to rare in CR and PA. **ID** Whitish belly. Male has broad *black mask bordered by pale gray supercilium*. Ad female has yellow throat and whitish belly. Some imm females from west NA have grayish throat. **HABITS** Understory at forest edge, second growth, marshes, scrub, mangroves, plantations, agricultural margins, and gardens. Forages actively inside cover of dense vegetation, but regularly appears in open at edges. Solitary. **VOICE** Call (1) a variable, dry *chedp* or *jierrk*.

Olive-crowned Yellowthroat *Geothlypis semiflava* 12.5 cm

CA and north SA. Uncommon resident in Caribbean lowlands and foothills (to 1200 m). Poorly known in east HN (Olancho, 442). **ID** *Olive above including crown*. Ad male has extensive black mask and forehead. Resembles Common Yellowthroat but note Olive-crowned's *unbordered black mask* (ad male) and uniform yellow-olive underparts. Masked Yellowthroat allopatric. **HABITS** Understory of damp grassy or brushy areas. Pairs or solitary birds skulk in dense vegetation. Often near water. Sings from elevated perch. **VOICE** Song (1) a long, slightly accelerating series of two- or three-note, rich, warbled phrases with rolling finish *wichay-chu wichaychu wichaychu witchetychay-chu witchety chay-chu witchety chay-chu witchety-chrrr*. Calls (2) a sharp *chip* or *kip* and (3) short, dry, downslurred chatter.

Masked Yellowthroat[29] *Geothlypis aequinoctialis* 12 cm

CA and SA. Uncommon and local resident in Pacific lowlands and foothills (to 1200 m) of CR (Puntarenas, 600, 341, 74) and west PA (Chiriquí, 659, 512). A report from NI is dubious (Río San Juan, 452). **ID** Y*ellow belly* and *gray (not whitish) forecrown*. Female has gray crown and auriculars. **HABITS** Understory of damp grasslands and marshes. Solitary or in pairs. Skulks in dense vegetation. **VOICE** Song (1) a long, accelerating series of three- to four-note warbled phrases that rise in pitch; series ends with several harder notes *tuwichywer tuwichywer tuwichywer tuweecha tuweecha chee-cheche-chit*. May give several songs without pause. Calls (2) a sharp, fine *stit* or *chip* and (3) scolding, nasal *jurrr* or *churr*.

Kentucky Warbler *Geothlypis formosa* 12.5 cm

Breeds east Nearctic. Winters mainly MX and CA. Fairly common transient and winter resident (Aug to Apr) in north Caribbean lowlands and foothills (to 1200, rarely to 1800 m). Rare in north Pacific. Uncommon in south. **ID** Fairly short tail. Black mask and *yellow supercilium*. Yellow below including long crissum. **HABITS** Floor and understory of semihumid to humid broadleaf forest, tall second growth, and shaded plantations. Walks deliberately over leaf litter. May ascend briefly to low perch. Solitary. Attends ant swarms. **VOICE** Call (1) a low-pitched *chuck*.

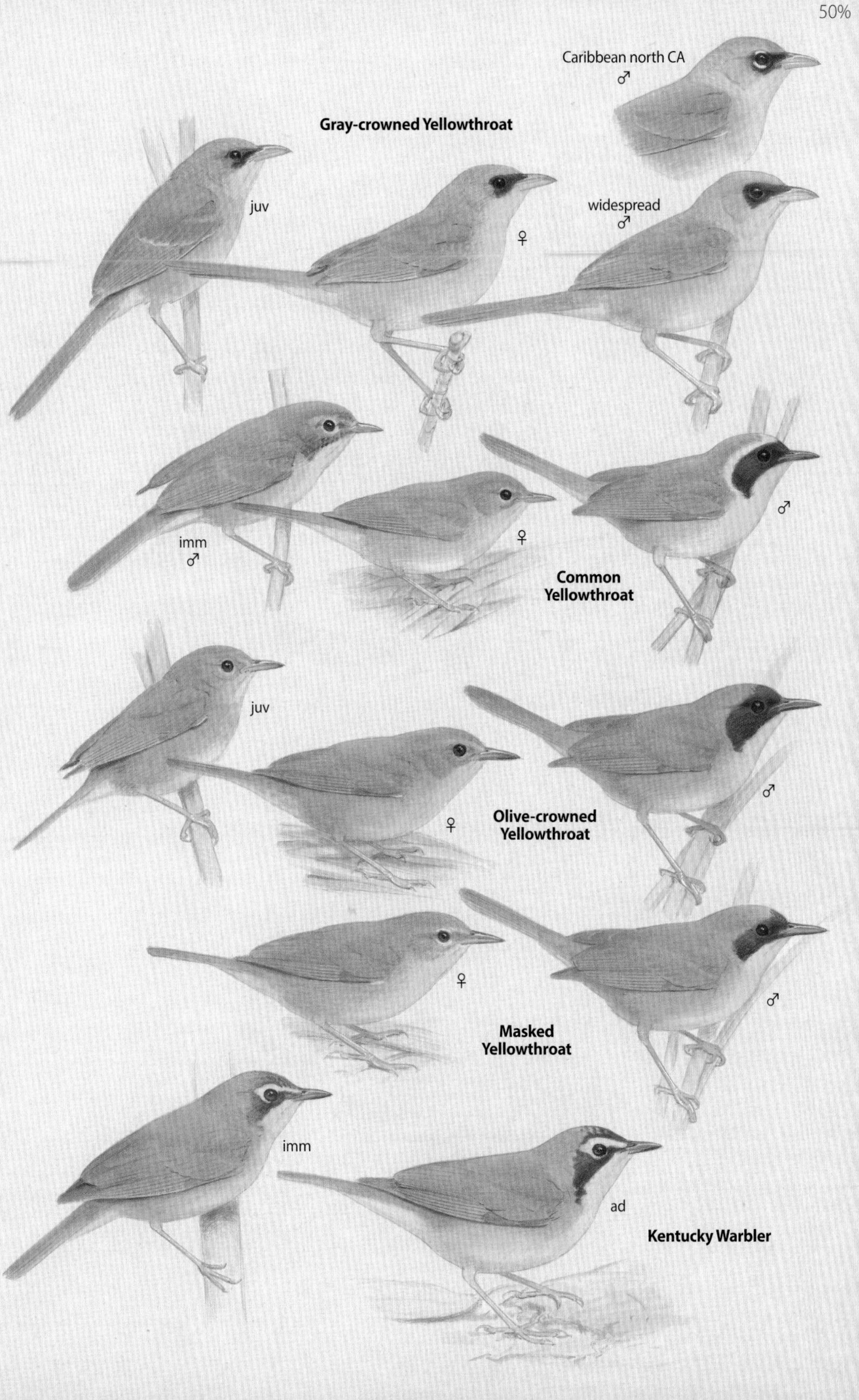

50%

Gray-crowned Yellowthroat

Caribbean north CA
♂

juv

♀

widespread
♂

imm
♂

♀

Common Yellowthroat

♂

juv

♀

Olive-crowned Yellowthroat

♂

♀

Masked Yellowthroat

♂

imm

ad

Kentucky Warbler

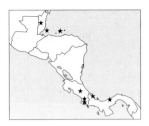

Connecticut Warbler *Oporornis agilis* 13 cm

Breeds Nearctic. Winters SA. Passage mainly in WI. Very rare vagrant (Mar to May and Sep to Oct) to BZ (Cayo, 346), CR (San José, Puntarenas, 600), and PA (Bocas del Toro, 303). Also Bay Islands (442) and BZ Cays (529). Poorly known but fall occurrence in west PA is based on specimen records (203, 659). **ID** *White eye ring.* Ad male has gray hood. Female and imm have brown hood. Long undertail coverts extend to near tip of tail. Mourning and MacGillivray's warblers have different head pattern and habits. Compare with Nashville Warbler. Note different structure, underparts, and habits. **HABITS** Floor, understory, and edge of semihumid to humid broadleaf forest, littoral woodland, second growth, scrub, plantations, and gardens. Reclusive. *Walks* deliberately on ground or low substrate. Solitary. Does not follow mixed flocks.

VOICE Call (1) a slightly squeaky *riip* or *eep*.

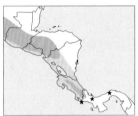

Mourning Warbler *Geothlypis philadelphia* 12.5 cm

Breeds Nearctic. Winters CA and SA. Widespread transient. Uncommon to locally common winter resident (Sep to May) mainly in south Caribbean lowlands and foothills (to 2500 m). **ID** Ad male has *dark gray hood* (no eye ring) and variable black patch on upper breast and throat. Ad female has *grayish-white breast and throat* (may have pale eye ring). Imm (Jul to Mar) usually has *yellowish throat* and indistinct grayish or brownish bib. Compare with MacGillivray's Warbler. Note that Mourning has slightly different structure with shorter tail. Usually separable from MacGillivray's by plain face but some Mourning Warblers (especially imm females) have narrow, pale whitish or yellowish eye ring (never broad white crescents). **HABITS** Understory of semihumid to humid forest edge, second growth, scrub, plantations, and gardens. Skulks in dense vegetation. Solitary. Does not follow mixed flocks. **VOICE** Call (1) a dry, flat, husky *pwich*.

MacGillivray's Warbler *Geothlypis tolmiei* 13 cm

Breeds west Nearctic. Winters MX and CA. Uncommon transient and winter resident (Sep to May) mainly in foothills and highlands (1000 to 3300 m). Rare in PA. **ID** *Broken white eye ring.* Ad male has dark gray hood with black mottling on throat and breast, and black lores connected across forehead. Ad female has gray bib. Imm (Jul to Mar) resembles female but may have browner, less distinct bib and grayish throat. Mourning Warbler has different head pattern. **HABITS** Understory to midstory of semihumid to humid broadleaf forest edge, second growth, scrub, plantations, and gardens. Solitary. Does not follow mixed flocks. **VOICE** Call (1) a hard, dry *chik* or *twik*. Sharper than Mourning Warbler. Also compare with call of Common Yellowthroat.

Hooded Warbler *Setophaga citrina* 13 cm

Breeds east Nearctic. Winters MX and CA. Fairly common transient and winter resident (mainly Aug to May) in lowlands and foothills (to 1200 m). Most common in north Caribbean. Rare in north Pacific. **ID** Spreads tail to display *white inner webs of rectrices.* Ad male has *black hood.* Variable female can have partial hood. Plain female resembles other mostly yellow warblers but has white on tail. **HABITS** Floor and understory of semihumid to humid broadleaf forest, tall second growth, gardens, and shaded plantations. Transients use a wide variety of arboreal habitats. Forages actively. Makes short sallies from ground to capture prey. Solitary. Does not follow mixed flocks. **VOICE** Call (1) a rich, sharp *chik.*

Wilson's Warbler *Cardellina pusilla* 11.5 cm

Breeds Nearctic. Winters MX and CA. Common transient and winter resident (mainly Sep to May) in foothills and highlands (SL to 3500, but mainly 800 to 2500 m). Uncommon in Caribbean lowlands. Rare south to central PA. **ID** Plain olive tail. *Yellow forehead contrasts with darker crown.* Male has *broad yellow supercilium* and *black cap.* Female has olive crown and yellow supercilium. Compare with female Yellow Warbler. Note different wing and head pattern. Also compare with Golden-browed Warbler (often syntopic). **HABITS** Understory to subcanopy and edge in pine, pine-oak and broadleaf forests, second growth, plantations, and gardens. Forages actively in foliage. Follows mixed flocks. **VOICE** May sing in spring passage. Song (1) a rising series *chichi-chi-chi-chi-chit.* Compare with songs of Golden-browed Warbler and Slate-throated Redstart. Call (2) a dry *chit.*

Canada Warbler *Cardellina canadensis* 12.5 cm

Breeds Nearctic. Winters mainly SA. Fairly common fall transient (Aug to Oct) on Caribbean slope and islands including BZ Cays. Spring passage (Apr to May) mainly in WI. Uncommon to rare in winter. **ID** Blue-gray upperparts and *yellow supraloral and eye ring.* Breeding male has *black streaks on breast.* Imm female has less extensive black markings. **HABITS** Midstory of humid broadleaf forest, tall second growth, shaded plantations, and gardens. Follows mixed flocks. **VOICE** Call (1) a sharp, dry, slightly squeaky *tyup.*

Connecticut Warbler

imm

breeding
♂

Mourning Warbler

imm

breeding
♀

breeding
♂

MacGillivray's Warbler

imm

breeding
♀

breeding
♂

♀

Hooded Warbler

♀

ad
♂

Wilson's Warbler

♀

♂

♀

♂

Canada Warbler

WARBLERS Parulidae

Mainly resident warblers found in lower levels of woodland or forest. Red-faced Warbler is a winter resident. Slate-throated Redstart is the most common and widespread and shows striking geographic variation in Central America.

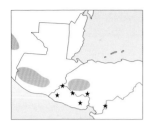

Red-faced Warbler *Cardellina rubrifrons*   13 cm

South USA to CA. Uncommon winter resident (mainly Sep to Apr) in north highlands (mainly 1500 to 3000, rarely or locally as low as 1000 m). Rare in SV (Santa Ana, Morazán, 296, 619, 341). **ID** Mostly gray and white. *Red face, neck, and throat* and black crown and auriculars. Single white wingbar. Imm slightly duller. **HABITS** Midstory and edge of semihumid pine-oak and semi-deciduous woodlands. Solitary or in pairs. Forages actively in foliage or by spiraling along branches. Makes spiraling sallies to seize prey from air or vegetation. Tail often cocked and flipped from side to side. Follows mixed flocks. **VOICE** Song (1) a variable, sweet, warbled series that often ends with a downslurred note *wi tsi-wi tsi-wi si-wi-si-wichu*. Call (2) a full, rich *tchip* or *tcheep*.

Pink-headed Warbler *Cardellina versicolor*   13 cm

South MX and CA. Uncommon to locally common resident in GT highlands (mainly 2200 to 3500 m, rarely lower). **ID** Ad mostly red with *pink nape, auriculars, and breast.* Juv mostly brown with two narrow pink wingbars. **HABITS** Understory to canopy and edge of semihumid to humid pine-oak, coniferous, and broadleaf forests. Local in humid broadleaf (cloud) forest. Forages actively by gleaning from foliage. In pairs or small groups. Follows mixed flocks. **VOICE** Song (1) a variable, rapid series of high-pitched notes and short trills *wee-tee-weecheep ch-ch-ch-ch*. May end with emphatic, upslurred note *wee-tee-weecheep ch-ch-ch-ch-wheer*. Compare with song of Golden-browed Warbler. Call (2) a two-syllable *tchlip*.

Painted Redstart *Myioborus pictus*   13.5 cm

South USA to CA. Uncommon resident in north highlands (500 to 3000, but mainly above 1500 m). Rare in SV (Morazán, 183). **ID** *Mostly black* with white markings on wings and long tail. Belly red. *White crescent below eye.* Juv drab dusky brownish **HABITS** Understory to midstory of humid pine-oak and oak woodlands. Locally in humid broadleaf (cloud) forest. Solitary or in pairs. Follows mixed flocks. Forages actively. Gleans from foliage or bark. Clings briefly to tree trunks with tail held cocked or spread. **VOICE** Song (1) a variable, rich warble. Often accelerates and ends abruptly with sharply downslurred note *wee-chee wee-chee wee-chee wee-chee wee-chee-cheewheet*. Calls (2) a sharply downslurred, slightly buzzy *sreeh* or *wsseu* or *sreeu* and (3) abrupt, two-syllable *chewee* or *chew'lee*.

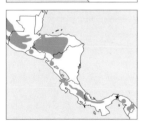

Slate-throated Redstart *Myioborus miniatus*   13 cm

MX to SA. Fairly common to common resident in foothills and highlands (700 to 3200 in north, mainly below 2000 in south, rarely or locally as low as 100 m). Also volcanic highlands of SV (Santa Ana, 183). Rare and local in north NI. **ID** Plain dark gray above with *white markings on long tail.* Dark gray throat contrasts with variably red or yellow lower underparts. **GV** Varies geographically in underparts color, ranging from red in GT to yellow with ochre breast in east PA. **HABITS** Understory to midstory and edge of humid broadleaf forest, second growth, and plantations. Locally in pine-oak forest and woodland in north. Forages actively. Makes short sallies to seize prey. Frequently cocks or spreads tail to flash white on rectrices. Follows mixed flocks. Often in pairs. Confiding. **VOICE** Song (1) a variable series of thin, slightly slurred, whistled notes. May accelerate at end *chee chewee chewee chee cheu* or *tew tsee tsew tsew-tseu-tsu-tsu tseweep* or a more complex *tsi-chew tsi-chew tsi-chew chwee chwee chew chwee chew*. In south compare with song of Collared Redstart. Calls (2) a sharp *pik* or *chip* and (3) drier *chet*.

Collared Redstart *Myioborus torquatus*   13 cm

CA endemic. Common resident in highlands (above 1500 m) of CR and west PA. **ID** *Yellow sides of head, forehead, and throat.* Yellow underparts with *dark breast-band.* Mostly black tail with extensive white on outer rectrices. Juv has gray breast. Slate-throated Redstart (lower elevations) has dark throat. **HABITS** Understory to lower midstory and edge of very humid broadleaf (cloud) forest, second growth, and plantations. In pairs or small groups. Follows mixed flocks. Forages actively. Spreads or flips tail from side to side to flash white markings. Makes short sallies to seize prey from air or vegetation. May drop to ground. Confiding. **VOICE** Song (1) similar to Slate-throated Redstart but longer, mellower, and more varied, and includes warbles and trills as well as slurred whistles. Call (2) a sharp *tchip* or *cheep* louder and richer than call of Slate-throated Redstart.

Red-faced Warbler

juv

Pink-headed Warbler

ad

juv

Painted Redstart

ad

GT ad

SV and HN ad

Slate-throated Redstart

CR and west PA ad

east PA juv

east PA ad

Collared Redstart

WARBLERS, OVENBIRD, AND WATERTHRUSHES Parulidae

Mainly Nearctic migrant warblers found in lower levels of woodland or forest. Buff-rumped Warbler is a resident species found near watercourses in humid broadleaf forest.

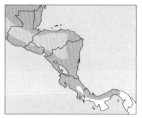

Worm-eating Warbler *Helmitheros vermivorum* 13 cm
Breeds east Nearctic. Winters MX, WI, and CA. Uncommon transient and winter resident (mainly Sep to Apr) in lowlands and foothills (to 1800 m, rarely or locally higher). Most common in north Caribbean slope. **ID** Long bill. Note *buff underparts* and *striped crown*. In south compare with Three-striped Warbler. **HABITS** Midstory of semihumid to humid broadleaf forest, tall second growth, and shaded plantations. Solitary birds follow mixed flocks that include antwrens, greenlets, and Nearctic migrant warblers. Clings or hangs to probe in suspended clusters of dead leaves. **VOICE** Usually quiet. Call (1) a loud, clear *chip*.

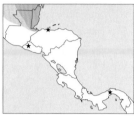

Swainson's Warbler *Limnothlypis swainsonii* 13 cm
Breeds east Nearctic. Winters mainly WI. Uncommon to rare transient and winter resident (Sep to Apr) in north BZ, BZ Cays (529, 667, 630, 343, 493), north GT (Petén, Izabal, 78), and Bay Islands. Very rare in mainland HN (Atlántida, Cortés, 442, 346), SV (Santa Ana, 341), and PA (Panamá, 341, 42). **ID** Long bill. Plain, dull buff underparts and *rufous-brown crown*. *Dull buff supercilium contrasts with dark eyeline.* Compare with Worm-eating Warbler. Note different head pattern and habits. **HABITS** Understory and floor of semihumid broadleaf and littoral forest, second growth, and scrub. Forages mainly on ground by probing in leaf litter or flipping leaves with bill. Solitary. Does not follow mixed flocks. **VOICE** Call (1) a loud, sharp, slightly squeaky *teep* or *tchip*.

Ovenbird *Seiurus aurocapilla* 14.5 cm
Breeds east Nearctic. Winters MX, WI, and CA. Uncommon to fairly common transient and winter resident (Aug to May) in lowlands and foothills (to 1500, rarely or locally to 2200 m). **ID** *Orange crown bordered with black* (sometimes raised in short crest). Note *pale eye ring* and black-and-white streaked underparts. *Parkesia* waterthrushes have plain crown. **HABITS** Floor, understory, and edge of semihumid to humid broadleaf forest, second growth, plantations, and gardens. Solitary. Walks deliberately over ground beneath shaded undergrowth. Takes elevated perch when disturbed. Solitary. **VOICE** Usually quiet. Call (1) a hard, unmusical note that varies from high-pitched, hard *chap* to low-pitched, flat *chup* or *dik*.

Northern Waterthrush *Parkesia noveboracensis* 14.5 cm
Breeds Nearctic. Winters MX, and WI to north SA. Common transient and winter resident (Aug to May) in lowlands and foothills (to 1500, rarely or locally to 2500 m). **ID** Brown above with heavy brown streaking on white or yellowish underparts. *Narrow, white or buff supercilium concolorous with flanks and narrowing behind eye.* Louisiana Waterthrush has longer, broader, whiter supercilium. **HABITS** Floor and understory of semihumid to humid broadleaf forest, second growth, plantations, mangroves, and gardens. Walks deliberately over ground near small streams, pools, or puddles. Bobs tail. Solitary. **VOICE** Call (1) a loud, hard *spik*.

Louisiana Waterthrush *Parkesia motacilla* 14.5 cm
Breeds east Nearctic. Winters MX, WI, and CA. Uncommon transient and winter resident (Jul to Apr) in foothills and highlands (to 3000 m, but mainly in highlands). **ID** Brown above with relatively sparse brown streaking on white underparts. Resembles Northern Waterthrush but *white supercilium is broader behind eye* and is whiter than buff flanks. **HABITS** Floor and understory of semihumid to humid broadleaf forest, second growth, plantations, and gardens. Walks deliberately over ground near small streams. Bobs tail. More closely associated with running water than Northern Waterthrush. Solitary. **VOICE** Call (1) a loud, hard *tsik*.

Buff-rumped Warbler *Myiothlypis fulvicauda* 14.5 cm
CA and north SA. Fairly common resident in humid lowlands and foothills (to 1500 m). **ID** *Buff rump and base of tail* (often fanned). Crown and upperparts brown. Note buff supercilium and dark eye stripe. Juv has dingy brown head and breast. **GV** Birds from east PA are deep buff below and on tail. **HABITS** Floor, understory, and edge of humid broadleaf forest and tall second growth. Favors margins of streams, rivers, and ponds and areas with flooded vegetation. Sallies from ground to seize prey in air. Takes low, exposed perch in vegetation or on streamside boulder when disturbed. Bobs tail to display bright rump. **VOICE** Loud song (1) a soft, warbled phrase followed by long, rapid, even-pitched or slightly descending series of clear whistles that increase in volume. Call (2) a hard, sharp *chut chut-it* or *chut-t-t*.

Worm-eating Warbler

Swainson's Warbler

Ovenbird

Northern Waterthrush

Louisiana Waterthrush

juv

Buff-rumped Warbler

widespread ad

east PA
ad

WARBLERS Parulidae

Resident warblers found at lower or middle levels in forest or woodland. Pairs or groups often follow mixed flocks. Golden-crowned and Rufous-capped warblers are both widespread and geographically variable species in Central America.

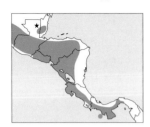

Rufous-capped Warbler *Basileuterus rufifrons* 12.5–13 cm

Mainly MX and CA. Common resident in north foothills and highlands (200 to 2200 m). Also Mountain Pine Ridge region of BZ, and reported from north GT (Petén, 78) where status uncertain. Also Isla Coiba off PA (Veraguas, 653, 470). **ID** Long tail typically cocked. Mostly olive above and yellow below. *Rufous crown and auriculars* separated by *white supercilium*. Juv mostly drab brownish-olive with narrow cinnamon wingbars and white supercilium. In north compare with Golden-browed Warbler (locally syntopic). **GV** Birds from west GT have whitish lower underparts and white malar. Birds from south CA have more extensively yellow underparts (including malar) and usually have white mark below eye. **HABITS** Understory to midstory and edge of deciduous and semihumid forest, scrub, open pine and pine-oak woodland. Hops deliberately through vegetation. **VOICE** Song (1) a variable, rapid series of loud, bright chip notes and squeaky, warbled phrases that accelerate in second half. Typically starts with one to three sharp notes and ends with several clear, slurred notes *chip, cheep, chaweechyweechyweechcha-cheweet*. Song in south GT more liquid. Call (2) an emphatic, metallic *chink* or *cheek* or *cheet*. Sometimes repeated.

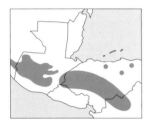

Golden-browed Warbler *Basileuterus belli* 13 cm

MX and north CA. Fairly common to common resident in north highlands (1200 to 3500 m). **ID** Mostly plain olive above and plain yellow below. Rufous crown, face, and auriculars separated by *broad yellow supercilium*. Tail usually held level, not as often cocked as with Rufous-capped Warbler. Compare with Wilson's Warbler. **HABITS** Understory to midstory of humid pine-oak and broadleaf forest. Pairs or small groups forage actively in foliage. **VOICE** Song (1) a variable, rapid series of high-pitched notes *chewi chewi tsee tsee tsee s-s-siiiii-up*. Becomes loudest in middle and typically ends with a buzzy, upslurred note. Compare with song of Pink-headed Warbler. Call (2) a very high-pitched, slightly buzzy *tzeeeet* or two-syllable *tsseeup*. Compare with call of Yellowish Flycatcher.

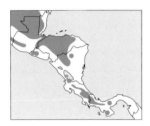

Golden-crowned Warbler *Basileuterus culicivorus* 12.5 cm

MX to SA. Fairly common resident in north lowlands and foothills (to 1600 m). Also volcanic range of SV (Santa Ana, 183). In south mainly foothills and highlands (300 to 2150 m) including Azuero Peninsula in PA (Herrera, Veraguas, 10). **ID** Tail often slightly raised. Olive or gray above and dull, pale yellow below. Note variable *orange- or yellow-and-black crown stripes*, grayish (or olive) auriculars, and broad, dull-yellow supercilium. Juv drab gray above and olive below with narrow, dull-cinnamon wingbars. **GV** Birds from CR and PA typically have more olive head and upperparts. **HABITS** Midstory of broadleaf forest, tall second growth, and adjacent shaded plantations. Pairs or small groups forage actively in foliage. **VOICE** Song (1) a series of three to five loud, whistled notes that rise rapidly in pitch. Last note loudest and strongly upslurred *chee wee wee weet?* or *cheuw cheuw chew weet weet?* Groups produce (2) a chorus of dry *chit* or *teht* notes.

Costa Rican Warbler[30] *Basileuterus melanotis* 13 cm

CA and north SA. Uncommon to common resident in foothills and highlands (1000 to 2200 m) of CR and west PA. **ID** Plain dull olive above with *dusky and buff crown stripes*. Note plain pale olive underparts. Golden-crowned Warbler has brighter yellow breast and different head pattern (usually with bright crown patch). **HABITS** Understory to midstory of very humid broadleaf (cloud) forest. In pairs or small groups. Forages actively in foliage. Sometimes drops to ground. Makes short sallies or hover-gleans to seize prey. **VOICE** Song (1) a rapid, staccato series of short, buzzy trills and sharp, high-pitched notes *tsss-t-t-t-siiii-t-t-t zeeeee . . .* Calls constantly while foraging, giving (2) very high-pitched, sharp *tsit* or *see*.

Tacarcuna Warbler[30] *Basileuterus tacarcunae* 12.5 cm

CA and north SA. Uncommon to common resident in foothills and highlands (400 to 2200 m) of east PA (Panamá, Kuna Yala, Darién, 659, 512). **ID** Plain dull olive above with *dusky and olive crown stripes*. Note plain pale olive underparts. Costa Rican Warbler allopatric. Golden-crowned Warbler has brighter yellow breast and different head pattern (usually with bright crown patch). **HABITS** Understory to midstory of very humid broadleaf (cloud) forest. Like Costa Rican Warbler. **VOICE** Poorly known but seems much like Costa Rican Warbler.

50%

Rufous-capped Warbler

west GT
ad

east GT
ad

juv

south CA
ad

Golden-browed Warbler

north CA
ad

juv

Golden-crowned Warbler

CR and PA
ad

Costa Rican Warbler

Tacarcuna Warbler

WARBLERS Parulidae

Black-cheeked Warbler[31] *Basileuterus melanogenys*   12.5–13.5 cm
CA endemic. Common resident in highlands (above 1600 m) of CR and west PA. An undescribed *Basileuterus* warbler has been reported from highlands of the Azuero Peninsula, PA (Veraguas, Los Santos, 425). **ID** *Rufous crown* and *black auriculars* separated by *long white supercilium*. Juv has narrow cinnamon wingbars. Pirre Warbler allopatric. **GV** Birds from central PA (Veraguas, Ngäbe-Buglé) have gray mantle and whitish underparts. **HABITS** Understory to midstory and edge of humid broadleaf forest, second growth, elfin forest, and bamboo stands in paramo. Pairs or small groups forage actively in foliage, moss clumps, and epiphytes. Follows mixed flocks. **VOICE** Song (1) a lisping, sputtering series of notes *tsi tsi wee tsi tsi wee*. Compare with longer song of Rufous-capped Warbler. Typical call (2) a high-pitched, thin *tsit* repeated rapidly and sometimes followed by a thin whistle *t-t-t-t-tew*. Also (3) a high-pitched *pit-tew*.

Pirre Warbler[31] *Basileuterus ignotus*   12.5 cm
CA endemic. Uncommon to rare and local resident in highlands (above 1200 m) of Pirre Massif and Tacarcuna Massif in east PA (Darién, 462, 519, 643). **ID** Brownish-olive above and dull whitish below. Rufous crown and dusky auriculars separated by *long yellowish-white supercilium*. Black-cheeked Warbler allopatric. **HABITS** Midstory of humid broadleaf (cloud) forest. Poorly known. Pairs or family groups sometimes follow mixed flocks. **VOICE** Song undescribed. Call (1) a penetrating *tseeut* or *tseeit*.

Fan-tailed Warbler *Basileuterus lachrymosus*   14.5 cm
MX and north CA. Uncommon to rare and local resident in Pacific foothills (recorded 50 to 1800, but mainly above 300 m). Rare and local in HN and NI. **ID** Long, white-tipped tail often fanned or cocked. Note yellow crown and *white eye crescents and white spot on lores*. Underparts mostly yellow becoming *tawny on breast*. **HABITS** Floor and understory of broadleaf forest, especially rocky areas in arid to semihumid (deciduous) forest, second growth, and adjacent scrub. Forages actively. Attends ant swarms. Solitary or in pairs. Does not follow mixed flocks. **VOICE** Song (1) a series of thin, high-pitched, warbled phases with downslurred ending *weesu weesu weesu chuu* or *suwee suwee suwee chu*. Compare with song of Golden-crowned Warbler. Calls (2) a thin, high-pitched, slightly tinny *sieu* or *tseein* or *seeeeu* and (3) shorter *sii*.

WRENTHRUSH Zeledoniidae

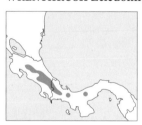

Wrenthrush *Zeledonia coronata*   11 cm
CA endemic. Uncommon to locally fairly common resident in highlands (above 1500 m) of CR and west PA. Reported east to Coclé. **ID** Rounded and short-tailed. Plain dark olive above and plain dark gray below with *cinnamon-orange median crown bordered laterally with black*. Compare with Silvery-fronted Tapaculo (often syntopic). Note different head pattern. **HABITS** Floor and understory of humid broadleaf (cloud and elfin) forest and paramo thickets. Favors bamboo stands. Pairs or solitary birds hop or creep over moss or leaf litter. May ascend to midstory to vocalize or when disturbed. Secretive. Usually detected by voice. **VOICE** Variable song (1) a short phrase of three to five high-pitched, piercing notes *see-see-suu seep* or *see-suu-seep* or *tsee-tuu-tseee*. May be repeated. Call (2) a high-pitched, thin, upslurred *pseeee* or *psssss*. Compare with lower-pitched calls of Black-billed Nightingale-Thrush and Timberline Wren.

YELLOW-BREASTED CHAT Icteriidae

Yellow-breasted Chat *Icteria virens*   17 cm
Breeds Nearctic. Winters mainly MX and CA. Uncommon transient and winter resident (Aug to May) in north Caribbean lowlands and foothills (to 1500 m). Rare in CR and PA (Panamá, 346, 659). **ID** Large and long-tailed with heavy bill. *Rich yellow breast* and *white spectacles*. **HABITS** Understory of semihumid to humid forest edge, second growth, riparian thickets, plantations, and gardens. Skulks in dense vegetation. Solitary. **VOICE** Song (1) rarely given in winter, a long, varied, strident series of clucks, rattles, scolds, mews, etc. Phrases typically repeated three to eight times with single mellow notes (suggesting a mimid) *chreeu chreeu chreeu chreeu, huit, hoooh cheh-chehcheh cheh-cheh-cheh, joyn-joyn-joyn . . .* Calls (2) a hard, dry *chak* or *cha-chak* and (3) dry, oriole-like chatter.

OLIVE WARBLER Peucedramidae

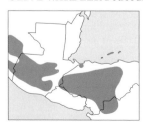

Olive Warbler *Peucedramus taeniatus*   13 cm
Southwest USA to CA. Fairly common resident in north foothills and highlands (1000 to 3800 m). **ID** *Notched tail* with extensive white on undersurface. Male has *deep orange hood* extending to breast and *black mask and lores*. Female and imm have deep yellow hood. Female (particularly imm) resembles various Nearctic migrant warblers. Note Olive Warbler's distinctive tail shape and unstreaked plumage. **HABITS** Subcanopy to canopy of pine and mixed pine-broadleaf forest. Pairs or small groups follow mixed flocks. Forages actively in terminal foliage of coniferous trees. **VOICE** Song (1) a variable, fairly rapid series of phrases on even pitch *eechu-eechu-eechu-eechu-eechu* or *tree-tree-tree-tree-tree-tree*. Compare with song of Grace's Warbler. Call (2) a soft *teu*.

CR and
west PA

Black-cheeked Warbler

central PA

Pirre Warbler

juv

Fan-tailed Warbler

ad

Wrenthrush

Yellow-breasted Chat

imm

ad

Olive Warbler

♀

♂

DICKCISSEL, CHATS, AND TANAGER Cardinalidae

Dickcissel *Spiza americana* female 14, male 16 cm
Breeds Nearctic. Winters mainly SA. Uncommon to (briefly) abundant transient (Mar to May and Aug to Nov). Uncommon and local winter resident on Pacific slope. **ID** Fairly heavy, conical bill. Note *chestnut on lesser wing coverts*. Breeding male (Apr to Aug) has variable *yellow supercilium* and malar and *black patch on breast*. Female and imm duller with black and yellow markings less extensive or lacking. Compare female with smaller female House Sparrow. Note different wing pattern and bill shape. **HABITS** Open grassy areas, marshes, hedgerows, and agricultural (especially grain) fields. Forages mainly on ground or low in weedy vegetation or crops. Forms large flocks at favored foraging or roosting sites. **VOICE** Call (1) often given in flight, a loud, husky, slightly buzzy *jeet*. Flocks call in jumbled chorus.

Red-breasted Chat *Granatellus venustus* 14 cm
South MX and CA. Uncommon and local resident in northwest GT (Huehuetenango, 229). **ID** Stout bill and *long tail* (often fanned or cocked) with *white on outer rectrices*. Male has black auriculars, sides of neck, and breast-band. Note *scarlet central breast and crissum* and broad white supercilium extending behind eye. Female gray above with *buff sides of head, supercilium, and breast*. Gray-throated Chat allopatric. **HABITS** Floor to subcanopy of arid to semihumid scrub and thorn or deciduous forest. Often in pairs. Does not follow mixed flocks. Forages actively. Flips tail from side to side. **VOICE** Variable, loud song (1) a short, slightly hoarse series *weeuw weeuw chee-weeucheeweeu* on steady pitch. Call (2) an emphatic *whit* or *vhit*.

Gray-throated Chat *Granatellus sallaei* 12.5 cm
South MX and north CA. Uncommon resident in lowlands (to 300 m) of north GT (Petén, Alta Verapaz) and BZ. Most common in north BZ. **ID** Stout bill and *long tail* (often fanned or cocked). Male has *scarlet central breast and crissum* and white supercilium extending behind eye. Female gray above with *buff sides of head, supercilium, and breast*. Red-breasted Chat allopatric. **HABITS** Floor to subcanopy of arid to semihumid scrub and semihumid broadleaf forest. Favors vine tangles in tall forest. Often in pairs. Does not follow mixed flocks. Forages actively. Flips tail from side to side. **VOICE** Loud, warbled song (1) ends with downslurred note *weechuchuweetseewuuu*. Call (2) an emphatic *whit* or *vhit*.

Rose-throated Tanager *Piranga roseogularis* 15.5 cm
South MX and CA. Uncommon to locally fairly common resident in Caribbean lowlands of north GT (Petén) and north BZ. **ID** Heavy gray bill and *whitish eye crescents*. Male mostly gray with *deep red crown, wings, and tail*. Throat, central underparts and crissum deep pink. Female has similar pattern with male's pink and red markings replaced by yellow and olive. Compare with Red-crowned and Red-throated ant-tanagers. Note different habits and head pattern. **HABITS** Midstory to subcanopy of semihumid (often deciduous or seasonally flooded) forest, tall second growth, and scrub. Often in pairs. Does not follow mixed flocks. **VOICE** Song (1) a halting series of short, rich, slightly hoarse, warbled phrases *chee-chu, cheeawee, cheeawee cheeuu . . .* Call (2) a nasal, coarse, whining *yaaaw* or *eeeaw*. Sometimes repeated persistently.

Dickcissel

imm
♀

breeding
♂

Red-breasted Chat

♀

♂

Gray-throated Chat

♀

♂

Rose-throated Tanager

♀

♂

TANAGERS Cardinalidae

Medium-sized, sexually dimorphic birds found mainly in upper levels of forest and woodland. Summer Tanager, a Nearctic migrant, is the most widespread and common.

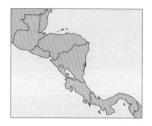

Summer Tanager *Piranga rubra* 18 cm

Breeds Nearctic. Winters south MX to north SA. Widespread and common transient and winter resident (mainly Sep to May) in lowlands and foothills (to 2500, but mainly below 1500 m). Vagrant to Isla del Coco (329). **ID** *Heavy, pale bill.* May appear slightly crested. Male *uniform red*. Female variable but typically *near-uniform dull yellow*. Compare with corresponding plumages of Hepatic Tanager. Note different head pattern and bill color. Female Scarlet Tanager has smaller bill and more rounded crown. **HABITS** Midstory to canopy in a wide variety of arboreal habitats including forest edge, second growth, mangroves, gardens, and plantations. Solitary. **VOICE** Call (1) a dry, emphatic *piti tuck* or *pit-uck*. Sometimes given in series. Compare with calls of Flame-colored, Western, and Hepatic tanagers.

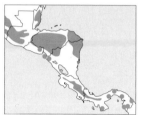

Hepatic Tanager *Piranga flava* 17.5–20.5 cm

Southwest USA to SA. Widespread in north foothills and highlands (400 to 2500 m). Also volcanic highlands in north NI (Chinandega, 413) and Caribbean lowlands (SL to 450 m) of BZ, HN (Gracias a Dios), and NI (RAAN). Uncommon resident in south foothills and highlands (600 to 1800 m). Nearctic breeding birds reach west GT as winter residents (229, 297). **ID** *Dark lores* and *heavy, dark gray bill.* Male variably near-uniform brick red to burnt orange. Female near-uniform dull yellow to greenish-yellow. Briefly held juv plumage (not shown) is drab and has buff underparts streaked with brown. Compare ads with Summer Tanager. Note different head pattern and bill color. **GV** Birds from resident breeding population in north CA have dusky or grayish auriculars. Birds from BZ (not shown) and from the Mosquitia region are smaller and darker with contrasting brighter throat and belly. Birds from Nearctic migrant population are larger and paler with grayish mantle and flanks. Birds from south CA highlands are darker and richer overall. **HABITS** Subcanopy to canopy of pine and pine-oak woodland (north CA, including Caribbean lowlands) and semihumid to humid broadleaf forest (CR and PA). Usually in pairs. Follows mixed flocks, especially in north. Habitually flicks tail. **VOICE** Song (1) a series of rich, slightly burry or squeaky warbled phrases of four to eight notes *chew-cheweecheer-cheeur-chuee* . . . Higher-pitched than song of Flame-colored Tanager. Calls (2) a rapid phrase of three to four sharp notes that rise in pitch *chu-chit-it* or *chudidit* and (3) shorter *chut* or *choot*.

Summer Tanager

imm ♂

♀

♀

ad ♂

Hepatic Tanager

♀

northern migrant

♂

♀

Mosquitia

♂

♀

north CA highlands

♂

♀

♂

south CA

45%

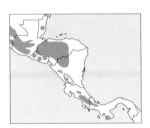

White-winged Tanager *Piranga leucoptera* 14 cm

MX to SA. Uncommon and local resident in foothills and highlands (mainly 1100 to 1850 m in CR, locally near SL in north). Also volcanic range in SV (Santa Ana, Morazán, 183) and highlands of Azuero Peninsula in PA (Herrera, 512, 425). **ID** Small. *Two bold white wingbars.* Male mostly red with black tail and wings, and *black mask.* Female greenish-olive above and yellow below. Compare female with larger female Western Tanager. Note different bill color. **HABITS** Subcanopy to canopy and edge of semihumid to humid broadleaf and pine-oak forest, adjacent tall second growth, and shaded plantations. Often in hilly terrain. Pairs follow mixed flocks. **VOICE** Song (1) a short, thin, whistled phrase *chuut swee-swee-eet* or *chut-weet, chut-weet weet* with last note slightly higher in pitch. Calls (2) an abrupt, thin, squeaky *pseewhee* or *ch'wee'wee* sometimes repeated and (3) soft *chick, chick* in flight.

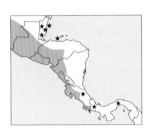

Flame-colored Tanager *Piranga bidentata* 19 cm

MX and CA. Uncommon to locally fairly common resident in north highlands (mainly 900 to 2850, locally or seasonally to 500 m). Local in highlands of SV (Santa Ana, Morazán, 183, 364) and in BZ at Mt. Margaret (Cayo, 343). Common in south highlands. May descend to lower elevations outside breeding season. **ID** Large and long-tailed. Note *streaked mantle, dusky auriculars,* and *bold white wingbars.* Ad male mostly deep orange-red. Female mostly yellowish-olive. Imm male may have orange head and breast. Smaller White-winged Tanager is deeper red with black mask and plain mantle. Compare female with male Western Tanager. **HABITS** Subcanopy to canopy and edge of pine-oak and broadleaf forest, second growth, plantations, and gardens. Pairs may follow mixed flocks. Sings from high in canopy. **VOICE** Song (1) a vireo-like series of three to six short, slurred, slightly hoarse or burry warbled phrases *chewee-very-vire, chewee-very-vire-very, cheery-cherewuu.* Call (2) a loud, abrupt *whi-t-deck* or *chi-t-dik.* Compare with call of Hepatic Tanager.

Western Tanager *Piranga ludoviciana* 17 cm

Breeds west Nearctic. Fairly common transient and winter resident (Sep to May) in Pacific and interior north (SL to 3000 m). Vagrant to BZ (Belize, 346) and PA (Chiriquí, Panamá, 512). **ID** Relatively short-tailed with rounded crown. *Two bold wingbars.* Breeding male (Mar to Aug) mostly yellow with black mantle and wings and mostly *red head.* Nonbreeding male has variable dusky markings on head and fine olive scaling on mantle. Female resembles other female *Piranga* but has *grayish mantle* contrasting with yellow rump and nape. Female's underparts variably yellow to gray, but always with yellow crissum. Female Scarlet Tanager sometimes shows wingbars, but has greenish upperparts with nape and mantle concolorous. Summer Tanager has heavier, paler bill. **HABITS** Midstory to canopy and edge of arid to semihumid broadleaf or pine-oak forest, second growth, plantations, and gardens. Transients may form small flocks. **VOICE** May sing in spring passage. Song (1) resembles song of Flame-colored Tanager. Call (2) a rolled, upslurred *pred-it* or *ched-it.* Compare with calls of Summer and Flame-colored tanagers.

Scarlet Tanager *Piranga olivacea* 17 cm

Breeds east Nearctic. Winters SA. Widespread transient (Sep to Nov and Apr to May) mainly in Caribbean lowlands and foothills (to 1200 m). May be briefly or locally very common in spring. Very rare in north Pacific. **ID** Relatively short-tailed with rounded crown. Breeding male (Mar to Aug) mostly *brilliant scarlet* with contrasting *black tail and wings.* Nonbreeding male mostly olive with contrasting *black tail and wings.* Female resembles female Summer Tanager but has bright greenish-yellow underparts and *smaller bill.* Imm male Scarlet Tanager has mostly grayish tail and wings with black confined to wing coverts. Compare with female Western Tanager. Note different mantle color. **HABITS** Midstory to canopy and edge of humid broadleaf forest, second growth, plantations, and gardens. Transients form small flocks and may occur in a wide variety of arboreal habitats. **VOICE** Call (1) a hard, two-syllable *chik-brr* or simple *chik.*

White-winged Tanager ♀

♂

imm
♂

Flame-colored Tanager ♀

♂

Western Tanager ♀

nonbreeding
♂

breeding
♂

Scarlet Tanager ♀

nonbreeding
♂

breeding
♂

TANAGERS AND ANT-TANAGERS Cardinalidae

Heavy-billed birds found in lower levels of broadleaf forest. Red-throated and Red-crowned ant-tanagers are both geographically variable. Details of head pattern are useful in separating these species where they occur together. Voice is also helpful.

Carmiol's Tanager *Chlorothraupis carmioli*   17.5 cm
CA endemic. Fairly common resident in humid lowlands and foothills (to 1000 m). Historical record from Pacific west PA (Veraguas, 659). **ID** Fairly heavy bill. *Near-uniform olive* becoming slightly paler and more yellowish below. **HABITS** Upper understory to midstory of humid broadleaf forest and adjacent tall second growth. Pairs or groups follow mixed flocks. Forages actively in foliage and epiphytes. Often noisy and conspicuous. **VOICE** Variable song (1) a very long, often accelerating series that begins with two notes alternating in pitch before suddenly switching to a rapidly repeated rich whistled note and then to a rapid series of short, grating or buzzy notes *wheechu wheechu wheechu wheechu wheechu chuu chuu chuu chuu chuu chu chu chu zee zee zee zee zee zee zee*. Calls (2) a high-pitched, piercing, slightly buzzy *seeet* or *seee-seeee*, (3) staccato *tik* or *tip* given in bursts, and (4) a nasal, scratchy or squeaky *nyaaaah* or *cheeyah* or *cheeea*. May be repeated rapidly.

Lemon-spectacled Tanager *Chlorothraupis olivacea*   17.5 cm
CA and north SA. Uncommon resident in lowlands and foothills (to 1200 m) of east PA (Darién). **ID** Fairly heavy bill. Near-uniform dark olive becoming slightly paler below. *Bold yellow eye ring* and supraloral and *yellow streaking on throat*. Carmiol's Tanager allopatric. **HABITS** Upper understory to midstory of humid broadleaf forest. Pairs or small groups follow mixed flocks. **VOICE** Often noisy. Calls (1) a rapid series of harsh, squeaky, high-pitched cries *he-he-he-he-hi-hi-hi* that often rise slightly in pitch, (2) a short, soft, high-pitched *pcheew* or *pseuu*, and (3) variable series of dull, low-pitched notes that may accelerate into a rattle.

Red-crowned Ant-Tanager *Habia rubica*   18–19 cm
MX to SA. Fairly common resident in lowlands and foothills (to 1500 m). Most common in north Caribbean. Mainly Pacific slope in south. **ID** Fairly long tail and heavy bill. Male's slightly brighter *red throat does not contrast strongly with sides of head*. Note *red crown bordered with blackish*. Female brownish-olive becoming paler below. *Yellowish throat contrasts only slightly with remaining underparts and sides of head*. Resembles Red-throated Ant-Tanager. Note different head pattern and voice. **GV** Individually and geographically variable (extremes are shown). Birds from PA are darker and have bold dark border to crown stripe. Birds from Pacific NI and west CR are palest. **HABITS** Understory and lower midstory of semihumid to humid broadleaf forest and tall second growth. Pairs or small groups often follow mixed flocks. Attends ant swarms, especially in north. **VOICE** Song (1) a variable series of two to four loud, clear, whistled phrases *choodoo choodoo choodoo*. Compare with more complex song of Red-throated Ant-Tanager. Calls include (2) noisy, scratchy, scolding notes that are higher-pitched and smoother than calls of Red-throated Ant-Tanager *chee cheche-heh che* or *chee-heh-hehehee*. Often accelerates into a staccato chatter. Also (3) a dry *chek-chek*.

Red-throated Ant-Tanager *Habia fuscicauda*   female 19, male 20 cm
South MX to north SA. Fairly common resident in lowlands and foothills (to 800, locally to 1300 m). Mainly Caribbean slope in south. **ID** Male dusky red with *contrasting red throat*. Note *dark face*. Female mostly olive becoming paler below with *contrasting yellow throat*. Imm male resembles female. Compare with Red-crowned Ant-Tanager. Note different head pattern and voice. **GV** Female from north CA has brown breast contrasting with yellow throat. Female from south CA is darker. Male from south CA is darker and grayer below and has more black on face and auriculars. **HABITS** Understory to lower midstory of semihumid to humid broadleaf forest and tall second growth. Pairs or small groups follow mixed flocks. Attends ant swarms, especially in north. **VOICE** Song (1) a series of rich, whistled phrases *whichoo chi choochoowee* or *choo-weechowooochooweechu-wu*. Sometimes repeated persistently. Compare with simpler song of Red-crowned Ant-Tanager. Call (2) a harsh, scolding *raaah* or *raaak*. Lower-pitched and coarser than call of Red-crowned Ant-Tanager.

Black-cheeked Ant-Tanager *Habia atrimaxillaris*   female 19, male 20 cm
CA endemic. Common resident in humid Pacific lowlands of Osa Peninsula and Golfo Dulce region in east CR (Puntarenas, 155). **ID** Gray above. *Pink throat and breast* contrast with *blackish face and malar*. Male has red central crown. **HABITS** Understory of humid broadleaf forest, second growth, and littoral scrub. Pairs or small groups follow mixed flocks. Gleans prey from foliage, dead leaf clusters, and arboreal litter. Attends ant swarms. **VOICE** Song (1) a repeated phrase of clear, slightly nasal whistles *cheeoo-huu-cheeoo-huu-cheeoo-huu* . . . Calls (2) a low-pitched, nasal *chit* or *chet* and (3) dry, harsh *rrak* or *rruk* like Red-throated Ant-Tanager but shorter and more clipped.

Carmiol's Tanager

Lemon-spectacled Tanager

Red-crowned Ant-Tanager

north CA
♀

north CA
♂

Pacific NI and
west CR
♂

PA
♀

PA
♂

north CA
♀

north CA
♂

Red-throated Ant-Tanager

south CA
♂

south CA
♀

♂

♀

Black-cheeked Ant-Tanager

GROSBEAKS Cardinalidae

Medium-sized, heavy-billed birds found in upper levels of forest or woodland. Rose-breasted Grosbeak, a Nearctic migrant, is the most common and widespread.

Rose-breasted Grosbeak *Pheucticus ludovicianus* 19 cm

Breeds Nearctic. Winters MX to SA. Widespread transient (Sep to May) and winter resident (SL to 3000 m). **ID** Heavy pinkish or whitish bill. Ad male boldly patterned with black and white wings and tail and *rose-red on breast*. Note white on base of primaries (conspicuous in flight). Nonbreeding female mostly pale buffy brown with two whitish wingbars and brown streaking on crown, breast, and dorsum. Female's dark auriculars contrast with *bold whitish supercilium*. **HABITS** Midstory to canopy and edge of humid broadleaf forest, second growth, gardens, and shaded plantations. Gregarious. Transients may form small flocks. **VOICE** Calls (1) a sharp, squeaky *iik* or *eek and (2) whistled phew*.

Black-headed Grosbeak *Pheucticus melanocephalus* 19 cm

Breeds west Nearctic. Winters mainly MX. Very rare vagrant to BZ (Cayo, 341), HN (Copán, 263), and CR (Guanacaste, Cartago, San José, Puntarenas, 602, 600, 341, 346). **ID** Heavy bill with dark culmen. Ad male has *orange-tawny neck, underparts, and postocular stripe*. Male has black sides of head, crown, and chin. Female and imm male closely resemble corresponding plumages of Rose-breasted Grosbeak but Black-headed has *tawny-cinnamon collar and breast*. Fresh-plumaged fall imm Rose-breasted Grosbeak may show cinnamon band on breast and fall Black-headed Grosbeak may be very pale below (some nearly white below). Note that Black-headed Grosbeak has mostly gray culmen (bill entirely pink or whitish in Rose-breasted). **HABITS** Similar to Rose-breasted Grosbeak. CA reports are mostly from arid to semihumid broadleaf forest, second growth, and scrub. **VOICE** Typical call (1) *kichk*, is lower-pitched and harsher than call of Rose-breasted Grosbeak. Both species give (2) whistled *phew*.

Yellow Grosbeak *Pheucticus chrysopeplus* 23 cm

MX and CA. Uncommon resident in Pacific foothills and highlands (300 to 3000 m) of west GT. Local on Caribbean slope in Motagua Valley, GT (El Progreso, Zacapa). **ID** Bulky with *very heavy, conical bill*. White wingbars and prominent white spots on tertials. Ad male has *deep orange-yellow head and underparts* and mostly black tail and wings. Note *white on base of primaries*. Female mostly deep yellow. Female's crown, nape, and mantle heavily streaked with dusky. Female's tail mostly gray with whitish tips on rectrices. Imm male resembles female but has darker (blackish) wings. Note blackish eye stripe, malar, and crown stripes. Black-thighed Grosbeak allopatric. **HABITS** Canopy of arid to humid broadleaf forest, tall second growth, and open areas with scattered trees. Solitary or in pairs. **VOICE** Variable song (1) a short, slightly hoarse series of whistled notes *weeu chee-wee chee-r weer weeuh* or *ch-reer wi-wi h'ree reee-e-eer*. Ends with a downslurred note. Call (2) a sharp, nasal or metallic *iehk* or *plihk*.

Black-thighed Grosbeak *Pheucticus tibialis* 21 cm

CA endemic. Uncommon to fairly common resident in highlands (1000 to 2600 m) of CR and west PA. **ID** Bulky with *very heavy, conical bill*. Note *white band on base of primaries* (conspicuous in flight). Mostly deep yellow with diffuse black facial mask and chin and black tail and wings. Mantle mottled with yellow and black. Yellow Grosbeak allopatric. Compare with Black-faced Grosbeak (mainly lower elevations). **HABITS** Subcanopy to canopy and edge of humid broadleaf forest, adjacent plantations, and clearings with scattered tall trees. Solitary or in pairs. Forages high in trees. Sluggish. Often difficult to locate in dense foliage. Usually detected by voice. **VOICE** Variable song (1) a series of high-pitched, clear, warbling and slurred phrases. Sometimes ends with repeated note and may accelerate into short trill *chuwee ch-chwee chuwee-oow chuwee chechecheche*. Call (2) a high-pitched, very sharp *pik* or *iik*. Compare with lower-pitched call of Rose-breasted Grosbeak.

Rose-breasted Grosbeak

imm
♂

♀

nonbreeding
♂

breeding
♂

♀

Black-headed Grosbeak

♂

imm
♂

♀

♂

Yellow Grosbeak

Black-thighed Grosbeak

BUNTINGS AND GROSBEAK Cardinalidae

Fairly small birds found mainly at lower levels in shrubby, nonforest habitats. Details of the wing and head pattern are useful in separating female *Passerina* buntings. The Nearctic migrant Indigo Bunting is the most common and widespread.

Varied Bunting *Passerina versicolor* 13 cm

South USA to north CA. Uncommon and local resident in Nentón Valley in west GT (Huehuetenango, 229) and on Caribbean slope in Motagua Valley (El Progreso, Zacapa, 164, 279, 376). **ID** Short bill with curved culmen. Breeding male mostly deep purple and blue (may appear all dark) with *red nape*. Note male's black chin and lores contrasting with *red eye ring*. Female mostly plain grayish-brown (grayer when worn) with *plain wings* (or very faint wingbars when worn). Note female's *plain brownish breast*. Female Indigo Bunting has faintly streaked breast, more distinct wingbars, and pale edgings on tertials. **HABITS** Understory to midstory and edge of deciduous or thorn forest and second growth. Forages mainly inside dense cover. Solitary or in pairs. **VOICE** Song (1) a rich, slightly scratchy warble *weesususeeweewuu*. Song may include or end with short, buzzy note *susweecheechuweetzzz*. Call (2) a liquid *plik* or *spik* like Indigo Bunting.

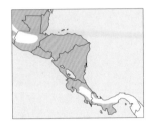

Painted Bunting *Passerina ciris* 14 cm

Breeds south USA to north MX. Winters mainly MX, WI, and CA (612). Uncommon transient and winter resident (mainly Nov to Apr). Most common in Pacific lowlands and foothills (to 1350 m). Rare in west PA (512) including records from Caribbean lowlands (Bocas del Toro, 392). Uncommon to rare transient and winter resident in north Caribbean (343). Vagrant to Isla del Coco (329). **ID** Ad male has blue head with red eye ring and *red rump and underparts*. Female and imm *mostly plain green above* and variably pale grayish-yellow to yellow below (brighter in imm male). All female and imm plumages have some *green on mantle or rump*. Some show traces of ad male's head pattern. Other *Passerina* buntings basically brown above and never have green or olive on upperparts. **HABITS** Understory, floor, and edge of arid to semihumid forest, second growth, scrub, gardens, and mangroves. Forages mainly on ground or at low levels beneath cover. Usually solitary. **VOICE** Call (1) a liquid *plik*.

Indigo Bunting *Passerina cyanea* 13.5 cm

Breeds Nearctic. Winters mainly MX, WI, and CA. Widespread transient and winter resident (mainly Oct to Apr) in lowlands and foothills (to 1500 m, higher in migration). Common to locally abundant. **ID** Breeding male (Mar to Aug) mostly plain, deep blue becoming darkest on head and breast. Nonbreeding male mostly brown (most have some blue on flight feathers and coverts). Female mostly brown becoming paler below with *cinnamon wingbars and soft streaking on breast*. Note *whitish throat*. Female Varied Bunting is relatively plain (unpatterned) and never shows whitish throat. Compare with Blue-black Grassquit. Note different bill shape. Also compare with Blue Grosbeak. Note different bill shape and wing pattern. **HABITS** Understory of open grassy areas including low second growth, scrub, agricultural margins, and roadsides. Forages near ground. Takes elevated perch when disturbed. May form large flocks. **VOICE** Calls (1) a sharp, slightly liquid *spic* and (2) buzzy *zzrt*.

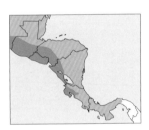

Blue Grosbeak *Passerina caerulea* 17.5 cm

USA to CA. Nearctic breeding and resident populations. Breeds in north Pacific lowlands and foothills (to 1500 m). Also widespread transient and winter resident (Oct to Apr) in lowlands and foothills. Uncommon to locally (or seasonally) abundant. Vagrant to Isla del Coco (329). **ID** May raise short, bushy crest. *Heavy bill* with pale mandible and *distinct wingbars*. Ad male has *rufous wingbars*. Otherwise rich blue (some show whitish fringing on underparts). Female and imm variably cinnamon to dull brown (when worn) becoming paler below. and have wingbars variably whitish to cinnamon. Some show streaking on underparts. Some ad females show mixture of blue and brown body plumage. Note pale lores and throat. Other CA finches with mostly blue or brown plumage are smaller with finer bills and none has similar wingbars. **HABITS** Understory to midstory of open grassy or brushy areas including forest edge, hedgerows, low second growth, grassy or weedy areas, scrub, and roadsides. Usually remains hidden inside cover. Solitary or in pairs. May form small flocks outside breeding season. Takes open perch when vocalizing or disturbed. Twitches tail from side to side. **VOICE** Song (1) a rich, slightly scratchy or buzzy warble like other *Passerina* buntings, but lower-pitched and perhaps buzzier. Calls (2) a sharp, metallic *chik* or *chink* and (3) buzzy *bzzir* or *zzir* often given in flight.

Varied Bunting

♀

nonbreeding
♂

breeding
♂

imm
♂

Painted Bunting

♀

ad
♂

Indigo Bunting

♀

nonbreeding
♂

breeding
♂

imm
♂

♀

Blue Grosbeak

♂

CARDINAL, GROSBEAKS, AND BUNTING Cardinalidae

Stout-billed birds found mainly in broadleaf forest and scrub. Blue-black and Black-faced grosbeaks are widespread and common.

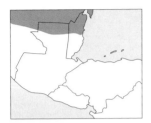

Northern Cardinal *Cardinalis cardinalis* 20 cm

USA to south MX. Uncommon resident in lowlands of north BZ (Corozal, Orange Walk) and north GT (Petén, 229). Also (perhaps introduced) resident on Swan Islands off Caribbean HN (34). **ID** Black face and throat and prominent, *pointed crest*. Ad has *heavy red bill* (blackish in juv). Ad male *near-uniform red*. Female mostly grayish-brown with red crest. **HABITS** Understory to midstory of arid to semihumid scrub, pine savanna, and second growth. Solitary or in pairs. Sings from elevated perch. **VOICE** Song (1) a series of loud, clear whistles sometimes followed by a lower-pitched series *chiiu chiiu chiiu chiiu chiiu chuk chuk chuk*. Call (2) a loud, metallic *pink* or *iink*.

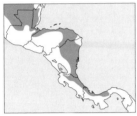

Black-faced Grosbeak *Caryothraustes poliogaster* 18 cm

South MX and CA. Fairly common resident in lowlands and foothills (to 1200 m). **ID** Heavy bill with curved culmen and short tail. *Black face and throat* and *yellow breast and forehead*. Mostly golden-olive with gray belly, rump, and scapulars. Yellow-green Grosbeak allopatric. **GV** Some birds from CR and PA (not shown) have less gray on scapulars and lower back. **HABITS** Subcanopy to canopy and edge of semihumid to humid broadleaf forest. Gregarious. Often in large, noisy groups. Also follows mixed flocks. **VOICE** Song (1) a series of three to six mellow but sharp whistles *chee-chee cheer che-chew* or *chew tee chu-chuweet* or *cheer-chee chu chu cher-weet-cher*. Calls (2) often given by several birds in chorus, a buzzy note followed by several sharp, downslurred whistles *prrrrt chew chew chew* or *prrr-cheweeweee* and (3) a staccato, sometimes metallic *chick* or *chip* often repeated.

Yellow-green Grosbeak *Caryothraustes canadensis* 17 cm

CA and SA. Uncommon resident in foothills (650 to 1200 m) of east PA at Pirre Massif and Serranía de Jungurudó (Darién, 462, 519, 45). **ID** Heavy bill with curved culmen and short tail. *Black face and throat*. Olive above and deep yellow below. Black-faced Grosbeak allopatric. **HABITS** Midstory to canopy of humid broadleaf forest and adjacent tall second growth. Groups sometimes form mixed flocks with various tanagers. Often noisy and conspicuous. **VOICE** Song (1) a burry *churwee chii-chii-chii-chii*. Loud calls include (2) a buzzy *ddzreet* followed by series of clear notes *chew-chew-chew-chew* or *tew-tew-tew-tew* (like Black-faced Grosbeak) and (3) shorter *pwee* or *pwit* or *see*.

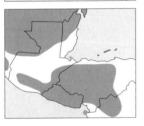

Blue Bunting *Cyanocompsa parellina* 13.5 cm

South MX and north CA. Fairly common resident in north lowlands and foothills (to 1800 m). Rare in north NI (Chinandega, 413). **ID** Tail near square (slightly notched). Ad male *deep blue with lighter ("frosted") forehead*, malar, forewing, and rump. Female uniform plain brown with *rufous rump*. Compare with female of larger Blue-black Grosbeak and with female Blue Seedeater. Note different bill shape. **HABITS** Understory and edge of semihumid broadleaf forest, second growth, and scrub. Forages at lower levels in dense vegetation. Solitary or in pairs. **VOICE** Song (1) a variable, sweet warble that rises slightly in pitch. Begins with one or two introductory notes and fades slightly at end *sweeu, sleeleeswee* or *seeu, seeusyeesu-eesi-si-see*. In north Caribbean compare with song of Gray-throated Chat. Call (2) a clear, metallic *teek* or *peek*. Compare with call of Hooded Warbler.

Blue-black Grosbeak *Cyanocompsa cyanoides* 17 cm

MX to SA. Widespread and common resident in lowlands and foothills (to 1200 m). Confined to Caribbean slope in north. **ID** *Very heavy bill* and broad, rounded tail. Ad male *uniform dark blue*. Female and imm male *uniform cocoa-brown* (becoming slightly paler on chin). Compare female with females of smaller Blue Bunting and Blue Seedeater. Note different bill. **HABITS** Understory and edge of broadleaf forest, tall second growth and shaded plantations. Solitary or in pairs. Reclusive and usually detected by voice. **VOICE** Both sexes sing. Loud song (1) composed of about six successively lower-pitched, rich whistles. Often ends with sharp, warbled phrase *see see seee sewee suwee sweet suuu*. Compare with song of Spot-breasted Wren. Call (2) a loud, sharp, hard *spek* or *piik*. Sometimes doubled. Often given persistently.

Northern Cardinal ♀ ♂

Black-faced Grosbeak

Yellow-green Grosbeak

Blue Bunting ♀ ♂

Blue-black Grosbeak ♀ ♂

SEEDEATER Cardinalidae

Blue Seedeater *Amaurospiza concolor*   12.5 cm

MX to SA. Rare and irregular resident (SL to 2850 m) in BZ (Belize, Orange Walk, Cayo, 313, 625), GT (Sololá, Suchitepéquez, Sacatepéquez, Escuintla, Alta Verapaz, San Marcos, 229, 226), SV (Santa Ana, Ahuachapán, 619, 341), HN (Cortés, Olancho, Copán, 442), and NI (Jinotega, Matagalpa, RAAN, Río San Juan, 413). Mainly highlands (1000 to 2200 m) in CR (Guanacaste, Alajuela, Puntarenas, Cartago, 65, 570, 600) and PA (Herrera, Veraguas, Panamá, 512, 162, 659, 512). **ID** *Fairly straight, gray, conical bill.* Male *near-uniform dark blue* becoming darker on face, chin, and lores. Female *uniform cinnamon-brown.* Female resembles females of Blue-black Grassquit and Slaty Finch. Note seedeater's *plain, unstreaked underparts.* Compare with female Thick-billed Seed-Finch. Note different bill shape. Also compare with Indigo and Blue buntings. **HABITS** Understory to midstory and edge of semihumid to humid broadleaf forest, bamboo thickets, and riparian edges. Forages near ground. Sings from elevated perch. Solitary or in pairs. **VOICE** Song (1) a short series of loud, rich, whistled notes and short warbles. May end with short, sputtering phrase *ch'swee ch'swee ch'switto ch'seeu ptr-r-r.* Compare with song of Slate-throated Redstart. Calls (2) a sharp *hu-tseet* or *chu-tsee* and (3) flat, slightly buzzy *vhit* or *chit* like *Passerina* bunting.

FINCHES AND FLOWERPIERCERS Thraupidae

Slaty and Peg-billed finch are generally rare but can be briefly or locally common where *Chusquea* bamboo is seeding. Bill shape is useful in identifying these. The two *Diglossa* flowerpiercers are common residents with allopatric, highland distributions in north and south Central America.

Slaty Finch *Haplospiza rustica*   13 cm

MX to west SA. Rare resident in highlands (above 1500 m) of GT (Baja Verapaz, Quetzaltenango, El Progresso, 229), SV (Santa Ana, Morazán, 619, 364, 346), HN (Ocotepeque, Copán, Francisco Morazán, 450, 442, 346), NI (Matagalpa, Granada, 411), CR (Alajuela, Cartago, Puntarenas, Heredia, 126, 285, 570, 474, 598, 667, 540, 346), and west PA (Chiriquí, Panamá, 160, 659). Perhaps nomadic. **ID** *Dark, slender, conical bill.* Male *uniform slaty gray.* Female brownish with *streaked underparts* including throat. Imm male gray with brownish wings. Compare with female Blue-black Grassquit (note different habits). Also compare with Slaty Flowerpiercer and Peg-billed Finch. Note different bill. **HABITS** Understory and floor of humid broadleaf forest and edge. Breeds in areas with seeding bamboo. Solitary, in pairs, or in small groups. Male sings from elevated perch. **VOICE** Variable song (1) a two- or three-part, very high-pitched, thin, slightly metallic trill. Last part higher-pitched *bzzzzzzziiiiiii* or *wee-zeeeeiiiiiii.* Compare with song of Chestnut-capped Brushfinch. Call (2) a very high-pitched, thin *seeep.*

Peg-billed Finch *Acanthidops bairdi*   13.5 cm

CA endemic. Rare to briefly or locally common resident in highlands (mainly above 1500 m) of east CR (Alajuela, Puntarenas, Cartago, 570, 474, 667, 600) and west PA (Chiriquí, 659). Perhaps nomadic. **ID** *Slender, bicolored bill.* Male uniform slaty gray. Female dull grayish-brown with *buff wingbars, pale supercilium,* and soft streaking below. Compare with Slaty Finch and Slaty Flowerpiercer. Note different bill. **HABITS** Understory to midstory and edge of very humid broadleaf (cloud) forest, second growth, and paramo thickets. May be locally common where bamboo is seeding. May follow mixed flocks. **VOICE** Buzzy song (1) begins with several high-pitched, squeaky notes and ends with lower-pitched note *chee-schee-schee-schee-bzzzzz.* Calls (2) a buzzy, low-pitched *zeert* and (3) flat, high-pitched *tseeeeet.*

Cinnamon-bellied Flowerpiercer *Diglossa baritula*   11.5 cm

MX and north CA. Fairly common resident in north highlands (above 1200, rarely as low as 800 m). Also volcanic highlands of SV (Santa Ana, San Miguel, 183). Rare in NI (Jinotega, Matagalpa, Madriz, 411). **ID** Small. *Upturned, hooked bill.* Male has *blackish head, blue-gray upperparts,* and *rufous underparts.* Female paler and duller. Imm female grayish-brown with indistinct streaking on underparts and variable pale wingbars. **HABITS** Canopy and edge of humid broadleaf and pine forest, second growth, scrub, gardens, and plantations. In pairs or small groups. Forages actively. Clings or hangs on flowers, piercing them at base to extract nectar. **VOICE** Variable song (1) a rapid, jumbled, high-pitched, squeaky series that drops slightly in pitch *chi-chii-chii sese sisisi* or *swii-swii-swi-chi-chuchuchu.* Call (2) a high-pitched, thin, sharp *tsik.*

Slaty Flowerpiercer *Diglossa plumbea*   11.5 cm

CA endemic. Fairly common resident in south highlands (above 1200 m). Perhaps undertakes local movements. **ID** Small. *Upturned, hooked bill.* Male slaty gray becoming darker on head and wings. Female dull grayish-brown becoming paler on belly with faint streaking on breast. **HABITS** Midstory and edge of humid broadleaf forest, second growth, and plantations. Like Cinnamon-bellied Flowerpiercer. **VOICE** Song (1) a variable, rapid series of high-pitched, thin, slurred whistles, short warbles, chips, and weak trills *see-chew see-chew, see chew seer seer surrtseep, tsee tsew tsewery tseer tsewry sewy tsink-tsink-tsink.* Calls (2) a high-pitched, thin, weak *tsip* and (3) piercing *tseep.*

♀

Blue Seedeater

♂

♀

Slaty Finch

♂

♀

♂

Peg-billed Finch

imm

ad
♀

♂

Cinnamon-bellied Flowerpiercer

♀

♂

Slaty Flowerpiercer

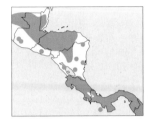

Cocos Finch *Pinaroloxias inornata* 12 cm

CA endemic. Confined to Isla del Coco where a common resident (571, 600). **ID** Short tail and *pointed, decurved bill*. Male *uniform black*. Female brownish with *dusky streaking and speckling on sides of head, crown, breast, and mantle*. Note female's cinnamon wingbars. Imm like female. **HABITS** Uses all strata in vegetation and occurs in every available terrestrial habitat. Forages actively by gleaning and probing. Typically in pairs or small groups. Confiding. **VOICE** Song (1) a buzzy phrase that rises in pitch. Often preceded by a high-pitched, metallic note *tseek ka-jeeuuuurrreek*. Calls (2) a burry, rough *djrr* that may be doubled and (3) whistled *tyew* that may be varied to a harsh *jeew* or *jeeak*.

Yellow-faced Grassquit *Tiaris olivaceus* 10 cm

MX to north SA. Locally common resident (SL to 2000, mainly above 200 m). Recently expanded into BZ (Cayo, Orange Walk, 313, 343). Local in north Pacific in GT (Suchitepéquez, 229), SV (San Vicente, 341), and NI (Managua, Masaya, 413). Also Isla Coiba (Veraguas, 653, 470). **ID** Small with *straight, conical bill*. Ad male mostly olive with *yellow throat, supercilium, and mark below eye*. Breast black. Ad female has reduced yellow markings and less extensive black. Imm uniform olive with faint suggestion of ad's head markings. **GV** Ad male from Isla Coiba has more extensive black on head and underparts. **HABITS** Floor and understory in open areas including roadsides, pastures, plantations, low scrub, and gardens. In pairs or small groups. **VOICE** Song (1) a high-pitched, thin, slightly metallic trill on steady pitch. Sometimes repeated. Call (2) a simple *tsik*.

Wedge-tailed Grassfinch *Emberizoides herbicola* 18 cm

CA and SA. Uncommon and local resident in Pacific foothills of east CR (Puntarenas, 65, 600) and PA (Chiriquí, Panamá, 659). **ID** *Long, ragged or pointed tail* and bicolored bill (black above and yellow below). Ad has streaked upperparts and plain breast. Note white lores and eye ring. Juv has dusky streaking on underparts. Compare with various female blackbirds. **HABITS** Understory to midstory in open areas including pastures, marshes, and savannas. Solitary or in pairs. Forages on ground or low in grass. Secretive, but sings from open, elevated perch in early morning or evening. When flushed flies short distance then quickly drops into cover. **VOICE** Song (1) a short, decelerating trill or rattle of four to six notes *chididididideeer*. Calls (2) a sharp, dry, metallic *spit* or *plit* sometimes repeated persistently and (3) soft, low *chip* or *chirp*.

Saffron Finch *Sicalis flaveola* 13.5 cm

CA and SA. Uncommon and local resident in central PA where introduced in 1951 (Colón, Panamá, 551, 389, 659). **ID** Stout bill. Ad has uniform yellow underparts and *orange-yellow crown*. Imm grayer and paler with fine, soft streaking on head, underparts and mantle. Compare with Grassland Yellow-Finch (not known to be syntopic). Note that Grassland Yellow-Finch never shows plain yellow head of ad Saffron Finch. **HABITS** Urban and suburban areas including parks, lawns, and gardens. Forages mainly on ground. Usually in pairs or small groups. **VOICE** Male's song (1) a persistently repeated series of squeaky, slurred notes *tzip-tzip-tzee-tzee . . .* or *tseu chip tseu tsee-tseeuu chip . . .*

Grassland Yellow-Finch *Sicalis luteola* 12 cm

MX to SA. Rare and local in GT (Sacatepéquez, Baja Verapaz, 229, 279, 646), BZ (Belize, Orange Walk, Stann Creek, 667, 625, 343, 250, 346), east HN (Gracias a Dios, 442), NI (Granada, Jinotega, RAAN, RAAS, 327), and PA (Chiriquí, Coclé, Panamá, 652, 551, 659, 40). Historical record from CR (Guanacaste, 570). Perhaps nomadic. **ID** Short, stout bill. Note streaked crown, yellow around eye, and grayish upperparts. Ad male has *clear yellow underparts*. Female has dusky crown and auriculars and duller breast. Juv has whitish throat and streaked breast. **HABITS** Grasslands, agricultural fields, marshes, and savannas. Forages mainly on ground. May perch on low shrub or fence post. Forms flocks outside breeding season. **VOICE** Song (1) a variable, high-pitched series of *chip* or *tsp* notes that accelerate into steady, insect-like trill *tsp tsp ttttttttttttttttttttt*. Trill usually even in pitch, but may rise or drop slightly in second half. Compare with higher-pitched, thinner trill of Yellow-faced Grassquit. Males give (2) a buzzy *dzzi dzzi . . .* or *dzzirr dzirr . . .* in flight display. Calls (3) a sharp *siik* or *syiik* and (4) longer *sii-sii chi* or *ss-siit*.

Cocos Finch

♀

♂

Yellow-faced Grassquit

Coiba
ad ♂

♀

imm
♂

widespread ad
♂

Wedge-tailed Grassfinch

ad

juv

Saffron Finch

juv

ad

Grassland Yellow-Finch

juv

ad
♀

ad
♂

SEEDEATERS Thraupidae

Tiny, stout-billed birds found mainly at lower levels in open areas. Often in flocks. Drab female and immature plumages can present identification problems. White-collared Seedeater is the most common and widespread.

White-collared Seedeater *Sporophila torqueola* 11 cm

South USA to CA. Common resident in lowlands and foothills (to 1500, locally to 2500 m). **ID** *Bold wingbars.* Male has white wingbars. Plumage variable with flanks sometimes buff and mantle varying from black to gray mottled with black. Some males from Pacific slope have black throat. Female has *two buff wingbars.* **HABITS** Open, grassy areas, savannas, plantations, pastures, roadsides, and gardens. **VOICE** Song (1) a variable series of clear, rich, whistled notes that usually drop in pitch and end with a dry, buzzy trill *swee-swee-swee-swee, tee chee chee tewtewtewtew* or *weedeedeedee chew-chew-chew*. Calls (2) a soft *cheep*, (3) harsher, more strident *preep*, and (4) nasal *cheea*.

Variable Seedeater *Sporophila corvina* 11.5 cm

MX to SA. Common resident in lowlands and foothills (to 1500 m, locally higher). Also Isla Coiba (Veraguas, 470). **ID** Ad male of widespread form is uniform black with *white mark on base of primaries.* Female of widespread form *near-uniform dark olive-brown* becoming slightly paler below. Females from east PA paler below. Compare with Thick-billed Seed-Finch. Note different bill and tail shape. **GV** Male from east Pacific CR and west PA has white rump and collar. Ad male from central and east PA has white throat and less black on breast. **HABITS** Open grassy or weedy areas, savannas, plantations, pastures, roadsides, agricultural margins, and gardens. Sings from elevated perch. **VOICE** Song (1) a long, varied warble with buzzy notes or brief trills *weecheecheweecheche-bzzz-treechea cha*. Calls (2) squeaky, slurred notes and (3) harsh, buzzy *jiir* or *chur*.

Lesson's Seedeater *Sporophila bouvronides* 11.5 cm

SA. Rare vagrant to east PA (Darién, 512, 48, Apr to Jun). **ID** Ad male has black throat and *white malar.* Female like female Variable Seedeater but has smaller, pale bill. Ad male Variable lacks Lesson's white malar. Female Variable has dusky bill. **HABITS** Open, grassy areas. **VOICE** Variable song (1) a short series of clear, rich notes followed by short, accelerating trill *chew-chew-chee-e-e-e-e* or (2) trill followed by several clear, staccato notes *trrrrrrr-chee-chee-chee.*

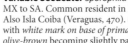

Slate-colored Seedeater *Sporophila schistacea* 12 cm

CA and SA. Rare and irregular resident in lowlands and foothills (SL to 1000 m) of BZ (Toledo, Orange Walk, Belize, 313, 343), GT (Alta Verapaz, 227), HN (Colón, Gracias a Dios, 401, 629, 346), and NI (RAAN, RAAS, Río San Juan, 413, 412, 548). More widespread in CR (600) and PA (512, 464, 605, 346). **ID** *Heavy bill.* Ad male has *yellow bill,* white malar, and white wingbar. Imm male more olivaceous and may lack white markings. Female pale below (especially on throat) with plain wings. **HABITS** Riparian woodland with extensive bamboo, humid broadleaf forest, marshes, and flooded agricultural fields. Sings from elevated perch or in brief flight. **VOICE** Song (1) a staccato series of high-pitched, buzzy notes. First one to three notes loud and clear *zeeee-eeeee-eeee tzee lee lee see-see-see-see-see* or *tiii-lee chew chew zitsi-tsi-tsi-tsi-tsi.* Calls (2) a thin *peep* or *tseet* and (3) metallic, upslurred *zheet.*

Yellow-bellied Seedeater *Sporophila nigricollis* 11.5 cm

CA and SA. Fairly common resident in south Pacific lowlands and foothills (to 1800 m). Also Pearl Islands (Panamá, 611, 651). Rare on Caribbean slope and Central Valley of CR (Alajuela, Cartago, 600). One report from NI (Río San Juan, 412). **ID** Small with gray bill. Ad male has pale bill. *Black throat and sides of head* and *yellowish-white lower underparts.* Female mostly dull ochre-olive (usually) including throat and upper breast. Some show contrasting pale lower underparts. Most differ from female Ruddy-breasted Seedeater in having *dark (not whitish) throat.* Pale or worn birds perhaps not separable from other female or imm *Sporophila.* **HABITS** Open grassy areas, savannas, plantations, pastures, roadsides, and gardens. **VOICE** Song (1) a series of clear, slurred whistles that end with slightly dry trill or buzzy note *see seeeu se seeuu seoo treeeee* or *seee-suurr-che-chew-chee-chee-cheuw-zezeze.* Compare with longer, sweeter song of White-collared Seedeater. Calls (2) a variety of dry chips. Harsher than Variable Seedeater.

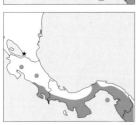

Ruddy-breasted Seedeater *Sporophila minuta* 10 cm

MX to SA. Uncommon to locally common resident. Mainly in Pacific lowlands. **ID** Small. Breeding male *bluish-gray above* (browner in south) with *rufous rump and underparts.* Note white mark at base of primaries. Female plain dull cinnamon-buff (grayer when worn) becoming paler below. Nonbreeding male resembles female, but has traces of rufous on rump. Imm male resembles female. **GV** Nonbreeding male in north CA resembles female, but has traces of rufous on rump. **HABITS** Open, grassy areas including marshes, savannas, plantations, pastures, roadsides, and gardens. **VOICE** Song (1) a series of clear, slurred whistles (often paired) *weeteer weeteer chercher teeaweet, weet weet cher-weet weet teeaweer.* Lacks buzzy notes of White-collared Seedeater. Call (2) a slurred *cheeeip.*

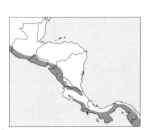

524

♀

**White-collared
Seedeater**

♂

♂

widespread
♂

widespread
♀

Pacific CR and
west PA
♂

central and
east PA
♂

♂

Variable Seedeater

east PA
♀

**Lesson's
Seedeater**

**Slate-colored
Seedeater**

imm
♂

♀

♂

**Yellow-bellied
Seedeater**

imm
♂

♀

♂

**Ruddy-breasted
Seedeater**

♀

north CA
breeding
♂

north CA
nonbreeding

south CA
♂

SEED-FINCHES AND GRASSQUIT Thraupidae

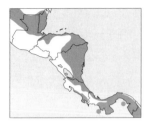

Thick-billed Seed-Finch *Sporophila funerea* 12 cm

MX and CA. Uncommon resident in lowlands and foothills (to 1100 m). Also Isla
Coiba and Pearl Islands (Veraguas, Panamá, 649, 470, 471). **ID** *Heavy, dark bill* and
long, rounded tail. Male black with *small white mark at base of primaries*. Female
uniform rich, deep brown (including crissum). Male Variable Seedeater similar.
Note different bill and tail shape. Female may suggest other female *Sporophila*
seedeaters but has larger bill and dark crissum. Compare female with female Blue-
black Grosbeak. **HABITS** Nests in open, wet or marshy areas (may use drier areas at
other seasons). Takes elevated perch when disturbed or vocalizing. Wags tail from side
to side. **VOICE** Variable song (1) a series of rich, slurred whistles and short warbles *seeu
seeeu wi chi che chi weeeu*. Compare with shorter, harsher song of Variable Seedeater.
Calls (2) an abrupt, slurred *tchew* or *cheeuw* and (3) shorter *dit* or *dik*.

Nicaraguan Seed-Finch *Sporophila nuttingi* 14.5 cm

CA endemic. Uncommon to rare and local resident in Caribbean lowlands and
foothills (to 1200 m) of NI (RAAN, Río San Juan, RAAS, 466, 511, 322, 326, 413), CR
(Guanacaste, Heredia, Alajuela, Limón, 172, 590, 594, 600), and west PA. Also Isla
Colón (Bocas del Toro, 659). **ID** *Very heavy conical bill*. Male black with *pale pinkish
bill*. Female uniform warm brown (grayer when worn) with dark grayish bill. Smaller
Thick-billed Seed-Finch has proportionally smaller, blackish bill. Compare with Blue-
black Grosbeak. Note different habits and bill color. **HABITS** Understory of marshes,
damp pastures, and borders of lakes, ponds, and wetlands. In pairs when breeding.
May form small flocks at other seasons. Sings from elevated perch or in flight.
VOICE Song (1) a series of rich, slurred whistles *chee, wheeu cheeu wee wee cheu cheuuu
ttttt*. Notes or phrases often doubled or tripled. Compare with faster, higher-pitched
song of Thick-billed Seed-Finch. Call (2) a short, sharp *chek*.

Large-billed Seed-Finch *Sporophila crassirostris* 14.5 cm

CA and north SA. Rare and local resident in lowlands of east PA (Panamá, Darién,
346, 43). **ID** *Very heavy conical bill*. Male black with faint bluish gloss, white mark at
base of primaries, and *whitish bill*. Female near-uniform brown (grayer when worn)
with dark bill. Compare with smaller Thick-billed Seed-Finch (may be syntopic).
Nicaraguan Seed-Finch allopatric. **HABITS** Damp, grassy marshes, pastures, and rice
fields. **VOICE** Song (1) a rapid series of short, rich, warbled phrases and brief trills *chee
wee cheeu wee cheuuu ttttt*. Call (2) a short, upslurred *choy*.

Blue-black Grassquit *Volatinia jacarina* 10.5 cm

MX to SA. Common resident in lowlands and foothills (SL to 2200 m). Also Isla
Coiba and Pearl Islands (Veraguas, Panamá, 649). **ID** Small with *pointed bill*. Ad male
uniform, glossy blue-black. Female brownish with *streaked underparts*. Imm male
mottled. Compare with Indigo Bunting. Note different bill shape. **HABITS** Open areas
including roadsides, marshes, agricultural fields, pastures, gardens, and plantations.
Forages mainly on or near ground. May perch prominently on low shrub or fence post.
Singing males fly vertically upward then flutter back to perch in display. **VOICE** Song (1)
a buzzy *b'zeeer* or *zi-zi-zheeer* or (2) simpler, plaintive *tssse-u* or *pssseeu*. Calls (3) a soft,
dry ticking and (4) high-pitched, sharp *peet* or *piik*.

Thick-billed Seed-Finch

♀ ♂

Nicaraguan Seed-Finch

♀ ♂

Large-billed Seed-Finch

♀ ♂

Displaying male
Blue-black Grassquit.

Blue-black Grassquit ♂

imm ♂

♀

SALTATORS Thraupidae

Fairly large, long-tailed and stout-billed birds found mainly at middle levels in forest edge or disturbed areas. Saltators are often common and conspicuous. Slate-colored Grosbeak is a secretive species found inside humid broadleaf forest. All have loud, conspicuous songs.

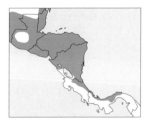

Black-headed Saltator *Saltator atriceps* 27 cm

South MX and CA. Common resident in lowlands and foothills (to 1800, locally to 2200 m). **ID** Largest CA saltator. Somewhat variable. Note black crown and blackish sides of head (in north CA). Buff-throated Saltator has olive crown. **GV** Individually variable in extent of black on the breast. Birds from north CA have black auriculars. **HABITS** Midstory to subcanopy of semihumid to humid broadleaf forest edge, second growth, scrub, plantations, gardens. In pairs or small groups. May join loose associations of edge-inhabiting tanagers, orioles, or honeycreepers. Noisy and often conspicuous. **VOICE** Pairs duet. Song (1) typically a series of loud, harsh, scratchy notes ending with a long, upslurred whistle *chaak ch-ch cher jur jur weeeee*. Calls (2) single harsh, squeaky, descending notes *chaak* or *chweer* or *week* or (3) several harsh notes followed by harsh, explosive chatter *week week, chchchrrrrrr*.

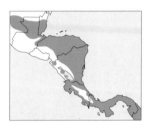

Buff-throated Saltator *Saltator maximus* 20–22 cm

MX to SA. Fairly common resident in lowlands and foothills (to 1500 m). **ID** *Buff throat* surrounded by black malar and (usually) black breast-band. Crown grayish-olive. Compare with Black-headed Saltator. Note different head pattern. **GV** Birds from east PA have black breast-band reduced or lacking. **HABITS** Midstory to canopy of semihumid to humid broadleaf forest edge, second growth, scrub, plantations, and gardens. Pairs may form loose foraging associations with edge-inhabiting orioles, tanagers, or honeycreepers. **VOICE** Pairs duet. Song (1) a variable series of soft, warbled phrases *cheer-chaweeu cheery* or *chee-cheera chee-cheera* or *cheer-cheerdle-chew*. Song phrases often combined with call notes. Call (2) a high-pitched, thin, sibilant *seeent* or *tseeeet*.

Grayish Saltator *Saltator coerulescens* 22–24 cm

MX to SA. Uncommon to fairly common resident in lowlands and foothills (to 1800, locally to 2000 m). Recently reported from Pacific east CR (Puntarenas, 346) and west PA (Chiriquí, Bocas del Toro, 346, 42). **ID** Ad *plain gray above* with dull buff lower underparts and short white supercilium. Juv more olive overall with yellowish supercilium and throat. Some have indistinct coarse streaking on breast (compare with Streaked Saltator). **HABITS** Midstory of second growth, scrub, plantations, and gardens. Often in pairs. **VOICE** Variable song (1) a short series of rich, slurred whistles, warbles, and short, sputtering notes. Usually ends with upslurred or downslurred whistle *cheechu cha wheeer?* or *pee-pipit pit-cheeew?* or *chick a chichreee?* Pairs may duet with shorter phrases. Call (2) a high-pitched, sharp *tsit* or *tseet*. Higher-pitched than call of Rose-breasted Grosbeak. Shorter and sharper than Buff-throated Saltator.

Streaked Saltator *Saltator striatipectus* 19.5 cm

CA and SA. Uncommon to locally common resident in lowlands and foothills (to 1200 m) of Pacific east CR and PA. Also Isla Coiba and Pearl Islands off PA (Veraguas, Panamá 649, 470). **ID** Olive above with *streaked underparts*. Most have yellow tip on mostly black bill. Usually has broken yellowish eye ring and yellow gape. **HABITS** Understory to midstory and edge of second growth, forest borders, gardens, and plantations. Solitary or in pairs. Retiring. **VOICE** Variable song (1) a series of loud, rich whistles. Often includes a slightly buzzy roll *chu chucheer cheeer-chew chrchrchrchr rerrr-chup* or *prrr-chow chow cheeer purrrrrit* or simpler *wheeer chowchow weeeer*. In flight, calls (2) *qua qua qua*. Other calls (3) a loud *spit* or *speet*, sharper and shorter than call of Buff-throated Saltator, (4) scratchy *cheu*, and (5) squeaky *whit-chaaaar* with second note a dry rattle.

Slate-colored Grosbeak *Saltator grossus* 21 cm

CA and SA. Uncommon resident in lowlands and foothills (to 1200 m). Confined to Caribbean slope in north. Rare in HN (Atlántida, Colón, Gracias a Dios, 401, 629). Historical record from central NI (Chontales, 537). **ID** Male *near-uniform dark slate-gray* with white central throat and *coral-red bill*. Female slightly browner with less black on head and breast. **HABITS** Upper understory to subcanopy of humid broadleaf forest and tall second growth. Solitary or in pairs. May follow mixed flocks. **VOICE** Song (1) composed of short, melodious but monotonously repeated phrases of rich whistles and warbles *ch'woo-ch'weeeu wheeeuu, ch'woo chuweet* or *peeeuw ch-chueew* that drop in pitch. Calls (2) a sharp, metallic *pick* or *spik* higher-pitched than call of Blue-black Grosbeak and (3) whining, nasal, slurred *nyaaaah* or *caaw*.

Black-headed Saltator

Buff-throated Saltator

south CA

north CA

east PA

widespread

Grayish Saltator

ad

juv

Streaked Saltator

♂

♀

Slate-colored Grosbeak

BANANAQUIT, CONEBILL, AND DACNIS Thraupidae

Small birds found in upper levels of humid broadleaf forest. Often with mixed flocks that may include *Tangara* tanagers.

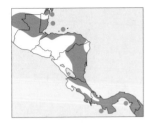

Bananaquit *Coereba flaveola*   10–11 cm

South MX and WI to SA. Uncommon to locally common resident in lowlands and foothills (to 1500 m). Also BZ Cays (343) and Isla Coiba, and Pearl Islands (Veraguas, Panamá, 59, 611, 455, 649, 653, 470). **ID** Small and short-tailed with *pointed, decurved bill*. Yellow breast. Broad white supercilium and *white spot at base of primaries*. **GV** Widespread mainland form is drab with pale upperparts. Birds from BZ Cays are larger, with white throat, dark upperparts, and yellow rump. Birds from Pearl Islands are dark above with yellow rump. **HABITS** Midstory to canopy and edge of broadleaf forest, second growth, littoral woodland, plantations, scrub, and gardens. Forages actively by gleaning from foliage. Takes nectar from flowers. On mainland, pairs follow mixed flocks that include tanagers and honeycreepers. **VOICE** Song (1) a high-pitched, thin, scratchy, insect-like *pseeeeu pzeeeeu pzeeeeu* or *tsee-tsee-tsee-tsee-tzzeew* (with last phrase becoming a buzzy trill) or *tzee zheeew-zheeew* (with two or sometimes more buzzy notes). Compare with song of Blue-gray Tanager. Call (2) a variable, high-pitched, sharp *tsip* or *tseep*. May be repeated in long series. Also (3) a sharp, metallic chipping.

White-eared Conebill *Conirostrum leucogenys*   9 cm

CA and north SA. Uncommon to locally fairly common resident in lowlands and foothills (to 450 m) of east PA. **ID** Small and warbler-like with fine, pointed bill. Male has *black cap and white auriculars*. Note rufous crissum. Female plain blue-gray above and plain dull buff below. Note female's pale lores. **HABITS** Subcanopy to canopy and edge of semihumid to humid broadleaf forest, second growth, and plantations. Pairs or small groups follow mixed flocks. Forages actively in terminal foliage. Visits flowering trees for nectar. **VOICE** Song (1) a series of high-pitched, thin, slurred phrases *tsing-le, tseet-e-tseet*. Calls (2) a slightly dry, emphatic, warbler-like *tcheep* and (3) short, rapid trill or rattle *tsi-tsi-tsi-tsi-tsi-eet*.

Scarlet-thighed Dacnis *Dacnis venusta*   12 cm

CA and north SA. Uncommon resident in south foothills (500 to 1500 m). May wander to lowlands outside breeding season. Rare in NI (RAAN, Río San Juan, 346, 626) where perhaps a seasonal visitor. **ID** Red eyes and dusky legs. Male has mostly blue head, mantle, and rump, black face and wings, and *entirely black underparts*. Scarlet tibials inconspicuous. Female has buff sides of head and rump and *plain grayish-buff underparts*. Compare female with Blue Dacnis. **HABITS** Subcanopy to canopy and edge of humid broadleaf forest, tall second growth, and shaded plantations. May descend to lower levels in vegetation at edges or gaps. Pairs or small groups follow mixed flocks. **VOICE** Usually quiet. Song (1) a repeated, short, rapid phrase that includes buzzy notes and short euphonia-like whistles *weee cha whee cheer bzzeet*. Calls (2) a buzzy, upslurred *vheet* or *wiit* or *wheit* and (3) shorter, scratchy *tzik*.

Blue Dacnis *Dacnis cayana*   12 cm

CA and SA. Uncommon to fairly common resident in lowlands and foothills (to 1200 m). Poorly known in east HN (Gracias a Dios, 401). **ID** Pink legs and red eyes. Male mostly blue with *black mantle, forehead, and throat*. Female *mostly green* with *turquoise head and whitish throat*. Compare female with female Green Honeycreeper (often in same mixed flock). Note different bill shape and head color. **GV** Male from Pacific CR and west PA is turquoise. **HABITS** Subcanopy to canopy and edge of humid broadleaf forest. May descend to lower levels at edges or gaps. Pairs or solitary birds follow mixed flocks. **VOICE** Usually quiet. Song (1) a rapid series of sharp notes followed by several longer, buzzy notes *t-t-t-t-t-t zeeeeee zeeeee zeeee*. Call (2) a high-pitched, thin, sharp *tsip* or *tseep* sometimes repeated or doubled.

Viridian Dacnis *Dacnis viguieri*   11 cm

CA and north SA. Uncommon to rare resident in lowlands and foothills (to 600 m) of east PA (Darién, 659, 512, 48). **ID** Pale yellow eyes. Male mostly *brilliant opalescent-green* with contrasting *black tail, primaries, and mantle*. Female near-uniform light olive (becoming paler below) with *blackish primaries*. Compare male with Blue Dacnis. Note Viridian's plain green throat. Compare female with female Scarlet-thighed Dacnis. Note female Viridian's plain, dull mantle. **HABITS** Poorly known. Subcanopy to canopy of humid broadleaf forest and adjacent tall second growth. Male may perch motionless for long periods on high, exposed twigs. Also forages actively in terminal foliage and blossoms. Pairs follow mixed flocks. **VOICE** Undescribed.

BZ cays

widespread

Pearl Islands

Bananaquit

♀

♂

White-eared Conebill

♀

♂

Scarlet-thighed Dacnis

♀

♂

widespread

Blue Dacnis

Pacific CR and west PA ♂

♀

♂

Viridian Dacnis

TANAGER AND HONEYCREEPERS Thraupidae

Small birds found mainly in canopy of humid broadleaf forest. Often with mixed flocks. Female *Cyanerpes* honeycreepers can be separated by head and underparts pattern. Red-legged Honeycreeper is the most common and widespread of the *Cyanerpes* honeycreepers in Central America.

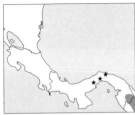

Swallow Tanager *Tersina viridis*   15 cm

CA and SA. Uncommon rare resident in lowlands and foothills (to 450 m) of east PA (Panamá, Darién). Vagrant to central PA (Panamá, 512). **ID** Broad, flat bill and upright posture. Male *turquoise-blue* with *black forehead, face, and throat* and black barring on flanks. Note white central underparts and crissum. Female mostly green with buffy gray face and chin, buff eye ring, and *green barring on yellow flanks*. Compare female with Green Honeycreeper. Note different bill shape and posture. **HABITS** Canopy and edge of humid broadleaf forest and adjacent clearings with scattered trees. Solitary birds, pairs, or small groups perch on high snags. May forage lower at edges or in clearings. Does not follow mixed flocks. **VOICE** Song (1) a series of high-pitched, lisping phrases. May suggest Blue-gray Tanager. Call (2) a high-pitched, buzzy *tzeet*.

Green Honeycreeper *Chlorophanes spiza*   13.5 cm

MX to SA. Uncommon resident in lowlands and foothills (to 1500 m). Most common in south Caribbean lowlands. **ID** *Long, slightly decurved, mostly yellow bill* (birds from south CA tend to have shorter bill). Eyes red. Male *brilliant green* with black crown and sides of head. Female *near-uniform yellow-green*. Compare with female Blue Dacnis. Note honeycreeper's green head and different bill. **HABITS** Canopy and edge of humid broadleaf forest, tall second growth and shaded plantations. Follows mixed flocks. Mobs predators such as snakes and pygmy-owls. Attracted to flowering trees. **VOICE** Calls (1) a repeated, sharp, dry *tsup, tsup, tsup* . . . (2) sharp, warbler-like *cheep* sometimes repeated persistently, and (3) high-pitched, piercing *pseet* or *tseet*.

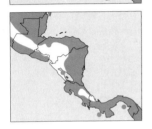

Red-legged Honeycreeper *Cyanerpes cyaneus*   11.5 cm

MX to SA. Fairly common to locally or seasonally very common resident in lowlands and foothills (to 1500 m). May undertake seasonal movements (183, 343). Also Isla Coiba and Pearl Islands (Veraguas, Panamá, 611, 649, 470). **ID** Red legs, relatively long tail, and long, decurved bill. Yellow underwings sometimes visible in flight. Breeding male *blue-violet* with *black mantle*, face, throat, and wings. Note pale blue crown. Nonbreeding male (Aug to Dec) mostly drab olive with black tail and wings. Female mostly olive with pale supercilium and diffuse whitish streaking on underparts. Imm male resembles female. Female Shining Honeycreeper has white throat.
HABITS Canopy and edge of semihumid to humid broadleaf forest, tall second growth, and shaded plantations. In pairs or small groups when breeding. At other seasons may form large flocks. Also follows mixed flocks. **VOICE** Rarely heard dawn song (1) a thin, high-pitched, repeated *tsip tsip chaa, tsip tsip chaa* . . . Calls (2) a high-pitched, thin, piercing *tseet* or *tsip* and (3) nasal, gnatcatcher-like *chaa* or *naaa* or *whaaa*. Compare with calls of Tropical and Blue-gray gnatcatchers.

Shining Honeycreeper *Cyanerpes lucidus*   10.5 cm

South MX to north SA. Uncommon resident in humid foothills (300 to 1500 m, seasonally or locally to near SL). Rare in BZ (Stann Creek, Cayo, Toledo, 529, 313) and GT (229). **ID** *Yellow legs*. Male *violet-blue including mantle* with black face, throat, and wings. Female has bluish crown, nape, and malar. Note female's mostly *whitish underparts with blue streaking*. Also note female's dusky lores and whitish throat. Compare with female Red-legged Honeycreeper. Note different leg color, underparts, and head pattern. **HABITS** Canopy and edge of humid broadleaf forest, tall second growth, and shaded plantations. In pairs or small groups. Follows mixed flocks. Not in large flocks like Red-legged Honeycreeper. **VOICE** Song (1) a long series of thin, high-pitched, notes *pit pit pit pit-pit pit-peet pit pit pit-peet pit pit* . . . Call (2) a high-pitched, very sharp *seeet* or *siiip* or *seeep*.

Purple Honeycreeper *Cyanerpes caeruleus*   10.5 cm

CA and SA. Rare and local resident in lowlands and foothills (to 600 m) of east PA (Darién, 659, 48, 426). **ID** *Yellow legs*. Male closely resembles male Shining Honeycreeper. Note more restricted black throat. Female resembles female Shining Honeycreeper but is more extensively streaked below (including flanks) and has green nape and crown. Note female's blue malar contrasting with *buff eye ring, lores, and throat*. Female Red-legged Honeycreeper has red legs and different head pattern. **HABITS** Canopy and edge of humid broadleaf forest, tall second growth, and shaded plantations. Pairs or small groups follow mixed flocks that often include various tanagers. **VOICE** Calls (1) a high-pitched, lisping *zzree* and (2) longer, slurred *sseeeup*

50%

Swallow Tanager
♀
♂

Green Honeycreeper
♀
♂

♀
nonbreeding ♂

Red-legged Honeycreeper

breeding ♂

♀
♂

Shining Honeycreeper

♀
♂

Purple Honeycreeper

TANAGERS Thraupidae

Small birds found mainly with mixed flocks in upper levels of humid broadleaf forest. Golden-hooded Tanager is the most common and widespread.

Plain-colored Tanager *Tangara inornata* 13.5 cm

CA and north SA. Uncommon to fairly common resident in south lowlands and foothills (to 750 m). **ID** Small. Mostly *gray* with *darker face, tail, and wings* and whitish belly and crissum. Blue on wing coverts inconspicuous. **GV** Birds from CR and west PA (west of Laguna de Chiriquí) are buffy white below. **HABITS** Subcanopy to canopy and edge of humid broadleaf forest, second growth, and shaded plantations. Small groups follow mixed flocks that include other *Tangara* tanagers and honeycreepers. **VOICE** Song (1) a variable, staccato series of high-pitched, thin whistles and short notes and sputters *tseee tsp tsp tseee tsp tsp tsp.* May be repeated persistently. Call (2) a high-pitched, thin *tsit* or *tseep* or *sip.* May be repeated or may accelerate to become a dry twitter.

Spangle-cheeked Tanager *Tangara dowii* 13.5 cm

CA endemic. Locally common resident in south highlands (1200 to 2750 m). **ID** Dark. Mostly black head speckled with pale green on auriculars and nape. Note *cinnamon lower underparts* and dark speckling on breast. Green-naped Tanager allopatric. **HABITS** Subcanopy to canopy and edge of humid, broadleaf (cloud) forest. Descends to lower levels at gaps or where fruit is available. Pairs or small groups follow mixed flocks. Forages actively in foliage and epiphytes. **VOICE** Call (1) a high-pitched, thin, penetrating *tsip* or *seek* often given in twittering series.

Green-naped Tanager *Tangara fucosa* 13.5 cm

CA and SA. Locally fairly common resident in highlands (mainly above 1350, rarely as low as 600 m) of east PA including Pirre Massif, Tarcarcuna Massif, and Serranía de Jungurudó (Darién, 659, 512, 45). **ID** Dark, with mostly black head and mantle. Note *speckled breast* and *pale cinnamon lower underparts.* Spangle-cheeked Tanager allopatric. **HABITS** Like Spangle-cheeked Tanager. **VOICE** Calls (1) a high-pitched *tsit* and (2) more squealing *tseet.* Given singly or in short, rapid series.

Azure-rumped Tanager *Tangara cabanisi* 16 cm

South MX and CA. Rare to locally fairly common resident in Pacific volcanic highlands (860 to 1900 m) of GT (San Marcos, Quetzaltenango, Sololá, Suchitepéquez, Chimaltenango, 223, 224, 229, 294, 304, 553). **ID** Large. Pale blue and green with *black speckling on breast, nape, and mantle.* Note *black mask,* chin, and sides of neck. Gray-and-gold Tanager allopatric. **HABITS** Midstory to canopy and edge of humid broadleaf forest and adjacent shaded plantations. In pairs or small groups. Does not follow mixed flocks. **VOICE** Variable calls include (1) a long, whistled phrase that rises, then falls, then finally rises again in pitch *fseeeee-ew-weeee?* (2) shorter falling and rising whistles, (3) an up- and downslurred call followed by sharp note *siiiuu-ti,* and (4) whistled phrases sometimes followed by rapid clicking *t-t-t-t-t* that may suggest Common Chlorospingus or Emerald-chinned Hummingbird. Also (5) a rapid, sputtering *p-p-p-pt-pt* and (6) rasping *rrrb-rrb-rrb* in aggressive interactions.

Gray-and-gold Tanager *Tangara palmeri* 16 cm

CA and north SA. Rare and local resident in foothills (450 to 1020 m) of PA (Panamá, Kuna Yala, Darién, 659, 512, 45). **ID** Large with heavy bill. Ad has black face, forehead, and chin. Otherwise mostly pale gray (becoming whitish on face and throat) with blackish tail and wings. Note *black speckling on breast, neck, and nape* and pale, opalescent yellow wash on breast and mantle. Juv lacks speckled breast-band. Azure-rumped Tanager allopatric. **HABITS** Subcanopy to canopy and edge of humid broadleaf forest, adjacent second growth, and shaded plantations. Most common in hilly terrain. Pairs or small groups forage independently but also follow mixed flocks. Less restless than other *Tangara* tanagers. Often perches in open. Sometimes noisy. **VOICE** Song (1) a loud, high-pitched *chup, chup-sweeeet* with last note upslurred. Call (2) a short, slightly dry *chep.* May be repeated.

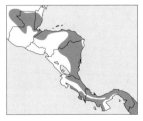

Golden-hooded Tanager *Tangara larvata* 13.5 cm

MX to north SA. Uncommon to fairly common resident in lowlands and foothills (to 1500 m). **ID** *Black breast and mantle* contrast with *yellow-buff hood* and white lower underparts. Note black face and chin and light blue-green wing coverts. Juv mostly olive-green with dark mask and whitish central underparts. Note juv's brighter nape contrasting with dark mantle. **HABITS** Subcanopy to canopy and edge of semihumid to humid broadleaf forest, tall second growth, and shaded plantations. In pairs or small groups. Follows mixed flocks. May linger on high, open perch. **VOICE** Often quiet. Song (1) a series of sharp notes that accelerate to become a dry trill or rattle *tsit tsit tsit tsitsitsitsit . . .* Drops slightly in pitch. Call (2) a high-pitched, scratchy, metallic *tsit* or *chik.*

50%

Plain-colored Tanager

CR and
west PA

PA

Spangle-cheeked Tanager

Green-naped Tanager

Azure-rumped Tanager

Gray-and-gold Tanager

Golden-hooded Tanager

ad

juv

TANAGERS Thraupidae

Brightly colored tanagers. These are usually found in pairs or small groups with mixed flocks in upper levels of humid broadleaf forest in foothills and highlands.

Silver-throated Tanager *Tangara icterocephala* 13.5 cm
CA and north SA. Uncommon to common resident in south foothills and highlands (600 to 1700 m). May descend to near SL outside breeding season (600, 92, 253). **ID** Ad male mostly yellow with variably white or gray throat contrasting with *black malar* and lores. Black-and-yellow streaked mantle. Female slightly duller. Juv mostly dull with olive throat. Compare with Emerald Tanager (sometimes in same mixed flock). **GV** Birds of both sexes in west central PA are darker and duller than widespread form. **HABITS** Subcanopy to canopy and edge of humid broadleaf forest, tall second growth, and shaded plantations. Forages actively in foliage and on epiphyte-laden branches. Leans forward to inspect undersides of branches. **VOICE** Calls (1) a dry, buzzy *bzeeet* or *zeeep* and (2) shorter, harsher, insect-like *zeet*.

Emerald Tanager *Tangara florida* 13.5 cm
CA and north SA. Uncommon resident in south foothills (350 to 1100 m). May descend to near SL outside breeding season (600, 92). **ID** Male mostly green grading to yellow on crown, nape and lower underparts. Mantle streaked with black and green. Note *black auriculars* and *black lores*. Female lacks ad male's yellow nape and crown. Compare with Speckled Tanager (often in same mixed flock). Note different underparts. **HABITS** Subcanopy to canopy of humid broadleaf forest and adjacent tall second growth. Forages actively in foliage and on epiphyte-laden branches. **VOICE** Song (1) a steady series of loud *cheet* or *chiip* notes. Call (2) a sharp *chip* or *tsip*. May be repeated and sometimes accelerates into a rapid twitter.

Speckled Tanager *Tangara guttata* 13 cm
CA and north SA. Uncommon resident in south foothills (400 to 1400 m). **ID** Ad mostly yellowish-green above spotted with black. Note *bold, dark spotting on whitish breast*. Dark wings with blue-green edging. Female less boldly spotted below. Compare with female Emerald Tanager. Note different underparts. **HABITS** Subcanopy to canopy and edge of humid broadleaf forest and adjacent plantations or second growth. May descend to midstory to feed at fruiting shrubs. Forages actively in foliage and on epiphyte-laden branches. **VOICE** Calls (1) a series of very thin, sharp *tse* or *sit* notes that may accelerate to a fine twitter, and (2) single, longer *tseet* notes.

Bay-headed Tanager *Tangara gyrola* 14.5 cm
CA and SA. Uncommon resident in south foothills (600 to 1500 m, occasionally or locally near SL). Rare in north NI (Nueva Segovia, Jinotega, Matagalpa, RAAN, 420, 412). Reports from Caribbean HN require confirmation (Atlántida, 346). **ID** *Turquoise-blue underparts* and rump and *brick-red hood, including chin*. Upperparts, including wings, green. Female slightly duller. Imm mostly green with dull-buff face and auriculars. Compare with Rufous-winged Tanager. Note different underparts. **GV** Birds from east PA (not shown) have less yellow on lesser wing coverts. **HABITS** Subcanopy to canopy and edge of humid broadleaf forest and adjacent tall second growth. Follows mixed flocks. Forages actively in foliage and on epiphyte-laden branches. **VOICE** Song (1) a series of four to six thin notes that drop successively in pitch *tseep, tsip-tsiptseuu . . .* Calls (2) a sibilant *tsip* or *tseeu* and (3) harsh, buzzy, squeaky *tzeeik* or *weeit*.

Rufous-winged Tanager *Tangara lavinia* 14 cm
CA and SA. Uncommon resident in foothills (mainly 250 to 900 m, locally near SL). Rare and poorly known in HN (Atlántida, El Paraíso, Olancho, Gracias a Dios, 63, 167, 442, 346) and NI (Jinotega, RAAN, Matagalpa, 537, 420, 332). Rare and poorly known in east PA (Darién, 659, 512, 426). **ID** *Mostly green below including throat*. Note blue central underparts and male's *brick-red wings* and hood. Upperparts including rump mostly green grading to yellow on mantle. Compare with Bay-headed Tanager. **GV** Birds from central PA (not shown) have less rufous on wings. Birds from east PA (Darién) have more extensive blue below (including throat) and more yellow on nape and mantle. **HABITS** Subcanopy to canopy and edge of humid broadleaf forest, tall second growth, and shaded plantations. Forages actively in foliage and on epiphyte-laden branches. **VOICE** Song (1) a rapid, staccato series on steady pitch *seet-t-t-t-t-t-t*. Calls (2) a high-pitched, thin, sharp *tseeup* or *tseep* and (3) piercing *zeek*.

west central PA
ad (dull extreme)
♀

widespread ad
♂

**Silver-throated
Tanager**

♂

**Emerald
Tanager**

♀

**Speckled
Tanager**

**Bay-headed
Tanager**
♀

♂

juv

**Rufous-winged
Tanager**
♀

widespread ad
♂

east PA
ad
♂

TANAGERS Thraupidae

Thraupis tanagers are found mainly in upper levels in disturbed or semi-open areas. Blue-gray Tanager is a widespread and familiar species. Blue-and-gold Tanager is scarce in humid foothill forests of south Central America.

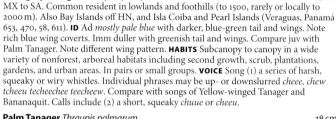

Blue-gray Tanager *Thraupis episcopus*   17 cm

MX to SA. Common resident in lowlands and foothills (to 1500, rarely or locally to 2000 m). Also Bay Islands off HN, and Isla Coiba and Pearl Islands (Veraguas, Panamá 653, 470, 58, 611). **ID** Ad *mostly pale blue* with darker, blue-green tail and wings. Note rich blue wing coverts. Imm duller with greenish tail and wings. Compare juv with Palm Tanager. Note different wing pattern. **HABITS** Subcanopy to canopy in a wide variety of nonforest, arboreal habitats including second growth, scrub, plantations, gardens, and urban areas. In pairs or small groups. **VOICE** Song (1) a series of harsh, squeaky or wiry whistles. Individual phrases may be up- or downslurred *cheee, chew tcheeu techeechee teecheew*. Compare with songs of Yellow-winged Tanager and Bananaquit. Calls include (2) a short, squeaky *chuue* or *cheeu*.

Palm Tanager *Thraupis palmarum*   18 cm

CA and SA. Common resident in south lowlands and foothills (to 1500 m). Also Isla Coiba off PA (Veraguas, 659). Rare in NI north of Río San Juan drainage (RAAN, RAAS, Río San Juan, Granada, 662, 452). Sight reports from east HN (Atlántida, Olancho, 100). **ID** Male drab grayish-olive. *Pale wing coverts* and olive base of primaries contrast with dusky flight feathers. Female more olive. Compare with Blue-gray Tanager (especially imm). Note different wing pattern. Smaller Plain-colored Tanager has different head pattern and habits. **HABITS** Midstory to canopy in a wide variety of arboreal habitats including forest edge, second growth, plantations, urban areas, scrub, and gardens. Often perches in the open. Usually in pairs. **VOICE** Song (1) a rapid series of high-pitched, buzzy phrases *su'suri su'suri su'suri sre sree su'suri susri . . .* Like Blue-gray Tanager but faster and with more distinct phrases. Call (2) a high-pitched, upslurred *zeeeeip*.

Yellow-winged Tanager *Thraupis abbas*   18 cm

MX and north CA. Uncommon to common resident in lowlands and foothills (to 1800, rarely to 2000 m). Rare in east NI (Jinotega, RAAN, RAAS, Río San Juan, 452) and CR (Cartago, Alajuela, Guanacaste, 600, 346, 115, 677). Perhaps expanding. **ID** Large and robust with short, deep bill. In all plumages, note *yellow band at base of dark primaries* and *dark face*. Ad has blue head, breast, and mantle. Sexes similar but female slightly duller. Juv still drabber with variably dull grayish head and less yellow on primaries. **HABITS** Subcanopy to canopy and edge of semihumid broadleaf forest, second growth, scrub, plantations, and gardens. Often in pairs. May perch conspicuously on high, bare limb. **VOICE** Song (1) a harsh trill that slows slightly near end. Often with one or two hissing introductory notes *shee iiiiiiiiiiirr*. Usually steady in pitch, but may be slightly upslurred or downslurred. Compare with song of Golden-hooded Tanager. Call (2) a high-pitched, hissing *sseeu* or *ssheeeup*.

Blue-and-gold Tanager *Bangsia arcaei*   16 cm

CA endemic. Uncommon and local resident in south humid foothills (mainly 400 to 1200 m). Recently reported from Colombian slope of Tacarcuna Massif (527). **ID** *Bulky and short-tailed* with deep bill. *Dark blue upperparts and throat* contrast with *rich yellow underparts*. Note red eyes and (variable) dark markings on flanks. Structure and yellow underparts may suggest a euphonia. Note Blue-and-gold Tanager's larger size and different underparts. **GV** Birds from CR are more orange below and have more extensive blue on flanks. **HABITS** Canopy of humid broadleaf forest and adjacent tall second growth. Pairs or small groups follow mixed flocks. Hops heavily through foliage and along limbs while foraging. Sometimes appears sluggish and may perch motionless for long periods. **VOICE** Song (1) a halting series of high-pitched, short, squeaky notes and thin, squeaky or wheezy whistles *tsip tseee tsup tseeeeur weeuwee tsip . . .* Calls (2) a high-pitched, piercing *zeek* or *keep* and (3) squeaky *spit* or *chit*.

Blue-gray Tanager

ad

juv

♂

Palm Tanager

♀

ad

juv

Yellow-winged Tanager

CR

PA

Blue-and-gold Tanager

TANAGERS Thraupidae

Tanagers confined in the region mainly to south Central America. Rosy Thrush-Tanager is a distinctive and enigmatic species with no close relatives.

Yellow-backed Tanager *Hemithraupis flavicollis* 12 cm

CA and SA. Uncommon resident in lowlands and foothills (to 1000 m) of east PA (Darién). **ID** Small and warbler-like with pink mandible. Male has *yellow throat, lower back, and rump* contrasting with otherwise black upperparts. Note *white on base of primaries*. Female resembles female Black-and-yellow Tanager but has *heavier bill, yellow eye ring, and whitish lower underparts*. Note female's yellow wingbars. **HABITS** Subcanopy to canopy and edge of humid broadleaf forest and adjacent tall second growth. In pairs or small groups. Follows mixed flocks. Forages actively in outer foliage. **VOICE** Song (1) a rapid, high-pitched series *si, si, si, si . . .* Call (2) a high-pitched *tsick* or *tut* or *tyoo tsick*.

Black-and-yellow Tanager *Chrysothlypis chrysomelas* 13 cm

CA endemic. Uncommon to locally fairly common resident in south foothills (mainly 600 to 1200, locally as low as 400 or as high as 1575 m). **ID** Small with fine *black bill*. Male has *yellow head* and underparts (including belly) contrasting with *black mantle, wings, and tail*. Female olive-green above and yellow below with gray belly and flanks. Compare female with female Yellow-backed Tanager. **GV** Female from central and east PA has entirely yellow-olive underparts. **HABITS** Subcanopy to canopy and edge of humid broadleaf forest and adjacent tall second growth. Usually in pairs or small groups. Follows mixed flocks. Forages actively in outer foliage. Often reaches, briefly hovers, or hangs to seize prey. Calls frequently while foraging. **VOICE** Call (1) a scratchy *tsew* or *tseerw*. Higher-pitched than call of Silver-throated Tanager.

Sulphur-rumped Tanager *Heterospingus rubrifrons* 15.5 cm

CA endemic. Uncommon to rare resident in lowlands and foothills (to 900 m) of east CR (Limón) and PA. Rare and local in CR. **ID** Robust with heavy bill. Sexes similar. Ad mostly gray with contrasting darker wings and tail. Note *yellow rump* and lower back and *white pectoral tufts*. Imm is darker above. In east PA (Darién) compare with darker and more uniform female Scarlet-browed Tanager. **HABITS** Subcanopy to canopy and edge of humid broadleaf forest, tall second growth, and shaded plantations. Pairs follow mixed flocks that may also include Black-faced Grosbeaks and Tawny-crested Tanagers. **VOICE** Calls (1) a sharp, buzzy *dzeet*, (2) higher-pitched, thinner *tseet* in flight, and (3) short, rapid chatter.

Scarlet-browed Tanager *Heterospingus xanthopygius* 17 cm

CA and north SA. Uncommon resident in Pacific lowlands and foothills (to 900 m) of east PA (Darién). **ID** Large and robust with heavy bill. Note yellow rump and white pectoral tufts. Male has narrow white supercilium and *long scarlet tuft extending from behind eye*. Female has plain gray head and is very similar to both sexes of Sulphur-rumped Tanager. Note female Scarlet-browed's darker and more uniform gray plumage. Sulphur-rumped Tanager (Caribbean slope) mainly allopatric. **HABITS** Midstory to canopy and edge of humid broadleaf forest and tall second growth. Pairs or small groups follow mixed flocks. Forages actively in foliage and epiphytes. **VOICE** Song (1) a complex, cascading series of high-pitched, slurred notes and harsh, buzzy phrases *cheer-cheer a-burr bzz bzz*. Frequent call (2) a loud, emphatic *zeep* or *dzeet* or *dziip*. Compare with call of Swallow Tanager.

ROSY THRUSH-TANAGER Rhodinocichlidae

Rosy Thrush-Tanager is a distinctive and enigmatic species with no close relatives.

Rosy Thrush-Tanager *Rhodinocichla rosea* 19.5 cm

MX, CA and north SA. Uncommon to rare and local resident in south Pacific lowlands and foothills (SL to 1200, rarely or locally to 1800 m) of Río Térraba region in CR (Puntarenas, 515, 566, 600) and PA (512, 659). Local on Caribbean slope in central PA (Colón). **ID** Broad tail and fairly long bill. Male has magenta-pink throat and breast. Note *magenta-pink supercilium with narrow white extension behind eye*. Female has underparts and supercilium orange-rufous. **HABITS** Understory, floor, and edge of semihumid broadleaf forest, second growth, plantations, and scrub. Often in pairs. Forages on ground. May scratch noisily in leaf litter. Secretive and usually detected by voice. Does not follow mixed flocks. **VOICE** Pairs sing in duet. Song (1) a variable series of four- to six-note phrases rapidly repeated several times. Rich tone may suggest an oriole or wren *cheer, cheer, cheerily cheer, cheeo-cheera cheerily cho*. Call (2) a mellow, querulous *kweeo, kyew*, or *querup* that may be repeated persistently. Pairs duet (3) with buzzy, accelerating and descending *pseeeer-zeeeer-zeeer-zeeer-zur*.

Yellow-backed Tanager

♀

♂

Black-and-yellow Tanager

CR and
west PA
♀

central
and east PA
♀

♂

Sulphur-rumped Tanager

♀

Scarlet-browed Tanager

♂

♂

Rosy Thrush-Tanager

♀

TANAGERS Thraupidae

Striking red or yellow and black–plumaged tanagers found mainly at middle levels in humid second growth or broadleaf forest edge. Usually in pairs or small groups. Most have distinctive deep-based, pale gray mandible. Often conspicuous. Passerini's Tanager is the most common and widespread.

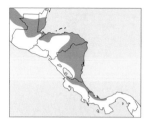

Crimson-collared Tanager *Ramphocelus sanguinolentus* 19 cm
South MX and CA. Uncommon resident in Caribbean lowlands and foothills (to 1200, locally to 1800 m). Local on Pacific slope in west CR (600). Rare in Caribbean west PA (Bocas del Toro). **ID** Sexes similar. Heavy, entirely pale gray bill. Mostly black with *crimson-red crown, nape, breast-band, and rump*. Imm (not shown) duller with mostly black breast. **HABITS** Midstory to subcanopy in forest edge, second growth, riparian thickets, plantations, and gardens. Follows prominently in the open. Follows mixed flocks that include various edge-inhabiting tanagers, orioles, or saltators. **VOICE** Song (1) a slow series of slightly squeaky, up- or downslurred whistles *tueee-tseew, chu-che-weee chew, teweee*. Calls (2) a thin, downslurred *tseweeu* and (3) sharply upslurred *chuweee*.

Passerini's Tanager *Ramphocelus passerinii* 17 cm
South MX and CA. Widespread and locally very common resident in lowlands and foothills (to 1200, but mainly below 800 m in north). **ID** Deep-based, bluish-gray bill with dark tip. Male velvety black with *brilliant scarlet rump and lower back*. Female ochre-olive (including rump) with *grayer head*. Cherrie's Tanager allopatric. **HABITS** Midstory at edge of humid broadleaf forest, second growth, riparian thickets, plantations, and gardens. Particularly numerous near water. Often active and conspicuous. Perches in outer boughs of foliage. May form loose associations with other edge-inhabiting birds such as Crimson-collared and White-shouldered tanagers or saltators. **VOICE** Song (1) a vireo-like series of one to three short, up- or downslurred whistles followed by a buzzy chatter of two to three notes *wiiu-wiiu-wiiu chichichi*. Calls (2) a sharp *ac* or *wac*, (3) dry, scratchy *chuck*, (4) dry *pzzt*, and (5) sharp *whip*.

Cherrie's Tanager *Ramphocelus costaricensis* 17 cm
CA endemic. Common resident in Pacific lowlands and foothills (to 1200 m) of east CR and west PA. **ID** Deep-based, bluish-gray bill. Male velvety black with *brilliant scarlet rump and lower back*. Female has *orange or scarlet rump* and *orange breast-band*. Flame-rumped and Passerini's tanagers allopatric. **HABITS** Like Passerini's Tanager. **VOICE** Song (1) a series of short phrases of three to four slurred notes *wheea wheuu wheea . . .* repeated persistently. Calls (2) a sharp *ac* or *wac*, (3) dry, scratchy *chuck*, (4) dry *pzzt*, and (5) sharp *whip*. Also (6) a sharp, descending chatter.

Flame-rumped Tanager *Ramphocelus flammigerus* 17.5 cm
CA and north SA. Common resident in lowlands and foothills (to 1200 m) of PA. **ID** Deep-based, bluish-gray bill. Male velvety black with *brilliant yellow rump and lower back*. Female mostly grayish-brown above with yellow rump and underparts. Passerini's and Cherrie's tanagers allopatric. **HABITS** Upper understory to midstory at edge of humid broadleaf forest, dense second growth, riparian thickets, and gardens. In pairs or small groups. Active and conspicuous. Perches in outer boughs of foliage. May form loose associations with other edge-inhabiting birds. **VOICE** Typical call (1) a simple nasal *ahr* or *ehr*. May be repeated.

Crimson-backed Tanager *Ramphocelus dimidiatus* 17 cm
CA and north SA. Fairly common resident in lowlands and foothills (to 1650 m) of PA. Also Isla Coiba and Pearl Islands (Veraguas, Panamá, 659, 470). **ID** Deep-based, bluish-gray bill. Male mostly *deep crimson-red becoming brighter on rump and lower underparts* with contrasting blackish tail and wings. Female slightly duller with brownish head and wings. **GV** Male from Isla Coiba and Pearl Islands has less black on central belly. Female from Isla Coiba is darker than mainland female. **HABITS** Midstory at edges of humid broadleaf forest, dense second growth, riparian thickets, plantations, and gardens. On islands reported to use forest interior. Usually in pairs or small groups. May follow mixed flocks. **VOICE** Dawn song (1) a repeated, clear, loud, whistled phrase *chewachee, chewachee, chewachee . . .* Calls (2) a short, nasal *wah* or *whanh* or *anh*, (3) a hoarse, upslurred *waah* or *wheeaah* or *zhawhee* that may be given in a series, and (4) high-pitched, loud *wheeeeet* or *zeeeeeet*. May be doubled.

45%

Crimson-collared Tanager

♀

Passerini's Tanager

♂

♀

Cherrie's Tanager

♂

♀

Flame-rumped Tanager

♂

Crimson-backed Tanager

widespread
♀

widespread
♂

Coiba
♀

Coiba
♂

TANAGERS Thraupidae

Mostly black or drab-plumaged tanagers found at middle levels in humid broadleaf forest and edge. Often seen in groups with mixed flocks. White-shouldered Tanager is geographically variable in Central America.

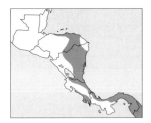

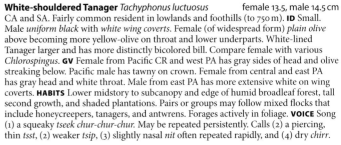

White-shouldered Tanager *Tachyphonus luctuosus*   female 13.5, male 14.5 cm
CA and SA. Fairly common resident in lowlands and foothills (to 750 m). **ID** Small.
Male *uniform black* with *white wing coverts*. Female (of widespread form) *plain olive*
above becoming more yellow-olive on throat and lower underparts. White-lined
Tanager larger and has more distinctly bicolored bill. Compare female with various
Chlorospingus. **GV** Female from Pacific CR and west PA has gray sides of head and olive
streaking below. Pacific male has tawny on crown. Female from central and east PA
has gray head and white throat. Male from east PA has more extensive white on wing
coverts. **HABITS** Lower midstory to subcanopy and edge of humid broadleaf forest, tall
second growth, and shaded plantations. Pairs or groups may follow mixed flocks that
include honeycreepers, tanagers, and antwrens. Forages actively in foliage. **VOICE** Song
(1) a squeaky *tseek chur-chur-chur*. May be repeated persistently. Calls (2) a piercing,
thin *tsst*, (3) weaker *tsip*, (3) slightly nasal *nit* often repeated rapidly, and (4) dry *chirr*.

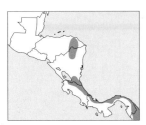

Tawny-crested Tanager *Tachyphonus delatrii*   female 15, male 16 cm
CA and north SA. Uncommon to locally fairly common resident in Caribbean
lowlands and foothills (to 1000 m). **ID** Male *uniform black* with *tawny-yellow erectile
crown patch*. Female *uniform dusky brown*. Compare with White-lined and White-
shouldered tanagers. **HABITS** Midstory to subcanopy of humid broadleaf forest and tall
second growth. Forages actively. Noisy and conspicuous. Pairs or groups sometimes
follow mixed flocks that may include woodcreepers, tanagers, and various tyrannids.
VOICE Calls (1) a metallic *tchit* or *zick*, (2) higher-pitched *tsip* or *tchewp*, and (3) high-
pitched, flat, thin, slightly buzzy *zeeet* or *pseeet* given singly or repeated in long series.

White-lined Tanager *Tachyphonus rufus*   female 17, male 19 cm
CA and SA. Uncommon to locally fairly common resident in south lowlands and
foothills (to 1400 m). **ID** Large. Fairly heavy, bicolored bill with pale gray mandible.
Male *uniform black*. Underwing coverts white (rarely visible). Male has (mostly
concealed) white on lesser coverts. Female *near-uniform cinnamon-brown* becoming
slightly paler below. Compare male with smaller male White-shouldered Tanager.
HABITS Midstory to canopy at edge of humid broadleaf forest, second growth, scrub,
and shaded plantations. In pairs or small groups. Forages actively, mainly in foliage or
epiphytes. Occasionally descends to ground to seize prey. Sometimes follows mixed
flocks that include other edge-inhabiting tanagers and honeycreepers. **VOICE** Song (1)
a long, irregular series of *chip* notes that may be upslurred or downslurred *chip cheep
cherp cherp cheet chep chep cherp chip chip . . .* Calls (2) a short *kchip* or *check* and (3)
weak, thin *seep*.

48%

widespread ♂

east PA ♂

Pacific CR
and west PA ♂

widespread ♀

Pacific CR and
west PA ♀

east PA ♀

White-shouldered Tanager

Tawny-crested Tanager

♀

♂

White-lined Tanager

♀

♂

TANAGERS Thraupidae

Lanio shrike-tanagers have heavy, hooked bill and are found with mixed flocks at middle levels in humid broadleaf forest. They typically perch upright on an open vine or branch. Gray-headed Tanager is a widespread species often found at army ant swarms.

Black-throated Shrike-Tanager *Lanio aurantius*　　　21 cm

South MX and CA. Uncommon resident in north Caribbean lowlands and foothills (to 800, locally to 1200 m). **ID** Hooked bill and long, square tail. Male *mostly yellow with black hood, wings, and tail*. Female has yellow lower underparts and grayish face, auriculars, and throat. Female may recall Gray-headed Tanager but note olive breast and flanks and *brownish wings*. White-throated Shrike-Tanager parapatric. **HABITS** Upper midstory of interior semihumid to humid broadleaf forest. Pairs or family groups follow mixed flocks that include woodcreepers, tanagers, and various tyrannids. Often conspicuous. Perches upright and motionless on exposed horizontal limb or looping vine. Makes abrupt, rapid sallies to seize prey flushed by other birds. **VOICE** Song (1) a short series of harsh, scratchy whistles that accelerate to become a rapid, high-pitched trill. Calls (2) an abrupt, loud whistle *cheer!* or *cheeeo!* and (3) loud, emphatic, two-syllable *whi-cheer!* or *chee-cheer!* often repeated in stuttering series. Also (4) a persistent, scolding *che-che-che-che-che . . .* or *chu-chu-chu-chu-chu . . .*

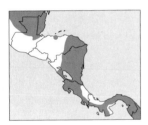

White-throated Shrike-Tanager *Lanio leucothorax*　　　21 cm

CA endemic. Uncommon to rare resident in lowlands and foothills (mainly 400 to 900 m, locally to near SL). Historical record from central NI (Chontales, 537). **ID** Hooked bill and long, square tail. Male *mostly yellow with white throat and black wings and tail*. Female variable, but generally dull brownish above with pale grayish throat and yellow lower underparts. Gray-headed Tanager has more contrasting pattern with entirely gray head. Black-throated Shrike-Tanager allopatric. **GV** Male from PA has black rump. Female from PA (not shown) has brown rump. **HABITS** Like Black-throated Shrike-Tanager. **VOICE** Calls (1) a two-syllable *cheh-chuu* or *ch'chu* that is slower and less emphatic than similar call of Black-throated Shrike-Tanager and (2) a short, rapidly accelerating trill *cheedtdtdtdt*. Also (3) a short series of loud, slightly burry notes that drop in pitch *cheeuw, cheer-churr-churr*.

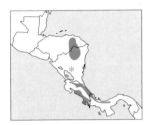

Gray-headed Tanager *Eucometis penicillata*　　　18.5 cm

MX to SA. Uncommon resident in lowlands and foothills (to 1200 but mainly below 800 m). **ID** Sexes similar. Olive-green upperparts and *yellow underparts contrast sharply with gray head*. Raises ragged crest in alarm or excitement. Juv has olive head and faint streaking on breast. In north compare with female Black-throated Shrike-Tanager. Note different underparts and habits. **GV** Birds from PA have whitish throat, clear yellow breast, and longer crest. **HABITS** Understory to lower midstory of semihumid to humid broadleaf forest. Pairs or solitary birds move deliberately through shaded undergrowth. Occasionally drops to ground. Does not follow mixed flocks. Attends army ant swarms, particularly in north. **VOICE** Song (1) a variable series of very high-pitched, thin notes and phrases *zreez-reeezeeepweer-wheuh* or *whichis whichis whicheery whichis whichu', tsee tseep seeur tsp-tsp tseeur tsp-tsp seeur ts-suur*. Calls (2) a squeaky, high-pitched, thin *pseeet* or *teet* or *tseeet* often repeated two or three times and (3) sharp, metallic, high-pitched *chip* or *pit*. Sometimes repeated persistently.

DUSKY-FACED TANAGER Mitrospingidae

Dusky-faced Tanager is a highly distinctive species with no close relatives in the region.

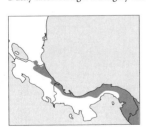

Dusky-faced Tanager *Mitrospingus cassinii*　　　19 cm

CA and north SA. Uncommon resident in south lowlands and foothills (to 600 m). One report from southeast NI (Río San Juan, 346). **ID** *Pale gray eyes*. Mostly dark gray with olive underparts, *bright olive-green crown and nape,* and black forehead, face, and chin. **HABITS** Understory of humid broadleaf forest and second growth. Favors shaded, wet areas along streams or tangled undergrowth in ravines. Usually in groups. Skulks in dense vegetation. Does not follow mixed flocks. Forages restlessly. Twitches wings and tail. **VOICE** Often noisy. Song (1) a sharp, high-pitched, emphatic *zeep zeep zeep zeep-it zeepity zeep* repeated persistently. Calls (2) a harsh, rolling, metallic *chrrrt* or *trrrrt*, (3) high-pitched, piercing *zeet* or *siiit*, and (4) sputtering chatter.